COREL
WordPerfect 8
TUTORIAL

Mary Alice Eisch
Appleton, Wisconsin

JOIN US ON THE INTERNET
WWW: http://www.thomson.com
EMAIL: findit@kiosk.thomson.com   A service of I(T)P®

South-Western Educational Publishing
an International Thomson Publishing company I(T)P®

Cincinnati • Albany, NY • Belmont, CA • Bonn • Boston • Detroit • Johannesburg • London • Madrid
Melbourne • Mexico City • New York • Paris • Singapore • Tokyo • Toronto • Washington

Copyright © 1999
by SOUTH-WESTERN EDUCATIONAL PUBLISHING
Cincinnati, Ohio

ALL RIGHTS RESERVED

The text of this publication, or any part thereof, may not be reproduced or transmitted in any form or by any means, electronic or mechanical, including photocopying, recording, storage in an information retrieval system, or otherwise, without the prior written permission of the publisher.

WZ23AA ISBN: 0-538-68533-6
WZ23AB ISBN: 0-538-68535-2
WZ23A8H881 ISBN: 0-538-68534-4
WZ23A8H882 ISBN: 0-538-68536-0

1 2 3 4 5 6 7 8 9 10 VH 06 05 04 03 02 01 00 99 98 97
Printed in the United States of America

I(T)P®

International Thomson Publishing

South-Western Educational Publishing is a division of International Thomson Publishing Inc. The ITP logo is a registered trademark used herein under License by South-Western Educational Publishing.

Corel® and WordPerfect® are registered trademarks of Corel Corporation or Corel Corporation Limited in Canada, the United States and/or other countries. Windows is a registered trademark of Microsoft Corporation. IBM is a registered trademark of International Business Machines Corporation. WordPerfect and Windows, together with the names of all other products mentioned herein, are used for identification purposes only and may be trademarks or registered trademarks of their respective owners.

Screen shots for this text were created using Collage Complete, a product of Inner Media, Inc., Hollis, New Hampshire.

Managing Editor:	Carol Volz
Project Manager:	Anne Noschang
Consulting Editor:	Judith Voiers
Content Reviewers:	Sue Ehrfurth, Linda Mallinson
Cover and Internal Design:	Grannan Graphic Design, Ltd.
Cover Illustration:	Grannan Graphic Design, Ltd.
Design Coordinator:	Mike Broussard
Production Services:	Electro-Publishing

THE SECRETS OF COREL® WORDPERFECT® SUITE 8 ARE OUT!

Our exciting new Corel WordPerfect Suite 8 series will provide everything needed to master the Corel WordPerfect Suite 8 software. The series includes the following products:

- *Corel WordPerfect 8 Complete Course,* by Mary Alice Eisch, is the most comprehensive instructional text available for learning the WordPerfect 8 software. It contains 75+ hours of instruction on the most widely used beginning through advanced features of WordPerfect 8.

- *Corel WordPerfect 8 Tutorial,* also by Mary Alice Eisch, covers the beginning through intermediate features of WordPerfect 8 in 30+ hours of instruction. The text is available in both hard cover spiral and softbound form.

- *Corel WordPerfect 8 QuickTorial,* also by Mary Alice Eisch, gives the user a quick introduction to the beginning through advanced WordPerfect 8 features and tools that make the software such a delight to use. It contains 12+ hours of instruction and is available in both hard cover spiral and softbound form.

- *Corel WordPerfect Suite 8 Integrated Course,* by Eisch, Baumann, and Blake, allows the user to learn the applications in Corel WordPerfect Suite 8 (WordPerfect, Quattro Pro, Presentations, and also Paradox), and learn how these applications can be integrated with each other to perform all the tasks needed in today's workplace. It contains 75+ hours of instruction.

A new feature available for each of these products is the *Electronic Instructor*, which includes a printed instructor's manual and a CD-ROM. The CD-ROM contains SCANS coverage, block scheduling, tests, lesson plans, all data and solution files, and more!

Product	ISBN
Corel WordPerfect 8 Complete Course	
Student Text (side spiral bound, hard cover):	
With data disk	0-538-68293-0
Without data disk	0-538-68291-4
Electronic Instructor	0-538-68545-X
Corel WordPerfect 8 Tutorial	
Student Text (side spiral bound, hard cover):	
With data disk	0-538-68534-4
Without data disk	0-538-68533-6
Student Text (perfect bound, soft cover):	
With data disk (*not sold without disk*)	0-538-68536-0
Electronic Instructor	0-538-68537-9
Corel WordPerfect 8 QuickTorial	
Student Text (side spiral bound, soft cover):	
With data disk	0-538-68550-6
Without data disk	0-538-68549-2
Student Text (perfect bound, soft cover):	
With data disk (*not sold without disk*)	0-538-68551-4
Electronic Instructor	0-538-68552-2
Corel WordPerfect Suite 8 Integrated Course	
Student Text (side spiral bound, hard cover):	
With data disk	0-538-68528-X
Without data disk	0-538-68527-1
Electronic Instructor	0-538-68529-8

South-Western Educational Publishing

To order
Corel WordPerfect Suite 8 software
or these South-Western products
Join Us on the Internet
WWW: http://www.swpco.com

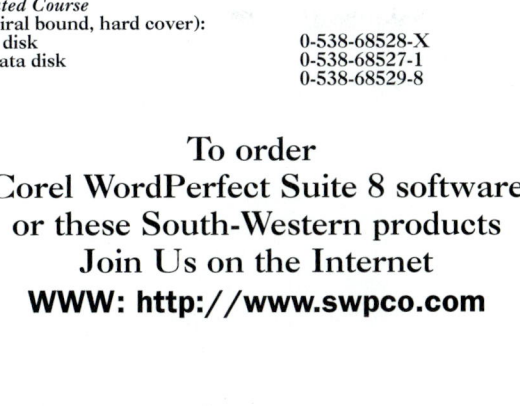

How to Use this Book

What makes a good applications text? Sound pedagogy and the most current, complete materials. That is what you will find in the new Corel WordPerfect Suite 8 series. Not only will you find a colorful, inviting layout, but also many features to enhance learning.

SCANS (Secretary's Commission on Achieving Necessary Skills)–The U.S. Department of Labor has identified the school-to-careers competencies. The five workplace competencies (resources, interpersonal skills, information, systems, and technology) and foundation skills (basic skills, thinking skills, and personal qualities) are identified in the exercises throughout the text. More information on SCANS can be found on the *Electronic Instructor*.

Notes– These boxes provide necessary information to assist you in completing the exercises.

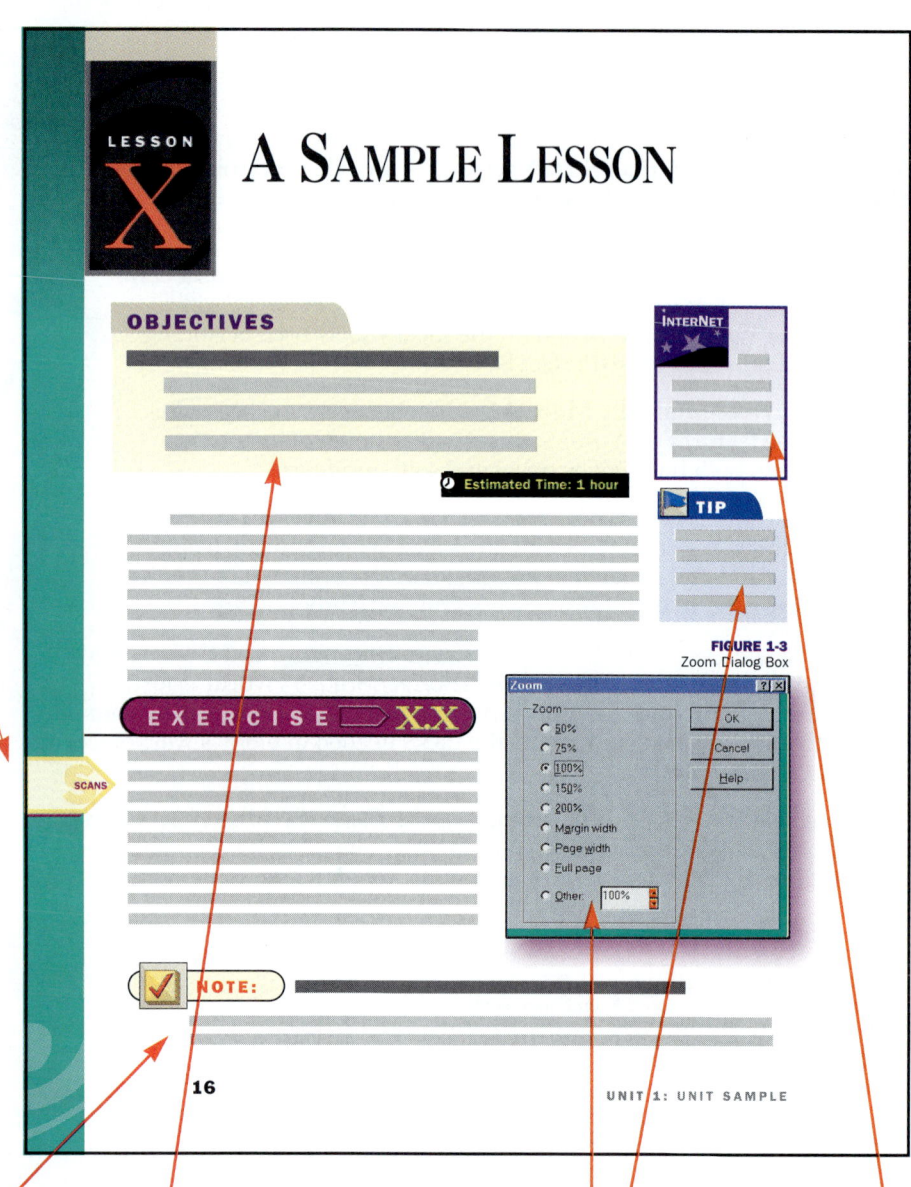

Objectives– Objectives are listed at the beginning of each lesson, along with a suggested time for completion of the lesson. This allows you to look ahead to what you will be learning and to pace your work.

Enhanced Screen Shots– Screen shots now come to life on each page with color and depth.

Tips– These boxes provide enrichment information about WordPerfect features.

Internet– Internet terminology and useful Internet information is provided in these boxes located throughout the text.

iv

How to Use this Book

Summary– At the end of each lesson you will find a summary to prepare you to complete the end-of-lesson activities.

Review Questions– Review material at the end of each lesson and each unit enables you to prepare for assessment of the content presented.

Lesson Projects– End-of-lesson hands-on application of what has been learned in the lesson allows you to actually apply the techniques covered.

Critical Thinking Activity– Each lesson gives you an opportunity to apply creative analysis to situations presented.

Command Summary– At the end of each unit, a command summary is provided for quick reference.

End-of-Unit Applications– End-of-unit hands-on application of concepts learned in the unit provides opportunity for a comprehensive review.

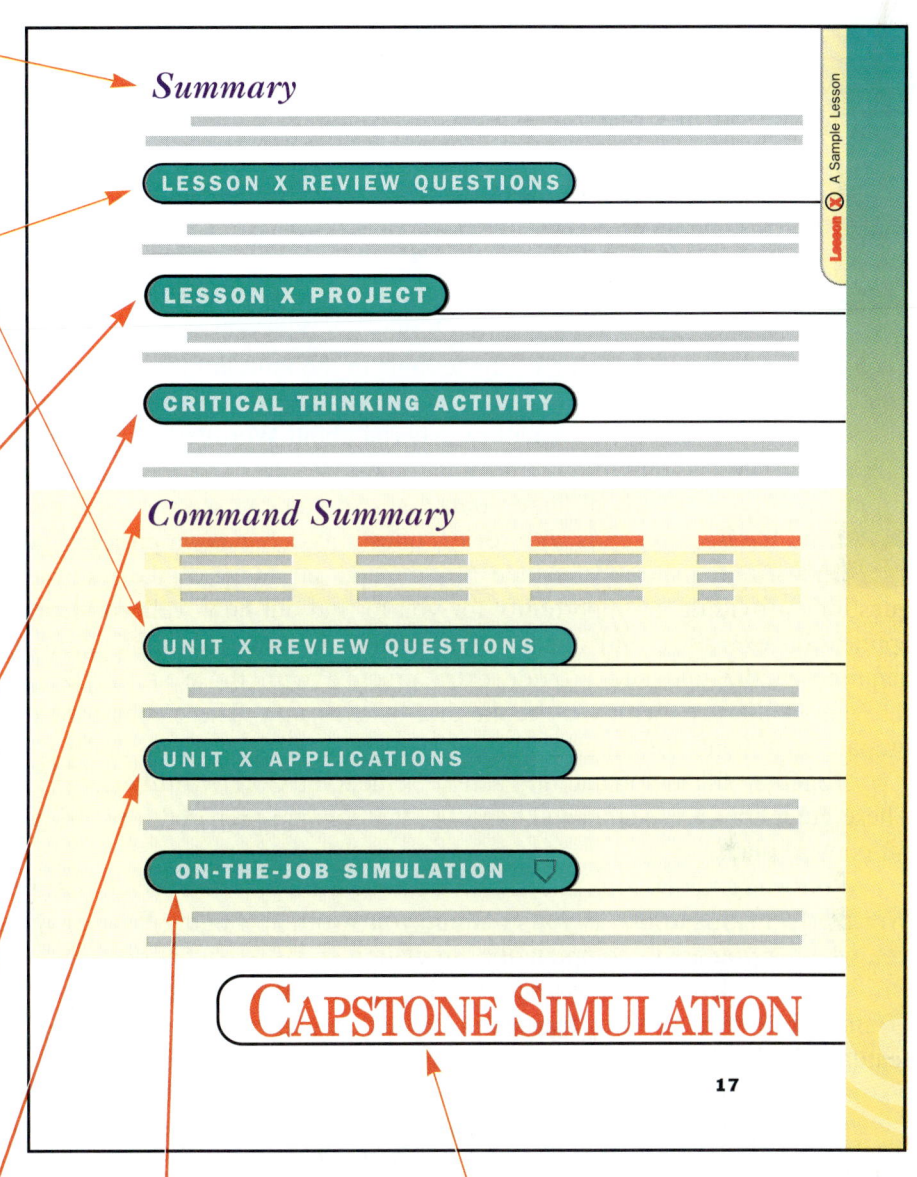

On-the-Job Simulation– A realistic simulation runs throughout the text at the end of each unit, reinforcing the material covered in the unit.

Capstone Simulation– Another simulation appears at the end of the text, to be completed after all the lessons have been covered, to give you an opportunity to apply all of the skills you have learned and see them come together in one application.

v

PREFACE

To the User

Congratulations on choosing to learn how to use Corel® WordPerfect® 8. At the end of the course, you should be proficient in the use of WordPerfect to prepare documents of all kinds.

Organization of the Text

Take a few minutes to page through this text. You will see that it is divided into units and lessons. Each unit begins with a listing of the lessons in the unit and the estimated time for completion of that unit.

The lessons contain explanatory material about WordPerfect features and tools, along with short exercises in which you will practice using those features and tools. At the beginning of each lesson is an introduction and a list of lesson objectives so you can see at a glance what you will be learning in the lesson. Each lesson ends with review questions, a hands-on project, and a critical thinking activity.

End-of-unit materials include a command summary of the tools learned in the unit, a set of questions providing an opportunity for you to find out how well you learned the material, a series of application exercises, and one or two simulation jobs. The applications review many of the skills acquired in the unit and provide extra practice with those skills. The on-the-job simulation runs throughout the text, with jobs at the end of each unit. These jobs provide additional review as you prepare documents for Singing Wheels Tours, a local charter and tour bus company.

Together, the lesson and unit activities meet the Corel WordPerfect Certification Exam guidelines. These guidelines are established to ensure that you are prepared for work using WordPerfect in today's office workplace.

Following the lessons is a short Capstone Simulation in which you get to put your considerable WordPerfect skills to use as you continue your work at Singing Wheels Tours. Your instructor will tell you whether you are to complete the simulation and, if so, what procedure to follow.

At the back of the text is a set of Quick Reference cards. These cards contain an alphabetical listing of all WordPerfect features learned in the text, together with information about how to choose those features from WordPerfect menus or how to access the features from the keyboard. In addition, the lesson number which covers that feature is listed, in case you wish to refer back to the lesson for review.

It is important that you proceed through the lessons in order. Do not skip around, or you will miss important information about WordPerfect tools. As you work through a lesson, read the information provided in the paragraphs carefully to get the background information for each of the WordPerfect tools. The exercises that provide practice in the use of the tools are printed in a different font face and have numbered steps that lead you though the use of the feature. Follow the steps carefully so you get the expected results with each exercise. Develop the habit of reading through an exercise before you begin it so you have an idea of the purpose of the exercise.

A suggested time is provided at the beginning of each lesson to give you a target time frame for the completion of the lesson. As indicated, this time is just an estimate. The time it will take for you to learn the contents of a lesson will depend on the following variables:

- Is this your first computer class?
- Have you had previous experience with Windows?
- Have you had previous training in WordPerfect?
- Are you learning in an independent setting or in an instructor-led classroom?

Obviously, if you've had extensive computer training, you will progress through the lessons more quickly than you would if this were your first computer class. If you are working in an individualized, self-paced classroom, work carefully and methodically so you don't miss any important information. See how well you can complete the exercises without help from your instructor.

Other Resources

A set of prerecorded documents is available to save keying time as you progress through the lessons. These documents are saved in what's referred to in the text as the student **datafile** folder. When you need to open a prerecorded file, your exercise instructions will clearly specify that the file is in the student **datafile** folder. (These files are available on the *Electronic Instructor* CD-ROM or in one of the text/data disk packages, ISBN 0-538-68534-4 or ISBN 0-538-68536-0.) Check with your instructor about the location of the student **datafile** files.

A Progress Record is located at the end of the text, just before the Quick Reference. The Progress Record lists each document you will be printing as you progress through the lessons. It provides a place for your instructor to check off your work as you complete each lesson. Check with your instructor to find out how you should use the Progress Record.

The WordPerfect reference for Corel WordPerfect 8 comes on CD-ROM. This reference may or may not be available in your classroom. Ask your instructor whether or not you may use the CD containing the reference.

Before You Begin

If you have never before used a computer, study Appendix A before beginning Lesson 1. In that appendix, you will find information about the sophisticated piece of equipment on which you will be working as you learn about WordPerfect and document production. This introduction to the equipment should make you feel more comfortable with the hardware that you will be using.

In addition, if this is your first experience with WordPerfect in the Windows environment, it is imperative that you study Appendices B, C, D, and G.

- Appendix B introduces you to the Windows environment and the many important parts of the WordPerfect working window. It also teaches you how to start and exit from WordPerfect, as well as how to create and save text. You are expected to know this information when you begin Lesson 1.

- Appendix C is an introduction to file management. You'll learn more about file management in some of your lessons.

- Appendix D introduces you to the intricacies of using a mouse.

- Appendix G introduces the Windows 95 environment. If you have not had an introduction to this operating system under which Corel WordPerfect 8 runs, take the time to read through it.

Once you are comfortable with all of the material in Appendices A, B, D, and G and have read through Appendix C, you will be ready to begin your work with Lesson 1.

If you work hard and concentrate as you progress through the material in this text, you are sure to complete the course with a good understanding of what WordPerfect is and how it can help you do your work. Happy learning!

To the Instructor

An *Electronic Instructor* is available to provide you with a variety of instructional materials to be used in the classroom. This *Electronic Instructor* includes a CD-ROM and a printed instructor's manual. On the CD-ROM you will find lesson plans, tests, the prerecorded **datafile** files, solution files, SCANS materials, and much more. You'll have all the materials you need in one convenient location. The materials on the CD-ROM may be copied onto your hard drive or on the classroom network server. The printed manual shows solutions to the hands-on exercises as well as other materials to help you guide users as they learn Corel WordPerfect 8.

Acknowledgments

Many thanks to Judy Voiers for her guidance, inspiration, and friendship as the consulting editor on this project. Thanks, too, to Anne Noschang for holding it all together. As always, much appreciation to Achim, Sara, Peter, Bea, and Chester for their love and support.

Mary Alice Eisch

TABLE OF CONTENTS

iv How to Use This Book
vi Preface
xiii New Features
xiv Start-Up Checklist

UNIT 1 — GETTING STARTED

2 Lesson 1: Introduction to Corel® WordPerfect®
- 2   Before You Begin
- 3   Starting Corel® WordPerfect®
- 3   Creating Text
- 4   Saving a Document
- 5   Viewing a Document
- 7   Printing a Document
- 8   Opening a Document

12 Lesson 2: Moving the Insertion Point and Correcting Text
- 13 Moving the Insertion Point
- 15 Inserting Text
- 16 Deleting Text
- 17 Path and Filename Code
- 18 Typeover
- 18 Select
- 19 Undo, Redo, and Undelete
- 22 Reveal Codes

27 Lesson 3: Text Enhancement
- 27 Caps Lock, Underline, Bold, and Italic
- 28 Fonts
- 31 Formatting Codes
- 32 Convert Case
- 33 Center and Flush Right
- 35 Dot Leaders
- 36 Tabs
- 39 Envelope

44 Lesson 4: Working with Documents
- 44 The Open File Dialog Box
- 47 Favorites
- 48 Insert
- 49 Mass Mailings Using Merge
- 50 The Default Template

UNIT 2 — COREL® WORDPERFECT® BASICS

64 Lesson 5: Text Entry Features
- 64 Deleting Commands
- 66 Indent, Hanging Indent, and Double Indent
- 67 QuickIndent
- 67 Creating Lists
- 68 Outline/Bullets & Numbering
- 69 New Page
- 70 Date
- 71 Center Page
- 73 Hyphen and Space Codes
- 75 Superscripts and Subscripts

79 Lesson 6: Editing Features
- 80 Find and Replace
- 83 Editing with Select
- 85 QuickMenus
- 86 Drag and Drop
- 87 Highlight

91 Lesson 7: Writing Tools
- 91 QuickCorrect
- 93 Spell-As-You-Go
- 94 Spell Check
- 96 Thesaurus
- 97 Grammatik

ix

103 Lesson 8: Windows Tools and File Management
- 103 Toolbar
- 105 Property Bar
- 106 Windows
- 107 File Management
- 109 Open as Copy
- 109 Recent Files
- 110 Printing

UNIT 3 — FORMATTING TOOLS

124 Lesson 9: Page and Paragraph Formatting
- 124 Formatting Defaults
- 125 Line Spacing
- 127 Justification
- 128 Margins
- 130 Tabs
- 131 The Ruler
- 134 Tab Types

139 Lesson 10: Document Formatting
- 140 Headers, Footers, and Watermarks
- 143 Page Numbering in Headers
- 145 Suppress
- 146 Widow/Orphan
- 146 Center Page(s)
- 147 Page Numbering
- 149 Change Page Number Value
- 150 Footnotes and Endnotes

158 Lesson 11: Miscellaneous Formatting Tools
- 158 Advance
- 160 Make It Fit
- 161 WordPerfect Symbols
- 163 QuickWords
- 165 QuickFormat
- 167 Block Protect
- 168 Double Clicking
- 169 Selecting Text
- 169 Default Font and Current Document Style
- 172 Shadow Pointer

176 Lesson 12: Advanced File Management
- 176 Working with Files
- 177 QuickFinder
- 178 QuickMark and Bookmark
- 181 Comment
- 182 File Transfer

UNIT 4 — SPECIAL LAYOUT TOOLS

198 Lesson 13: Tables
- 199 Table Terminology
- 199 Create a Table
- 201 Add Rows; Join Cells
- 202 Adjust Column Width
- 203 Format a Table
- 207 Table Formulas
- 212 Recalculation
- 212 More Formulas
- 215 Table SpeedFormat
- 216 Floating Cells
- 217 Sources of Tables

223 Lesson 14: Outlining and Text Columns
- 223 Outlining
- 227 Text Columns
- 228 Balanced Newspaper Columns
- 229 Hyphenation
- 231 Editing Column Sizes

237 Lesson 15: Forms
- 237 Forms with Tabs
- 240 Divide Page
- 241 Forms with Tables
- 247 Orientation

x

252 Lesson 16: Macros
- 252 Settings
- 253 Record a Macro
- 254 Play a Macro
- 256 Edit a Macro
- 257 Macro with Pause
- 259 Information About Macros

UNIT 5 — MERGE TOOLS

272 Lesson 17: Merge
- 272 Merge Terminology
- 273 Data Files
- 276 Form Documents
- 278 Merging the Files
- 279 Editing a Data File
- 279 Multiple-Line Fields
- 281 Envelopes
- 283 Table Data File
- 284 Troubleshooting a Merge
- 284 Keyboard Merge
- 286 Viewing File Extensions

292 Lesson 18: Putting Merge to Work
- 292 Planning Data Files
- 293 Missing Data
- 296 Merge Options
- 297 POSTNET Bar Codes
- 299 Merge into Tables
- 301 Document Assembly
- 304 Address Book

311 Lesson 19: Sort, Extract, and Select
- 311 Types of Sort
- 312 Line Sort
- 316 Paragraph Sort
- 317 Merge Sort
- 319 Table Sort
- 319 Extract
- 321 Select Records

326 Lesson 20: Labels
- 327 Labels for Mailing
- 330 Name Badges
- 332 Numbered Tickets

UNIT 6 — GRAPHICS TOOLS

346 Lesson 21: Graphics Boxes
- 346 Insert an Image
- 347 Selecting, Moving, and Sizing Boxes, and Adding Captions
- 350 Graphics Box Styles
- 351 Border/Fill
- 352 Customizing a Caption
- 353 Wrap
- 354 Position
- 356 Text Box
- 357 Drag to Create
- 359 Image from File

364 Lesson 22: Working with Images
- 364 Sources of Images
- 366 Image Tools Palette
- 368 Box Styles
- 370 Grouping and Arranging Graphics Boxes

374 Lesson 23: Graphics Lines, Borders, and Fill
- 374 Graphics Lines
- 378 Shapes
- 379 Borders
- 384 Fill

388 Lesson 24: Feature Bonanza
- 389 TextArt
- 391 Drop Cap
- 392 Equation Editor
- 394 Rotate Text
- 395 Line Numbering
- 395 Redline and Strikeout
- 397 Compare
- 397 Booklet Printing

- **411** Capstone Simulation
- **425** Appendix A: The Hardware
- **427** Appendix B: The Corel® WordPerfect® Environment
- **443** Appendix C: File Management
- **447** Appendix D: Using a Mouse
- **450** Appendix E: Codes
- **452** Appendix F: Working with Type
- **454** Appendix G: Introduction to Windows 95
- **461** Glossary
- **469** Index
- **480** Progress Record
- Quick Reference

NEW FEATURES

The Corel WordPerfect 8 software includes the following new features:

- The Power Bar has been replaced with a series of context-sensitive Property Bars to provide the tools needed for the current application.
- The Status Bar has been replaced with the Application Bar which shows, in addition to the usual Status Bar information, the names of all open documents.
- A large number of context-sensitive Toolbars have been added.
- QuickTasks, templates, and Coaches have been combined into a feature called PerfectExpert projects that WordPerfect remembers from one use to another.
- The PerfectExpert panel provides button access to designing and formatting tools for completion of projects.
- The Address Book has been improved, making it possible for you to enter business and home information about your contacts.
- HTML support has been improved to help with the preparation of Web documents.
- A drawing layer has been added that enables you to draw graphics directly into your text, group the objects, and specify the order of the graphics layers.
- TextArt can now be displayed in either 2-D or 3-D format.
- Tools have been regrouped into the menus in a more logical manner.
- The Bullets & Numbering feature now contains full Outline flexibility for creation and editing of outlines.
- The Prompt-As-You-Go feature helps you with spelling and grammatical errors and provides help with finding the correct word (thesaurus).
- The Abbreviations feature is now called QuickWords and has expanded capabilities, allowing you to automate the insertion of frequently used, formatted text.
- The Tables tool includes features that make it easy to split cells and columns and add formatting to your tables.
- The Clipart Scrapbook enables you to drag the desired image into your document. Tens of thousands of graphics images are available on the Corel WordPerfect 8 CD-ROM.

START-UP CHECKLIST

HARDWARE

Minimum Configuration

- ✓ PC using 486 processor operating at 66 MHz
- ✓ 8 Mb RAM
- ✓ Hard disk with at least 50 Mb free disk space
- ✓ VGA monitor with graphics adaptor
- ✓ Mouse or tablet
- ✓ Printer

Recommended Configuration

- ✓ PC using 486 or Pentium processor operating at 66 MHz (faster preferred)
- ✓ 16 Mb RAM (32 Mb preferred)
- ✓ Hard disk with at least 120 Mb free disk space
- ✓ CD-ROM drive, 4x or faster
- ✓ VGA monitor with graphics adaptor
- ✓ Mouse or tablet
- ✓ Printer

SOFTWARE

- ✓ Microsoft Windows 95 or Windows NT 4.0
- ✓ Corel WordPerfect Suite 8 or WordPerfect 8

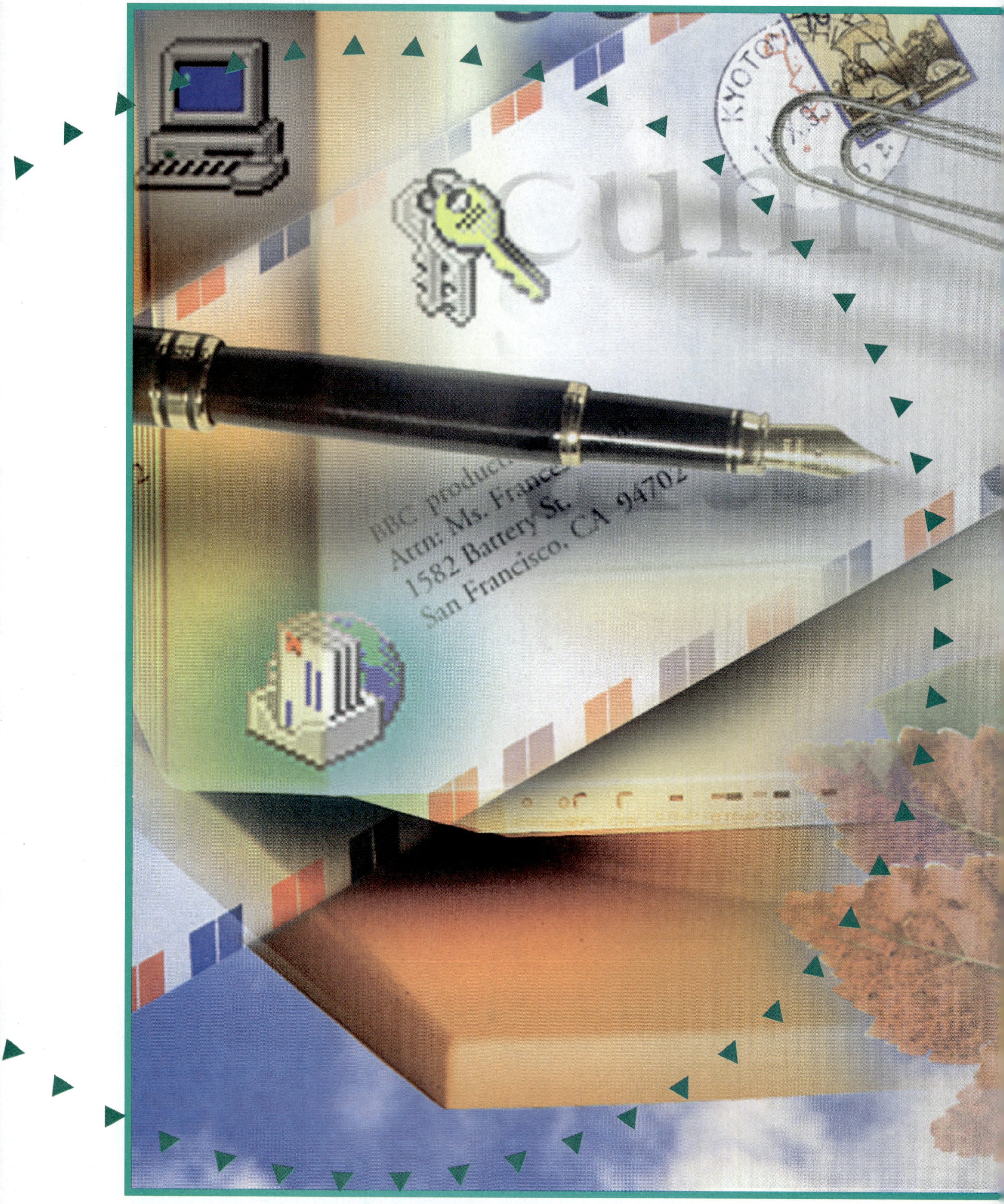
1582 Battery St.
San Francisco, CA 94702
KYOTO

GETTING STARTED

UNIT 1

lesson 1 — 1 hr.
Introduction to Corel® WordPerfect®

lesson 2 — 1.5 hrs.
Moving the Insertion Point and Correcting Text

lesson 3 — 1.5 hrs.
Text Enhancement

lesson 4 — 1 hr.
Working with Documents

Estimated Time for Unit 1: 5 hours

LESSON 1
INTRODUCTION TO COREL® WORDPERFECT®

OBJECTIVES

Upon completion of this lesson, you will be able to:

- Start Corel® WordPerfect® 8.
- Create and save a document.
- View a document in a number of ways.
- Print a document.
- Open a document.
- Use Save As.
- Close a document.
- Exit from WordPerfect.

⏱ **Estimated Time: 1 hour**

You are about to embark on the process of learning to use Corel® WordPerfect® 8 to create, save, and modify files (also known as documents). In addition, you will learn many ways to make your work easier, as well as ways to create attractive documents.

The first thing you need is to be good at starting the program, creating text, saving a file, and closing that file. You need to know how to open a file that has been saved, make changes to that file, and then save it again, either with the same name or with a different name.

Before You Begin

If you have never before used a computer, study Appendix A now to get information about the sophisticated piece of equipment you are using.

In addition, if this is your first experience with WordPerfect for Windows, it is imperative that you study the following appendices:

- Appendix B introduces you to the Windows environment and the WordPerfect working window. It includes exercises to help you learn how to start and exit from WordPerfect and how to create and save text.

- Appendix C is an introduction to file management. Read it. You'll learn more about file management in some of your lessons.

UNIT 1: GETTING STARTED

- Appendix D introduces you to the intricacies of using a mouse.
- Appendix G introduces the Windows 95 environment. If you have not had an introduction to the operating system under which Corel WordPerfect 8 runs, read it.

Assuming you are familiar with the material in the appendices, you can begin by starting WordPerfect and creating a document.

Starting WordPerfect

Beginning at the Windows 95 desktop, start WordPerfect using either a shortcut on the desktop or the Start menu. Your instructor may have some special instructions for starting WordPerfect on your computer.

When the WordPerfect window is showing, compare it with Figure B-2 in Appendix B to see if it looks approximately the same. You should see the Title Bar, Menu Bar, Toolbar, Property Bar, Application Bar, vertical scroll bar, and the insertion point at the guidelines in the upper left corner. The Application Bar should report that you are on *Pg 1*, at *Ln 1"* and *Pos 1"*. When your window looks like the window in Figure B-2, you are ready to begin.

Creating Text

Now let's practice creating a document. Follow the steps in the exercise carefully.

EXERCISE 1.1

1. Key the paragraph illustrated in Figure 1-1. If you misspell or make an error keying a word, WordPerfect will probably underline the word in red. Don't worry about errors! Do NOT press **Enter** at the ends of the lines.

   Just let your text *wrap* to the next line if it doesn't fit on the line above.

2. When you reach the end of the paragraph, press **Enter** twice and continue reading to learn how to save your first document.

NOTE: Keep in mind two important things when keying text:

- When you key text in paragraphs, press **Enter** only at the end of the paragraph or when you purposely want to go to a new line. Allowing the text to wrap to the next line is a very important part of working with computers. If you press **Enter** at the ends of lines within paragraphs, you will cause yourself a great deal of trouble when you try to edit your documents.

- Space twice on the space bar following the punctuation that comes at the end of a sentence. If you are keying work that will be published using desktop publishing or some other electronic method, one space following ending punctuation is preferred. For office work, two spaces are used for readability.

FIGURE 1-1
Text for Exercise 1.1

> Perhaps more than ever before, American public education is an issue of national concern. Major studies have focused on the weaknesses in our education system. These studies cite statistics that appear to reflect a degeneration of teacher and student performance as well as apathy on the part of parents.

Saving a Document

When you have created a document, the first step is to proofread your work. Then you should save it before printing it. If you are going to continue to work with the document, you may keep it open. Otherwise, you will close the document.

You learned to save a document in Appendix B. This involves giving the document a name and selecting the disk or folder where the document is to be saved. All of this takes place in the Save File dialog box.

INTERNET The Internet is a telecommunications system that connects many different networks of computers. The Internet is often called a "network of networks."

When you open the Save File dialog box, the *File name* text box contains *.wpd which is selected, or displayed in reverse video.

It is best to begin by specifying the location for the document. Then provide the name for the document. Let's save this document on your disk in Drive A. (If your instructor specifies a different location, you will have to make the appropriate adjustments to this exercise and all of the exercises that follow.)

For this training, each of your document names will have either three or four parts, with each part separated from the others by a space. The parts will always appear in the same order. You will be asked to include the following:

- A word that briefly describes the subject of the document.

- A set of numbers that identify the lesson and exercise.

- Two or three letters that represent your initials (shown as *xxx* in the exercises).

- WordPerfect's default setting adds the *.wpd* extension to all documents saved in WordPerfect 8 format. Usually that extension does not show with the document name, but it is assumed because when the *File name* text box contains *.wpd,* all of your documents will be listed.

Except for very rare instances, the names of the files will always be given to you in the exercises.

EXERCISE 1.2

1. Open the **File** menu and choose **Save**. The Save File dialog box will open, looking somewhat like Figure 1-2.

2. In the *Save in* text box near the top of the dialog box, look for *3½ Floppy (A:)*. If it doesn't already show there, click the arrow at the right end of the text box and select it from the list. (You might need to use the scroll bar.)

3. At the bottom of the box, in the *File name* text box, key **education 1-2 xxx**, replacing the *xxx* with your initials.

4. When everything is appropriately set, press **Enter** or click the **Save** button at the right of the dialog box.

5. Keep the paragraph in the window as you read on.

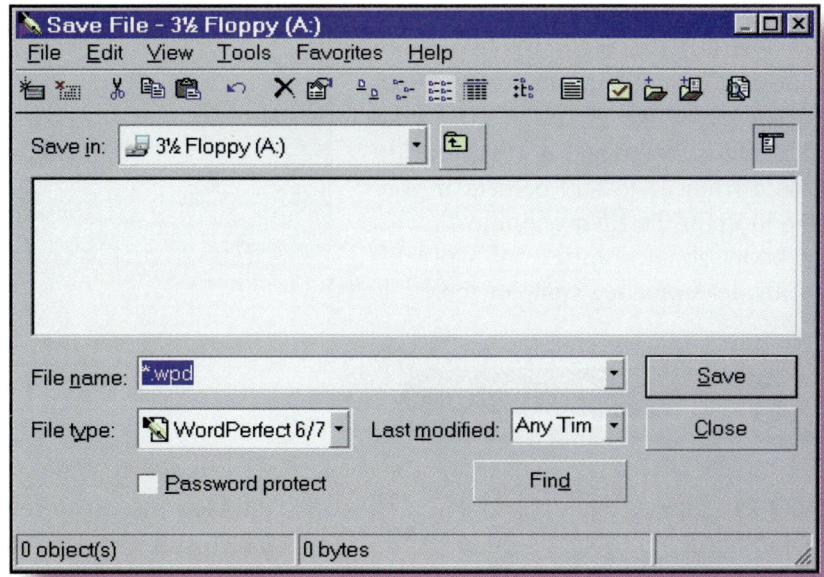

FIGURE 1-2
Save File Dialog Box

Viewing a Document

When working in Corel WordPerfect 8, you may work in one of three views. These views are described in the following list.

- Draft view — shows the text almost exactly as it will appear when printed. Headers, footers, watermarks, footnotes, and margin spaces do NOT show.

- Page view — shows the text exactly as it will appear when printed. Items such as headers, footers, and watermarks appear as they will on the printed page, and the margin spaces are also displayed in Page view. For now, don't worry if you're not familiar with headers, footers, or watermarks.

5

- Two Pages view   shows the document as it appears in Page view, except two small consecutive pages are displayed side by side in the same document window.

The view you choose for your work depends on what you are doing. If you are formatting headers (information that is repeated at the top of each page) or footers (information that is repeated at the bottom of each page), you will probably want to work in Page view so you can see how the headers or footers appear on the page. Draft view responds more quickly as you move through your document, because time is not required to display headers, footers, and other document parts that appear in Page view. In addition, in Draft view you don't have to look at the bottom and top margin spaces of your pages.

Two Pages view is most useful for checking the layout of your documents before printing. The text is so small in Two Pages view that it would be virtually impossible for you to actually edit normally unless you were working with very large letters.

Zoom

If you need more options regarding how you view your documents, you can use Zoom. Zoom can be chosen from the View menu or from the Toolbar. The Zoom button on the Toolbar gives you a list of zoom choices from which to select. Choosing Zoom from the View menu opens a dialog box that looks like Figure 1-3. As you can see, the normal viewing percentage is 100 percent, although you can zoom from 25 to 400 percent if you choose Other at the bottom of the right column.

FIGURE 1-3
Zoom Dialog Box

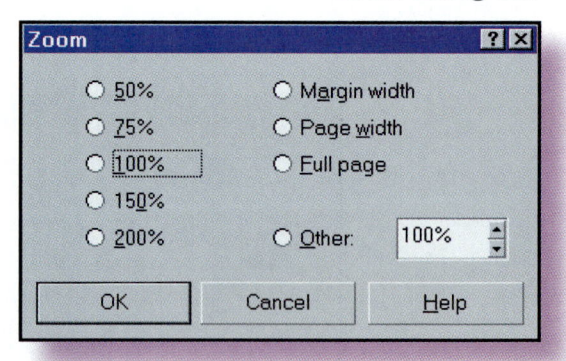

Now that you know about a variety of ways to look at your documents, let's practice some of them.

EXERCISE 1.3

1. With **education 1-2 xxx** showing in the window, press **Ctrl+Home** to make sure your insertion point is at the top of the document. Can you see about an inch of white space (the top margin) above the top margin guideline? If so, you are in Page view.

2. Open the **View** menu and choose **Draft** to go to Draft view. The top margin should disappear. (Ctrl+F5 also selects Draft view.)

3. Open the **View** menu and choose **Two Pages**. Now you should be able to see side-by-side pages of the document.

4. Open the **View** menu and return to **Page** view. (Alt+F5 also selects Page view.)

5. Click the Zoom button on the Toolbar and choose **200%**. Then return to **Zoom** and choose **Full Page**.

6. Finally, use **Zoom** to return to **100%**.

6

UNIT 1: GETTING STARTED

Printing a Document

It is usually a good idea to view your document using Full Page view before printing. Then you can see how the text fits on the page. Viewing this paragraph was less interesting than if you were viewing a letter or a heavily formatted document. In future exercises, you'll see how a longer or fancier document looks using Two Pages view. How you are viewing a document will not affect the way the document looks when it is printed.

Printing in WordPerfect is simple. As with just about anything else you do in WordPerfect, there are a number of ways to print. The method you will probably use the most is to print the full document currently showing in the window.

Print can be chosen from the File menu, the Toolbar, or the Application Bar. On the default Toolbar, the Print button is the fourth button. Whether you choose File, Print, or you click the Print button on the Toolbar or Application Bar, a Print dialog box that looks like Figure 1-4 appears. (You can also choose Print by pressing Ctrl+P.)

Look at the dialog box. At the top you'll see tabs for various print options. Be sure the *Print* tab is chosen. Next you'll see the printer driver for the currently selected printer. If you are working with several printers, you may click the arrow button in the dialog box to change to a different printer before sending the document to be printed.

FIGURE 1-4
Print Dialog Box

At the left in the dialog box are buttons enabling you to choose how many of your pages are to be printed. *Full document* is the default setting. When you choose the Print button, your entire document is sent to the printer. This dialog box provides a number of other options. You'll learn about them in a later lesson. For now, let's print the full document.

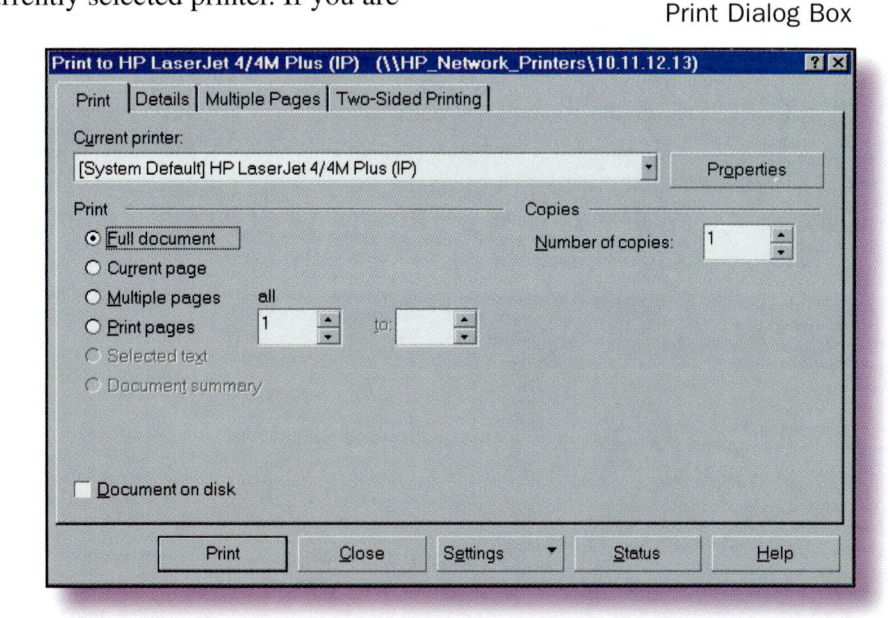

EXERCISE 1.4

1. With **education 1-2 xxx** still showing in the window, choose **File**, **Print**, or click the **Print** button on the Toolbar or on the Application Bar.

2. Compare your dialog box with the one illustrated in Figure 1-4. Your dialog box may show a different printer driver.

(continued on next page)

EXERCISE 1.4 CONTINUED

3. Make sure the printer described at the top of the box matches the printer to which you are connected. You may need to check with your instructor regarding what you need to know about classroom printers.

4. Finally, when everything is ready, click the **Print** button near the bottom of the dialog box (or press Enter because the Print button is selected).

5. Close your document without saving it again. Then retrieve your printed copy from the printer. Congratulations! You have your first document to take home and put on the refrigerator!

Opening a Document

After a document has been saved and closed, you may open it and edit it. You will learn about editing in Lesson 2. Open can be chosen from the File menu or by clicking the second button on the default Toolbar. (The icon on the Open button looks like a small yellow file folder.) When you make either of those choices, the Open File dialog box will appear, looking much like the Save File dialog box—it displays your disk drives or folders and a list of the files saved in each. You can also display the Open File dialog box by pressing Ctrl+O.

In the next exercise we'll open the document you just saved and printed and add your name to it. Then we'll learn about Save As so you can save the document with a different name.

EXERCISE 1.5

1. Open the **File** menu and choose **Open**, or click the **Open** button on the Toolbar.

2. Look at the Open File dialog box. In the *Look in* section at the top, you need to see $3^1/_2$ *Floppy (A:)* because that is where your work is stored. If a different drive or folder appears, click the down arrow and use the scroll bar, if necessary, so you can select $3^1/_2$ *Floppy (A:)*.

3. Look in the large white box in the center. Does your **education 1-2 xxx** document appear?
   a. Yes? Click the icon to the left of the document to select the document.
   b. No? Look at the *File name* text box at the bottom. If it shows **.wpd*, double click to select **.wpd* and change it to **.** (the asterisks represent all files with all extensions). Press **Enter**. Does the file appear now? Click to select the **education** file.

4. With the desired file highlighted, open the file using one of these three methods. Then keep the file open as you read on.
   a. Point to the file and double click to open the file.
   b. Press **Enter** to open the file.
   c. Click the **Open** button at the bottom right of the dialog box.

UNIT 1: GETTING STARTED

With the old document appearing in the window, we'll make a change to the document. Then we'll give it a new name and save it again.

EXERCISE 1.6

1. With your insertion point at the top of the document, key your entire name and then press **Enter** three times. (The paragraph is pushed down on the page when you press Enter.)

2. Open the **File** menu and choose **Save As** to display the Save As dialog box. WordPerfect should remember the name of the current file (displayed in the *File name* box near the bottom of the dialog box) and the location of the current file (in the *Save in* box near the top of the dialog box).

3. Click to the right of the *2* in the document name. Backspace once to delete the *2* and replace it with **6**.

4. Click the **Save** button at the bottom right of the window. The document will be saved in the same location but with a different name.

5. Open the **File** menu and choose **Close**. Your document should be closed without any prompts because you had already saved it.

Summary

Congratulations! You've completed your first lesson! In this lesson you learned a number of important things. You learned that:

- Word wrap puts words that don't fit on one line onto the next line.
- You must use the Save File dialog box to name and save files.
- You close documents using the File menu.
- You can view a document in Draft, Page, or Two Pages view.
- To open a document, you must identify the document and the location of the document.
- Your printer description must match the printer you're using before you print.
- If you close a document that has been modified, WordPerfect will ask if you would like to save it again.
- You can save a document with a different name using Save As.

The skills learned in this lesson will be used many times throughout your training. If you have any questions about anything covered in this lesson, ask your instructor to help you with it before you go on to Lesson 2. Before you do that, however, it is time to review your skills with the Lesson 1 Project.

At the end of each lesson is a short project to review the skills learned in the lesson. As you complete each of the projects, work carefully and thoughtfully. See how much you can do on your own—without having to look back in the lessons for help.

LESSON 1 REVIEW QUESTIONS

TRUE/FALSE

Circle the T if the statement is true. Circle the F if it is false.

(T) F 1. When you are keying text, you do not need to press Enter at the end of each line because your text will automatically wrap to the next line.

T **(F)** 2. To save a document for the first time, you must first name your document and then open the Save File dialog box.

(T) F 3. When working in Corel WordPerfect 8, you may work in one of four views.

(T) F 4. You can choose Zoom from the View menu or press the Zoom button on the Toolbar.

T **(F)** 5. How you view a document will affect the way a document looks when it is printed.

(T) F 6. The icon on the Open button looks like an opening file folder.

WRITTEN QUESTIONS

Write your answers to the following questions.

7. When you start WordPerfect, name at least four features you see in your window.
Title bar, Toolbar, Menu bar, Property bar, Application

8. What does the Application Bar indicate as your position when you start WordPerfect?
Pg 1, at Ln 1" and Pos 1"

9. To what location have you been instructed to save your documents? *3½ floppy.*

10. What are the four ways you can choose Print?
From the File menu, the Application bar, the Toolbar or the Print button.

LESSON 1 PROJECT

SCANS

1. Key the paragraph in Figure 1-5. Remember to let the text wrap at the ends of the lines.

2. At the end of the paragraph, press **Enter** two times. This leaves a double space between the paragraph and any text that might follow it.

3. When you finish, save the document as **matter proj1a xxx**.

4. Print your paragraph.

5. Close the document.

10

UNIT 1: GETTING STARTED

FIGURE 1-5
Text for Lesson 1 Project

> Everything in the universe is made up of matter. This includes all living things, from amebas to whales, from the smallest bacteria to giant sequoias. Matter is anything that occupies space and has mass. Mass is the quantity of matter held by an object. The pull of gravity on the mass of an object gives the object weight.

6. Beginning in a new document window, open **matter proj1a xxx**.

7. Key your name at the top and press **Enter** four times to separate your name from the paragraph.

8. Use **Save As** to save the document again, this time as **matter proj1b xxx**.

9. Print the new version of the document and close it.

CRITICAL THINKING ACTIVITY

SCANS

You are beginning to realize how useful WordPerfect is going to be to you in many ways, especially in completing your assignments for all your other courses. Think about how you will start naming the documents you will be preparing and make a list of possible names you will give them. Make sure you develop a system that will be easy for you to use and remember.

LESSON 2

MOVING THE INSERTION POINT AND CORRECTING TEXT

OBJECTIVES

Upon completion of this lesson, you will be able to:

- Move the insertion point using several methods.
- Delete text using several methods.
- Insert text into existing documents.
- Insert the Path and Filename code into your documents.
- Use Typeover to replace old text with new text.
- Select text for deletion.
- Use Undo, Redo, and Undelete.
- Use the Reveal Codes feature to help you with editing.

Estimated Time: 1½ hours

Editing in WordPerfect is accomplished by moving the insertion point, using the Backspace and Delete keys in a combination of ways, and inserting new material. In this lesson you will learn how to do simple editing, and you'll have several little exercises for practice.

Don't try to learn everything at once. Read the material carefully. Work through the exercises. Make a note of the fact that Lesson 2 is a place you can return to for review later when some of these features may have more meaning. To get the feel of the various keys and features as you study this lesson, you should have some text showing in the window. We'll use a practice document that has been prepared and saved in the student **datafile** folder for you. To open this file, you must know where the data files are saved and how to access them. Your instructor may need to help you open this first file from the student **datafile** folder.

EXERCISE 2.1

1. Open the **File** menu and choose **Open**.

2. Check the *Look in* text box to see if the student **datafile** folder is displayed. If it is not, click the arrow beside the text box and move to the folder containing the data files.

3. Locate the file named **nasa** and open the file, using one of the methods you learned in Lesson 1.

4. When the document appears in your window, open the **File** menu and choose **Save As**.

5. Change the name of the file to **nasa 2-1 xxx**, where *xxx* represents your own initials. For example, if your name is Sara Anne Stewdent, the file name will be **nasa 2-1 sas**. Choose **Save** or press **Enter**.

6. Open the **View** menu and choose **Two Pages** to see how a multiple-page document looks in Two Pages view.

7. Change back to **Page** view, and keep the document in the window as you read on.

Moving the Insertion Point

In order to edit your documents, you need to move the insertion point to the point of correction. WordPerfect 8 offers you a number of ways to move the insertion point in your document. You can move the insertion point with the keys on the keyboard, or you can move the insertion point with the mouse. Let's look at both methods.

Using the Keyboard

THE ARROW KEYS

The up, down, right, and left arrow keys on your keyboard can be used to move the insertion point a line or a space at a time. If Num Lock is turned off, the Number Pad keys 8 and 2 move your insertion point up and down a line at a time. Number Pad keys 4 and 6 move your insertion point left and right a space at a time.

In the set of keys beside Enter and Backspace are four more keys useful for moving the insertion point.

- **Page Up** moves your insertion point backward through your text a full window at a time.

- **Page Down** moves your insertion point forward through your text a full window at a time.

- **Home** moves your insertion point to the beginning of the line on which it is currently located.

- **End** moves your insertion point to the end of the line.

In addition to these single keystrokes for moving the insertion point, a number of keystroke combinations can be used to move from one place on a page of type to another place. Figure 2-1 lists a number of these combinations. The plus between the keystrokes indicates that the first key is held while the other is pressed. For example, with Ctrl+Home, you hold Ctrl while you press Home. This combination always takes your insertion point to the beginning of the document.

EXERCISE 2.2

1. Press **Ctrl+End** to move your insertion point to the end of the document. Look at the *Pg* indicator on the Application Bar. It should report that you are on page 3 of the document.

2. Press **Ctrl+G** and key **3** in the *Page number* text box. Click **OK**. Your insertion point should be moved to the top of the third page.

3. Change to **Two Pages** view and go to the end of the document with **Ctrl+End**.

4. Press **Alt+Page Up** twice to return to the beginning of the document.

5. Return to **Page** view and practice all of the keystrokes in Figure 2-1.

6. When you are comfortable with these keystrokes, move the insertion point to the beginning of page 1 and read on.

FIGURE 2-1
Keystrokes for Moving the Insertion Point

End	moves to the end of the line	Ctrl+→	moves one word to the right
Home	moves to the beginning of the line	Ctrl+←	moves one word to the left
		Ctrl+↑	moves up one paragraph
Page Up	moves to the top of the window	Ctrl+↓	moves down one paragraph
		Alt+Page Up	moves to the first line on the previous page
Page Down	moves to the bottom of the window	Alt+Page Down	moves to the first line on the next page
Ctrl+Home	moves to the beginning of the document	Ctrl+G	Go To enables you to move to a specific page.
Ctrl+End	moves to the end of the document		

Using the Mouse

You can click the insertion point into a new position by positioning it and clicking the left mouse button. If the desired location doesn't show in the window, you can use the scroll bars to move forward or backward in the document until you can see the desired location. Then point and click to position the mouse in that position.

It is important to note that when you move around in a document using the keyboard, the insertion point moves with you. When you use the scroll bars to move in the document, the insertion point remains in its original location until you click it into place.

Look at the vertical scroll bar at the right of your window. It has an arrow at the top and an arrow at the bottom. Between the arrows is a box that indicates how far through a document you are. When the box is at the bottom of the bar, you are looking at the bottom of the document—regardless of the length of the document. When the box is at the top of the bar, you are looking at the top of the document.

The two buttons below the bottom arrow are page turn buttons. The top one moves your view of the document to the top of the previous page. The bottom one moves your view of the document to the top of the next page.

Let's practice moving the insertion point with the mouse.

EXERCISE 2.3

1. With the insertion point at the top of your document, click the **Next Page** button to go to the top of page 2. Click it again to go to page 3.

2. Press the right arrow key on the keyboard. You will be returned to the top of the document because the insertion point remained at that location while you were looking through the document with the page turn buttons.

3. Point to the scroll box and drag it to the bottom of the bar. You should see the white space at the bottom of page 3.

4. Click in that white space. Your insertion point will be positioned at the bottom of the final paragraph of the document.

5. Click on the scroll bar ABOVE the scroll box. You should now see a page break.

6. Click above the scroll box again. Check the Application Bar. It will report that your insertion point is still at the end of the document, on page 3.

7. Click at the end of the side heading *Insulin Infusion Pump*. Look at the Application Bar. It should now report that you are about 7" from the top of page 2.

8. Click the **Previous Page** button so you can see the top of the document. Click to position the insertion point near the top of the page.

9. Practice moving around in the document using the scroll bar and the page turn buttons. Then keep the document open as you read on.

When using the mouse to position the insertion point at the beginning of a line, MAKE SURE THE INSERTION POINT LOOKS LIKE A LARGE "I" BEFORE YOU CLICK. If a fat white arrow is pointing to the right, clicking will tell WordPerfect to select the entire sentence. When selected, the sentence will be displayed in reverse video (white letters on a black background). If that happens, click in that black area to deselect the line and try again.

Inserting Text

It is very easy to insert letters, spaces, and words into text that has already been keyed. To do this, simply position the insertion point at the point immediately following the location for the added material and key the new text. Let's try it. (Are you remembering to read all the way through each exercise before beginning it?)

EXERCISE 2.4

1. With **nasa 2-1 xxx** showing in the window, use **Save As** to save your file as **nasa 2-4 xxx**, remembering to replace *xxx* with your initials.

2. Check to be sure the word *Typeover* isn't showing in the Application Bar. If it is, turn it off by pressing the **Insert** key.

3. Position the insertion point at the end of the word *Administration* in the first line of the first paragraph of the document.

4. Space once and key **(NASA)**. Include the parentheses. Check the spacing around the added text.

5. Position your insertion point between the word *disasters* and the period at the end of the *Weather Forecasting* paragraph. Space once and key **such as hurricanes**. Check the spacing around the added text.

6. Save the document again with the same name. Keep it open while you learn to delete text.

Deleting Text

Text can be deleted with either the Backspace key or the Delete key. Figure 2-2 lists the delete keystrokes and how they may be used in WordPerfect.

FIGURE 2-2
Delete Keystrokes

Backspace removes text to the left of the insertion point, one character or space at a time. Hold down this key to delete several characters quickly. The text to the right of the insertion point will shift to the left to close up the space as you press the Backspace key.

Del and **Delete** are used to delete characters following the insertion point. Again, if you hold the key down, characters will be deleted as they scroll in from the right.

Ctrl+Backspace deletes the word in which the insertion point is located. If you hold the Ctrl key and press Backspace several times, you will delete several consecutive words.

Ctrl+Delete deletes from the insertion point to the end of the line.

EXERCISE 2.5

1. Working with the document you have in your window, try each of the four delete methods listed in Figure 2-2.

2. Watch what happens as you use each method of deletion. Don't worry about destroying the document.

3. When you finish, open the **File** menu and choose **Close**. Do NOT save the changes to the document.

> **TIP**
> If you do something you didn't really mean to do, you can undo it with Ctrl+Z. You must do this immediately.

16

UNIT 1: GETTING STARTED

Now that you know how to insert and delete text, let's make corrections to a document that was keyed and saved with lots of errors. As you will see when the document is open, WordPerfect underlines in red words that might be misspelled. A quick way of correcting those underlined words is available. Because you are learning to insert and delete text, however, you should make the corrections to this paragraph manually.

EXERCISE 2.6

SCANS

1. Beginning in a new document window, go to the student **datafile** folder and open the document named **foreign**. Use **Save As** to save the file with your documents using **foreign 2-6 xxx** as the name, substituting your initials for *xxx* in the file name.

2. Comparing the document in your window with the copy in Figure 2-3, correct the spelling in the words that are displayed in bold.

3. When you finish, keep the document open in the window and read on.

FIGURE 2-3
Text for Exercise 2.6

```
An increasing number of American companies are doing business with
overseas companies.  Most Americans are at a disadvantage in foreign
business negotiations because we are ignorant of their cultural
differences and value systems.  In many cases, foreign business people
have all the power because they have studied our culture and our
language.
```

Path and Filename Code

WordPerfect provides an easy way for you to identify your documents. You can tell the program to insert the file path and file name with the insertion of a simple code. Let's add the code to the document that's open in the window.

EXERCISE 2.7

SCANS

1. Use **Save As** and the procedure in this step to save the file as **foreign 2-7 xxx**, remembering as always to replace *xxx* with your initials. (The Save As procedure listed in Steps a-c saves much unnecessary keying.)

    a. In the *File name* box near the bottom of the Save File dialog box, click the insertion point next to the character to be changed—in this case, the *6*.

    b. Delete the number with either **Backspace** or **Delete**—depending on the location of your insertion point.

    c. Then key **7** in its place. Click **Save**.

    (continued on next page)

Lesson 2 Moving the Insertion Point and Correcting Text

17

EXERCISE 2.7 CONTINUED

2. Move the insertion point to the end of the document and press **Enter** twice.

3. Open the **Insert** menu and choose **Other**. In the cascading menu, choose **Path and Filename**.

4. Look at the information that was added to your document. Note that it was added at the location of the insertion point.

5. Print your file. Then close it, saving it again as you close.

Typeover

While it isn't exactly a delete function, *Typeover* is used to key new text over existing text. You can turn Typeover on by pressing Ins, or Insert. (That may seem backwards, but remember that the Insert mode is the default in WordPerfect.) When you press Insert, the word *Typeover* appears just to the right of center on the Application Bar at the bottom of the window.

When you've made your correction and press Insert again, you return to the Insert mode and the word *Insert* reappears at the bottom of the window. Don't leave Typeover on when you are formatting your documents. Typeover may give you some results that are quite different from what you expect. Let's try a quick practice with Typeover.

EXERCISE 2.8

1. Key the following sentence:

   The dog jumped over the moon and the cat laughed.

2. Position the insertion point to the left of the *d* in *dog*. Press **Insert** and key **cow**.

3. Move the insertion point to the *c* in *cat* and key **dog**. Press **Insert** to return to Insert mode.

4. Close the practice exercise without saving it.

Select

Text can also be deleted by first *blocking,* or *selecting,* it. When text is selected, it shows in reverse video (white on a black background). WordPerfect provides several ways to select text. Once text is selected, you can delete it with either the Delete or Backspace key.

You can select text with the keyboard or mouse in the following ways:

■ Position the insertion point at one end of the text to select, press F8, and use the arrow keys to extend the selection to the desired ending point.

■ Position the mouse pointer at the beginning of the text to select, depress and hold the left mouse button, and drag the pointer to the end of the desired text.

If you make a mistake in selecting text and you still have the mouse button pressed, you can move the pointer around until the correct text is selected. If you have already released the button with the incorrect text selected, you can deselect the text by clicking the left mouse button and beginning again.

The following QuickSelect options are available with the mouse:

- **Word**. Select a word by pointing to it and double clicking.
- **Sentence**. Select a sentence by pointing to it and triple clicking.
- **Sentence**. Point in the left margin opposite the sentence and click once.
- **Paragraph**. Select a paragraph by pointing to it and quadruple clicking.
- **Paragraph**. Point in the left margin opposite the paragraph and click twice.

EXERCISE 2.9

1. Open **education 1-2 xxx**. Point to the word *American* in the first line. Double click to select it.

2. Click once to deselect the word.

3. Point to the word *American* again and double click to select it. Press either **Backspace** or **Delete** to delete the word.

4. For practice, point to the last sentence and triple click to select that sentence. Click to deselect it. Then triple click to select it again and delete it.

5. Finally, point anywhere in the paragraph and quadruple click to select it. Deselect it by clicking once.

6. Close the document without saving it.

Undo, Redo, and Undelete

WordPerfect has several features that enable you to fix certain kinds of mistakes you might make.

Undo (Undo from the Edit menu or Ctrl+Z). You can reverse the last change you made to your document by choosing Undo from the Edit menu or by pressing Ctrl+Z. For example, if you have deleted text from your document and moved the insertion point to a different location, you can use Undo to put the text back in the original location. Undo must be used immediately.

Redo (Redo from the Edit menu or Ctrl+Shift+R). You can reverse the last Undo action by choosing Redo. To see a "history" of your edits using Undo and Redo, choose Undo/Redo History from the Edit menu. WordPerfect will display a list of up to 300 edits in a document. You can reverse several revisions at a time.

Undelete (Ctrl+Shift+Z). If you incorrectly delete text from your document, the deletion is not automatically lost. WordPerfect remembers the last three deletions. You can display the deletions one at a time and restore the proper one at the location of the insertion point when you choose Undelete.

The next two exercises give you an opportunity to practice Undo, Redo, and Undelete. When you finish, be sure you can distinguish among the features. All three features will be useful to you in your work.

NOTE:

- As you key the paragraphs in Exercise 2.10, you may notice that some words are underlined in red and that some of your errors are automatically corrected. Two WordPerfect features that you'll learn about later are responsible for this. Don't worry about it for now.

EXERCISE 2.10

1. Key the paragraphs illustrated in Figure 2-4. Press **Enter** twice following the first paragraph.

2. Choose **Save** from the **File** menu.

3. Save the document as **working 2-10 xxx**, replacing *xxx* with your initials.

4. Press **Enter** twice at the bottom of the document. Then open the **Insert** menu and choose **Other**. Choose **Path and Filename** to identify your file.

5. Choose **Save** from the **File** menu to save the document again.

6. Print the document. Then keep it open for the next exercise.

FIGURE 2-4
Text for Exercise 2.10

```
When you key a document on the computer, key carefully so you don't
make many mistakes.  Most people can "feel" a mistake when they make
it.  Learn to press the Backspace key by touch to correct your errors
as you proceed.

Develop the habit of proofreading all of your work while it is showing
in the window.  At the same time, you might also decide to do some
editing.  Use the skills you learned in this section to move around in
your work quickly and efficiently.
```

Now let's practice using different methods of deleting text and putting the deleted text back into your document. Follow along carefully.

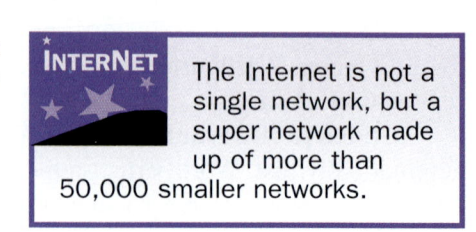

INTERNET
The Internet is not a single network, but a super network made up of more than 50,000 smaller networks.

20

UNIT 1: GETTING STARTED

EXERCISE 2.11

1. Point to the word *proofreading* in the first line of the second paragraph. Double click to select it and press **Delete** or **Backspace** to delete it.

2. Press **Ctrl+Shift+Z**. The text will appear in reverse video with a dialog box that looks like Figure 2-5. The dialog box asks if you'd like to **Restore** or look at the **Previous** deletion. Click **Restore** to put the word *proofreading* back into place.

3. Click to position the insertion point to the left of the word *proofreading*, and space once to fix the spacing between words.

4. Press **Enter** six times after the word *proofreading*. Then choose **Undo** or press **Ctrl+Z** to remove those lines.

NOTE:

No prompt appears with **Undo** because WordPerfect will undo only the LAST change made, as opposed to **Undelete** that remembers the LAST THREE deletions made.

5. Choose **Redo** from the **Edit** menu to put the blank lines back into the text. Then use **Undo** to remove them again.

6. Depress the left mouse button and drag the pointer across any three words in the paragraph. Delete the words. Then choose **Undo** to return the words to their proper location.

7. Delete five consecutive words from anywhere in the document. Then click the insertion point in a different location. Choose **Undo** to return the words to their former location.

8. Delete five consecutive words again. Click the insertion point in a different place in the document and use **Undelete** and then **Restore**. What happens to the five words?

9. Click once to position the insertion point in any word of the paragraph. Watch the window as you press **Ctrl+Backspace** twice to delete that word and the one following it. (This is a method of deletion you used earlier in the lesson.)

10. Practice a little more on these paragraphs. Then close the document without saving. It is probably a mess anyhow.

FIGURE 2-5
Undelete Dialog Box

Reveal Codes

Hidden behind the characters of any word processing text are codes for bold, tab changes, center, temporary margins, etc. You can see the entire text, including the codes, with the Reveal Codes feature. *Codes* are revealed by pressing Alt+F3 or by choosing Reveal Codes from the View menu. When your codes are revealed, the window is split with a gray section at the bottom, as illustrated in Figure 2-6.

The text at the top is separated from the text at the bottom with a double line. The text below the line contains formatting codes, with the codes in boxes that look like buttons.

When you move the insertion point in your document (in the top portion of the window), the insertion point moves in the Reveal Codes view of the document. The insertion point in Reveal Codes is a small red box. Let's work with Reveal Codes.

FIGURE 2-6
Document with Codes Revealed

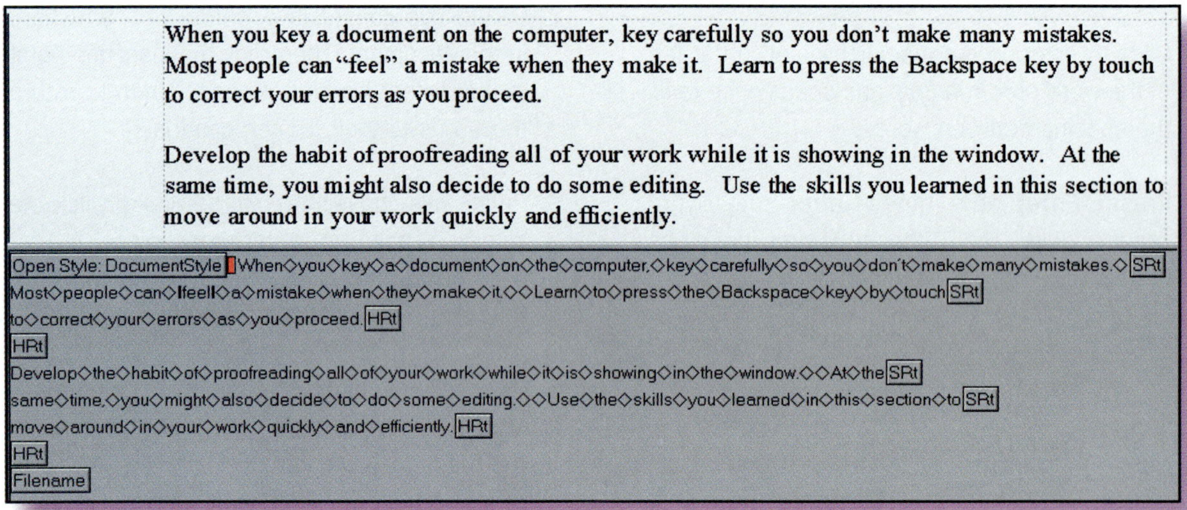

EXERCISE 2.12

1. Open **working 2-10 xxx** again. With the insertion point at the top of the document, choose **Reveal Codes** from the **View** menu, or press **Alt+F3** to reveal your codes.

2. Look at the text in Reveal Codes. The document code [Open Style: DocumentStyle] appears at the beginning of each document. Notice that a diamond character appears between each of the words of text representing the spaces you keyed.

3. Use → to move the insertion point a few characters to the right. Watch the insertion point in both windows as you do this.

4. Look at the [SRt] codes at the ends of the lines. These are the returns that WordPerfect puts at the end of each line when text is wrapped to the next line. These are called *soft returns*.

22

UNIT 1: GETTING STARTED

5. Look at the two *Hard Return* [HRt] codes between the two paragraphs. A Hard Return code is put into your text each time you press **Enter**.

6. Using the form in Appendix E, begin a list of the codes you've seen in your documents. (So far you have seen only the [Open Style: DocumentStyle], [Filename], [SRt], and [HRt] codes.)

7. Close the Reveal Codes window by choosing **Reveal Codes** from the **View** menu or by pressing **Alt+F3**. Then close the document. If you are asked about saving it again, choose **No**.

You can also reveal your codes by pointing to the tiny button above the up arrow at the top of the scroll bar. When your insertion point becomes a two-headed arrow, press the left mouse button and drag the top of the Reveal Codes window to the desired position. That two-headed arrow can also be used to size the Reveal Codes window after Reveal Codes is displayed.

Because the use of Reveal Codes is so important to the editing of your documents, you will be using this feature regularly. Most of the codes are easy to figure out. While you don't need to memorize the codes, you should make a conscious effort to learn to work with them.

Summary

In this lesson you learned the important skills of moving through your document and editing it. For example, you learned that:

- There are a number of different ways to move the insertion point from one location to another in your document.
- The Path and Filename code identifies a document and its location on your disk.
- You can use QuickSelect options to select chunks of text of varying sizes.
- Text can be deleted using a variety of methods.
- You can insert text by positioning the insertion point and keying.
- You can replace text by using Typeover.
- Reveal Codes helps you to see how your document is formatted.

LESSON 2 REVIEW QUESTIONS

MULTIPLE CHOICE

Circle the best answer to each of the following statements.

1. To move your insertion point to the end of the document, press
   - **A.** End
   - **B.** Page Down
   - **C.** Ctrl+End
   - **D.** Ctrl+

(continued on next page)

2. You can delete from the insertion point to the end of the line with the _____ keystroke combination.
   A. Ctrl+Backspace
   B. Ctrl+Delete
   C. Ctrl+End
   D. Ctrl+

3. The Delete key deletes _____ at the insertion point.
   A. characters
   B. words
   C. sentences
   D. lines

4. The QuickSelect option allows you to select a sentence by pointing to it and
   A. double clicking.
   B. triple clicking.
   C. quadruple clicking.
   D. clicking once.

5. You can reverse the last change you made to a document by choosing _____ from the Edit menu.
   A. Undo
   B. Redo
   C. Undelete
   D. Reverse

MATCHING

Write the letter of the term or phrase from Column 2 that best matches the description in Column 1.

Column 1

_C_ 6. Used to restore a deletion at the location of the insertion point.

_A_ 7. Used to key new text over existing text.

_G_ 8. Used when text shows in reverse video.

_D_ 9. Used to see the entire text, including the codes.

_B_ 10. Used by pressing Ctrl+Z.

Column 2

A. Typeover
B. Undo
C. Undelete
D. Reveal Codes
E. Redo
F. Insert
G. Select
H. Path and Filename Code

LESSON 2 PROJECT

SCANS

Let's review some of the skills you learned in Lesson 2. We'll work with a document you used in this lesson.

1. Open **nasa 2-4 xxx**. Use **Save As** to save the file as **nasa proj2 xxx**.

2. Press **Ctrl+End** to move the insertion point to the end of the document. Press **Enter**, if necessary, to add blank lines so you can position your insertion point a double space below the last line of text.

3. Insert the Path and Filename code.

4. Select and delete the paragraph that tells about MRI equipment.

5. Select and delete the side heading for the paragraph you just deleted.

6. Position the insertion point just above the side heading about *wheelchairs*. Use **Undelete** to replace the paragraph in your document. (You'll need to click the **Previous** button to find the paragraph.)

7. Position the insertion point above the paragraph and **Undelete** the side heading for the MRI paragraph. Use **Enter** or **Delete** to make any necessary adjustments to vertical spacing, both in the new location of the MRI section and the old location of that section.

8. Move to the section about *Scratch-Resistant Glasses*. Delete the words *visibility-reducing* in the last line of the sentence. At the end of the sentence, add the words **that reduce visibility for the wearer.**

9. Move to the section about *Flame-Resistant Materials*. In the second line of the second paragraph, insert the word **have** between the words *cable* and *spread*.

10. Save the document again with the same name. (You can do this by simply clicking the Save button on the Toolbar.)

11. Print the document and close it.

2 5

CRITICAL THINKING ACTIVITY

SCANS

You have just come into class and turned on your computer. As soon as you start WordPerfect, you open a document that you worked on yesterday and begin keying new material to add to the first paragraph.

Instead of the new text being added, you see that it is replacing the old text. Determine what is causing this problem. *Duh! The Application bar is set to "type over" instead of "Insert"*

UNIT 1: GETTING STARTED

TEXT ENHANCEMENT

LESSON 3

OBJECTIVES

Upon completion of this lesson, you will be able to:

- Use Bold, Underline, Italic, and Caps Lock to display text attractively.
- Choose fonts from the Font dialog box.
- Discuss the kinds of codes used in formatting your documents.
- Change the case of text with Convert Case.
- Center between margins.
- Align text at the right margin with Flush Right.
- Use dot leaders to lead your attention to text at the right.
- Discuss the use of tabs to indent text.
- Use the tools in the lesson to create a formatted letter, complete with an envelope.

Estimated Time: 1½ hours

Often when you are creating a document, you need a way to make a word or two, or fifteen, stand out from the remainder of the text. You must be careful when you do this so that you don't have so many words "standing out" that the formatting is distracting and the text is difficult to read. With that warning in mind, let's look at some of the ways you can enhance the words in your documents to give them emphasis.

Caps Lock, Underline, Bold, and Italic

Caps Lock, Underline, Bold, and Italic are tools you'll use in your work to add interest to your documents. Except for Caps Lock, these formatting tools can be chosen in a variety of ways. In the section below you'll learn only one method—one that is easy to remember. You'll learn about some of the alternate methods shortly. Don't worry about them for now.

All of these formatting tools must be turned on at the beginning of the text to be formatted. After you have keyed the text, the format must be turned off—usually the same way it was turned on.

Caps Lock. Find the Caps Lock key on your keyboard. The Caps Lock key, as well as the AB button on the Application Bar may be used to tell WordPerfect you want all letters keyed to be capitals. On most keyboards, a light tells you when you have Caps Lock turned on. The AB button also appears to

27

be depressed when Caps Lock is on. Caps Lock affects only alphabetic keys. It doesn't enable you to key symbols, such as $, #, or %. The use of Caps Lock does NOT put any codes in your documents.

Underline. An easy way to turn Underline on is to hold the Ctrl key while you key U. When you have Underline on, your text will be underlined as you key it. To stop underlining, press Ctrl+U again. The Underline code is [Und].

Bold. Press Ctrl+B for bold. When Bold is turned on, any text you key will show in bold. Bold is turned off the same way you turned it on—by pressing Ctrl+B. The Bold code is [Bold].

Italic. Italic can be turned on and off with Ctrl+I. Any text you key while Italic is turned on will appear in italic. The code for italic is [Italc].

EXERCISE 3.1

1. Press the **Caps Lock** key and key your name. Don't worry if a red underline appears. Press **Caps Lock** again to turn it off, and press **Enter** two times.

2. Save your exercise as **appearance 3-1 xxx**.

3. Key your name again in all lowercase letters. Choose **Reveal Codes** from the **View** menu and note that there is no code for capital letters.

4. Press **Enter** twice. (Keep your codes revealed so you can see them as you add to this document.)

5. Press **Ctrl+U** to turn on Underline. Key your name using "initial caps" (that's a capital letter at the beginning of each "word" in your name). Press **Ctrl+U** again to turn off Underline. Press **Enter** twice. Look at the Underline codes that surround the Underlined text.

6. Press **Ctrl+B** to turn on Bold. Key the words **WordPerfect Word Processing**. Notice that the words show in bold in your document. Press **Ctrl+B** to turn off Bold again, and press **Enter** twice. Look at the Bold codes.

7. Press **Ctrl+I** to turn on Italic. Key your name one more time and turn Italic off. Press **Enter** two more times. Key your name one final time so you can compare the normal text with the text formatted with **Italic**, **Bold**, and **Underline**. Press **Enter** twice.

8. Save the file. Keep it in the window for the next exercise.

As you can see, it is very easy to format characters as you key them by using what are known as *keyboard shortcuts*. Now let's look at another place where you can make changes to the appearance of your text.

Fonts

One way to change the appearance of text in WordPerfect is by changing the font face or the font size. If you have never before worked with fonts or if your knowledge of fonts is sketchy, Appendix F provides you with terminology and information important to the use of fonts. Please study that appendix before leaving Lesson 3.

The default font for Corel WordPerfect 8 is 12-pt. Times New Roman. However, a wide variety of both serif and sans serif fonts are available through Windows, WordPerfect, and through your printer driver.

You can change fonts in the following ways:

- Open the Format menu and choose Font to open the Font dialog box.
- Select the font from the Property Bar drop-down menu. As you browse through this list, WordPerfect provides a preview of each font.
- Press F9 to open the Font dialog box. The appearance of each font is previewed here, too.
- Choose recently used fonts from the QuickFonts list.

Let's explore fonts.

EXERCISE 3.2

1. With **appearance 3-1 xxx** showing in the window, use **Save As** to save the file as **appearance 3-2 xxx**.

2. Press **Ctrl+End** to be sure your insertion point is at the bottom of your document.

3. Look at the Font Face button on the Property Bar. It is probably the first button. What is the name of the font that is listed? Look at the next button. What font size is chosen?

4. Open the **Format** menu and choose **Font**. It's at the top of the menu. The Font dialog box should open, looking much like Figure 3-1.

5. Look at the font face listed in the *Font face* portion of the dialog box. Is it Times New Roman, or is your computer set for a different font?

6. Does the selected font size match the size on the Property Bar button? It is probably set at 12 pt., but something different might be chosen.

7. Without making any changes, click **OK** and key a sentence naming the font face and font size using the following sample: **The current font is 12-pt. Times New Roman. Press Enter** twice.

8. Open the Font dialog box again. This time do it by pressing **F9**. The font faces are listed alphabetically. Scroll through the list of font faces until you find *Arial*. Click to highlight **Arial** and change the font size to **20 pt**.

9. Look at the following parts of the dialog box:
   a. The preview area at the bottom of the dialog box. It should show a sample of Arial Regular 20-pt. type.
   b. The Appearance section where you can choose Bold, Italic, Underline, and a number of other attributes.
   c. The other features, such as color, in the right section of the dialog box.

10. Click **OK** to close the dialog box.

11. Key another sentence identifying the new font face and size. (If you have forgotten what you chose, look at the Property Bar buttons.)

12. Press **Enter** twice. Save the file and keep it open for your next exercise.

(continued on next page)

FIGURE 3-1
Font Dialog Box

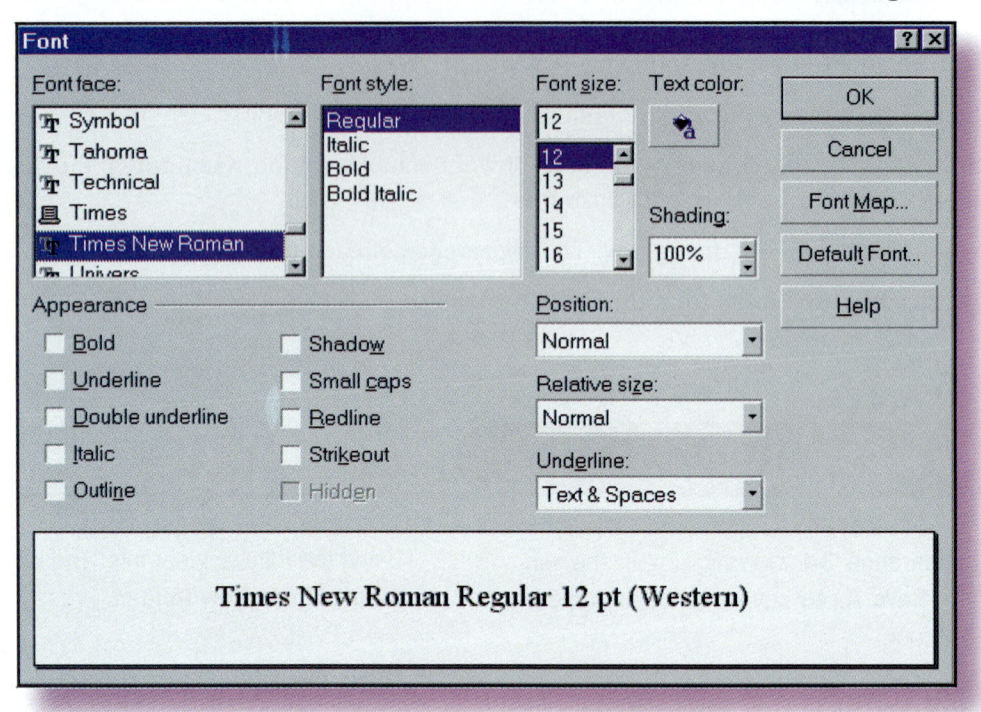

QuickFonts

The QuickFonts button on the default Property Bar compiles a list of the most recent 10 font faces and sizes that you have used. As you use more fonts, the oldest will "fall off" from the bottom of the list. QuickFonts saves you time in going back to frequently used font faces and sizes. Let's see how easy it is to use QuickFonts.

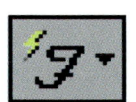

EXERCISE 3.3

1. With **appearance 3-2 xxx** showing in the window, use **Save As** to save the file as **appearance 3-3 xxx**.

2. With your insertion point a double space below the second sentence you keyed in Exercise 3.2, click the **QuickFonts** button on the Property Bar. (If your Property Bar has been edited and the QuickFonts button has been removed, you will not be able to do Steps 2–4 of this exercise.)

3. Find *Times New Roman 12* (not italic) in the drop-down list and select it.

4. Key your name one more time and press **Enter** three times.

5. Look at all of the codes in your document. Add them to the list you are keeping in Appendix E.

6. Add the Path and File name code to the bottom of your document. Then print it.

7. Close the file, saving it one more time.

30

UNIT 1: GETTING STARTED

Formatting Codes

Formatting codes fall into two categories—open codes and paired codes. Open codes are codes that appear in the document at the beginning of the text to be formatted. With open codes, the format continues in effect until another code is entered to change that particular format.

Paired codes "enclose" the text they format. Bold, Underline, and Italic are paired codes. You probably noticed that they point toward the text to be formatted. If you delete one of the pair, both codes will be removed, and the text will return to a normal format.

The exercise you just printed was fine to introduce changes in appearance. But the examples were not quite what you would have in a normal document. Let's key a short paragraph using your new knowledge.

EXERCISE 3.4

1. Beginning in a new document window, key the paragraph illustrated in Figure 3-2. Use **Caps Lock**, **Bold**, **Italic**, and **Underline**, as shown. Substitute the name of your school for the name in the paragraph.

2. When you finish keying, save the document as **appearance 3-4 xxx**. Then press **Enter** twice and insert the Path and File name code.

3. Press **Ctrl+Home** to return to the beginning of the document. Reveal your codes.

4. Look at the [Bold] codes, the [Italc] codes, and the [Und] codes. Do you see any [HRt] codes? The only ones should be at the end of the paragraph.

5. Turn off Reveal Codes.

6. Position the insertion point at the end of the paragraph. Press **Enter** twice so the insertion point is halfway between the paragraph and the Path and File name code.

7. Press **F9** to open the Font dialog box. In the Appearance section, choose **Bold**, **Underline**, and **Italic**. Click **OK** to close the dialog box.

8. Key the name of your school.

9. Finally, print your document and close it, saving it again with the same name.

FIGURE 3-2
Text for Exercise 3.4

WINCHESTER BUSINESS COLLEGE provides all kinds of classes on computers for eager students. One of the popular areas of training is **word processing** training since **word processing** is widely used in the *Fox River Valley* area. This is a course using the **COREL WordPerfect 8 for Windows** word processing program. Students find that WordPerfect is <u>easy to learn</u> and <u>easy to use</u>.

FIGURE 3-3
Property Bar Bold, Italic, and Underline Buttons

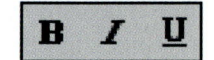

So far, you know that you can use keyboard shortcuts for Bold, Italic, and Underline and that you can make those choices from the Font dialog box. These attributes can also be chosen from the Property Bar. Figure 3-3 illustrates the buttons for these choices. To use the Property Bar buttons, simply click the Bold button to turn on Bold. Click it again to turn off Bold. Use the same procedure for Italic and Underline. We'll use these buttons in your next exercise.

Applying Attributes to Selected Text

As you've worked with Bold, Underline, and Italic, you've been instructed to turn the attribute on, key the text, and turn the format off. It is possible to format something that has already been keyed without having to delete the text and rekey it. To do so, you must first select the text.

In Lesson 2 you learned several ways of selecting text for the purpose of deleting that text. Deleting is only one of many things you can do with selected text. Let's practice adding appearance attributes to selected text.

EXERCISE 3.5

1. Open **foreign 2-7 xxx**. Use **Save As** to save the file as **foreign 3-5 xxx**.

2. Click to position the insertion point in the word *American* in the first line. Then click the **Bold** button on the Property Bar to bold the word. Bold the word *Americans* in the second line using the same procedure.

3. Position the insertion point in the word *companies* and click the **Italic** button to italicize the word. Repeat the procedure for the other occurrence of *companies*.

4. Point to the last sentence of the paragraph and triple click to select it. Click the **Underline** button on the Property Bar to add underline to that sentence.

5. Use the mouse to drag across the words *cultural differences*. Add both **Bold** and **Italic** to the selected text. Repeat the procedure with *value systems*.

6. Click the **Save** button on the Toolbar (the third button from the left), but keep the document open for the next exercise.

Convert Case

Occasionally, you'll key something in lowercase that should be in uppercase. Or you'll key something in uppercase that should be in lowercase. It is time-consuming to delete and rekey the text correctly. WordPerfect offers you a feature called *Convert Case* that enables you to change the case of selected text.

Convert Case is chosen from the Edit menu. Let's practice on our little practice document. (It already is jammed full of special effects!)

UNIT 1: GETTING STARTED

EXERCISE 3.6

1. With **foreign 3-5 xxx** open in the window, use **Save As** to save the file as **foreign 3-6 xxx**.

2. Drag across the words *foreign business people* to select them.

3. Open the **Edit** menu. Choose **Convert Case** and then **UPPERCASE**.

4. Select the word *American* in the first line. Return to **Convert Case** and choose **UPPERCASE** for the word at the insertion point.

5. Do the same for *Americans* in the second line.

6. Position the insertion point in the word *FOREIGN* that is in uppercase letters and press **Ctrl+K**.

7. Select the word *AMERICAN* in the first line. Go to **Convert Case** and choose **Initial Capitals**. Do the same with *AMERICANS* in the second line.

8. Print the practice document. Then close it, saving it again with the same name. (Are you remembering to put your initials in the *xxx* locations?)

Note that to change the appearance of text with bold or italic, you didn't need to select the text. You only needed to position the insertion point in the word. With Convert Case you don't need to select the text if you use the keyboard shortcut (Ctrl+K). If you use the Edit menu, the text must be selected.

Also, in the sentence that you underlined, you triple clicked to select the sentence. That included the period at the end of the sentence. Normally the ending punctuation isn't underlined. To select the sentence and NOT the period before applying the underline, you would need to use the mouse to drag across the words in the sentence to select them—up to the period. Then apply the underline attribute. You can practice more with that at your leisure.

Center and Flush Right

As you learned in the previous sections, text can be enhanced with character formatting such as bold or italic. The location of the words on the page can also make a difference in how text is perceived. For example, centering text or aligning it at the right margin makes some kinds of text stand out from the other text on the page.

Center. You can automatically center a line of text between the margins by pressing Shift+F7 or by opening the Format menu, choosing Line, and then choosing Center. You can give the command before you key the text, or you can position the insertion point at the beginning of the line to be centered and give the command. Press Enter to end centering.

Flush Right. To make a short line end even with the right margin *(flush right)*, press Alt+F7 or open the Format menu, choose Line, and then choose Flush Right. If you give the command before you key the text, it will "back up" from the right margin as you key. If you give the command after the text has been keyed, the insertion point must be at the left of the text to be formatted with Flush Right. Press Enter to end flush right.

EXERCISE 3.7

1. Press **Shift+F7** and key your full name. End by pressing **Enter**. Is your name centered between the guidelines?

2. Beginning at the left margin, key your name again. Press **Enter**.

3. Position the insertion point at the beginning of the first letter of the name at the left margin. Press **Shift+F7** to center the name again. Press **Ctrl+End** to go to the end of the "document."

4. Press **Alt+F7** and key today's date. Press **Enter**. Does the date end at the guideline for the right margin?

5. Key the date beginning at the left margin. Position the insertion point at the left of the date and press **Alt+F7** to move the date to the right margin.

6. Look at the Center and Flush Right codes in Reveal Codes. Add them to your list. Then close the document without saving it.

Now let's use your new skills with Center and Flush Right on a real exercise. Work quickly and efficiently. Then we'll practice printing from the disk rather than from the window.

EXERCISE 3.8

1. Center the title of the exercise in Figure 3-4 on page 35. Format the title with **Bold** and **Caps Lock**. Press **Enter** three times after the title. (This is a *triple* space. You will be using triple spaces often.)

2. Key the name of the character at the left. Then give the command for Flush Right and key the name of the actor or actress.

3. Insert the Path and File name code a double space below the last line of the exercise. NOTHING WILL SHOW because your document does not yet have a name.

4. Save the document as **music 3-8 xxx** and close it.

5. Open the **File** menu and choose **Open**. Click once to highlight the file named **music 3-8 xxx**. In the Open File dialog box, open the **File** menu and choose **Print**. Close the Open File dialog box.

> **INTERNET**
>
> Users of the Internet include schools, government agencies, businesses, libraries, colleges and universities, military bases, and more. Every year, in addition, more and more people can access the Internet from their homes.

FIGURE 3-4
Text for Exercise 3.8

```
                        CAST
Professor Harold Hill                    Charlie Stowe
Marian Paroo                              Sally Martin
Mrs. Paroo                               Lindsey Chang
Winthrop Paroo                           Phil Holverson
Mayor Shinn                              Jeff Rodriguez
Eulalie Mackeckine Shinn                 Doris Derkson
Tommy Washburn                           James Timanez
Zeneeta Shinn                          Brianna Boscobel
```

Dot Leaders

Dot leaders can easily be added to material that is formatted with Flush Right. Simply press Alt+F7 twice (instead of only once) before keying the text at the right. The result will be a document that looks like this small section of the exercise above.

Professor Harold Hill . . . . .Charlie Stowe
Marian Paroo. . . . . .Sally Martin

You can also add dot leaders to text that has already been keyed. Reveal your codes and align the insertion point at the beginning of the text following the Flush Right command. Press Alt+F7 and watch the dot leaders appear. Let's try dot leaders.

EXERCISE 3.9

1. Key **Marian Paroo** at the left margin. Press **Alt+F7** twice and key **Sally Martin**. See the leaders? Press **Enter** twice.

2. Key **Marian Paroo** at the left margin again. Press **Alt+F7** and key **Sally Martin**.

3. Position the insertion point just to the left of *Sally* and press **Alt+F7** again. Voila!

4. Close your practice without saving.

Dot leaders are very useful in drawing your attention from one side of the page to another. They are often used in financial statements and in programs like the one in Exercise 3.8.

Lesson 3 Text Enhancement

Tabs

The Tab key is located next to the letter *Q*. It is normally used to indent the first line of a paragraph. WordPerfect's tabs are preset at each half inch. These tab stops can easily be changed. You'll learn to do that in a later lesson.

ALWAYS use the Tab key instead of the space bar to indent lines from the left margin so each paragraph is indented an even amount of space. Sometimes you may need to press the Tab key several times to move the insertion point to where you want it to be.

The Tab key can also be used to tab to the left. To do so, you must hold the Shift key while you press Tab. That's why the Tab key often has an arrow pointing to the left along with the arrow pointing to the right.

Let's create a short four-paragraph document. Each of the paragraphs should be indented with Tab.

EXERCISE 3.10

SCANS

1. Key the four short paragraphs illustrated in Figure 3-5. At the beginning of each paragraph, press **Tab** once and begin keying. Key each paragraph continuously. Press **Enter** twice between paragraphs.

2. When you finish the last paragraph, press **Enter** twice.

3. Proofread carefully and correct any errors that you detect. Save your document as **gifts 3-10 xxx**.

4. Insert the Path and File name code a double space below the final paragraph.

5. Print your file and close it, saving it again as you close it.

FIGURE 3-5
Text for Exercise 3.10

```
    Regardless of the country where you are presenting a gift to a
host or business associate, there are some general guidelines regard-
ing international gift giving.

    Flowers are acceptable in most cultures, but in many countries you
should avoid red roses because they signify romantic interest.  Also,
in most European countries, white flowers and chrysanthemums are given
only for condolences or sympathy.  Avoid giving an even number of
flowers, and unwrap the flowers before presenting them to the recipi-
ent.

    Chocolates or gifts of candy are usually appropriate.  Be careful
not to give candy manufactured in a rival country.

    Gifts with company logos are usually acceptable, providing the
logo is small and unobtrusive.  In some countries, caps and T-shirts
with logos are considered souvenirs, not gifts.
```

UNIT 1: GETTING STARTED

Now let's create a letter that uses Tab. The letter is longer than one page. When you are about two-thirds of the way through the letter, a line will appear across the window that separates page 1 from page 2. (This line is called a *soft page break*.) If you are working in Page view, you will also see the bottom margin space on the first page and the top margin space on the second page. Don't worry about the location of the page break or a second page heading. We'll return to this letter later and fix it.

The first thing we'll do in this document is give it a 2" top margin. We'll do this by adding extra space at the top of the letter with the Enter key. You can watch the *Ln* indicator in the Application Bar so you know when you've pressed Enter enough times. This is called "giving your document a 2" top margin." You'll be doing it often!

Then we'll use Tab to move the date to a location near the center. The same procedure will be used to position the closing lines of the letter.

EXERCISE 3.11

SCANS

1. Prepare the letter in Figure 3-6 on page 38. Press **Enter** until the *Ln* indicator says approximately *2"* to give your letter a 2" top margin.

2. Press **Tab** as many times as necessary to move the insertion point to **Pos 4"** and key the current date. Spell out the date; e.g., **July 1, 199x**. Follow the date with a quadruple space (press **Enter** four times).

3. Key the inside address and the greeting at the left margin.

4. Use **Center** and **Bold** for the subject line.

5. Use **Tab** to indent each line of the display matter in the body of the letter. (QuickCorrect will cause the *T* of *Time difference* to appear as a capital letter. Use **Backspace** to delete the *T* and change it to lowercase. It may take two tries.)

6. At the end of the letter, tab to **Pos 4"** for the complimentary closing. Press **Enter** four times after the closing and key your name, again at **Pos 4"**.

7. Save the letter as **sasoot 3-11 xxx**. Press **Enter** two more times below the enclosure notation and insert the Path and File name code at the left margin.

8. Open the **View** menu and choose **Two Pages** so you can see the entire document at once. Then proofread the letter carefully and print it.

9. Whoops! The list in the letter should have been in bold. Select the entire list and give the Bold command to change the items to bold.

10. Print the letter and save the letter again. Keep it open for the next exercise.

(continued on next page)

FIGURE 3-6
Text for Exercise 3.11

(Current Date)

Mr. Antonio Larsen
Suite 334
789 Embassy Drive
Sasoot 3G76H
GRAPHIA

Dear Mr. Larsen:

Subject: International Awareness

We are aware that there has been an increase in the amount of trade between businesses in your country and ours. We are launching a project to learn more about some of the differences and similarities between our homelands.

Our project will begin with some geographic basics that will provide our company's administrative assistants with information needed for international communications and to arrange for international travel. Some of the topics about which we'd like information are listed below:

    time difference
    currency used
    exchange rate
    telephone prefix
    climate
    language spoken
    type of government
    location of international airport
    housing opportunities
    cultural practices affecting trade
    major products of your country

Your name and address were provided by a mutual friend who has traveled to Graphia. He was certain you would be willing to pass this request on to someone who could provide some answers to help us with our project.

Also, if you have any brochures describing your country, please send them. A map of Graphia, as well as a map of Sasoot or any of your other major cities, would be wonderful! Information of this type is extremely valuable in visualizing a place never visited. I am enclosing a brochure about our city that you may share with your coworkers.

Thank you for your help with this endeavor.

                Sincerely,

                (Your Name)

Enclosure

Envelope

Since you're not likely to hand deliver this letter to Sasoot, you need an envelope in which to mail it. WordPerfect has made the preparation of envelopes easy, providing you have a printer that will print envelopes. Most ink jet and laser printers will print envelopes if you hand-feed them. For one envelope at a time, that shouldn't be too bad.

To create an envelope, simply choose the Envelope feature from the Format menu. WordPerfect will do the rest of the work for you. We'll try it in an exercise. Before you begin the exercise, check with your instructor to see if you can print envelopes on the classroom printer. Your instructor may wish to give you special instructions.

EXERCISE 3.12

1. Open the **Format** menu and choose **Envelope**. A dialog box will open that looks much like Figure 3-7. (Printer differences might affect some of the envelope settings.) You'll see that WordPerfect picked up the inside address from the letter and inserted it into the *Mailing addresses* location in the dialog box.

2. Click in the *Return addresses* box and key your own name and return address to be printed in the upper left corner of the envelope.

(continued on next page)

FIGURE 3-7
Envelope Dialog Box

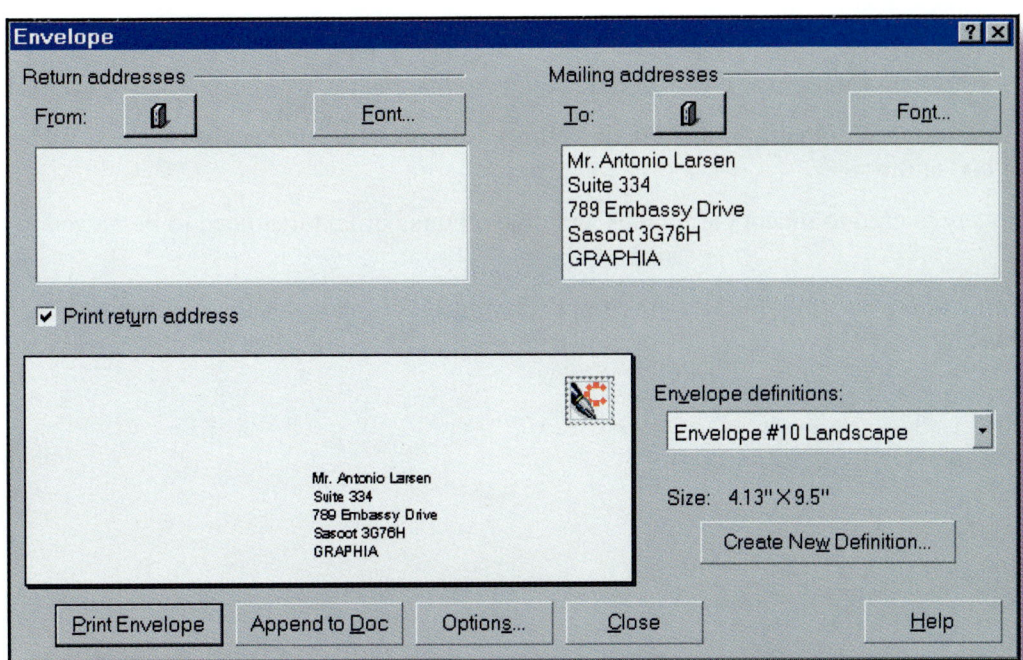

> **EXERCISE 3.12 CONTINUED**

3. Click the **Print Envelope** button at the bottom of the dialog box. Your printer may prompt you when it is ready to print the envelope. You may do one of the following to print the envelope:
   a. Insert a regular envelope.
   b. Cut a piece of paper to measure 9.5" x 4" and feed that into your printer in place of the envelope.
   c. Turn your letter over and print the "envelope" on the back of the page.

4. After printing, close your document without saving it again.

Summary

As you learned in this lesson, WordPerfect makes it easy for you to enhance your text in a number of ways. You learned that:

- You can use attributes such as Caps Lock, Bold, Underline, and Italic to make sections of text stand out from the rest of the document.
- A wide variety of font faces and sizes are readily available.
- Some formatting codes come in pairs that format the text between the pairs.
- Some formatting codes affect the document forward from the point where they are inserted.
- You can apply appearance attributes to text that has already been keyed by first selecting the text to be formatted.
- Convert Case enables you to change text between uppercase and lowercase.
- Short lines of text can easily be centered between the margins.
- Text can be aligned at the right margin, sometimes using dot leaders between the text at the left and the text at the right.
- The Tab key is used to indent paragraphs and other chunks of text that need to be moved to the right.
- WordPerfect automatically formats envelopes for your letters and adds the mailing address in the proper location.

LESSON 3 REVIEW QUESTIONS

MULTIPLE CHOICE

Circle the best answer to each of the following statements.

1. To turn on Bold, you can press the Bold button on the Property Bar, or you can press
   - **A.** Caps Lock+B
   - **B.** Shift+B
   - **(C.)** Ctrl+B
   - **D.** Alt+B

2. If you wish to turn on Italic along with several other Appearance attributes, you can do it in the _____ dialog box.
   - **A.** Format
   - **(B.)** Font
   - **C.** Appearance
   - **D.** Print

3. Formatting codes fall into two categories which are
   - **A.** open codes and closed codes
   - **B.** closed codes and double codes
   - **C.** single codes and double codes
   - **(D.)** open codes and paired codes

4. Which of the following ways is NOT a way to change fonts?
   - **(A.)** Open the Format menu and choose QuickFormat
   - **B.** Use the QuickFonts list
   - **C.** Select from the Property Bar drop-down menu
   - **D.** Press F9 to open the Font dialog box

5. The QuickFonts feature compiles a list of the _____ most recent font faces and sizes you have used.
   - **A.** five
   - **(B.)** ten
   - **C.** fifteen
   - **D.** twenty

FILL IN THE BLANKS

Complete each of the following statements by writing your answer in the blank provided.

6. To add attributes to text that has already been keyed, you must first __select__ it before applying the attribute.

7. WordPerfect offers you a feature called __Convert Case__ that enables you to change the case of selected text.

(continued on next page)

8. By pressing Alt+F7, you will format text with <u>right margin justified</u>.

9. ALWAYS use the <u>Tab</u> key to indent lines from the left margin so each paragraph is indented an even amount of space.

10. To create an envelope in WordPerfect, simply choose the Envelope feature from the <u>Format</u> menu.

LESSON 3 PROJECT

SCANS

Let's test your understanding of the features learned in Lesson 3. Work quickly and efficiently. How much can you do without referring to the instructions in the lesson?

1. Key the paragraphs illustrated in Figure 3-8. **Center** and **Bold** the title.

2. Use **Tab** to indent the first line of each paragraph. Use **Bold**, **Underline**, and *Italic*, as shown in the figure. (The two hyphens in the first line may change to a dash. That's OK.)

> **NOTE:**
>
> Be careful when you use Bold, Underline, or Italic near the end of a sentence. The period at the end of the sentence should not be formatted with the same formatting applied to the words preceding it.

FIGURE 3-8
Text for Lesson 3 Project

The Skeleton

The SKELETON is composed of two parts--the **axial skeleton** and the **appendicular skeleton**. The **axial skeleton**, consisting of about **80** bones, includes the <u>spine, ribs, sacrum, sternum, and cranium</u>. The **appendicular skeleton**, which contains **126** bones, includes the bones of the <u>arms, legs, pelvis, and shoulders</u>.

Bones are made up of both *organic* and *inorganic* material. The tough outer membrane of the bone is called the periosteum (*per-ee-ahs-tee-um*). If you want to study more about the skeleton, read THE HUMAN FRAME.

---

3. When you finish keying, save the document as **skeleton proj3 xxx**.

4. Position the insertion point a double space below the second paragraph and insert the Path and File name code.

UNIT 1: GETTING STARTED

5. Select the title and use **Convert Case** to change the title to all uppercase letters.

6. Click in the word *periosteum* in the second line of the second paragraph and change it to **Bold** and **Italic**.

7. Select *THE HUMAN FRAME* in the last line and add **Italic** to the formatting.

8. Press **Ctrl+Home** to move the insertion point to the beginning of the document. Change the font face to **Arial** or some other sans serif font. Change the font size to **14 pt.**

9. Print your document and close it, saving it again with the same name.

CRITICAL THINKING ACTIVITY

SCANS

The small group assignment for your Environmental Science Class is to research and write a report on the endangered species of Florida's Everglades. Everyone in your group has worked hard searching the Internet for information, as well accumulating material from the library and other sources.

You have offered to key the report using your knowledge of WordPerfect. The report is now 50 pages long, and you want to make it look very professional. What are some of the attributes you could add to enhance the text of your report, and where would you apply them?

LESSON 4

WORKING WITH DOCUMENTS

OBJECTIVES

Upon completion of this lesson, you will be able to:

- Discuss the addition of the *.wpd* extension to your document names.
- Change viewing options in the Open File dialog box.
- Delete items from the Favorites list.
- Add items to the Favorites list.
- Insert one document into another.
- Perform a simple Merge operation.
- Discuss the WordPerfect default template.

Estimated Time: 1 hour

In the previous three lessons you've created text, named documents, and saved them. You've opened documents and resaved them with the same name, as well as saved them with a different name. All of this has taken place while you were learning other things—inserting, deleting, selecting, changing case, aligning with Center and Flush Right, and a variety of other skills.

In this lesson you'll reinforce some things you already know and learn a little more about working with the dialog box that enables you to open and save documents. In addition, you'll learn how to join two documents together, and you'll learn about what's known as the default template—the settings that give you a good-looking document every time.

The Open File Dialog Box

In Appendix B and all of the lessons in this unit, you have been working with the Open File dialog box. You've also worked with the Save File dialog box, and you probably noticed that the two dialog boxes are almost identical. While one is used for saving and the other is used for opening, the two boxes have the same features and work in much the same way.

The illustration in Figure 4-1 shows one version of the Open File dialog box. We will explore this box in the next few pages. Remember that what you learn about the Open File dialog box also applies to the Save File dialog box.

You are about to learn that many of the features showing in the figure are optional; that is, you can choose to display them or not. Let's address the issues one at a time.

Features at the Bottom

The .wpd Extension. As you learned in Lesson 1, documents are automatically saved with the .wpd extension unless you specify in the Settings dialog box that .wpd should not be used. The .wpd extension identifies the files as WordPerfect text files. You need not key .wpd as part of the file name. When you list your files, WordPerfect will list all files with all extensions, signified by *.* in the *File name* box.

Last Modified. Near the bottom of the Open File dialog box, note the *Last modified* box. While it normally reports *Any Time*, you can use this option to tell WordPerfect to list only those files modified yesterday, last week, last year, or a variety of other choices. This feature is especially useful when looking for a file for which you can't remember the exact name but you can remember the date on which it was last modified.

FIGURE 4-1
Open File Dialog Box

File Type. While WordPerfect saves different types of files and attaches different extensions to those types, when *.* is listed in this box, WordPerfect will show all files.

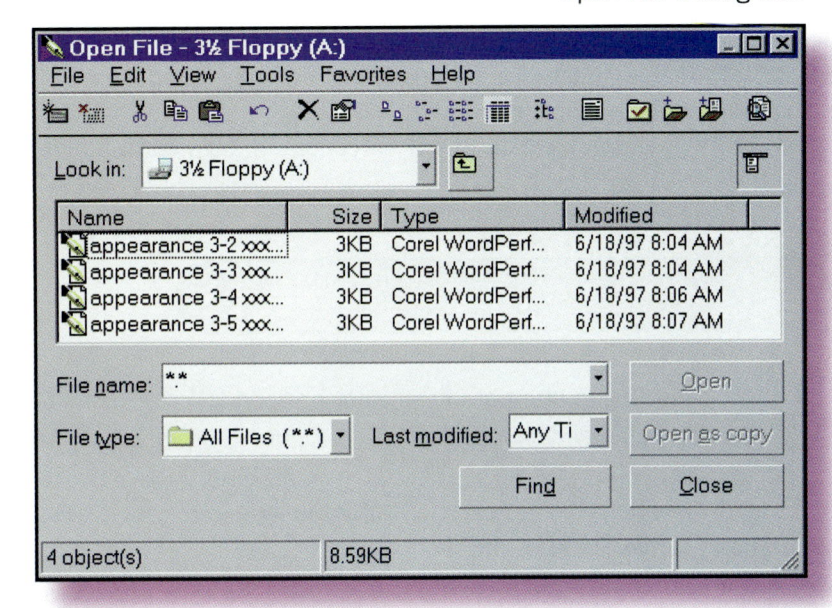

View Options

Study the Open File dialog box illustrated in Figure 4-1. You'll see that the following options have been chosen:

- The Menu Bar is displayed. (A button at the right of the *Look in* box controls whether or not the Menu Bar shows.)

- The Toolbar is displayed below the Menu Bar.

- The Status Bar is displayed at the bottom. (This may need to be chosen in the View menu.)

- Preview is deselected. (The button does not appear to be depressed.)

- Details are displayed in the list.

- Files are listed alphabetically by name.

All of these items can be chosen from the View menu. Some can be chosen from the Toolbar. We'll learn about the parts of the View menu and then practice with them.

Toolbar. Note that the Toolbar looks much like the Toolbar in your normal working window. It contains different tools, but you can preview what each button will do by pointing to the button with the mouse pointer and holding it until the QuickTip appears.

Status Bar. The Status Bar tells you how many objects (files) are in the displayed folder, how much space they take (in terms of bytes or kilobytes), and how much room remains on the disk.

Preview. When selected, Preview displays a miniature version of any document in the list that is highlighted. Preview tends to slow WordPerfect down when you are opening the dialog box, so you probably will not use Preview except in special circumstances.

View. Four choices are provided in the View menu. You can look at your list of files by displaying small icons, large icons, a list, or "details" (as shown). Details lists the name of the file, the size of the file in bytes or kilobytes, the type of file, and the date and time the file was last saved. Sometimes this information is of value to you. Other times, you might not need to see all of that information.

A fifth view option is the Tree view, which can be toggled on and off. The Tree view shows folders and subfolders on your computer.

Arrange Icons by. You can list your files alphabetically by name, by size, by date, or by type of file. The default is to list them by name. Others prefer to see their files in descending order by date—in other words, the most recently opened file will be listed first. For classroom purposes, it would be best to list the files in alphabetic order.

Now that you have all of that information, let's learn how to make changes to this dialog box.

EXERCISE 4.1

1. Click the **Open** button on the Toolbar or open the **File** menu and choose **Open**.

2. If *3½ Floppy (A:)* isn't selected, click the little down arrow beside the *Look in* text box. Compare your Open File dialog box with the one illustrated in Figure 4-1. The list of files should be similar.

3. If your dialog box doesn't display a Menu Bar, click the Menu toggle button at the right.

4. Open the **View** menu in the dialog box and compare it with Figure 4-2.
   a. Notice that at the top of the menu in the figure, **Toolbar** and **Application Bar** are both selected. If your two bars are not selected, choose them. You'll have to do it one at a time.
   b. Click the **Preview** choice. Note that you can preview content only, or you can choose Page view. Choose **No Preview**.
   c. Note the choice of large or small icons, the list, or the list with details. In the figure, **Details** is chosen. Make that choice.
   d. Return to the **View** menu and click **Arrange Icons**. Look at the choices. Choose **by Date**. Look at your list. Are the most recent files at the top? Return to **Arrange Icons** and choose **by Name** again.

5. Look at the second button to the right of the black *x* on the Toolbar. If you display the Quick Tip, you'll learn that this cluster begins with *Large Icons*. Beginning with *Large Icons*, click the next four buttons to see how your list varies with each. Set it at **Details**.

FIGURE 4-2
Open File Dialog Box View Menu

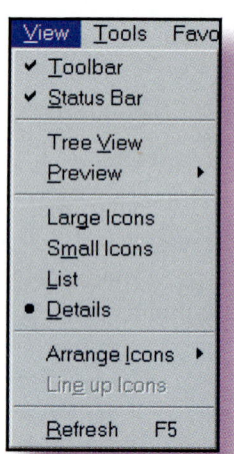

6. Point to the right side of the Open File dialog box. When a two-headed black arrow appears, drag the side of the box to the right so it is larger. Then drag it back so the box is a little wider than the one in Figure 4-1.

7. Point to the bottom of the box and look for a similar black arrow. Drag the bottom of the box down so you can see at least eight files in the list.

8. Keep the Open File dialog box open as you read on.

Favorites

One way to speed up finding your files when you wish to open one is to add the disk (or folder) you use regularly to the Favorites list. This is an easily customizable list that opens with a click of the Favorites button. When it is set up, Favorites can also be used to identify the folder to which your files should be saved.

In Exercise 4.2 it is assumed that you are saving your work on a disk in Drive A of the computer. If you are saving your work in a different folder on the hard drive, please substitute the location for your work whenever reference is made to $3\frac{1}{2}$ Floppy (A:).

EXERCISE 4.2

SCANS

1. With the Open File dialog box still displayed, click the button near the right on the Toolbar that shows a file folder with a red check mark. (This is the Favorites button.)

2. Look at the list of favorites. If no one has changed the list, you might see folders for graphics, macros, and personal files in the list.

3. Look for *$3\frac{1}{2}$ Floppy (A:)* in the list. If it is there, continue with this exercise. If it is not there, skip to Step 5.

4. Position the highlight on *$3\frac{1}{2}$ Floppy (A:)* and open the **File** menu. Choose **Delete**. At the prompt asking if you would like to delete $3\frac{1}{2}$ Floppy to the Recycle Bin, answer **Yes**. (YOU ARE ONLY DELETING A SHORTCUT!) Was the *$3\frac{1}{2}$ Floppy* item removed? It should have been. Now let's put it back.

5. Click the down arrow beside the *Look in* text box near the top. Use the scroll bar, if necessary, to find the *$3\frac{1}{2}$ Floppy (A:)* item in the list. Click to highlight it.

6. With the $3\frac{1}{2}$ Floppy item highlighted, click the **Add to Favorites** button. (It is just to the right of the Favorites button.)

7. Click **Yes** at the question about the *.* filter. You want all files listed.

8. Close the Open File dialog box and read on.

Lesson 4 Working with Documents

47

With the *3½ Floppy (A:)* item in your Favorites list, all you have to do when you wish to open a file from that disk or save a file onto that disk is open the Open File dialog box, click the Favorites button, double click the folder containing your documents, and proceed to open or save your file. You won't need to be fishing around in the *Look in* portion of the dialog box for the correct disk or folder.

> **NOTE:**
>
> When working with Favorites, you must double click the folder to be opened. If you don't, the highlight might be on the folder to be opened, but WordPerfect will still have a different folder selected. Learn to check the *Look in* box just above the names of the files to make certain you are in the correct folder before saving or opening.

As you can see from Exercise 4.2, it is easy to add folders to the Favorites list or remove those folders when they are no longer the most important folders for your work. As you progress throughout this course, the folder that contains your lesson exercises will be used frequently. So you'll want to keep it in the Favorites list. When you are on the job, however, you'll add folders to the list that you are using regularly. That list might change from day to day as the kind of work or the boss for whom you're working changes.

Insert

Occasionally, you wish to join one document to another. This is accomplished by opening one document and positioning the insertion point where you would like the other document to appear. Then you will open the Insert menu, choose File, and choose the file to be inserted.

Let's practice by keying a couple of introductory paragraphs. Then we'll insert a document you created in Lesson 3 at the end of the new document.

EXERCISE 4.3

SCANS

1. Key the paragraphs illustrated in Figure 4-3. Indent the first line of each paragraph with **Tab** and press **Enter** twice following each paragraph.

2. When you finish keying, proofread your work carefully. Then save it as **gifts 4-3 xxx**.

3. Position your insertion point a double space below the last paragraph.

4. Open the **Insert** menu and choose **File**. (It's near the bottom.) This will open your Insert File dialog box.

5. Locate the file named **gifts 3-10 xxx**. Double click the file to insert it, or click it once and then click the **Insert** button.

6. Print your file and close it, saving it again as **gifts 4-3 xxx**.

FIGURE 4-3
Text for Exercise 4.3

> Customs vary around the world with regard to when to give gifts to business associates, what to give, what is quite improper, when the gift should be presented, and whether or not the gift should be wrapped.
>
> In some countries, it is in very bad taste to arrive giftless. In Japan, you are ALWAYS expected to give a gift. Japan is followed closely in that regard by the countries in the Middle East and the Pacific Rim countries such as Korea, China, Taiwan, Thailand, Malaysia, and Hong Kong. In the Latin American countries, gift giving is quite acceptable but not imperative.

In Exercise 4.3 you inserted the text from the previous lesson at the end of the new file. As mentioned earlier, you can insert text anywhere in a document. When you use Insert, the text is inserted at the location of the insertion point. This is a very useful skill. It saves rekeying!

Mass Mailings Using Merge

Most word processing programs enable you to combine a list of names and addresses with a standard document to prepare identical letters for all of the people on the list. This is sometimes referred to as mass mailing. In WordPerfect it is called Merge. Most of Unit 5 is dedicated to learning about Merge, but Exercise 4.4 will provide you with a brief introduction to the feature.

EXERCISE 4.4

1. Go to the student **datafile** folder and open **seasons.dat** and study the document. This grid contains mailing information for potential customers. You will send letters to these people.

2. Note the Merge Feature Bar (Figure 4-4) below your Property Bar (or Ruler, if it is displayed). Click the **Go to Form** button. In the Associate dialog box, click **Create** since you are about to create the standard letter. A new document window will appear, with a different Feature Bar at the top.

3. Press **Enter** until you are about 2" from the top of the page. Key today's date at the left margin. Press **Enter** four more times.

4. Click the **Insert Field** button on the Feature Bar. This will list the titles of the two columns of the grid. Point to *correspondent* and double click. A red FIELD code with parentheses will appear.

(continued on next page)

FIGURE 4-4
Merge Feature Bar

EXERCISE 4.4 CONTINUED

5. Press **Enter** twice and double click the *greeting* title. Press **Enter** twice.

6. Open the **Insert** menu and choose **File**. In the student **datafile** folder, find **Jacobson.wpd** and insert it. Save your letter as **seasons.frm**. Keep it open in the window.

7. Click the **Merge** button on the Feature Bar and then click **Merge** again. Your list of names and addresses will be combined with the letter, and your insertion point will be at the bottom of the fourth letter.

8. Use **Page Up** to go back through the letters, looking at the names and addresses and greetings on each. Save your letters as **seasons 4-4 xxx**. Print the letters and close all files.

That's how simple Merge is. This sample had only four people in the list, but the list could contain hundreds of names. There are many variables with WordPerfect Merge. As mentioned above, you'll learn the terminology and what makes Merge work when you get to Lesson 17.

The Default Template

Every document you create in WordPerfect is formatted by what's known as a *template*. A template is a preformatted document design. If you start a document on a new, blank window, your document will be managed by the default template. That template contains some settings that make it easy for you to begin your document without having to worry about margins, line spacing, tab stop locations, font face and size, and a huge number of other options. Study this list of settings that you'll learn about early in your training.

Margins:	1 inch on all sides—top, bottom, left, and right. The guidelines show you where your margins are.
Tabs:	Set at every half inch.
Line Spacing:	Single
Justification:	Left
Font:	Times New Roman 12 pt.

You should note a couple of things in this list. The one-inch margins support the fact that when your insertion point is at the margin guidelines at the beginning of a document, both the *Ln* and *Pos* indicators report *1"*. Also, when you indented your work with Tab, each time the text was indented a half inch. The font name and point size are the first two items on the default Property Bar. Justification (Left) appears in the middle of the default Property Bar.

As you work with features and formatting in WordPerfect, you will also learn what the default settings are for each feature. It will soon become obvious to you that this program is designed to help you with your work.

Summary

When working with any kind of information processing program, document control is imperative. You need to be able to save your files confidently, knowing exactly where they should go so you can find them when they are needed. In WordPerfect 8 the Open File dialog box is your key to saving and opening files.

In this lesson you learned that:

- WordPerfect automatically identifies your documents as WordPerfect documents with the *.wpd* extension.

- You can customize the Open File dialog box with a Toolbar, Status Bar, Preview Area (not recommended), and a variety of ways to list your files.

- If you include folders that are used frequently in the Favorites list, you will save time locating those folders.

- All WordPerfect documents are formatted by a template. The default template provides margins, font face and size, and a number of other settings to make your documents attractive.

- Mass mailings may be produced with WordPerfect's Merge feature.

LESSON 4 REVIEW QUESTIONS

TRUE/FALSE

Circle the T if the statement is true. Circle the F if it is false.

(T) F   1. The Open File dialog box and Save File dialog box are almost identical, having the same features and working in much the same way.

T **(F)**   2. If the Menu bar in your Open File dialog box does not display, you need to reinstall your software and specify this choice.

T **(F)**   3. One way to speed up finding your files when you wish to open one is to add the file to your Favorites list.

(T) F   4. When working with Favorites, you must double click the folder to be opened.

T **(F)**   5. If you wish to add one document to another, you can do so by opening the File menu and choosing Insert.

(T) F   6. Mass mailings are easy to prepare using WordPerfect's Merge feature.

(continued on next page)

WRITTEN QUESTIONS

Write your answers to the following questions.

7. The .wpd extension identifies files as what type of files? *Word Perfect Doc's*

8. What are four ways you can list your files in the Open File dialog box?
By Name, Type, size or date/last modified.

9. Where should your insertion point be when you join one document to another?
Where you want the document to appear.

10. What feature in WordPerfect formats every document you create with a preformatted document design? *The Default Template.*

LESSON 4 PROJECT

In this project we will build on a document with which you have been working. Work carefully and efficiently.

1. Key the paragraphs in Figure 4-5. Use **Tab** and **Enter**, as shown in the figure.

FIGURE 4-5
Text for Lesson 4 Project

> Be cognizant of the culture of the country in which you are visiting. In most Arab countries, you would avoid giving alcohol. In India, you would not want to give leather objects since cows in India are sacred.
>
> Be sensitive of the correct time for the exchange of gifts. It shouldn't always be the first thing you do upon meeting an associate from another country. Also, don't push for the gift to be opened immediately. In some countries, the gift is opened in private later.
>
> To be safe, carry the gift in a shopping bag or some other way that's not too obvious. Then hand the gift to the associate with both hands (never with the left hand). It is also a good idea to wrap the gift in subdued colors, since gifts in bright colors in some cultures are considered vulgar.
>
> In some cultures, the best gift is a dinner at a restaurant. In Spain and a number of other Mediterranean countries, however, dinner may not be served until 10:30 or 11 p.m. Be careful when you eat in the home of an associate from another country. In some countries, it is rude to clean your plate. In others, it is rude NOT to clean your plate!

2. When you finish, insert the Path and File name code a double space below the final paragraph.

3. Save your file as **gifts proj4a xxx**. Keep it open in the window.

4. Press **Ctrl+Home** to move your insertion point to the beginning of your document.

5. Open the **Insert** menu and choose **File**. Insert **gifts 4-3 xxx**.

6. Delete the Path and File name code that is in the middle of the document. (Use **Reveal Codes**, if necessary, to find the code.) Adjust the spacing so all paragraphs are separated by a double space.

7. Save the file again, this time as **gifts proj4b xxx**.

8. Check your work over once more. Then print the project and close the file.

CRITICAL THINKING ACTIVITY

SCANS

You can't remember the exact name of a document, but you can remember when you worked on it. Where would you go in WordPerfect and what would you look at to find this document?

Command Summary

UNIT 1 REVIEW

FEATURE	MENU CHOICE	KEYBOARD	LESSON
Bold	Format, Font (Property Bar)	Ctrl+B or F9	3
Caps Lock	—	Caps Lock	3
Center	Format, Line	Shift+F7	3
Close	File	Ctrl+F4	1, Appendix B
Convert Case	Edit	—	3
Delete Line	—	Ctrl+Delete	2
Delete Word	—	Ctrl+Backspace	2
Dot Leaders	—	Alt+F7, Alt+F7	3
Draft View	View, Draft	Ctrl+F5	1
Envelope (Single)	Format, Envelope	—	3
Exit	File	Alt+F4	1, Appendix B
Favorites	File, Open (Toolbar)	F4 or Ctrl+O	4
Flush Right	Format, Line	Alt+F7	3
Font Face	Format, Font (Property Bar)	F9	3
Font Size	Format, Font (Property Bar)	F9	3
Full Page Zoom	View, Zoom (Toolbar)	—	1
Go To	Edit	Ctrl+G	2
Help	Help, Help Topics	F1	Appendix B
Insert	—	Insert	2
Insert File	Insert, File	—	4
Italic	Format, Font (Property Bar)	Ctrl+I or F9	3
Merge	Tools, Merge	Shift+F9	4
Open	File (Toolbar)	F4 or Ctrl+O	1, Appendix B
Page View	View, Page	Alt+F5	1
Path and Filename	Insert, Other	—	2
Print	File (Toolbar)	Ctrl+P	1
QuickMenu	—	—	Appendix B
Redo	Edit (Toolbar)	Ctrl+Shift+R	2
Reveal Codes	View	Alt+F3	2
Save	File	Shift+F3	1, Appendix B
Select Text	Edit, Select	F8	2
Soft Page Break	Automatic	—	3

FEATURE	MENU CHOICE	KEYBOARD	LESSON
Tab	—	Tab	3
Two Pages View	View, Two Pages	—	1
Typeover	—	Insert	2
Undelete		Ctrl+Shift+Z	2
Underline	Format, Font (Property Bar)	Ctrl+U or F9	3
Undo	Edit (Toolbar)	Ctrl+Z	3
View Page	View	Alt+F5	1
Zoom	View (Toolbar)	—	1

DELETING TEXT

KEY	ACTION
Backspace	Erases text to the left of the insertion point one character or space at a time. Hold down this key to delete several characters quickly. The text to the right of the insertion point will shift to the left to close up the space as you press the Backspace key.
Del and Delete	Deletes characters following the insertion point. If you hold the key down, characters will be deleted as they scroll in from the right.
Ctrl+Backspace	Deletes the word in which the insertion point is located. If you hold the Ctrl key and press Backspace several times, you can delete several consecutive words.
Ctrl+Delete	Deletes from the insertion point to the end of the line.

SELECTING TEXT

ACTION	RESULT
double click	selects a word
triple click	selects a sentence
quadruple click	selects a paragraph
click with large white arrow in left margin	selects a sentence
double click with large white arrow in left margin	selects a paragraph

MOVING THE INSERTION POINT

KEY	ACTION	KEY	ACTION
→	one character to the right	↓	one line down
←	one character to the left	Ctrl+↑	up one paragraph
Ctrl+→	one word to the right	Ctrl+↓	down one paragraph
Ctrl+←	one word to the left	Home	to the beginning of the line
End	to the end of the line	Page Down	to the bottom of the window
Page Up	to the top of the window	Alt+Page Up	to the first line on the previous page
Ctrl+Home	to the top of the document	Alt+Page Down	to the first line on the next page
Ctrl+End	to the bottom of the document		
↑	one line up		

UNIT 1 REVIEW QUESTIONS

FILL IN THE BLANKS

Complete the following statements by keying the correct answers on a page to be submitted to your instructor. Center *Unit 1 Review Questions* at the top of the page and triple-space. Number your answers.

1. The ____home____ key moves your insertion point to the left margin.

2. The view that shows your document, complete with top and bottom margins, is ____page____ view.

3. In Reveal Codes [HRt] is the code for a ____hard return____.

4. If you want to add a document on the disk to a document showing in the window, you open the ____Insert____ menu and choose ____File____.

5. The periods that connect a column at the left with a column at the right are known as ____dot leaders____.

WRITTEN QUESTIONS

Key your answers to the following questions. Number your answers and double-space between answers. Use complete sentences and good grammar.

6. What is the difference between Save and Save As? *Save only allows you to save to the last location/filename, whereas Save As allows you to save in a new location and/or under a new filename.*

7. When you move around in the text using the scroll bar, what happens to the insertion point? *It remains at its last point.*

8. List two different keystrokes that can be used for deleting text and tell what each of them does. *Backspace ⇒ deletes the last character or if held down continues to delete previously entered information. Control+delete ⇒ deletes from the insertion point to the end of the line.*

UNIT 1: GETTING STARTED

9. Briefly describe the difference between Undo and Undelete. *Undo reverses an action & can reverse several while undelete will only restore the last two deleted items.*

10. Open Help and choose **Help Topics**. Key **template** and open the Help section entitled *about*. What three features from previous versions have been combined into the PerfectExpert feature? What are some of the PerfectExpert projects available?
   → *Templates, QuickTasks, and Coaches.*
   → *Any doc, spreadsheet, template, macro, or application that can be opened when you click File ▸ New.*

UNIT 1 APPLICATIONS

SCANS

Estimated Time: 1 hour

APPLICATION 1

1. Key the memo illustrated in Figure APP-1. Before beginning, press **Enter** until your insertion point is on approximately *Ln 2"*.

2. Center and bold **Memorandum** and triple space.

3. After keying **TO:**, watch the *Pos* indicator on the Application Bar while you tab to **2"** to key **Hubert Ramon**.

4. Follow the procedure in Step 3 for the other heading lines.

FIGURE APP-1
Text for Application 1

```
                        Memorandum

TO:        Hubert Ramon
FROM:      (key your name)
DATE:      (key the current date)
RE:        Self-Directed Teams

We're off to a good start with Total Quality Management in our
organization.  Thank you for volunteering to help with the initial
planning meetings for our staff training.

As you know, our goal down the pike is to completely convert our
workforce to self-directed teams.  Your training in this area will be
of great value to our company.
```

5. When you finish keying the memo, check your work carefully. Then save the Unit 1 Application 1 memo as **quality u1ap1a xxx**, substituting your initials for the *xxx* as always.

6. Insert the Path and Filename code a double space below the last paragraph of the memo.

(continued on next page)

57

7. Print your document.

8. Position your insertion point following the word *goal* in the first line of the second paragraph. Delete the words *down the pike* and replace them with **for the future**.

9. Following the word *training* in the second paragraph, add the words **and experience**.

10. Select *Memorandum* at the top and use **Convert Case** to change it to all uppercase letters.

11. Following the words *Total Quality Management* in the first line, add **(TQM)**, complete with parentheses.

12. Save the document again as **quality u1ap1b xxx**. Print it and close it.

APPLICATION 2

Figure APP-2 illustrates some of the most frequently used proofreaders' marks. Study the marks. Then follow the steps listed to make corrections to a document you've already prepared.

1. Open **gifts proj4b xxx**. Save the file as **gifts u1ap2 xxx**.

FIGURE APP-2
Proofreaders' Marks

Change	Mark	Example	Result
Capitalize	≡	word processing is fun.	Word processing is fun.
Close up	⌒	Word Perfect	WordPerfect
Delete	℮	Your work work is good.	Your work is good.
Insert	∧	Word processing fun.	Word processing is fun.
Insert comma	⌢	apples potatoes and peas	apples, potatoes, and peas
Insert space	#	Wordprocessing is fun.	Word processing is fun.
Insert period	⊙	Key the memo	Key the memo.
Lowercase	/lc	Word Processing is fun. lc	Word processing is fun.
New paragraph	¶	¶ Please call me Tuesday.	Please call me Tuesday.

58   UNIT 1: GETTING STARTED

2. Using Figure APP-3 as a guide, make the corrections indicated to your document. (Note that the document is shown with expanded line spacing in Figure APP-3. The extra line spacing is so you can read the proofreaders' marks. You do not need to change line spacing.)

3. When you finish, check your work carefully. Print the revised document and close it, saving it again as **gifts u1ap2 xxx**.

FIGURE APP-3
Corrections for Application 2

Customs vary around the world with regard to when to give gifts to business associates, what to give, what is ~~quite~~ improper, when the gift should be presented, and whether or not the gift should be wrapped.

In some countries, it is in very bad taste to arrive giftless. In Japan you are ALWAYS expected to give a gift. Japan is followed closely in that regard by the countries in the Middle East and the Pacific Rim countries such as Korea, China, Taiwan, Thailand, *and* Malaysia, ~~and Hong Kong.~~ In the Latin American countries, gift giving is quite acceptable but not imperative.

Regardless of the country where you are presenting a gift, to ~~a host or business associate,~~ there are some general guidelines regarding international gift giving.

Flowers are acceptable in most cultures, *however,* ~~but~~ in many countries, you should avoid red roses because they signify romantic interest. Also, in most European countries, white flowers and chrysanthemums are given only for condolences or sympathy. Avoid giving an even number of flowers, and unwrap the flowers before presenting them to the recipient.

Chocolates or gifts of candy are usually appropriate. Be careful not to gove candy manufactured in a rival country.

Gifts with company logos are usually acceptable, providing the logo is small and unobtrusive. In some countries, caps and T-shirts with logos are considered souvenirs, not gifts.

(continued on next page)

FIGURE APP-3 (continued)
Corrections for Application 2

> *is important. You should be aware that*
>
> /lc ~~Be cognizant of~~ the culture of the country in which you are visiting. ⁞In most Arab countries, you would avoid giving alcohol. In India, you would not want to give leather objects since cows in India are sacred.
>
> *is also important.*
>
> ~~Be sensitive of~~ the correct time for the exchange of gifts. It shouldn't always ⁞be the first thing you do upon meeting an associate from another country. Also, don't push for the gift to be opened immediately. In some countries, the gift is opened in private later.
>
> *It is in good taste to*
>
> ~~To be safe,~~ carry the gift in a shopping bag or some other way that's not too obvious. Then hand the gift to the associate with both hands (never with the left hand). It is also a good idea to wrap the gift in subdued colors, since gifts *wrapped* in bright colors in some cultures are considered vulgar.
>
> *in many places*
>
> ~~In some cultures,~~ the best gift⁞is a dinner at a restaurant. In Spain and a number ⁞of other Mediterranean countries, however, dinner may not be served until 10:30 or 11 p.m. Be careful when you eat in the home of an associate from another country. In some countries it is rude to clean your plate. In others, it is rude NOT to clean your plate! *Follow the example of your host or hostess when dining.*

APPLICATION 3

Go to the student **datafile** folder and open the document named **canada**. Use **Save As** to save the document as **canada u1ap3 xxx**. Format by selecting text and adding the following appearance attributes:

■ Format all dates using **Italic**.

■ Format the names of all explorers using **Bold**.

■ Each time the word *Canada* appears, format it with **Bold** and **Italic**.

■ Underline the following: *Newfoundland, Atlantic Coast, St. Lawrence River* (twice), and *Hudson Bay*.

When you finish, add the Path and Filename code a double space below the second paragraph. Then save the file again with the same name. Print the file and close it.

ON-THE-JOB SIMULATION

You have been hired part time to work for Singing Wheels Tours, a local charter and tour bus company, for a few hours each week. Your boss, Mr. Charlie Becker, knows you are just learning how to use WordPerfect, so he has planned your responsibilities to progress from simple to more difficult. Several exercises will be included for you at the end of each unit. See how much of the work you can do without special instructions.

JOB 1

Mr. Becker has handed you the paragraphs illustrated in Figure J1. Key the paragraphs and correct all errors. Save the file as **schedule job1 xxx**. (The On-the-Job exercises will be numbered consecutively throughout the text.) Then insert the Path and Filename code a double space below the second paragraph and print the document. Close the document.

FIGURE J1
Text for Job 1

```
    We are sorry for the delay in notifying you of your scheduled
trips for August.  As you know, recent flooding in the Midwest has
necessitated a change in many of our scheduled tours.

    The August schedule will be posted later in the week.  Please
check your assignments and make your personal arrangements for the
tours on which you will be serving.
```

JOB 2

Mr. Becker has prepared a tentative list of tours for the first three months of next year. Press **Enter** to space to *Ln 2"* for the heading. Triple space following the heading. Using your knowledge of Flush Right and dot leaders, prepare the short document illustrated in Figure J2.

When you finish, check your work carefully and save the job as **schedule job2 xxx**. Add the Path and Filename code a double space below the document, print it, and close it.

FIGURE J2
Text for Job 2

```
                      EARLY 199x TRIPS
Southwest Area  . . . . . . . . . . . . . . . . . . . . . . . . January
Branson . . . . . . . . . . . . . . . . . . . . . . . . . . . . January
Pacific Northwest . . . . . . . . . . . . . . . . . . . . . . February
Southern California . . . . . . . . . . . . . . . . . . . . . February
Phoenix and Flagstaff . . . . . . . . . . . . . . . . . . . . .  March
Key West  . . . . . . . . . . . . . . . . . . . . . . . . . . .  March
```

61

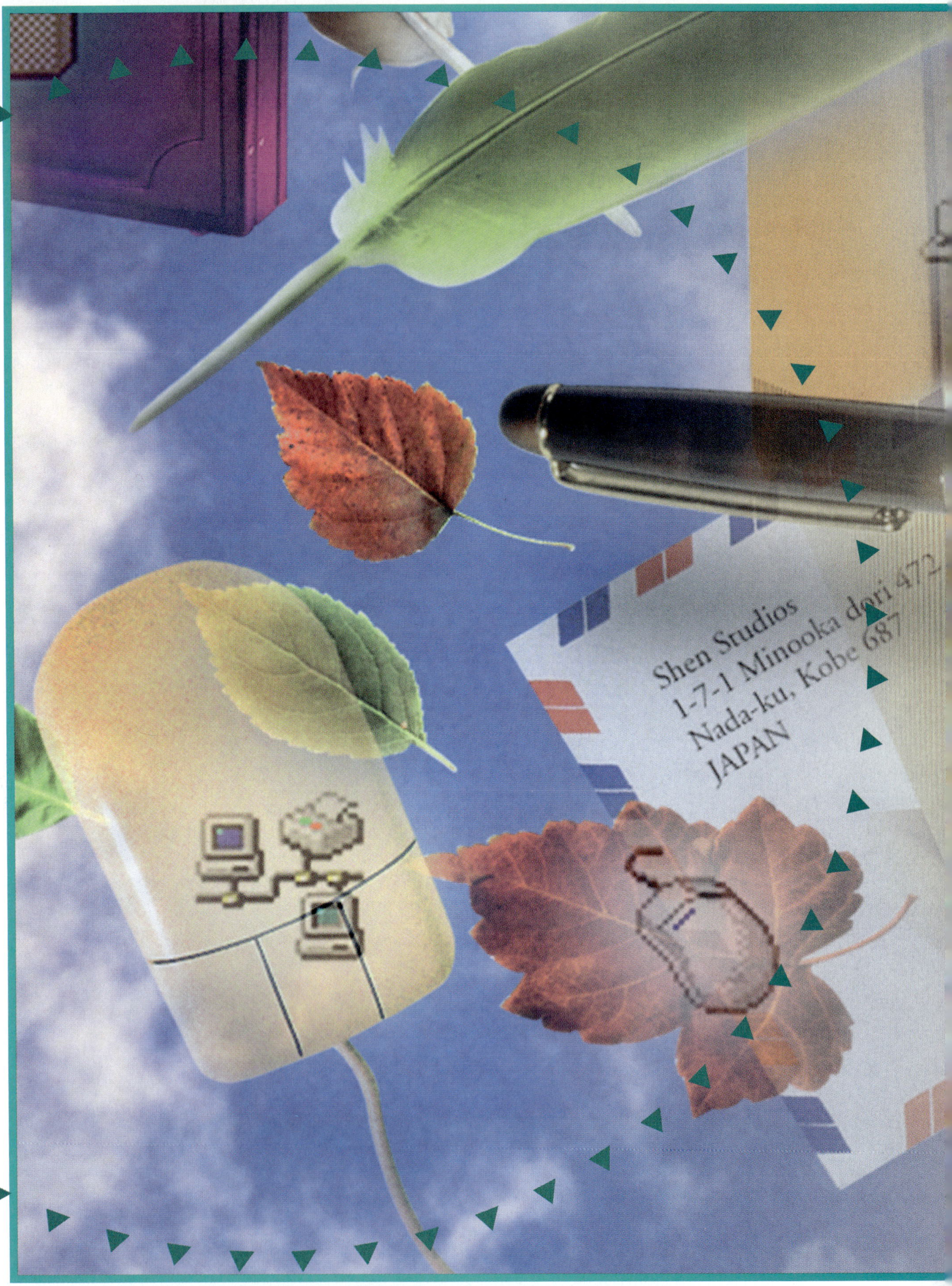
Shen Studios
1-7-1 Minooka dori 472-
Nada-ku, Kobe 687
JAPAN

Corel® WordPerfect® Basics

UNIT 2

lesson 5 — 1 hr.
Text Entry Features

lesson 6 — 1 hr.
Editing Features

lesson 7 — 1 hr.
Writing Tools

lesson 8 — 1 hr.
Windows Tools and File Management

Estimated Time for Unit 2: 5 hours

LESSON 5
TEXT ENTRY FEATURES

OBJECTIVES

Upon completion of this lesson, you will be able to:

- Use various methods of deleting commands.
- Format text with Indent, Hanging Indent, and Double Indent.
- Use QuickIndent to format paragraphs.
- Use the WordPerfect method of creating lists.
- Create lists with the Outline/Bullets & Numbering feature.
- Start a new page using a hard page break.
- Use the WordPerfect Date feature.
- Center text vertically with the Center Page command.
- Format numerals with superscript and subscript.
- Work with various hyphen and space codes.

Estimated Time: 1 hour

Deleting Commands

Sometimes you make a mistake in choosing a menu, dialog box, or feature, and you wish to change your mind. There are different methods of deleting the commands you make in error. For example:

- **Menu.** To close a menu without making a choice, click outside of the menu, press Alt, press Esc, or open a different menu.

- **Dialog box.** To close a dialog box without making any changes, press Esc, click the *x* in the upper right corner, or, if there is a Cancel button, click Cancel.

Commands like Bold, Italic, and Underline don't open a menu. Nor do they display a dialog box. Instead, they put a code in your document. Some may be removed with the Backspace key. Others can be removed by immediately giving the same command again. Let's try a short practice.

EXERCISE 5.1

1. Read all three steps in this exercise. Beginning in a new document window, reveal your codes. Watch your codes as you give each of the commands in Figure 5-1. Then delete the command with one of the following: **Esc**, **Delete**, **Backspace**, or by repeating the command.

2. For each item in the list, jot down which method you used to successfully delete the codes. (The items are numbered for your convenience.)

3. When you finish, check to be sure no codes are remaining in the Codes part of your window except the Initial Style code.

FIGURE 5-1
Practice Instructions for Exercise 5.1

1. Press Ctrl+B (Bold)
2. Open the File menu
3. Press F5 (Print)
4. Open the File menu and choose Print
5. Press Shift+F3 (Save)
6. Press Tab
7. Press F4 (Open)
8. Press Ctrl+U (Underline)
9. Press Caps Lock
10. Open the File menu and choose Open

You can also delete codes that affect your text, such as the Bold, Italic, and Underline formatting codes, by dragging them out of the Reveal Codes window or by using Backspace or Delete. Let's create some text and try these skills.

EXERCISE 5.2

1. Turn on **Bold** and key your name. Turn Bold off and press **Enter** twice.

2. Turn on **Underline** and key your name. Turn Underline off and press **Enter** twice.

3. Reveal your codes. Point to one of the Bold codes with the mouse pointer and press the left mouse button. Drag that Bold code up and out of the gray Reveal Codes area. Your name should no longer be bolded.

4. Point to one of the Hard Return codes between the two occurrences of your name. Drag that code up and out of the Reveal Codes area.

5. Use **Backspace** or **Delete** to remove one of the Underline codes. Then close your document without saving it.

Indent, Hanging Indent, and Double Indent

You learned in Lesson 3 that Tab is used to indent the first line of a paragraph. The Indent feature may also be used to indent, although the result is quite different. In addition, you can indent with Double Indent and Hanging Indent. Using this variety of tools, you can format your work to make it more easily read or more attractive. While all three of the indent formats can be chosen from the menu that appears when you choose Format and then Paragraph, using keystrokes is easier.

Indent is chosen by pressing F7.
Hanging Indent is chosen with Ctrl+F7.
Double Indent is chosen with Ctrl+Shift+F7.

Let's practice.

EXERCISE 5.3

1. Beginning in a new document window, open the **Format** menu. Choose **Paragraph**. Look at the indent formats chosen there. Click outside of the menu to close it.

2. Press **F7**. Key the first paragraph in Figure 5-2. Use **Bold** and *Italic* as shown. Double space between paragraphs.

3. Press **Ctrl+F7** and key the second paragraph in Figure 5-2.

4. Press **Ctrl+Shift+F7** and key the third paragraph in Figure 5-2.

5. When you finish, reveal your codes and look at the codes that format your paragraphs. Add the codes and a description of each to your list in Appendix E.

FIGURE 5-2
Text for Exercise 5.3

> This paragraph is indented with **F7**. This format is simply called *Indent*. It causes all lines to be indented from the left margin the distance of the first tab stop, which is set by default at one-half inch. Indent is canceled when I press the **Enter** key.
>
> This paragraph is indented with **Ctrl+F7**. This is called *Hanging Indent*. All lines except the first will be indented from the left margin to the first tab stop. This format, too, is canceled when I press the **Enter** key.
>
> This paragraph is indented with **Ctrl+Shift+F7**. With *Double Indent*, all lines are indented from the left margin to the first tab stop. The lines are indented an equal amount from the right margin. Pressing **Enter** ends the format. The results of this format don't show very well with left justification.

6. Press **Ctrl+Home**. With your codes revealed, press **Delete** to delete the [Hd Left Indent] code that formats the paragraph. Then press **F7** to reformat the paragraph.

7. Look at the second paragraph in Reveal Codes. Use your mouse pointer to drag the two Hanging Indent codes up and out of the gray window. Your paragraph should look like a normal paragraph. Press **Ctrl+F7** to reformat the paragraph with the same format.

8. Check your work carefully and save it as **indent 5-3 xxx**. Insert the Path and Filename code a double space below the Double Indent paragraph.

9. Print the document and close it, saving it as you close it.

QuickIndent

The QuickIndent tool helps you create the indented formats you want for your documents. To use it, press Tab at the beginning of any line of the paragraph except the first.

- If the first line of the paragraph is already indented with Tab, all lines will be aligned with the beginning of the first line.

- If the first line of the paragraph is not already indented with Tab, QuickIndent will cause a Hanging Indent format. Let's practice with this timesaving tool.

EXERCISE 5.4

1. Open **online** from the student **datafile** folder. Use **Save As** to save the file as **online 5-4 xxx**.

2. Position the insertion point at the beginning of the second line of the first paragraph and press **Tab**. Watch as the remaining lines are indented.

3. Delete the [Hd Left Indent] code at the beginning of the first line of the first paragraph. Position the insertion point at the beginning of the second line. Press **Tab**. Watch as your paragraph is given a Hanging Indent format.

4. Insert the Path and Filename code a double space below the final paragraph. Print the file and close it, saving it again as you close.

This was a quick introduction to QuickIndent. It is a tool you are sure to find useful. It's actually quicker and easier to remember than the tools you practiced in the first three exercises of this lesson. You may practice QuickIndent more at your leisure. Let's move on.

Creating Lists

Indent is useful for formats like the numbered steps in the exercise you just completed. Imagine how much more difficult it would be to follow the steps if the second and third lines of the steps wrapped to the left margin.

WordPerfect makes it easy for you to create lists like the numbered steps. All you need to do is key a numeral, a period, and press the Tab key and WordPerfect knows you're beginning a list. It inserts a style that automatically inserts the numbers until you delete a number to tell WordPerfect the list is ended. Let's practice.

EXERCISE 5.5

1. Beginning in a new document window, reveal your codes so you can watch what happens. Key **1.** and press **Tab**. Note that WordPerfect adds three codes to your document. (Add them to your list in Appendix E.)

2. Key the first item in Figure 5-3. At the end of the item, press **Enter** twice and key the second item. Note that WordPerfect automatically inserts your second number and indents the text.

3. After Item 2, press **Enter** twice. Since this is the end of the list, press **Backspace** once to delete the numeral. Then key the closing paragraph in the figure.

4. Press **Enter** three times. Save your practice as **numbers 5-5 xxx** and keep the document open as you read on.

FIGURE 5-3
Text for Exercise 5.5

```
1.   This is the beginning of a list that was indented with the
     Tab key.  WordPerfect knew from the format that the text was
     to be indented as if I'd used F7 for indent.

2.   This is the second item in the list.  This text, too, will
     wrap at the tab stop so my list is easy to read.

This sentence indicates that the list is ended.  If I had wanted, I
could have indented this line with Tab and had a normally indented
paragraph.
```

Outline/Bullets & Numbering

The style WordPerfect entered when you began your little list in Exercise 5.5 automatically takes you to the Outline/Bullets & Numbering feature in the Insert menu. When you use this feature, you have a choice of symbols for your list. This includes a number of bullet shapes, as well as a variety of number types.

An interesting facet of this feature is that it "reads" the location of your insertion point when you begin the list and starts the list at that location. For example, if you wanted your numerals to be indented to begin at the first tab stop, you would press Tab to get to that location before beginning the list.

If you lose the format because you accidentally backspace out a number or a bullet, return the insertion point to the end of the previous formatted paragraph and press Enter to restore the numbered or bulleted format. Then you can use Delete to get rid of any extra blank lines and bring your text up to the correct location.

Let's experiment a little more with the bullets. You'll work with the much more powerful outlining tool in Lesson 14.

EXERCISE 5.6

1. With **numbers 5-5 xxx** open, use **Save As** to save the file as **numbers 5-6 xxx**. With the insertion point at the left margin a triple space below the paragraph, open the **Insert** menu and choose **Outline/Bullets & Numbering**.

2. Click the **Bullets** tab and choose a small bullet. In the *Numbering* section at the bottom, click the button that tells WordPerfect to start a new outline or list. Click OK.

3. Key a two-line sentence (or two) describing how you got the bullet and indent to begin your list. Then press **Enter** twice and key the Item 2 sentence from Figure 5-3. (It's showing at the top of your window.)

4. Press **Enter** twice and then press **Backspace** once to delete the bullet. Key the final paragraph from Figure 5-3.

5. Press **Enter** three times. Then press **Tab** once to move your insertion point to the first tab stop.

6. Return to the Outline/Bullets & Numbering dialog box and choose a different bullet shape (you get to choose!). Click the **Start New...** button and then **OK**. Note that the bullet is indented from the left margin at the position of the insertion point when you chose the feature.

7. Key the same text for the first bullet as you keyed in Step 2.

8. Press **Enter** twice and then **Backspace** once. Whoops! You wanted that bullet. Fix it as follows:
   a. Press **Backspace** until your insertion point is at the end of the first item.
   b. Press **Enter** twice to restore the bullet.
   c. Then key the text for the second bullet and the ending paragraph that you keyed in Steps 3 and 4 of this exercise. (Note that you need to press **Backspace** twice to get the insertion point back to the left margin for the final paragraph because you are working with an indented format.)

9. Save your exercise again as **numbers 5-6 xxx**. Insert the Path and Filename code a double space below the final paragraph. Print the exercise. Keep the document open.

New Page

You learned in Lesson 1 that when a page is full, WordPerfect automatically moves the text to a new page. When this happens, a *soft page break* is inserted. Regardless of how full you have a page, you can begin a new page wherever you want by inserting a *hard page break*. You do this by pressing Ctrl+Enter.

Hard page breaks can be removed simply by positioning the insertion point at the beginning of the new page and pressing Backspace, or by revealing your codes and deleting the [HPg] code. Let's work with hard and soft page breaks.

EXERCISE 5.7

1. With **numbers 5-6 xxx** open in the window, use **Save As** to save the file as **numbers 5-7 xxx**. Press **Ctrl+Home** twice to move your insertion point to the beginning of your document, above all codes.

2. Press **Enter** until the *Ln* indicator in the Application Bar says you are about *5"* from the top of the page.

3. Press **Ctrl+End** to check the bottom of your document. One paragraph and the Path and Filename code should be on page 2.

4. Look at the soft page break and the top and bottom margins separating that final paragraph from the rest of your document.

5. Open the **View** menu and choose **Draft** to see the single line that identifies a soft page break in Draft view. Then change back to **Page** view.

6. Position your insertion point in the line space above the first bulleted item on the first page of your document. Hold **Ctrl** while you press **Enter**. Note that you are now on page 2.

7. Look at the hard page break. It has a black line along with the colored line. Change to **Draft** view to see the double line that indicates a hard page break in Draft view.

8. Page through your document. Note that the final paragraph and the Path and Filename code are still on page 2 because there is enough room for them on that page.

9. Reveal your codes. Find the [HPg] code above the first bulleted item. Remove the code to return the bulleted text to page 1.

10. Close your document without saving it again.

Date

Most computers have an internal clock that keeps track of the date and time. That time is recorded along with the date when you save your documents. You saw the results of that when you looked at *Details* in the Open File dialog box in Lesson 4. Because your computer knows the date, you can insert it into your documents by opening the Insert menu and choosing Date/Time. The dialog box in Figure 5-4 will be displayed. As you can see, this dialog box lists a variety of formats and enables you to customize your format. To insert the date, choose the format and click the Insert button. You may enter the date in a WordPerfect document in one of two ways:

FIGURE 5-4
Date/Time Dialog Box

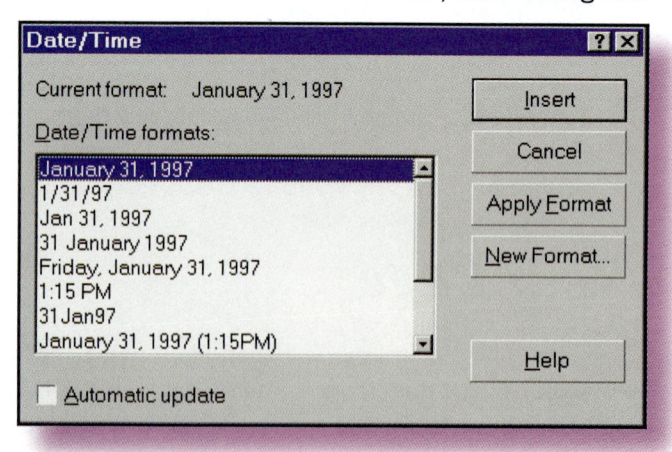

■ **Date Text** enters today's date at the location of the insertion point as a permanent part of your document. You can also accomplish this by pressing Ctrl+D.

70   UNIT 2: COREL WORDPERFECT BASICS

- **Date Code** enters the date as a code that changes to the current date each time the document is opened. In other words, if you enter the code in a document created today and open the document a week from today, the date on which the document is opened will be the date showing in the document. You can also enter the Date Code with Ctrl+Shift+D.

EXERCISE 5.8

1. Beginning in a new document window, press **Ctrl+D** to enter today's date into your window. Is the date correct? If not, have your instructor help you change the date in your computer.

2. Press **Enter** twice and press **Ctrl+Shift+D** to insert the Date Code. Again, the date will appear, but it is entered as a hidden code. Press **Enter** twice.

3. Reveal your codes and look at the two dates. Enter the appropriate code(s) in your list in Appendix E.

4. Open **indent 5-3 xxx**. With the insertion point at the top of the document, use **Date Text** to enter the current date. Press **Enter** twice.

5. Save the document as **indent 5-8 xxx** and close it. Your previous date practice should be showing. It was hiding behind the **indent** document.

6. Save your "dates" practice as **dates 5-8 xxx**. Keep the file open for the next exercise.

Center Page

Up to this point, whenever you wanted extra space at the top of a document, you've pressed Enter until the insertion point was the prescribed distance from the top of the page. There's a better way for certain situations. When you have a short document that you'd like centered between the top and bottom margins, you can use the Center Page command. Let's use the Center Page command to move your dates to the center of the page.

EXERCISE 5.9

1. With **dates 5-8 xxx** open in the window, use **Save As** to save the file as **dates 5-9 xxx**. Move your insertion point to the top of the document.

2. Open the **Format** menu and choose **Page**. Then choose **Center**. The dialog box illustrated in Figure 5-5 will appear.

3. Choose **Current page** and click **OK**.

4. Click the **Zoom** button on the Toolbar and choose **Full Page** to see how your dates look with even top and bottom margins. Use **Zoom** again to return to 100%.

(continued on next page)

EXERCISE 5.9 CONTINUED

5. Position the insertion point at the bottom of the document, a double space below the second date.

6. Insert the Path and Filename code. Print the file. Then close it, saving it when you close it.

FIGURE 5-5
Center Page(s) Dialog Box

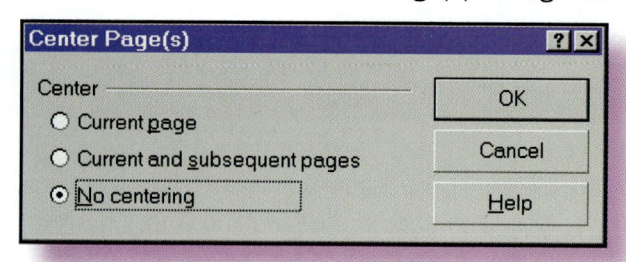

Now that you know how to insert dates and use Center Page, let's put these features to work in a letter. We'll also use Double Indent in this letter.

EXERCISE 5.10

1. Beginning in a new document window, open the **Format** menu and choose **Page**. Choose **Center** and then **Current page**.

2. Press **Tab** to **Pos 4"**. Open the **Insert** menu, choose **Date/Time**, select the format for *January 31, 1997*, and click **Insert**. Press **Enter** four times.

3. Key the inside address and greeting in Figure 5-6 in the usual manner, leaving a blank line above and below the greeting.

4. Use **Tab** to indent the first line of the first, second, and fourth paragraphs. Use **Double Indent** for the third paragraph.

5. Tab to **Pos 4"** for the two closing lines, leaving a quadruple space between them. Press **Enter** twice after the name and key **Enclosures** at the left margin.

6. Press **Enter** twice. Save the document as **sasoot 5-10 xxx**. Insert the Path and Filename code.

7. Prepare an envelope. Then print the letter and the envelope. Close the document, saving it again as you close it.

INTERNET An Internet address is a set of numbers or words that identifies a unique user or computer. Every user and computer on the Internet must have a different address so that the system knows where to send electronic mail and other data.

72　　UNIT 2: COREL WORDPERFECT BASICS

FIGURE 5-6
Text for Exercise 5.10

```
                                             (Current Date)

Mr. Paul Weigel
P.O. Box 8760
Beaver Dam, WI 53916-8760

Dear Mr. Weigel:

    It is a pleasure to reply to your inquiry about Sasoot, Graphia.
We are quite proud of our city and of our country and are delighted to
have an opportunity to inform people from other countries about our
people, our products, and our beautiful land.

    The enclosed report will provide you with much of the information
you have requested about Sasoot.  Several brochures are also enclosed
that cover these topics:

    climate, currency used, exchange rate, major cities,
    type of government, housing opportunities, manufacturing, and
    agricultural products

    If we can be of further help, please do not hesitate to write to
me.  If you decide to visit beautiful Sasoot, please look me up for a
personal tour of the city.

                                             Sincerely,



                                             Reiko Onodera

Enclosures
```

Hyphen and Space Codes

In addition to the formatting tools you've been exploring, WordPerfect has a series of codes that are mostly designed to help at the end of the line. These codes include some special hyphen codes and a special space code. Let's learn about them.

Hyphen. A normal hyphen is used for joining words that always contain a hyphen—words like jack-in-the-box or self-esteem. These hyphens are keyed in the normal way, and they always show as part of a word. If they fall at the end of the line, WordPerfect will automatically divide the parts of the word at the hyphen.

Hyphen Character. A hyphen character is used to join two words that are NOT to be divided at the end of the line. The best example is when a hyphen is used as a minus sign in a formula. Key a hyphen character by holding Ctrl while you key the hyphen (Ctrl+-).

73

Dash. In typography, a dash is known as an *em dash*. It is longer than a hyphen. Where a hyphen is used to join two closely related words, a dash is used as a pause or break in thought, as illustrated in the Hyphen paragraph about the jack-in-the-box. A dash may occur anywhere on the line. You can create a dash using a shortcut. Key three hyphens (---) and continue keying. A dash never has a space before it or following it.

Hard Space. A hard space works like a hyphen character. It keeps two words from being divided at the end of a line. For example, when a date like January 5, 2001, comes at the end of the line, your keyboarding rules tell you that you may (if you must) divide that date after the comma. Keyboarding rules dictate that you should NEVER divide the date between *January* and *5*. Like hyphen characters, a hard space will fool WordPerfect into thinking *January 5* is all one word, and if it falls at the end of the line, the entire "word" will drop to the next line.

Key a hard space using the same procedure as a hyphen character—holding Ctrl while you press the space bar. Hard spaces are used in formulas to keep an entire formula on one line. Look at Figure 5-7. If you key the paragraph in the normal manner, half of the formula will be on one line and half will be on the other. This would make the formula very hard to read. Let's see if we can key it so everything "hangs together." Study all parts of Step 1 before beginning.

> **TIP**
> All of these codes may be chosen from a dialog box (Format, Line, Other Codes).

EXERCISE 5.11

1. Beginning in a new document window, key the sentences illustrated in Figure 5-7. Use the following instructions:
   a. For each dash, press **Ctrl+W**. When a dialog box full of symbols appears, press the **Hyphen** key twice and press **Enter**. Do NOT space before or after the dash.
   b. In the formula, press **Ctrl+space bar** between each of the letters and characters. Key the minus sign with **Ctrl+–**.
   c. For the date, press **Ctrl+space bar** between *January* and *5*.

2. Reveal your codes and check the document against the solution of the document in Figure 5-8. Then add the codes to your list. (The codes for the dashes won't show unless you position your insertion point to the left of them.)

3. Save your paragraph as **codes 5-11 xxx**. At the end of the document, press **Enter** twice and insert the Path and Filename code.

4. Print your document and save it again with the same name. Keep it open.

FIGURE 5-7
Text for Exercise 5.11

```
The scientists discovered that the best formula—the one that will
solve your problem—is a + b - c = x + y.  This spectacular formula
was developed in Chester, West Virginia, on January 5, 1924.
```

FIGURE 5-8
Sentences with Codes

```
The scientists discovered that the best formula[|: 4, 34]the one that
will solve your problem[|: 4, 34]is
a[HSpace]+[Hspace]b[HSpace]-[HSpace]c[HSpace]=[HSpace]x[HSpace]+
[HSpace]y.  This spectacular formula was developed in Chester, West
Virginia, on January[HSpace]5, 1924.
```

NOTE:

The results of this exercise may vary according to computer and printer description. If keyed properly, however, the formula and date will remain together on the line.

You no doubt found that inserting all of those dashes, hyphen characters, and hard spaces took some concentration. The result is that you can reformat the text as many different ways as you wish, and the formula and date will both remain intact.

All of the codes you used in this portion of the lesson are available from a dialog box. To display it, open the Format menu, choose Line, and then choose Other Codes. You'll also find quite a number of additional commands in the Other Codes dialog box. You may explore that dialog box at your leisure.

Superscripts and Subscripts

In Lesson 3 you learned about the Font dialog box. The *Position* section of this dialog box enables you to insert superscripted or subscripted numerals in your documents. The formula in Exercise 5.11 provides an excellent opportunity for you to try out this feature.

EXERCISE 5.12

1. With **codes 5-11 xxx** showing in the window, position the insertion point immediately following the *a* in the formula. Key a **2** and drag the mouse pointer over the numeral to select it.

2. Open the **Format** menu and choose **Font** (or press F9) to open the Font dialog box. Near the center, find the Position feature.

3. Click the arrow and choose **Superscript**. Click **OK**. The 2 should now be small and raised.

4. Position the insertion point immediately following the *x* in the formula. Key a **3**, select it, and format it with **Subscript**. It should be small and below the line.

5. Close the document without saving it again.

While a few other applications use superscripts and subscripts, this feature is most frequently used in mathematical calculations and formulas.

75

Summary

This lesson has provided you with a number of small but important tools for use in creating WordPerfect documents. Some are nice, some are wonderful, and some may not be useful to you at all. You get to choose. In this lesson you learned that:

- There are a variety of ways to delete commands.
- You can indent your text with Indent, Hanging Indent, and Double Indent, as well as with the Tab key.
- The QuickIndent tool is a quick way of formatting indented paragraphs or paragraphs formatted with Hanging Indent.
- The Outline/Bullets & Numbering feature helps you create lists.
- You can begin a new page anywhere you wish in your documents.
- WordPerfect can be told to insert the current date or a code that displays the current date each time a document is opened.
- The Center Page command enables you to vertically center the text of a document.
- Hyphens, hyphen characters, dashes, and hard spaces are useful in protecting your documents from unwanted breaks at your line endings.
- Numerals may be formatted with superscript and subscript using the Font dialog box.

LESSON 5 REVIEW QUESTIONS

FILL IN THE BLANKS

Complete each of the following statements by writing your answer in the blank provided.

1. The _QuickIndent_ tool helps you create indented formats.

2. The indented format which has all lines indented from the left margin and the right margin an equal amount is called _Double Indent_.

3. An easy way to create a numbered list is to key a numeral, a period, and press the _enter_ key.

4. You choose the Outline/Bullets & Numbering feature from the _Insert_ menu.

5. Regardless of how full you have a page, you can begin a new page by inserting a _hard page break_.

6. To insert a Date Code into your document, you can open your Insert menu, choose Date/Time, and then choose the format, or you can press the key combination of _Ctrl + Shift + D_.

MATCHING

Write the letter of the term or phrase from Column 2 that best matches the description in Column 1.

Column 1

_F_ 7. The feature used to refer to the position of a character that is printed above the normal line of print.

_E_ 8. This is the feature you would use to keep a date such as October 11, 2001, together on one line.

_A_ 9. Use this feature when you want a short document centered between the top and bottom margins.

_C_ 10. You can create this feature by keying three hyphens.

Column 2

A. Center Pages
B. Hyphen
C. Hyphen Character
D. Dash
E. Hard Space
F. Superscript
G. Subscript

LESSON 5 PROJECT

This project will have two unrelated parts so you can practice several of the skills learned in this lesson. You'll begin with adding numbers to the most recent version of the **gifts** document.

PROJECT 5A

1. Open **gifts u1ap2 xxx**. Use **Save As** to save the file as **gifts proj5a xxx**. Position the insertion point at the left margin beside the paragraph that begins with the word *Flowers*. It is the fourth paragraph.

2. Press **Delete** once to delete the tab that indents the first line of the paragraph. Then press **Tab** and key **1.** followed by **Tab** again. The entire paragraph should move to align at an inch from the left margin (*Pos 2"*).

3. Position the insertion point after the word *recipient* at the end of the same paragraph. Press **Enter**. Then press **Delete** until the *Chocolates* item lines up with the *Flowers* item.

4. Follow the procedure in Step 2 to add numerals to all of the remaining "gift" paragraphs of the document. (There should be seven in all.)

5. Print the document and close it, saving it again with the same name.

Now let's format a document that has been created and saved for you.

PROJECT 5B

1. Go to the student **datafile** folder and open **online**. Use **Save As** to save the file as **online proj5b xxx**. With the insertion point at the top of the document, press **Enter** to add some line spaces above the first paragraph.

2. Move your insertion point to the top again. Use **Flush Right** and key your full name at the right margin. Press **Enter** and use **Flush Right** and **Date Text** to position the date below your name.

3. Double-space following the date, and center the title in **Bold** and **Caps** as shown below. Use **20-pt. Arial** for the title.

COMMUNICATIONS ONLINE

4. Adjust the spacing so one blank line separates the title from the first line of the first paragraph.

5. Return to the top of the document and use the **Center Page** command to center the document vertically.

6. Use **Double Indent** for the second paragraph. Select that paragraph and apply **Bold** to the entire paragraph.

7. In the last sentence, select *free speech*. Change those two words to **Italic**. Do the same with *full exchange of ideas*.

8. Insert the Path and Filename code a double space below the last paragraph. Check your work carefully. Then print it and close it, saving it again with the same name.

CRITICAL THINKING ACTIVITY

SCANS

As you practice using the Date Text and Date Code features, think about when one would be more appropriate than the other. Make a list of the types of documents in which you would insert Date Text. Make another list of the types of documents in which you would insert a Date Code.

EDITING FEATURES

LESSON 6

OBJECTIVES

Upon completion of this lesson, you will be able to:

- Use Find to search for unique strings of text.
- Use Replace to replace existing text with different text.
- Use Select for cutting, copying, moving, and pasting text.
- Highlight text to call attention to it with the Highlight tool.
- Use Drag and Drop for editing selected text.

⏱ **Estimated Time: 1 hour**

You have already learned quite a number of ways to edit your text. You learned that to edit, you can:

- Use Backspace to delete text to the left of the insertion point.
- Use Delete to delete text to the right of the insertion point.
- Use Ctrl+Delete to delete from the insertion point to the end of the line.
- Use Ctrl+Backspace to delete the word at the insertion point.
- Delete formatting codes (such as Indent) with the Backspace or Delete keys, depending on where the insertion point is located.
- Delete formatting codes by dragging them out of the Reveal Codes window.
- Select a chunk of text and delete it with the Backspace or Delete keys.
- Select a chunk of text and key new text over the selected text.
- Use Typeover to key new text over existing text.

As you can see, you've learned a lot in five short lessons about how to manipulate the text showing in your window. One of the basic premises of any word processing program is that you should "edit—don't rekey."

In this lesson you will learn about several other powerful features that help support you with this idea of editing. Work carefully in this lesson so you master the concepts covered. They are critical!

Find and Replace

The *Find and Replace* feature enables you to tell the computer to look through the open document to locate specific words, phrases, or codes. It can also be used to replace one piece of text or code with another. Find and Replace can be chosen from the Edit menu, by pressing F2, or by pressing Ctrl+F.

We'll learn about Find and Replace with a couple of simple exercises, beginning with Find.

EXERCISE 6.1

1. Open **pc-tv** from the student **datafile** folder. Use **Save As** to save the document as **pc-tv 6-1 xxx**. Keep the insertion point at the top of the file.

2. Open the **Edit** menu and choose **Find and Replace**. The Find and Replace dialog box should open, looking much like Figure 6-1.

3. With the insertion point in the *Find* text box, key **morp** and click **Find Next** or press **Enter**. (The word you are searching for is much longer than what you keyed, but you have enough unique characters so you know WordPerfect will take you directly to the text for which you're searching.)

4. Your insertion point should be moved directly to the word *morphing*.

5. Click outside of the Find and Replace dialog box to make your document window the active window. Press **Ctrl+Home** to return to the beginning of the document.

6. Point to *morp* in the dialog box and click to activate the dialog box. Double click to highlight *morp* in the *Find* text box. Key **tv** in lowercase letters. Then click the **Find Next** button.

7. WordPerfect will stop at the first occurrence of *tv*. Click **Find Next** again. Continue the procedure, counting the number of times *tv* appears in the document. When WordPerfect can find no more occurrences of *tv*, a warning box will tell you that. Click **No** at the Begin again question. Did you find five occurrences?

8. Click outside of the dialog box and return to the top of the document. Keep the document open as you read on.

FIGURE 6-1
Find and Replace Dialog Box

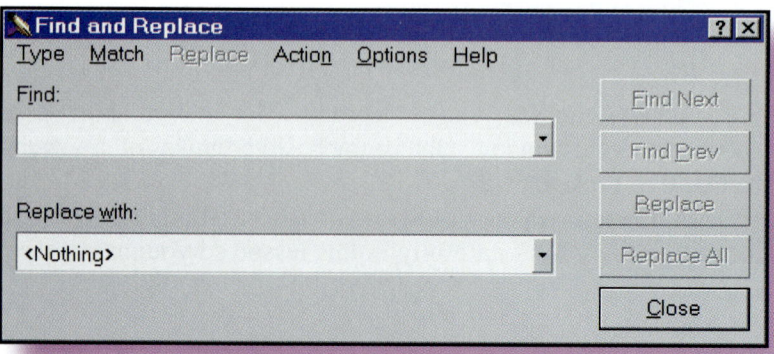

UNIT 2: COREL WORDPERFECT BASICS

Some of the more important Find and Replace options come from the Match menu. Let's look at the following Match options:

- **Whole Word**. If you choose Whole Word, WordPerfect will not find the specified text when it is part of another word. For example, if you search for *the* and you don't choose Whole Word, WordPerfect will stop at *weather, them, further, these,* etc.

- **Case**. In Exercise 6.1 you keyed *tv* in lowercase and Find found it. That's because the default for Find is not case-sensitive. We'll experiment with this shortly.

- **Font**. This menu choice opens a dialog box where you may choose the font code or appearance attribute for which you're searching.

- **Codes**. The final choice in the Match menu provides a long list of codes for which you may search.

Now that you have an introduction to these features, let's experiment.

EXERCISE 6.2

1. With your insertion point at the beginning of the document and the Find and Replace dialog box open, open the **Match** menu.

2. Choose **Whole Word**. See how many times WordPerfect will stop at the word *tv* this time. (It should be four times because it won't find the occurrence with the *s*.)

3. Return to the top of the document and choose **Case** from the **Match** menu. Then press **Enter** or click **Find Next**. How many occurrences of *tv* did WordPerfect find? What happened?

4. Return to the top of the document. In the **Match** menu, deselect **Whole Word**. (Case is still selected.)

5. In the *Find* text box, change the text from *tv* to **TV**. Now use **Find Next** to go through the document. Did you find five occurrences of *TV*? Return your insertion point to the top of the document.

6. In the **Match** menu, deselect **Case**. Open the **Match** menu again and choose **Codes**. The resulting dialog box should look much like Figure 6-2.

7. Scroll way down in the list until you find *Hd Left Ind*. Click the code to select it. Then click the **Insert & Close** button. (If *TV* is still in the *Find* box, delete it.)

8. Click **Find Next**. Did Find take you directly to the beginning of the indented paragraph?

9. Close the Find and Replace dialog box, but keep your document open as you read on.

FIGURE 6-2
Find and Replace Codes Dialog Box

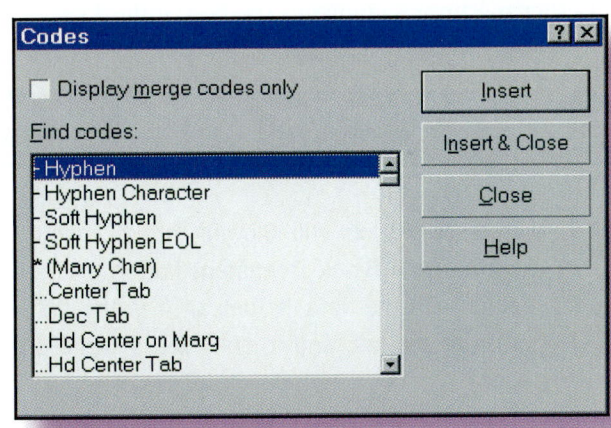

You're doing well. You have already practiced the main parts of Find. Now let's learn about Replace.

Replace uses Find to locate the text that needs to be replaced.

EXERCISE 6.3

1. With your insertion point at the top of the **pc-tv 6-1 xxx** document, open the Find and Replace dialog box.

2. In the *Find* box, key **tv**. Press **Tab**.

3. In the *Replace with* box, key **bicycle**. (OK. So it's corny. But it's good practice!)

4. Click the **Find Next** button. When Word-Perfect stops at the first occurrence of *TV,* click **Replace**. (Note that because *TV* had a capital letter at the beginning, the replacement—*Bicycle*—will also have an initial cap.)

5. WordPerfect will stop at the next occurrence of *TV,* waiting for you to confirm the replace-ment. This time, click **Replace All**. The remaining four replacements should be made in a jiffy! (Can you count better than WordPerfect can?)

6. Click outside of the Find and Replace dialog box and press **Ctrl+Home** to return to the beginning of your document. Can you use **Replace** to change *Bicycle* back to *TV* on your own?

7. Close the Find and Replace dialog box. Keep your document open in the window as you read on.

While you can easily use Replace All to replace each occurrence of one word with another, it usually isn't safe. Sometimes you need to see the surrounding text to know if other repairs need to be made. For example, assume you had a long document containing the names of Mary Christensen and Harry Christianson. When you keyed the document, you spelled Harry's name like Mary's—Christensen. You can use Replace to fix the error, but you must confirm every replacement so you can look at the surrounding text to see if it is referring to Mary or Harry.

WordPerfect helps you to maintain good grammar with the Word Forms choice in the Type menu. Let's try a little exercise to see how it works.

EXERCISE 6.4

1. With **pc-tv 6-1 xxx** still showing in the window, click the **New Blank Document** button on the Toolbar. (On the default Toolbar, it is the first button at the left, and it looks like a piece of paper.)

2. Key the little paragraph in Figure 6-3. Then return the insertion point to the beginning of the document.

3. Open the Find and Replace dialog box. Open the **Type** menu and click **Word Forms**.

4. In the *Find* text box, key **fly**. In the *Replace with* text box, key **swim**.

5. Click the **Replace All** button. Study your sentences. Note that WordPerfect was smart enough to spell *swimming* correctly.

6. Close the Find and Replace dialog box, and close your document without saving it. The **pc-tv 6-1 xxx** document should still be showing in your window. (It was hiding under the other document.) Keep it open and read on.

FIGURE 6-3
Text for Exercise 6.4

```
I have always wanted to learn to fly.  To me there couldn't be
anything more delightful than flying freely with no stop signs.
```

You'll find lots of opportunities to use Find and Replace. You will also find that it is a great time-saver, both for locating specific places in your documents and for replacing text.

Editing with Select

In Lesson 2 you learned that you can select a block of text and delete it all at once. In Lesson 3 you learned that you can select a block of text and format it with appearance attributes such as Bold, Italic, or Underline. It shouldn't come as any surprise to you that you can select blocks of text and move them around in your documents.

You learned that text can be selected using the mouse. You can also turn on Select with F8 or choose it from the Edit menu and use the arrow keys to define the size of a block of text. In this lesson we'll practice both methods, although it is usually faster to select text using the mouse.

We will also use the Windows Clipboard. Whenever you are working in one of the many Windows programs, you can use the Windows Clipboard for cutting, moving, and pasting selected text.

Cut

As you know, once text has been selected, you can cut it from your document with Delete. When you do this, it goes into the Delete holding space—the place that holds three deletions that can be restored, if you wish, with Undelete.

The text can also be cut to the Windows Clipboard in the following ways:

- By using the Ctrl+X shortcut.
- By clicking the Cut button (scissors icon) on the Toolbar.
- By choosing Cut from the Edit menu.

When you cut text to the Windows Clipboard, it remains there until you cut something else or until you close WordPerfect. Usually when you cut text, your intention is to move the insertion point to a different location where you will choose to paste the text.

Paste

Paste is used to place text that is on the Clipboard back into your document. You can paste from the Clipboard in the following ways:

- By pressing Ctrl+V.
- By clicking the Paste button (clipboard icon) on the Toolbar.
- By choosing Paste from the Edit menu.

Before you paste, you must position the insertion point where you want the text to be pasted. Cutting and pasting is a great way to move text from one location to another. Let's practice. We'll begin by selecting text with yet another method. Position the insertion point at the beginning of the block of text to be selected, hold the Shift key, and click at the end of the block of text to be selected.

EXERCISE 6.5

1. With **pc-tv 6-1 xxx** still showing in your window, move the insertion point to the beginning of the document.

2. Press **F8**. Press the down arrow key until the first paragraph is selected, along with the line separating the first two paragraphs.

3. Press **Ctrl+X** to cut the paragraph. It will disappear from the document.

4. Press **Ctrl+End** to move the insertion point to the end of the document, a double space below the final paragraph. Press **Ctrl+V** to paste the paragraph at the bottom.

Now we'll move a different paragraph with the mouse and the **Edit** menu.

5. Point to the paragraph in the middle and quadruple click to select the paragraph, together with the blank line following the paragraph.

6. Open the **Edit** menu and choose **Cut**. Press **Ctrl+Home** to move the insertion point to the top of the document. Open the **Edit** menu and choose **Paste** to paste the paragraph at the top.

Let's use the Toolbar to do the same thing.

7. Position the insertion point at the left margin of the first line of the indented paragraph. Hold the **Shift** key while you point with the mouse to the left margin opposite the first line of the next paragraph. Click once to select the paragraph and the line following it.

8. Point to the Cut tool on the Toolbar—the scissors icon—and click to cut the paragraph. Move the insertion point to the end of the document and click the Paste tool on the Toolbar—the clipboard icon—to paste the paragraph at the end of the document.

9. Keep your document open in the window as you read on to learn the difference between cutting and copying. You'll also read about yet another way to perform these activities.

Copy

Copy is like Cut except that the text you select and place on the Clipboard will also remain in its original position in the document. You might use Copy to copy a phrase, sentence, or paragraph to a different location in a document. Or it is more likely that you would copy a block of text onto the Clipboard so that it could be used in a different document.

Like Cut and Paste, Copy can be selected in the following ways:

- By pressing Ctrl+C.
- By clicking the Copy button (with two "pages") on the Toolbar.
- By opening the Edit menu and choosing Copy.
- From the QuickMenu.

Let's use the same three paragraphs to practice Copy. This time we'll use the QuickMenu.

QuickMenus

As you know, QuickMenus are displayed by clicking the right mouse button. If you have never worked with QuickMenus, you should read about them in Appendix B. The tools available in a QuickMenu depend on where you are pointing and what is happening in your window when you right click.

If text is selected, the QuickMenu includes Cut, Copy, and Paste. It also includes some other tools about which you've been learning. We'll use the QuickMenu in Exercise 6.6.

EXERCISE 6.6

1. With **pc-tv 6-1 xxx** still showing in the window, save the file as **pc-tv 6-6 xxx**. Position the insertion point at the beginning of the paragraph in the middle.

2. Select that paragraph (be sure to include the line following the paragraph). Right click to display the QuickMenu. It should look like Figure 6-4. Choose **Copy** to copy the paragraph to the Clipboard.

3. Press **Ctrl+End** to move the insertion point to the end of the document. Point below the final paragraph and right click to display the QuickMenu again. Choose **Paste** to paste the paragraph into place. Now your document should have two paragraphs exactly alike.

FIGURE 6-4
QuickMenu

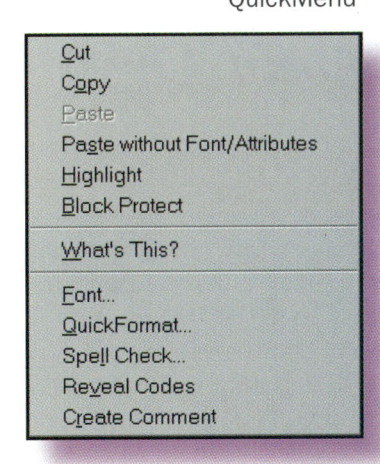

Cut
Copy
Paste
Paste without Font/Attributes
Highlight
Block Protect
What's This?
Font...
QuickFormat...
Spell Check...
Reveal Codes
Create Comment

(continued on next page)

EXERCISE 6.6 CONTINUED

4. Study the QuickMenu in Figure 6-4. Notice that it contains some additional features about which you've already learned—Cut, Paste, Font, and Reveal Codes.

5. Double click to select any word in the document. Right click to display the QuickMenu and choose **Highlight**. Reveal your codes and look at the Highlight code. Add it to your list. (We'll discuss this feature shortly.)

6. Practice cutting, copying, and pasting until you are comfortable with the procedure. Then insert the Path and Filename code a double space below the last paragraph.

7. Print your messed-up document and save it again with the same name. Keep it open.

Vertical Spacing

Whenever you use Cut, Copy, and Paste, you should always check the vertical spacing of your document after you've completed the move. It's easy to leave an extra hard return in the old location or end up with two pieces of text too close together in the new location. When that happens, you must add or delete hard returns to make the text correctly spaced. ALWAYS visually check your work when you edit. You'll save yourself much time and frustration.

Methods of Editing

Also, this is a good time to observe that while you normally learn only one way to perform a task, this time you learned FOUR of them! The method you use will depend on where your hands are when you need a feature, and it will also depend on personal preference. Whichever method(s) you choose to use, you will become quite skilled at cutting, copying, and pasting text. It helps you with the "don't rekey" mentality that needs to be developed with word processing. It also helps you save time and errors.

Drag and Drop

One more editing tool deserves mention here. This tool is called *Drag and Drop*. The procedure is to select text to be moved or copied and then use the mouse to drag that selected text to its new position.

If the place where you wish to drag the text is below the text showing in the window, simply drag your mouse pointer into the Application Bar at the bottom. WordPerfect will scroll up in the window until you can see the desired location for the text.

Drag and Drop can be used to move text or to copy text. To move, simply drag it and drop it. To copy, hold the Ctrl key while you drag and drop the text. Let's try it.

> **INTERNET**
> The Internet can be found on all seven continents, including Antarctica. A host at the South Pole sends out scientific and weather information.

EXERCISE 6.7

1. With **pc-tv 6-6 xxx** showing in your window, save the file as **pc-tv 6-7 xxx**.

2. Select the indented paragraph—wherever it is in your document. Point to the selected text and depress the left mouse button. Hold it down and move the mouse slightly. The move icon should appear—an arrow with a page attached to the tail.

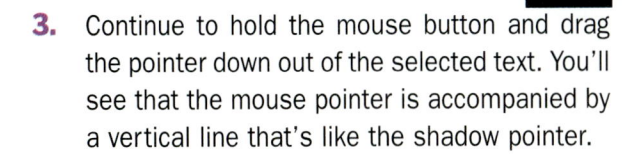

3. Continue to hold the mouse button and drag the pointer down out of the selected text. You'll see that the mouse pointer is accompanied by a vertical line that's like the shadow pointer.

4. Move the shadow pointer until it is a double space below the final paragraph of the document, just in front of the Path and Filename code. Release the mouse button. The paragraph should be moved to that position. (Repair the spacing around the paragraph and at the top, if necessary.)

5. To copy a paragraph, select the paragraph that is currently second in your document. Hold the **Ctrl** key while you point to the selected text and depress the left mouse button. Hold **Ctrl** and the mouse button as you move the mouse slightly. The copy icon will change from a pointer with two copies of a page to a pointer with a plus sign.

6. Move the mouse and the shadow pointer so the pointer is to the left of the final paragraph and release the mouse button to drop the paragraph there.

7. Practice copying and moving words, sentences, phrases, or paragraphs using the Drag and Drop procedure until you are comfortable with it. Don't worry about messing up the document.

8. When you finish, close the document without saving it.

Highlight

You used Highlight to paint text yellow in Exercise 6.6. Highlight is a way of marking text for shared documents. You can change the color of highlighting and use several colors in the same document. You can also hide the highlighting so it doesn't show in the window or on the printed copy, but the codes remain in the copy so the highlighting can be displayed again.

When you practiced Highlight in Exercise 6.6, you selected the text before selecting Highlight from the QuickMenu. If you prefer, you can turn Highlight on and highlight text by dragging the mouse pointer over text in your document. You probably noticed that highlighted text prints with a shaded background.

Highlight can also be chosen from the Toolbar (the icon near the middle that looks like a yellow marker) or from the Tools menu. In fact, if you wish to change any of the Highlight options, you must choose Tools and then Highlight.

You may explore Highlight at your leisure. Be sure to change it back to the defaults when you finish—with the color as yellow and with Print/Show Highlighting selected.

Summary

In addition to Find and Replace, the major thrust of this lesson had to do with selected text. In this lesson you learned that:

- You can use Find to move the insertion point to a unique string of characters.
- Replace enables you to find text to be replaced and replace it automatically. Text can be replaced one occurrence at a time or globally.
- There are a number of ways to cut or copy text to the Clipboard.
- There are an equal number of ways to paste from the Clipboard.
- If you cut and paste text, it is deleted from the original location.
- If you copy and paste text, you'll have two copies of that chunk of text.
- You can select text and drag or copy it to a new location.
- Text can be marked with Highlight to make it stand out for the attention of others.

LESSON 6 REVIEW QUESTIONS

WRITTEN QUESTIONS

Write your answers to the following questions.

1. Describe the functions of the Find and Replace feature. *To locate specific words or phrases and, where necessary, replace them with new text.*
2. What three ways can text be cut to the Windows Clipboard? *Ctrl+X shortcut; by clicking the "Cut" (scissors) button; selecting "Cut" on the Edit Menu.*
3. In order to display the QuickMenu that includes features such as Cut, Copy, and Paste, what must be done with your text? *Select the text before Right Clicking the mouse to bring the Quick Menu up on screen.*
4. The Drag and Drop feature can be used two ways. Name them. *To move or copy text.*
5. What is the name of the feature that can be used as a way of marking text for shared documents and can be chosen from the Toolbar with an icon that looks like a yellow marker? *"Highlight"*

TRUE / FALSE

Circle the T if the statement is true. Circle the F if it is false.

(T) F 6. The default for Find is not case sensitive.

T **(F)** 7. Once you paste text that is on the Clipboard back into your document, it is removed from the Clipboard.

T F 8. Copy is like Cut except the text you select and place on the Clipboard will also remain in its original position.

T F 9. When using Drag and Drop to copy text, hold the Ctrl key while you drag and drop.

T **F** 10. You can change the color of highlighting as long as you maintain that same color throughout your document.

LESSON 6 PROJECT

Let's try some of the features you learned in this lesson on a document that has been keyed and saved for you. As always, remember to read through the entire exercise before beginning. Work efficiently and carefully.

1. Open **gifts proj5a xxx**. Use **Save As** to save the file as **gifts proj6 xxx**. (If you make a mess of the project and need to start again, close this file without saving. Open **gifts proj6 xxx** and begin again.)

2. Use **Find and Replace** to replace the word *vulgar* with the word **offensive**.

3. Using either **Cut and Paste** or **Drag and Drop**, rearrange the first three items in the list into the following order. (Read Step 4 before you begin.)

    1. *Chocolates . . .*
    2. *Gifts with company logos . . .*
    3. *Flowers . . .*

4. Note that the items are automatically renumbered. If you lose a numeral with:
    a. **Drag and Drop:** Click the **Undo** button on the Toolbar and start again. (When positioning the shadow pointer to "drop" the item into place, point in the left margin, opposite the margin guideline. That puts the insertion point in front of the numeral.)
    b. **Cut and Paste:** Position the insertion point at the end of the last line above the missing numeral and press **Enter**. Then delete the spaces to bring the text up to the numeral. (The best way to paste an item before a numbered item so you don't lose a numeral is to first click on the line where the item is to be pasted. Then press **Home** twice to get the insertion point to the left of all codes on the line. Finally, paste the item into place.)

5. Exchange items 4 and 5.

6. Position the insertion point at the beginning of the *Be careful . . .* sentence in the final item. Press **Enter** to give it a number and make it item 8 in the list.

7. Exchange items 7 and 8.

8. Save the file again with the same name. Then print it and close it.

CRITICAL THINKING ACTIVITY

SCANS

One of the members of your small group helping with your Environmental Science Class report just realized she gave you an incorrect spelling of one of the endangered species about which you wrote. The other members have also suggested that the order of the information needs to be changed with some additions and deletions. What are some of the features you learned to use in this lesson that could be put to use with this report?

WRITING TOOLS

LESSON 7

OBJECTIVES

Upon completion of this lesson, you will be able to:

- Discuss the QuickCorrect feature.
- Fix words marked with the WordPerfect Spell-As-You-Go feature.
- Use Spell Check to find errors in your document.
- Use the WordPerfect Thesaurus to help you find the right word.
- Use Grammatik to check the grammar in your documents.
- Use Prompt-As-You-Go

Estimated Time: 1 hour

WordPerfect has several tools to help you with spelling and keying as you enter your text. Those tools are Spell-As-You-Go, Prompt-As-You-Go, QuickCorrect, WordPerfect Spell Check, the WordPerfect Thesaurus, QuickWords, and a grammar checker called Grammatik.

Let's learn about QuickCorrect, Spell-As-You-Go, and Prompt-As-You-Go, and then we'll learn about some of the other tools. QuickWords will be covered in Lesson 11.

QuickCorrect

You learned in an earlier lesson that WordPerfect automatically corrects some of your errors as you key. The program contains dozens of commonly misspelled or miskeyed words, as well as some odd things like ordinals (the *th* in 6th and $^{1}/_{2}$). It also makes some changes to capitalization—sometimes they are changes you don't want. When QuickCorrect capitalizes a letter that should remain a lowercase letter, fix it with Backspace or Delete. Sometimes it takes two tries. Let's practice by keying some of the errors QuickCorrect fixes.

INTERNET The communications structure of the Internet is the global telephone system, which is a network of networks working together. By using the phone system, the Internet has worldwide coverage and significant potential for growth.

EXERCISE 7.1

1. Watch your window as you key the sentence in Figure 7-1, complete with errors.

2. When you finish, close the practice without saving it.

FIGURE 7-1
Text for Exercise 7.1

```
THe dog adn cat are in teh barn.
```

You probably noticed that the correction was made when you pressed the space bar following the word with the error.

QuickCorrect can be customized to fix errors you make frequently. You can also add shortcuts for words and phrases you use often. Then when you key the shortcut, the longer version will appear. Let's try a quick exercise in customizing QuickCorrect.

EXERCISE 7.2

1. In a new document window, open the **Tools** menu and choose **QuickCorrect**. The Quick-Correct dialog box should appear, looking much like Figure 7-2.

2. Use the scroll bar to look through the list at the kinds of mistakes QuickCorrect fixes.

3. Browse through the other four tabs and look at the choices available there. Do not make any changes to the options unless your instructor tells you to. Return to the Quick-Correct tab.

4. In the *Replace* text box at the upper left, key **wp**. Tab to the next box. Key **WordPerfect**. Click the **Add Entry** button and then click **OK**.

5. In your document window, key the paragraph illustrated in Figure 7-3. Each time you come to *WordPerfect*, key **wp** and press the space bar. At the end of the paragraph, press **Enter** twice. Did the word expand like you expected it to?

FIGURE 7-2
QuickCorrect Dialog Box

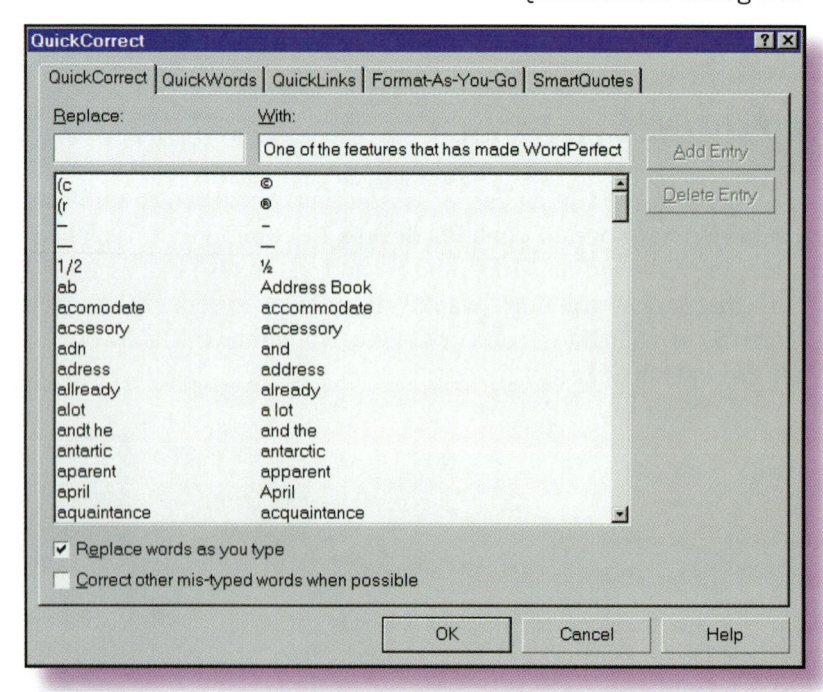

92

UNIT 2: COREL WORDPERFECT BASICS

6. Return to the QuickCorrect dialog box. Scroll through the list until you find the *WordPerfect* entry. Highlight it and click the **Delete Entry** button to delete it. Then click **OK** to close the dialog box.

7. Save your paragraph as **fix 7-2 xxx**.

8. Keep the document open in the window as you read on.

FIGURE 7-3
Text for Exercise 7.2

```
    I am in the process of learning about WordPerfect word processing
on a computer.  In the few lessons I have completed, I've learned that
WordPerfect is a great computer application program.  I certainly hope
that when I get a computer at work, I will have a choice of word
processing programs so I can use WordPerfect.
```

Obviously, the shortcut you use must be a unique set of characters. Also, the expanded text is limited to about 125 characters. Do NOT make any changes to QuickCorrect in the classroom unless your instructor gives you permission to add entries. On the job, however, this feature should be of great value to you.

Spell-As-You-Go

Another feature that helps you identify errors in your documents is Spell-As-You-Go. This is the feature that underlines in red words that aren't in the WordPerfect dictionary. Up to this point, you probably have been manually correcting those underlined words. A couple of alternatives are available.

When the insertion point is in a word that is underlined in red, that word is shown in red in the text box at the right of the Property Bar. (Words that are spelled correctly show in black in that box.) The feature is referred to as Prompt-As-You-Go, and it fits together with the Spell-As-You-Go feature. Spell-As-You-Go offers the following two choices:

- When the insertion point is in the incorrect word and the word is red in the Prompt-As-You-Go box, you can click the arrow beside the box and choose the correct spelling of the word.

- When a word is underlined in red, regardless of the position of the insertion point, you can point to it and right click. This displays a short list of possible spellings, as well as some additional options. You can choose the correct spelling from the list.

Let's try a short exercise so you can see how Spell-As-You-Go and Prompt-As-You-Go work.

EXERCISE 7.3

1. With **fix 7-2 xxx** showing in the window, use **Save As** to save the file as **fix 7-3 xxx**.

2. Position the insertion point at the end of the document and key the sentence in Figure 7-4.

   Do not correct the misspelled words as you key. (Keep an eye on the Prompt-As-You-Go box.)

   (continued on next page)

9 3

EXERCISE 7.3 CONTINUED

3. When you finish, click to position the insertion point in *WordPerfct* and click the arrow beside the Prompt-As-You-Go box on the Property Bar. Choose the correct spelling of WordPerfect.

4. Point to *underlning* and right click. Look at the options at the bottom of the menu. Then choose the correct spelling of *underlining* from the list at the top.

5. Use either method to fix *speled*.

6. Read your sentence carefully. Did Spell-As-You-Go find all of the errors? Why do you suppose it missed *sem*? Fix the word.

7. Insert the Path and Filename code a double space below the last paragraph. Click the **Save** button on the Toolbar to save your document again as **fix 7-3 xxx**.

8. Print the two-paragraph document and close it.

FIGURE 7-4
Text for Exercise 7.3

```
WordPerfct helps you by underlning words that don't sem to be speled
correctly.
```

Spell Check

Spell Check uses the same WordPerfect dictionary as Spell-As-You-Go for checking the words in your document. With Spell Check, however, you will probably check the document after you've finished it. Like Spell-As-You-Go, Spell Check helps you build supplementary dictionaries to fill specific needs.

Spell Check can be chosen from the Tools menu or the Spell Check button on the default Toolbar. It pictures a book with a red *s*. Perhaps the best way to get a feel for Spell Check is to try it on a document containing errors. After practicing, some of the features and cautions regarding Spell Check will be discussed.

EXERCISE 7.4

1. Open **errors** from the student **datafile** folder. Use **Save As** to save the file as **errors 7-4 xxx**.

2. Select the parenthetical information in the first line and key your name in its place. Do the same at the bottom of the document. Select the parenthetical information about the school and key the name of your school in that location.

3. Click the **Spell Check** button on the Toolbar or open the **Tools** menu and choose **Spell Check**. A dialog box will open that looks like Figure 7-5. Note that the Spell Checker tab is chosen. WordPerfect may stop at your name. If it does, click **Skip All**, because you probably spelled your name correctly.

4. Next, WordPerfect will stop at *lerning*. WordPerfect prompts you to replace the word with *leaning*. Click *learning* in the Replacements box and then click **Replace**. When WordPerfect stops at *WordPerfek*, no suggested spelling is available. In the *Replace with* text box, delete the *k*. Then *WordPerfect* will be prompted in the Replacements box. Click the correct spelling and then you can click the **Replace** button.

5. Continue through the document correcting the misspelled words.
   a. If the correct word appears in the *Replace with* text box, click the **Replace** button.
   b. If the correct word is in the list below, click it to select it and then click the **Replace** button.
   c. Some errors may have to be fixed manually. When that occurs, make the correction in the *Replace with* text box and click the **Replace** button. (You can also make the correction right in your text and click the **Resume** button when you are ready to continue spell checking your document.)

6. When WordPerfect tells you that all errors are corrected, confirm that Spell Check should be closed.

7. Proofread your document carefully. Did Spell Check find the missing capital letter at the beginning of the last sentence? Did it know that *corse* was not correct? Fix both errors.

8. Add the Path and Filename code a double space below your name and print the document. Save it again with the same name and keep it open.

FIGURE 7-5
Spell Checker Dialog Box

What did Spell Check do when it came to your name at the bottom of the document? Because you chose Skip All at the top, it should have skipped the one at the bottom without even highlighting it.

This document was filled with foolishly misspelled words that you would have caught and corrected if you had been asked to proofread. Many times, however, even if you've proofread, it's a good idea to run Spell Check to be certain that all of the words are correctly spelled.

You didn't use all of the choices in the dialog box. Following is a brief explanation of the main buttons in the dialog box:

■ **Replace.** Replaces the word or phrase with the text in the Replace with box. You can select one of the suggested replacements or edit the word or phrase in the text box.

95

- **Resume**. Lets you continue an incomplete spell check if you click in the document while the Spell Checker is displayed.

- **Skip Once**. Skips the current occurrence of the word or phrase.

- **Skip All**. Skips every occurrence of the word or phrase during the current spell check.

- **Add**. Adds the current replacement word or phrase to the user word list showing in the Add to drop-down list. We won't make any changes to the lists in the classroom. If you were on the job, however, you might add your name and your boss's name, and perhaps, the name of your company or city.

- **Auto Replace**. Enables you to define automatic replacements for words as you key them.

- **Undo**. Backs you up to the previous correction.

- **Options**. Gives you some choices regarding how the document is checked. Figure 7-6 shows the Options menu. The User Word Lists choice enables you to go into the word list to delete items. In addition to the multiple user word lists, you can purchase additional main word lists and various language modules. The check marks in the figure show the default settings. If you deselect Auto start, for example, WordPerfect will wait for you to click a Start button before spell checking begins. Don't change any of the options unless your instructor asks you to do so.

FIGURE 7-6
Spell Options Menu

Miscellaneous Spell Check Notes

Following is a review and some additional information about Spell Check:

- The document to be checked should be showing in the window.
- Click Close if you wish to discontinue checking.
- Sometimes Spell Check takes a moment to find the next word. Be patient.
- You can check a block of text by first selecting the text in the usual manner. Then start Spell Check.
- Spell Check doesn't recognize an incorrect word if the word is spelled correctly. It can't distinguish, for example, between the correct usage of *house* and *horse*.

YOU MUST PROOFREAD YOUR WORK CAREFULLY, even when you use Spell Check.

Thesaurus

In addition to Spell Check, WordPerfect contains a Thesaurus. The Thesaurus helps you find just the right word when you're unsure how to say something. It does this by providing a list of synonyms (words that have the same meaning). You may have noticed the Thesaurus tab when you were using Spell Check. WordPerfect also offers a list of synonyms for any word that shows in black in the Prompt-As-You-Go box. Let's try the Thesaurus on the corrected document you used for Spell Check.

EXERCISE 7.5

1. With **errors 7-4 xxx** showing in the window, use **Save As** to save the file as **errors 7-5 xxx**.

2. Position the insertion point in the word *beautiful* in the last line of the first paragraph.

3. Click the arrow beside the Prompt-As-You-Go box on the Property Bar and look at the list of possible synonyms for *beautiful*. Press the **Esc** button to close the list.

4. Open the **Tools** menu and choose **Thesaurus**. Look at the dialog box. It looks much like the Spell Checker dialog box. In fact, it is the third tab of the Spell Check dialog box. (See Figure 7-7.)

5. The word *beautiful* appears above a list of synonyms. Use the scroll bar beside the list of synonyms for *beautiful* and look through the words. What are two of the antonyms (opposites) for *beautiful*? Now scroll back to the top of the list.

6. Point to *lovely* in the list and double click. A list of synonyms for *lovely* will appear.

7. Point to *elegant* and click once. Then choose **Replace** to replace *beautiful* in your document with *elegant*. When you make a replacement, the Thesaurus is closed.

8. Print the document. Save it again as **errors 7-5 xxx**. Keep it open.

FIGURE 7-7
Tabs in Writing Tools

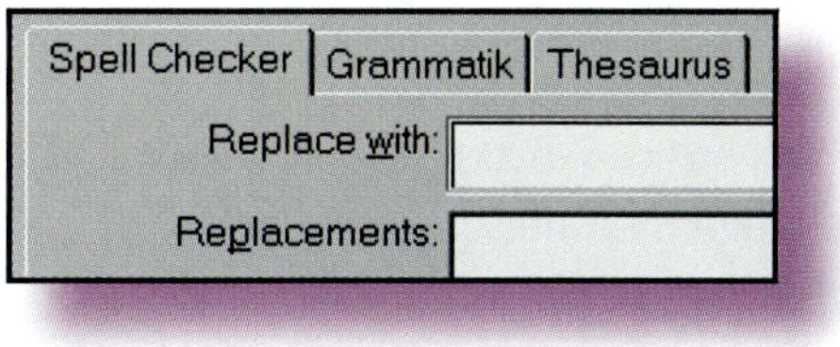

You can close the Thesaurus dialog box at any time by clicking the Close button. Sometimes you may wish to look up a word in the Thesaurus but not make any replacement in your document. Whether you use the Thesaurus dialog box or the Prompt-As-You-Go drop-down menu, the Thesaurus should be a great help in your writing.

Grammatik

The third tab in the dialog box is a grammar checker called Grammatik. This tool looks for grammar, punctuation, and style flaws in your documents. Even if you have a good command of the English language and write well, Grammatik can help you find ways to improve the way you put your words together.

Let's try a short Grammatik exercise so you can see how it works. This exercise contains your name and the name of your school. Grammatik probably won't find those names in the dictionary. If it doesn't and those names are highlighted, click Skip All.

EXERCISE 7.6

1. With **errors 7-5 xxx** showing in the window, open the **Tools** menu and choose **Grammatik**. Look at the dialog box. It is the second tab of the dialog box. (If a dialog box appears asking if you'd like the grammar checker closed, click **No**.)

2. Choose **Options** and then **Checking Style**. If Quick Check isn't selected, choose it.

3. Click **Skip All** for any names that are highlighted. If you are asked if you'd like the grammar checker closed, click **No**.

Grammatik allows you to check your work using a variety of writing styles. Obviously, using Quick Check, the sentences were complete and everything was OK. Let's check the paragraphs using one of the other styles.

EXERCISE 7.7

1. With **errors 7-5 xxx** still showing in the window, change the Checking style from Quick Check to **Student Composition**. Click **Select**.

2. After it gets past your name and school (click Skip Once if either of these is highlighted), Grammatik will highlight the phrase *in the process of*. Look at the explanation. It says the phrase is wordy, but neither of the suggested solutions fits.

3. Click somewhere in the phrase and delete all of the words that were highlighted. Your sentence will read *I am learning . . . .* Then click the **Resume** button. (If you are asked if you'd like to close Grammatik, choose No.)

4. Grammatik may or may not highlight some of the other sentences or phrases in the paragraphs. If it does, see if you can work your way through the solution without help.

5. Try a couple of other styles to see if Grammatik finds anything else it doesn't like.

6. Change the Checking style back to Quick Check. Then read on to see what else Grammatik can do for you.

The Prompt-As-You-Go box shows words in blue when WordPerfect identifies a grammatical error. When that happens, the drop-down list provides some possible "fixes." This document didn't have any screaming errors. Grammatik is good at finding incomplete sentences, subject-verb agreement errors, incorrect punctuation, etc. Whenever you do any original writing of your own, you may wish to use this tool to help make your documents easier to read.

One of the other things you can do with Grammatik is check the statistics for your document. When you check for statistics, Grammatik will provide lots of information about the document—the number of words, the number of syllables, and reading grade level. Let's check **errors 7-5 xxx**.

EXERCISE 7.8

1. With **errors 7-5 xxx** still showing in the window and the Grammatik dialog box displayed, click the **Options** button and choose **Analysis**.

2. Then choose **Readability**. Look at the dialog box that is displayed. The **errors 7-5** document will probably be compared with a Hemingway short story. Note that the short story has a grade 4 level, while the **errors** paragraphs have about a grade 9 level. Check the vocabulary comparison.

3. Click the **Basic Counts** button at the bottom of the dialog box. Note the number of words, etc.

4. Finally, click the **Close** button in Basic Counts and the **Close** button for Grammatik. Then close your document without saving it.

This was a very quick introduction to Grammatik. The tool has a number of additional features. For example, you can create a custom writing style for specific documents. You may wish to explore this tool further at your leisure.

Summary

In this lesson you reviewed a couple of WordPerfect tools you learned about earlier, and you were introduced to some additional tools. All of them were designed to help you create documents with few, if any, errors. You learned that:

- QuickCorrect repairs some of your keying errors. Entries can be added to help you with your work.

- Spell-As-You-Go identifies words that may need to be fixed. WordPerfect makes suggestions regarding the correct spelling of those words.

- Spell Check can be used to check your document after you've finished keying. It finds words that aren't in the WordPerfect dictionaries.

- The Thesaurus may be used to look for the "right" word.

- Grammatik is a grammar checker that can count your words, as well as find errors in your punctuation and sentence structure.

- Prompt-As-You-Go can help you with spelling, grammar, and finding the right word. It is a feature on the Property Bar.

LESSON 7 REVIEW QUESTIONS

FILL IN THE BLANKS

Complete each of the following statements by writing your answer in the blank provided.

1. The QuickCorrect dialog box is opened from the _Tools_ menu.

2. The feature, _Spell-as-you-go_, refers to the text box at the right of the Property Bar that shows incorrectly spelled words in red.

3. The feature that underlines in red words that aren't in the WordPerfect dictionary is known as _Spell-as-you-go_.

4. Clicking the icon on the Toolbar that looks like an open book with an s will begin the _Spell Check_.

5. The _Thesaurus_ provides a list of synonyms to help you find the right word to use.

6. The tool that looks for grammar, punctuation, and style flaws in your documents is called _Grammatik_.

7. When WordPerfect identifies a grammatical error, the word in the text box on the right side of the Property Bar is shown in _Prompt as you go_.

MULTIPLE CHOICE

Circle the best answer to each of the following statements.

8. All of the following are WordPerfect tools that help you with spelling and keying as you enter text EXCEPT
    A. Spell Check.
    B. Thesaurus.
    C. QuickWords.
    D. CheckWords.

9. QuickCorrect would not correct
    A. hose for house.
    B. adn for and.
    C. sem for seem.
    D. teh for the.

10. When a word is underlined in ____, it means that WordPerfect thinks the word is misspelled.
    A. blue
    B. red
    C. green
    D. yellow

UNIT 2: COREL WORDPERFECT BASICS

LESSON 7 PROJECT

SCANS

Let's practice a couple of the features with which you worked in Lesson 7. We'll begin with Spell-As-You-Go to correct the errors in a document that has been prepared and saved for you.

PROJECT 7A

1. Open **japanese gifts** from the student **datafile** folder. Use **Save As** to save the file as **gifts proj7a xxx**. This document has a number of misspelled words which Spell-As-You-Go has underlined in red.

2. One at a time, point to an underlined word and click the right mouse button. Select the correct spelling of each word.

3. When you finish, check your work over carefully and insert the Path and Filename code a double space below the paragraph.

4. Return the insertion point to the top of the document. Press **Enter** three times. Then press **Ctrl+Home** again to move the insertion point above the hard returns.

5. Use **Flush Right** to move the insertion point to the right of the line. Then use the **Date Code** feature to insert the date.

6. Print the file and close it, saving it again with the same name.

Now let's use some of the other tools on the same document.

PROJECT 7B

1. Open **japanese gifts** from the student **datafile** folder again. Use **Save As** to save the file as **gifts proj7b xxx**. Insert the Path and Filename code a double space below the paragraph.

2. Start **Spell Check** and correct all of the words in the paragraph. When asked if you would like to close Spell Check, choose **No**.

3. Position the insertion point in the word *relish*. Click the **Thesaurus** tab to start the Thesaurus. Find a better word to replace *relish*.

4. Click the **Grammatik** tab and choose **Analysis**. Key the answers to all of the following questions below the Path and Filename code. What is the reading grade level? In which ONE area does the Hemingway comparison show a higher percentage? How many words are in the document?

5. Print your document and close it, saving it again with the same name.

CRITICAL THINKING ACTIVITY

You have started keying one of your documents and notice that your QuickCorrect feature is not correcting some of the common errors you normally make. What is the problem and how do you fix it?

QuickCorrect is turned off. Go into the Tools menu, then click on QuickCorrect to turn it on again.

Windows Tools and File Management

LESSON 8

OBJECTIVES

Upon completion of this lesson, you will be able to:

- Customize the Toolbar.
- Discuss the default Property Bar.
- Manage your files by creating folders and moving files.
- Discuss the Open as copy feature.
- Work with the various printing options.

Estimated Time: 1 hour

Quite a number of tools are available in your window at all times to help you with your work. You've already worked with the Menu Bar, the Toolbar, the Property Bar, the scroll bars, QuickMenus, and the Application Bar. You've also practiced using the Next Page and Previous Page buttons to move from page to page.

With the Toolbar and the Property Bar, you've used a few of the buttons as you've learned about a particular feature. But the Toolbar and Property Bar are powerful tools that you will probably customize when you use WordPerfect on the job.

Let's briefly explore those two tools and then we'll look at some other Windows features that will make your work easier.

Finally, you'll learn to manage your files. You've already created quite a number of files, and a full folder is difficult to use. You learned file management basics in Appendix C. You worked with the Open File dialog box in Lesson 4. Now you will create folders into which you can move your files so the basic storage location is more tidy. You'll also learn to delete files that are no longer needed.

Toolbar

You've already used a number of tools on the Toolbar. If you're using the default WordPerfect 8 Toolbar, you've learned the following tools: New Blank Page, Open, Save, Print, Cut, Copy, Paste, Undo, Redo, Highlight, Zoom, and Spell Check. Can you find each of those buttons?

Other Toolbars. WordPerfect 8 comes with no less than 13 other Toolbars—each for a specific purpose. You can display the list of Toolbars by pointing anywhere on the Toolbar and right clicking.

Location. The Toolbar can also be located in a number of places in your window. To move it, point to a space on the Toolbar. When the four-headed pointer appears, press the left mouse button and hold it while you drag the Toolbar to the desired location.

Customizing. You can create your own Toolbar that contains buttons for the features you use most often. One way to do this is to name a Toolbar and start from scratch. Another way is to edit one of the existing Toolbars. If you are working in the classroom, you should NOT edit the Toolbar selected for your computer unless you receive permission from your instructor. In the next exercises, we'll explore Toolbar options. Then we'll create and name a Toolbar. We'll add only a couple of buttons. Then we'll delete the practice Toolbar.

Scroll Bars. The resolution of your video display terminal controls a number of things. One of those is the size of the buttons on the Toolbar and how much space they take. If your Toolbar takes more space than the window allows, a tiny scroll bar will appear at the right of the Toolbar so you can look at the next part of the Toolbar. It is recommended that when you create a Toolbar, you include only as many buttons as will appear in the first window.

Now let's practice all of these Toolbar features.

EXERCISE 8.1

1. Point to the Toolbar and right click. Look at the list of available Toolbars. Which one has a black check mark at the left? That's the Toolbar to which you'll return at the end of this exercise.

2. Choose one of the other Toolbars. Note that the original Toolbar remains displayed with the new one below it. Try a different one. Then, one at a time, deselect all Toolbars except the original one.

3. Point to a blank gray area on the Toolbar. When the four-headed pointer appears, press the left mouse button and drag the Toolbar to each of the following locations and release it:
   a. To the middle of the window.
   b. To the lower right corner of the window.
   c. To the left until a long vertical box appears.
   d. To the top until a long horizontal box appears. Leave it at the top.

4. Point to the Toolbar and right click to display the menu. Choose **Settings**. The Customize Settings dialog box will appear (see Figure 8-1).

FIGURE 8-1
Customize Settings Dialog Box

5. Click the **Create** button. Name your Toolbar **practice** and click **OK**. Note that a new, empty bar is displayed between the normal Toolbar and the Property Bar.

6. Look at the Toolbar Editor dialog box. The list of features displayed are from the **File** menu. Click **Close All** and then click the **Add Button** button. See the new button on the Toolbar?

7. In the lower right corner is a separator. Double click it to insert a space between buttons.

8. Change the arrow beside the *Feature categories* text box and choose **Edit**. In that list, choose **Case Toggle**. Either double click the feature to add it to your Toolbar or click it once and click the **Add Button** button. Insert another spacer.

9. Change Feature Categories to **View**. Add a button to the practice Toolbar for Draft.

Now that you have a practice Toolbar, let's learn to rearrange the buttons and delete buttons. Then we'll close the Toolbar Editor dialog box and delete your practice Toolbar.

EXERCISE 8.2

1. Point to the Close All button on your practice Toolbar and drag it to the right, so it becomes the third button.

2. Drag the Case Toggle button down and off the Toolbar. You'll see the wastebasket when you "throw it away."

3. Close the Toolbar Editor dialog box. When you return to the Customize Settings dialog box, the **practice** Toolbar will be highlighted. Click the **Delete** button to remove the practice Toolbar from the list.

4. Be sure only the original Toolbar is chosen and close the dialog box.

As mentioned earlier, unless your instructor tells you to do so, you shouldn't make any permanent changes to your Toolbars. Now let's see what can be done with the Property Bar.

Property Bars

WordPerfect 8 comes with more than three dozen Property Bars which are said to be "context sensitive." This means that the choices available on the Property Bar change according to what you are doing. The main Property Bar is the *Text* Bar, although several bars can be displayed at one time, just as with Toolbars. If you wish to choose a particular Property Bar, go to the same menu you used when creating a Toolbar and choose the Property Bars tab.

No practice is included for Property Bars, because you'll be using many of them as you learn about various WordPerfect features.

Windows

Working with Windows provides you with a number of other features. For example, you can look at more than one document at a time using either *Cascade* or *Tile*. You also can move between open documents—a total of nine documents can be open at any given time. All of these choices come from the Window menu.

In addition, the Application Bar at the bottom enables you to switch from one document to another without even opening a menu. WordPerfect 8 enables you to drag selected text through the Application Bar to move it from one document to another. Let's explore.

EXERCISE 8.3

1. Beginning in a clear document window, click the **Open** button on the Toolbar.

2. Choose the folder containing your files. Hold the **Ctrl** key while you click each of the following files to highlight it: **music 3-8**, **pc-tv 6-1**, and **skeleton proj3**. Click the **Open** button to open all three files.

3. Open the **Window** menu and choose **Cascade**. Note that each of the documents has its own separate window. Also note that the active file (**music 3-8**) has a blue Title Bar. The others are gray.

4. Point to the Title Bar of **music 3-8** and drag the window down and to the right. Click to make **pc-tv 6-1** the active file.

5. Select the first paragraph in **pc-tv 6-1** and copy that paragraph to the Clipboard. Make **music 3-8** the active file. Position the insertion point a double space below the Path and Filename code in **music 3-8**. Paste the paragraph from **pc-tv 6-1** in that location.

6. Open the **Window** menu and choose **Tile Top to Bottom**. (You probably wouldn't tile more than three files this way.) Now open the **Window** menu and choose **Tile Side by Side**.

7. Click the **Maximize** button (the middle button of the three buttons in the upper right corner) of the **music 3-8** document window.

8. Open the **Window** menu and look at the list of three documents at the bottom of the menu. Change to **pc-tv 6-1**.

9. Find the names of the three documents on the Application Bar at the bottom of the window. Click **skeleton proj3** to make it the active document.

10. Select the second paragraph. When it is selected, point to the paragraph. Press and hold the left mouse button. Drag the mouse pointer to the **music 3-8** button on the Application Bar. Hold the mouse button until **music 3-8** appears. Continuing to hold the

NOTE:

If you don't do Step 10 right, a warning box will tell you that you can't copy to the Application Bar. Click **OK** and try again, remembering to hold the mouse button until you've positioned the insertion point in the **music** document where you'd like the paragraph to be inserted.

mouse button, drag the pointer to the beginning of the Path and Filename code in **music 3-8**. When you release the mouse button, the *bones* paragraph should be at the end of the **music** document.

11. Look at the two sets of Minimize/Maximize/Restore buttons in the upper right corner of the window. The top set is for WordPerfect. The lower set is for the document. Close all three documents without saving by clicking the lower *x* for each document.

12. Open your **Window** menu one more time. The documents should no longer be listed. Close the menu and read on.

File Management

Most file management takes place in the File menu of the Open File dialog box. You have already explored much of the Open File dialog box. Now it's time to work with copying, moving, and deleting files. You will also learn to create folders to hold certain groups of files.

Deleting Files

Quite a number of the documents you've saved in the lessons have no future value. Many of them were interim saves of documents that received more formatting later. Others were simply practice. In the next exercise you will select the files that have no further value and delete them. If you can't find some of these files in your list, don't worry about it. You may have forgotten to save them. Work carefully so you don't delete some files that may be needed later.

EXERCISE 8.4

SCANS

1. Go to the Open File dialog box and open the list of files you have saved.

2. Hold the **Ctrl** key while you click to select the files listed in Figure 8-2.

3. Press the **Delete** key on the keyboard. WordPerfect will ask if you want to send the selected files to the recycle bin. Answer **Yes**.

FIGURE 8-2
Files to be Deleted

appearance 3-1	fix 7-2	gifts proj4b	numbers 5-5
appearance 3-2	fix 7-3	gifts proj5a	numbers 5-6
appearance 3-3	foreign 2-6	gifts proj7a	numbers 5-7
appearance 3-4	foreign 2-7	gifts proj7b	online 5-4
codes 5-11	foreign 3-5	indent 5-3	pc-tv 6-1
dates 5-8	foreign 3-6	indent 5-8	pc-tv 6-7
dates 5-9	gifts 3-10	matter proj1a	quality u1ap1a
education 1-6	gifts 4-3	nasa 2-1	working 2-10
errors 7-4	gifts proj4a	nasa 2-4	

107

Creating Folders and Moving Files

Now that we've gotten rid of all of the extra files, we'll divide the remaining files into three folders. We'll prepare a folder for the regular documents in Units 1 and 2. Then we'll prepare a folder for Applications and another for Mr. Becker's files created in the On-the-Job Simulation. Finally, we'll move the remaining files into the correct folders.

EXERCISE 8.5

1. With your Open File dialog box showing in the window, open the **File** menu and choose **New**. Then choose **Folder**. A New Folder icon will appear at the bottom of the list with a box around the words *New Folder*. Key **Units 1 and 2** and press **Enter**. Click away from the folder to deselect it.

2. Hold **Ctrl** while you click to select the files listed in Figure 8-3.

3. Open the **File** menu and choose **Move to Folder**. Locate the **Units 1 and 2** folder and double click to select it. Click the **Move** button at the bottom of the dialog box.

4. Back in your regular folder, follow the procedure in Step 1 to create a new folder named **Becker**. Select **schedule job1** and **schedule job2** and move them into the **Becker** folder.

5. In your regular folder, create a folder named **Applications**. Select **canada u1ap3**, **quality u1ap1b**, and **gifts u1ap2** and move them into the **Applications** folder.

6. Look at your regular folder. It should be empty. If it isn't, check the remaining files.
   a. If they are junk that you saved accidentally while you were working on the lessons, delete them.
   b. If they are files that you have created for other classes or personal work, have your instructor help you transfer them to a different location.

7. If you completed the exercises in Appendix B, your folder will include **move b-9 xxx** and **move2 b-9 xxx**. Delete those files.

8. Finally, close your Open File dialog box and read on.

FIGURE 8-3
Files to Move to the **Units 1 and 2** Folder

education 1-2	online proj5b
errors 7-5	pc-tv 6-6
gifts proj6	sasoot 3-11
matter proj1b	sasoot 5-10
music 3-8	skeleton proj3
nasa proj2	

Miscellaneous

A couple of things need to be noted from Exercise 8.5.

- Do NOT save any personal work or work for other classes with the files for this class. Your disk will be too full for you to complete the course if you do. Instead, if you are saving files for other purposes, save them on a different disk.

108 UNIT 2: COREL WORDPERFECT BASICS

- This exercise utilized the File menu in the Open File dialog box. The menu illustrated in Figure 8-4 shows the File menu when no files are selected. This is the way it looked when you created the file folders. Figure 8-5 shows the File menu when files are selected. As you can see, you can move as well as copy files. You can also rename files. The other useful tool in the menu illustrated in Figure 8-5 is the *Print File List* item. This choice actually sends a list of the file names, sizes, and dates to the printer for the folder that is open when the selection is made. You'll have an opportunity to print a file list in Lesson 12.

- "Cleaning out" your folders periodically is very important. This topic is covered in Appendix C. If you have not yet studied Appendix C, take time to do it before you begin Unit 3.

FIGURE 8-4
File Menu in Open File Dialog Box

FIGURE 8-5
File Menu in Open File Dialog Box (with Files Selected)

Open as Copy

One of the tools that appears on both of the illustrations of the File menu in Figures 8-4 and 8-5 and is a button at the bottom of the Open File dialog box is the *Open as copy* feature. If you have a document open and try to open it again, a message box will appear telling you the document is either in use or specified as read-only. It goes on to tell you that you can open the document, but you'll have to save it with a different name. In other words, if you choose to continue, you will be opening a copy of the document.

When you choose to open a document as a copy, the part of the document that contains the filename is not included. You can look at the document. You can edit the document, and you can save the document, but it must be saved with a different name.

The *Open as copy* warning message most often serves to remind you that you already have that particular file open in one of your windows.

Recent Files

Another option that is sure to be useful is the list of files at the bottom of the File menu when you are working in your normal document window. WordPerfect remembers the last nine documents with which you have worked. Those documents are listed consecutively in the File menu. If you have recently worked with a file and need to reopen it, the easiest place to go for that file is the File menu.

By selecting the file from the list, you can bypass the Open File dialog box and save yourself a great deal of time.

INTERNET The World Wide Web is a subnetwork of computers that display multimedia information, including text, graphics, sound, and video clips. Web documents also contain special connections that allow users to switch to other documents that could be on computers anywhere in the world.

Lesson 8 Windows Tools and File Management

1 0 9

Printing

FIGURE 8-6
Choices for Printing

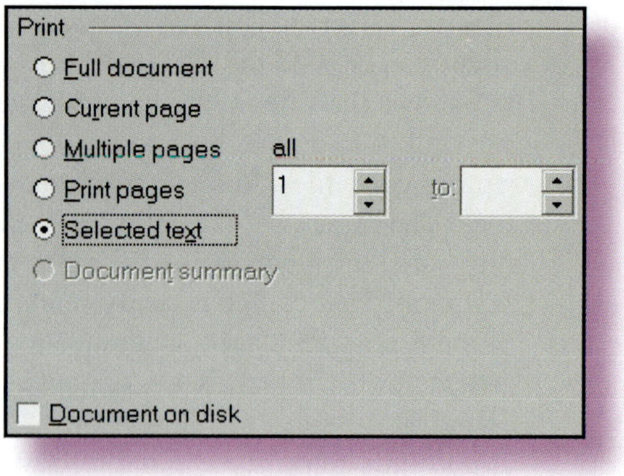

Back in Lesson 1 you learned to print the file showing in the window. In a later lesson, you learned that you can print directly from the file list. In addition to those two methods of printing entire documents, a number of other options are available for special circumstances.

Look at Figure 8-6. It shows the choices for printing. Let's discuss the options.

- **Full document**. This is the choice you've used for all of your printing up to this point. This choice sends the document you are viewing in your window to the printer.

- **Current page**. To print a single page of a document, position the insertion point on the page to be printed and make this choice.

- **Multiple pages**. This choice also enables you to specify pages to be printed. To print pages 1, 3, and 6, choose the Multiple pages tab, and key *1, 3, 6* in the *Page(s)/label(s)* text box before clicking Print. To print from page 5 to the end of a document, choose Multiple pages, and key *5-* before clicking Print. Multiple pages also enables you to print by chapter or volume.

- **Print pages**. With this choice, you can print several consecutive pages of a document. For example, you can tell WordPerfect to print pages 2, 3, and 4 by keying *2* in the *from* box and *4* in the *to* box. In this case, WordPerfect will actually make the Print pages choice for you.

- **Selected text**. To print a chunk of text, select it and choose Print. WordPerfect will automatically make the Selected text choice.

- **Document summary**. You'll learn about document summaries in a later lesson.

- **Document on disk**. If you need a quick printout of a document other than the one on which you're working, you can choose Document on disk and choose the document to be printed.

At the right in the Print dialog box is the place where you can tell WordPerfect how many copies you want of the document to be printed. You can specify whether the documents should be collated or not.

Among the other things you can do with the Print dialog box is check the status of a print job. Click the Status button at the bottom of the dialog box for a list of the last several documents sent to the printer.

With that overview, let's try a few of the features you will probably use when printing your documents.

EXERCISE 8.6

1. Click the **Open** button on the Toolbar. In the folder that should contain the names of your documents, you'll see the three folders you created to hold the documents from Lessons 1 through 7.

2. Point to the **Units 1 and 2** folder and double click to open that folder.

3. Locate **nasa proj2 xxx** and open the file. Position the insertion point somewhere on page 3.

4. Click **Print** on the Toolbar. Choose **Current page**. On the right of the dialog box, change the number of copies to **3**.

5. Then click the **Print** button at the bottom of the dialog box to send the document to the printer.

6. Go to page 2 and select the side heading about flame resistant materials, as well as the paragraphs in that section.

7. Choose **Print** from the Toolbar again. Note that the drop-down menu now suggests **Selected text**. Click **Print** to send the paragraphs to the printer. (If you have text selected and wish to print the entire document anyhow, you can choose Full document and override the Selected text setting.)

Now let's explore a little further.

EXERCISE 8.7

1. Open the Print dialog box again. At the lower left, choose **Document on disk**. Since no document is specified, click the button with the tiny file folder to open the Document on disk dialog box (see Figure 8-7).

2. Locate **canada u1ap3 xxx** in the **Applications** folder and double click to select it.

3. When the document name is showing in the Document name portion of the Print dialog box, click **Print**. Your document will be sent to the printer.

FIGURE 8-7
(Print) Document on Disk Dialog Box

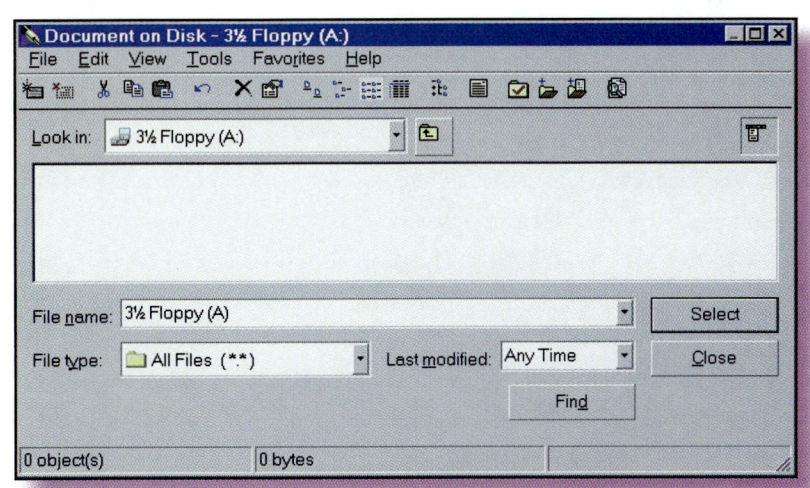

(continued on next page)

111

EXERCISE 8.7 CONTINUED

4. As soon as you can, return to the Print dialog box and click the **Status** button. Because the **canada** document is so short, you'll see it listed at the top of the Status dialog box as completed.

5. Close the Status dialog box and the Print dialog box. Then close the **nasa** document without saving it.

You should now be more familiar with the Print dialog box and the options available there. You'll be learning more about it later.

Summary

This lesson had less to do with the creating and formatting of documents and more to do with how you work with the Windows environment and how you print your files. In this lesson you learned that:

- You can customize the Toolbar and choose alternate Toolbars for specific projects.
- Several Property Bars are available for specific tasks.
- You can create and name file folders and move files into those folders.
- It is easy to delete a group of selected files.
- The Open as copy feature reminds you when you try to open a document that is already open.
- WordPerfect keeps a list at the bottom of the File menu of the last nine documents with which you've worked.
- You can print parts of a document instead of the whole document.
- You can use the Print dialog box to print in a variety of ways.

All of these skills will be useful to you as you progress with your WordPerfect training.

LESSON 8 REVIEW QUESTIONS

MATCHING

Write the letter of the term or phrase from Column 2 that best matches the description in Column 1.

Column 1

_E_ 1. You can use this feature to switch from one document to another without even opening a menu.

_F_ 2. If you have more than one document opened at a time, this arranges your documents so they overlap.

_C_ 3. WordPerfect comes with more than three dozen of these, which are said to be "context sensitive."

_D_ 4. Tools such as Cut, Copy, Redo, Highlight, and Zoom can be found on the bar.

_I_ 5. Most file management takes place in this dialog box.

_G_ 6. Use this feature if you want your open documents on top of each other but not overlapping.

Column 2

A. Toolbar
B. Property Bar
C. scroll bars
D. Menu Bar
E. Application Bar
F. Cascade
G. Tile Top to Bottom
H. Tile Side by Side
I. Open File dialog box
J. Save As dialog box

FILL IN THE BLANKS

Complete each of the following statements by writing your answer in the blank provided.

7. The print choice that sends the document you are viewing in your window to the printer is ___Full Document___ printing.

8. To print a chunk of text, select it and choose Print. WordPerfect will automatically make the ___Selected Text___ choice for printing.

9. If you want to print pages 6, 7, and 8, choose ___Print Pages___ in the Print dialog box.

10. Choose ___Document on disk___ if you need a quick printout of a document other than the one on which you are working.

113

LESSON 8 PROJECT

In this project you will manipulate your files and practice some of the printing options you learned to use in this lesson.

1. Open **errors 7-5 xxx**, **nasa proj2 xxx**, and **schedule job1**. (The first two files listed are in the **Units 1 and 2** folder, and the last one is in the **Becker** folder.)

2. Open the **Window** menu and choose to cascade the documents.

3. Open the **Window** menu and choose **Tile Side by Side**.

4. Open the **Window** menu and choose **Tile Top to Bottom**.

5. Select the first sentence in **errors 7-5 xxx** and copy it to the Clipboard.

6. Paste the sentence at the bottom a double space below the Path and Filename code of each of the other two documents.

7. Use **Save As** to save **nasa proj2 xxx** in the folder where you normally save your files as **proj8a xxx** (no *nasa*). Print only the final page (**Current page**) of the file and close it.

8. Use **Save As** to save **schedule job1 xxx** in the folder where you normally save your files as **proj8b xxx** (no *schedule*). Print the file and close it.

9. Close **errors 7-5 xxx** without saving it.

CRITICAL THINKING ACTIVITY

In Exercises 8.1 and 8.2 you practiced customizing a Toolbar with specific instructions. Now write a list of the tools you would add to your own customized Toolbar and explain why you made those choices.

Command Summary

UNIT 2 REVIEW

FEATURE	MENU CHOICE	KEYBOARD	LESSON
Bulleted List	Insert, Outline/Bullets & Numbering	—	5
Cascade Windows	Window, Cascade	—	8
Center Page(s)	Format, Page	—	5
Copy	Edit (Toolbar)	Ctrl+C	6
Create Folder	File, Open	Ctrl+O	8
Cut	Edit (Toolbar)	Ctrl+X	6
Dash (em dash)	—	---	5
Date Code	—	Ctrl+Shift+D	5
Date Text	Insert, Date/Time	Ctrl+D	5
Double Indent	Format, Paragraph	Ctrl+Shift+F7	5
Drag and Drop	—	—	6
Find	Edit, Find	F2 or Ctrl+F	6
Grammatik	Tools	Alt+Shift+F1	7
Hanging Indent	Format, Paragraph	Ctrl+F7	5
Hard Page Break	Insert, Page Break	Ctrl+Enter	5
Hard Space	Format, Line, Other Codes	Ctrl+space bar	5
Highlight	Tools (Toolbar)	—	6
Hyphen Character	Format, Line, Other Codes	Ctrl+ –	5
Indent	Format, Paragraph	F7	5
New Blank Page	(Toolbar)	Ctrl+N	6
Open as Copy	File, Open	Ctrl+O	8
Outline/Bullets & Numbering	Insert	—	5
Page Break	Insert, New Page	Ctrl+Enter	5
Page Print	File, Print	—	8
Paste	Edit (Toolbar)	Ctrl+V	6
Prompt-As-You-Go	(Property Bar)	—	7
Property Bar	View	—	8
QuickCorrect	Tools	Ctrl+Shift+F1	7
QuickMenu	—	—	6
Replace	Edit, Find and Replace	F2	6
Soft Page Break	(Automatic)	—	5
Spell Check	Tools (Toolbar)	Ctrl+F1	7

115

FEATURE	MENU CHOICE	KEYBOARD	LESSON
Spell-As-You-Go	Tools (Property Bar)	Alt+Ctrl+F1	7
Subscript	Format, Font	F9	5
Superscript	Format, Font	F9	5
Thesaurus	Tools	Alt+F1	7
Tile Windows	Window, Tile	—	8
Toolbar	View, Toolbars	—	8
Windowing	Window	—	7

UNIT 2 REVIEW QUESTIONS

MATCHING

Match the correct term in Column 2 to its description in Column 1 by keying the name of each term on a page to be submitted to your instructor. Center *Unit 2 Review Questions* at the top of the page and triple-space. Number your answers.

Column 1

1. The current date is inserted each time the document is accessed.

2. All lines are indented from the left to the first tab stop, and they are indented from the right an equal distance.

3. All lines of a paragraph are indented from the left to the first tab stop.

4. The current date is placed in the document and that date is a permanent part of the document.

5. All lines, except the first, are indented from the left to the first tab stop.

Column 2

Indent

Hanging Indent

Double Indent

Date Code

Date Text

WRITTEN QUESTIONS

Continuing on the same page, key your answers to the following questions. Number your answers and double-space between answers. Use complete sentences and good grammar.

6. What is the name of the feature that enables you to tell WordPerfect to look through the open document for a unique string of characters?

7. List the four ways you can copy selected text to the Clipboard.

8. How do you make QuickCorrect fix your errors?

9. After you have selected a list of files to be moved to a different location, how do you tell WordPerfect to move the files?

10. Open Help and key **print**. In the print section, find multiple pages. Read about page ranges and keying page numbers. If you want random pages of a document printed and you don't key the numbers to be printed in chronological order, what will happen? Open the Page dialog box and click the Help button. Click to view print job progress and About Print Status and History. How do you cancel a print job?

UNIT 2 APPLICATIONS

SCANS

Estimated Time: 1 hour

APPLICATION 1

1. Key the short memo illustrated in Figure APP-1. Use the **Tab** key to tab as many times as necessary to align the information as shown.

FIGURE APP-1
Text for Application 1

```
TO:         Juan Hernandez
FROM:       (key your name)
DATE:       (use the Date Text feature)
RE:         Quality Training

You have been scheduled for Phase 2 of your quality training.  Here are
the particulars about your class:

    Duration:   6 weeks
    Day:        Monday
    Time:       9 to 10:30 a.m.
    Location:   Room A116
    Beginning:  Next Monday

There is no assignment for this first class session.  Please be
prompt.
```

2. When you finish, use **Spell Check** to check your document and make any necessary corrections. Then save the memo in your regular document folder as **quality u2ap1 xxx**.

3. Check the document with Grammatik set to check at the **Student Composition** level. Correct the document as follows:
   a. Use **Skip All** on the comment about *You*.

(continued on next page)

117

b. For the *You have been scheduled* problem, click the green *active voice* words at the bottom and read about why Grammatik highlighted the sentence. Click the *x* to close the Active Voice window. Fix the passive voice by choosing the second replacement—*We have scheduled you*—and clicking the **Replace** button.
c. Fix the *Six* weeks.
d. Continue through the document until Grammatik is finished. You decide how to fix the errors pointed out by Grammatik. Then close Grammatik.

4. When you finish, insert the Path and Filename code a double space below the last line of the memo.

5. Print and close the document, saving it again as **quality u2ap1 xxx** when you close it.

APPLICATION 2

1. Open **desktop** from the student **datafile** folder. Save the file as **desktop u2ap2a xxx**.

2. Note that the first line in four of the paragraphs are not indented. Select those four paragraphs (all at once) and open the **Insert** menu. Choose **Outline/Bullets & Numbering**. Then choose **Bullets** and the **Diamond** bullet style and click **OK**.

3. At the beginning of each of those bulleted paragraphs is a word or two followed by a period. Beginning with *Graphics*, select the word and format it with **Bold** and **Italic**. Do the same with *Layout*, etc. Be careful not to format the periods.

4. Select the title. Change it to **20-pt. Bold**. Center the title.

5. Press **Ctrl+Home** twice to get above all codes and press **Enter** to add some line spaces. **Flush Right** your name in the upper right corner. Use **Date Text** to put the current date on the line below your name, also using **Flush Right**. Adjust the spaces so two blank lines separate the date from the title of the document.

6. Insert the Path and Filename code a double space below the last paragraph. Save the file again as **desktop u2ap2a xxx** and print it.

7. Use **Cut and Paste** or **Drag and Drop** to move the bulleted items around so the paragraphs are in the following order:
   a. Well-written material
   b. Layout
   c. Graphics
   d. Typography

8. Use **Save As** to save the file again, this time as **desktop u2ap2b xxx**. Print it and close it.

APPLICATION 3

Open **quality u2ap1 xxx**. Use **Save As** to save the file as **quality u2ap3 xxx**. The document is illustrated in Figure APP-2 with corrections. Make the indicated corrections. Then check your work. When you finish, the Path and Filename code should remain a double space below the *Attachment* line. When the file is perfect, print it and close it, saving it again as **quality u2ap3 xxx**.

FIGURE APP-2
Corrections for Application 3

```
TO:        Juan Hernandez
FROM:      (key your name)
DATE:      (use the Date Text feature)
RE:        Quality Training

You have been scheduled for Phase 2 of your quality training.  Here
are the particulars about your class:

    Duration:      6 weeks
    Day:           ~~Monday~~ Tuesday
    Time:          ~~9 to~~ 10:30 a.m. to noon
    Location:      ~~Room A116~~ Conference Room A
    Beginning:     Next ~~Monday~~ Tuesday

~~There is no assignment for this first class session.  Please be
prompt.~~
```

Attached is an article that will be discussed at the first class session. Read the article and make a list of questions and comments to bring for discussion. Also be on the lookout for magazine and/or newspaper articles dealing with the aspect of quality discussed in the attached article.

Please be prompt.

Attachment

APPLICATION 4

Key a short paragraph or two, telling how you feel about your training in WordPerfect so far. Which features do you like the best? Which do you like the least? With which features do you have the most problems?

Use any of the formatting features you have learned thus far. When you finish your paragraph, proofread it carefully and save it as **opinion u2ap4 xxx**. Insert the Path and Filename code a double space below the last line of the document. Finally, print a copy of your work for your instructor. Close the document, saving it again as you close it.

APPLICATION 5

The documents that you've created and saved in the Unit 2 applications need to be moved to the **Applications** folder. Select **quality u2ap1 xxx**, **desktop u2ap2a xxx**, **desktop u2ap2b xxx**, **quality u2ap3 xxx**, and **opinion u2ap4 xxx**. Move them to the **Applications** folder. When your lesson has been approved by your instructor, delete **proj8a** and **proj8b**.

ON-THE-JOB SIMULATION

SCANS

JOB 3

Mr. Becker has finalized the tour assignments for September. Please key the opening lines illustrated in Figure J3. Tab to **Pos 2"** for *Drivers and Guides* and the related information in the opening lines. Save the file in your normal folder as **schedule job3 xxx**.

With the insertion point a double space below the *SUBJECT:* line, use **Insert** to insert **schedule job1 xxx** into the open document. (The file is in your **Becker** folder.) Make the corrections illustrated in Figure J4. (The text is spread to make room for the corrections. Do not leave extra space between the lines of your document.)

Add the schedule at the bottom of Figure J4. Proofread and print the document. Then close it, saving it as **schedule job3 xxx**.

FIGURE J3
Beginning Text for Job 3

```
TO:        Drivers and Guides

FROM:      Charlie Becker

DATE:      (use Date Text)

SUBJECT:   September Schedule
```

FIGURE J4
Corrections and New text for Job 3

~~We are sorry for the delay in notifying you of your scheduled trips for August.~~ As you know, recent flooding in the Midwest has necessitated a change in many of our scheduled tours ¶ *for September and cancellation of a number of others.* The ~~August~~ *September* schedule ~~will be posted later in the week.~~ *is listed below.* *note the dates you will be working* Please ~~check your assignments~~ and make your personal arrangements for ~~the tours you will be serving.~~ *your*

```
Sept. 1-4:   Mall of America in Minneapolis; Dennis & Karen
Sept. 6-7:   Fireplace Theater in Madison; Michael & Janie
Sept. 12-28: Vancouver, B.C.: Eric & Shelley
Sept. 14-25: New England; Greg & Karen
Sept. 15-19: Amana Colonies in Iowa; Fred & Janie
Sept. 18-23: Washington, D.C.: Al & Stacey
Sept. 20-27: Branson, Missouri; Tom & Anne
```

120   UNIT 2: COREL WORDPERFECT BASICS

JOB 4

Mr. Becker has asked you to write a letter to his good friend, Andrew A. Pitchur, 4561 River Road, Houston, TX 63225. Mr. Becker said, "Tell him I will be in Houston for three days beginning on September 6. I would like to take Andrew to dinner on either the 6th or 7th. Tell Andrew I'll be staying at the Van Gogh Inn on Gallery Drive and that he should call me at my hotel at around 4 p.m. on the 6th to make arrangements."

Spell check your letter and check the writing with Grammatik. Then prepare an envelope, print the letter and the envelope, and close the document, saving it as **houston job4 xxx**.

JOB 5

Mr. Becker tried to find his work on your computer—the work you have saved in the **Becker** folder. He says he never thought to try **Becker**. He was looking for something with the company name. You've decided to change the name of the folder to **Singing Wheels**. While you're at it, you will move the work from Jobs 3 and 4 into that folder.

1. Open the Open File dialog box and locate the **Becker** folder. Click once to highlight it, but don't double click to open it.

2. Using the mouse pointer, point to the highlighted folder and right click to display the QuickMenu.

3. Choose **Rename** from the QuickMenu. The folder name will be enclosed in a box with the words highlighted. Key **Singing Wheels** and press **Enter**.

4. Select **houston job4 xxx** and **schedule job3 xxx**. Move the files to the **Singing Wheels** folder.

5. Check your **Singing Wheels** folder. It should contain the four **job** files.

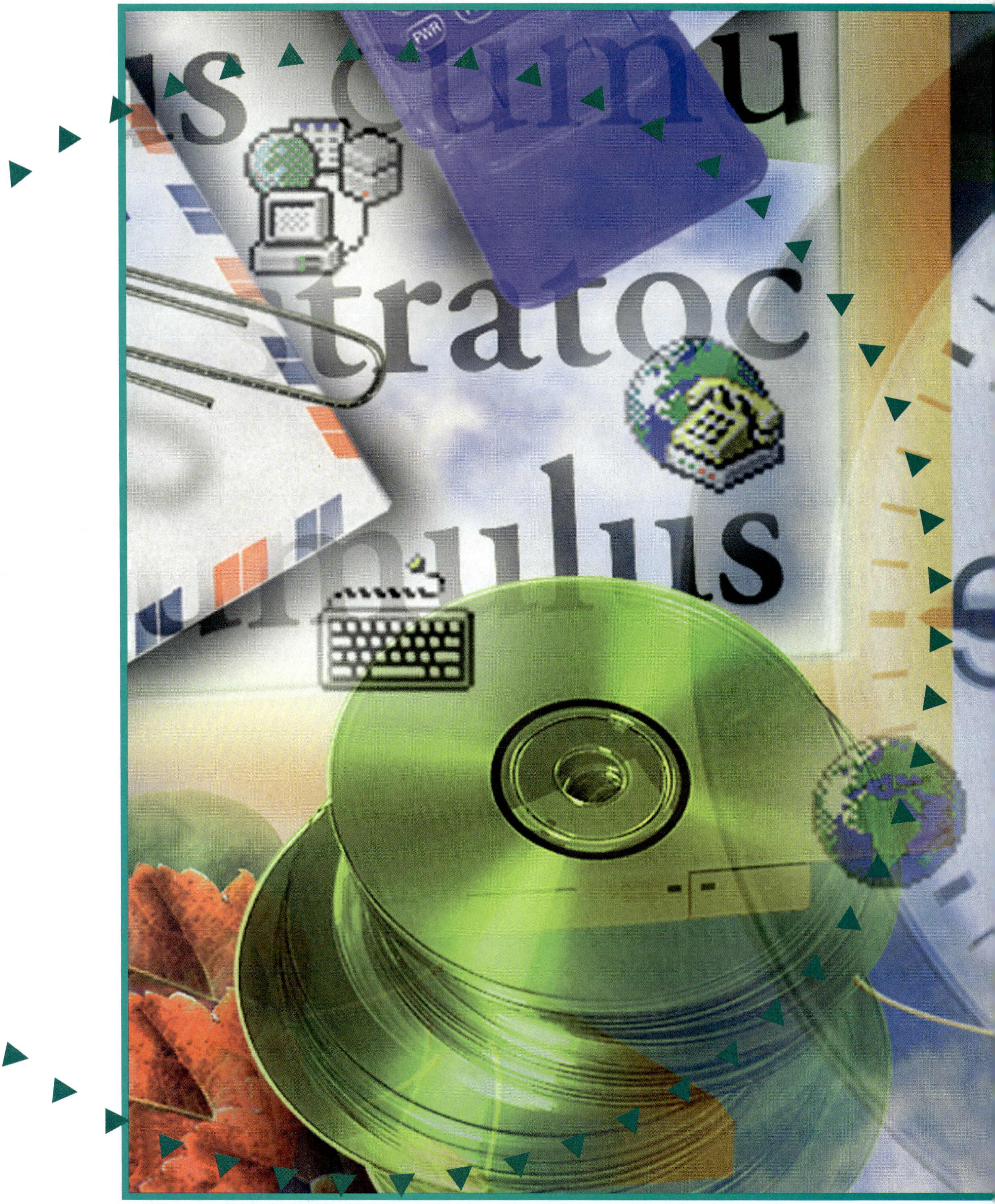

FORMATTING

UNIT 3

lesson 9 — 1.5 hrs.
Page and Paragraph Formatting

lesson 10 — 2 hrs.
Document Formatting

lesson 11 — 1.5 hrs.
Miscellaneous Formatting Tools

lesson 12 — 1 hr.
Advanced File Management

Estimated Time for Unit 3: 8 hours

LESSON 9

PAGE AND PARAGRAPH FORMATTING

OBJECTIVES

Upon completion of this lesson, you will be able to:

- Discuss the WordPerfect 8 formatting defaults.
- Adjust the line spacing in your documents.
- Work with the five kinds of justification.
- Adjust the margins of your documents.
- Change tab settings to give your documents the right look.
- Use the Ruler for indents, margins, and tabs.

Estimated Time: 1½ hours

If you've taken a keyboarding or typing class, you've learned to change the appearance of your documents with line spacing, margins, and tab stops. So far in this course, your documents have looked pretty good because the margin, tab stop, line spacing, and justification settings in the default template are designed to give you a good-looking document for most purposes.

In Lesson 9 you will learn to change the most common of those settings. Work carefully and think about what you're doing as you progress through the lessons so that when you finish, you'll be comfortable changing the same defaults on your own.

Formatting Defaults

The formatting with which you'll be working in this lesson is set as follows:

- **Line Spacing**: set to single spacing.
- **Justification**: set to left.
- **Margins**: set so you have equal 1" margins on all sides.
- **Tab Stops**: set with a tab stop at each half inch.

All of these settings can be changed easily so your documents will look exactly as you'd like. Following are some general formatting guidelines:

- Formatting changes that affect an entire document should be inserted at the beginning of a document.

- Formatting changes affect the text forward from the point where the change is made. The text prior to the change is not affected.

- Formatting changes remain in effect until another change to the same format is made. Then only the text following the change is affected.

- WordPerfect automatically positions formatting codes in the proper locations. Paragraph codes are placed at the beginning of the paragraph, and page formatting codes are placed at the beginning of the page.

- The default formats will work for most documents. Use them.

- The default formats are part of the default template. If you find that you are repeatedly changing certain formats, consider creating a customized template that contains the settings you use. WordPerfect Help contains lots of material about templates. In addition, you'll learn more about templates in a later lesson.

- Formatting codes become a permanent part of the document template and are saved with the document. When you close a document, you are returned to the default template.

Line Spacing

So far, everything you've keyed has been single-spaced unless you pressed Enter twice to add a blank line. There will be many times when you want all or part of a document double- or triple-spaced. WordPerfect allows you to space your document using a variety of settings.

It is very important when you want to use spacing other than single for a paragraph that you set line spacing rather than add the extra spaces by pressing Enter twice at the end of the line. When you press Enter, you insert a hard return that makes it impossible for WordPerfect to wrap your text to the next line. This makes quite a mess when you edit the paragraph.

Line spacing is set by choosing Format, Line, and then Spacing to open the dialog box.

EXERCISE 9.1

FIGURE 9-1
Line Spacing Dialog Box

1. Open **record** from the student **datafile** folder. Use **Save As** to save the file as **record 9-1 xxx**, replacing the *xxx* with your initials as usual.

2. With the insertion point at the beginning of the document, open the **Format** menu, choose **Line**, and then choose **Spacing**. The dialog box in Figure 9-1 should appear.

3. Key **2** and press **Enter**.

(continued on next page)

EXERCISE 9.1 CONTINUED

4. Look through your paragraphs. Observe the large amount of space between paragraphs. The blank line between the paragraphs was doubled, too, when you chose double spacing.

5. Reveal your codes. Position the insertion point to the left of the Line Spacing code. Note that it tells you what spacing is set. Enter the Double Spacing code on your list in Appendix E. Keep your codes revealed.

6. Move the insertion point to the beginning of the document and use the arrow buttons in the Line Spacing dialog box to change to **1.5** spacing. Look at the code in Reveal Codes. Use the mouse to drag the Line Spacing code out of the document and return the document to single spacing.

7. Position the insertion point at the beginning of the SECOND paragraph. Set double spacing for that paragraph. Keep the paragraphs showing as you read on.

Single, double, and 1.5 spacing are quite common. WordPerfect also lets you set odd spacing in increments of a tenth of an inch for special documents.

EXERCISE 9.2

SCANS

1. With **record 9-1 xxx** showing in the window, use **Save As** to save the file as **record 9-2 xxx**.

2. Move the insertion point to the beginning of the first paragraph. Open the Line Spacing dialog box and use the arrow keys to change line spacing to **1.3**. Then click **OK**.

3. Look at the paragraphs. Can you see the difference between the **1.3** spacing and the **2.0** spacing in the second paragraph? What kind of spacing do you suppose formats the line between paragraphs? (If you were on the first line of the second paragraph when you applied the 2.0 spacing, the space between paragraphs is formatted by the 1.3 spacing.)

4. Go to the end of the document and insert hard returns, if necessary. Press **Enter** twice after the second paragraph and insert the Path and Filename code.

5. Save and print the file. Keep it open for the next exercise.

In Exercise 9.2 you saw how the Line Spacing code at the beginning of the first paragraph formatted the document up to the Line Spacing code at the beginning of the second paragraph. This illustrates the theory explained at the beginning of the lesson, and is the way formatting works in WordPerfect. Let's learn about another kind of formatting.

> **INTERNET**
> "Netiquette" is an Internet phrase that refers to the rules of conduct and behavior on the Net. For example, don't send unwanted advertising, do keep your messages brief and to the point, and don't use ALL CAPS unless you mean to shout.

Justification

WordPerfect offers five kinds of justification, as illustrated in the sample paragraphs in Figure 9-2.

FIGURE 9-2
Samples of Justification

Full:
Researchers have been working on developing a technology that will enable you to not only watch TV on your computer, but also to capture images from the TV to be used in other computer programs.

Center:
Mary had a little lamb.
Its fleece was white as snow,
and everywhere that Mary went,
the lamb was sure to go.

Left:
Researchers have been working on developing a technology that will enable you to not only watch TV on your computer, but also to capture images from the TV to be used in other computer programs.

Right:
Jack and Jill went up the hill
to fetch a pail of water.
Jack fell down and broke his crown
and Jill came tumbling after.

All:
W   o   r   d   P   e   r   f   e   c   t
W   o   r   d   P   r   o   c   e   s   s   i   n   g

- With *Full justification*, all lines begin and end at the margins, except for a short line at the end of the paragraph. This is commonly used for documents.

- With *Center justification*, all lines are centered between the margins. This style is used for display purposes.

- *Left justification* causes all lines to begin at the left margin and appear ragged at the right. (This is the WordPerfect default setting and is also commonly used for documents.)

- *Right justification* causes all lines to be ragged at the left and to end at the right margin. This is used for special kinds of documents.

- Finally, *All justification* causes each line to spread from margin to margin, no matter how short the line might be. Again, All justification is used for special situations.

Justification can be chosen from the Format menu, from the Property Bar, or with keyboard shortcuts. Let's use the Property Bar to practice justification in Exercise 9.3.

EXERCISE 9.3

1. With **record 9-2 xxx** showing in the window, use **Save As** to save the file as **record 9-3 xxx**.

2. Position the insertion point at the beginning of the first paragraph. Watch the right side of the paragraphs as you use the **Justification** button on the Property Bar to change from Left to **Full**.

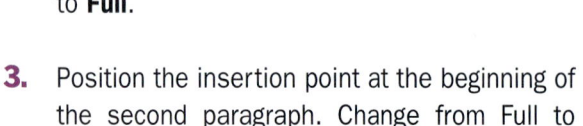

3. Position the insertion point at the beginning of the second paragraph. Change from Full to **Right**.

4. Move the insertion point to the end of the second paragraph and press **Enter** twice. Key your name and address on three or four lines the way you normally key your name and address. It should also be aligned at the right margin, just above the Path and Filename code.

5. Click to position the insertion point at the beginning of the second paragraph again. This time open the **Format** menu and choose **Justification**. Choose **Center**. This setting should affect everything in the document except the first paragraph.

6. Position the insertion point at the beginning of the first paragraph and choose **Left** justification.

7. On your own, can you change the second paragraph to **Full** justification, your name and address to **Center** justification, and the Path and Filename code to **Left** justification?

8. Change your name and address to single spacing.

9. When you finish, print your document and save it again as **record 9-3 xxx**.

In addition to choosing justification from the Format menu or the Property Bar, keyboard shortcuts have been assigned to all kinds of justification except All. If you wish, you may use the following:

Ctrl+J = Full   Ctrl+L = Left
Ctrl+R = Right   Ctrl+E = Center

Margins

While WordPerfect provides you with a number of ways to set margins, the easiest is to move the guidelines to the desired locations. No doubt you have seen the tool that moves the guidelines when you've been trying to position the insertion point close to one of the margins. It looks like an intersection with arrows pointing to the left and right (for left and right margins) or up and down (for top and bottom margins).

When you change the margins with the guidelines, the margins will move in increments of about a sixteenth of an inch. You'll know where your margin is at any time because a small box will appear as you're moving the margin, displaying the current position.

For the left and right margins, the margin is set forward from the place on the page where you grab the guideline to adjust the margin. Let's practice.

EXERCISE 9.4

1. With **record 9-3 xxx** showing in the window, use **Save As** to save the file as **record 9-4 xxx**.

2. Point to the left margin just to the left of the beginning of the second paragraph. When the tool with the right/left arrows appears, press the left mouse button and hold it. Watch the box giving you the position of the margin and drag the margin to **2"**.

3. Look at your document. You should see a couple of things.
   a. The first paragraph wasn't affected when you changed the margin.
   b. Everything below the second paragraph was affected—even the centered lines. They are centered between the margins.

4. Reveal your codes. Position your insertion point to the left of the [Lft Margin] code and see where your margin is set. It should report 2".

5. Grab the left margin guideline between your address and the Path and Filename code. Move it back to **1"**.

6. Grab the top margin and drag it to **2"** from the top of the page.

7. Print the document and save it again as **record 9-4 xxx**.

Sometimes you want to set all four margins or, occasionally, you can't get the exact setting you want by dragging the guidelines. In those instances, you should use the Margins portion of the Page Setup dialog box. Let's use it to change your margins.

EXERCISE 9.5

1. With **record 9-4 xxx** showing in your window, use **Save As** to save the file as **record 9-5 xxx**.

2. Press **Ctrl+Home** to move the insertion point to the top of the document.

3. Open the **Format** menu and choose **Margins**. The Margins portion of the Page Setup dialog box will look like Figure 9-3.

4. Are the margins correct? They should report that all of the margins except the top margin are at 1". The top margin should be set at 2".

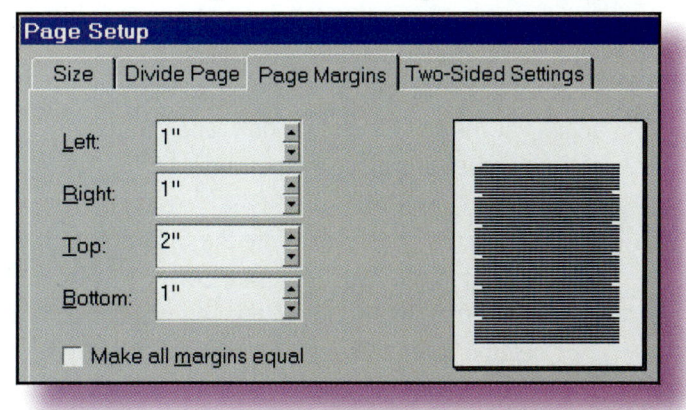

FIGURE 9-3
Margins Portion of Page Setup Dialog Box

(continued on next page)

129

EXERCISE 9.5 CONTINUED

5. Key **0** (zero) in the text box for the left margin. Press **Tab** and key **0** again. Continue until you've keyed **0** into each box. (The numbers will change to something else rather than staying at *0*.) Click **OK**.

6. Print your document and save it again as **record 9-5 xxx**. Close the document.

Each printer has what's known as a *no-print zone*. That's an area near the edges of the page where text or graphics can't be printed. When you set the margins at zero and they changed to a different number, that number reported in the Margins portion of the Page Setup dialog box represented the no-print zone on that edge of the paper. These no-print zones range from 0.2" to 0.5" or more, and they might be different on the various sides of your page.

Look at your document. How many Margin Set codes do you have in your document now? (You may reveal your codes and count, if you'd like.) You should have four of them. Add any new codes to your list.

Tabs

As you know, the default tab stops are set at each half inch. You can set one, three, or all tab stops in the Tab Set dialog box. You can also set a variety of tab types. The default type is the Left tab, meaning that when you tab to a location and key text, the text will begin at the tab stop and continue to the right.

Let's first try an exercise where you change all of the tab stops. Then we'll look at how they can be adjusted and work with the different types of tabs.

EXERCISE 9.6

1. Beginning in a new document window, open the **Format** menu and choose **Line**. Then choose **Tab Set**. The dialog box illustrated in Figure 9-4 should be opened, and a ruler will appear at the top of your window. Look at the half-inch tabs (triangles) on the Ruler.

2. Briefly study the dialog box. Note the following:
   a. At the top, the type is set for Left.
   b. Below that, the button in the *Tab position* section that is chosen tells WordPerfect to measure the locations for the tabs from the left margin. (This is so when you change the margin, you don't have to reset your tabs.)
   c. At the right is a set of buttons.

3. Click the **Clear All** button. Note that all of the tabs are removed.

4. Halfway down at the left, click the **Repeat every** box and key **1.35** in the text box just to the right. Click **OK** to return to your document window.

5. Key the text in Figure 9-5. Begin at the left margin with *corn*. (WordPerfect will capitalize the first letter. Backspace to replace it with a lowercase **c**. It may take two tries.)

6. Tab once and key **eggplant**. Tab once and key **potatoes**. Continue in the same manner, working across and pressing **Enter** at the end of each line.

7. Save your work as **salad 9-6 xxx**. Keep it open as you read on.

FIGURE 9-4
Tab Set Dialog Box

FIGURE 9-5
Text for Exercise 9.6

corn	eggplant	potatoes	beans	zucchini
okra	cucumbers	lettuce	onions	peppers
peas	broccoli	celery	beets	radishes
yams	tomatoes	sprouts	carrots	cabbage

Look at your work. Because you set evenly spaced tabs and some columns have longer words than the others, the space between columns does not appear to be equal. WordPerfect enables you to reset the tabs to make your columns more attractive. The easiest way to do that is with the Ruler.

The Ruler

The Ruler that appeared when the Tab Set dialog box was opened is another tool you can use for setting and adjusting tabs. It can be used to set margins and indents, too. Look at the left portion of the Ruler, illustrated in Figure 9-6. Observe the following parts:

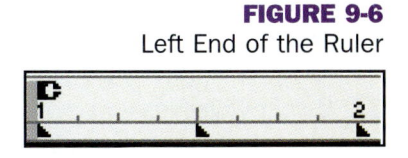

FIGURE 9-6
Left End of the Ruler

- The top part is for setting margins.

- The heavy black marker at 1" is the left margin.

- The two little triangles beside the margin marker are for indents. The top one can be set to automatically indent the first line of a paragraph. The bottom one works like the Indent feature that you learned about in Lesson 5. It indents the entire paragraph.

- The middle part is a scale marked in eighths of an inch.

131

- The bottom part is for setting tabs.
- The right triangles at each half inch are Left tabs.

FIGURE 9-7
Right End of the Ruler

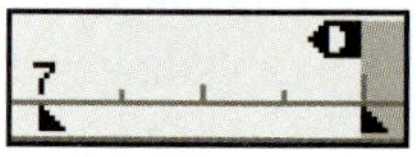

The right portion of the Ruler is illustrated in Figure 9-7. It has a margin marker and only one indent triangle. The triangle is for indenting the right side of a paragraph.

Let's fix our columns of veggies using the Ruler. Then we'll work with the margins and indents.

EXERCISE 9.7

1. With **salad 9-6 xxx** showing in the window, use **Save As** to save the file as **salad 9-7 xxx**.

2. If the Ruler is not displayed, open the **View** menu and choose **Ruler**.

3. Press **Ctrl+Home** to move your insertion point to the top of the document. Using your mouse pointer, grab the black triangle tab stop that is near 2½" on the scale. Drag it to the left and drop it at the **2⅛"** marker. Watch the column of vegetables move.

4. Using the same procedure, adjust the tab stops until your columns appear to have equal space between them.

5. When you finish, insert the Path and Filename code a double space below the columns. Then print the document and close it, saving it again with the same name.

Now let's open a partial document and reset the tabs. Then we'll complete the document using the new tabs.

EXERCISE 9.8

1. Open **hostas** from the student **datafile** folder. Use **Save As** to save the file as **hostas 9-8 xxx**.

2. If your Ruler isn't displayed, open the **View** menu and select the **Ruler**.

3. Drag the tab stop that's at 1.5" one notch on the scale to the left. Drag the next tab stop two notches to the left. Point to the bar where the tab triangles are located and click a third tab stop three notches from the one you just moved (at 2⅛"). The first four tabs should be evenly spaced.

4. Move your insertion point to the bottom of the document. Key the text in Figure 9-8, beginning the first line at the left margin and using **Tab** to indent the lines as shown.

5. When you finish keying and proofreading, return the insertion point to the top of the document and use either the guidelines or the Ruler to change the margins to **2"** on each side (that's **2"** at the left and **6½"** at the right). Note that when you move the left margin, the tabs you set move along with the margin.

6. Insert the Path and Filename code a double space below the document. Print the document and close it, saving it again as you close.

FIGURE 9-8
Text for Exercise 9.8

```
Large plants (more than 20 inches tall)
   High-priced varieties (more than $10 each)
      Blue Angel
      Fluctuans variegated
   Low-priced varieties (less than $10 each)
      Frances Williams
      Gold Regal
      Gold Standard
```

Now let's use the Ruler to experiment with margins and indents. Then we'll learn about the types of tabs available for your documents.

EXERCISE 9.9

1. Open **record 9-2 xxx**. Use **Save As** to save the file as **record 9-9 xxx**.

2. Remove the tab that indents the first line of each of the paragraphs. Move the insertion point to the beginning of the first paragraph.

3. Drag the heavy black margin marker to **2"** on the Ruler. Note how your text rearranges itself. Now drag the margin marker back to **1"**.

4. Point to the tiny top triangle beside the left margin marker. Drag it to **1½"** on the scale. Note that both paragraphs are indented as though you pressed Tab at the beginning of the first line.

5. Now point to the tiny bottom triangle. Drag it to **1½"** on the scale. Both paragraphs should now be indented a half inch from the left margin. The first line indents are still in place, a half inch farther than the other lines.

6. Point to the triangle beside the right margin marker and drag it a half inch to the left. Both sides of the paragraphs should now be indented.

7. Reveal the codes and record all three new codes on your list. Then print the document and save it again as **record 9-9 xxx**.

8. Play with the margins and indents until you are comfortable with what they do. (Remember that the insertion point must be above text you wish to format.) When you are comfortable with the features, close the document without saving it again.

The indents you just set from the Ruler will remain in effect until you change them. Note that for the entire document to be affected, you had to have your insertion point at the top of the document. You can use these tools on individual paragraphs, if you wish, but indenting with F7 and Ctrl+Shift+F7 is probably easier for small parts of a document.

Tab Types

FIGURE 9-9
Tab QuickMenu

As mentioned earlier, you can set a variety of types of tabs. Those choices can be made from the Tab Set dialog box. They can also be made from the Tab QuickMenu. The Tab QuickMenu is illustrated in Figure 9-9. You can set Left, Center, Right, and Decimal tabs. In addition, you can set the same selection of tabs to be preceded by dot leaders. The QuickMenu can be used to clear all tabs, reset the default tabs, hide the Ruler, or open the Tab Set dialog box.

The various types of tabs provide you with different kinds of formatting, as illustrated in Figure 9-10. Note that each kind of tab has a different shape marker.

- **Left Tab**. This common tab aligns text at the left. The names at the left are aligned with a Left tab set at $1^{1}/_{4}$" on the scale.

- **Decimal Tab**. This tab type automatically aligns figures at the decimal point. In this case, the series of dots under the tab set marker tell you that dot leaders were included with the tab setting at $2^{3}/_{4}$".

- **Center Tab**. Everything is centered around a Center tab. Minerva, Carlos, and Hue are aligned on the Center tab set at $3^{1}/_{2}$".

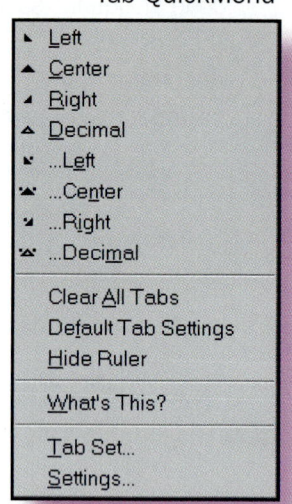

FIGURE 9-10
Tab Type Samples

- **Right Tab**. Everything ends at the location of a Right tab. The Right tab in Figure 9-10 is set at $4^{3}/_{4}$".

Now that you are familiar with the types of tabs, let's go through the steps to create the sample in Figure 9-10.

EXERCISE 9.10

1. Beginning in a new document window, display your Ruler.

2. Point to the tab portion of the Ruler (the area below the scale) and right click to display the QuickMenu. Choose **Clear All Tabs**. Point to the area just below the $1^{1}/_{4}$" mark and click to set a Left tab.

3. Display the QuickMenu and choose **...Decimal** (with dot leaders—it's the last choice above the line). Click at $2^{3}/_{4}$" to set a tab stop there.

4. Use the QuickMenu to change to a Center tab. Click the Ruler to set a Center tab stop at $3^{1}/_{2}$".

5. Change to a Right tab and set one at $4^{3}/_{4}$". Save your practice document as **Mildred 9-10 xxx**.

6. Beginning at the left margin, press **Tab** once and key **Mildred**. Tab and key the dollar amount for Mildred. Tab and key **Minerva**. Tab and key **Maryland**.

134   UNIT 3: FORMATTING

7. Press **Enter** and do the same for the Charlotte row and then the Hank row.

8. At the bottom of the document, double space and insert the Path and Filename code. Your document is squished to the left. With the insertion point at the top of the document, adjust the columns as follows:
    a. Move the Right tab to **7¼"**.
    b. Move the Center tab to **5¼"**.
    c. Move the Decimal tab with dot leaders to **3½"**.

9. Print the document and close it, saving it again with the same name.

Most of your work with changing tab settings in this lesson has been done with the Ruler. You had only a brief introduction to the Tab Set dialog box. While you can set different kinds of tabs in any location using the Tab Set dialog box, doing it that way is awkward and laborious. The Ruler and QuickMenu make the job much easier.

You may have noticed that setting both tab stops and margins using the Ruler is somewhat approximate. If you want precise settings, you must use the Tab Set dialog box for tabs and the Margins portion of the Page Setup dialog box or guidelines for margins.

Summary

This lesson covered a lot of territory with regard to changing default settings for your documents. The theory learned in this lesson will be practiced throughout the rest of your course as you learn to work with different kinds of documents that need different margins, line spacing, justification, and tabs. As a quick review, in this lesson you learned that:

- Settings such as line spacing, justification, margins, and tab stops format forward from the point where they are inserted.
- While the default line spacing is single, you can easily change to different spacing using the Line Spacing dialog box.
- Full and Left are the most common justification choices for business documents.
- Center justification may be used when several lines in a row need to be centered.
- Right and All justification are rarely used in business documents, unless some kind of display is needed.
- Margins may be set by moving the guidelines, keying the desired numbers into the Margins portion of the Page Setup dialog box, or by moving the margin markers on the Ruler.
- Tabs may be set from the Tab Set dialog box or on the Ruler.
- WordPerfect provides you with a variety of tab stops to fit your document creation needs.
- Tab stops can be adjusted after the document has been keyed. (To do this, remember to move your insertion point to the beginning of the text to be adjusted.)

While this lesson wasn't particularly long, you can see from the bulleted list that it contained a wealth of information about margins, tabs, line spacing, and justification. You probably won't remember all of the information in the lesson unless you review it after you finish. It would make good at-home reading!

LESSON 9 REVIEW QUESTIONS

MATCHING

Match the tab types to the sample below. Put the letter of the tab type from Column 2 in the blank provided in Column 1.

Column 1

A 1.
F 2.
D 3.
H 4.
E 5.
B 6.

Column 2

A. Left tab
B. Decimal tab
C. Center tab
D. Right tab
E. Left tab with Leaders
F. Decimal tab with Leaders
G. Center tab with Leaders
H. Right tab with Leaders

1.	2.	3.
Fax Machine	Office	$299.95 .... 20% off
Color Printer	Office & Personal	325.00 .... Free with purchase
Answering Machine	Office	39.50 .... $5 rebate
Cellular Phone	Car	20.00 .... Monthly lease

4.	5.	6.
Betty	van	Town & Country $31,000.00
Judith	sedan	Avalon 29,900.75
Barbara	convertible	Sebring 23,650.00

MULTIPLE CHOICE

Circle the best answer to each of the following statements.

7. The default formats are a part of
   A. the Tools menu.
   (B.) the default template.
   C. Reveal Codes.
   D. the Property Bar.

136 UNIT 3: FORMATTING

8. All lines begin and end at the margins, except for a short line at the end of a paragraph with _____ justification.
   A. Full
   B. Center
   C. Right
   D. All

9. In addition to setting tabs, the Ruler can be used
   A. to set margins.
   B. to set indents.
   C. to adjust tabs.
   D. all of the above.

10. Line spacing is set by opening the _____ menu, and choosing Line and then Spacing to open the dialog box.
    A. Insert
    B. Format
    C. Tools
    D. Edit

LESSON 9 PROJECT

SCANS

Create the short document illustrated in Figure 9-11 as follows:

1. Use **Center Current Page** to center the document vertically on the page. Center the title and key it in all caps and using **16-pt. Bold** and **Italic**. Key all dashes by keying three hyphens.

2. Press **Enter** three times following the title.

3. Double-space both paragraphs and single-space the list. Use **Full** justification.

4. Set the side margins at **1$\frac{1}{2}$"**.

5. For the list, set a Left tab at **3"** and a Right tab with dot leaders at **5$\frac{1}{2}$"**.

6. Following the list, choose **Default Tab Settings** from the QuickMenu so you can indent the first line of the paragraph in the normal way.

7. When you finish, save the file as **cheese proj9 xxx.** Insert the Path and Filename code a double space below the last paragraph. Print the document and close it, saving it again when you close it.

(continued on next page)

FIGURE 9-11
Text for Lesson 9 Project

```
            WISCONSIN—NOT JUST FOR CHEESEHEADS

    Wisconsin has long been known as the Dairy State.  While other
states may rank higher in overall production of dairy products,
Wisconsin is number one when it comes to making cheese—producing a
whopping 32 percent of all cheese made in the U.S.  In a recent
attempt to rank the states in the nation, the following Wisconsin
statistics were assembled:

        American . . . . . . . . . . . . . . . . . . First
        Blue . . . . . . . . . . . . . . . . . . . . First
        Brick  . . . . . . . . . . . . . . . . . . . First
        Italian  . . . . . . . . . . . . . . . . . . First
        Limburger  . . . . . . . . . . . . . . . . . First
        Muenster . . . . . . . . . . . . . . . . . . First
        Swiss  . . . . . . . . . . . . . . . . . . . Third

    In addition to those overwhelming numbers, enough processed cheese
is manufactured in Wisconsin each year to feed each resident of
Wisconsin 15 grilled cheese sandwiches every day. Enough mozzarella
cheese is produced in Wisconsin each year to make over 1 billion
pizzas.  Are you a cheese lover?  If so, Wisconsin is the place to go!
```

CRITICAL THINKING ACTIVITY

SCANS

You have been using WordPerfect 8 for a while now for both classroom and personal use. Most of the formatting defaults have worked just fine, but you are beginning to realize that you are repeatedly changing certain formats. Consider creating a customized template. What settings would you include?

Document Formatting

LESSON 10

OBJECTIVES

Upon completion of this lesson, you will be able to:

- Format your documents with headers, footers, and watermarks.
- Suppress page numbering and headers on certain pages.
- Use Widow/Orphan protection to give your documents better page breaks.
- Use Center Page(s) in report-type documents.
- Use page numbering in your documents.
- Adjust the page number value.
- Add footnotes to your documents.
- Include endnotes in your document and format the endnote page.

Estimated Time: 2 hours

Look at the book in front of you. Turn to a page that isn't the first page of a lesson and notice the information included at the bottom of the pages. These pieces of information are known as *footers*.

The left-hand page is *always* the even-numbered page. In this book the footer includes a page number positioned all the way to the left. Next to the page number is the number and name of the unit. The right-hand page is *always* the odd-numbered page. In this book only the page number appears in the footer on this page.

Much of the work you do when you create multiple-page documents will be formatted differently from what you see here. This is because most business documents aren't printed with facing pages. Instead, the documents are printed on one side of a page and fastened together at the left. Therefore, you don't need to worry about odd and even footers.

WordPerfect provides many options for how a page will print. All of the options presented in this lesson have default settings that software developers thought would be most practical. In most cases, you can use those settings. The features with which we'll work in this lesson come from either the Insert menu or the Format menu.

This is another lesson that contains many useful skills. Don't try to do it all at once. When you come to a stopping point, you might want to give yourself a mini-break and relax for a moment. When you finish, be sure to review the lesson as at-home reading. It will be difficult to remember everything in this lesson after just one trip through it.

Headers, Footers, and Watermarks

As you learned at the beginning of the lesson, footers are the text that appears at the bottom of pages to tie a document together. The footers may identify the page, document, chapter, etc. Headers are similar text printed at the top of the pages.

Watermarks are a little different. While they are inserted into your document much like headers and footers, watermarks are used to dress up the appearance of a document or to impart some special information. Watermarks might include logos, headlines, art images, or words like *Confidential* printed behind the text on a sheet. While the technical aspect of including watermarks in your documents is much like that for headers and footers, the actual usage is quite different. We'll deal with headers and footers first. Then we'll learn about watermarks.

Headers and Footers

Following are some important facts about including headers and footers in your WordPerfect documents:

- If you are working in Draft view, headers and footers don't show in your window.

- You may have two headers and two footers (a total of four) in one document. With two, you can include different information on facing pages, like the information in the footers in this book. If you don't have facing pages, you probably won't use more than one header or footer in a document.

FIGURE 10-1
Headers/Footers Dialog Box

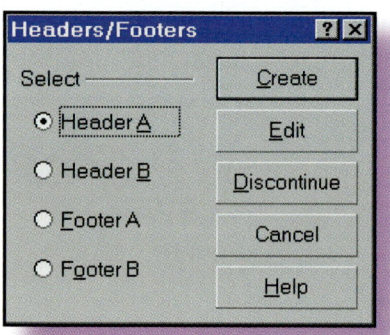

- Headers and footers are added to your documents by choosing Header/Footer from the Insert menu. When you make that choice, the dialog box illustrated in Figure 10-1 appears.

- In Draft view you are taken to a special header/footer editing window where the rest of your document doesn't show. In Page view your insertion point will be placed in an area enclosed in a dotted line—at the top for a header or at the bottom for a footer. The Header/Footer Property Bar tools (see Figure 10-2) will appear at the top of the window.

FIGURE 10-2
Header/Footer Property Bar Tools

You will enter the text of the header or footer in the special window. When you are finished with the header or footer, choose Close on the Property Bar to return to your document. In Page view you may click anywhere away from the area enclosed in gray to return to your document.

- Many WordPerfect features, such as Margin Set, Center, font changes, and Flush Right may be used in headers and footers.

- A header or footer may exceed one line in length. The first line of a header will begin at the top margin. The last line of a footer ends before the bottom margin.

- WordPerfect automatically adjusts the available space on a page to make room for headers and footers. Both headers and footers are automatically separated from the text by the equivalent of one blank line.

- You can use Suppress to prevent a header or footer from appearing on a particular page.

- While in the header/footer edit area, you can define a location for page numbering, and you can tell WordPerfect if you want the header or footer to appear on all pages, odd pages, or even pages.

- You need to enter the header or footer information only once for a document. It will then affect all of the pages of the document from the point where it is inserted.

- Headers and footers are spell checked along with your document.

- Headers and titles are two entirely different things. Here are definitions of each. Do not confuse them.

A *title* is the name of the document. It appears only on the first page of the document, where it is usually keyed two inches from the top of the page. Traditionally, the title is keyed in all capital letters and is separated from the body of the text by a quadruple or triple space. The title is considered to be part of the text.

A *header* may use the same words as the title of the document, but headers rarely appear on the first page of a document. (You'll soon learn how to suppress the header on the first page.) The header appears instead on other pages of the document, and it is frequently keyed in lowercase letters with the first letter of important words capitalized.

Now let's apply what you've learned about headers and footers in a short exercise. We'll work with both a header and a footer in the exercise.

EXERCISE 10.1

1. Open **pcug** from the student **datafile** folder. Use **Save As** to save the file as **pcug 10-1 xxx**, substituting your initials for *xxx* as always.

2. With the insertion point at the beginning of the document, change to double spacing. Remove the extra return between the paragraphs so the document has double spacing throughout. If you are not in Page view, open the **View** menu and choose **Page**.

3. Open the **Insert** menu and choose **Header/Footer**. You should see a dialog box that looks like Figure 10-1.

4. Leave **Header A** as the setting and choose **Create**. The Header/Footer tools will be added to the Property Bar. The insertion point will be in the header area that is outlined by dotted lines.

5. This header consists of two pieces of information, as illustrated in Figure 10-3. Key **PC User Group Meeting** at the left. Give the command for Flush Right (Alt+F7) and press **Ctrl+D** to insert the Date Text. Click the **Close** button on the Header/Footer Property Bar to return your insertion point to the document window.

FIGURE 10-3
Text for Header

```
PC User Group Meeting                                    (Current date)
```

(continued on next page)

EXERCISE ▶ 10.1 CONTINUED

6. Open the **Insert** menu and choose **Header/Footer** again. This time choose **Footer A**. Click **Create**. With the insertion point in the footer area outlined in gray, center and key the two lines illustrated in Figure 10-4 as the footer for your document. Click the **Close** button to return to your document.

7. Insert the Path and Filename code a double space below the second paragraph. Then Zoom to **Full Page** to view the document, complete with header and footer. Return to **100%**.

8. Reveal your codes and add the Header and Footer codes to your list.

9. Save your document again as **pcug 10-1 xxx** and print it.

FIGURE 10-4
Text for Footers

```
        For Discussion Purposes Only
                CONFIDENTIAL
```

As you can see, headers and footers are easy to add to your documents. You'll have more practice with them in later exercises. Let's try a watermark.

Watermarks

Watermarks are lightly shaded images behind the print on your document. Watermarks don't show in the window in Draft view. We'll learn about watermarks as we add one to the **pcug** document.

EXERCISE ▶ 10.2

1. With **pcug 10-1 xxx** showing in the window, use **Save As** to save the file as **pcug 10-2 xxx**.

2. Open the **Insert** menu and choose **Watermark**. Then choose **Create**. The Watermark tools (see Figure 10-5) will be added to the Property Bar.

3. Open the **Insert** menu and choose **Graphics**, Then choose **Clipart**.

4. The Scrapbook dialog box will appear. Drag the box on the scroll bar about three-fourths of the way to the bottom. Find **watrm061.wpg**. Drag that image out of the dialog box onto your page.

5. Click the **X** in the upper right corner of the Scrapbook dialog box to close it. Then point to the *Confidential* image on your page and drag it so the dotted lines surrounding the image are aligned with the margin guidelines.

6. Click outside of the image (in the margin of the document) to deselect the image. Then click the Close button on the Property Bar to return to your document.

7. Save the document again as **pcug 10-2 xxx** and print it. Then close it.

FIGURE 10-5
Watermark Property Bar Tools

142

UNIT 3: FORMATTING

Even though you used an image designed to be used as a watermark in this exercise, any image can be used for a watermark. In addition, watermarks can be edited in a number of ways since they are a graphics application. You'll learn about working with graphics images in Unit 6.

Page Numbering in Headers

WordPerfect is always counting your pages. If you request it, the page number can be printed on the page. You have some choices regarding page numbering. One of those choices is where the page number will be located on the page. Another choice is whether you'll include the page number as part of the header or as a separate feature.

In the next exercise we'll work with a longer document. This one will have a header that includes page numbering and a watermark.

EXERCISE 10.3

1. Key the beginning of the document, as illustrated in Figure 10-6.
   a. Press **Enter** until the insertion point is at approximately **2"** from the top of the page for the title.
   b. Center the title in all caps, and press **Enter** three times for a triple space following the title.
   c. Set justification at **Full** and line spacing at **Double**.
   d. Use **Tab** to indent the first line of the first paragraph.
   e. Press **Enter** following the last line of the paragraph.

2. Proofread and correct any errors. Then open the **Insert** menu, choose **File**, and insert **wind** from the student **datafile** folder.

3. Save your document as **wind 10-3 xxx**.

4. Move your insertion point to the top of the document and open the **Insert** menu. Choose **Header/Footer** and **Create** for Header A.

5. Create a header for your document that looks like Figure 10-7. Use **Bold** for the header. Follow these steps:
   a. Key **Wind Power** at the left.
   b. Press **Alt+F7** for Flush Right and key **Page**.

FIGURE 10-6
Text for Exercise 10.3

```
                    THE POWER OF WIND
    In this age of ecology consciousness, we hear more and more about
the best way to provide power to the billions of people inhabiting the
earth.  Power from fossil fuels has long been considered the most eco-
nomical way of producing electricity. Coal, however, is expensive and
dangerous to mine, and the supply is not unlimited.  What's more,
environmentalists are forever attacking the use of fossil fuels
because of the pollution caused by power plant emissions.
```

(continued on next page)

c. Space once and click the **Number** button on the Header/Footer Feature Bar. Choose **Page Number**. A *1* should appear in your document.

d. Click below the header (in the document) to exit the header editing window.

6. Check the appearance of your document using **Two Pages** view. Does the header appear at the top of both pages? Return to **Page** view.

7. Save your document again as **wind 10-3 xxx** and keep it open as you read on.

FIGURE 10-7
Header for **Wind** Document

| Wind Power | Page 1 |

When you used the Header/Footer Property Bar to enter the page number, you actually entered a code telling WordPerfect to number all pages of your document at the location of the insertion point. You don't have to include the word *Page* with your numbers. In fact, pages are usually numbered without any identifying words.

You can put a page number anywhere in a document, even without the Header/Footer feature. Let's take a side trip to learn to do that. Then we'll return to the formatting of the **wind** document.

EXERCISE 10.4

1. Position your insertion point in the middle of the word *harvesting* in the last sentence of the document.

2. Open the **Format** menu, choose **Page**, and then choose **Insert Page Number**. This will open the Insert Page Number dialog box, as illustrated in Figure 10-8.

3. The settings are fine. Click the **Insert** button and then click **Close**.

Now let's return to the **wind** document. First, we'll add a watermark. The best place for codes that format the entire document is at the top of the first page.

Text can be used for a watermark. We'll use an image from a previous version of WordPerfect for our watermark.

4. Look at your document. A number *2* should appear in the word *harvesting*.

5. Reveal your codes. Move the insertion point to the left of the code. Add the code to your list. Then remove the number from the document. You don't really want a page number in the middle of the word.

FIGURE 10-8
Insert Page Number Dialog Box

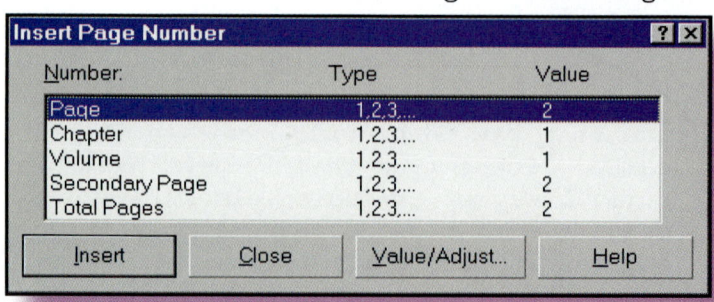

Number:	Type	Value
Page	1,2,3,...	2
Chapter	1,2,3,...	1
Volume	1,2,3,...	1
Secondary Page	1,2,3,...	2
Total Pages	1,2,3,...	2

Insert | Close | Value/Adjust... | Help

144

UNIT 3: FORMATTING

EXERCISE 10.5

1. With **wind 10-3 xxx** open in your window, use **Save As** to save the file as **wind 10-5 xxx**.

2. With your insertion point at the top of the first page, open the **Insert** menu and choose **Watermark**. Then choose **Create**.

3. Click the **Image** button on the Watermark Property Bar. When the list of images appears, click your **Favorites** button and change to the drive or folder that contains the **datafile** documents.

4. Find **Windmill.wpg** and double click to select it.

5. Click outside of the image (in a margin) and then click the **Close** button. Look at both pages. Is the windmill watermark there? (It won't show if you are in Draft view.)

6. Save your document again as **wind 10-5 xxx**. Insert the Path and Filename code a double space below the last paragraph. Keep the file open.

Suppress

Sometimes you don't want your headers or your page numbers to appear on certain pages. The **wind** exercise is a good example. The header looks strange on the top of the first page. You can turn off headers, footers, page numbering, and watermarks by placing the insertion point on the page where you don't want the header, footer, watermark, or page number to appear and by inserting a Suppress code.

Suppress affects only the page on which you place the code. It is accessed by choosing **Format**, **Page**, and then **Suppress**. The Suppress dialog box allows you to select all features to be suppressed on that page. Let's suppress the header on the **wind** document.

NOTE:

If your page number is included as part of the header, as in the wind document, the page number is suppressed when you suppress the header. It can't be suppressed individually.

EXERCISE 10.6

1. With **wind 10-5 xxx** open in the window, use **Save As** to save the file as **wind 10-6 xxx**.

2. Move your insertion point to the top of the first page (not in the header area). Open the **Format** menu and choose **Page**. Then choose **Suppress**.

3. Choose **Header A** and click **OK**. You will be returned to your document. Use **Two Pages** view to see if the header still shows on the second page but not the first.

4. When you are satisfied that everything looks as it ought to look, save your document again as **wind 10-6 xxx**. Keep it open.

Widow/Orphan

If you are using the default font—12-pt. Times New Roman—your document still has something wrong with it. Good document formatting rules dictate that a single line of a paragraph should never be by itself at the bottom or the top of a page. Renegade lines of paragraphs are called *widows* and *orphans*.

The Widow/Orphan feature controls those renegade lines. It may be accessed by opening the **Format** menu, and choosing **Keep Text Together**. The Widow/Orphan feature is handy because you need to insert it only once, like headers, footers, and watermarks, to take care of an entire multiple-page document.

If your document doesn't have a bad page break, you can use the Widow/Orphan feature anyhow, as a precaution. Let's see how easy it is to add this code to your document.

EXERCISE 10.7

1. With **wind 10-6 xxx** open, use **Save As** to save the file as **wind 10-7 xxx**.

2. Position your insertion point near the top of the first page. Open the **Format** menu and choose **Keep Text Together**. This opens the Keep Text Together dialog box, as illustrated in Figure 10-9.

3. Click the box below Widow/Orphan. Then click **OK** to close the dialog box and return to your document.

4. Use whatever view best displays your document. Check the watermark, the header, and the page end breaks.

5. If everything looks good, print the document. Save it again as **wind 10-7 xxx** and keep it open.

FIGURE 10-9
Keep Text Together Dialog Box

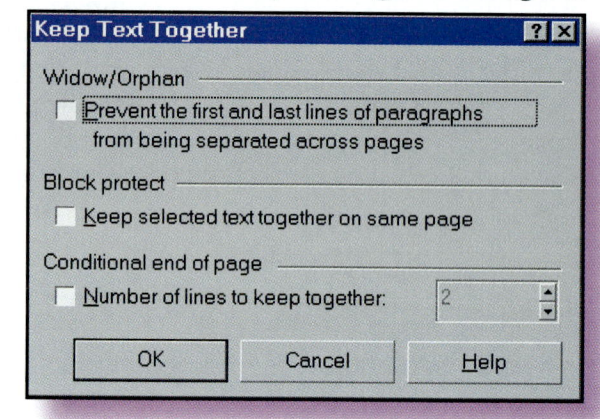

Center Page(s)

Remember the Center Page(s) command? It centers the text from top to bottom on the page. You used it in a couple of earlier documents. We'll use it here to prepare a title page for the **wind** document.

> **INTERNET**
> Many Internet connections from schools and homes are dial-in connections. With a dial-in connection, the Internet tools and programs are located on a host computer; your desktop computer can only display what the host processes.

EXERCISE 10.8

1. Press **Ctrl+Home** twice to position your insertion point at the top of your document, above all codes. Press **Ctrl+Enter** to add a new page at the beginning of the document. Press **Ctrl+Home** again to position the insertion point on the new page.

2. Open the **Format** menu and choose **Page**. Then choose **Center**. Choose the first button—to center the **Current page**. Click **OK**.

3. Back in your document window, click the **Justification** button on the Property Bar and choose **Center** justification.

4. Key the title page information, as shown in Figure 10-10. All lines will be centered, and the text will have even top and bottom margins. Change the title to **24 pt.** and format the name of the course with bold.

5. Zoom to **Full Page** to look at your lovely title page.

FIGURE 10-10
Text for Title Page

```
          THE POWER OF WIND
(press Enter 8 times)
                  by
(press Enter twice)
            (Student Name)
(press Enter 8 times)
        Beginning WordPerfect
(press Enter twice)
            (Current date)
```

6. Check through the document to make sure everything looks OK. If there are any problems, fix them. Save the document as **wind 10-8 xxx**. Print the title page only.

7. Keep the document open as you use another document to learn about page numbering. We'll come back to it in a moment.

Page Numbering

As mentioned earlier in the lesson, page numbering can be a separate feature. For some documents, you'll want page numbering but no header or footer. Let's work with page numbering in a document from a previous unit.

EXERCISE 10.9

1. Go to your **Units 1 and 2** folder and open **gifts proj6 xxx**. Use **Save As** to save the file as **gifts 10-9 xxx**. Be sure you are in Page view.

2. Press **Enter** a number of times to position the title about **2"** from the top of the page. Center the title **GLOBAL GIFT GIVING**. Follow the title with a triple space.

(continued on next page)

EXERCISE 10.9 CONTINUED

3. Position the insertion point at the beginning of the first paragraph.
   a. Set **1.5** line spacing for the introductory paragraphs.
   b. Change to **Full** justification.

4. Go through the document and remove the extra blank line between paragraphs so the entire document is formatted with 1.5 line spacing.

5. Position the insertion point at the beginning of the numbered items and set line spacing at **1.0**. Look through the document and make sure everything is correctly formatted.

6. Return the insertion point to the top of the document. Open the **Format** menu and choose **Page** and then **Numbering** to display the Select Page Numbering Format dialog box (see Figure 10-11).

7. Click the **Position** button at the top. After looking at the choices, return to **Bottom Center**.

8. Look at the *Page numbering format* section. The highlighted format is fine. Click **OK**.

9. Look at the bottom of both pages. (You'll have to use the scroll bar to see the bottom of page 2.)

10. Save the file again with the same name. Then keep it open as you read on.

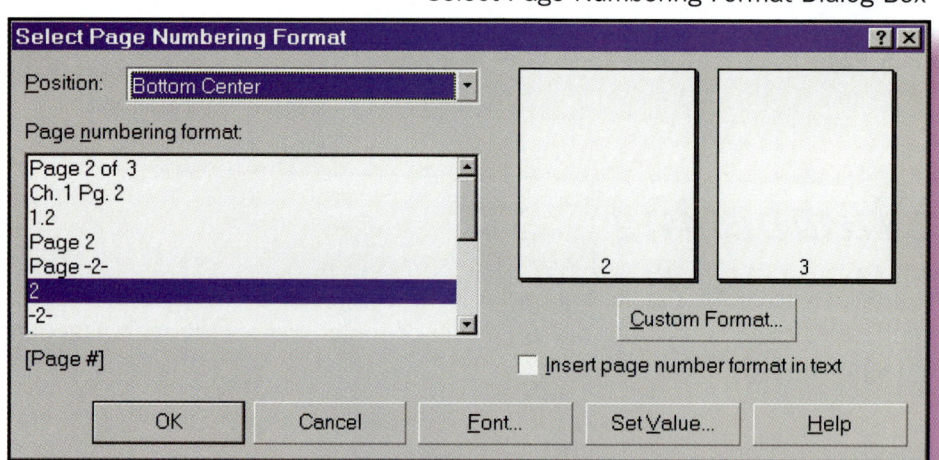

FIGURE 10-11
Select Page Numbering Format Dialog Box

Because the page number is in the document area, you might want to extend the length of your page by changing the bottom margin. It is customary to have a half-inch bottom margin when the page numbers are at the bottom of the page.

Let's drag the guideline for the bottom margin down to a half inch to give your document more room and decrease that unsightly BIG bottom margin.

148

UNIT 3: FORMATTING

EXERCISE 10.10

1. With **gifts 10-9 xxx** showing in your window, use **Save As** to save the file as **gifts 10-10 xxx**.

2. Move the document so you can see the bottom margin on the first page. Using the mouse pointer and the crosshair drag tool, drag the bottom margin guideline down until the little box reports **0.5"**. Release the guideline.

3. Return to the beginning of the first paragraph and display the Ruler. Move the tab marker at $1^1/_2$" to the left so it's between the $1^1/_4$" and the $1^3/_8$" marks. Click to insert an extra tab stop at $1^5/_8$". (Be sure it's a Left tab. You may need to change the type.)

4. Look through your document. In all likelihood, only one or two lines will be on the second page.

5. Return to the beginning of the document and insert a **Widow/Orphan** code (Format, Keep Text Together).

6. Save your document again as **gifts 10-10 xxx**. Print it and close it. (Your **wind** document should be showing now.)

Change Page Number Value

If you looked carefully at your **wind** document after adding the title page, you probably noticed that WordPerfect counted the title page as the first page of the document. Therefore, the second page of text is numbered as page 3. Technically, the title page shouldn't be counted, so the second page of text should be numbered as page 2.

WordPerfect has a feature that enables you to change the value of the page number. WordPerfect will continue numbering from that new page number value. This choice is made in the Select Page Numbering Format dialog box about which you just learned. We'll set the number for the first page of text (after the title page) to 1.

EXERCISE 10.11

1. With **wind 10-8 xxx** showing in the window, use **Save As** to save the file as **wind 10-11 xxx**.

2. Position the insertion point at the top of the first page of text (following the title page). The insertion point will be at the center because you set Center justification on the title page. Change justification to **Left**.

3. Open the **Format** menu and choose **Page** and then **Numbering**. Click the **Set Value** button.

4. The Values dialog box will open, looking like Figure 10-12. Click in the *Set page number* text box and change from *2* to **1**. Click **OK**.

5. Click **OK** again to return to your document.

(continued on next page)

EXERCISE 10.11 CONTINUED

6. Check the header at the top of the second page of text. It should now report that you are on page 2.

7. Print only the last page of the document. Then close it, saving it again as **wind 10-11 xxx** as you close it.

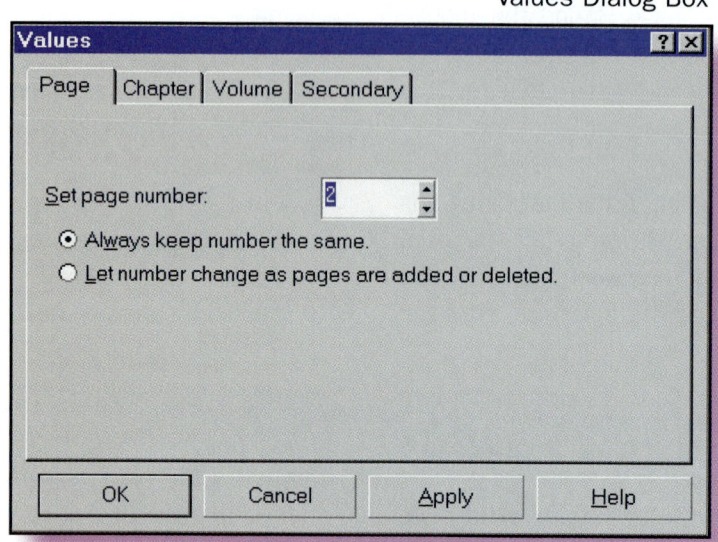

FIGURE 10-12
Values Dialog Box

Footnotes and Endnotes

In technical writing, footnotes and endnotes are used to identify the sources of the information used in a report and provide additional information to the reader. Footnotes are usually numbered consecutively, and each footnote appears at the bottom of the page where the resource is referenced. Footnotes are different from footers, where the same text appears at the bottom of each page.

Endnotes provide the same kind of information as footnotes. The major difference between them is that endnotes are usually at the end of a document—often on a page by themselves. Endnotes, too, are usually numbered consecutively.

WordPerfect helps you create and format footnotes. Numbering is automatic, and footnotes are properly placed and formatted. The same is true of endnotes.

Footnotes

When you are ready to insert a footnote into your document, open the Insert menu and choose Footnote/Endnote. Then choose Create. In Draft view, the reference number will be entered into your document and you will be taken to a special footnote window. In Page view, the reference number will be entered, and you will be moved to the bottom of the page where the footnote is to be keyed next to the footnote number. Both the reference and the footnote numbers are automatically superscripted (small reference numbers raised above the line).

FIGURE 10-13
Footnote Property Bar Tools

The tools for the Footnote Property Bar appears when you are in the footnote area (see Figure 10-13). The buttons on the bar enable you to restore the note number in case you accidentally lose it, as well as browse through existing notes. The Close button returns you to your document window when you finish keying the note.

Following are some miscellaneous considerations for you as you insert footnotes and edit text containing footnotes:

- WordPerfect automatically inserts the footnote numbers. Do not key the number in the text or in the footnote.

- If you want the reference number in the manuscript to appear tight against the preceding text, DON'T SPACE before inserting your footnote.

- WordPerfect indents the first line of each footnote one-half inch.

- WordPerfect inserts the line that divides the footnote from the text on the page.

- Do not press Enter at the end of a footnote. WordPerfect automatically inserts one blank line between footnotes.

- Footnotes do not show in the document in Draft view. When working with footnotes, it is best to work in Page view.

- Footnotes can be inserted as you create the document. You can also go back and insert them after the document is finished.

- If editing affects the footnotes in the document, WordPerfect will automatically renumber and rearrange the footnotes.

- When keying a footnote, you can use most of the features you use with regular text entry, such as Italic, Underline, and Bold.

- Titles of published materials, such as newspapers, magazines, and books, should be italicized.

Let's try a short exercise to see how footnotes work.

EXERCISE 10.12

1. Key the short paragraph in Figure 10-14. Set line spacing at **Double** at the beginning of the document and indent it as a normal paragraph.

2. When you come to the footnote reference number, don't key the numeral. Instead, create a footnote using these steps:
   a. Open the **Insert** menu and choose **Footnote/Endnote**. Be sure Footnote is selected, and click **Create**.
   b. Key the text of the footnote, as illustrated at the bottom of Figure 10-14. Key the name of the book in italic.
   c. Click the **Close** button on the Property Bar when you finish the footnote. Then complete the paragraph.

   (continued on next page)

EXERCISE ▷ 10.12 CONTINUED

3. Use **Two Pages** view or Zoom to **Full Page** to see how your footnote looks on the page. (You could also use the scroll bar to see the bottom of the page.)

4. Save your document as **footnote 10-12 xxx**. Insert the Path and Filename code a double space below the paragraph.

5. Print the document and save it again. Keep it open.

FIGURE 10-14
Text for Exercise 10.12

```
   This is a paragraph that contains a footnote.  The footnote number
is here.¹  This is the sentence that follows the footnote. It is a
thrill to discover how easy creating footnotes can be! Now I can use
footnotes in all my school papers.
_____

   ¹Mary Makebelieve.   Practice Footnotes, (Larsen:  Ann Street
Press, 199x), p. 85.
```

Editing Footnotes

Creating the footnote was pretty simple. Editing is just as simple. Let's make a couple of changes to the little document you just created.

EXERCISE ▷ 10.13

1. With **footnote 10-12 xxx** open in your window, use **Save As** to save the file as **footnote 10-13 xxx**.

2. In Page view, use the scroll bar to go to the bottom of the document so you can see the footnote. Click in the word *Mary* to enter the footnote editor.

3. Change *Mary* to **Maria**. Then change the page number from *85* to **25**.

4. Click in the document, above the footnote dividing line, to exit from the footnote editor.

5. Print the document and close it, saving it again as you close it.

Endnotes

As mentioned earlier, endnotes are created and edited much the same as footnotes. The major difference is location. When you put endnotes on a page by themselves at the end of a document, you must add that blank page and format it for the endnotes. Also, endnotes aren't formatted like a paragraph. Instead, they have a kind of hanging indent format, where the number is at the left margin and all other lines are indented. Let's practice.

EXERCISE 10.14

1. Open **wind 10-11 xxx**. Use **Save As** to save the file as **wind 10-14 xxx**.

2. With your insertion point at the top of the first page of text, reveal your codes and remove the Watermark code. (The watermark isn't necessary for this exercise, and it slows you down as you move through the document.)

3. Position your insertion point at the end of the paragraph about the *wind turbines in California*.

4. Open the **Insert** menu and choose **Footnote/Endnote**. Click the **Endnote** button and then **Create**. Your insertion point will be moved to a new line following the Path and Filename code at the end of your document. Endnote number **1.** will be there, with your insertion point next to the number.

5. Press **F7** to indent the text and key the **Melanie Malson . . .** endnote in Figure 10-15. Click the **Close** button on the Property Bar.

6. Position the insertion point at the end of the next paragraph (the one about the *eight-year payback*). Follow the procedure in Steps 4 and 5 to insert the **Donald Swenson . . .** endnote.

7. Experiment with trying to move the insertion point using the arrow keys on the keyboard while it is in an endnote.

8. Click to position the insertion point in the last paragraph of the document. Then click the **Save** button on the Toolbar to save the document with the same name. Keep the document open as you read on.

FIGURE 10-15
Endnotes for Exercise 10.14

[1]Melanie Malson, "The Winds of Tehachapi," *Journal of Power Resources*, February, 199x, p. 66.

[2]Donald Swenson, "That Great, Breezy Midwest," *Wisconsota Farm Journal*, November, 199x, p. 23.

As you no doubt discovered, each endnote is an entity. When you try to move the insertion point, you can go left and right, but you can't get to the other endnote, and you can't get to the text of the document. To get out of the endnote "window," use your mouse to click into the document or click the Close button on the Property Bar. Also, when you're in the document, Ctrl+End will take you to the end of the *text* of the document, but it won't take you into the endnote section. You must use the scroll bar to see the endnotes.

Now that the endnotes have been inserted into the document, let's format the documents so the endnotes are on a page by themselves at the end of the document.

EXERCISE 10.15

1. With **wind 10-14 xxx** showing in the window, use **Save As** to save the file as **wind 10-15 xxx**. Position your insertion point at the end of the Path and Filename code.

2. Press **Ctrl+Enter** for a new page. Press **Enter** several times to move your insertion point to somewhere near **2"** on the *Ln* indicator. (Double spacing is still in effect. Unless you change to single spacing, you won't hit exactly 2". It doesn't matter.)

3. Give the Center command (Shift+F7) and key the word **ENDNOTES** in bold and all caps.

4. Reveal your codes and look through the document at the new codes inserted when you created the endnotes. Add those codes to your list.

5. Print the document. Then close it, saving it again as you close it.

A number of options are available for working with footnotes and endnotes. If these features are important to the work you do, you may wish to spend some time exploring them further. WordPerfect Help contains information about formatting and changing options for both footnotes and endnotes.

Summary

Most of the features you studied in this lesson are primarily useful for documents of more than one page, although all of them can be used in single-page applications. In this lesson you learned that:

- Headers are information put at the top of the page to give a document continuity and to identify the pages.
- Footers provide the same services but are placed at the bottom of the page.
- Watermarks are lightly shaded images in the background on your pages.
- The codes for headers, footers, and watermarks only need to be entered once at the beginning of a document to format the entire document.
- The Widow/Orphan feature prevents a single line of a paragraph from appearing at either the bottom or the top of a page.
- Page numbering can be entered as a separate code, or the header can contain the command to number the pages.
- The value of the page number can easily be adjusted.
- Footnotes are used to identify references. WordPerfect formats footnotes automatically and even provides the reference numbers.
- Endnotes are like footnotes except they appear at the end of the document. If you want your endnotes on a separate page, you can format it after the document has been prepared.

All of the features presented in this lesson have options where you can change from the default settings to achieve an appearance that might be more to your liking. You learned the basics of each of the features. If you wish to explore further, you may do so at your leisure.

LESSON 10 REVIEW QUESTIONS

TRUE/FALSE

Circle the T if the statement is true. Circle the F if it is false.

(T) F 1. Headers and footers are similar except that headers appear at the top of a page and footers appear at the bottom.

T **(F)** 2. If you are working in Draft view, headers will show in your window, but footers will not.

T **(F)** 3. If you do not want your header to appear on the first page of your document, you must insert the header at the top of your second page.

(T) F 4. Suppress is accessed by choosing Format, Page, and then Suppress.

T **(F)** 5. Single lines of a paragraph at the bottom or top of a page are called leftovers.

T **(F)** 6. In preparing footnotes in Draft view, the reference number will be entered into your document and you will be taken to a special footnote window.

WRITTEN QUESTIONS

Write your answers to the following questions.

7. What is the difference between a footer and a footnote?
Footers identify the page, doc, chapter etc. Footnotes identify the sources of info used in a report & provide additional info.

8. How do you get out of the endnote "window"?
Click at the end of the last para.

9. Describe a watermark and list the type of things you might use as a watermark.
A lightly shaded image behind the print in a document. Any image can be used as a watermark. Currency/Money, Photos, clipart, etc.

10. What command did you use to prepare the title page in Exercise 10.8?
Ctrl + Enter.

LESSON 10 PROJECT

A relatively long document has been created and saved for you to format. It needs a header and some footnotes. You will do more formatting of this document at the end of Lesson 11. Let's get it started here.

1. Beginning in a new document window, open **pc care** from the student **datafile** folder. Use **Save As** to save the file as **pc proj10a xxx**.

(continued on next page)

155

2. Give the document a header, with **PC Care** in bold at the left and **Page** and the page number in bold at the right.

3. Suppress the header on the first page.

4. Use **Widow/Orphan** to protect the document against awkward page breaks.

5. Go to the bottom of the first page. With the mouse pointer, grab the bottom margin guideline and drag it down to **0.75"**. (That change will affect both pages.)

6. Return to the top of the document. Give the commands to insert a footer that contains the Path and Filename code. Format the footer with **Flush Right** and **8-pt. Arial**.

7. Insert four footnotes into the document. The footnotes are shown in Figure 10-16. Position the footnotes as follows:
   a. Footnote 1 at the end of the first paragraph in the section about *Equalizing the Power*.
   b. Footnote 2 following the sentence about *commercial screen savers* in the second paragraph of *Prevent Burn-in*.
   c. Footnote 3 following the sentence telling about the *15,000 volts*. (You'll need to change the *P* for the page number to lowercase. It may take a couple of tries.)
   d. Footnote 4 following the second paragraph under *Make Backups*.

8. When you finish, check your work over carefully. If everything is OK, print the document and save it again as **pc proj10a xxx**. If it isn't correct, fix whatever is wrong before printing.

9. You just discovered that you were given an incorrect page number for the second footnote. Change the page number from *61* to **16**. Print only the page containing the correction.

10. Save the file again, this time as **pc proj10b xxx**, and close it.

FIGURE 10-16
Footnotes for Lesson 10 Project

```
1.  Freddy Keelowatt, "Power Up," PC Prognosticators, April 199x,
    p. 42.
2.  "Pixel Protectors," Timely Technology, July 199x, p. 61.
3.  Keelowatt, Op. Cit. p. 37.
4.  Hiam Halpa, "Better Backups," Timely Technology, January
    199x, p. 61.
```

CRITICAL THINKING ACTIVITY

You learned many features in this lesson that you will be using in formatting your documents. You will use some of these features, such as footnotes, page numbering, headers, and footers, frequently, but others have great potential for personal and professional use. Get a multiple-page report from your library, off the Internet, or from a local business. List as many document formatting features as you can find used in that report.

LESSON 11
Miscellaneous Formatting Tools

OBJECTIVES

Upon completion of this lesson, you will be able to:

- Use Advance to set the beginning point in a document.
- Make your document fit the page with Make It Fit.
- Use WordPerfect Symbols for characters not on the keyboard.
- Create and use QuickWords.
- Format portions of your text with QuickFormat.
- Use Block Protect to keep critical pieces of text together on a page.
- Double click parts of the WordPerfect window to open selected dialog boxes.
- Change the default font for documents.
- Use Current Document Style to format the entire document.
- Position text on the page using the Shadow Pointer.

Estimated Time: 1½ hours

WordPerfect has a variety of tools to help you with your work. Some of them are powerful tools that are used with great regularity. Others are tools that perform a small task but are invaluable when needed. In Lessons 9 and 10 you have worked with tools that are important parts of text editing. Tools such as headers, footers, margins, line spacing, and justification are standard tools and belong in the tool case for everyday use. In Lesson 11 you'll learn about a variety of small but useful tools. They don't fit together. In fact, this lesson may seem like a potpourri of features. Some are new; most are old; but all are useful sometimes.

Advance

The Advance tool enables you to position your text anywhere you'd like it on the page. You can use Advance to place text a certain distance from the current location of the insertion point, or you can place text at a specific location on the page measured from the edges of the paper. Usually you will measure from the edges of the paper. Let's try it.

EXERCISE 11.1

1. Beginning in a new document window, open the **Format** menu. Choose **Typesetting** and then **Advance**. The dialog box illustrated in Figure 11-1 will appear.

2. In the *Horizontal position* section, click **From left edge of page**. Key **4.25"** into the *Horizontal distance* box.

3. In the *Vertical position* section, click **From top of page**. In the text box, key **5.5"**. Press **Enter** or click **OK**.

4. Key your name. Zoom to **Full Page** to see where your name begins. It should be at the exact center of the page.

5. Print your document and fold it in half in both directions. Does your name begin at the center of the page?

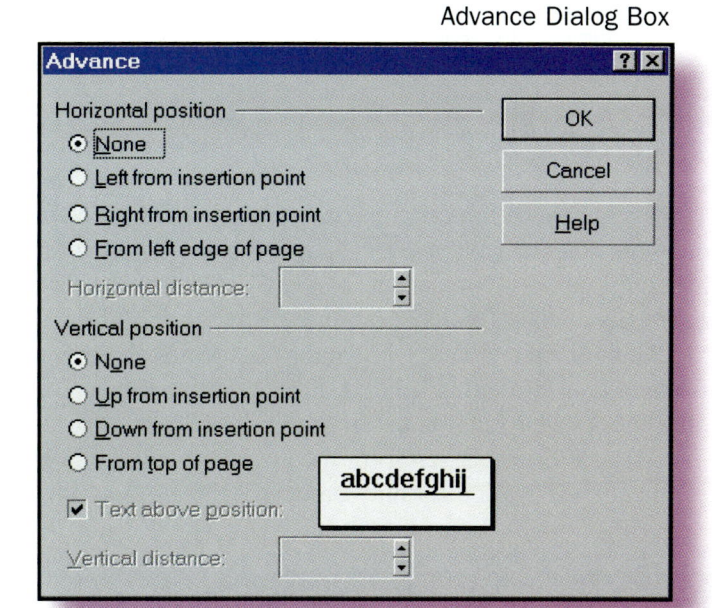

6. Close the document without saving it.

FIGURE 11-1
Advance Dialog Box

Now that you see how it works, let's use Advance to set the top margin of the first page of a document with which you've been working.

EXERCISE 11.2

SCANS

1. Open **gifts 10-10 xxx**. Then use **Save As** to save the file as **gifts 11-2 xxx**.

2. Reveal your codes and remove all of the [HRt] codes above the title of the document.

3. Open the **Format** menu and choose **Typesetting**. Then choose **Advance**.

4. In the *Vertical position* section, click **From top of page**. In the text box, key **2.25"**. Click **OK**.

5. Position your insertion point on the title of the document. The Application Bar should report that you are slightly more than 2 inches from the top of the page.

6. Save the document again as **gifts 11-2 xxx** and keep it open.

159

Near the bottom of the Advance dialog box is a check box for *Text above position*. If you click to deselect this option, the advanced text will be below rather than above the position measured from the top of the page. That explains why you set Advance at 2.25" and the Application Bar measured only 2.05". In many of the exercises you will complete in this course, you will be asked to advance from the top of the page 2". It will actually turn out to be about 1.8". Don't be concerned about what seems like a discrepancy in distance.

Make It Fit

If you looked through the document in your window, you probably noticed that very little of the document extended to the second page. If you fiddled with the margins, the line spacing, or the font size, you could get it to fit on one page. WordPerfect has a feature called *Make It Fit* that adjusts your documents so they fit on the number of pages you wish.

Make It Fit can make a number of changes in your document to make it fit in the desired amount of space. The formatting it looks at by default are font size and line spacing. You know how to change both of those items, but it's easier to let WordPerfect adjust your documents for you.

Make It Fit is chosen from the Format menu. Let's learn about Make It Fit as we adjust this **gifts** document so it fits comfortably on one page.

EXERCISE 11.3

SCANS

1. With **gifts 11-2 xxx** showing in your window, use **Save As** to save the file as **gifts 11-3 xxx**.

2. Open the **Format** menu and choose **Make It Fit**. The dialog box illustrated in Figure 11-2 will appear.

3. Note that WordPerfect is telling you that the document is currently *2* pages long. Be sure *Desired number of pages* is set at **1**.

4. Note also that none of the items in the left column are selected. Only Font size and Line spacing should be checked. If necessary, fix the *Items to adjust* section so it matches Figure 11-2.

5. Click the **Make It Fit** button. WordPerfect will take a minute to complete your task.

6. When WordPerfect finishes squishing your document, it will be on one page. Look at the following things:
   a. Look at the font size reported on the Property Bar. It is now smaller than the default of 12 pt.
   b. Position your insertion point in the first paragraph. Go the the Line Spacing dialog box and check the spacing. It should be less than 1.5.
   c. Look at line spacing with the insertion point in the enumerated items. It should report spacing of less than single (1).

7. Print the document and save it again as **gifts 11-3 xxx**.

Make It Fit also works in the opposite direction. If your report is a little short, you can tell WordPerfect to make it fill a little more space. Exercise judgment with this feature. The request must be reasonable. It would have been unreasonable, for example, to have asked WordPerfect to expand the **gifts** document to two pages. If you had, you would have ended up with a gigantic font and very wide line spacing. You may practice more with this feature at your leisure.

Make It Fit is a feature you'll use frequently in this training.

FIGURE 11-2
Make it Fit Dialog Box

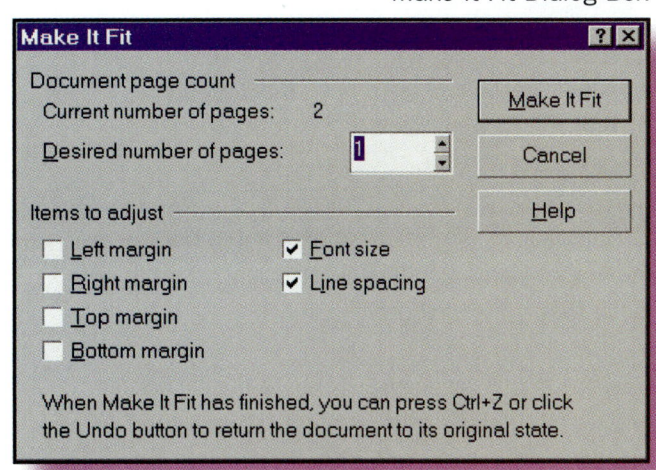

WordPerfect Symbols

You learned earlier that you can create an em dash by keying three hyphens. That was one of a few shortcuts available in WordPerfect Symbols. Another way to get different symbols is by using the 15 sets of symbols provided in WordPerfect.

To access special symbols, position the insertion point where you would like the symbols to appear and press Ctrl+W, click the Symbol button on the Property Bar, or choose Symbols from the Format menu. In each case a window will open, illustrating a set and waiting for you to choose the desired symbol. The buttons at the bottom of the dialog box offer choices regarding inserting the symbol and closing the dialog box.

FIGURE 11-3
WordPerfect Symbols Dialog Box

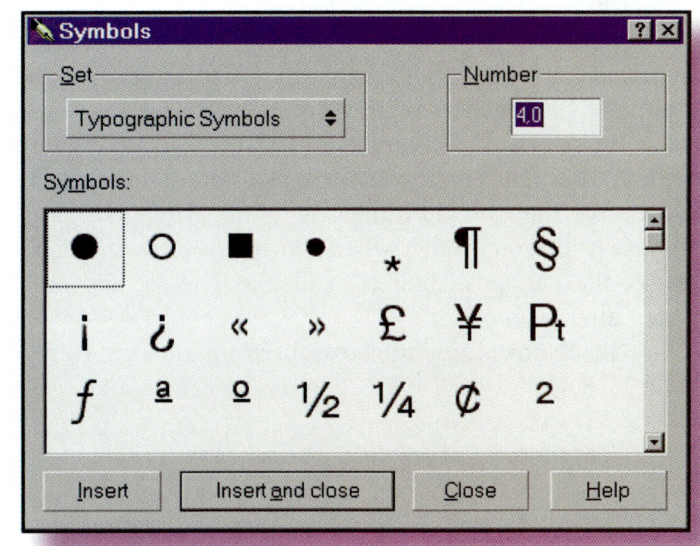

Look at Figure 11-3. It shows the WordPerfect Symbols dialog box and Set 4, the set of symbols you'll probably use most frequently.

161

EXERCISE 11.4

1. Beginning in a new document window, press **Ctrl+W**. Key the numbers **4,67**, with no space following the comma.

2. The number you keyed will appear in the box in the upper right corner. The highlight should move to the $^3/_8$ fraction.

3. Use the scroll bar in the Symbols dialog box and look at some of the symbols. Then return the highlight to $^3/_8$ and click the **Insert and close** button at the bottom of the dialog box. The $^3/_8$ should appear at the location of your insertion point in your window.

4. Zoom to **200%** so you can see your fraction. Stay at 200% temporarily.

5. Press **Ctrl+W** again. Note that WordPerfect remembered that the last symbol you used was $^3/_8$, so if you wanted $^3/_8$ again, you would only need to press Enter to put the fraction in your document and close the dialog box.

6. Use the scroll bars, if necessary, to find the $^1/_2$ fraction. Double click it to put it into your document. Then click the **Close** button.

7. Press **Enter** twice to prepare for the next exercise.

Bullets and Check Boxes

Many of the symbols in the 15 sets of symbols are not symbols you will use with regularity. Bullets and check boxes are examples of symbols you might find useful.

You worked with bullets in Lesson 5. If you want a bullet with a different look, you can use WordPerfect symbols to customize the Outline/Bullets & Numbering list, or you can choose a different bullet when starting your own list. Here is a list of the variety of bullets available. The set and number are listed after each bullet.

◦ 2,27	◦ 4,45
• 4,0	☻ 5,8
◦ 4,1	◦ 6,33
• 4,3	◦ 6,36
● 4,44	▶ 6,27

Check boxes are little boxes used for choices. Here is how you might use the check box that occurs with 4,38.
 ☐ Yes or ☐ No
 ☐ Male or ☐ Female

Additional choices for check boxes are ☐ (4,48) and ☐ (5,24). If you think all of these are too small, you can vary the sizes of the check boxes (and all other symbols) by changing the font size. When you do this, extra space might be added between your lines.

While it seems like quite a job to change font size and choose a symbol from the set, you can create the symbol(s) with all the desired changes. Then copy it to the Windows Clipboard and paste it into your document each time you need it.

EXERCISE 11.5

1. Press **Ctrl+W** and browse through the sets. Practice making some bullets and check boxes. See if you can find a check mark. Vary the sizes of your check boxes and symbols.

2. Zoom to **100%** and press **Enter** twice.

3. Key the sentences in Figure 11-4. Double-space between the sentences. Insert the required symbols using the numbers in parentheses for reference. You do not need to key the numbers in parentheses.

4. When you finish, save your exercise as **char 11-5 xxx**. Insert the Path and Filename code in a footer. Print the document and close it, saving it again when you close it.

FIGURE 11-4
Sentences for Exercise 11.5

```
It might cost $1.70 or more to buy £ of British money. (4,11)
The cake was baked in a 350° oven. (6,36)
"¿Dónde está su niña?" (4,32) (4,8) (1,59) (1,27) (1,57) (4,31)
I can create check boxes with 4,38 ☐ and 4,48 ☐.
```

WordPerfect symbols open a whole new set of doors for document creation. Look for opportunities to use special symbols.

QuickWords

QuickWords may be used for abbreviations that expand into the complete text when you key the QuickWord and then expand it by pressing the space bar, Enter, or Tab. QuickWords work much like QuickCorrect. QuickWords, however, can contain formatting such as Bold, Italic, Underline, and font changes, in addition to a number of formatting features about which you have not yet learned. We'll practice QuickWords here. Then we'll work with it again when you've learned some of those other features.

EXERCISE 11.6

1. Beginning in a new document window, key your entire name. Select the name and format it with **Bold**, **Italic**, and **24-pt. Arial**.

2. Below your name, key your address using **10-pt. Arial** (no Bold or Italic).

3. Select the entire name and address. Then open the **Tools** menu and choose **QuickWords**. The dialog box illustrated in Figure 11-5 will appear.

(continued on next page)

EXERCISE ▶ 11.6 CONTINUED

FIGURE 11-5
QuickWords Section of the QuickCorrect Dialog Box

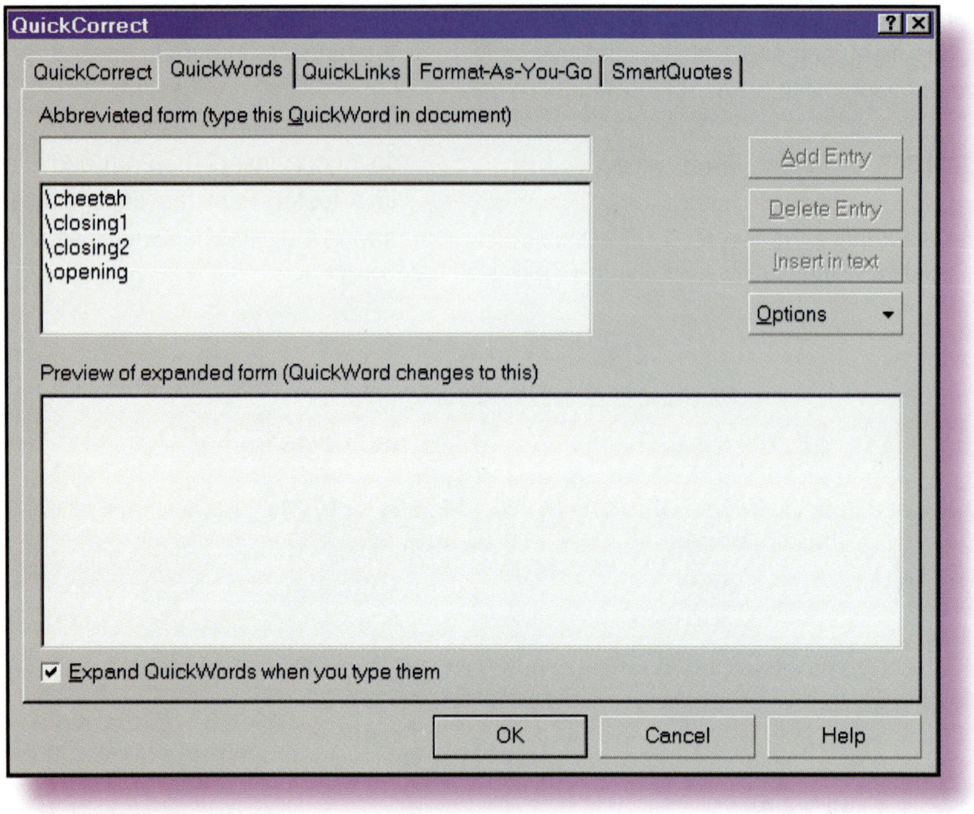

4. In the QuickWords portion of the QuickCorrect dialog box, key the characters that you will use for an abbreviation for your name. If your initials are unique characters, like *dk* for *Donald R. Knowles*, use them.

5. Click **Add Entry**, which closes the dialog box.

6. Back in your document window, move your insertion point to a double space below your formatted name. Key the abbreviation and press the space bar. Watch your name and address appear, complete with formatting.

7. Close your document without saving it.

As you discovered in Exercise 11.6, you aren't limited to one or two words with QuickWords. In fact, you aren't even limited to a single line, as you are with QuickCorrect. You can create as many QuickWords as you wish, and you can use them as often as they are needed. When a QuickWord is no longer needed, you can use Delete to remove it from the list.

Now let's learn about another "Quick" formatting tool.

164

UNIT 3: FORMATTING

QuickFormat

QuickFormat is a tool you may use to copy the format from one chunk of text in your document to other chunks of text. You can copy font face, font size, and appearance attributes (such as bold, underline, and italic). For paragraphs, you can also copy spacing, indentation, and borders.

When you choose QuickFormat from the Toolbar or from the Format menu, you have the choice of copying characters or headings. This is an important distinction. We'll review by adding some special formatting to the document. Then we'll practice QuickFormat, trying it both ways.

EXERCISE 11.7

1. Open **pc proj10b xxx**. Save the file as **pc 11-7 xxx**.

2. Position the insertion point at the beginning of the first paragraph. Change line spacing to **1.5**. Then go through the document and delete the extra blank line above and below each of the side headings.

3. Move the insertion point to the top of the document and use **Advance** to set the first line of the document at **1.5" From top of page**.

4. Select the first side heading (*Equalize the Power*) and format it with Bold, Italic, and Underline.

5. Position the insertion point somewhere in the side heading and click the **QuickFormat** button on the Toolbar. The QuickFormat dialog box, illustrated in Figure 11-6, will appear. Note that WordPerfect knows you're working with a chunk of text surrounded by hard returns, so Headings is selected.

6. Click **OK**. Move your mouse and look at the pointer. It should look like an I-beam with a paint roller.

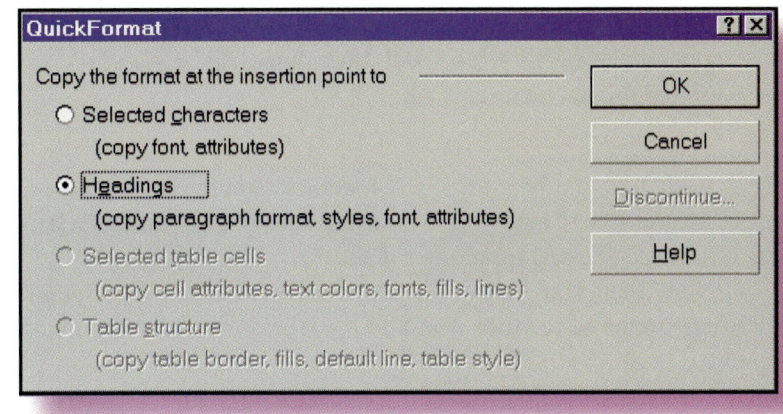

FIGURE 11-6
QuickFormat Dialog Box

7. Use **Page Down** to move through your document and find the next side heading. Point in the left margin opposite that side heading (your pointer will be a fat white arrow) and click once. The format from the first side heading should be painted onto the second one.

8. Find the other four side headings in the document and paint the format on in the same way. Then click the **QuickFormat** button on the Toolbar to turn QuickFormat off.

9. Check your work over carefully. Then print it and save it again as **pc 11-7 xxx**. Keep it open in the window.

When QuickFormat is used to format paragraphs (headings), it creates a style for those headings. They are all tied together. This is a big advantage, because if you later decide you don't like the style, you only need to change one of the occurrences of the style, and WordPerfect will change all the rest. Let's practice that with the document in the window.

EXERCISE 11.8

SCANS

1. With **pc 11-7 xxx** showing in your window, use **Save As** to save the file as **pc 11-8 xxx**.

2. Position the insertion point in any one of the side headings.

3. Press **F9** for the Font dialog box. In the *Appearance* section, deselect **Underline** and choose **Small caps**. Click **OK**.

4. Look through the document. All of the side headings should be formatted with Bold, Italic, and Small caps.

5. Click the **Save** button on the Toolbar and keep the document open in the window as you read on.

With the side headings tied together as a style, you can change the formatting of those lines as often as you like. That "style" is saved with the document when you save it and close the document. It cannot be transferred to another document.

Now that you know what a fine formatting tool QuickFormat is, let's look at the *Selected characters* part of the tool. With the QuickFormat Selected characters choice, the selected formatting is "painted" onto additional text.

EXERCISE 11.9

SCANS

1. With **pc 11-8 xxx** open, use **Save As** to save the file as **pc 11-9 xxx**.

2. Click to position the insertion point in the word *computer* in the first paragraph.

3. Click the **Bold** button on the Property Bar. With the insertion point in the bolded word, click the **QuickFormat** button on the Toolbar.

4. Choose **Selected characters** and click **OK**. Your insertion point should now look like a skinny paintbrush.

5. Look through the document. Each time you find the word *computer* or *computers*, double click to select and format that word. Then move to the next occurrence of the word. The word occurs 15 times!

6. When you finish, turn QuickFormat off by clicking the **QuickFormat** button on the Toolbar again.

7. Position the insertion point in any occurrence of *computer* and change from Bold to **Italic**. (All occurrences should change.)

166   UNIT 3: FORMATTING

8. Reveal your codes. Look at the codes by the side headings that are formatted with QuickFormat. Look at the *Auto QuickFormat* codes. Add them to your list. (Auto QuickFormat1 for the side headings and Auto Quickformat2 for the *computer*.)

9. Move your insertion point so it is to the left of one of the side heading Auto QuickFormat codes. Note that it lists all of the appearance attributes you've used to format the side headings.

10. Print your document. Then save it again as **pc 11-9 xxx**. Keep it open.

In this exercise you could select the text to be formatted by double clicking because it was only one word. If you want to add the format to two or more consecutive words, you must select and format the words by dragging across them with the mouse pointer.

Block Protect

If your document has the specified 1.5 line spacing, Widow/Orphan, and an Advance code positioning the title 1.5" from the top of the page, you probably have a side heading at the bottom of one page and the beginning of the paragraph for that side heading on the next page. Look through your document and find the *Prevent Burn-in* side heading. Widow/Orphan keeps paragraphs together very well, but it doesn't keep TWO paragraphs together (the side heading and the following paragraph).

You can deal with those situations individually as they occur using a tool called *Block Protect*. With Block Protect, you select the text to be kept together on a page, give the proper command, and WordPerfect will keep the text together. Since WordPerfect never violates a margin, it will move the entire block of text to be protected to the next page. Let's try it on the **pc** document.

EXERCISE 11.10

1. With **pc 11-9 xxx** showing in the window, use **Save As** to save the document as **pc 11-10 xxx**.

2. Move your document in the window so you can see the *Prevent Burn-in* side heading and at least two lines of the next paragraph. (If you prefer to go to Draft view so the footnote and header don't interfere, it will probably be easier to see what you're doing.)

3. Beginning with the side heading, select the side heading, all of the first line of the next paragraph, and at least a portion of the second line.

4. Point to the selected text. Right click to display the QuickMenu and then choose **Block Protect**. You'll see the side heading move to the top of the second page so it is together with the following paragraph.

5. Save the document again as **pc 11-10 xxx** and print it. Keep it open.

Double Clicking

A couple of other features should be mentioned here that you might find useful when you are formatting your documents. Both of them have to do with double clicking parts of the WordPerfect window.

Property Bar

If you double click the QuickFonts button on the Property Bar, WordPerfect will display the Font dialog box.

Ruler

As you know, if you point to one of the tab set markers on the Ruler and right click, the menu listing the kinds of tabs appears. If you point to one of those markers and double click (with the left mouse button, of course), the Tab Set dialog box will appear.

Pointing anywhere in the margin portion of the Ruler and double clicking will open the Margins portion of the Page Setup dialog box.

Codes

When your codes are revealed, you can point to most of the codes and double click to open the related dialog box. For example, double clicking the Bold, Italic, or Underline code or any of the font codes will open the Fonts dialog box. Double clicking any Tab code will open the Tab Set dialog box. Double clicking the Hard and Soft Return codes will open the Paragraph Format dialog box, where you can set such things as indents and spacing between paragraphs.

Application Bar

If you double click anywhere in the *Pg*, *Ln*, *Pos* portion of the Application Bar, the Go To dialog box will open. The Application Bar can be customized. Many users add the current date to the Application Bar. If your Application Bar includes the date, double clicking that date will add the current date to your document at the position of the insertion point.

Let's use the document showing in your window to practice this double clicking. Don't worry about spoiling the document. You'll throw it away when you're finished.

EXERCISE 11.11

1. Point to each of the following items and double click. When the appropriate dialog box appears, look it over and then close it. Some of the dialog boxes may be closed with **OK**. Others may be closed with **Close** or **Cancel**. All of them may be closed by clicking the *x* in the upper right corner.
   a. **QuickFonts** button on the Property Bar.
   b. *Pg, Ln, Pos* portion of the Application Bar.
   c. Margin markers on the Ruler. (You may have to choose the Ruler from the View menu to display it.)
   d. Indent triangles in the margin portion of the Ruler. (Paragraph Format dialog box)
   e. Tab set marker on the Ruler.
   f. A font code in Reveal Codes.
   g. Hard Return [HRt] code in Reveal Codes.
   h. **Left tab** code in Reveal Codes.

2. When you've explored this alternate method of displaying dialog boxes and closed those dialog boxes, close the document without saving it.

Selecting Text

While you're learning about miscellaneous formatting tools, one other procedure should be reviewed and expanded. This has to do with selecting odd pieces of text with the mouse. As you know, you can double click to select a word, triple click to select a sentence, or quadruple click to select a paragraph. Or, if you use the fat white arrow in the left margin, you can select sentences and paragraphs with fewer clicks.

It is not uncommon, however, to need to select text that doesn't fall into one of those neat packages (like a word or sentence). Then you are most likely to use the mouse to drag across the text to select it.

If the text to be selected begins at the margin, like the side heading in the Block Protect exercise earlier, it's sometimes difficult to get the first letter of the text without grabbing the margin guideline. In situations like those, it might be easier for you to begin at the opposite end of the text to select it. In the case of the Block Protect exercise, you would have begun in the middle of the second line of the paragraph and dragged the mouse pointer up and to the left until the entire side heading was included in the selected text.

As you work with WordPerfect and edit your documents, practice alternate methods in all you do. You'll soon develop a style that works for you and helps you to be efficient in your work.

Default Font and Current Document Style

In Lesson 10 you learned about formatting whole documents, including extended document parts such as headers, footers, footnotes, and page numbers. In most of those exercises you worked with the default font face and the default margins. Consequently, you didn't have any problems with odd fonts or margins in your documents.

When you change the font face or the margins, the change only applies to the body of the document. It does NOT extend to the parts of the document in the special editing windows. You must format those document parts separately. A better way is to put the format for the entire document in the Document Default Font or the Current Document Style. Let's look at these two features.

Document Default Font

This tool is for setting a new font for the entire document. The dialog box is opened by choosing File, Document, and then Default Font, or by choosing Default Font in the Font dialog box. When you set the font for a document using the default font, the headers, footers, footnotes, and page numbering will all have the same font. Let's try it.

EXERCISE 11.12

1. Open **pcug 10-1 xxx**. Use **Save As** to save the file as **pcug 11-12 xxx**.

2. With the insertion point at the beginning of the first paragraph, change the font of the text to **Arial**.

3. Check the header and footer. Note that those two parts are still formatted with Times New Roman. Remove the Arial font code you just inserted.

(continued on next page)

EXERCISE 11.12 CONTINUED

4. With the insertion point at the beginning of the first paragraph, open the **File** menu, choose **Document**, and then choose **Default Font**. The dialog box that opens should look like Figure 11-7.

5. Note the check box at the bottom. If you wished to permanently change the font for ALL documents, the box should contain a check. If not, the change is for the current document only. Be sure NO check mark is in the box now.

6. Choose **Arial** and click **OK**.

7. Check the header and footer. Note that those parts are now formatted with the same font as the text of the document.

8. Save the file again as **pcug 11-12 xxx**. Keep it open as you read on.

FIGURE 11-7
Document Default Font Dialog Box

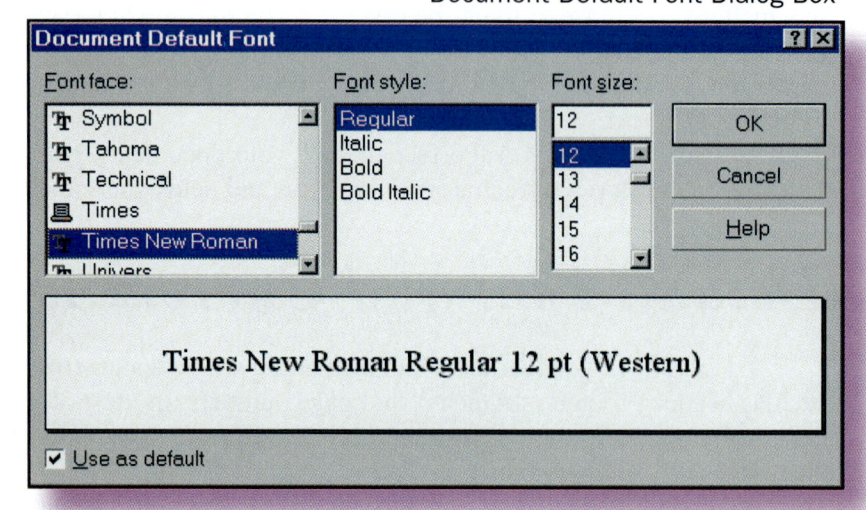

As you can see, if you wanted to change the font of the entire document, it is much easier to do it with Default Font than it would be to have to change the font of the header, the footer, page numbering, or the footnotes individually.

While Default Font is used to change the font face and font size of a document, you can make other changes with the Current Document Style feature.

Current Document Style

Current Document Style may be used for changing fonts, as well as a wide variety of other formats that you want to carry through your entire document. A good example is margins. We'll practice that in Exercise 11.13.

EXERCISE 11.13

1. With **pcug 11-12 xxx** showing in the window, use **Save As** to save the file as **pcug 11-13 xxx**.

2. Position the insertion point at the beginning of the first paragraph. Use either the Ruler or the Margins portion of the Page Setup dialog box to make **2"** margins on both the left and right.

170   UNIT 3: FORMATTING

3. Look at the header in your document. Look at the guidelines surrounding the footer space. As you can see, both of those parts are still governed by the default margin setting.

4. Return the insertion point to the beginning of the first paragraph. Use Reveal Codes so you can see to remove the Left and Right margin settings.

5. Open the **File** menu, choose **Document**, and then choose **Current Document Style**. The Styles Editor dialog box should appear (see Figure 11-8). This is a dialog box you'll see often as you progress through your work.

6. In the Styles Editor dialog box, open the **Format** menu and choose **Margins**. Set the Left and Right margins at **2"**.

7. Click **OK** to close the Margins portion of the Page Setup dialog box and again to close the Styles Editor dialog box.

8. Look at the header and the guidelines surrounding the footer space. As you can see, the margins in those areas now match the margins in the remainder of the document.

9. Save your document again as **pcug 11-13 xxx**. Print it and close it.

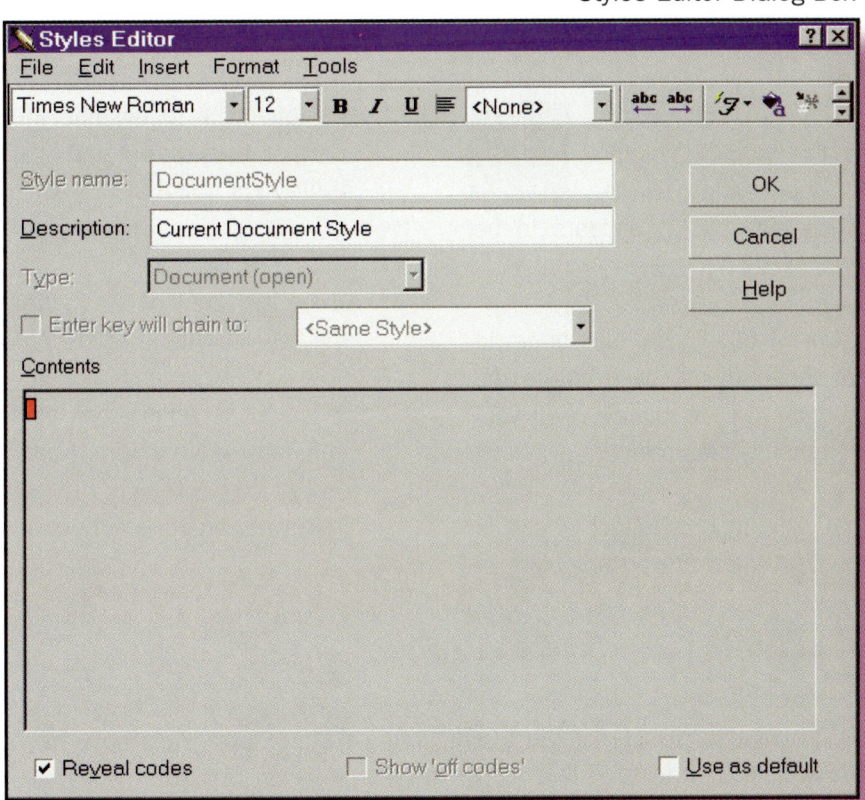

FIGURE 11-8
Styles Editor Dialog Box

Exercises 11.12 and 11.13 were short and somewhat exaggerated. But they should have given you a good idea of the value of Document Default Font and Current Document Style. Obviously, both of these tools are valuable when you work with documents that contain extra parts like headers and footers. As mentioned earlier, these features also work for footnotes, endnotes, page numbers, etc.

171

Shadow Pointer

Earlier in your training, you were told to leave the Shadow Pointer button on the Application Bar in the UP position. That means that your insertion point always looks like an *I*. The Shadow Pointer is actually a very useful tool for certain applications. When it is selected, you can

- point near the middle of the page. If you click when the pointer has an arrow in both directions, the text you key will be centered.

- point near the right of the page. If you click when the point has an arrow pointing to the left, the text you key will be formatted with Flush Right.

- point anywhere on the page where you would like text to begin. When you click, the insertion point will be positioned at that location, and the space between that location and the previous text will be filled with as many [HRt] and [Left Tab] codes as necessary to position the text.

Let's practice with the Shadow Pointer (sometimes referred to as the *Shadow Cursor*).

EXERCISE 11.14

1. Beginning in a new document window, click the Shadow Pointer tool on the Application Bar to select it. (When selected, it appears to be depressed.)

2. Anywhere in your window, move the pointer to the horizontal center of the page. When the arrow points right AND left, click. Key your entire name. It should be centered.

3. Point near the right margin (either above or below your name). When the arrow points to the left, click to position the insertion point there and key your name again. It should end at the right margin.

4. Move the pointer to a location on the page where the arrow points to the right. Click there and key your name again.

5. Reveal your codes. Look at all the [HRt] and [Left Tab] codes inserted by WordPerfect.

6. Close your practice without saving it.

Summary

As promised at the beginning of the lesson, lots of interesting tools have been discussed and practiced in this lesson. You've learned that:

- With the Advance tool, you can begin your text anywhere you'd like on the page.

- Make It Fit can be used to compress or expand a document onto a prescribed number of pages.

- WordPerfect Symbols is a tool that enables you to insert a wide variety of symbols and icons into your documents—symbols that don't appear on the keyboard.

- QuickWords can be set up to save you keystrokes. Text entered using QuickWords can contain a wide variety of formats.

UNIT 3: FORMATTING

- QuickFormat has two settings.
  - If you choose Headings, a style is prepared that you can apply to similar parts of the document.
  - If you choose Selected characters, you can paint the format onto words or phrases in the document.
- Block Protect is a tool that enables you to keep chunks of text together on a page. Block Protect must be applied each time it is needed.
- You can point to a variety of places in your window and double click to open related dialog boxes.
- You can use Document Default Font to insert a font setting that formats all parts of your document.
- Current Document Style is a tool that enables you to make formatting changes that format your entire document.
- The Shadow Pointer enables you to key anywhere on a page.

> **INTERNET** The federal government has plans to link schools, government agencies, colleges, and universities to a network that will be much faster than the current Internet. This new network is called the National Research and Education Network (NREN).

LESSON 11 REVIEW QUESTIONS

MULTIPLE CHOICE

Circle the best answer to each of the following statements.

1. The tool that enables you to position your text anywhere you'd like it on a page is called
   - **A.** Advance.
   - **B.** Make It Fit.
   - **C.** QuickFormat.
   - **D.** Center Page(s).

2. The Make It Fit feature looks at the following default settings:
   - **A.** margins and font size.
   - **B.** font size and line spacing.
   - **C.** line spacing and line length.
   - **D.** line length and margins.

3. WordPerfect 8 provides _____ sets of symbols.
   - **A.** five
   - **B.** ten
   - **C.** 15
   - **D.** 20

(continued on next page)

4. To change the size of check boxes and all other symbols, you can change
   - **A.** the font size.
   - **B.** to a different symbol.
   - **C.** to a different font face.
   - **D.** by adding Bold.

5. QuickWords may be used for abbreviations that expand into the complete text by pressing any of the following EXCEPT
   - **A.** the space bar.
   - **B.** Enter.
   - **C.** Tab.
   - **D.** Ctrl+Enter.

TRUE/FALSE

Circle the T if the statement is true. Circle the F if it is false.

T F 6. In order to change the font for an entire document, including headers and footers, you can put the format in the Document Default Font or the Current Document Style.

T **F** 7. QuickFormat is chosen from the Property Bar or the Format menu.

T **F** 8. If you double click on one of the tab set markers on the Ruler, a Left tab will be set.

T F 9. QuickFormat can copy font face, font size, and appearance attributes.

T F 10. Block Protect is used to keep headings and following paragraphs together.

LESSON 11 PROJECT

SCANS

Follow the steps below to format the **nasa** document you used for practice in Lesson 2.

1. Open **nasa** from the student **datafile** folder. Use **Save As** to save the file as **nasa proj11a xxx**.

2. Use **Advance** to move the title to **2"** from the top of the page.

3. Center the title. Select the title and format it as follows:
   - a. Use **Bold**.
   - b. Select a **20-pt**. font size.
   - c. Go to the Font dialog box and choose **Small caps**.

4. With your insertion point at the beginning of the document, open the **Format** menu and choose **Keep Text Together**. Choose **Widow/Orphan**.

5. Select the first side heading (*Weather Forecasting*). Format it with Bold and Small caps.

6. Use **QuickFormat** to copy the format in Step 5 to the other ten side headings.

7. Look through the document. If any of the side headings are separated from the following paragraphs by a page break, use **Block Protect** to keep the side headings with the following paragraph.

8. Insert a footer that contains the Path and Filename code.

9. On the bottom of the first page, grab the bottom margin guideline (below the footer) and drag it to approximately **0.75"**.

10. Save the document again as **nasa proj11a xxx** and print it.

11. Use **Make It Fit** to make the document fill three pages. Then adjust the document as follows:
    a. After it is expanded, you may need to reset the title at 20 pt.
    b. Look through the document and see if Block Protect is needed anywhere.
    c. If your edits cause the document to stretch to four pages, use **Make It Fit** again.

12. Check your work a final time. Then print it again and save it again as **nasa proj11b xxx**.

CRITICAL THINKING ACTIVITY

SCANS

The report you are keying is going to be bound at the top, so you have set Advance for a top margin of $2\frac{1}{2}$". When you begin keying, you notice that the Application Bar is showing Pos 2.3". What do you need to do to make the top margin exactly $2\frac{1}{2}$"?

LESSON 12

ADVANCED FILE MANAGEMENT

OBJECTIVES

Upon completion of this lesson, you will be able to:

- Change the listing order of your files.
- Use QuickFinder to locate files containing specified text.
- Use QuickMarks to help you find your place in a document.
- Use Bookmarks to mark certain parts of the document.
- Work with comments in your documents.
- Save a document in a format different from that of Corel WordPerfect 8.

Estimated Time: 1 hour

In Lesson 8 you learned to create folders, rename folders, delete folders, rename files, and delete files, as well as copy or move files from one folder to another. In Appendix B you learned more about file management. By now you should be quite comfortable with the Open File dialog box and how it may be used for most of your work with files. But there is more to learn.

Working With Files

You learned in Lesson 4 that you can change the order in which the files are listed in the Open File dialog box, and you practiced rearranging the files. You learned that this tool might help you find a misplaced file according to the date on which it was created.

You also learned that the files can be listed in a number of ways. Let's review and try a few more things in the Open File dialog box.

EXERCISE 12.1

1. Beginning in a new document window, open the Open File dialog box. On the Toolbar, you have the choice of listing the files with Large Icons, Small Icons, List, and Detail. One at a time, choose each of those four buttons on the Open File dialog box Toolbar. End with Small Icons. What is the difference between using Small Icons and List?

2. Click the **Tree View** button. Scroll through the tree view. This is a toggle button. Click it again to deselect it.

3. Select the student **datafile** folder that contains your prerecorded documents. Put the insertion point on **ball.wpd**. Click the **Preview** button on the Toolbar. If you get Page view, the document will be very small.

4. Open the **View** menu and choose **Preview**. You can choose between Page view (tiny type) and Content (large type, but with no formatting). Select **No Preview**.

5. Close the dialog box.

WordPerfect remembers how you arranged the files. If they are arranged in order by date or size when you exit from the program, they will be in that same order the next time you start the program. Sometimes another user might leave the setting at something other than Name. If that happens, you might have trouble finding the desired files. You can simply change it back.

QuickFinder

Another way WordPerfect helps you find a file is with QuickFinder. This tool can quickly scan a disk or folder to find files containing a specified word or phrase. It can also look through your folders to find a file by name.

In addition to all of that, QuickFinder Manager is a powerful tool that can also prepare a Fast Search file that indexes all of the words in the documents on your disk or in a folder so that searches can be performed much more quickly.

The Fast Search file can be named. You can prepare different lists of the files in different folders, and choose the particular list you wish to search when you are performing a search. We will not practice with the indexing feature in this text. We will, however, practice finding a file or files that contain specified text. Let's see how it works.

EXERCISE 12.2

1. Beginning in a new document window, open the Open File dialog box. Choose the folder or disk that contains your practice files for Unit 3.

2. On the Toolbar, make sure the **List** button is chosen. Make sure Preview is not chosen.

3. Be sure the *File type* lists "All Files." Key **hostas** in the *File name* box. Click the **Find** button at the bottom of the dialog box. QuickFinder should quickly tell you that **hostas 9-8 xxx** is the only file containing the word *hostas*.

(continued on next page)

EXERCISE 12.2 CONTINUED

4. Click the **Back** button to return to your original list.

5. Click in the *File name* text box again and replace *hostas* with **computer**. Click **Find**. WordPerfect will search and list the files that contain that word. It should find more than 20 of then. (Apparently, lots of the documents are about computers!)

6. Close the Open File dialog box and read on.

If you wish to search for a phrase rather than a word, you must put quotation marks around the phrase when you key it in the *Content* text box. For example, if you key **pc care** without quotation marks, WordPerfect will list all files containing *pc* as well as all files containing *care*, but none of the files might contain the words *pc care* consecutively.

QuickFinder can be used to locate files by name and by pattern. For example, you can ask to list all files where the name begins with *pc*. QuickFinder will also locate files with a date range—for example, all files created between January 1 and January 5.

QuickMark and Bookmark

WordPerfect enables you to move quickly from one place in your document to another by using QuickMarks and Bookmarks. Both of these tools are used to mark a specific point in the text. They have similarities—yet they are different.

QuickMark

A document may contain only one QuickMark. The QuickMark doesn't need a name, and if you set a new QuickMark, the old one disappears. You might use a QuickMark while editing a lengthy document to mark your place while you go to a different place to check something or to get additional information. After finding the information, you can use the QuickMark to return quickly to the point of edit.

To set the QuickMark, open the Tools menu, choose Bookmark, and click the Set QuickMark button. An easier way is to press Ctrl+Shift+Q. To return to the place where the QuickMark is set, either press Ctrl+Q or open the Tools menu, choose Bookmark, and click Find QuickMark. Let's try this simple procedure using the keyboard shortcuts.

EXERCISE 12.3

1. Beginning in a new document window, open **nasa proj11b xx**.

2. Use **Ctrl+G** for Go To and key **3** to go to page 3. Find the side heading *Wheelchairs*. Position the insertion point immediately after that side heading.

3. Press **Ctrl+Shift+Q** to set a QuickMark. Then **Ctrl+End** to go to the end of the document.

4. Press **Ctrl+Q** to return to the QuickMark. You should be after the word *Wheelchairs* again.

5. Press **Ctrl+Home** to go to the beginning of the document. Press **Ctrl+Q**. Are you back to *Wheelchairs* again?

6. Now set a QuickMark at the end of the first paragraph. Go to the end of the document with **Ctrl+End**. Press **Ctrl+Q**. Did you return to *Wheelchairs* or the end of the first paragraph?

7. Keep the document open as you read on.

As you can see, when you set a new QuickMark, the old one is removed. You can also see how quickly WordPerfect takes you to the place where the QuickMark is set.

Bookmark

A Bookmark is much like a QuickMark because it marks a specific location so you can return to that location quickly. Bookmarks, however, are named. You may have as many bookmarks in a document as you wish.

You can set a bookmark by selecting the text for the bookmark, choosing Create in the Bookmark dialog box, and clicking OK. If you prefer, you can select the text for the bookmark and give the bookmark a different name in the dialog box. There are times when you might choose either of those methods. In Exercise 12.4 you'll give the bookmarks a different, more meaningful name because you might not remember the text that was selected for the bookmark.

When you tell WordPerfect to search for a bookmark, you can tell WordPerfect to not only find the text marked with the bookmark, but also to automatically select the text when it is located. Then you can copy the selected text to the Clipboard for insertion at a different point in the document.

EXERCISE 12.4

1. With **nasa proj11b xxx** showing in the window, use **Save As** to save the file as **nasa 12-4 xxx**.

2. Click in the left margin opposite the first side heading to select that side heading.

3. Open the **Tools** menu and choose **Bookmark**. The Bookmark dialog box will open. Click **Create** to display the Create Bookmark dialog box with the side heading displayed as the Bookmark name (See Figure 12-1).

4. Click **OK** to return to your document. Look at the Bookmark code in Reveal Codes. Move your insertion point to the left of the code. Note that the code identifies the name of the bookmark.

5. Follow the procedure beginning in Step 2 to mark the following side headings as bookmarks: *Water Recycling, Dental Braces, Wheelchairs,* and *Anti-Corrosion Paint.*

6. Save the document again as **nasa 12-4 xxx** and keep it open.

FIGURE 12-1
Create Bookmark Dialog Box

Now that the document has been marked with bookmarks, you can use those bookmarks to jump from one part of the document to another. We'll practice using the bookmarks shortly. This is especially useful in lengthy documents where you need to move between sections frequently.

At the point where you clicked OK to create the bookmark, you had the option of giving the bookmark a name other than the name of the selected text. For example, you could put bookmarks in documents for your coworkers. Then when the coworker opens the document, he or she can use the bookmark(s) to go to the section of the document you've tagged for that person. Let's rename a bookmark, then we'll see how they work.

EXERCISE 12.5

1. With **nasa 12-4 xxx** showing in the window, use **Save As** to save the file as **nasa 12-5 xxx**.

2. Open the **Tools** menu and choose **Bookmark**. Your Bookmark dialog box should look like Figure 12-2. Point to the *Weather Forecasting* bookmark and double click to move to that portion of the document. Note that the text is selected by default.

3. Open the **Tools** menu and choose **Bookmark** again. Point to *Anti-Corrosion Paint* and click once. Then click the **Go To** button. This time the text shouldn't have been selected.

4. Open the **Tools** menu and again choose **Bookmark**. Point to *Water Recycling* and click once. Then click the **Rename** button in the dialog box. Key the name of a friend and click **OK**. Close the dialog box.

5. Press **Ctrl+Home** to return to the top of the document. Then open the **Tools** menu and choose **Bookmark**. Double click your friend's name to go to the section about *Water Recycling*.

6. Save the document again with the same name. Keep it open.

FIGURE 12-2
Bookmark Dialog Box

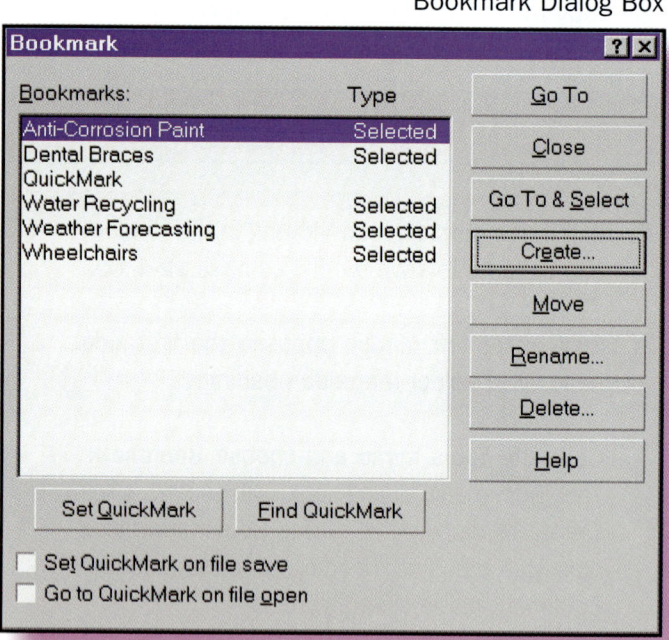

This has been only a sample of how you can use the Bookmark feature in your work. If you are creative, you'll think of lots of ways to use bookmarks to save time and effort in your work.

Comment

A comment is nonprinting text in your document. A comment may give you information about the document, or it may remind you or a coworker to do something with the document. Comments are not printed when you print a document.

Comments don't show in Page view. Instead, a Comment icon appears at the left edge of the left margin. If you click the icon, the text of the comment will appear in a "bubble." In Draft view, a comment shows with a shaded background so you know that the text is a comment.

When you put a comment in a document, a Comment code is inserted. Let's insert a comment telling your friend to read the paragraph about water recycling where you inserted your friend's name as a bookmark.

EXERCISE 12.6

1. With **nasa 12-5 xxx** showing in the window, use **Save As** to save the file as **nasa 12-6 xxx**. Position your insertion point in the line space below the *Water Recycling* side heading. Be sure you are in **Page** view.

2. Open the **Insert** menu, choose **Comment**, and then choose **Create**. You will be taken to a special Comment editing window. Note the Comment tools on the Property Bar. Key the text in Figure 12-3 as the comment for your friend.

3. Click the **Close** button on the Property Bar to return to your document window. Look for the icon in the left margin that indicates the presence of a comment. (You may need to use the horizontal scroll bar to see more of the left margin.)

4. Point to the icon with the mouse pointer and click to display the comment. Click the icon again to close the comment.

5. Change to **Draft** view and look at the comment in the document. Return to **Page** view. Save the file and keep it open as you read on.

FIGURE 12-3
Text for Comment

```
Please check the wording in this section about Water Recycling. If you
have suggestions for rewording, please key them into the text using
italic.  Thanks, (your name).
```

Comments can be edited or converted to text. Both of those changes are made from the Insert menu. You can also open the Comment editing window by pointing to the comment or the icon and double clicking. If a comment is no longer needed, it can be removed. To remove a comment, simply delete the Comment code. We'll edit the comment, change it to text, change it back to a comment, and delete it in the next exercise.

EXERCISE 12.7

1. With the insertion point near the comment in **nasa 12-6 xxx**, point to the Comment icon and double click. You will be taken to the Comment editing window.

2. Change the word *italic* in the last line to **bold**. Close the editing window.

3. With the insertion point near the comment, open the **Insert** menu, choose **Comment**, and then choose **Convert to Text**. Look at how the comment now becomes part of your document.

4. Select the text that was the comment in your document. Open the **Insert** menu, choose **Comment**, and then choose **Create**. Now the text is a comment again.

5. Reveal your codes and locate the [Comment] code. For practice, open the **Insert** menu, choose **Comment**, and choose **Edit**. You should have been taken to the Comment editing window.

6. Close the editing window. Then use your mouse to drag the Comment codes out of the Reveal Codes portion of the window. Your comment has now been deleted.

7. Close your document without saving it again.

File Transfer

With Corel WordPerfect 8, you can open files created in earlier versions of WordPerfect, as well as files created in other kinds of software. WordPerfect checks the file you are opening and converts the file to a WordPerfect file with little interference on your part.

If you have created a file in Corel WordPerfect 8 and wish to use that file in an earlier version of WordPerfect, you must take special steps. Earlier versions of WordPerfect are not able to read some of the WordPerfect 8 codes. For that reason, you must save the file in the format of the version in which you'll be opening it.

In addition, earlier versions of WordPerfect are constrained by DOS filenames. The names you've been using for your files are not acceptable to WordPerfect 6.1 for Windows, for example. DOS conventions allow you eight characters for the filename and a three-character extension following a period. If your WordPerfect 8 name is longer than that and you try to find it in a list of files in WordPerfect 6.1, the name will be shortened, and a tilde (~) will appear wherever the WordPerfect 8 name had spaces.

EXERCISE 12.8

1. Beginning in a new document window, open **footnote 10-12 xxx**.

2. With the document showing in the window, choose **Save As**.

3. In the *File name* text box of the Save As dialog box, change the word *footnote* to **6-1foot**. (Do not change the remainder of the document name.)

4. Click the arrow beside the *File type* text box. Look at all the different formats you can choose to save your WordPerfect 8 documents. (WordPerfect 6/7/8 should normally be chosen.)

5. Choose either **WordPerfect 5.0** or **5.1/5.2**. Click **Save** to complete the save and close the document.

6. If your classroom has any copies of WordPerfect 5.0 or 5.1 available, carry your file disk to that machine, start the older version of WordPerfect, and see if you can retrieve the **6-1foot 10-11 xxx** file. (Not all of the name will show in the WordPerfect file list.)

As mentioned earlier, if you want to use a document created in WordPerfect 8 in an earlier version of the program, it is critical that you save it in the format for that version. If you wish to use a document created in WordPerfect 8 in a different word processing program, it would also be a good idea to choose the program from the *File type* list when you save the document. The developers at WordPerfect have tried to provide a good cross section of programs to which you can take your WordPerfect 8 documents.

Summary

This lesson was primarily about working with files. If you are going to be good at WordPerfect or any other word processing program, you have to be able to find your files when you need them. In this lesson you learned that:

- You can look at your files listed by name, date, size, and type.
- You can use QuickFinder to locate files containing specified text or by name.
- QuickMarks help you return to a particular place in the document after you have browsed through it.
- You can have as many bookmarks in a document as you wish.
- Bookmarks may be named by selected portions of text, or they can be given different names.
- Nonprinting comments can be put in your documents as reminders or as additional information about the document.
- If you wish to open a WordPerfect 8 document in a different version of WordPerfect or a different word processing program, you should save the document in that format.

LESSON 12 REVIEW QUESTIONS

MATCHING

Write the letter of the term in Column 2 that best matches the description in Column 1.

Column 1

_____ 1. The place where you can change the order in which files are listed

_____ 2. A feature used to move quickly from one place to another, which is not named

_____ 3. The tool that is used to quickly scan a disk or folder to find files containing a specified word or phrase

_____ 4. Nonprinting text in your document

_____ 5. A feature used to tell WordPerfect not only to find text, but also to automatically select the text when it is located

_____ 6. In searching for a phrase, you would put quotation marks around the phrase when you key it in this box.

Column 2

A. Bookmark

B. Open File dialog box

C. QuickFinder

D. Bookmark dialog box

E. Comment

F. QuickMark

G. Save As dialog box

H. Content text box

WRITTEN QUESTIONS

Write your answers to the following questions.

7. Why is it important to save your files in the format of the version of WordPerfect in which you will be opening those files?

8. What are the two ways to set a Bookmark?

9. What are your four choices on the Toolbar of the Open File dialog box for listing files?

10. If you are working in Page view, how can you tell if a Comment has been added to a document?

LESSON 12 PROJECT

SCANS

Because of the nature of this lesson, the project will consist of a series of small exercises. As you advance in your training, instructions in the Projects and Applications will contain less detail, allowing you to apply your knowledge and skill.

PROJECT 12A

The first exercise reviews the View portion of the Open File dialog box.

1. Open the Open File dialog box and choose the folder that contains your documents. The answers are at the end of the project.
   a. Arrange the files by **Date**. What are the last two files you saved in your folder?
   b. Arrange your files by **Size**. What are the largest two files in your folder?
   c. Arrange the files by **Name**. Which two files are at the top of the list? (Notice that WordPerfect lists files with numerical names before files with alphabetic names.)

2. Close the Open File dialog box.

PROJECT 12B

Now let's work with the Bookmark and QuickMark features.

1. Open **pc proj10b xxx**. Use Save As to save the file as **pc proj12 xxx**.

2. Select the first side heading. With the side heading selected, create a bookmark named **David**.

3. Follow the procedure in Step 2 to create a bookmark for each of the side headings, as listed in Figure 12-4.

FIGURE 12-4
Bookmarks for Project 12B

SIDE HEADING	BOOKMARK
Keep Your PC Clean	Hue
Prevent Burn-in	Jessica
Defuse Static Electricity	Sandra
Make Backups	Tim

4. Open the Tools menu and choose Bookmark. Click once to position the insertion point on *David* and click Go To.

5. With the insertion point by the *David* bookmark, create a comment for David that says: **Read this paragraph. Then research surge suppressors and make a recommendation for surge suppressors in our company.**

6. Follow the procedure in Steps 4 and 5 to create comments near the text for the bookmarks in Figure 12-5.

7. Convert each of the comments into text. Print the file and save it as **pc proj12a xxx**.

(continued on next page)

185

8. Convert each of the comments in the document back to comments.

9. Invite your instructor to watch you use the bookmarks to move through the document and display the comments.

10. Close the document, saving it again as **pc proj12b xxx**.

FIGURE 12-5
Comments for Project 12B

BOOKMARK	COMMENT
Tim	Prepare a memo to go to all employees reminding them of the importance of backing up all important company documents on diskettes. The backup diskettes may be stored in the company vault on the first floor.
Jessica	Read this paragraph. Then check the Internet to find a small selection of inexpensive screen savers from which our employees may choose.
Hue	Read this paragraph. Then compose a memo to go to all employees reminding them of the company policy regarding food and drink at company computers.

Answers to Project 12A
Question 1a: **6-1foot 10-11 xxx** and **nasa 12-6 xxx**
Question 1b: **wind 10-8 xxx** and **wind 10-11 xxx**
Question 1c: **6-1foot 10-11 xxx** and **char 11-6 xxx**

CRITICAL THINKING ACTIVITY

SCANS

You have decided that it would be easier to find the files you need if they were listed in the order of the date you worked on them. Describe the steps you would take to arrange your files this way. What might be a reason you would choose this arrangement of files?

Command Summary

UNIT 3 REVIEW

FEATURE	MENU CHOICE	KEYBOARD	LESSON
Advance	Format, Typesetting	—	11
All Justification	Format, Justification (Property Bar)	—	9
Block Protect	Format, Keep Text Together	—	12
Bookmark	Tools, Bookmark	—	12
Center Justification	Format, Justification (Property Bar)	Ctrl+E	9
Comment	Insert, Comment	—	12
Current Document Style	File, Document	—	11
Default Font	File, Document	—	11
Endnote	Insert, Footnote/Endnote	—	10
Find QuickMark	Tools, Bookmark	Ctrl+Q	12
Footers	Insert, Header/Footer	—	10
Footnote	Insert, Footnote/Endnote	—	10
Full Justification	Format, Justification (Property Bar)	Ctrl+J	9
Headers	Insert, Header/Footer	—	10
Justification	Format, Justification (Property Bar)	—	9
Left Justification	Format, Justification (Property Bar)	Ctrl+L	9
Line Spacing	Format, Line	—	9
Make It Fit	Format	—	11
Margins	Format, Margins	Ctrl+F8	9
New Page Number	Format, Page, Numbering	—	10
Page Numbering	Format, Page, Numbering	—	10
QuickFinder	File, Open	Ctrl+O	12
QuickFormat	Format, QuickFormat (Toolbar)	—	11
QuickMark	Tools, Bookmark	Ctrl+Shift+Q	12
QuickWords	Tools	—	11
Right Justification	Format, Justification (Property Bar)	Ctrl+R	9
Ruler	View, Ruler	Alt+Shift+F3	9
Shadow Pointer	(Application Bar)	—	11
Spacing	Format, Line	—	9
Suppress	Format, Page	—	10
Symbols	Insert	—	11
Tab Set	Format, Line (Ruler)	—	9

FEATURE	MENU CHOICE	KEYBOARD	LESSON
Watermark	Insert, Watermark	—	10
Widow/Orphan	Format, Keep Text Together	—	10
WordPerfect Symbols	Insert, Symbol	Ctrl+W	11

UNIT 3 REVIEW QUESTIONS

TRUE/FALSE

On a separate page, for each statement below key True if the statement is true or False if it is not. Center *Unit 3 Review Questions* at the top and triple-space.

1. The default setting for margins is 1" on all sides of the page.

2. Using the Ruler, you can set up to four different types of tabs.

3. Page numbering at the top of a page must be set by choosing Page Numbering from the Format menu.

4. Widow/Orphan tells WordPerfect not to leave a single line of a paragraph alone at either the top of the page or the bottom of a page, and it affects the entire document, beginning with the page on which it is inserted.

5. The Headings choice in QuickFormat cannot be applied without selecting the text.

WRITTEN QUESTIONS

Key your answers to the following questions. Number your answers and double-space between them. Use complete sentences and good grammar.

6. How would you describe the difference between a header and a title in a document?

7. What does Make It Fit adjust (default settings) when you are compressing or expanding your documents?

8. What happens when you point to a code in Reveal Codes and double click?

9. What is the difference between a Bookmark and a QuickMark? How many Bookmarks can you have in your document? How many QuickMarks can you have?

10. Open the list of Help topics and find QuickFinder. Double click QuickFinder to look at the list of topics. How many topics are included in that section? Double click to open About QuickFinder (File Open System Help). This section describes Fast Searches. What does QuickFinder do in a Fast Search? What are the three criteria that help you decide whether or not you should use Fast Search?

UNIT 3 APPLICATIONS

Estimated Time: 2 hours

APPLICATION 1

1. Open **sasoot 3-11 xxx** from the **Units 1 and 2** folder. If you remember, this is the two-page letter with the awkward page break.

2. Use Save As to save the letter as **sasoot u3ap1 xxx**. Look through the letter to remind yourself of how it looks. Then format it as follows:
   a. Insert a Widow/Orphan code at the top of the letter.
   b. Give the letter a header, with the name of the recipient of the letter at the left, the automatic page number code at the center, and the current date (text) flush right, as shown in Figure APP-1.

FIGURE APP-1
Header for Application 1

```
Mr. Antonio Larsen                    1                    (current date)
```

   c. Suppress the header on the first page.
   d. Delete the Path and Filename code at the end of the document.
   e. With the insertion point at the end of the document, insert a footer that contains the Path and Filename code. (Because your insertion point is on the last page of the document, the code will appear only on that page.)

3. Page through the letter, checking the header, the footer, and the page break. (The only way you can see the footer on the last page is to use the vertical scroll bar and scroll all the way to the bottom.)

4. Print the letter and save it again as **sasoot u3ap1 xxx**. Close the file.

APPLICATION 2

1. Open **lighthouses** from the student **datafile** folder. Use Save As to save the file as **lighthouses u3ap2 xxx**. Page through the document to see what's included. Then format it as follows:
   a. Remove the 14 pt. code at the beginning of the document.
   b. Use Advance to advance the title at the top of the first page to 2" from the top of the page.
   c. Center the title and format it with 20-pt. Arial. Quadruple-space following the title.
   d. Select the first side heading. Format it with Bold, 16-pt. small caps.
   e. Use QuickFormat to copy that format to the other side headings.
   f. Beginning with the first paragraph, set 1.5 spacing for the entire document.
   g. Remove the extra hard return above and below each of the side headings.
   h. Return to the top and set Widow/Orphan.
   i. If necessary in your copy, use Block Protect to tie the *Illumination* side heading to the paragraph following it.

(continued on next page)

j. Create a footer that centers the word **Page** followed by the page number at the bottom of each page.
k. Change the bottom margin of all pages to approximately 0.6".
l. Create another footer (Footer B) that inserts the Path and Filename code. Position the code flush with the right margin and set it for an 8-pt. Arial font. (Both footers will print on both pages. Actually, all of the information in both footers could be combined in one footer.)

2. Do an interim save of your work. (Develop the habit of saving frequently when you are working with lots of formatting.)

3. With the insertion point above all codes on the first page, press Ctrl+Enter to insert a page at the top of the document. Create a title page as follows:
   a. With the insertion point on the new page at the top, use Center Page(s) to center the text vertically on the current page only.
   b. Set Center justification and key the lines in Figure APP-2. Use **Enter** to space the lines attractively.

FIGURE APP-2
Information for Application 2 Title Page

```
                        LIGHTHOUSES
                  (A History of Development)
                             by
                      (enter your name)
     (enter the name of the course in which you are learning WordPerfect)
                    (enter your school name)
                       (current date)
```

4. With the insertion point at the beginning of the first page of text, reset the page number value to **1** so the title page isn't included in the page count.

5. Also at the beginning of the first page of text, change from Center justification to Left justification.

6. Position the insertion point at the beginning of the title page and give the document a watermark.
   a. Click the Image button on the Watermark Property Bar and go to the student **datafile** folder.
   b. Find the file named **Lighths** and insert it as the watermark into your document.
   c. Move your insertion point to the beginning of the first page of text and return to the Watermark dialog box. Click the Discontinue button so the watermark appears only on the title page.

7. On the first page of text, insert the same subtitle that's on the title page below the title of the document. Position it a double space below the title, and leave only a triple space between the subtitle and the first line of the first paragraph.

8. Insert the footnotes in Figure APP-3. Position them as follows:
   a. Put the first one following the first sentence in the *History* section.
   b. Put the second one following the third sentence in the *Illumination* section.

190 UNIT 3: FORMATTING

c. Put the third one at the end of the first sentence of the third paragraph in the *Illumination* section.

FIGURE APP-3
Footnotes for Application 2

> [1]Henry McKinnon, *The Seven Wonders of the World*, (London: Plentiful Book Press, 1939), p. 44.
>
> [2]Alfredo Gutierrez, *Lighthouse Lenses*, (New York: Banta, 1989), p. 16.
>
> [3]Mary Madson, "The Fresnel Lense," *Lighthouse Journal*, July 199x, p. 55.

9. Check your work over for accuracy. When it is perfect, print it and save it again as **lighthouses u3ap2 xxx**. Close the file.

APPLICATION 3

1. Beginning in a new document window, key the chart of charges for your bank, as shown in Figure APP-4. Set up the document before keying as follows:
   a. Go to Document Default Font and change to Arial.
   b. Go to Current Document Style and set the side margins at 2".
   c. Use the Center Page(s) feature to give the chart even top and bottom margins.
   d. Display your Ruler and clear all tabs.
   e. For *Price in Dollars*, use Flush Right.
   f. Set a Left tab at 2.25" and a Right tab with dot leaders at 6.25".

2. Center all three titles in bold, all capital letters. Format all three titles using the 14-pt. font size.

FIGURE APP-4
Text for Application 3

> **SAFE-DEPOSIT BOX ANNUAL**
> **RENTAL FEES**
>   **Price in Dollars**
> 3" x 5" box 25.00
> 4" x 5" box 35.00
> 5" x 5" box 45.00
> 5" x 10" box 80.00
> 10" x 10" box 125.00
>
> **MISCELLANEOUS SAFE-DEPOSIT**
> **BOX FEES**
> Lost Key 20.00
> Drill Fee 100.00
>
> **MISCELLANEOUS FEES**
> Cashier's Check 3.50
> Certified Check 5.00
> Lost Passbook or CD 10.00
> Money Order 2.00
> Overdraft Charge 25.00
> Stop Payment 25.00
> Return Check Charge 25.00
> Wire Transfers
>   Domestic 20.00
>   International 30.00

(continued on next page)

3. Key the description at the left margin. Tab once to key the prices at the right.

4. Save your file as **boxes u3ap3 xxx**.

5. Insert a footer that contains the Path and Filename code formatted in 8-pt. Times New Roman.

6. Print the file and close it, saving it again as you close it.

APPLICATION 4

It's time to make room in the main folder on your disk for your work in Unit 4. Let's move some files and delete some others.

1. Display your Open File dialog box and hold the Ctrl key as you click the files listed in Figure APP-5 for deletion. If you accidentally click one that is not on the list, continue to hold Ctrl as you click that file again to deselect it. Then continue selecting those to be deleted.

FIGURE APP-5
Files to be Deleted

6-1foot 10-11	nasa 12-5	pcug 10-2	record 9-9
char 11-5	nasa proj11b	pcug 11-12	salad 9-6
footnote 10-12	pc 11-7	pcug 11-13	wind 10-14
footnote 10-13	pc 11-8	record 9-1	wind 10-3
gifts 10-9	pc 11-9	record 9-2	wind 10-5
gifts 11-2	pc proj10a	record 9-3	wind 10-6
gifts 11-3	pc proj12a	record 9-4	wind 10-7
nasa 12-4	pcug 10-1	record 9-5	wind 10-8

2. After highlighting the files to be deleted, press the Delete key on the keyboard and confirm that the files are to be deleted.

3. With the Open File dialog box showing in your window and $3^{1}/_{2}$ *Floppy (A:)* showing in the gray bar above the list of files, open the File menu and choose New. Then choose to create a new folder. Name the new folder **Units 3 and 4**.

4. Select the files listed in Figure APP-6. Open the File menu and choose Move to folder. Choose the **Units 3 and 4** folder and complete the move.

5. Select the following files and move them to the **Applications** folder: **sasoot u3ap1**, **lighthouses u3ap2**, and **boxes u3ap3**.

6. Check any odd files that might be remaining in your main folder. If they are files you need to save for some reason, move them to a different location. If they are junk, delete them, so your main folder is empty as you go to the On-the-Job exercises that follow.

FIGURE APP-6
Files to Move to the **Units 3 and 4** Folder

cheese proj9	pc 11-10
gifts 10-10	pc proj10b
hostas 9-8	pc proj12b
Mildred 9-10	salad 9-7
nasa 12-6	wind 10-11
nasa proj11a	wind 10-15

8. Use Page Numbering to center the page number at the bottom.

9. In the first line, change *2-1/2* to 2^1/$_2$ using Symbol 4,17 for the ^{1}/$_2$. Do the same for the *3-1/2*.

10. Use Find and Replace to replace all instances of two hyphens (--) with an em dash (4,34).

11. Return to the top of the document and set Widow/Orphan.

12. Use Make It Fit to make the document fill two pages. (You may need to change the title back to the 24-pt. font after using Make It Fit.)

13. Check your document over. If it looks good, print it. Then close it, saving it again as **coach job7 xxx**.

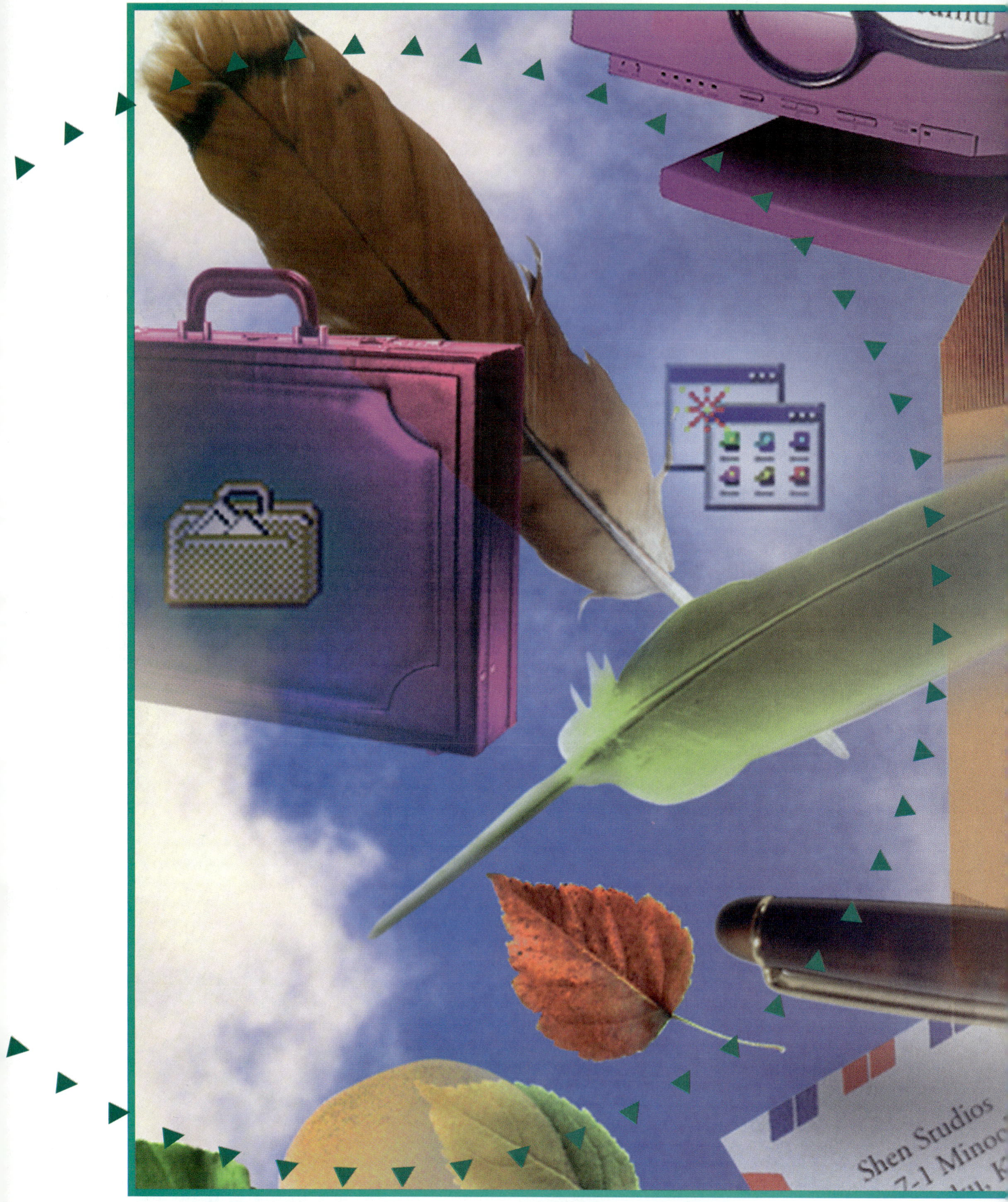
Shen Studios

Special Layout Features

UNIT 4

lesson 13 — 2 hrs.
Tables

lesson 14 — 1.5 hrs.
Outlining and Text Columns

lesson 15 — 2.5 hrs.
Forms

lesson 16 — 2 hrs.
Macros

Estimated Time for Unit 4: 9.5 hours

LESSON 13
TABLES

OBJECTIVES

Upon completion of this lesson, you will be able to:

- Discuss table terminology.
- Create a table.
- Add rows to a table.
- Join cells in the table.
- Adjust the width of table columns.
- Use a number of methods of formatting your table.
- Do calculations in a table using table formulas.
- Recalculate after a table has been completed.
- Use different means of calculating in a table.
- Use SpeedFormat to format your tables.
- Use floating cells to reference cells in your tables.
- Change tabular text into a table.

Estimated Time: 2 hours

In Lesson 9 you learned to use tabs to arrange your work in columns. You cleared old tab stops, set new tab stops, and rearranged your work when you had finished keying the text if the columns weren't spaced exactly right.

In this lesson you will be introduced to Tables, a more powerful relative of tabs. The WordPerfect Tables feature offers another way to arrange text in columns, but it includes some advantages that the Tab feature doesn't have.

One of the advantages of using the Tables feature to organize your columnar data is that it is faster to set up. It is also easier to add or delete columns than with tabs. Not only that, but you can perform calculations within tables so they can be used for such applications as invoices and time cards. Some documents are composed of several tables that are combined. Many of the documents that use tables won't even look like a table when you finish. You will enjoy working with WordPerfect's Tables feature.

This is a long lesson. You will probably not be able to do it all at once. In addition, there is much to learn. As you read the information and proceed through the exercises, concentrate and think about what you're doing so when you're faced with some of the same kinds of projects, you won't wonder WHAT to do and HOW to do it.

Table Terminology

A WordPerfect table looks and works much like a spreadsheet. The terminology is also similar. The following terms are peculiar to the use of tables and spreadsheets:

- **Spreadsheet**. A spreadsheet is a grid made up of columns and rows. The columns and rows contain data and/or formulas. Many offices use spreadsheet programs such as Lotus 1-2-3, Excel, or Quattro Pro.

- **Columns**. Vertical collections of information are called *columns*. Columns are labeled with letters (e.g., A, B, C).

- **Rows**. Information is arranged horizontally into *rows*. Rows are labeled with numbers.

- **Cells**. The point at which a row meets a column is called a *cell*. The address of a cell is identified by the column and row. For example, the cell where Column B meets Row 3 is called Cell B3. This location is reported in the Application Bar at the bottom of the window.

Create a Table

You can begin a table by opening the Insert menu and choosing Table, or by clicking and dragging the Tables button on the Toolbar until you have the desired size of the table. Since it is so easy, we'll use the Toolbar method in Exercise 13.1. When you finish, your table will look like Figure 13-3. Pay attention. You'll learn as you go.

EXERCISE 13.1

1. In a new document window, point to the **Tables** button on the Toolbar. Drag across and down the grid that appears until the table size is 3 x 2, as illustrated in Figure 13-1.

2. When the table is the right size, release the mouse button. When you do that, your table should appear, looking like Figure 13-2. If you don't get it right, click the **Undo** button and try again.

3. Keep your table in your window as you learn how to key text into the table.

FIGURE 13-1
Table Grid

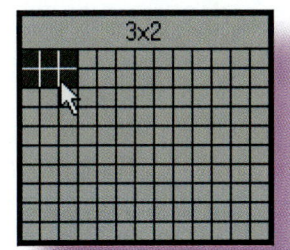

FIGURE 13-2
3 x 2 Table

199

Before keying text, you need to know how to move around in the table. When you key text, move from cell to cell with the Tab key. Do not press Enter, even at the end of a row. When you press Enter, you simply enlarge the cell in which your insertion point is currently located.

After the text has been keyed, you can move the insertion point in the table by clicking with the mouse or by using the following keystrokes:

Tab	Moves the insertion point to the next cell.
Shift+Tab	Moves the insertion point to the previous cell.
Home, Home	Moves the insertion point to the first cell in the row.
End, End	Moves the insertion point to the last cell in the row.

FIGURE 13-3
Finished Table of Times

WORLD TIMES
At 12:00 noon Eastern Standard Time, U.S.A.

Bombay	India	10:30 p.m.
Capetown	South Africa	7:00 p.m.
London	England	5:00 p.m.
Manila	Philippines	**1:00 a.m.
Moscow	Russia	7:00 p.m.
Munich	Germany	6:00 p.m.
Paris	France	5:00 p.m.
Rio de Janeiro	Brazil	2:00 p.m.
Tokyo	Japan	**2:00 a.m.
Vancouver	Canada	9:00 a.m.

**Morning the following day.

Obviously, your table isn't big enough for all the data in Figure 13-3. When you are working in a table and your insertion point is in the final cell, simply press Tab to add another row to the table. We'll skip the heading rows until later. Also, when you key text into your table, it won't be formatted like Figure 13-3. That will come later, too. Let's enter the data into the table.

EXERCISE 13.2

1. Key **Bombay** and press **Tab**. Key **India** and press **Tab**. Key **10:30 p.m.** and press **Tab**. Do NOT press Enter. If you press Enter by accident, use Backspace to delete it.

2. Continue keying the text in Figure 13-3. Move from cell to cell with the **Tab** key. When you finish, all of the text on the final line will be crowded into the first cell. Also, the information in the third column will be aligned at the left.

3. Reveal your codes and move around in the table. Find the Table Definition code and add it to your list. Notice that instead of [HRt] codes and [SRt] codes, the table has [Cell] and [Row] codes. Add them to your list, too. Which of these two codes comes between rows?

4. Look at the Application Bar, where *Insert* is usually reported. This section of the Application Bar will always report the location of the insertion point in your table. Move the insertion point to Cell B2. Does the prompt at the bottom agree with where you thought you were in the table?

5. Save your table as **Bombay 13-2 xxx**. This is an interim save in case you goof up and need to begin again at this point.

UNIT 4: SPECIAL LAYOUT FEATURES

Setting up the table was easy, wasn't it? The best part was that you didn't have to do any figuring. The columns were automatically spaced evenly, but there is much that can be done to make it more attractive. We'll learn how to make adjustments to the table shortly.

Add Rows; Join Cells

Before we change the formatting of the table, let's add a couple of rows for the headings. Then we'll join the cells in the rows so your headings can be centered. We will choose both of those options from the Table QuickMenu, illustrated in Figure 13-4. Follow along carefully.

FIGURE 13-4
Table QuickMenu

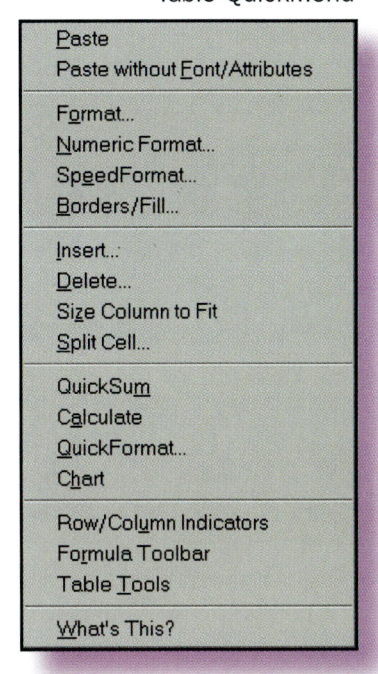

EXERCISE 13.3

1. With your insertion point somewhere in the top row of the table, point to the table with your mouse pointer and RIGHT click to display the Table QuickMenu.

2. Choose **Insert** from the QuickMenu to open the dialog box illustrated in Figure 13-5. Note that **Rows** is selected. At the bottom, WordPerfect reports the current size of your table. Note that Placement is set at Before. That means the rows will be added before the location of the insertion point.

3. Change the number in the text box from *1* to **2** and click **OK**. Your table should now have two empty rows at the top.

4. Point to the first row of the table and use the mouse to drag across all three cells to select them. When the cells are selected, they will appear to be black.

FIGURE 13-5
Insert Columns/Rows Dialog Box

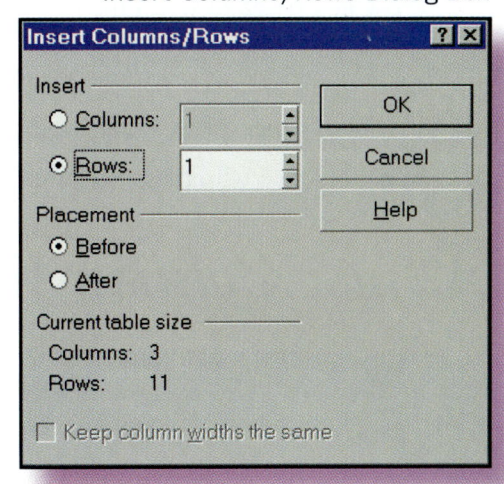

5. Right click to display the Table QuickMenu again. This time, choose **Join Cells**. All of the cells in Row 1 will be joined to form one large cell.

(continued on next page)

201

EXERCISE 13.3 CONTINUED

6. Point to the QuickJoin button on the Table Property Bar and click to select the tool. With the special join cell pointer drag across the cells in Row 2 to join them. Click the QuickJoin button to deselect the tool. (This is a toggle button.)

7. Click to position the insertion point in Row 1. Press **Shift+F7** for Center and key **WORLD TIMES**.

8. In Row 2, center the following:

    At 12:00 noon Eastern Standard Time, U.S.A.

9. Use **Save As** to save the file as **Bombay 13-3 xxx**.

You can add rows or columns anywhere in your tables. When you do this, be certain to position the insertion point appropriately and make the correct choices in the Insert Columns/Rows dialog box.

Cells can also be joined as needed. You'll learn more about this later, but you've already learned two ways to make two or three cells into one cell.

When you joined the cells in Rows 1 and 2, you selected the cells to be joined by dragging across them with the pointer. WordPerfect provides another tool to help with selecting text in tables. If you have a steady hand when you point to the top or left side of a cell with the mouse pointer, the pointer will change into a fat white arrow. When the pointer is a fat horizontal arrow, you can select text as follows:

- ← Click **once** to select the cell.
- ← Click **twice** to select the row.
- ↑ Click **once** to select the cell.
- ↑ Click **twice** to select the column.

With either arrow, click **three** times to select the table.

We'll practice with these select tools shortly.

Adjust Column Width

To adjust the width of the columns, simply drag the line separating the two columns. The sizing tool is the same crosshair you used when you adjusted your document margins by moving the guidelines. Let's adjust the width of the columns and practice selecting cells.

EXERCISE 13.4

1. With **Bombay 13-3 xxx** open in the window, use **Save As** to save the file as **Bombay 13-4 xxx**.

2. Point to the left line in the final row of the table (the row containing the asterisks and the *morning* message). When the fat arrow appears, double click to select the entire row.

202 UNIT 4: SPECIAL LAYOUT FEATURES

3. With the row selected, right click and choose **Join Cells** from the QuickMenu.

4. Use the crosshair pointer to drag the line between the first two columns so it is snug after *Janeiro*. (If you get too close, the word will wrap to the next line. If that happens, grab the table line and drag it a little farther away.)

5. Drag the line between the second and third columns so it is near the end of *South Africa*. Finally, drag the line at the right of the table so it is near the end of the text in the third column.

6. Point to the top of the table. When the fat white arrow appears, triple click to select the entire table. Change the font to **10-pt. Arial**.

7. Drag over Rows 1 and 2 to select both rows. With the rows selected, choose **Bold** from the Property Bar.

8. Point to the line at the left of Row 1. When the fat white arrow appears, click once to select the row. Choose **20 pt.** from the **Font Size** button on the Property Bar.

9. Press **Ctrl+End** to move the insertion point out of the table. Press **Enter** a couple of times to add some space and insert the Path and Filename code. Then save the file as **Bombay 13-4 xxx**. Print it and keep it open as you read on.

As you can see, creating tables and making adjustments to them are easy. You've only begun.

Format a Table

The QuickMenu is only one of the sources of tools when you're working with a table. Let's learn about some of the others. Then we'll do more with this practice table.

Normal Formatting Tools

As you've already learned, many of the formatting tools you use in your normal documents work very well in tables. You've used Center and Bold. You've changed font face and font size. While those choices may also be made from the special tables formatting sources listed below, it's fine to use the tools with which you're familiar whenever they are available.

Table Gridlines

On some computers or when working with very complicated tables, you may notice that you have to wait while your table lines "redraw" in the window. You can speed up this process by using what are called *table gridlines*. Table gridlines are dotted lines surrounding your table cells. With them, you can move around in tables much more rapidly.

The Table Gridlines option is chosen from the View menu. When they are used, the dotted lines simply take the place of the regular lines for viewing purposes. When you print your table, the lines will be printed as usual. We'll work with table gridlines shortly.

Table Property Bar

You may have noticed that when you were working in your table, the Property Bar changed. The 15 buttons to the right of the Justification button are tools for table formatting and editing. You've already used the QuickJoin button. Some of the others that are useful for certain applications include the two to the right of the QuickJoin button–QuickSplit Row and QuickSplit Column. The next is the Insert Row button. You'll use that shortly.

When text is selected, the tools available on the Property Bar change. With your insertion point in your table, periodically check the Quick Tip of the buttons that aren't familiar to you. Some of the tools available on the Property Bar aren't available from any menu (such as QuickSplit Row and QuickSplit Column).

Table Menu

One of the buttons on the Property Bar opens is the Table menu. That menu contains many of the same tools available in the Table QuickMenu or the Table Property Bar.

With all of these sources of tools available, it might be confusing about where you should go to select your tools. Actually, it doesn't matter. In the next few exercises you'll be given specific instructions about which source to use so you have an opportunity to try them all. When you create and format your own tables, however, you'll have favorite sources of tools that you'll use for most of your work. And your favorites might be different from everyone else's favorites.

Now let's add some additional formatting to your table. In the process, we'll explore all of the formatting sources listed in this section.

EXERCISE 13.5

1. With **Bombay 13-4 xxx** open in the window, position the insertion point anywhere in the table.

2. Look at the Property Bar. Beginning with the button to the right of the Justification button, point to each of the tables buttons to see what they do. Many of the tools are new to you. You'll learn about them later in the lesson.

3. Click the **Table** button on the Property Bar. Note that Insert and Join are in that menu as well as the QuickMenu, along with Delete (the opposite of Insert) and Split (the opposite of Join).

4. Open the **View** menu and choose **Table Gridlines**. Look at how the gridlines appear in your table. Return to the **View** menu and deselect **Table Gridlines**.

5. Press **Ctrl+End** to move your insertion point below the table. Press **Enter** three times to add some space. Then create a 2 x 2 table below your current table.

6. Click the **QuickSplit Column** button. Your insertion point will have two arrows and will be accompanied by a dotted line, as well as a box telling your location.

7. Move the pointer in one of the cells of your practice table until the box reads *1.5" 1.75"* as shown in the illustration. Click once to add a vertical line at that location. Click the **QuickSplit Column** button again to deselect the feature.

8. Use the **QuickSplit Row** button to split a cell vertically. Note that only one cell is split. Deselect the option.

9. Select your entire practice table and the extra spaces below the Bombay table and delete it. Keep your document open as you read on.

Properties for Table Format

Now that you have a good idea of the sources of tools, let's finish formatting the *World Times* table. The Properties for Table Format dialog box will be used for the following exercises. This dialog box is like some others that we've used, in that it has several kinds of formatting combined into one dialog box, complete with tabs. The Cell tab, for example, can be used to format a single cell or a group of selected cells. The Table portion has to do with formats that affect the entire table. You'll learn about these choices as you go.

We'll begin by centering the table between the margins.

EXERCISE 13.6

1. With **Bombay 13-4 xxx** open, save it as **Bombay 13-6 xxx**.

2. With your insertion point anywhere in the table, click the **Table** button on the Property Bar, and choose **Format**. The Properties for Table Format dialog box (from now on to be called Table Format dialog box) will open, looking like Figure 13-6.

3. Look at the tabs across the top of the dialog box. Click the **Table** tab.

4. In the lower left corner is a *Table Position* section. Click the button and choose **Center**.

5. Click **OK** to close the dialog box. Your table should now be centered between the margins.

6. Save the document again as **Bombay 13-6 xxx** and keep it open.

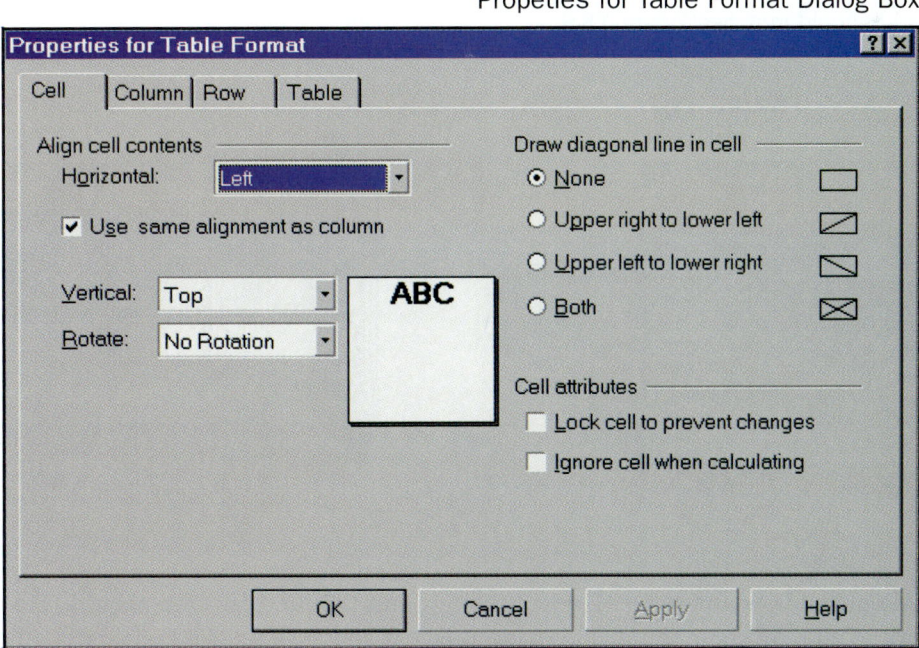

FIGURE 13-6
Propeties for Table Format Dialog Box

Lesson 13 Tables

205

Now we'll add shading (fill) to the subtitle row and align the times in Column 3 at the right.

EXERCISE 13.7

1. Save **Bombay 13-6 xxx** as **Bombay 13-7 xxx**.

2. Point to the left edge of the row containing the subtitle. When the fat white arrow appears, click to select the row.

3. Click the **Table** button on the Property Bar and choose **Borders/Fill**. A large dialog box will appear, showing choices for lines at the left and fill and a preview area at the right.

4. Click the **X** button beside *Fill*. In the grid of fill patterns that appears, click the second button to the right of the *X*. The grid will look like Figure 13-7. Note that at the bottom, it tells you that you've selected *10% Fill*. This is a common choice because it prints well.

5. At the left of the dialog box, click the button for *Top* and choose the big **X** to tell Word-Perfect you don't want a line at the top of the selected cell. The grid should look like Figure 13-8.

6. Click **OK** to close the dialog box. Click away from the selected row to deselect it. Does it look like you expected it to look?

7. Point to the top of the column listing the times (in the cell listing 10:30 p.m. for Bombay). Click the **Select Table Column** button on the Property Bar.

8. Right click to display the QuickMenu and choose **Format**. In the Table Format dialog box, click the **Cell** tab.

9. Locate the *Align cell contents* section. Then click the button to display the pop-up menu and choose **Right**. Click **OK** to close the dialog box. All of the times should now be aligned at the right side of the column.

10. Print your table. Save it again as **Bombay 13-7 xxx** and close it.

FIGURE 13-7
Fill Grid

FIGURE 13-8
Lines Grid

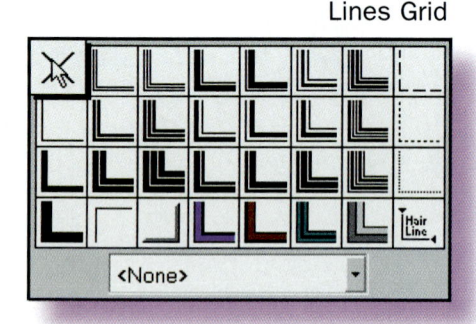

You've completed your first table. Does it look wonderful? Perhaps you should take it home and put it on the refrigerator. More importantly, however, is that you have touched on nearly all of the basics with regard to formatting tables in only seven short exercises.

You can do many more things with tables. For example, as mentioned at the beginning of the lesson, tables can be used like spreadsheets to perform calculations. Let's learn about table formulas. In the process, you will create another table and review many of the things you've learned so far about tables.

Table Formulas

The table you will create in the next series of exercises shows the first- and second-quarter sales for the top five sales representatives in the company. We'll begin with the raw data. Then we'll learn about tables as we manipulate the table and use the Spreadsheet feature to provide some of the figures for us.

We'll begin this table with only part of the cells needed for the finished product so you can review adding to a table by adding rows and a column. Finally, you'll add quite a lot of formatting. Pay attention to the changes in the appearance of the table as you go. Also, don't ignore the dialog boxes and menus you use to format your table. Soon you'll need to find these features on your own.

EXERCISE 13.8

SCANS

1. Open the **Insert** menu and choose **Table**. Fill in the text boxes to tell WordPerfect to create a table with **3** columns and **1** row. Click **Create**.

2. Using **Tab** to move from cell to cell, fill your table with the text in Figure 13-9. (Remember that when you press Tab at the end of a row, a new row is added.) When you finish, check your work carefully.

3. Whoops! We forgot to allow for the midyear sales figures. We'll add a column at the right. Position your insertion point somewhere in Column C.

4. Choose **Insert** from the QuickMenu. In the Insert Columns/Rows dialog box, change the setting to **Columns**. Change Placement to **After**. Click **OK** to close the dialog box. (Your table now has 4 columns and 5 rows. The spacing of the columns will not be even. Don't worry about it.)

FIGURE 13-9
Text for Exercise 13.8

Johnnie Jacks	499.25	540.00
Phillipe Darling	35.89	648.12
Yang Lin	625.88	569.12
Esther Flores	385.90	485.40
Diane Jones	485.00	1,146.50

5. Follow the Insert procedure to add 2 more rows at the top and 1 more row at the bottom of the table.

6. Select and join the cells in Row 1. Key the title in Row 1 all on one line at the left. Use all caps but do not use Bold.

   QUARTERLY AND MIDYEAR SALES EARNINGS

7. In Row 2, key the column headings, again at the left. Do not use Bold. Key the four column headings:

   Salesperson   First   Second   Midyear

   (continued on next page)

207

EXERCISE 13.8 CONTINUED

8. Key the word **Totals** in Cell A8. Then save the table as **sales 13-8 xxx**. It should look much like Figure 13-10. Keep it open in the window.

   Now that you have the basic table created, we'll format the number columns using the Properties for Table Numeric Format dialog box. Figure 13-11 illustrates that box. Quite a variety of number types are available. The columns in this exercise are money columns, so we'll choose Currency. This choice will add dollar signs to the numbers.

FIGURE 13-10
Example of **Sales 13-8 xxx** Document

QUARTERLY AND MIDYEAR SALES EARNINGS			
Salesperson	First	Second	Midyear
Johnnie Jacks	499.25	540.00	
Phillipe Darling	35.89	648.12	
Yang Lin	625.88	569.12	
Esther Flores	385.90	485.40	
Diane Jones	485.00	1,146.50	
Totals			

EXERCISE 13.9

1. Point to Cell B3 (499.25). Hold the left mouse button down while you drag to select the cells from Cell B3 to the lower right corner (Cell D8). All three columns (below the column headings) should be selected when you release the mouse button.

2. Display the QuickMenu and choose **Numeric Format**. The Properties for Table Numeric Format dialog box should appear, looking much like Figure 13-11.

FIGURE 13-11
Properties for Table Numeric Format Dialog Box

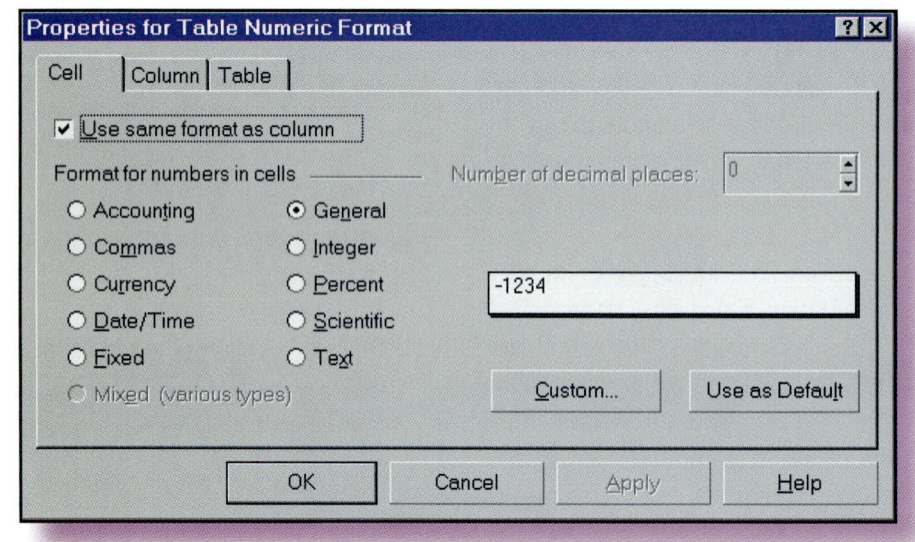

208

UNIT 4: SPECIAL LAYOUT FEATURES

3. In the *Format for numbers in cells* section, choose **Currency**. Click **OK** to close the dialog box.

4. Select the first two rows of the table. Press **F9** to display the Font dialog box and choose **Bold** and **Small caps**. Close the dialog box.

5. With the first two rows still selected, open the Table Numeric Format dialog box and choose **Text**. Close the dialog box.

6. Select Row 3 (any row with all four columns would do) and choose the **Equal Columns** button on the Property Bar.

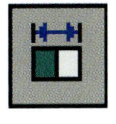

7. Press **Ctrl+End** to move your insertion point out of the table and press **Enter** twice. Insert the Path and Filename code.

8. Save your document as **sales 13-9 xxx**. Save it, and keep it open.

Formatting the first two rows to Text was done as a precaution. It really doesn't affect this exercise because the title and column heads contain only words. Sometimes, however, you might have numerals in the column heads (such as *1st quarter*). If you don't change those column heads to Text formatting, WordPerfect might include the numerals in the column totals.

Now we'll total the columns with the SUM formula and create a formula that will add the first and second quarter amounts for each sales representative, giving the midyear sales.

EXERCISE 13.10

1. With **sales 13-9 xxx** open, save it as **sales 13-10 xxx**.

2. Position your insertion point in Cell B8. Click the **QuickSum** button at the right of the Property Bar. The total of the numbers in Column B should appear. Repeat the same procedure for Column C and Column D. (WordPerfect will add the totals of Columns B and C for a total in Column D!)

3. Beginning in Cell D7, work UP the column, clicking the **QuickSum** button for each of the horizontal totals.

4. Save your table again as **sales 13-10 xxx** and close it.

In Exercise 13.10, you learned that you can use the QuickSum button to add all of the numbers above a cell. You also used the QuickSum button to add horizontally across the row. It is important to note that WordPerfect adds vertically before it adds horizontally. Had you added the numbers for Johnnie Jacks before the numbers for Phillipe Darling, for example, WordPerfect would have copied Johnnie's midyear total into the cell for Phillipe. That's why you worked UP Column D rather than down the column.

Another way to handle a table such as this would be to select all of the numeric columns. With the columns selected, you can click the QuickSum button for a quick horizontal and vertical total.

EXERCISE 13.11

1. Open **sales 13-9 xxx**. Use **Save As** to save the file as **sales 13-11 xxx**.

2. Position the insertion point in Cell D3. Then choose **Formula Toolbar** from either the **Table** button or the QuickMenu.

3. Click to position the insertion point in the text box just to the right of the blue check mark, and key **b3+c3** to add Johnnie's first- and second-quarter sales. Click the blue check mark to complete the calculation.

4. With the insertion point still in Cell D3, click the **Copy Formula** button on the Formula Bar. Click **Down** and then key **5** into the text box. Your dialog box should look like Figure 13-12.

5. Click **OK**. Look at Column D. Note that in Row 8 there were no numbers to add, so you have only zeros.

6. Use **QuickSum** (the Formula Toolbar also has a QuickSum button) to add Columns B and C. If necessary, click the **Calculate** button on the Formula Toolbar. The Cell D8 total should be filled in automatically.

7. Save your document again as **sales 13-11 xxx**. Keep it open.

FIGURE 13-12
Copy Formula Dialog Box

Adjusting Column Size

Most of the time you will let WordPerfect size your columns for you, or you will grab the column margins and size the columns by eye. Sometimes you might want specific sizes for the columns. You can use the Ruler to help you with that task, or you can look at the little boxes that appear beside the column margins when you are making an adjustment. Two buttons on the Tables Property Bar also help you size selected columns. The Equal Columns button makes the selected columns equal in width. The Size Column to Fit button makes a column larger to accommodate a complete word or number.

Let's make the first column in the exercise wider and the others a little narrower using the size boxes. Then we'll make one of the column headings a two-line heading and align the remaining headings at the bottom.

EXERCISE 13.12

1. Point to the line between Columns A and B. When the crosshair pointer appears, click and hold it for a minute and look at the two numbers that appear. The first number tells the size of the column to the left of the border and the second number tells the size of the column to the right.

210 UNIT 4: SPECIAL LAYOUT FEATURES

2. Drag the line so Column A is **1.75"**. Column B will become **1.5"**. Adjust Columns C and D so they are both **1.5"** like Column B. Your table won't quite reach from margin to margin.

3. Change *Salesperson* to **Sales Representative**. It will wrap to a second line.

4. Select all of Row 2. Open the **Format** menu and choose **Cell**. In the *Alignment, Vertical* section, click the button and choose **Bottom**. Change Horizontal Alignment to **Center**.

5. Return to your table. The column headings should look like Figure 13-13.

6. With Row 2 still selected, click the **Cell Fill** button on the Property Bar and choose the third choice in the first row.

7. Position your insertion point in Row 1. Go to the Table Format dialog box and choose the **Row** tab. Change Row height to **Fixed** and set it at **0.75"**.

8. With the Table Format dialog box still displayed, click the **Cell** tab and change both Vertical and Horizontal Alignment to **Center**. Click **OK** to return to your table. Change the font size of the title of the document to **20 pt**.

9. With the insertion point still in Row 1, go to **Borders/Fill**. Set the line for *Left* to **X**. Do the same with the lines for *Right* and *Top*. Close the dialog box and deselect Row 1 so you can see what the row looks like without lines. (A dotted line will remain to show you the row boundaries.)

10. Select Cells B3 through D8 and set Horizontal Alignment at **Decimal Align**.

11. Save your document as **sales 13-12 xxx**. Then print it and keep it open.

FIGURE 13-13
Column Headings Row in Sales Exercise

SALES REPRESENTATIVE	FIRST	SECOND	MIDYEAR

Let's take time for a recap on some of the things you did in Exercise 13.12.

- You sized the columns by dragging the column margins.

- You set vertical alignment so the column headings were aligned at the bottom of the cells. The default is for text to be aligned at the top of the cells.

- You specified a measured row height. Normally the row height is determined by the font size, with an 0.083" margin above the text and an 0.04" margin below the text. (You'll work with row margins in a later lesson.)

- You set vertical alignment so the main heading was centered in the space allowed for the heading.

- You added fill to the row containing column headings. Some printers do better with fill than others.

- You were directed to use the Table menu from the Property Bar, the Table QuickMenu, and buttons on the Property Bar as the sources of your formatting choices. In most of the exercises that follow, you can choose formatting from any of the sources. You get to decide!

- You turned off the lines surrounding the title of the table. The row containing the title remains part of the table, but it appears to stand out by itself above the table.

All of this formatting is easy to perform, and if you spend any time at all with tables, you will find that it becomes second nature to you.

Recalculation

Performing the calculations in the table was easy. In the same way, it is easy to tell WordPerfect to recalculate the table when a change is made. Phillipe wasn't on vacation during the first quarter. Instead, incorrect information was provided. His first-quarter sales should have been $1,035.89, not $35.89. In the next exercise we'll correct the amount and recalculate so all of the totals are correct. Then we'll remove the lines from the table so you can see what a table looks like without any lines.

EXERCISE 13.13

1. With **sales 13-12 xxx** open, save it as **sales 13-13 xxx**.

2. Click in Cell B4 between the dollar sign and the 3. Key **1,0** to change the amount to $1,035.89.

3. Click the **Calculate** button on the Formula Toolbar. Mentally calculate the totals to see if the affected ones increased by $1,000.

4. Use the fat white arrow at the top of any cell and triple click to select the entire table.

5. Choose **Borders/Fill** from one of the several sources. Change *Outside* lines to **None**. Change *Inside* lines to **None**.

6. Save the document again and print it. Keep it open to learn more about formulas.

More Formulas

WordPerfect can do more than add. A wide variety of formulas are available—all of the formulas and functions needed for spreadsheet preparation have been included in this powerful word processing program. Let's look at a couple of others and see how easy they are to use.

EXERCISE 13.14

1. Select the total in Cell B8 and delete it. Then delete the formula in the text box to the right of the blue check mark in the Formula Toolbar. Position your insertion point in Cell B8.

2. Click the **Functions** button on the Formula Toolbar and double click to choose **AVE(List)**. The *List* portion of the formula tells you that WordPerfect wants to know what cells to average. You could key **B3:B7**. (The colon is

used between cell addresses to designate a *range* of cells.) It's easier to use the mouse.

3. Drag down over the numbers in Cells B3 through B7 to select all of them. (If Word-Perfect asks about deleting a formula, confirm the deletion.) The formula should now read **AVE(B3:B7)**. If it is correct, click the blue check mark to complete the calculation. Did you get $606.38?

4. Delete the contents of Cell B8 again. Then delete the formula in the text box.

5. Position the insertion point in Cell B8 again. Click the **Functions** button again. This time find **PRODUCT(List)**. Double click to choose it.

6. Drag the insertion point over Cells B3 through B4 only to multiply those two numbers. When the text box reads **PRODUCT(B3:B4)**, click the blue check mark. Did you get $517,168.08?

7. Close your table document without saving it.

In Exercise 13.14, you worked with formulas provided by WordPerfect to calculate in your document. You learned that you can key the range of cells to be included in the calculation, or that you can drag the mouse pointer across the cells (if they are contiguous) to tell WordPerfect which cells to include in the calculation.

Sometimes it's easier to simply key the desired formula. Four symbols are generally used for calculating on the computer, since the keyboard doesn't provide you with symbols for calculations. Following are the computer symbols for calculating:

- *   Multiply
- /   Divide
- +   Add
- –   Subtract

When you multiplied the contents of Cell B3 times Cell B4 in Exercise 13.14, you could have simply keyed B3*B4 in the formula text box and not bothered with the PRODUCT function. If you wished to divide the contents of Cell B3 by the contents of Cell D4, you would key B3/D4 in the formula text box. To subtract the contents of Cell B3 from the contents of Cell D4, key D4-B3. In all cases, be sure to double check the formula before clicking the blue check mark to complete the calculation.

Now let's practice with WordPerfect functions in a new table.

EXERCISE 13.15

1. Prepare the table illustrated in Figure 13-14. Don't bother adjusting the sizes of the cells. Display the Formula Toolbar.

2. Position the insertion point in Cell B4 and click the **QuickSum** button on the Table Formula Toolbar. Repeat the procedure in Cells C4 and D4. Do a quick mental check to see if the sums are correct.

3. Position the insertion point in Cell E1 to enter a formula that adds all three of Patty's numbers. Click the **Functions** button on the Formula Toolbar and key **sum** to move the highlight to the SUM formula. Click the **Insert** button.

(continued on next page)

EXERCISE 13.15 CONTINUED

4. Either key **b1:d1** or drag to select Cells B1 through D1. Click the blue check mark to get the sum (105).

5. Position the insertion point in Cell E2 and click in the formula text box. Key **b2+c2+d2**. Click the blue check mark to get the sum (130).

6. Follow any procedure you'd like to get Sue's total (95).

7. Use **QuickSum** to total Column E.

8. In Column F, compute the average for Patty. It should be an average of the numbers in Columns B, C, and D. DO NOT include the amount in Column E in the average.

FIGURE 13-14
Text for Exercise 13.15

Patty	30	25	50		
Fred	25	45	60		
Sue	15	35	45		
Totals					

9. Compute the averages for the other three rows. If you wish, you can copy the formula in Row 2 down as you did in Exercise 13.11. Your averages will have many decimal places. We'll work with formatting the numbers shortly.

10. Save your work as **patty 13-15 xxx**. Keep it open for additional formatting.

Now that the calculations are complete in your table, let's add rows for headings and format the table.

EXERCISE 13.16

1. With **patty 13-15 xxx** open in the window, use **Save As** to save the file as **patty 13-16 xxx**.

2. Using the **Insert Row** button on the Property Bar, insert two rows at the top of the table. Join the cells in Row 1 and key the title: **QUARTERLY SALES FIGURES**. Format it in any way you wish.

3. In Cell A2, key **Sales Representative**. Select the cell and find the **Size Column to Fit** button on the Property Bar. Click it. Column A should expand to accommodate the entire column heading.

4. Key **January** in Cell B2. Select Cells B2, C2, and D2. Find the **QuickFill** button on the Property Bar. Click it. *February* and *March* should automatically appear in Cells C2 and D2.

5. Key **Quarter** in Cell E2 and **Monthly Average** in Cell F2.

UNIT 4: SPECIAL LAYOUT FEATURES

6. Select all of Row 2. Format it as follows:
   a. Align the text at the bottom of the row.
   b. Use **Center** justification for the column headings.

7. Select all of the money columns and format them as follows:
   a. Change the Numeric Format to **Currency**. (That will take care of the extra decimal places in the averages.)
   b. Decimally align the numbers.

8. Insert the Path and Filename code a double space below the table.

9. Save your file again as **patty 13-16 xxx**. Print it and keep it open.

Let's briefly review what you did in Exercise 13.16 and learn a little more about some of the features.

- You learned that the Size Columns to Fit feature will make the column wide enough for the largest entry in the column. This feature doesn't work on the column to the right unless you have room within the margins for it to work. For example, the monthly average can't be spread across the column unless you extend the right margin.

- You used the QuickFill button to fill in a pattern of information. This feature works in a wide variety of applications. For example, it fills in consecutive numbers, numbers in a particular sequence (if you give the sequence), or quarterly dates (if you begin the sequence of dates).

- You learned that QuickFill and Size Columns to Fit are available from the Table menu and from the QuickMenu, as well as from the Table Property Bar.

- You aligned text at the bottom of the cells.

- You formatted and aligned the numbers as in previous exercises.

Table SpeedFormat

Table SpeedFormat can take a boring-looking table and format it with a wide variety of formats. Some of the formats are especially good for certain kinds of tables, depending on the information in the table and whether it has main headings, column headings, or totals. Let's look at Table SpeedFormat and use it to format your table.

EXERCISE 13.17

1. With **patty 13-16 xxx** showing in your window, use **Save As** to save the file as **patty 13-17 xxx**.

2. Position the insertion point somewhere in the table.

3. Choose **SpeedFormat** from either the Table QuickMenu or the Table menu on the Property Bar. At the left is a list of available formats.

(continued on next page)

215

EXERCISE ▷ 13.17 CONTINUED

4. Click some of the formats and look at the preview area to see how they work.

5. Go down the list quite a ways and find **Fancy Fills**. Choose that format for your table and click **Apply**.

6. Back in your document window, evaluate the format. Do you like it?

7. Print the file and save it again as **patty 13-17 xxx**. Keep the file open.

As you discovered when you looked through the list of formats, quite a number of them are available. You can try other styles at your leisure. If you like the WordPerfect styles, this feature can save you lots of formatting time.

Floating Cells

WordPerfect has a feature called *floating cell* that allows you to create a tiny table referencing certain cells of a table. The floating cell may not be in the table. Instead, it is usually in the text either above or below the table.

For example, in Figure 13-15, the sentence below the table contains a floating cell that references the total profits. If any of the amounts in the profits column change, total profits change. When total profits change, the total in the text below the table will be updated.

Let's add a floating cell to the exercise with which you have been working.

FIGURE 13-15
Sample Table with Floating Cell

Location of Office	Fourth-Quarter Profits
New York	$40,500.00
Houston	$32,600.00
San Francisco	$37,800.00
Miami	$28,500.00
Total	$139,400.00

The total fourth-quarter profits from all offices amount to $139,400.00.

EXERCISE ▷ 13.18

SCANS

1. With **patty 13-17 xxx** showing in the window, save the file as **patty 13-18 xxx**.

2. Make some space between the bottom of the table and the Path and Filename code. Then position the insertion point a double space below the table.

3. Key the sentence in Figure 13-16. When you come to the asterisks (**), don't key them.

FIGURE 13-16
Text for the Floating Cell Sentence

The table above illustrates our sales for the first quarter. Notice that total sales for the quarter amount to **.

4. Open the **Insert** menu and choose **Table**. The Create Table dialog box will appear. Click to select the **Floating cell** button. The dialog box will look like Figure 13-17. Click **Create**.

216

UNIT 4: SPECIAL LAYOUT FEATURES

5. Reveal your codes and look at the two Floating Cell codes. Your insertion point should be between them.

6. Click to position the insertion point in the formula text box on the Formula Toolbar. Then click in Cell E6 ($330) to tell WordPerfect to reference that cell in the floating cell.

7. Click the blue check mark. After a moment, *330* should appear in the floating cell position. It is not formatted as currency. Key a period at the end of the sentence.

8. Position the insertion point in the floating cell. Change the Numeric Format to **Currency**.

FIGURE 13-17
Create Table Dialog Box

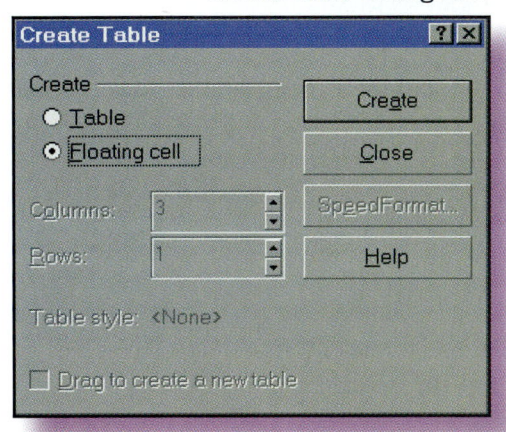

9. Save your document again as **patty 13-18 xxx**. Reveal your codes and add the table codes to your list of codes. Keep the file open.

Sue has come up with a plan that should increase her monthly sales by an estimated $20. This would have a positive impact on all of the figures in the table. For the sake of projection, let's increase Sue's sales for January through March and recalculate the table.

EXERCISE 13.19

1. Save **patty 13-18 xxx** as **patty 13-19 xxx**.

2. Manually increase Sue's sales for January by $20.00. Do the same for her February and March sales.

3. Click the **Calculate** button on the Formula Bar. The floating cell should now show a total of $390.00.

4. Print your final table. Then close it, saving it again.

Sources of Tables

Tables can be constructed from a number of sources. Let's look briefly at two of the most common.

Text

Text that has been keyed in columns can be converted to table format. The procedure is simple. Select the text you wish to have in your table. Open the Table menu and choose Create. Let's try it.

217

EXERCISE 13.20

1. Open your **Units 3 and 4** folder and open **salad 9-7 xxx**.

2. Select all of the text in the columns. (Do not include the Path and Filename code.)

3. Open the **Insert** menu and choose **Table**. Click **OK** to affirm that you are creating the table from tabular columns.

4. Look at your table. Each vegetable is in a separate cell. This table can be formatted like all of the others with which you've worked in this lesson.

Now let's turn the text back to tabular columns.

5. Reveal your codes. Find the code that defines the table. Delete the code. The dialog box illustrated in Figure 13-18 will appear. Choose to delete the **Table structure**, leaving the text. The text should be returned to the way it was before you turned it into a table.

6. Close the document without saving it.

FIGURE 13-18
Delete Table Dialog Box

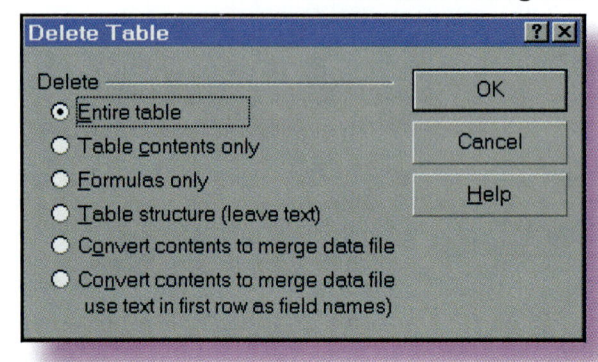

Spreadsheets

WordPerfect has made it possible for you to *import* work sheets prepared in popular spreadsheet programs such as Lotus 1-2-3, Excel, or Quattro Pro. Spreadsheets can also be *linked* to your WordPerfect documents so that as the spreadsheet is updated, it will also update your WordPerfect document. While this sounds difficult, it is really pretty easy. Let's import a simple Quattro Pro work sheet to see how it looks in WordPerfect.

EXERCISE 13.21

1. Beginning in a new document window, go to the student **datafile** folder and open the file named **office.wb3**. The Import Data dialog box illustrated in Figure 13-19 will appear.

2. Look at what the dialog box is telling you. You are importing a spreadsheet in table format. The range of cells is listed. Click **OK**.

3. Look at the table that appears. It certainly isn't beautiful, but it can easily be formatted. You could do it on your own with no trouble.

4. Close the document without saving it.

It's that simple to bring a work sheet created in a spreadsheet program into WordPerfect. It's nice to know that you can add work sheets or portions of work sheets to your WordPerfect documents.

FIGURE 13-19
Import Data Dialog Box

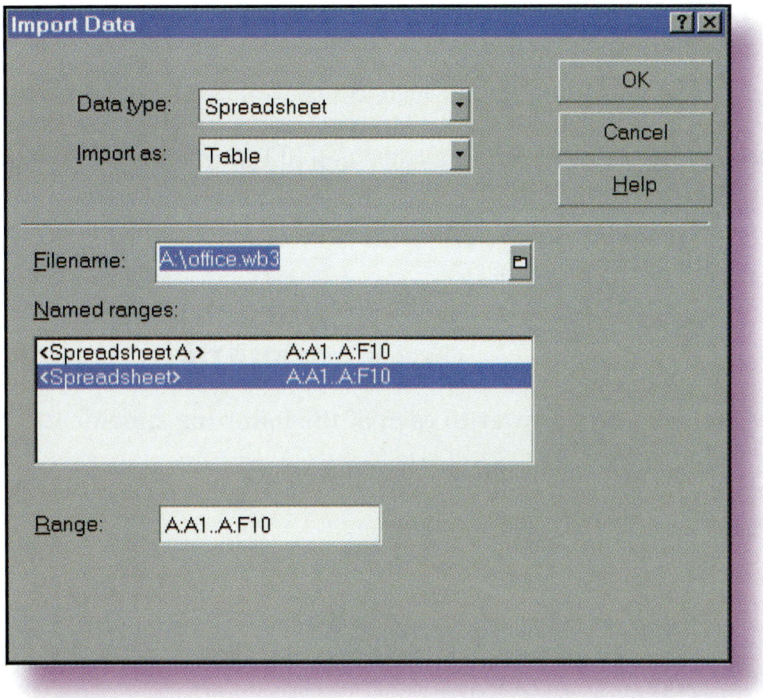

Summary

As promised, this was a long lesson. It included all of the basic information about working with tables. In this lesson you learned that:

- Tables can be created from the Toolbar or from the Insert menu.

- You can increase the size of a table by adding columns and rows.

- Many sources of commands are available for table formatting.

- Tables can be used to perform calculations.

- If the numbers in a table calculation change, you can update the entire table with the Calculate button.

- You can reference a table somewhere else in the document using a floating cell.

- Tables can be created from tabular columns or from spreadsheets created in other programs.

Many more things can be done with tables. They can be part of a larger document, as you'll practice in the Lesson 13 Project. They can be used for forms, as you'll learn in Lesson 15. They can be used to combine standard text with lists of names and addresses or other items. You will use tables in many of the lessons that follow, so you'll get plenty of opportunities to practice your skills with tables.

LESSON 13 REVIEW QUESTIONS

FILL IN THE BLANKS

Complete each of the following statements by writing your answer in the blank provided.

1. A __Row__ is a collection of information arranged horizontally in a table.

(continued on next page)

2. You can begin a table by opening the _Insert_ menu and choosing Table Create.

3. You can also begin a table by dragging the Tables button on the _Toolbar_.

4. The location of a cell, such as Cell B3, is reported on the _Application Bar_.

5. A _Column_ is a collection of information arranged vertically in a table.

6. To display the _Table Quick Menu_, point to the table with your mouse pointer and right click.

MULTIPLE CHOICE

Circle the best answer to each of the following statements.

7. To move the insertion point to the previous cell in a table, press
   - A. Tab.
   - **B.** Shift+ Tab.
   - C. Home, Home.
   - D. End, End.

8. To select the entire table, point to the top or left side of a cell, and when the pointer changes into a fat white arrow, click
   - A. once.
   - B. twice.
   - **C.** three times.
   - D. four times.

9. Which of the following is NOT a button on the Table Property Bar?
   - A. QuickJoin
   - B. QuickSplit Row
   - C. QuickSplit Column
   - **D.** QuickTip

10. The computer symbol for multiplying is
    - A. +.
    - B. /.
    - **C.** *.
    - D. -.

LESSON 13 PROJECT

SCANS

Prepare the following letter that contains a listing of medical costs and a floating cell. See how much of it you can do without referring back to the exercises in the lesson.

1. Beginning in a new document window, use Advance to set the beginning line of text 2" from the top of the page. Insert the date text.

220 UNIT 4: SPECIAL LAYOUT FEATURES

2. Key the text in Figure 13-20 as the beginning of a letter to Mrs. Sheri Schneider. Press Enter twice and create a 2-column by 1-row table. Key the table data, as illustrated in Figure 13-21.

3. With the insertion point in Cell B6, do the following:
   a. Display the Formula Toolbar and total the column with QuickSum.
   b. Use Size Columns to Fit.

4. Size Column A to fit.

FIGURE 13-20
Beginning of Lesson 13 Project

```
Mrs. Sheri Schneider
Box 814
Cranberry Creek, NY 12117

Dear Mrs. Schneider:

Below is a summary of the bill from St. Elizabeth Hospital for your
stay following your automobile accident on July 4, 199x.  As the party
responsible for this accident, you are financially responsible to
remit payment in full to the hospital for these services.
```

5. Select all of Column B and format it as follows:
   a. Change Numeric Format to Accounting.
   b. Set Alignment at Decimal Align. (Note that the dollar signs are aligned at the left, whereas when you used Currency they were directly in front of each number.)

6. Go to the Table Format dialog box and set the table Position at Center.

7. Insert a row at the top containing the following column headings: **Item** and **Amount**.

8. Move your insertion point below the table and key the sentence in Figure 13-22 a double space below the table. When you come to the asterisks (**), don't key them. Instead, create a floating cell that references Cell B7. Change the Numeric Format for the floating cell to Accounting.

9. Add the period following the floating cell and key the text in Figure 13-23 to end the letter.

10. Check your work carefully. When it is perfect, save the file as **schneider proj13a xxx**.

FIGURE 13-21
Table for Lesson 13 Project

Pharmacy	4.90
Medical Surgery Supplies	33.50
X rays	131.00
CT Scan/Head	933.50
CT Scan/Body	1245.00
Total	

FIGURE 13-22
Sentence with Floating Cell

```
As you can see, the total
for the bill is **.
```

(continued on next page)

11. Add a footer that inserts the Path and Filename code at the bottom of the letter. Print the letter and save it.

12. Change the amount of the X rays to $331.00. Recalculate the table.

13. Use Table SpeedFormat to apply Double Border Bold.

14. Save the file again, this time as **schneider proj13b xxx**. Print the file again and close it.

FIGURE 13-23
End of Lesson 13 Project Letter

```
If you have any questions
regarding this bill, please
contact my office.

Sincerely,



(Your Name)
Account Representative
```

CRITICAL THINKING ACTIVITY

SCANS

You have prepared a table to record the number of minutes you spend each week studying. Across the top of the table, you have named your eight columns—Days, 8 a.m., 9 a.m., etc., up to 10 p.m. Down the side you have labeled the rows with the days of the week. At the bottom, you've inserted another row to total the number of minutes per week per class you've spent studying. Since you have a class scheduled during the 8 a.m. time frame, you know the total in that column will be zero. However, when you clicked the QuickSum button, an 8 was inserted into the cell. What would cause that to happen and how would you fix it?

You inadvertently included that cell in the calculation. Adjust the calculation so that it excludes that particular cell.

Outlining and Text Columns

LESSON 14

OBJECTIVES

Upon completion of this lesson, you will be able to:

- Use the WordPerfect Outline tool to create outlines.
- Edit a WordPerfect outline.
- Arrange documents in text columns.
- Use balanced newspaper columns.
- Adjust the widths of the columns.
- Use Hyphenation to fill the lines.
- Discuss the use of one space or two at the ends of sentences.

Estimated Time: 1½ hours

In Lesson 5 you learned that you can create numbered and bulleted lists using the Outline/Bullets & Numbering feature. You also found that WordPerfect automatically continued a list that you began manually with bullets or numbers.

The Outline feature actually is much more sophisticated. We'll find out how powerful it is in this lesson.

Another feature that helps you arrange your text is the Text Columns feature. This is a different kind of columns than tabular columns or table columns. You'll also learn about the Text Columns feature in this lesson.

Outlining

One of the biggest areas where Outline is more sophisticated than Bullets & Numbering is with regard to levels. WordPerfect outlines can have as many as eight levels, all numbered differently.

The default outline style is Paragraph. Let's create a short three-level outline in that style.

EXERCISE 14.1

1. Beginning in a new document window, press **Ctrl+H** to begin a list. The first numeral should appear, and the Outline tools will appear on your Property Bar.

2. Key the text in Figure 14-1.
   a. To change from the first level to the second, press **Tab**. To change to the third level, press **Tab** again.
   b. To return to a higher level from a lower level, press **Shift+Tab**.

3. At the end of the outline, press **Enter** once and backspace once to end the outline and remove the numeral.

4. Check over your work to see that it matches the figure and that everything is correct.

5. Save the file as **outline 14-1 xxx**.

6. Give your file a footer that inserts the Path and Filename code. Save and print the file. Keep it open.

FIGURE 14-1
Text for Exercise 14.1 Outline

```
1.  Level one of the outline.  (This is the first item at this level.
    Note that it is aligned automatically when it wraps.)

2.  Second item at the first level.

3.  Third item at the first level.

    a.  Level 2 item.
    b.  Second item at Level 2, the first indented level.
        i.  First item at Level 3.  (It, too, will wrap automatically
            because the outline style includes Indent after each
            numeral.)
        ii. Last item at Level 3.  (Now I will press Enter twice and
            then Shift+Tab twice to return to Level 1 to put in the
            final item.)

4.  Final item of the outline.  (Note that this outline has double
    spacing before and after the first level lines and single spacing
    elsewhere.  This is the customary spacing for outlines.)
```

Look at the Outline tools on the Property Bar. It is illustrated in Figure 14-2. This bar contains a number of useful tools.

FIGURE 14-2
Outline Tools on Property Bar

224

UNIT 4: SPECIAL LAYOUT FEATURES

When an item in an outline contains indented items, the entire numbered item in the outline is referred to as a *family*. For example, all of Item 3 in your outline is considered a family. This is important, because you can edit entire outline families, rather than a line at a time.

At the left are four arrows. The first two may be used to change the level of indent for an item. The next two enable you to move a line up or down in the outline. The two buttons with yellow squares allow you to close up an item in the outline, hiding the lower level items in a family and displaying only the first-level items. The final button is similar—it allows you to show as many levels as you wish, rather than all or just one, and it affects the entire outline.

Sometimes an outline contains unnumbered text within the outline. This is called *body text*, and whether it shows or not is controlled with the button that looks like a page. The button with the Roman numerals allows you to change the numbering, and the following button enables you to change the style of the outline.

Finally, the button that looks like a green book is used to display or hide level icons–fat white numbers–in the margin area at the left of the outline. These icons indicate whether an outline item has second- or third-level items and are useful for editing. Let's try some of these buttons.

EXERCISE 14.2

1. Save **outline 14-1 xxx** as **outline 14-2 xxx**. Position the insertion point somewhere in the second item of the outline. Click the **Show Levels** button and choose **1**. Only the first-level items will show (and the spacing between them may not be equal).

2. Click the **Show Levels** button again. Choose **3**. All of the outline should reappear.

3. Click the **Show/Hide Body** button twice—once to take the blank lines out and again to put them back in. (The blank lines are considered text.)

4. With the insertion point still in the second item, click the black arrow that points to the right. The item should be changed to a second-level item. Now click the arrow that points to the left to return it to a first-level item.

5. If the Show Icons button is not depressed, click it and look at the icons.

6. Point at the *1-* at the left of Item 3 and look at the white double-headed arrow. Click once. The entire item should be selected. With the white arrow still in the area of the fat numbers, press the left mouse button and drag the entire section up until the horizontal line across the page is just above Item 2. Release the mouse button.

7. Use the same procedure to return Item 3 to its third-place position.

8. Change some of the other items around and then return them to their original locations. (If you were to leave some of them in their new positions, you would have to do some repair of blank lines.)

9. Keep the outline in the window as you read on.

225

Ending an Outline

You learned in Exercise 14.1 that you can discontinue an outline by backspacing to remove the final number. This worked with Bullets, too. However, if you want a new list later in the same document, the numbering will pick up where you left off in the earlier list. To begin a new outline, you may key the first number and let WordPerfect pick it up from there, or you may specify that you'd like a new outline in the Bullets & Numbering dialog box.

EXERCISE 14.3

1. Position your insertion point at the end of the final item in the outline. Press **Enter** twice. Then backspace to remove the *5*.

2. Key **This is a line of text in the document that isn't part of the outline**. Press **Enter** twice.

3. Press **Ctrl+H** to begin outlining. The number *5.* should appear. Assume you wanted the new number to be *1*. Backspace to remove the *5*.

4. Position your insertion point at the end of the original outline again. Click the **Options** button on the Feature Bar and choose **End Outline**. The *5* should become a *1*.

5. Keep the outline open in the window as you read on.

In Exercise 14.3 you began outlining with Ctrl+H. You can do that anytime you wish to start an outline. Although the default is Paragraph numbering, if you have used a different style, WordPerfect will remember that style when you begin an outline with Ctrl+H.

Adding and Deleting Outline Items

You can add text to the outline or delete text from the outline, and WordPerfect will adjust the numbers to accommodate your changes. That is the major reason that outlines are so nice to use for any kind of listing—they are so easy to edit. Let's practice.

EXERCISE 14.4

1. Position your insertion point at the end of the second item in the outline. Press **Enter** twice. You should get a new *3.* and the items below the new number should be increased by one.

2. Key **This is a new Item 3**.

3. Point to the fat *1-* to the left of the new item. Click once to select the new item. Press the **Delete** key.

4. Your outline should now be back to the original four items. Keep it open as you read on.

Outline Styles

WordPerfect comes with several outline styles. As you know, the Paragraph style is the default. Let's apply some of the others to the outline in your window so you can see how they look.

EXERCISE 14.5

1. Select your entire outline. Open the **Insert** menu. Choose **Outline/Bullets & Numbering**. Look at the **Numbering** section near the bottom where you may choose a new outline.

2. Choose one of the other styles and note the style name in the gray area near the top of the box. Click **OK**.

3. Select your text again and try some additional styles. Note that some of them don't indent the levels.

4. Close your document without saving it again.

That's enough about outlining for now. Practice will make you better with it. Now let's learn about text columns.

Text Columns

You've already learned a couple of ways to arrange your text in columns. You've learned to do the following:

- Set tabs.
- Create tables.

In both of those cases, the text needed to be arranged horizontally as well as vertically.

A category of WordPerfect columns called *Text Columns* allows you to format your text in columns that snake from one column to the next. Let's explore this feature.

EXERCISE 14.6

1. Beginning in a new document window, open **columns** from your student **datafile** folder. Use **Save As** to save the file with your working files as **columns 14-6 xxx**.

2. Study the contents of this document. It gives you lots of important information about newspaper columns, balanced newspaper columns, and parallel columns.

3. Point to the Columns button on the Toolbar and choose **2 Columns**.

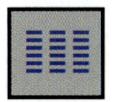

4. Your document should be formatted into columns. Zoom to **Full Page** and compare your document with Figure 14-3. Then return to 100%.

5. With your insertion point at the top of the file, create a footer that inserts the Path and Filename code. Save your document again as **columns 14-6 xxx**. Keep it open.

(continued on next page)

EXERCISE ▸ 14.6 CONTINUED

6. Reveal your codes. Look at the [Col Def] code. Add it to your list of codes. Then delete the code to return the document to its original form.

FIGURE 14-3
Zoom of Columns Document

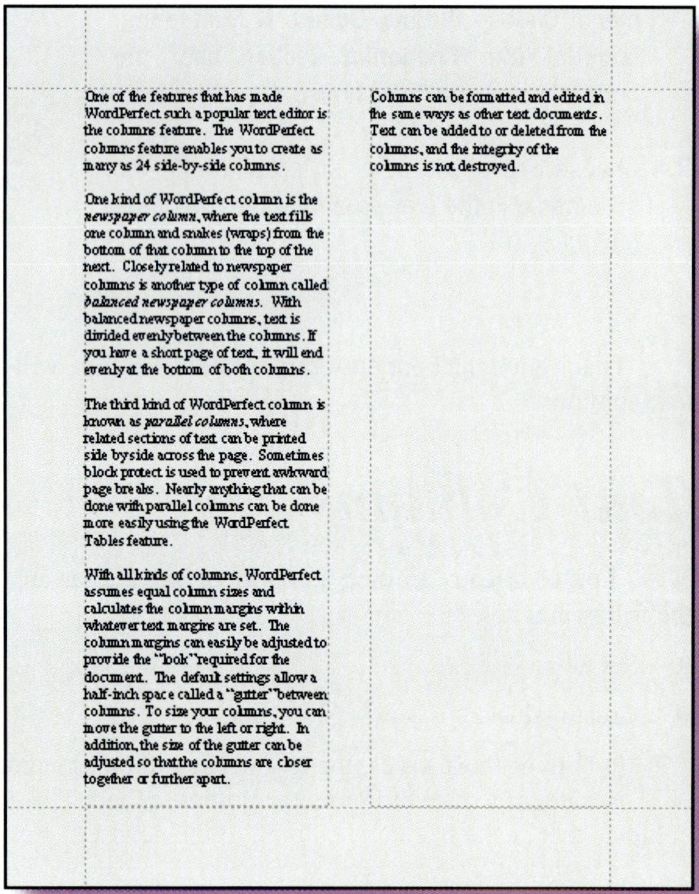

Balanced Newspaper Columns

With a short document, sometimes it looks better to have the columns end evenly on the page. WordPerfect will end the columns evenly if you choose balanced newspaper columns. Let's convert this document to balanced newspaper columns. We will need to go to the Columns dialog box to do this. The feature can be accessed by opening the Format menu, choosing Columns, and then choosing Define, or by choosing Format from the little menu that appears when you click the Columns button on the Toolbar.

228 UNIT 4: SPECIAL LAYOUT FEATURES

EXERCISE 14.7

1. With **columns 14-6 xxx** showing in the window, use **Save As** to save the file as **columns 14-7 xxx**. Position the insertion point at the top.

2. Click the **Columns** button on the Toolbar and choose **Format** to open the Columns dialog box (see Figure 14-4).

3. Look at the parts of the dialog box. Then click **Balanced newspaper** in the *Type of columns* section. Click **OK**.

   Look at your text. Before you changed to Full justification, your columns were quite ragged at the right—especially noticeable with the short line lengths. All of that excess space at the right was moved into the lines when you changed to Full justification. Either way, the text isn't particularly attractive.

4. How do your balanced columns look? Using the **Justification** button on the Property Bar, change from Left to **Full** justification.

5. Print the document. Then save it again as **columns 14-7 xxx**. Keep it open.

FIGURE 14-4
Columns Dialog Box

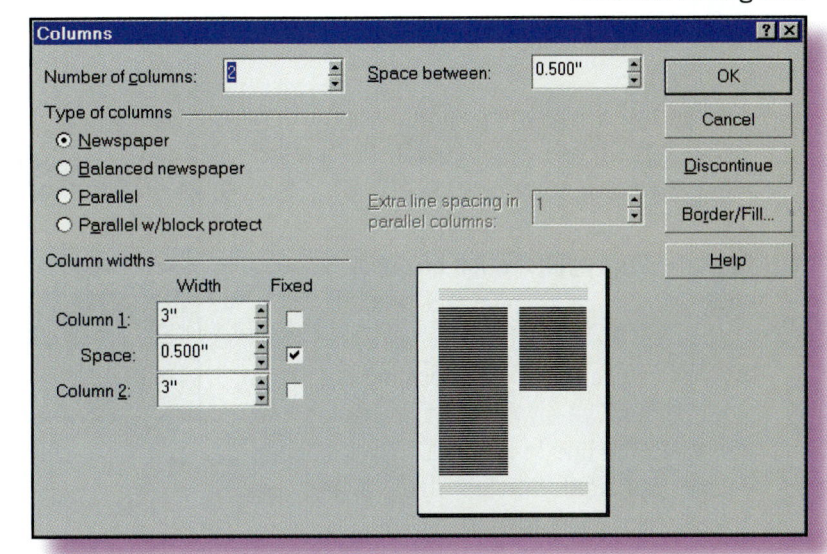

Hyphenation

One way to even up the line endings and get rid of that "spacey" look is to use Hyphenation. Hyphenation compares the word that falls at the end of the line with the Word-Perfect dictionary in which the words have been divided into syllables. WordPerfect then decides whether a word may or may not be divided at the end of the line. If so, the hyphen is inserted and the word is divided.

The hyphen placed in the word is a soft hyphen. When you reformat the text and the word containing the hyphen no longer falls at the end of the line, the hyphen doesn't show. When hyphenation is taking place, WordPerfect may ask you for some help regarding where hyphens should go in and which words may be hyphenated. Figure 14-5 contains a few of the major word division rules, in case you need help in that area.

Let's use Hyphenation in your document.

FIGURE 14-5
Word Division Rules

WORD DIVISION RULES
Divide words only between syllables.
Carry at least three letters to the next line.
Avoid dividing words with fewer than six letters.
Avoid dividing proper nouns.
Avoid dividing more than two lines in a row.
Avoid dividing the last word on a page or in a paragraph.

EXERCISE 14.8

1. With **columns 14-7 xxx** showing in the window, use **Save As** to save the file as **columns 14-8 xxx**.

2. With the insertion point at the beginning of the first column, open the **Tools** menu, choose **Language**, and then choose **Hyphenation**. The Line Hyphenation dialog box that should appear is illustrated in Figure 14-6.

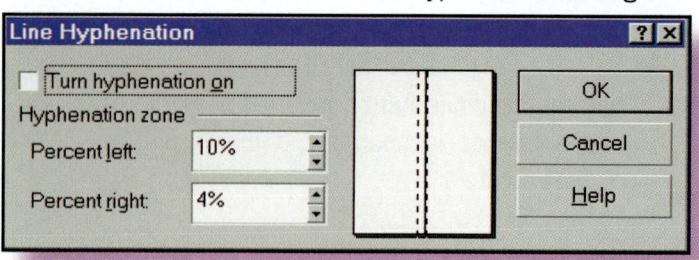

FIGURE 14-6
Line Hyphenation Dialog Box

3. Look at the Hyphenation zone portion of the dialog box. Those settings will be fine for most of your work.

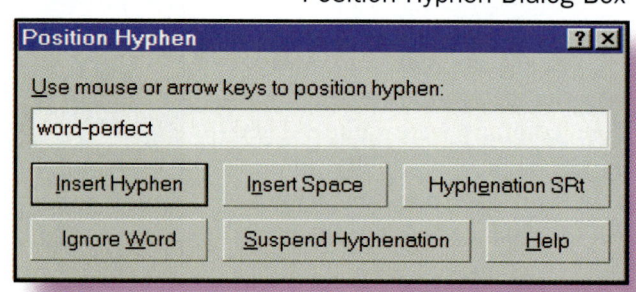

FIGURE 14-7
Position Hyphen Dialog Box

4. Click the **Turn hyphenation on** check box and click **OK**.

5. If WordPerfect has trouble deciding whether a word should be hyphenated, a dialog box similar to the one in Figure 14-7 will appear. Follow the word division rules if you are asked about hyphenation.

6. Look through your document at the hyphenation decisions. Does the document look less ragged?

7. Save the document again as **columns 14-8 xxx** and print a copy.

8. Reveal your codes and use the mouse pointer to drag the [Hyph] code out of your document to turn Hyphenation off. Most of the hyphens will be removed from your text. Keep the document open.

Soft Hyphens

If you wish to even some line endings but don't want to turn on Hyphenation for an entire document, you can manually add hyphens in specific places. This is done by positioning the insertion point and pressing Ctrl+Shift+– using the hyphen key next to the zero in the number row.

WordPerfect relies on you to identify the words that need to be divided with soft hyphens. Soft hyphens are great, because if text is edited so a word no longer falls at the end of the line, the hyphen does not appear.

In Exercise 14.9, you will use the soft hyphen to hyphenate some of the words in the document.

EXERCISE 14.9

1. With **columns 14-8 xxx** open in your window, use **Save As** to save the file as **columns 14-9 xxx**.

2. Position your insertion point after the *l* in *columns* at the beginning of the fourth line of the first paragraph. Hold the **Ctrl** and **Shift** keys while you press **–**. The word should be hyphenated at the indicated location.

3. If it will help your document, put soft hyphens in the following words. (If your line endings are different, find other words to which you can add soft hyphens to fill the lines better.)
   a. Paragraph 2, *col-umns* at the beginning of the sixth line.
   b. Paragraph 2, *bal-anced* at the beginning of the eighth line.

4. Save the file again as **columns 14-9 xxx** and print it. Keep it open.

Editing Column Sizes

While you have the capability of creating as many as 24 columns across the page, you will probably not use more than three or four columns on a standard sheet of paper. WordPerfect automatically spaces the columns evenly across the page. You may have noticed in the Columns dialog box that WordPerfect leaves a half inch between columns. This space is called the *gutter*.

You can edit columns within the Columns dialog box, on the Ruler, or using the column margin guidelines. Let's see how easy it is to change column widths with the guidelines.

EXERCISE 14.10

1. With **columns 14-9 xxx** open in the window, use **Save As** to save the file as **columns 14-10 xxx**.

2. Point to the gutter (space between margins). Your pointer will change to a double crosshair pointer.

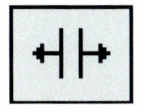

3. Press and hold the left mouse button. The little measurement box will tell you that both columns are 3" wide. Drag the gutter to the left until the left column is **2"** and the right column is **4"**. Deal with any hyphenation decisions that need to be made.

4. Drag the gutter back to the right to make both columns **3"** wide.

5. Drag the right column margin of the first column until the column is **3.25"** wide and the gutter is **0.25"** wide.

6. Display your Ruler and use the margin marker to change the right margin of the first column back to **4"**.

(continued on next page)

231

EXERCISE 14.10 CONTINUED

7. Use the little first-line indent triangle in the margins portion of the Ruler to give the paragraphs a quarter-inch indent. (Drag it to 1.25".)

8. Turn the Ruler off again and Zoom to **Full Page** to check your document. Is it beautiful?

9. Print your document. Then save it again as **columns 14-10 xxx**. Keep it open.

Columns in Part of the Document

Sometimes only a portion of the document should be formatted in columns. You can select the text to be in columns and turn columns on, or you can turn on columns at the beginning of the columnar portion and off at the end. Let's try it both ways in your document.

EXERCISE 14.11

1. With **columns 14-10 xxx** showing, save it as **columns 14-11 xxx**.

2. Reveal your codes and remove the [Col Def] code at the beginning of the document.

3. Position your insertion point at the beginning of the second paragraph. Open the **Format** menu and choose **Columns**. Choose **Balanced newspaper**. Return to your document.

4. Position your insertion point at the beginning of the final paragraph. Click the **Columns** button on the Toolbar and choose **Discontinue**. Look at your document. The first and last paragraph should extend across the page. The center portion of the document should be in columns.

5. Remove the [Col Def] code at the beginning of the second paragraph to return all lines to full length.

6. Drag across the three paragraphs in the middle of the document to select them.

7. Click the **Columns** button on the Toolbar and choose **Format** to open the Columns dialog box. Choose **3** and **Balanced newspaper** columns. Return to your document and deselect the text.

8. With your insertion point at the beginning of the text in columns, choose **Tools, Language**, and then **Hyphenation**. Turn **Hyphenation** on and look at the document. You may need to make some hyphenation decisions.

9. Save the document again as **columns 14-11 xxx**. Print it and close it.

You can adjust your columns in a number of other ways. You'll be able to work it out when you have the need. WordPerfect Help will guide you when you need additional information.

The third kind of text columns—Parallel columns—is not covered in this text because tables work so well for the same kind of work. If you want to try Parallel columns on your own, check WordPerfect Help for that topic, too.

Spaces Following Periods

In Lesson 1 you learned that you should space twice following the period at the end of a sentence. For business documents, it is the best plan because it makes documents easier to read.

In some arenas, however, only one space following end-of-sentence punctuation is used. In the printing and publishing industry, for example, the rule is to space only once at the end of the sentence because the goal is to get as much text on the line as possible.

The **columns** document, as well as the rest of the prerecorded documents you've been using throughout your training, was prepared using the business standard—two spaces. Those two spaces at the end of each sentence were responsible for some of the unsightly spaces in the columns with which you've been working in this lesson. The extra space is magnified with Full justification and short line lengths.

Normally you should develop the habit of spacing twice at the end of a sentence. When it adversely affects a document as described above, you can use Find and Replace to find instances of a period followed by two spaces and replace them with a period and only one space. It will make your document appear to be more professionally prepared.

Summary

This lesson consisted of two main parts—outlines and columns. You learned about hyphenation along the way. In this lesson you learned that:

- WordPerfect has a number of predefined outline formats.
- Outlines are easy to create and to edit.
- Outlines can be collapsed when you don't want all of the levels to show.
- When using text columns, you can fill one column and allow the text to snake to the next, or you can choose Balanced newspaper columns so the columns end evenly on the page.
- It is easy to adjust the sizes of the columns and the size of the gutter.
- Hyphenation helps fill the lines when they are too spacey.
- Soft hyphens can be inserted when you want control of where the hyphens will be located.
- You should space twice following punctuation at the end of a sentence unless you're working with narrow columns and Full justification, or when you're working in the printing and publishing industry.

LESSON 14 REVIEW QUESTIONS

MATCHING

Write the letter of the term or phrase from Column 2 that best matches the description in Column 1.

Column 1	Column 2
____ 1. First Level 2 item.	A. 1. Xxxxxxxxxxxxxxxxxxxxxxxxxx
____ 2. Third item at the first level.	B. 2. Xxxxxxxxxxxxxxxxxxxxxxxxxx
____ 3. First item at Level 1 of the outline.	C. a. Xxxxxxxxxxxxxxxxxx
____ 4. Second item at Level 3.	D. i. Xxxxxxxxxxxxxx
____ 5. Second item at the first level.	E. ii. Xxxxxxxxxxxxxx
	F. iii. Xxxxxxxxxxxxxx
	G. b. Xxxxxxxxxxxxxxxxxx
	H. 3. Xxxxxxxxxxxxxxxxxxxxxxxxxx

TRUE/FALSE

Circle the T if the statement is true. Circle the F if it is not.

T F   6. WordPerfect outlines can have as many as six levels, all numbered differently.

T F   7. When an item in an outline contains indented items, the entire numbered item in the outline is referred to as a community.

T F   8. On the Outline Tools Property Bar, the button that looks like a green book is used to display or hide level icons.

T F   9. Sometimes only a portion of a document should be formatted in columns.

T F   10. To discontinue a column, simply backspace to remove the final hard return.

LESSON 14 PROJECT

SCANS

PROJECT 14A

1. Open **wind** from the student **datafile** folder. Save the document as **wind proj14 xxx**.

2. Position the insertion point at the beginning of the second paragraph. Press Enter once to add a blank line between the first two paragraphs.

3. At the beginning of the second paragraph, tell WordPerfect you want two balanced newspaper columns.

4. Turn on Hyphenation and answer the questions about which words should be divided according to good word division rules.

5. Go to the beginning of the document and set a tab stop that changes the indent of the paragraphs from $^1/_2$" to $^1/_4$".

6. Open the Edit menu and choose Find and Replace. In the *Find* text box, key a period and two spaces. In the *Replace with* text box, key a period and one space.

7. Use Advance to move the first line of text 3" from the top of the page.

8. Insert a footer that puts the Path and Filename code at the bottom of the document. Format the footer with 8-pt. Arial.

9. Print your document and save it again as **wind proj14 xxx**. Close the document.

PROJECT 14B

1. Turn on Paragraph numbering and key the outline illustrated in Figure 14-8.

2. When you finish, check your work and end the outline.

3. With the insertion point at the top of the document, clear all tabs. Set tabs to be spaced evenly at 0.4".

4. Save the file as **nasa proj14a xxx**. Insert the Path and Filename code a double space below the last line of the outline.

5. Print the file.

6. Change to *Outline* style.

7. Move the *Anticorrosion paint* item so it is the second first-level item in the outline.

8. Collapse the outline to only two levels.

9. Save the document again as **nasa proj14b xxx**. Print it and close it.

FIGURE 14-8
Text for Project 14B

1. Environmental

    a. Improved methods for weather forecasting
    b. Water recycling

2. Medical

    a. Insulin infusion pump
    b. Vehicle controller for the handicapped
    c. Wheelchairs
        i. New materials to reduce weight
        ii. Mechanism for voice control
    d. Scratch-resistant glasses
    e. Speech autocuer for the hearing impaired
    f. Reading machine for the blind
    g. Laser heart surgery
    h. Flexible metal for dental braces

3. Breathing system for firefighters

4. Flame-resistant materials for mass-transit vehicles

5. Anticorrosion paint

6. Advanced turboprop

CRITICAL THINKING ACTIVITY

SCANS

You are proofreading a research paper for a friend and notice that several times in the document you come across a word in the middle of a line that has a hyphen inserted, such as circum-stance. You ask your friend why, and he doesn't know. What do you think caused this? How can he fix his document?

FORMS

LESSON 15

OBJECTIVES

Upon completion of this lesson, you will be able to:

- Use the Underline Tabs feature in creating forms.
- Divide your pages for creating documents smaller than the normal size.
- Construct forms using the Tables feature.
- Change the orientation of the page.

Estimated Time: 2½ hours

The preparation of forms is a part of the job that has caused headaches for many office workers. Some forms are prepared and completed all at once. Other forms are prepared for information to be filled in later by hand, by typewriter, or by the computer.

In this lesson you will learn several methods of preparing some sample forms. Pay close attention to the procedure so that when you need to prepare forms of your own, you'll have the necessary skills.

Forms with Tabs

Many forms used in the office consist of words asking for information and blanks where that information can be written in. To create forms using underlined blanks, set tab stops for the text within the form and tell WordPerfect to underline when you tab. The Underline Tabs feature is set in the Font dialog box. We'll begin with a little practice.

EXERCISE 15.1

1. In a new document window, check to see if your Ruler is displayed. If it isn't, open the **View** menu and choose **Ruler**. Clear all tabs.

2. Set a Left tab at **1¼"** and another at **4½"**. Press **Enter** twice. (You'll use this space later.)

(continued on next page)

EXERCISE 15.1 CONTINUED

3. Press **F9** or open the **Format** menu and choose **Font** to open the Font dialog box. In the lower right section of the Font dialog box, find *Underline*. Choose **Text & Tabs** and then click **OK**.

4. In your document window, key **Name**. Space once, turn on **Underline**, and press the **Tab** key. Turn **Underline** off and press **Enter** twice.

5. Key **Telephone**, space once, turn on **Underline**, and press the **Tab** key. Turn **Underline** off and press **Enter** twice.

6. Repeat the same procedure for the *Address* line and the *City, State ZIP* line. When you finish, your little form will look like Figure 15-1.

7. Save your practice as **intake 15-1 xxx**. Insert a footer containing the Path and Filename code.

8. Keep the document open.

FIGURE 15-1
Exercise 15.1 Sample Form

Name _____

Telephone _____

Address _____

City, State ZIP _____

The Underline Tabs code is positioned in the document at the location of the insertion point when the option is chosen. If you want this feature available for the entire document, your insertion point must be at the top of the document when you choose the feature.

Many forms contain check boxes. You learned to make check boxes when you learned about Symbols. Now you get to use some. Let's finish the form.

EXERCISE 15.2

1. With **intake 15-1 xxx** showing in the window, use **Save As** to save the form as **intake 15-2 xxx**.

2. Go to the top of the form and center **PATIENT INTAKE FORM** in bold, capital letters. Press **Enter** twice.

3. Press **Tab** twice (to the tab stop at $4^1/2"$) and key **COMPLAINTS:** in capital letters.

4. Go to the bottom of the form and complete the form, using the copy in Figure 15-2 for

FIGURE 15-2
Text for Exercise 15.2

Birth Date _____
    Male ☐   Female ☐
    Married ☐   Widowed ☐   Divorced ☐
Insurance Company _____
Policy Number _____
Time Admitted _____
Admitting Clerk _____
Blood Pressure _____
Pulse _____
Temperature _____

238   UNIT 4: SPECIAL LAYOUT FEATURES

the information. Double-space between all lines. For the indented sections:
a. Tab once, key **Male**, space once, press **Ctrl+W**, and insert check box **4,38**. Space three times and do **Female**.
b. Repeat the procedure for the *Married/ Widowed/Divorced* line.

5. Complete the form. Remember that you must turn **Underline** on and off for each line.

6. Check your work over carefully. Then save the form again as **intake 15-2 xxx**. Print it and close it.

Using Tab to insert the lines up to a tab stop when you've chosen to underline the tabs works well. When you wish to underline all the way to the right margin, however, a better method is to use Alt+F7 (Flush Right).

Also make it a habit of spacing once before and after each underline. If you don't put in those spaces, your form will look crowded and unfriendly. Let's create the form in Figure 15-3. This form contains the same information but is arranged in a half-page format.

EXERCISE 15.3

1. Beginning in a new document window, clear all tabs and set tabs at **1¼"** and **4½"**.

2. Set all four margins at **0.6"**.

3. Create the form in Figure 15-3, as follows:
   a. Double-space between all lines.
   b. Use **Tab** to insert the underlines that go to the middle of the page.
   c. Use **Alt+F7** to insert the underlines that extend to the right margin. (Remember that in each case, you must first turn Underline on and then turn it off after the line has been inserted.)
   d. Use WordPerfect symbol **4,38** for the check boxes.
   e. For the *Married/Widowed/Divorced* line, tab after the check box for *Female*. Then space once so all of the lines are aligned.

4. Complete the form. Check your work and save the form as **intake 15-3 xxx**.

5. With the insertion point at the top of the document, give it a footer that positions the Path and Filename code flush right. Format the footer with **8-pt. Arial**.

6. Zoom to **Full Page** to look at your form. How could you change the document so the footer is aligned with the rest of the text at the right? If you answered *Initial Codes Style*, you are right. Let's fix the footer margins. Zoom to **100%**.

7. Return to the top of the document. Open the **File** menu, choose **Document**, and then choose **Current Document Style**. In the Styles Editor, open the **Format** menu, choose **Margins**, and set all four margins at **0.6"**.

8. Return to your document window. Reveal your codes and move the insertion point all the way to the left at the top of the document. The [Open Style: DocumentStyle] code will show the margins, and the regular margin codes will be removed from the top of the document.

9. Save the file again as **intake 15-3 xxx**. Keep it open.

FIGURE 15-3
Text for Exercise 15.3

```
                        PATIENT INTAKE FORM
    Name _____      Date of Birth _____
    Telephone: Home _____      Work _____
    Address _____      City, State ZIP _____
           Male ☐   Female ☐           Married ☐  Widowed ☐  Divorced ☐
    Insurance Company _____      Policy Number _____
    Time Admitted _____      Blood Pressure _____
    Pulse _____      Temperature _____
    COMPLAINTS:
```

With this new arrangement of information, the form is obviously too large for a full sheet of paper. In fact, it would fit very well on a half sheet of paper. You could copy the text to the Windows Clipboard and paste it again on the same page. Then add spaces to push the two halves apart. If you do that, you'll only have the footer on one "page" of forms, and the two halves probably won't be equal. A better way is to use a feature called *Divide Page*.

Divide Page

The WordPerfect Divide Page feature enables you to divide a page into equal sections. You can divide a page by columns or rows. WordPerfect thinks of each section of the page as a *logical page*, while the actual sheet of paper is referred to as a *physical page*.

When you divide a page, you can use nearly any combination of columns and rows. In Exercise 15.4, you'll divide the page into two rows, which gives you the effect of two half pages, one over the other.

Usually when you use Divide Page, you will create your form or document in one of the pages. Then you will copy the form from the first logical page to the second, so that you will have two identical pages. After printing, all you need to do is go to the paper cutter and cut it in half for your two half-page forms.

EXERCISE 15.4

1. With **intake 15-3 xxx** showing in the window, use **Save As** to save the file as **intake 15-4 xxx**.

2. With the insertion point still at the top of the document, open the **Format** menu. Choose **Page** and then **Page Setup**. Click the **Divide Page** tab. The Divide Page dialog box will appear, looking like the section in Figure 15-4.

3. Change *Number of rows* to **2** and click **OK**.

4. Zoom to **Full Page** again to look at your document. Return to **100%**.

5. Open the **Edit** menu and choose **Select** and then **All**. (This is a good way to select the entire document as well as any codes at the beginning.)

6. Copy the selected text to the Clipboard. Press **Ctrl+End** to get to the bottom of the document and **Ctrl+Enter** to go to the next page.

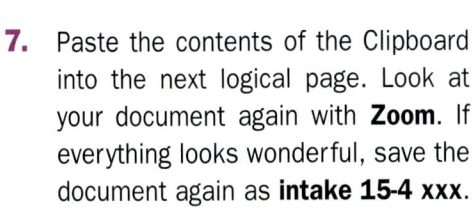

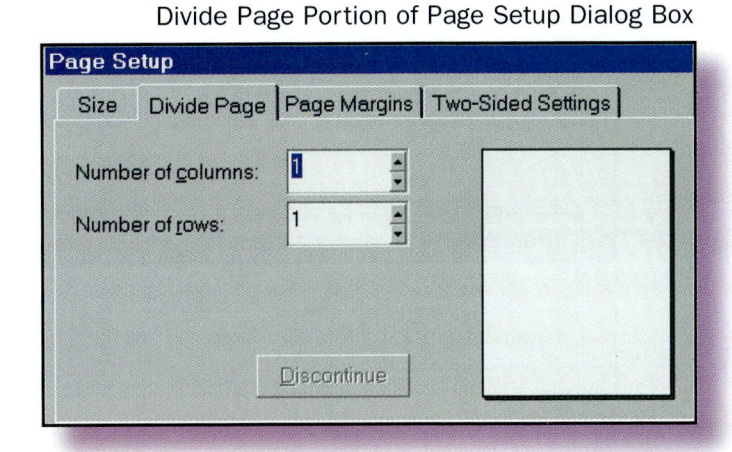

7. Paste the contents of the Clipboard into the next logical page. Look at your document again with **Zoom**. If everything looks wonderful, save the document again as **intake 15-4 xxx**.

8. Print your file and close it.

FIGURE 15-4
Divide Page Portion of Page Setup Dialog Box

As you saw when you looked at the physical page after pasting the form from one logical page to the next, both pages were formatted with margins and the footer. Using Divide Page is a clean way of reproducing a document when you want an exact duplicate.

Now let's learn another way to create forms.

Forms with Tables

After your work in Lesson 13 with the Tables feature, it should be no surprise to you that forms can be created with Tables. Study Figure 15-6. This is the shortened version of a form made up of two tables—one directly above the other. In Exercise 15.5 you will create a similar form. Follow along carefully.

EXERCISE 15.5

1. Create a table consisting of 2 columns and 4 rows. Join the cells in the first row and center **DAILY TIME SHEET** in bold, capital letters.

2. Join the cells in Row 2 and key **Employee:** at the left.

3. Adjust the location of the line separating the columns for Rows 3 and 4 and fill in the information shown in Figure 15-5 for those rows.

4. With the insertion point in the top row, go to **Borders/Fill** and set Left, Right, and Top lines at **X**.

5. Select Rows 2, 3, and 4. Set Left, Right, and Top lines at **Double** (just to the right of *X*). Set Bottom at **X**. When you finish, your table should look like Figure 15-5.

(continued on next page)

241

EXERCISE 15.5 CONTINUED

FIGURE 15-5
Top of Time Sheet Form

DAILY TIME SHEET	
Employee:	
Department:	Date:
Company:	Total Hours:

6. Press **Ctrl+End** to move your insertion point out of the table. Create a new table with 7 columns and 3 rows.

7. In Row 1 of the new table key **Job No.**, **Kind of Work**, and **Hours**, as shown in Figure 15-6. Join cells C1 and D1 and key **Began**. Join Cells E1 and F1 and key **Finished**. Select the row and set **Center** alignment.

8. Working in the order listed, size the columns as follows. (Do not change the side margins of the table.)

   a. Job No. = **0.75"**
   b. Hours = **0.75"**
   c. Column F in Row 2 = **0.5"**
   d. Column E in Row 2 = **0.5"**
   e. Column D in Row 2 = **0.5"**
   f. Column C in Row 2 = **0.5"**

9. Save your evolving table as **time 15-5 xxx**. Insert the Path and Filename code in a footer, formatted with **8-pt. Arial** and positioned at the right. Save the file again and keep it open.

FIGURE 15-6
Time Sheet Form

DAILY TIME SHEET					
Employee:					
Department:			Date:		
Company:			Total Hours:		
Job No.	Kind of Work		Began	Finished	Hours

Instructions: Enter the type of work on each job, listing the exact time you started and finished that job. List "Miscellaneous" for time not billable.

Just a note of explanation is necessary about Step 5 of Exercise 15.5. You set the bottom line of the first table at None. If you don't do this when you use two tables to look like one table, the lines from the bottom of the first table and the lines from the top of the second table pile on top of each other to make an unusually dark line show when you print your form. It looks patched.

Your form is coming along nicely. Now let's finish it up and make it fill the page.

EXERCISE 15.6

1. With **time 15-5 xxx** in the window, save it as **time 15-6 xxx**.

2. Select all three rows of the new table. Go to **Borders/Fill** and set the Left, Right, Top, and Bottom lines at **Double**.

3. Position the insertion point in Cell G3 and press **Tab** to add a new row.

4. Select the cells in the new row and join them. Then, with the insertion point in the new row, go to **Borders/Fill** and set the Outside lines at **X**. Key the text at the bottom of the table in Figure 15-6.

5. Position the insertion point in either Row 2 or 3 of the second table. Right click to display the QuickMenu and choose **Insert**. Insert 18 rows into your table. It should now fill the page.

6. Check your work carefully. If everything looks good, save it as **time 15-6 xxx**. Print it and close it.

Now that we've created forms for a medical job and a piecework job, let's create an invoice for a law office. We'll use the Tables feature for the invoice.

EXERCISE 15.7

SCANS

1. Prepare the document in Figure 15-7 as an invoice for work performed by Manuel Tovar, Attorney at Law.

2. Format the top of the invoice using your choice of fonts and arrangement of information. Figure 15-7 provides the information and a suggested layout.

3. Create a table consisting of 5 columns. Within the standard margins, size all of the columns except the *Description* column at **0.75"**.

4. Format the column headings as follows:
   a. Use Bold.
   b. Align the text at the bottom.
   c. Put a double line below the column headings.
   d. Set the rest of the lines around and between the headings at **X**.

5. Key the information into the table as shown. (You don't need to key the dollar signs.)

6. Format the columns as follows:
   a. Select the five cells containing the number of hours and set **Center** alignment.
   b. Select Cells D2 through E6. Set Numeric Format at **Currency** and set **Decimal Align**.
   c. Select Cells E7 through E9. Set Numeric Format at **Currency** and set **Decimal Align**.

(continued on next page)

243

EXERCISE 15.7 CONTINUED

7. In Row 7, join cells A7 through D7. Do the same for Row 8. Set Alignment for the joined cells in all three rows at **Right**.

8. Check your work for accuracy. If everything looks OK, save the file as **estate 15-7 xxx**. Keep it open.

FIGURE 15-7
Text for Exercise 15.7

MANUEL TOVAR
Attorney at Law
123 Main Street
Victoria, NJ 08344

INVOICE

(Current Date)   Billing Period: June 1, 199x to July 1, 199x

Mr. & Mrs. Homer Corretja
Box 44
Victoria, NJ 08344

Date	Description	Hours	Per Hour	Total
6/1/9x	Introductory meeting with Mr. & Mrs. Corretja	2	$95.00	
6/4/9x	Planning meeting with Mr. & Mrs. Corretja	1.5	$95.00	
6/13/9x	Library research on tax laws	1.75	$80.00	
6/18/9x	Meeting with Mr. & Mrs. Corretja	1.5	$95.00	
6/22/9x	Will signing session	.5	$95.00	
			Total Fees	
			State Tax at 5%	
			Total Charges	

Your invoice is complete except for the formulas and the calculations. Let's finish it up.

EXERCISE 15.8

1. With **estate 15-7 xxx** open in your window, save the file as **estate 15-8 xxx**.

2. Display your Formula Toolbar. In Cell E2 enter a formula that multiplies **C2*D2**. Copy the formula down four times.

3. Complete the calculations as follows:
   a. Use **QuickSum** in Cell E7 to add the numbers above the cell.
   b. In Cell E8 multiply **E7*0.05** to compute the 5% tax.
   c. In Cell E9 add **E7+E8**. The total should be $695.63.

4. Adjust the lines in the table as follows:
   a. Select everything below the double line beneath the column headings. Set all Inside lines at **X**. Set Left, Right, and Bottom lines at **X**.
   b. Select Cell E6. Set the Bottom line at **Single**.
   c. Select Cell E8. Set the Bottom line at **Single**.
   d. Select Cell E9. Set the Bottom line at **Double**.

5. Give the document a footer containing the Path and Filename code. Print the document and save it again as **estate 15-8 xxx**. Close the file.

Organizational Charts

One of the toughest pen and pencil jobs in the days prior to good word processing programs was the preparation of organizational charts. The job still takes some time but, using WordPerfect tables, it is much easier and the results are more gratifying.

Whether or not you use organizational charts, the skill used for this application can be transferred to other applications. We'll prepare a sample organizational chart to get the idea of how it works.

Figure 15-8 illustrates where the organizational chart will begin, although your table will be wider than the figure. It is simply a 5 x 4 table. The first thing you'll do is size the columns. In this example you'll be given the figures to use. If you were preparing the job on your own, you'd have to do a little mathematics before beginning. The chart in Figure 15-8 has three boxes across that contain text. Each box will be 2" wide. On a $6^1/_2$" line, that leaves $^1/_2$" to be divided for the space between the boxes. Follow along carefully.

EXERCISE 15.9

1. In a new document window, create a 5 x 4 table. Size the columns as follows:
   a. Drag the line between Columns A and B to the right so Column A is 2" wide.
   b. Drag the line between Columns B and C so Column B is 0.25" wide.
   c. Make Column C 2" wide.
   d. Make Column D 0.25" wide.
   e. Column E should be 2" wide.

2. Key the text illustrated in Figure 15-8 into your table. If you'd like, you can substitute your name and names of your friends in the table. Are you the boss?

(continued on next page)

EXERCISE 15.9 CONTINUED

3. Display the Tables QuickMenu and choose **Format**. Select the **Table** tab and set Alignment at **Center**.

4. Save the interim table as **boss 15-9 xxx**. Then give the document a footer that contains the Path and Filename code and save the file again.

FIGURE 15-8
Beginning of Organizational Chart

	Top Level Big Boss	
Second Level Boss 1	Second Level Boss 2	Second Level Boss 3

Now that the basic table is created, let's work with the lines. We'll make the lines for the organizational chart double lines and remove all of the remaining lines. When you finish, your chart will look like Figure 15-10.

EXERCISE 15.10

1. Save **boss 15-9 xxx** as **boss 15-10 xxx**. Position the insertion point in the first cell containing text.

2. Go to the Borders/Fill dialog box and set Outside lines at **Double**. Do the same for each of the other cells containing text.

3. Position the insertion point in the cell above *Boss 1*. Use the **QuickSplit Columns** button to split the cell into 2 equal columns.

4. Split the following cells:
   a. Above Boss 2.
   b. Above Boss 3.
   c. Below Big Boss.

5. Select the four-cell square between the Big Boss and Boss 2.

6. Change all Inside lines to **Double**.

7. Continue selecting cells and changing lines to **Double** until your chart looks like Figure 15-9.

8. Select blocks of cells and set all remaining lines at **X**. If you make a mistake, click the **Undo** button and redo it so the lines finally look like those in Figure 15-10.

FIGURE 15-9
Carved Out Organizational Chart

UNIT 4: SPECIAL LAYOUT FEATURES

9. Select all of Rows 2 and 3. Go to the Format dialog box. Choose the **Row** tab and set Row Height at **Fixed**. Change the amount to **0.15"** so the space between the boxes used isn't so great.

FIGURE 15-10
Final Organizational Chart

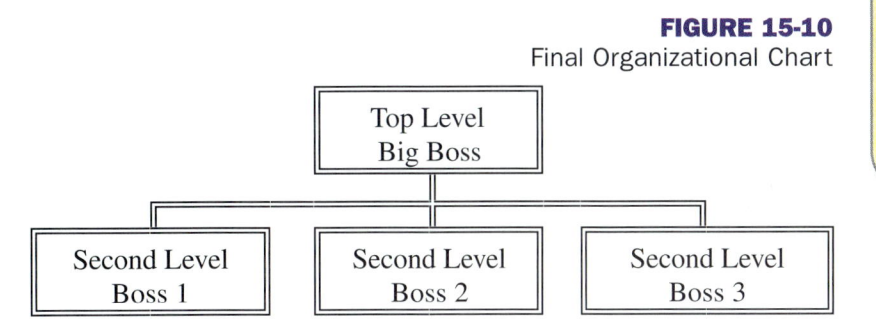

10. Save your final organizational chart again as **boss 15-10 xxx**. Print the file and close it.

FIGURE 15-11
Sample with Crooked Line

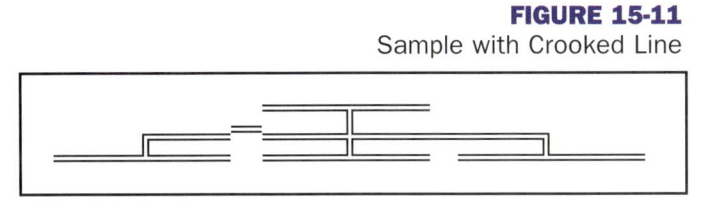

In an application like the one you just completed, sometimes your lines don't line up. A frustrating jag appears where the lines should be straight. Look at Figure 15-11. It is a sample taken from the table you just completed that illustrates the kind of trouble you can get into when you are formatting table lines.

The raised line that makes the joining line look crooked was applied to the *bottom of the top cell*. The other lines were applied to the *top of the bottom cells*. Obviously, when something like this happens, you know enough about tables and lines that you can go back and fix the problem. Practice with formatting lines will help you in situations such as this.

In WordPerfect tables not all lines are equal. When you have a choice regarding the formatting of the lines between two cells that are above one another, you'll usually be better off formatting the top of the lower cell rather than the bottom of the upper cell. Does that make sense? Practice, practice, practice will make you good at tables!

Orientation

M any times a document doesn't fit on the page in the normal manner—with the 8½-inch sides at the top and bottom and the 11-inch sides at the left and right. That normal orientation of the page is called *portrait* orientation.

WordPerfect makes it possible for you to turn the page so the long edges are at the top and bottom and the short edges are at the sides. This arrangement is called *landscape* orientation. WordPerfect can direct most printers to print using landscape orientation. Figures 15-12 and 15-13 illustrate a page in landscape and portrait orientation. Both are divided in two rows and two columns.

FIGURE 15-12
Landscape Orientation Page Divided in Two Columns and Two Rows

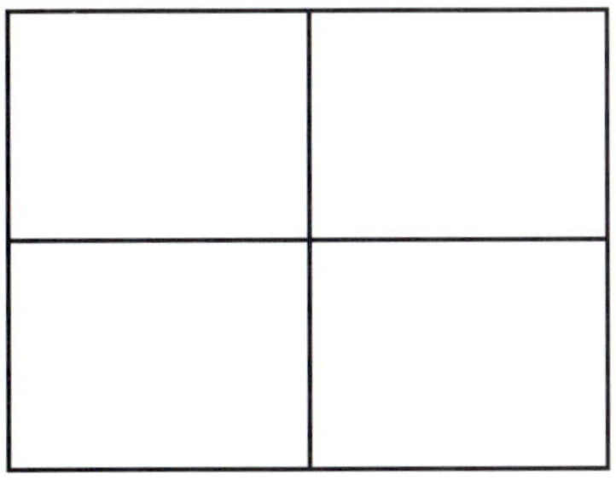

FIGURE 15-13
Portrait Orientation Page Divided in Two Columns and Two Rows

247

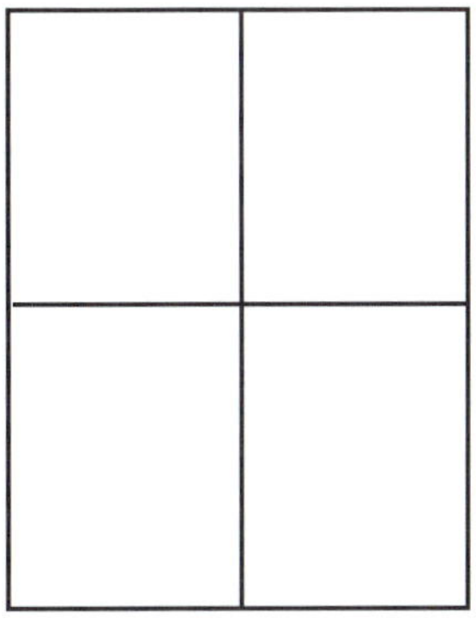

Landscape orientation can be used for any number of applications. Let's use it to create a large table form.

EXERCISE 15.11

1. Beginning in a new document window, open the **Format** menu and choose **Page**. Then choose **Page Setup**. Click the **Size** tab. The Size portion of the Page Setup dialog box will look like Figure 15-14.

2. With the **Portrait** button selected, look at the available sizes of paper and the orientations listed.

3. Choose **Landscape** and look at the view of the orientation at the right. Then click **OK**.

FIGURE 15-14
Size Portion of Page Setup Dialog Box

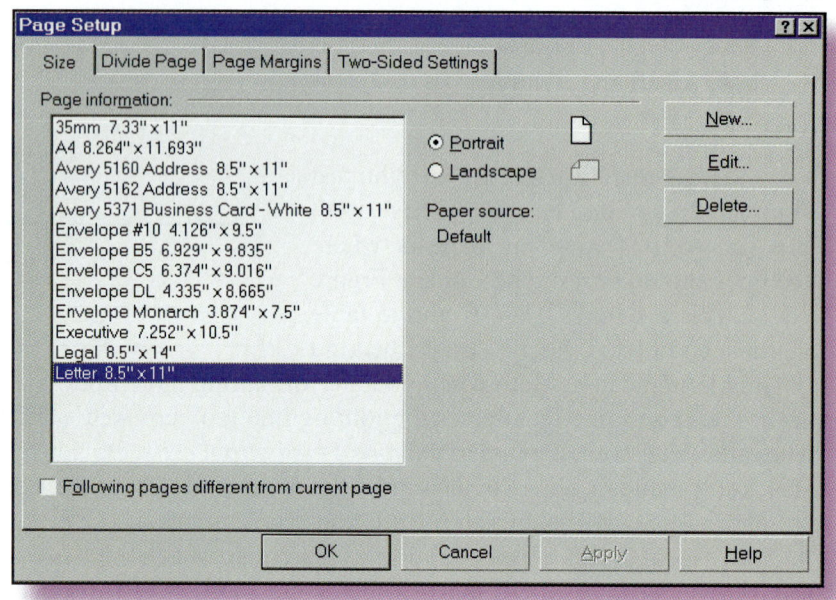

4. Back in your document window, zoom to **Full Page** so you can see the entire page. Zoom to **75%** so you can see most of the page.

5. Create the beginning of an organizational chart—just enough so it looks like Figure 15-8—with six bosses at the second level. Here's a start:
   a. Create a table that's 11 columns by 4 rows.
   b. Join Cells E1, F1, and G1 for the Top Level Boss.
   c. Size the odd columns—those which contain text—at about **1.3"** wide.
   d. Size the columns between the cells containing text at about **0.3"** wide.
   e. Set the entire table for **Center** alignment.

6. Spend no more than 10 minutes on this project. It is just practice.

7. Save the practice table as **landscape 15-11 xxx**. Insert the Path and Filename code a double space below the table.

8. Print the practice table and close it, saving it again as you close it.

248 UNIT 4: SPECIAL LAYOUT FEATURES

When you were in the Size portion of the Page Setup dialog box, you probably noticed that WordPerfect enables you to work with paper in a variety of sizes—nearly all of the sizes commonly available on the market today. Changing the orientation or size of the page doesn't change the other WordPerfect defaults. For example, when you choose Legal or Legal Landscape, the default margins will still be one inch and the tabs will be set at each half inch.

This was just a quick introduction to working with landscape orientation. You'll have another opportunity to use that tool in the project at the end of the lesson.

Summary

You created a number of forms in this lesson. All were sample forms designed to give you the skills needed to create your own forms when the need arises. In this lesson you learned that:

- You can tell WordPerfect to underline the space from one tab stop to another so your lines begin and end at a given location.

- The physical page can be divided into a number of logical pages for forms of different sizes.

- Tables is an ideal tool for the creation of forms.

- You have choices with regard to the size of paper you use for your documents and which way the text is printed on the page.

LESSON 15 REVIEW QUESTIONS

FILL IN THE BLANKS

Complete each of the following statements by writing your answer in the blank provided.

1. The Underline Tabs feature is set in the _____ dialog box.

2. The WordPerfect _____ feature enables you to divide a page into equal sections.

3. WordPerfect thinks of each section of a divided page as a _____ page.

4. When you arrange a page so that the long edges are at the top and bottom, this arrangement is called _____ orientation.

5. The best tool to use to create forms is the _____ feature.

WRITTEN QUESTIONS

List at least five features used to create the form shown on page 250 in Figure 15-15, Form for Lesson 15 Project.

LESSON 15 PROJECT

Create a quarter-page phone message form.

1. Open the Format menu and choose Page, Page Setup, and Size. Choose Letter Landscape.

2. Open the Format menu again. Choose Page, Page Setup, and Divide Page. Choose 2 columns and 2 rows for the quarter-page look.

3. Zoom to Full Page to look at the layout on the page. Then return to the normal view.

4. Go to Current Document Style and change all four margins to 0.3".

5. Save your form as **message proj15 xxx**.

6. Create a table consisting of 2 columns and 12 rows. The table will not all fit on one page. Select the entire table. Open the Table Format dialog box, choose Row, and set Row Height at Fixed. Change the row height to 0.3" to make the table fit on the quarter page.

7. Look at Figure 15-15. See how quickly you can duplicate this form in your window following these suggestions:
   a. Use a 10-pt. sans serif font for the text.
   b. Join cells where necessary. In the first row the cell containing *Urgent* was created using the QuickSplit Column feature. Notice the different line style around this cell.
   c. Use symbol 4,38 for the check boxes.

8. After *Signed:* in the last row, use Flush Right for the Path and Filename code. Format it with an 8-pt. font size.

9. For an added touch, use reverse video for the *WHILE YOU WERE OUT* cell. Follow these steps:
   a. Select the row and choose Borders/Fill.
   b. Choose the last fill pattern in the second row of patterns. It is black. Close the dialog box.
   c. While the row is still selected (it now looks white and the type doesn't show at all), open the Font dialog box and choose *Text Color* near the top. In the color palette that appears, choose the white square.

FIGURE 15-15
Form for Lesson 15 Project

UNIT 4: SPECIAL LAYOUT FEATURES

      d. In the *Appearance* section at the top, choose Bold.

      e. Return to the form and deselect the row.

10. When your form is beautiful, open the Edit menu and choose Select All. Press Ctrl+C to copy the form to the Clipboard.

11. Position the insertion point in the next logical page (the next quarter page) and press Ctrl+V to paste the form into that quarter.

12. Repeat Step 11 until the form is in all four quarters of the landscape page. (You may zoom to Full Page to see your page as you complete this step.)

13. Check your work over carefully. When it is perfect, save it again as **message proj15 xxx**, print it, and close it.

CRITICAL THINKING ACTIVITY

SCANS

    A form has been given to you that was created by joining two tables. The first table contains the heading, and the rest of the form has been formatted into the second table. The printed form looks patched with an unusually dark line below the heading. What is causing this problem and how do you fix it?

251

LESSON 16

MACROS

OBJECTIVES

Upon completion of this lesson, you will be able to:

- Set preferences.
- Record a macro.
- Play a macro.
- Edit a macro.
- Add a pause to a macro.
- Discuss miscellaneous information about macros.

Estimated Time: 2 hours

In most jobs there are some sets of keystrokes that are repetitive. You key the same thing over and over and wish for some way to streamline the task. WordPerfect provides you with such a feature. You can create what's known as a *macro* to save a series of keystrokes. Then you can play that macro whenever needed to repeat the keystrokes.

WordPerfect macros may be used to save frequently used phrases, paragraphs, or complicated formats. Before you begin this section on macros, you need to set WordPerfect so it can find macros you save on your data disk in Drive A. This setting may have already been made by a previous student. If so, you'll simply check to make sure it has been made. Then we'll learn how to record and play macros.

Settings

In Appendix B you learned that most of the WordPerfect default settings work well, but that they can be changed, if necessary. Working with macros is one of those times, if you are learning in a classroom. The default setting is for macros to be saved in the **Macros** folder.

If you were on the job, had your own computer for your work, and didn't have to share the computer with anyone else, you wouldn't make any changes to the location of your macros. They would automatically be saved along with the WordPerfect system macros in the **Macros** folder.

As a student, however, you want your macros available wherever you are doing your work. If you are saving your work on a diskette in Drive A, your macros should be saved on Drive A. In Exercise 16.1 it will be assumed the macros are to be saved on Drive A. You will be setting that location as the supplemental location for your macros.

EXERCISE 16.1

1. Open the **Tools** menu and choose **Settings**. The dialog box illustrated in Figure 16-1 will appear.

2. Point to **Files** and double click to open the Files Settings dialog box. Click the **Merge/Macro** tab to display the settings for macros and merge (see Figure 16-2).

3. Look at *Supplemental macro folder*. It should say *a:*. If it doesn't, key that information in that text box.

4. When your dialog box is set to look like Figure 16-2, click **OK** to close the dialog box and return to your document window.

FIGURE 16-1
Settings Dialog Box

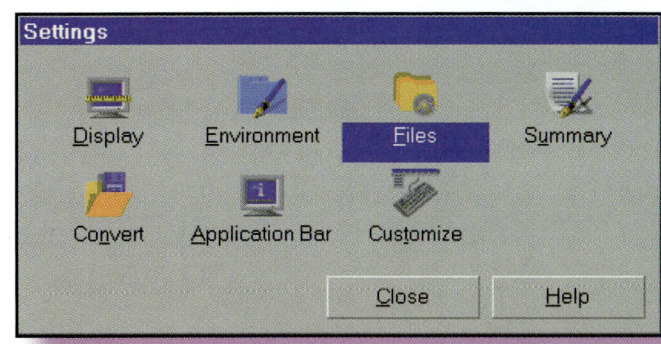

FIGURE 16-2
Files Settings Dialog Box

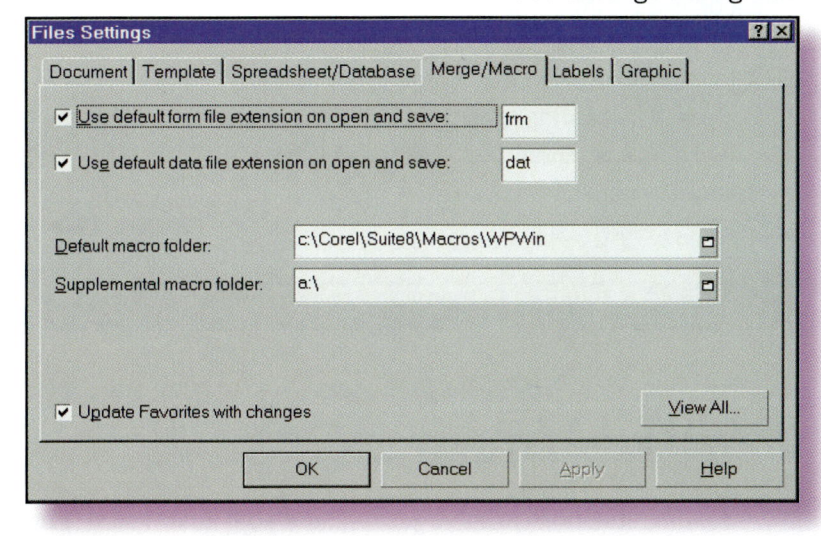

If you have any problem with Exercise 16-1, be sure to have your instructor help you. It is important that these settings be correct. Otherwise, either your macros will be mixed up with those of other students, or WordPerfect won't even be able to find your macros after you record them. When you create your macros, you will send them automatically to the disk in Drive A by including *a:* at the beginning of each macro.

Record a Macro

Assume that you work for a company named Cranberry Creations, and your boss, Francine Berry, likes the company name in the closing lines. You can speed up the preparation of your letters by creating a macro that contains the entire closing of the letters. Let's create the closing macro.

253

EXERCISE 16.2

1. Beginning in a new document window, open the **Tools** menu and choose **Macro**.

2. Click **Record**. The Record Macro dialog box should open, looking much like your Open File dialog box.

3. Key **a:\close** as the name of your macro and press **Enter**. Move your mouse. The pointer should look like a circle with a line through it.

4. Look at the Macro Feature Bar that is showing just below the Property Bar or Ruler. It should look like Figure 16-3.

5. Key the information in Figure 16-4. Double-space between the closing and the company name. Press **Enter** five times following the company name.

6. Press **Enter** twice at the end of the macro so the insertion point is in position for the instances where you need to add an Enclosure notation.

7. When you finish, open the **Tools** menu and choose **Macro**. Deselect **Record** to end the recording of the macro.

8. Close the document window without saving the document.

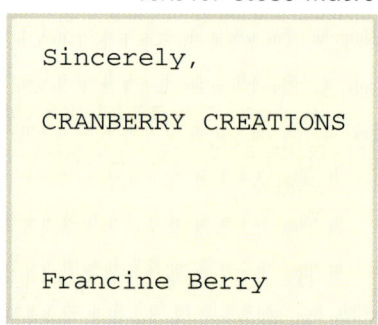

FIGURE 16-3
Macro Feature Bar

FIGURE 16-4
Text for **Close** Macro

```
Sincerely,

CRANBERRY CREATIONS




Francine Berry
```

Play a Macro

Congratulations. You've just created your first macro. Let's play the macro. To play it, you can use one of the following methods:

- Open the Tools menu, choose Macro, and then choose Play. Key the name of the macro—in this case, **close**.

- Open the Tools menu, choose Macro, and then choose Play. Locate the macro on disk and double click the name. (This involves clicking the Favorites button and identifying $3^1/_2$ *Floppy (A:)*.)

- Press Alt+F10 and key **close**.

When working with a Windows word processing program, it is normally more natural to use the mouse and the menu system for accessing features. In a case like this, if you know the name of the macro, you will probably choose either the first or third method listed above—and the third one is obviously fastest. We'll play the macro using all three methods. Then you can decide which you prefer.

254   UNIT 4: SPECIAL LAYOUT FEATURES

EXERCISE 16.3

1. Beginning in a new document window, open the **Tools** menu, choose **Macro**, and then choose **Play**.

2. In the Play Macro dialog box, locate *3½ Floppy (A:)* and then locate the **close** macro. Either click the macro name once and click **Play**, or double click the macro name.

3. Look at the results of the macro in your window. Close the document without saving.

4. Open the **Tools** menu, choose **Macro**, and then choose **Play**. Key **close** and press **Enter**.

5. Look at the results of the macro in your window. Close the document without saving.

6. Press **Alt+F10** and key **close**. Look at the results of the macro in your window. Close the document without saving.

As you can see, playing this little macro is easy. The same is true of all macros, regardless of the length or complexity of the macro. Let's create another macro that you can use frequently as you progress through your learning. Then we'll prepare a document that will use both macros.

EXERCISE 16.4

1. Beginning in a new document window, open **pcug** from the student **datafile** folder. (The document is totally unrelated to the exercise. You just need a document in the window that has a name so you can see your macro as it is prepared.)

2. With the insertion point at the top of the page, open the **Tools** menu, choose **Macro**, and choose **Record**.

3. Key **a:\pf** for the name of the macro and press **Enter** to begin the recording.

4. Give your document a footer that contains the Path and Filename code. Format the footer with **8-pt. Arial**. Close the Footer Property Bar.

5. Open the **Tools** menu, choose **Macro**, and deselect **Record**.

6. Use the scroll bar to go to the bottom of the document. Check to see if the footer is in place and looks like you expect it to look.

7. Close the document without saving it.

Now let's prepare a short letter and use the **close** macro for the closing and the **pf** macro for the Path and Filename code at the bottom.

EXERCISE 16.5

1. Beginning in a new document window, use the **Center Page(s)** command to vertically center the current page. (Remember? It's Format, Page, Center.)

2. Use **Date Text** to insert the date at the left margin. Press **Enter** four times.

3. Key the mailing address and greeting illustrated in Figure 16-5. When you finish, press **Enter** twice and insert **berry** from the student **datafile** folder. (Remember? It's Insert, File, and then identify the filepath and file.)

4. At the end of the letter, position the insertion point a double space below the last paragraph, and use one of the methods you practiced in Exercise 16.3 to play the **close** macro.

5. With your insertion point at the bottom of the letter, key **Enclosures**.

6. Save your document as **berry 16-5 xxx**. Return the insertion point to the top of the document and play your **pf** macro to put the Path and Filename code in a footer.

7. Prepare an envelope to go with your letter. (Remember? It's Format, Envelope.) Check your work over carefully. Then print both the letter and the envelope.

8. Close the document, saving it again when you close.

FIGURE 16-5
Opening LInes for Exercise 16.5

```
Mr. Joseph Anderson
776 Fourth Street
Blythedale, MD 21903-1918

Dear Mr. Anderson:
```

Edit a Macro

After you got the letter and envelope printed, your boss informed you that she has changed the name of her company to Franberry Creations and that she doesn't need so much room to sign her name. You know that you could recreate the macro incorporating the changes. Macros can be edited, however, so you decide to edit the **close** macro.

EXERCISE 16.6

1. Click the **Open** button on the Toolbar. Go to your disk and open **close** as a regular document. It will look like Figure 16-6.

2. Look at the format of the macro. Anything that is keyed is identified with the word *Type* and then *Text*. The text is enclosed in parentheses, and the actual words have quotation marks around them. Note that the Hard Return codes also are followed by parentheses.

3. Change *CRANBERRY* to **FRANBERRY**.

4. Delete one of the *HardReturn()* lines between the company name and Ms. Berry's name.

256

UNIT 4: SPECIAL LAYOUT FEATURES

5. Click the **Save & Compile** button on the Macro Feature Bar. (WordPerfect will check to make certain everything in the macro is in order.)

6. Click the **Options** button on the Macro Feature Bar and choose **Close Macro**.

7. In a new WordPerfect window, test your revised macro. If it looks good, close the document and read on. If it has a problem, fix that problem before continuing.

FIGURE 16-6
Close Macro in Editing Window

```
Application (WordPerfect;
"WordPerfect"; Default; "EN")
Type (Text: "Sincerely,")
HardReturn ()
HardReturn ()
Type (Text: "CRANBERRY CREATIONS")
HardReturn ()
HardReturn ()
HardReturn ()
HardReturn ()
HardReturn ()
Type (Text: "Francine Berry")
HardReturn ()
HardReturn ()
```

If you know the macro language, macros are easy to edit. If you don't know the macro language, you can delete items from a macro with ease. Adding them is more difficult. In those cases, you might want to create a small macro that contains the new commands to be added and then copy them to the old macro. In other situations, you may choose to completely redo the macro.

Macro with Pause

You can set up a macro to stop for you to enter information. Then it will continue again. We'll use a fax cover sheet as an example of how you might do this with a macro. Later in your training you'll learn another way to create this same kind of cover sheet.

As you create this macro, note that you don't have full use of the mouse for selecting text and moving the insertion point. You must use the keyboard for these tasks. Work carefully and thoughtfully when you create macros. Remember that the recorder is on, recording all of your actions!

EXERCISE 16.7

1. Beginning in a new document window, create a macro named **a:\fran fax**. Key the beginning of the macro using the information in Figures 16-7 and 16-8. Stop when you come to the *To:* line. Note the following things about the form:
   a. The phone numbers are on the same line as the first two lines of the return address—positioned with **Flush Right**.
   b. Switch to **20 pt.** for the words *FAX TRANSMITTAL*. Switch back to **12 pt.** following the words.

2. Key **Date:** followed by two spaces with the space bar. Press **Ctrl+Shift+D** to insert the date code. Press **Enter** twice.

3. Key **To:** as illustrated in Figure 16-8. Press the space bar twice and click the **Pause** button on the Macro Feature Bar. Click the **Pause** button again. (To pause and restart the recording of the macro, you must always click the Pause button twice.)

(continued on next page)

EXERCISE 16.7 CONTINUED

FIGURE 16-7
Beginning of Form for **fran fax** Macro

FRANBERRY CREATIONS   Phone: 814-555-4545
123 Sixth Street   Fax: 814-555-4343
Cranberry Ridge, PA 18201

FAX TRANSMITTAL

4. Follow the same procedure to enter the information in Figure 16-8 for the rest of the macro.
   a. Space twice after each colon and add a Pause code.
   b. Press **Enter** twice between each of the lines and at the end.

5. When you finish, look your work over and make any necessary corrections. Open the **Tools** menu, choose **Macro**, and deselect **Record**.

6. Close the document window in which you were working. Do not save the document. (It has already been saved as a macro.)

FIGURE 16-8
Section of **fran fax** Macro with Pause Codes

```
Date:

To:

At Fax Number:

From:

At Fax Number:

Number of pages (including this
page):
```

Now that the fax form is created, you need to send some information to Joseph Anderson in Blythedale about the craft workshop Francine is attending. Use your fax form to transmit the information.

EXERCISE 16.8

1. Start the **fran fax** macro. The date should be entered automatically.

2. Key **Joseph Anderson** in the *To:* location. Press **Enter**. Key Mr. Anderson's fax number, **301-555-9811**, and press **Enter**.

3. Can you decide what goes in the next two blanks? The number of pages (including the cover sheet) should be **4**.

FIGURE 16-9
Note for Fax Cover Sheet

```
Here is the setup information
you wanted for my booth at the
craft workshop.  If you have
any questions, please let me
know.

F. Berry
```

258

UNIT 4: SPECIAL LAYOUT FEATURES

4. After the macro is finished, key the brief note a double space below the *Number of pages* line. The text for the note is in Figure 16-9.

5. Check the transmittal sheet over carefully. If everything looks good, save it as **fax 16-8 xxx**. Then play your **pf** macro. Print the document

Information about Macros

Following are some important things you should know about macros:

- The WordPerfect macro language is a type of programming language. The first time you play a macro, it takes a little longer because WordPerfect has to *compile,* or check, the macro for programming errors. If you have an error, a warning box will appear, telling you which line of the macro to check for an error.

- Programming commands such as CHAIN, LABEL, IF, NEXT, and ENDIF are included in the WordPerfect macro language. These commands enable you to record powerful macros that can take care of just about any circumstance in your work.

- You may *chain* a macro to the end of a different macro to combine them and save more time. The chained macro plays as soon as the original macro finishes.

- WordPerfect automatically applies the *.wcm* extension to your macro names.

- When you are recording a macro, the words *Macro Record* appear on your Application Bar.

- Macros from WordPerfect 6.1 and 7 do not need to be converted to run in WordPerfect 8. A few commands, however, function differently in WordPerfect 8. You can get information about those commands in the macros portion of Help.

- A number of macros come with the WordPerfect program. The **Checkbox** macro, for example, inserts a box into which you can add an *X* by simply clicking the box. You may explore the **Macros** folder at your leisure.

- If you make a mistake when creating a macro, you may redo or edit it. If you redo it, WordPerfect will display a warning box telling you that a macro already is saved with that name and asking if you would like to record over the top of the existing macro.

- You can map your keyboards, assigning specific tasks to key combinations. A macro can be assigned to a key combination.

- A macro can be added as a button on the Toolbar or the Property Bar.

Summary

This lesson introduces you to macros. Macros are wonderful, but you must remember to create them and use them. Whenever you find yourself doing something repetitive, that might be a time for you to record a macro and put it to work for you. You can do it because in this lesson you learned that:

- You can set the location where WordPerfect looks to find macros.

- Macros can be named just like you name your regular files.

- Macros automatically get a *.wcm* extension.

- Macros can be played as many times as needed.
- Macros can be edited.

You learned how to create some simple macros. If you really get into the macro language, you can create macros that will do wonderful things in helping you with your work.

LESSON 16 REVIEW QUESTIONS

TRUE/FALSE

Circle the T if the statement is true. Circle the F if it is false.

(T) F 1. The WordPerfect macro language is a type of programming language.

T **(F)** 2. If you have an error in your macro, the first time you play the macro your screen will remain blank until you correct the error.

T **(F)** 3. Link is the term used to connect a macro to the end of a different macro.

(T) F 4. WordPerfect automatically applies the .wcm extension to macro names.

(T) F 5. When you are recording a macro, the words Macro Record appear on your Property Bar.

T **(F)** 6. Macros from WordPerfect 6.1 and WordPerfect 7 must be converted to run in WordPerfect 8.

T **(F)** 7. There is a Macro button on the default Property Bar.

WRITTEN QUESTIONS

Write your answers to the following questions.

8. Why would you want to create a macro? *To save time & resources when drafting repetitive text in documents.*

9. From which menu do you choose Macro? *Tools Menu*

10. If you edit your macro, what must you do before you close the macro? *click on "save & compile"*

LESSON 16 PROJECT

SCANS

In the world of business, many letters consist of more than one page. A second-page heading is necessary to give continuity to the pages and to make sure they are assembled in the correct order. Let's record a macro that can be used to automatically supply the correct information at the top of all of the pages of a letter except the first page. We'll work with the short letter you created in this lesson, since it's easier to create the macro with a letter open.

PROJECT 16A

1. Open **berry 16-5 xxx**. Position the insertion point at the end of the word *Enclosures* and press Ctrl+Enter to add a new page.

2. Return your insertion point to the beginning of Mr. Anderson's name in the mailing address.

3. Create a macro named **a:\header hor** (for *horizontal*). Follow these steps to record your macro:
   a. Press F8 to turn on Select. Press End to move the insertion point to the end of the line. (You have selected the name of the recipient.)
   b. Press Ctrl+C to copy the selected text to the Clipboard.
   c. If the text is still selected, press F8 again to turn Select off.
   d. Create a header.
   e. When the header window appears, press Ctrl+V to paste the name of the recipient at the left margin. Choose Center from the QuickMenu.
   f. Key **Page**, space once, and click the Number button on the Header Property Bar. Choose Page Number.
   g. Choose Flush Right from the QuickMenu. Press Ctrl+D to insert the date.
   h. Click Close on the Header Property Bar to close the header.
   i. Suppress the header on the first page of the letter.

4. End the macro. Press Alt+Page Down to look at the top of the second page of the document (the fake page you added in Step 1). Is the header there? Is Mr. Anderson's name at the left? Is the page number centered? Is the date at the right? If everything looks good, close the document without saving it.

PROJECT 16B

1. Open **sasoot 3-11 xxx**. It is in your **Units 1 and 2** folder. Use Save As to save the file with your Unit 4 files (not in the **Units 1 and 2** folder) as **sasoot proj16 xxx**.

2. Position the insertion point at the beginning of the name of the recipient of the letter—Mr. Antonio Larsen.

3. Play your **header hor** macro. Check the second page of the letter to see if the horizontal header appears as you expected.

4. Position the insertion point at the top of the letter and choose Widow/Orphan. (Remember? It's Format, Keep Text Together.)

5. Print the letter and close it, saving it again as you close it.

CRITICAL THINKING ACTIVITY

SCANS

You begin keying a document in class and attempt to play a macro you recorded a couple of days ago, but nothing happens. You open the folder containing your personal macros that you have saved on a disk in Drive A, but cannot find the macro you want. Where is the next place you should look?

Command Summary

UNIT 4 REVIEW

FEATURE	MENU CHOICE	KEYBOARD	LESSON
Balanced Newspaper Columns	Format, Columns (Toolbar)	—	14
Columns	Format, Columns (Toolbar)	—	14
Create Macro	Tools, Macro	Ctrl+F10	16
Create Outline	Insert	Ctrl+H	14
Create Table	Insert (Toolbar)	F12	13
Divide Page	Format, Page, Page Setup	—	15
Edit Macro	Tools, Macro, Edit	—	16
Edit Table	Table, QuickMenu	Ctrl+F12	13
Hyphenation	Tools, Language, Hyphenation	—	14
Macro, Edit	Tools, Macro	—	16
Macro, Play	Tools, Macro	Alt+F10	16
Macro Record	Tools, Macro	Ctrl+F10	16
Newspaper Columns	Format, Columns (Toolbar)	—	14
Newspaper Columns, Balanced	Format, Columns (Toolbar)	—	14
Outline	Insert	—	14
Page Size	Format, Page, Page Setup	—	15
Pause Macro	Tools, Macro	—	16
Play Macro	Tools, Macro	Alt+F10	16
Record Macro	Tools, Macro	Ctrl+F10	16
Select All	Edit, Select	—	15
Settings	Tools, Settings	—	16
Soft Hyphen	Format, Line, Other Codes	Ctrl+Shift+–	14
Table, Create	Insert, Table (Toolbar)	—	13
Underline Tabs	Format, Font	F9	15

UNIT 4 REVIEW QUESTIONS

MULTIPLE CHOICE

Select the best response that fits the following statements. Key your answers on a separate page with the heading, *Unit 4 Review Questions*, centered at the top followed by a triple space.

1. When working in tables, you can get formatting commands from the following source:
   - **A.** Tables Property Bar.
   - **B.** QuickFormat.
   - **C.** Create a Table dialog box.
   - **D.** Applications Bar.

2. The correct formula to use to divide the contents of Cell B3 by the contents of Cell D3 is
   - **A.** B3:D3.
   - **B.** D3:B3.
   - **C.** B3/D3.
   - **D.** D3/B3.

3. When keying an outline, you use _____ to go from a higher level of the outline to a lower level.
   - **A.** Ctrl+Tab
   - **B.** Shift+Tab
   - **C.** Alt+Tab
   - **D.** Tab

4. The Underline Tabs feature is chosen from which dialog box?
   - **A.** Tab Set dialog box
   - **B.** Font dialog box
   - **C.** Page Setup dialog box
   - **D.** Typesetting dialog box

5. If your macro isn't exactly right, you can either _____ it or _____ it.
   - **A.** edit, revise
   - **B.** copy, delete
   - **C.** edit, recreate
   - **D.** delete, recreate

WRITTEN QUESTIONS

Key your answers to the following questions. Number your answers and double-space between them. Use complete sentences and good grammar.

6. At the beginning of Lesson 13 you were introduced to the terms related to WordPerfect tables as well as spreadsheets. What is the relationship between columns, rows, and cell addresses?

7. Describe a floating cell and its relationship to the table in the document.

(continued on next page)

8. How would you describe the difference between Newspaper columns and Balanced newspaper columns?

9. Describe the difference between Landscape and Portrait orientation.

10. Go to Help Topics and read about Divide Page. What is the orientation of the sample divided page that is illustrated? Now go to the section about Booklet, Print. WordPerfect will organize and appropriately number the pages of your booklet as it is being printed. What does Help say must be done before you can print a booklet? How many logical pages must you have on a physical page to print a booklet?

UNIT 4 APPLICATIONS

SCANS

⏱ **Estimated Time: 1 hour**

APPLICATION 1

In Project 16 you created a header for continuing pages of multiple-page letters. The letter you used when you created the macro was a block style letter—with all lines beginning at the left margin. The letter to which you applied the header when you played your macro was a modified block style—with the date and closing lines beginning at approximately center and the paragraphs indented.

Your header was the correct style for the **sasoot** letter. It would not be correct for a block style letter. Use the **berry** letter, if you'd like, as you create another macro to be used with block style letters. Name this one **header ver** (for *vertical*). When you finish, it should contain the lines in Figure APP-1.

FIGURE APP-1
Vertical Letter Header

```
Mr. Antonio Larsen
Page (page number code)
(date code)
```

When you finish recording the header, open **sasoot 3-11 xxx**. Save the file with your Unit 4 files as **sasoot u4ap1 xxx**. Play the **header ver** macro. Then play the **pf** macro. Delete the Path and Filename code in the closing lines of the letter. Print the file and close it, saving it again when you close it.

APPLICATION 2

Sometimes Francine Berry uses a fax transmittal sheet on which she writes the information required. Only a half sheet is needed for this form. A suggested sample is illustrated in Figure APP-2.

FIGURE APP-2
Sample Fax Form for Application 2

```
FRANBERRY CREATIONS                    Phone: 814-555-4545
123 Sixth Street                       Fax: 814-555-4343
Cranberry Ridge, PA 18201

                    FAX TRANSMITTAL

Date: _____

To: _____    At Fax Number: _____

From: _____    At Fax Number: _____

Number of pages (including this page): _____
```

264   UNIT 4: SPECIAL LAYOUT FEATURES

1. Prepare for the half-page form as follows:
   a. Divide your page into two rows and one column.
   b. Display the Ruler and clear all tabs. Set a Left tab at 4".
   c. Go to the Current Document Style and change all four margins to 0.8".
   d. Turn on the Underline Tabs option.
   e. Save the file as **fax form u4ap2 xxx**.

2. Create the form illustrated using Underline Tabs, Underline, Tab, and Flush Right.

3. Use your **pf** macro to put the Path and Filename code at the bottom of the form.

4. Check your work carefully. When it is perfect, open the Edit menu, choose Select, and then choose All. Copy the form to the Clipboard.

5. Move your insertion point to the next logical page (go to the end of the form and press Ctrl+Enter) and paste the form onto that page.

6. Save your document again. Print your two half-page forms and close the file.

APPLICATION 3

Figure APP-3 illustrates a portion of a form for the release of medical records. Study it. Then see if you can create a form that is similar. Some suggestions are listed following the sample form. Read through all of the instructions before you begin. It will help you to see the big picture of the formatting.

FIGURE APP-3
Sample Medical Release Form

Leiser-Gunby Clinic

Patient History # _____

Home Chart Location _____

I HEREBY AUTHORIZE

Name of Physician/Health Care Facility
_____

Street Address
_____

City, State ZIP Code
_____

TO RELEASE TO

Name of Physician/Health Care Facility
_____

Street Address
_____

City, State ZIP Code
_____

Send Attn:
_____

Date Needed By:
_____

INFORMATION TO BE RELEASED

☐ All Clinic Records
☐ Electrocardiogram
☐ Immunization Records
☐ X Ray Films

☐ Lab Reports
☐ Allergy Records
☐ X Ray Reports
☐ Other (Specify) _____

(continued on next page)

FIRST SECTION

1. Clear all tabs. Set a Left tab at 4.5".

2. Use Underline Tabs to insert the lines for the two pieces of information.

3. Save the form as **release u4ap3 xxx**.

SECOND SECTION

1. Create a 3 x 6 table. Adjust the columns so the first column is 3" wide, the second is 0.5" wide, and the third is 3" wide.

2. Set the lines as follows:
    a. Select Column B and choose X for all lines (Inside and Outside).
    b. Select Column A and choose X for the Left lines.
    c. Select Column C and choose X for the Right lines.
    d. Select Cells A5 and A6. Choose None for the Inside and Bottom lines.

3. Key the text in all of the cells of the table.

4. Select Cell A1. Set the Font Color at White. Set Fill at 100%. Do the same with Cell C1.

5. Select the remainder of the table. Go to the Format menu and apply the following formats:
    a. Click the Column tab. Set the Left Column Margin at 0.02".
    b. Click the Row tab. Set Row Height at Fixed. Make it 0.35" high. Set the Top Row Margin at 0.02".
    c. Set the Font Size at 7 pt.

THIRD SECTION

1. Create a one-cell table. Format it with the same colors as Cells A1 and C1 of the other table.

2. Create the check boxes with Symbol 4,38. Tab to the existing tab stop for the second column of check boxes. Underline Tabs is still on for that final underline.

FINISHING UP

1. Select the entire form. Change the font face to Arial.

2. Proofread your form and check the appearance of the parts. Make any necessary adjustments.

3. Use your **pf** macro to put the Path and Filename code in the footer.

4. Print the form and close it, saving it again as you close.

APPLICATION 4

1. Open **online** from the student **datafile** folder. Save the file with your Unit 4 work as **online u4ap4 xxx**.

2. Remove the blank lines between the paragraphs.

3. Format the document in two Balanced newspaper columns.

4. Drag the left column margin of the second column so Column 2 is 2.5" wide. Drag the right column margin of the first column so the columns are separated by 0.25".

5. Use Find and Replace to replace all instances of a period followed by two spaces with a period followed by one space.

6. Turn on Hyphenation to help fill the lines of the document. Make any hyphenation decisions requested by WordPerfect.

7. Set Full justification.

8. Play your **pf** macro to identify the document. When everything is correct, print the file and close it, saving it again as **online u4ap4 xxx** when you close it.

APPLICATION 5

It's housekeeping time again—time to clear your main folder to make room for your Unit 5 work. Work carefully and confidently. You've done this kind of thing several times before.

1. Display your Open File dialog box and delete the files listed in Figure APP-4.

FIGURE APP-4
Files to be Deleted

berry 16-5	columns 14-7	nasa proj14a	sales 13-11
Bombay 13-2	columns 14-8	online u4ap4	sales 13-12
Bombay 13-3	columns 14-9	outline 14-2	sales 13-8
Bombay 13-6	estate 15-7	patty 13-15	sales 13-9
boss 15-9	fax 16-8	patty 13-16	sasoot u4ap1
columns 14-10	intake 15-1	patty 13-17	time 15-5
columns 14-11	intake 15-3	patty 13-18	time 15-6
columns 14-6	landscape 15-11	sales 13-10	

2. Move the files in Figure APP-5 to the **Units 3 and 4** folder.

3. Move **fax form u4ap2** and **release u4ap3** to your **Applications** folder.

(continued on next page)

4. No files should be remaining in your main folder except your macros. Leave them there so WordPerfect can find them when they are needed. If you have extra files that are unnecessary, delete them. If you have other work in your main folder, move it to a different location where it will be out of your way.

FIGURE APP-5
Files to be Moved to the **Units 3 and 4** Folder

Bombay 13-4
Bombay 13-7
boss 15-10
estate 15-8
intake 15-2
intake 15-4
message proj15
nasa proj14b

outline 14-1
patty 13-19
sales 13-13
sasoot proj16
schneider proj13a
schneider proj13b
wind proj14

ON-THE-JOB SIMULATION

SCANS

JOB 8

Mr. Becker is looking for other formats for posting the schedules for the drivers and tour guides. Since you're now an expert at preparing tables, you suggested that perhaps a table format would look good. Now he wants to see how it would look.

Illustrated below is the schedule portion of the memo you prepared in Job 3. It is illustrated as an unformatted table. Begin by preparing the table below. Then format it so it looks MUCH better than the illustration. Use your **pf** macro to insert the Path and Filename code as a footer. Print it and save the document in your **Singing Wheels** folder as **schedule job8 xxx**.

SEPTEMBER TOURS		
Dates	Destination	Driver & Guide
Sept. 1-4	Mall of America in Minneapolis	Dennis & Karen
Sept. 6-7	Fireplace Theater in Madison	Michael & Janie
Sept. 12-28	Vancouver, B.C.	Eric & Shelley
Sept. 14-25	New England	Greg & Karen
Sept. 15-19	Amana Colonies in Iowa	Fred & Janie
Sept. 18-23	Washington, D.C.	Al & Stacey
Sept. 20-27	Branson, Missouri	Tom & Anne

JOBS 9 AND 10

Mr. Becker is still not happy with the appearance of the coach policies list you prepared in Job 7. He has asked you for suggestions regarding other formats.

You've suggested that the items in the list could be numbered, or the list could be prepared in columns. He has asked for samples of both.

1. Open **coach job7 xxx** from your **Singing Wheels** folder. Use Save As to save the file in the **Singing Wheels** folder as **coach job9 xxx**.

2. Change the first-line indent so it is no more than $3/8$". Beginning with the first paragraph, change the font face and size to 12-pt. Times New Roman.

3. Display the Columns dialog box and choose 2 Balanced newspaper columns. In the lower left corner of the box, set the distance between columns at 0.25". Return to your document.

4. Include additional formatting as follows:
   a. Change to Full justification.
   b. Turn on Hyphenation.
   c. Use Block Protect so no item begins in one column and extends to another.
   d. Use Find and Replace to replace all occurrences of a period followed by two spaces to a period followed by one space.
   e. Move the *Memorize your luggage tag* item so it is the last one in the list. Make any necessary adjustments to spacing.

5. Save your document again in the **Singing Wheels** folder as **coach job9 xxx**. Print it. Keep it open.

Now let's return the file to a single-column format and add numbers to the items.

1. With **coach job9 xxx** showing in the window, use Save As to save the file as **coach job10 xxx**.

2. Position the insertion point at the beginning of the first item. Reveal your codes and remove the [Col Def] code and the [First Ln Ind] code.

3. The insertion point should still be at the beginning of the first item. Open the Insert menu and choose Outline/Bullets & Numbering. Choose Paragraph numbering.

4. One at a time, position your insertion point at the end of the final numbered item. Press Enter twice. Then press Delete twice to move the text up to the line with the numeral.

5. Check your work over carefully. When everything looks good, print the document and close it, saving it again as you close it.

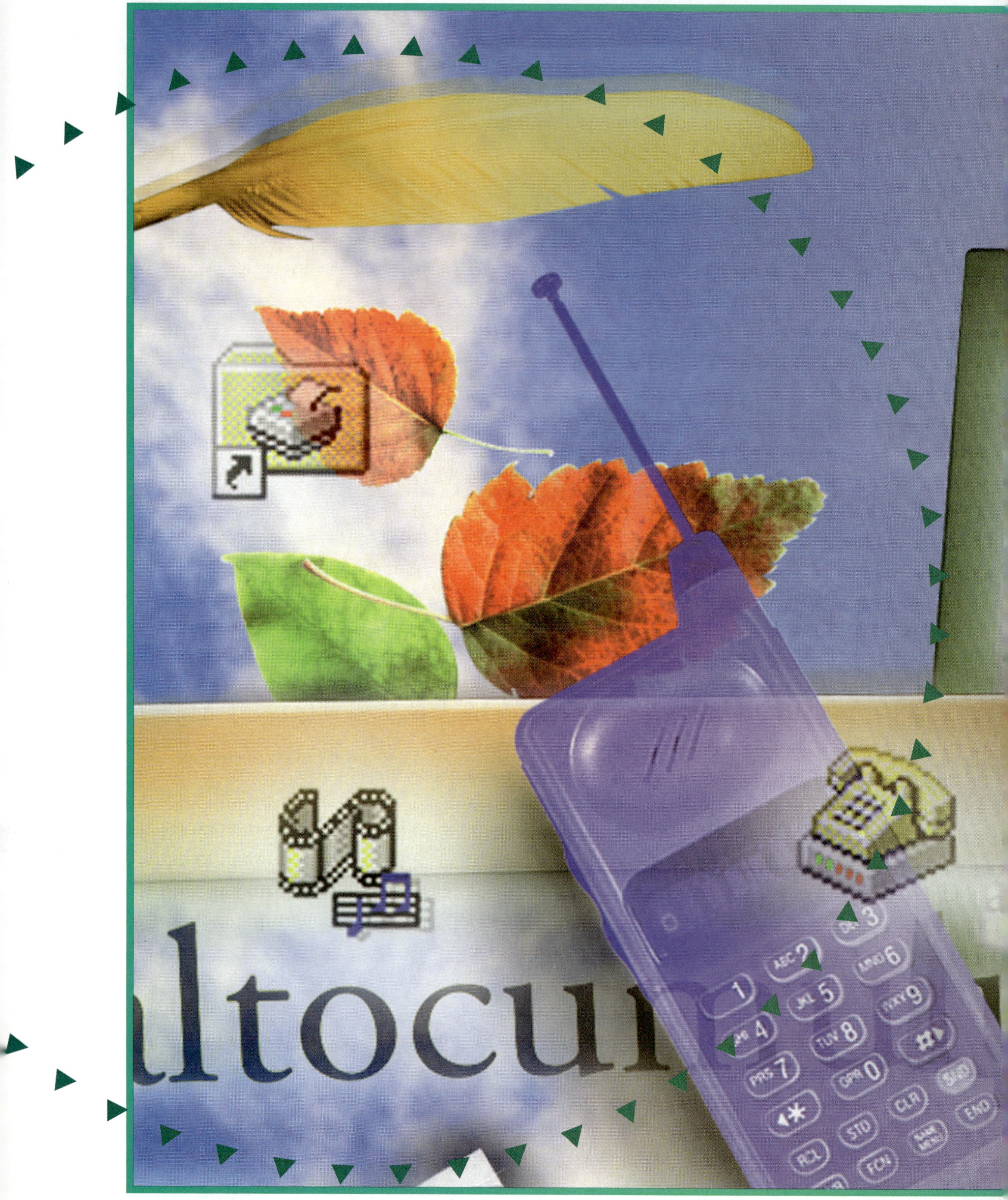

MERGE TOOLS

UNIT 5

lesson 17 — 2 hrs.
Merge

lesson 18 — 3 hrs.
Putting Merge to Work

lesson 19 — 2 hrs.
Sort, Extract, and Select

lesson 20 — 2 hrs.
Labels

Estimated Time for Unit 5: 10½ hours

LESSON 17

MERGE

OBJECTIVES

Upon completion of this lesson, you will be able to:

- Discuss Merge terminology.
- Create a data source.
- Create a form document.
- Merge a data source and a form document.
- Edit a data source.
- Work with multiple-line fields.
- Create envelopes using Merge.
- Use the table style of data file.
- Solve problems that occur in a merge.
- Work with Keyboard Merge.
- Discuss viewing file extensions.

Estimated Time: 2 hours

No doubt you've received a number of sweepstakes mailings addressed specifically to YOU and telling you that you might be the first person in (your city name) to win $1,000,000. Have you wondered how much work it must be to send a personalized letter to the millions of people who have probably received the same letter? (There must be millions. Why else can't you win??)

In Lesson 4 you learned that the procedure of preparing personalized letters for a number of people is referred to as *merge, mail merge,* or *mass mailing*. In this lesson we will call it *Merge*, and you will discover how easy it is to prepare any number of personalized letters.

Merge Terminology

Every merge requires a *form document*. This is the main form containing text and merge codes. A form document can be merged with information from the keyboard or a *data source* (such as an address list), or a combination of these. In order to work with Merge, you should be comfortable with the terminology.

- **Merge Codes**. Dozens of special codes can be used to help WordPerfect perform merges. The most common are FIELD, ENDFIELD, and ENDRECORD codes.

- **Record**. A record is one complete entry in the list or data file. If you have a list of names, addresses, and phone numbers for a group of people, the complete information for one person is a record. An ENDRECORD code identifies the end of the record. A Hard Page code always follows an ENDRECORD code.

- **Field**. A field is one piece of data in a record. Each of the following could be a field:

    Name
    Street Address
    City, State ZIP
    Telephone

FIGURE 17-1
Sample Record

```
Mr.ENDFIELD
FrankENDFIELD
WeigelENDFIELD
Weigel Wire WorksENDFIELD
453 Rummer RoadENDFIELD
Brunswick, ME 00834ENDFIELD
COM systemsENDFIELD
340-555-1200ENDFIELD
ENDRECORD
```

There is no limit to the number of lines in a field. The first three lines in the above list might be combined into one field and the telephone number might be a second field. Dividing records into more fields with smaller chunks of information makes your data files more versatile. An ENDFIELD code marks the end of a field. It is always accompanied by a hard return. Look at Figure 17-1. Notice how this record has been divided into eight fields.

- **Form Document**. This is the document prepared to be merged with a list. Sometimes it is called a *form file*, or a *main*, or *shell, document*. In earlier versions of WordPerfect it was called a *primary file*. Often it is a letter to be sent to a number of people, although there are no restrictions on the format you might choose to use for a form document.

- **Data Source**. The data source for Merge in WordPerfect may be information from the Address Book, a file from a database program such as Paradox, a data file created in a different word processing program, a data file created in WordPerfect, or a number of other sources. When the data source is created in WordPerfect, these learning materials will refer to that source as a *data file*.

The data source is generally made up of some kind of list containing records. In WordPerfect the number of records in a data file is unlimited. Each record may consist of as many as 255 fields. Figure 17-1 illustrates one record of a WordPerfect data file. As mentioned above, this record contains eight fields, and it is a sample of what you will create in this lesson.

Data Files

The first data file you will create will be a text data file with named fields. It will be a list of potential customers who have inquired about a product. As always, read through the entire exercise before beginning.

EXERCISE 17.1

1. In a new document window open the **Tools** menu and choose **Merge**. The Merge dialog box will appear, looking like Figure 17-2.

2. Click the **Create Data** button. The Create Data File dialog box (see Figure 17-3) appears and asks for the names of the fields in your data file.

3. Enter the field names as follows:
   a. Key **title** and press **Enter**. The first field name will be added in the *Fields used in merge* box.
   b. Key **first name** and press **Enter**.
   c. Key each of the remaining names shown in the following list, pressing **Enter** after each:
      last name
      business
      street
      city, state ZIP
      area of interest
      phone

FIGURE 17-2
Merge Dialog Box

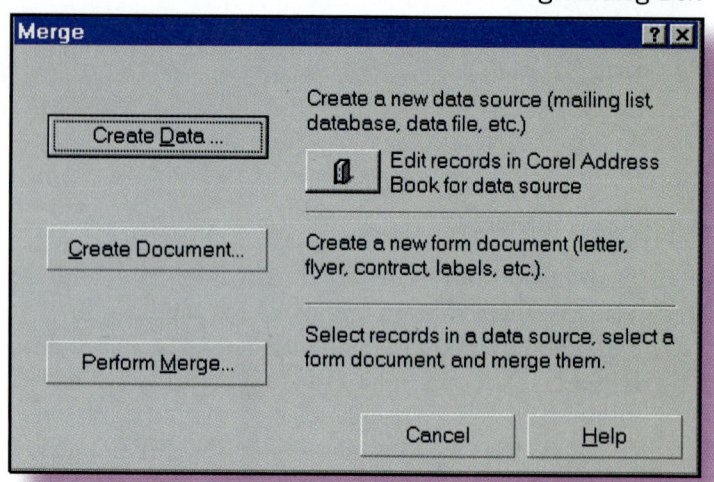

4. When you've keyed *phone* and pressed Enter, click **OK** to tell WordPerfect you are done naming fields. The Quick Data Entry dialog box will appear. Look at the data portion of that dialog box in Figure 17-4.

FIGURE 17-3
Create Data File Dialog Box

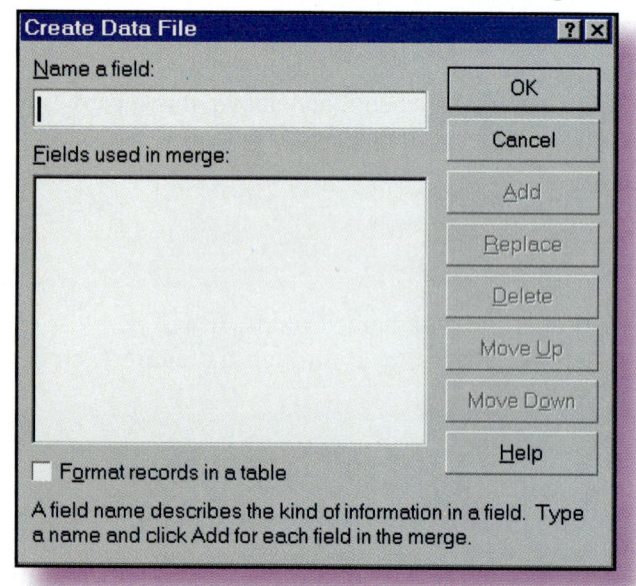

FIGURE 17-4
Data Portion of Quick Data Entry Dialog Box

274

UNIT 5: MERGE TOOLS

5. Key **Mr.** and press **Enter**. Key **Frank** and press **Enter**. Key **Weigel** and press **Enter**.

6. Turn back to Figure 17-1 and key the remaining information for Mr. Weigel. Follow the prompts to the left of the text boxes so you get the correct information in the correct boxes.

7. When you've pressed **Enter** after Mr. Weigel's phone number, WordPerfect should complete the record and put all of the information for Mr. Weigel in the file behind the dialog box.

You have entered the information for the first customer, or *record*, in your first data file. WordPerfect is now prompting you to enter information for the first field of the second record. Let's continue with this process and save your data file.

EXERCISE 17.2

1. The insertion point is in position for you to enter the next record. Enter the data for the potential customers in Figure 17-5.

2. After you have finished with the information for Ms. Oppermann and pressed **Enter** following her phone number, click the **Close** button of the dialog box.

3. WordPerfect will ask if you'd like to save the file. Click **Yes**.

4. Check the folder to be sure you will be saving to your main folder. Key **micro 17-2 xxx** and press **Enter**. WordPerfect will add *.dat*, which identifies the file to WordPerfect as a data file. Click **Save**.

5. Keep the file open in the window as you read on.

FIGURE 17-5
Customers for Exercise 17.2

```
Mr.                         Ms.
Berndt                      Dorothee
Helmke                      Oppermann
Celle Engineering           Opperthee Sporting Goods
6678 Celle Lane             782 N. Kassel Street
Hamburg, VT 09221           Landeau, ME 00884
micrographics               image printers and plotters
442-555-9866                341-555-7639
```

After saving, the file remains in your window. Study the file, looking for the following:

- Look at the FIELDNAMES code at the top.

- Look at the ENDFIELD codes. Does each record have eight of them? This is very important! If you don't have information for a field, the ENDFIELD code must still be included on a line by itself. If you inadvertently miss an ENDFIELD code, weird things will happen when you try to merge the file with a form document.

- Look at the ENDRECORD codes. Is there one at the end of each of the three records, as well as at the end of the field names?

- Does a Hard Page code separate the records?

- Look at the Data File Merge Bar that shows below your Property Bar. It should look like Figure 17-6. If you wish to get back into the Quick Data Entry dialog box, merely click the Quick Entry button on the Merge Bar. If you wish to edit and need to add ENDFIELD or ENDRECORD codes, those buttons are available. We'll explore other parts of the Merge Bar later.

FIGURE 17-6
Data File Merge Bar

Form Documents

Form documents take all shapes. Some are letters, and others are forms similar to those you created in Lesson 15. The one thing that form documents have in common is that they contain merge codes where variable information, such as the information in a data source, will be inserted when the files are merged.

You can start from scratch, creating a form document by choosing Merge from the Tools menu and then clicking the Create Document button. However, if your data file is showing in the window, WordPerfect has made it easy for you to simply click the Go to Form button on the Data File Merge Bar. When you do this, WordPerfect will create a link between the data file showing in the window and the new form document, and also provide the field names.

Let's learn about this process as you create a form document to match your data file. This form document will be a letter, and it will contain much of the same kinds of formatting you have used for your letters in earlier lessons.

EXERCISE 17.3

1. With **micro 17-2 xxx** showing in the window, click the **Go to Form** button on the Merge Bar. Figure 17-7 illustrates the Associate dialog box that will appear.

FIGURE 17-7
Associate Dialog Box

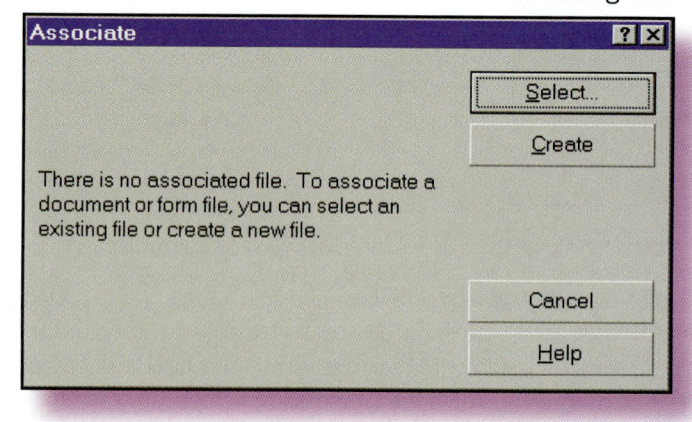

2. Click **Create**. A new blank window will open. Look at the buttons on the Form File Merge Bar.

3. Set **Advance** to move the first line of the document **2"** from the top of the page.

4. Click the **Date** button on the Merge Bar to put a red DATE code in your letter.

UNIT 5: MERGE TOOLS

5. Press **Enter** four times and click the **Insert Field** button on the Merge Bar to display the Insert Field Name or Number dialog box (see Figure 17-8). Note that it identifies your data file and lists the names of the fields in your data file.

6. Point to **title** in the dialog box and double click to enter that field name. Press the **space bar** once and double click **first name**. Press the **space bar** once and double click **last name**. Press **Enter**.

7. Double click **business** and press **Enter**. Double click **street** and press **Enter**. Double click **city, state ZIP** and press **Enter** twice.

8. Close the dialog box containing the field names and save your file as **micro 17-3 xxx.frm**.

FIGURE 17-8
Insert Field name or Number Dialog Box

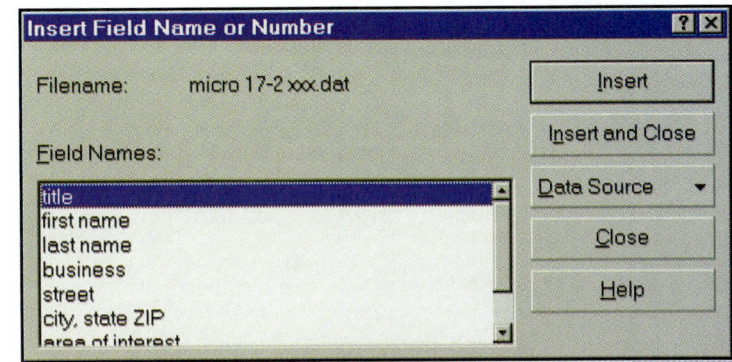

You've just entered the form document codes for the inside address portion of your letter. We'll finish the letter in a moment. In the meantime, let's look at what you have done so far.

The form document contains FIELD codes that match the fields in the data file. When you complete the merge, you will combine the data file with this form document. WordPerfect will know what to put in each "blank" because you've identified the field that contains the desired information.

When entering the FIELD codes for the inside address, be careful with spacing. For example, if you neglected to space between the items on the first line of the mailing address, the names will run together during the merge. This is true whenever you use FIELD codes in documents. Let's finish the form document and put some FIELD codes in one of the paragraphs.

EXERCISE 17.4

1. With the insertion point a double space below the mailing address of **micro 17-3 xxx**, key **Dear** and space once.

2. Click the **Insert Field** button on the Merge Bar to open the Insert Field Name or Number dialog box again. Double click **title**.

3. Space once and double click **last name**. Key a colon and press **Enter** twice.

4. Open the **Insert** menu and choose **File**. Go to the student **datafile** folder and insert the file named **image**.

5. Add a paragraph between paragraphs 1 and 2 using the information in Figure 17-9. When you come to the location for the first FIELD code, double click **area of interest** in the Insert Field Name or Number dialog box.

(continued on next page)

EXERCISE 17.4 CONTINUED

FIGURE 17-9
Text for New Paragraph 2

```
In your letter, you mentioned
FIELD(area of interest) as the
technology you would like to
research in your effort to
begin using imaging in your
office. In response to that
request, I am enclosing
several brochures on FIELD(area
of interest).
```

6. Continue keying the paragraph and insert the same FIELD code where required. Make sure the spacing is correct above and below the inserted paragraph.

7. Close the Insert Field Name or Number dialog box.

8. Near the bottom of the letter, substitute your name where required. Position your insertion point at the top of the letter and use your **pf** macro to add the Path and Filename code at the bottom of the letter.

9. Check the letter over carefully to make sure everything looks good. Then save the letter again, this time as **micro 17-4 xxx**. (Be sure it has the *.frm* extension.) Keep it open in the window.

Merging the Files

Now that your data file and form document have been prepared, you are ready to combine them into three (in this case) letters customized for the recipients. You'll be pleased to learn how easy it is to merge the two files.

EXERCISE 17.5

1. With **micro 17-4 xxx** showing in the window, click the **Merge** button on the Merge Bar. The dialog box illustrated in Figure 17-10 will appear.

2. Look at the dialog box. Notice the following:
   a. Form document should say Current Document.
   b. The Data source is **micro 17-2 xxx**.
   c. Output tells you that the merged file will go to New Document.

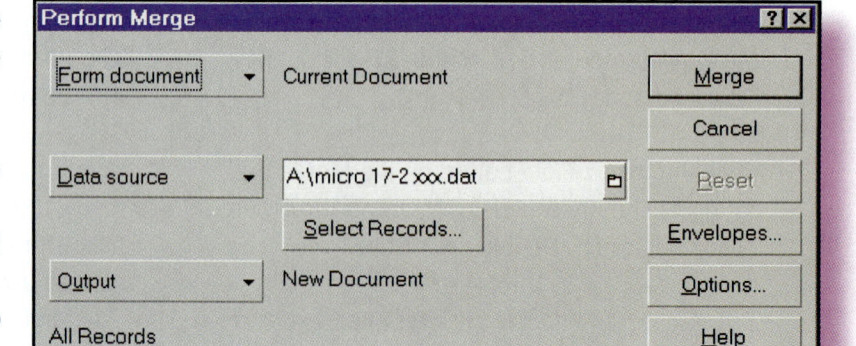

FIGURE 17-10
Perform Merge Dialog Box

3. Click the **Merge** button to complete the merge. When the merge is finished, your insertion point will be at the end of the final letter.

4. Use **Page Up** to go through the letters. Look at the following:
   a. The Path and Filename code location is empty because the merged file has not yet been saved.
   b. The second paragraph contains the area of interest designated for each potential customer.
   c. The mailing address area is complete with customer name and address. Check the spacing around the parts of the name. (If one letter is spaced correctly, all of the letters probably will be.)
   d. The current date should show on all three letters.

5. Save your letters as **micro 17-5 xxx**. Then print the three letters. Close the document. (The form document should appear. It was hiding behind the merged file.) Close the form document, and the data file will appear. Keep it open.

Editing a Data File

Occasionally you will want to add a record to a data file or remove one. Or perhaps you may want to update a record or make a correction of some type. WordPerfect makes it very easy for you to add, delete, or edit records in an existing data file.

With the data file open, choose Quick Entry from the Data File Merge Bar. Follow these steps to edit your file:

- **Add**. To add a record, move to the end of the file using the Last button and then choose New Record.
- **Delete**. To delete a record, move to the record you wish to delete and choose Delete Record.
- **Edit**. To edit a record, move to the record you wish to edit and make the appropriate changes.

When you close the Quick Data Entry dialog box, you will be prompted to save the changes.

Multiple-Line Fields

Sometimes the information for a field takes more than one line. For example, a street address might consist of the following two lines:

Suite 982
921 Plymouth Court

When you are in the Quick Data Entry dialog box, you can't press Enter to add the extra line because Enter takes you to the next field. Instead, whenever you need to add a new line to a field, press Ctrl+Enter. The field text boxes only display one line of a field. Use the up or down arrows to the right of the field box (see Figure 17-4) to view the additional lines.

Let's practice by editing an existing record and adding a new one.

EXERCISE 17.6

1. Only **micro 17-2 xxx.dat** should still be open in your window. This is your data file. Use **Save As** to save the file as **micro 17-6 xxx**.

2. Position the insertion point somewhere in the second record (Berndt Helmke). Click the **Quick Entry** button on the Merge Bar. The Helmke record will appear in the Quick Data Entry dialog box.

3. Position your insertion point at the beginning of the street address and key **Suite 6B**. Press **Ctrl+Enter** to force the street address to the next line.

4. Use the little arrows at the right of the street address to see the two lines of text in the box. (This is a single field that contains two lines of text.)

5. Click the **Last** button at the bottom of the dialog box. (This moves you to the end of the file.) Now click the **New Record** button and enter the information for the potential customer in Figure 17-11.

6. Press **Enter** after the phone number, and close the Quick Data Entry dialog box. Choose **Yes** to save the file again as **micro 17-6 xxx.dat**.

7. Close the newly revised data file.

FIGURE 17-11
New Record for Data File

```
Mr.
Jacob
Noschang
JN Communications
821 Kingsway Road
Blackwell, ME 04950
micrographics
341-555-7654
```

In addition to being able to merge by clicking the Merge button while the form document is showing, you can merge two files that are saved on the disk or in a folder.

EXERCISE 17.7

1. Beginning in a new document window, open the **Tools** menu and choose **Merge**. Then click the **Perform Merge** button at the bottom of the dialog box.

2. The Perform Merge dialog box will appear, asking for the names of the files to be merged. Click the folder button beside the *Form document* text box. Note that only form documents are listed, even though your folder contains several other files. Choose **micro 17-4 xxx**.

3. Click the folder button beside the *Data source* text box. Note that only data files are listed. Locate **micro 17-6 xxx** and double click to choose it for your merge.

4. Click the **Merge** button to complete the merge. When the merge is completed, check to see if the changes made to the data file were included.
   a. Check the Application Bar. Are you on page 4?
   b. Use **Page Up** to see if that fourth letter is to Jacob Noschang.
   c. Press **Ctrl+G** and key **2** to go to the second page. Is the suite number listed for Mr. Helmke?

d. If all of your answers aren't *Yes*, go back and repeat Exercise 17.6.

5. Save the merged file as **micro 17-7 xxx** and keep it open.

6. Print only Letters 2 and 4 by opening the Print dialog box, choosing the **Multiple Pages** tab, and keying **2,4** (no space after the comma). Click **OK** and then click **Print**.

7. Close the document without saving it again.

Envelopes

You learned in an early lesson that WordPerfect will automatically position the address of your letter on the envelope when you are working with individual letters. The program will also prepare envelopes to go with your letters when you merge a form document and a data file.

To prepare envelopes, you must insert the FIELD codes in the envelope format. Then as the merge is completed, an envelope will be prepared to match each letter. After the merge, the insertion point will still be at the end of the final letter. The envelopes will be in the same order as the letters, and will follow the letters.

When you print envelopes in the office, you may have a printer designated just for envelopes. In other cases, the envelopes might be loaded in a specified drawer that you will choose when you wish to print an envelope. In the classroom, those conditions are probably not present and you'll need to print your envelopes using the same printer used for your other work. If that is the case, the printer will probably prompt you to insert the envelope to be printed. You have the following choices:

- Your instructor may have a supply of inexpensive envelopes with which you may practice.
- You may be instructed to cut paper to the correct size for envelopes (4.13" x 9.5").
- You can reinsert the letter and print the envelope on the back of the page.

Check with your instructor to see what procedure you should follow for the printing of envelopes. Now let's perform the same merge as in Exercise 17.7 and prepare envelopes for the potential customers.

EXERCISE 17.8

1. Choose **Tools**, **Merge**, and then **Perform Merge**. WordPerfect will probably remember the files you were using. If not, choose **micro 17-4 xxx** for the Form document and **micro 17-6 xxx** for the Data source.

2. Click the **Envelopes** button at the right of the dialog box to display the Envelope dialog box (see Figure 17-12).

3. Look at the left side of the dialog box. If *Print return address* contains a check mark, click to deselect it.

4. Click in the *Mailing addresses* box. Then click the **Field** button to display a list of the field names. Enter the mailing address as follows, clicking the **Field** button before inserting each part of the address.
   a. Double click **title** and space once.

(continued on next page)

EXERCISE 17.8 CONTINUED

    b. Double click **first name** and space once.
    c. Double click **last name** and press **Enter**.
    d. Double click **business** and press **Enter**.
    e. Double click **street** and press **Enter**.
    f. Double click **city, state ZIP**.

5. Look at the address in the preview box at the lower left. Only the field names are illustrated.

6. Click **OK** to close the Envelope dialog box, accepting all settings. Then click the **Merge** button to complete the merge. When the merge is finished, your insertion point will be at the bottom of the final letter. The envelopes will follow the letters. Use **Page Down** to see the envelopes.

7. Zoom to **Full Page** to look at an envelope. Then return to **100%**.

8. Print only one envelope—the one to Jacob Noschang. Save your document as **micro 17-8 xxx** and close it.

FIGURE 17-12
(Merge) Envelope Dialog Box

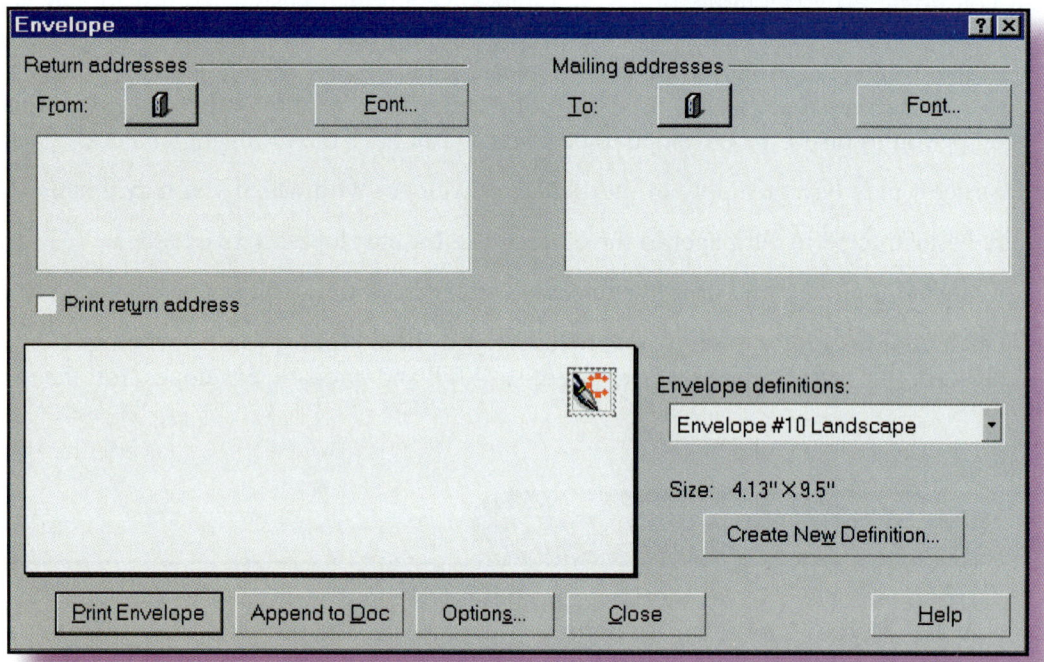

If you looked at the results of this merge carefully, you noticed that the first three letters contained the footer with the path and filename. The footer did not appear on the fourth letter. WordPerfect turns the footer off for the envelopes (the Footer End code is at the bottom of the final letter), and for some unknown reason, that command takes effect already on the fourth letter.

Table Data File

When you prepare the data file, you have the choice of formatting it in text format, as you did in Exercises 17.1 and 17.2, or in table format like the data source you used in Lesson 4. When you use table format, the fields are named and the information is entered in the same way, but it appears spread across the page in a table rather than along the left margin with ENDFIELD and ENDRECORD codes.

In the next exercise you will prepare a short table data file using the same information you used for Exercise 17.2.

EXERCISE 17.9

1. Beginning in a new document window, open the **Tools** menu, choose **Merge**, and then choose **Create Data**. Key the field names listed in Figure 17-13 into the Field Names dialog box, pressing Enter after each name.

2. At the bottom of the dialog box, click the *Format records in a table* check box. Click **OK** to display the Quick Data Entry dialog box.

3. Prepare the data file for the two prospective customers in Figure 17-14. When you finish, close the Quick Data Entry dialog box and save the file as **micro 17-9a xxx**. WordPerfect will add the *.dat* extension.

4. Look at your file. It should look much like Figure 17-15. Close the file.

5. Beginning in a new document window, merge **micro 17-4 xxx** (the form document) with **micro 17-9a xxx** (the data source in table format).

6. Check your two letters. If they look good, print them and close the file, saving it as **micro 17-9b xxx**. If something isn't right, close the document and go back to the data file to make the necessary repairs. Then merge again and finish the exercise. Close all files.

FIGURE 17-13
Field Names

```
title
first name
last name
business
street
city, state ZIP
area of interest
phone
```

FIGURE 17-14
Customers for Exercise 17.9

```
Mr.                    Ms.
Frank                  Dorothee
Weigel                 Oppermann
Weigel Wire Works      Opperthee Sporting Goods
453 Rummer Road        782 N. Kassel Street
Brunswick, ME 00834    Landeau, ME 00884
COM systems            image printers and plotters
340-555-1200           341-555-7639
```

(continued on next page)

FIGURE 17-15
Table Data File

title	first name	last name	business	street	city, state ZIP	area of interest	phone
Mr.	Frank	Weigel	Weigel Wire Works	453 Rummer Road	Brunswick, ME 00834	COM systems	340-555-1200
Ms.	Dorothee	Oppermann	Opperthee Sporting Goods	782 N. Kassel Street	Landeau, ME 00884	image printers and plotters	341-555-7639

Troubleshooting a Merge

When merging, sometimes your files don't turn out exactly the way you planned. The only way you'll know that is to look through your merged documents to see if the correct information is in the right place. It is costly in terms of time and resources to print your letters or other merged documents before really looking at them. If you find an error, you'll have to print again after fixing that error. Too often, the error occurs on ALL letters, not just one or two.

When something doesn't work, check both the data source and the form document. You can open both of them and choose Tile from the Window menu so you can see both documents at one time. Check to see if the FIELD codes in both documents match. Check to be sure you keyed the correct information in each of the fields. If you find something wrong in either the data source or the form document, make the correction and save the document again before performing the merge again.

Sometimes in a merge, you'll end up with a "blank" form document at the end of your merged letters or other forms. Usually that is the result of an extra hard return or code of some kind following the final Hard Page code in the data file. If that happens, open your data file, reveal your codes, and be sure the [HPg] code is at the end of the file.

You've done well with your merges so far. We'll look at one more kind of merge in this lesson.

Keyboard Merge

Merging form documents and data files is a good way to produce customized documents when you have a number of them to prepare at one time. Another kind of merge is available for situations where you need to prepare only one or two letters or forms at a time. In cases like that, it's not efficient to create a data file for the merge.

A better method is to prepare what's known as a *keyboard merge*. With Keyboard Merge, you prepare only the form document. During the merge you key the variable information. A different merge code is used for a keyboard merge. It is a KEYBOARD code that stops the merge while you key the information. When you've finished keying at that location, you start the merge again with Alt+Enter and WordPerfect will move to the next KEYBOARD code.

You can tell WordPerfect to prompt you with the kind of information to be entered at each stop in the keyboard merge, although the prompts aren't necessary to make the merge work. Let's try a short sample to see how Keyboard Merge works.

EXERCISE 17.10

1. Beginning in a new document window, set line spacing at **2.0** for double spacing.

2. Open the **Tools** menu and choose **Merge**. Click **Create Document** and tell WordPerfect to use the active window. Click **OK**.

3. In the Associate Form and Data dialog box, click **No association** and then **OK**. Look at the buttons on the Form File Merge Bar. Find the **Keyboard** button. You'll use that button in this exercise.

4. Key the paragraph in Figure 17-16. At the location of the first KEYBOARD code, click the **Keyboard** button on the Merge Bar.

5. In the Insert Merge Code dialog box, key **patient name**. (The prompts are shaded in Figure 17-16.) Press **Enter** to insert the code and prompt into your document. Space once.

6. Continue keying until you come to the next KEYBOARD code. Click the **Keyboard** button and key the prompt. Repeat the process until you have keyed the entire paragraph. The variable information is shown as shaded text in Figure 17-16 to help you pick it out. In your window, the text will appear as normal text with the KEYBOARD codes in red.

7. When you finish, save the document as **referral 17-10 xxx**.

8. Return your insertion point to the top of the document. Play your **pf** macro. Then close the document, saving it again as you close it.

FIGURE 17-16
Text for Exercise 17.10

```
This is a referral of KEYBOARD(patient name) to your care.
KEYBOARD(He/She) lives at KEYBOARD(street address) in KEYBOARD(city,
state and ZIP code). KEYBOARD(patient name) is a KEYBOARD(male/
female) who is KEYBOARD(age) years old. KEYBOARD(He/She) has a blood
pressure of KEYBOARD(blood pressure) and is suffering from
KEYBOARD(symptoms). A complete medical chart is available upon
request.
```

Look at Figure 17-17. It contains the variable information for two patients who are being referred to a specialist. Let's see how easy it is to prepare a document using Keyboard Merge.

FIGURE 17-17
Data for Keyboard Merge

```
Patient 1:                      Patient 2:
Isabella Legg                   Harley Hartmann
333 Erie Street                 77 Yoman Court
Epsonville, IA 49876            Yaleston, IA 49879
Female                          Male
Age: 33                         Age: 77
Blood Pressure: 98/58           Blood Pressure: 180/95
Symptoms: dizziness             Symptoms: chest pains
                                          and shortness
                                          of breath
```

EXERCISE 17.11

1. Open the **Tools** menu and choose **Merge**. Then choose **Perform Merge**. In the location for the Form document, fill in **referral 17-10 xxx**. Look at the *Data source* text box. If it doesn't say *None*, click the **Data source** button and choose **None**. (This merge does not require a data file.)

2. Click the **Merge** button. When your document appears, the insertion point will be in the location for the first piece of variable information. Key **Isabella Legg**.

3. Click the **Continue** button on the Merge Bar or press **Alt+Enter** to move the insertion point to the next variable. Following the prompt, fill in the correct information from Figure 17-17.

4. Work carefully. After the final KEYBOARD code, click **Continue** or press **Alt+Enter** one more time to end the merge.

5. Check your work. Then save it as **referral 17-11 xxx**. Position the insertion point at the end of the paragraph and press **Ctrl+Enter** to go to a new page.

6. Open the **Tools** menu, choose **Merge**, and then choose **Perform Merge**. In the Perform Merge dialog box click the **Output** button and change it to **Current Document**.

7. Continue the merge procedure in Steps 1-4 to complete the referral for Mr. Hartmann.

8. Print your two referrals and save them again with the same name. Close the file.

This was a brief introduction to Keyboard Merge. You'll have a number of additional opportunities to work with this feature in future lessons.

Viewing File Extensions

Up to this point, you have learned that most of your documents have a *.wpd* extension. Macros have a *.wcm* extension, form documents have a *.frm* extension, and data files have a *.dat* extension. These extensions identify the particular file types to WordPerfect. They also help you to identify your files when you see them in the Open and Save As dialog boxes.

Your computer might be set up so that the extensions don't show. This is a choice that's made in the Windows 95 desktop. It is not a WordPerfect setting. If you have been able to see all of the extensions on your document names as you've progressed through your training, that's good. If you haven't been able to see the extensions, check with your instructor to find out whether or not you should do Exercise 17.12. In this exercise we will go to the Windows 95 desktop and change the settings so your extensions show. Being able to see the extensions will help you a lot as you continue to work with Merge.

EXERCISE 17.12 (optional)

1. Check with your instructor to see if you should proceed with this exercise!

2. Click the dash button in the upper right corner of your WordPerfect window to minimize WordPerfect to a button on the Windows 95 Task Bar.

3. Find the **My Computer** button on the desktop. Double click to open the My Computer dialog box, if it isn't already open.

4. Open the **View** menu and choose **Options**. Then click the **View** tab.

5. At the bottom of the dialog box, be sure the final choice is deselected (Hide MS-DOS file extensions for file types that are registered).

6. Check to make sure that none of the other options are chosen.

7. Click **OK** to close the dialog box. Close the My Computer dialog box. Then click the **Corel WordPerfect** button on the Task Bar to maximize your WordPerfect window again.

8. Display the Open dialog box and see if the extensions now show on your documents. If not, check with your instructor to see if something else needs to be done to display the extensions.

Summary

This has been an introduction to Merge and the kinds of tasks that can be completed using this feature. In this lesson you got the basics. You learned that:

- Merge is sometimes referred to as "mail merge."
- A data file contains the variable information for a merge.
- Every merge must have a form document.
- WordPerfect helps you insert the fields for your form document by making the data source field names readily available.
- To join a data source with a form document, all you need to do is tell WordPerfect to merge and then name the files to be merged.
- Data files can be in text format or table format.
- Data files can be edited after they have been created.
- You can prepare an envelope for each letter as part of a merge.
- Keyboard Merge is used for situations where a small number of letters or forms are prepared at one time.

In the next three lessons you will continue to work with Merge and explore some of the ways you can put it to work for you.

LESSON 17 REVIEW QUESTIONS

MATCHING

Write the letter of the term or phrase from Column 2 that best matches the description in Column 1.

Column 1

_C_ 1. One complete entry in a list.
_E_ 2. The document prepared to be merged with a list.
_B_ 3. Dozens of special codes used to help WordPerfect perform merges.
_D_ 4. One piece of data in a record.
_H_ 5. Press Alt+Enter to start this merge again.
_F_ 6. A file generally made up of some kind of list.

Column 2

A. Mail merge
B. Merge codes
C. Record
D. Field
E. Form document
F. Data source
G. Table Data File
H. Keyboard merge
I. Keyboard codes

MULTIPLE CHOICE

Circle the best answer to each of the following statements.

7. A data source may consist of as many as ____ fields.
   A. 25
   B. 255
   C. 55
   D. 555

8. A form document contains ____ codes.
   A. ENDFIELD
   B. ENDRECORD
   C. FIELD
   D. FILE

9. The default is to merge all documents
   A. onto one page.
   B. onto as few pages as possible.
   C. onto two pages per record if possible.
   D. onto one page per record.

10. When a merge is completed between a form letter and mailing list, the insertion point will be
    A. at the beginning of the first letter.
    B. at the end of the first letter.
    C. at the beginning of the last letter.
    D. at the end of the last letter.

288 UNIT 5: MERGE TOOLS

LESSON 17 PROJECT

This project will consist of several small tasks. Work carefully but efficiently. How much can you do without referring back to the lesson?

PROJECT 17A

Create a memo form with KEYBOARD codes. It should look like Figure 17-18 when you finish. The instructions will help you set up your form.

1. Create a form document. There is no associated data source. Center the heading in bold, all capital letters with a 20-pt. type size. Use a font face of your choice.

2. Display the Ruler and remove the tab stop at 1.5". Set a Right tab at 1.75". Tab once and key **TO:**. Tab again and insert the KEYBOARD code as shown. Press Enter twice to separate the parts of the opening lines with a double space. Follow the same procedure for the four opening lines. Use the DATE button on the Merge Bar for the date.

3. After inserting the KEYBOARD code for the body of the memo, save the file as **memo** (with the *.frm* extension). Return the insertion point to the top of the memo and play the **pf** macro. Then close the file, saving it again as **memo.frm**.

FIGURE 17-18
Memo Form

MEMORANDUM

TO: KEYBOARD(memo recipient)
FROM: KEYBOARD(memo author)
DATE: DATE
SUBJECT: KEYBOARD(subject of memo)

KEYBOARD(body of memo)

PROJECT 17B

Create a data file using the data in Figure 17-19. Use the following field names: *customer, greeting, area of interest, representative, time, date*. In this data file the entire customer name and address will be

FIGURE 17-19
Records for Project 17B

```
Mr. Miguel Zedillo                    Mr. Kim Lee
Bits and Chips                        Lee Electronics
441 Main Street                       42 Leeward Way
Springvale, ME 04083ENDFIELD          Leeds, ME 04263
Mr. ZedilloENDFIELD                   Mr. Lee
multimediaENDFIELD                    COM
Andreas WernerENDFIELD                Pedro Costilla
2 p.m.ENDFIELD                        8:30 a.m.
Thursday, March 23ENDFIELD            Monday, March 20

Mrs. Rosemary Waldman
Wally's Wallpaper Shop
554 Walnut Street
Waldo, ME 04915
Mrs. Waldman
image printing and plotting
Marcus Schmidt
1 p.m.
Friday, March 24
```

(continued on next page)

289

keyed into one field. That means you must press Ctrl+Enter following the customer name, the name of the business, and each line of the mailing address. After the ZIP code, press Enter to move the insertion point to the text box for the greeting. Follow the usual procedure to enter the data for the three records. Note that the ENDFIELD codes are shown for the first record only. When you finish, check your work. Each record should have six ENDFIELD codes, with the first one following the ZIP code number. Make any necessary corrections, and save the file as **im spec proj17b xxx**.

PROJECT 17C

Click the Go to Form button on the Merge Bar and choose Create. Create the form document illustrated in Figure 17-20. Begin by giving the Center Page(s) command to center the current and subsequent pages. Press Enter four times following the date. Click the Insert Field button on the Merge Bar to help you in entering the FIELD codes.

When you finish, save the file as **im spec proj17c xxx**. Then play the **pf** macro to add the Path and Filename code in the footer. Save the file again.

FIGURE 17-20
Form Document for Project 17C

```
DATE

FIELD(customer)

Dear FIELD(greeting):

Thank you for choosing Image Specialists to install imaging equipment
in your company.  As we agreed in our phone conversation yesterday,
part of our service to your company is to provide training for those
employees who will be using the imaging equipment.

Our consultant for FIELD(area of interest) equipment,
FIELD(representative), will meet you at your company at FIELD(time) on
FIELD(date) to discuss your company's needs and how the installation
of the FIELD(area of interest) equipment will be handled.  At that
time, arrangements for the training of your employees will be made.

Again, the staff of Image Specialists would like to thank you for your
confidence in our organization.  We are looking forward to providing
you with the best in FIELD(area of interest) equipment and service.

Sincerely,



(your name)
Imaging Manager
```

PROJECT 17D

Click the Merge button on the Form File Merge Bar to merge your form document and data file. Click the Envelopes button in the Perform Merge dialog box. You'll only need to enter one FIELD code—*customer*—for the mailing address on the envelopes.

Complete the merge. Check the letters and envelopes carefully. If everything looks good, print all three letters and envelopes. If the spacing around the variable information is incorrect or if something is wrong with the format of your letter, make the appropriate corrections to the form document or data file, save the files again, and then merge again, printing the letters and envelopes. Save the merged file as **im spec proj17d xxx** and close all files.

CRITICAL THINKING ACTIVITY

SCANS

You have just completed a merge between a letter (form document) and the mailing list of all club members (data source). As you proofread the merged documents, you notice that the names in the inside address run together. What is the first thing you should check and how would you fix this problem?

Lesson 18: Putting Merge to Work

SKIP

OBJECTIVES

Upon completion of this lesson, you will be able to:

- Discuss different arrangements of data files.
- Deal with missing data in merge records.
- Put POSTNET bar codes on envelopes.
- Merge into a table format.
- Use Merge for document assembly.
- Create an Address Book and use it to merge.

Estimated Time: 3 hours

In Lesson 17 you learned the terminology associated with Merge and the basics of creating form documents and data files. You learned to combine those form documents and data files into finished documents. Best of all, you learned that a great deal of time can be saved by using Merge to streamline your work.

In Lesson 18 you will learn that there are a number of things you can do to expand the power of Merge in your work. None of the applications here are difficult, providing you take the time to think about what you are doing and how you are being asked to do it. What's more, these applications might give you some ideas about how you can use Merge in your work.

Planning Data Files

While you can break up your data files into as many parts as you wish, you learned in Lesson 17 that the smaller the pieces of information in each field, the more flexible your data file will be.

Usually you know ahead of time how the information in a data file will be used. You can configure the fields in the records so that they will best fit your needs. In designing a data file, it is important to remember that all records in the entire file must be prepared in the same way. Figure 18-1 illustrates four possible schemes that might be used for a data file. All four schemes include the same information.

Look at Scheme 4. Notice that the entire name and address section is one field. This arrangement doesn't allow you to work individually with the parts of a person's name. The same is true of Scheme 2. Note that the title is separate, but the entire name is in one field.

You could debate the advantages of each of the schemes. Each of the illustrated schemes is best for a certain situation. Most important is that you understand the options so you can make an educated choice when asked to create a data file.

FIGURE 18-1
Data File Schemes

	Scheme 1	Scheme 2	Scheme 3	Scheme 4
Field 1	title	title	title	mailing address
Field 2	first name	name	first name	telephone
Field 3	middle initial	company	last name	
Field 4	last name	street address	company	
Field 5	company	city	street address	
Field 6	street address	state	city, state ZIP	
Field 7	city	ZIP	telephone	
Field 8	state	telephone		
Field 9	ZIP			
Field 10	telephone			

Missing Data

Notice that in Scheme 1 a separate field is used for the middle initial. If you don't know the initial, an ENDFIELD code must still be included for that field. You must have the same number of ENDFIELD codes in each record of a file.

It is not unusual to not know all of the information called for in a data file. The way you deal with the missing data differs, however, depending on what information is missing and where it should be positioned when the merge is completed.

- **Data on a line by itself**. If the missing data is a company name, for example, it will usually fall on a line by itself. WordPerfect is set to delete a line if it doesn't include any information. You can change this setting in the *Options* portion of the Perform Merge dialog box.

- **Data between other variables**. If the missing data is a middle initial as discussed above, additional merge codes need to be inserted to deal with it. If you don't, WordPerfect will leave two spaces between the adjacent words. In this case, it would be the space before AND AFTER the missing initial.

Let's create a data file where each record has 13 fields. Then we'll experiment with the way the data can be used in several kinds of merges.

EXERCISE 18.1

1. Beginning in a new document window, create a new data file. Use the following field names: *account number, title, first name, middle initial, last name, company, street, city, state, ZIP, phone, amount due, months overdue*.

2. Enter the three records for this data file using the data in Figure 18-2. Save the file as **flowers 18-1 xxx.dat**.

(continued on next page)

293

EXERCISE 18.1 CONTINUED

3. Use **Go to Form** to create a form document that looks like Figure 18-3. Save the form document as **flowers 18-1 xxx.frm**.

4. Click the **Merge** button on the Form File Merge Bar to display the Perform Merge dialog box. It should show that you are merging the current document with **flowers 18-1 xxx.dat**. Complete the merge.

5. When your merge is finished, all three addresses will be on separate pages. Open the **View** menu and choose **Draft** so you can see all three at once.

6. Look at the three sets of information. Note the following:
   a. No blank line was left for Mr. Bloom's missing company name.
   b. Look at the extra space between first and last names for the other two customers. This space is so large because you spaced before and after the FIELD code for the middle initial, which isn't included for either of those customers.

7. Close the file without saving. You will be returned to your form document. Keep the form document and the data file open.

FIGURE 18-2
Records for Exercise 18.1

account number	3349	2399	5488
title	Mr.	Mrs.	Ms.
first name	Bill	Daisy	Pearl
middle initial	B.		
last name	Bloom	Ditson	Poppy
company		Dixie's Dilemma	Puppies and Pets
street	543 Bixby Street	7632 Ann Street	6732 Polk Street
city	Bloomington	Dixonville	Pittsburgh
state	OK	DE	WI
ZIP	74562	19811	54461
phone	405-555-9975	302-555-1490	715-555-4453
amount due	789.56	45.39	125.90
months overdue	1	4	2

FIGURE 18-3
Form Document for Exercise 18.1

```
FIELD(title) FIELD(first name) FIELD(middle initial) FIELD(last name)
FIELD(company)
FIELD(street)
FIELD(city), FIELD(state) FIELD(ZIP)

FIELD(amount due)
```

Let's address the problem of the missing middle initial, first. Then we'll learn about some other options. The WordPerfect Merge language contains a large number of powerful commands, each designed for a particular job. Two of those commands can solve the problem of the missing middle initials.

Figure 18-4 illustrates the same portion of a form document illustrated in Figure 18-3. The IFNOTBLANK and ENDIF commands tell WordPerfect that if the initial is there, it should be included. If it is not included, the FIELD code for the middle initial should be ignored. The black dots indicate where the spaces should go. (Note that because the merge commands take so much room, the first line of the form document is wrapped to the next line. It will be OK when you merge.)

FIGURE 18-4
Form Document with IFNOTBLANK and ENDIF Codes

```
FIELD(title)•FIELD(first name)•IFNOTBLANK(middle initial)FIELD(middle
initial)•ENDIF FIELD(last name)
FIELD(company)
FIELD(street)
FIELD(city),•FIELD(state)•FIELD(ZIP)

FIELD(amount due)
```

Let's amend the **flowers 18-1 xxx.frm** file to include the IFNOTBLANK and ENDIF codes.

EXERCISE 18.2

1. With **flowers 18-1 xxx.frm** showing in the window, use **Save As** to save the file as **flowers 18-2 xxx.frm**.

2. Leave the space following the *first name* field, and delete to the end of the line with **Ctrl+Del**.

3. Click the **Merge Codes** button on the Form File Merge Bar to open the Insert Merge Codes dialog box. It should look like Figure 18-5. If necessary, point to the dialog box name and drag the box down so you can see your work.

4. Key **ifn** to move the highlight to **IFNOTBLANK**. Click the **Insert** button.

5. WordPerfect will ask you for the field in question. Key **middle initial** and press **Enter**.

6. Click the **Insert Field** button to open the Insert Field Name or Number dialog box. Drag this box down beside the other one. Then double click **middle initial** to enter a FIELD code for the middle initial.

FIGURE 18-5
Insert Merge Codes Dialog Box

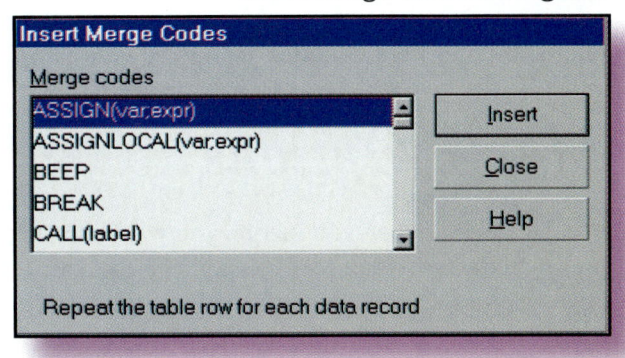

7. Space once with the space bar. Click in the Insert Merge Codes dialog box to activate it. Scroll back through the codes to find the **ENDIF** code. Click **Insert** to insert it. Then click **Close** to close the dialog box.

(continued on next page)

295

EXERCISE 18.2 CONTINUED

8. Double click **last name** in the Insert Field Name or Number dialog box to insert the FIELD code for the last name. Close the dialog box.

9. Compare your form document with Figure 18-4. Do you have a space only in the places marked with a dot in the figure? When everything is correct, save your file again as **flowers 18-2 xxx.frm**. Keep it open.

Now let's merge the two files and see if the extra space in the name has been taken care of.

EXERCISE 18.3

1. Click the **Merge** button on the Merge Bar to merge the current file with **flowers 18-1 xxx.dat**. (You may need to go to your files to select the data file.) Complete the merge.

2. Change to **Draft** view so you can compare the three merged pages. Reveal your codes, if necessary, to be sure that the first and last names for Mrs. Ditson and Ms. Poppy have only one space separating them.

3. Close the file without saving it. Keep the form document and the data file open.

Now that you've learned how to remove that extra space when information is missing on the same line with other FIELD codes, let's look at some of the options available during a merge.

Merge Options

Usually when you merge, you want each record to end up on a page by itself. Letters would look pretty funny, for example, if one began where the other left off, all on the same page. Sometimes, however, you want the records to merge onto one page. It would have been easier to compare the records in the merge you just completed if all three sets of information had been on one page.

The Merge Options dialog box offers you the place to change that setting. It also allows you to make multiple copies of a merge, and it allows you to tell WordPerfect not to remove the blank line that results from a missing field if you should want it to appear.

Let's try our merge one more time and work with all of these options.

EXERCISE 18.4

1. Check the bottom of your form document. The FIELD code for Amount Due should be followed by two hard returns. If the hard returns aren't there, please add them.

2. Click the **Merge** button on the Merge Bar to display the Perform Merge dialog box. Then click the **Options** button to open the Perform Merge Options dialog box (see Figure 18-6).

3. Click the **Separate . . .** item at the top to deselect it.

4. Change Number of copies . . . to **2**.

5. Change the *Remove Blank Line* button to **Leave Blank Line**. Click **OK**.

6. Back in the Perform Merge dialog box, click **Merge**.

7. Save your merged file as **flowers 18-4 xxx**. Print it and keep it open as you read on.

FIGURE 18-6
Perform Merge Options Dialog Box

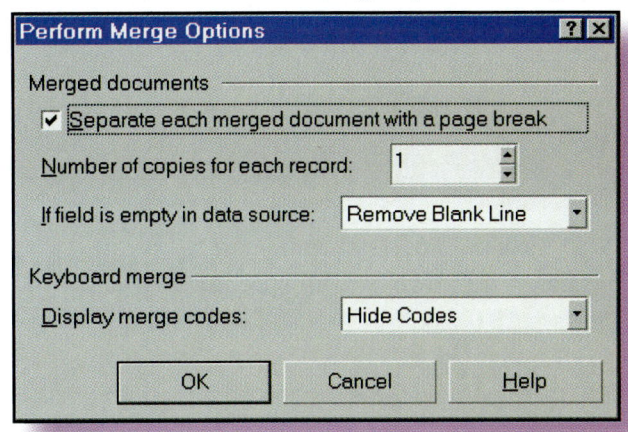

Look at your merged file. Notice the following things about the file:

- Each person appears twice. You asked for two of each in the Perform Merge Options dialog box.

- All six records appear on the same page. You requested that, too.

- Note that Mr. Bloom has a blank line in both occurrences of his address. What's supposed to be in that blank line? If you answered that the company name is missing, you are correct. In your earlier merges that blank line was suppressed. You told WordPerfect to leave the blank line in this merge.

After you've changed some of the options in a merge, it is important that you remember to click the Reset button if you wish to return to the default settings. Since your next merge will be quite different from this one, let's finish up the previous exercise and take care of Reset.

EXERCISE 18.5

1. Close **flowers 18-4 xxx**. You don't need to save it again.

2. Back in the form document, click the **Merge** button on the Merge Bar. Click the **Reset** button and then the **Close** button.

3. Keep the form document and the data file open for the next exercise.

POSTNET Bar Codes

POSTNET bar codes can be added to any of your envelopes. If you are working with a single letter and are creating an envelope, you only need to go to Options and tell WordPerfect where you'd like the bar code—above or below the address.

297

When you merge, you must have the ZIP code in a field by itself to add bar codes to your envelopes. In the next exercise we'll convert your **flowers** form document into a brief letter. Then we'll merge. We'll include envelopes, and we'll add POSTNET bar codes to the envelopes.

EXERCISE 18.6

1. With **flowers 18-2 xxx.frm** showing in the window, use **Save As** to save the file as **flowers 18-6 xxx.frm**.

2. Delete the *Amount Due* section from the form. Replace it with a greeting that begins with **Dear** and includes the title and last name. Put a colon at the end of the greeting.

3. Return to the top of the document and tell WordPerfect to center the current and subsequent pages. Insert the DATE merge code and press **Enter** four times.

4. Position the insertion point a double space below the greeting and prepare the rest of the letter, using the information in Figure 18-7.

5. When you finish, check your work over carefully. Play the **pf** macro, and save your document again as **flowers 18-6 xxx.frm**.

FIGURE 18-7
Text for Exercise 18.6

```
SUBJECT: Account #FIELD(account number)

It has been a great pleasure doing business with you for a number of
years.  In all likelihood, the business relationship between our
companies has benefitted both our company and yours.

We are concerned, however, about your overdue account in the amount of
$FIELD(amount due).  Your account is now FIELD(months overdue) months
overdue, and we will have to put you on our cash-only account list if
we don't hear from you within 10 days.

Please maintain your good credit and send us a check for $FIELD(amount
due) today.

Sincerely,

GAILLARDIA GARDEN SUPPLY


Gabby Gaillardia, Account Manager
```

Now let's prepare the merge and tell WordPerfect to put the POSTNET bar code on each envelope. We'll set the option and then identify the field that contains the ZIP code number.

EXERCISE 18.7

1. With **flowers 18-6 xxx.frm** showing in your window, click the **Merge** button on the Merge Bar to open the Perform Merge dialog box.

2. Choose **Envelopes** and enter the FIELD codes to address the envelope. Do NOT include the middle initial, because there is no way on the envelope to deal with missing fields.

3. Look for the POSTNET box below the mailing address. If it is there, skip to Step 6. If it isn't there, click the **Options** button to open the Envelope Options dialog box (see Figure 18-8).

4. Click the third choice in the bottom section—**Position bar code below address**. Then click **OK** to return to the Envelope dialog box.

5. Position the insertion point in the POSTNET bar code box below the *Mailing Address* area. Click the **Field** button and double click **ZIP** to put the ZIP field in the box.

6. Click **OK** to close the Envelope dialog box and complete the merge.

7. Look at your letters and envelopes. Is the spacing correct around the variables in the letters? Do the envelopes contain the POSTNET bar codes below the addresses? If not, close the merged file without saving. Can you go back and think your way through the problem?

8. Read through the letter to Bill Bloom. Can you find an error that needs to be corrected?

9. When your letters and envelopes are correct, save the merged file as **flowers 18-7 xxx**. Print all three letters and envelopes and close all three files without saving again.

FIGURE 18-8
Envelope Options Dialog Box

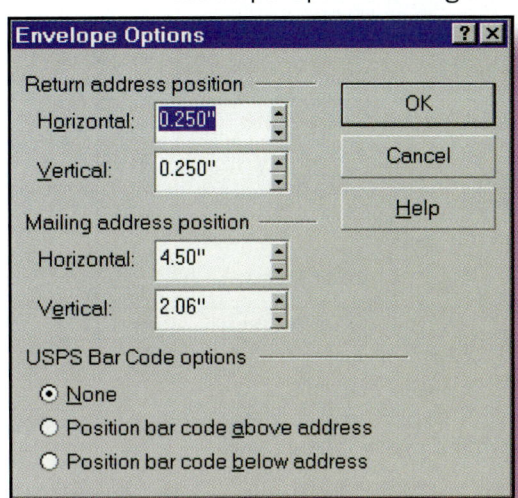

Merge into Tables

A different set of commands is used if you wish to merge into a table format. When you do this, you begin with a table that's too small to contain all of the records. WordPerfect will make the table the correct size for the merge.

Look at Figure 18-9. The following three new codes are chosen from the Merge Codes list on the Merge Bar:

- **LABEL(top)** tells WordPerfect where to loop back to in merging the records. It should be placed in the first cell of merged text. Put the first FIELD code directly after the LABEL code.

299

- **NEXTRECORD** must be in the cell with the final FIELD code. It tells WordPerfect to go to the next record (Obviously!).
- **GO(top)** tells WordPerfect to loop back to the *top* label with the information for the next record.

FIGURE 18-9
Form Document for Merge into Table Format

Name	Amount Due	Months Overdue
LABEL(top)FIELD(title) FIELD(first name) IFNOTBLANK(middle initial)FIELD(middle initial) ENDIF FIELD(last name)	FIELD(amount due)	FIELD(months overdue)NEXTRECORD
GO(top)		

Let's perform a merge using this form document so you can see how the LABEL and NEXTRECORD codes work.

EXERCISE 18.8

1. Beginning in a new document window, create a 3-column by 3-row table. Key the column headings, as shown in Figure 18-9, and position the insertion point in Cell A2.

2. Open the **Tools** menu, choose **Merge**, and then choose **Create Document**. Tell WordPerfect to convert the file in the active window to a form document. Use **flowers 18-1 xxx.dat** as the associated data source.

3. Click the **Merge Codes** button to open the list of merge codes from which you may choose the LABEL, NEXTRECORD, and GO codes. For both the LABEL and GO codes, key **top** in the label box. Click the **Insert Field** button to get the fields for the names, the amount overdue, and the number of months overdue. Insert the spaces between the name codes as before.

4. When you finish creating the form document so it looks somewhat like Figure 18-9, save the file as **flowers 18-8 xxx.frm**.

5. Merge the form document with **flowers 18-1 xxx.dat**. Check your final table. Is the spacing between the parts correct?

6. Format the table to make it attractive. Give it the title **OVERDUE ACCOUNTS**.

7. Save the finished document as **accounts 18-8 xxx**. Use your **pf** macro to insert the Path and Filename code. Print the file and save it again.

8. Close all open files.

Exercise 18.8 provided a small example of how you can use tables as form documents for merges. Regardless of the size of the table or the number of records, the three special merge codes that made Exercise 18.8 work will be the same.

Document Assembly

Another way you can use Merge to speed up the preparation of documents is to put information that is used repeatedly into the fields of a data file, and retrieve those pieces of text to make up a customized document. This prerecorded text is sometimes called *standard text,* or *boilerplate.*

A data file to be used for document assembly doesn't have named fields. In fact, you never really HAVE TO name your fields as you have done for your previous data files. You can let WordPerfect number the fields and just work with field numbers.

Let's begin to learn about document assembly by creating a data file. Then we'll learn how to use the information in that data file.

EXERCISE 18.9

1. Beginning in a new document window, open the **Tools** menu and choose **Merge**. Then choose **Create Data**.

2. In the Create Data File dialog box click **OK**. In the Number of Fields dialog box click **Cancel**. Click on the blank page to position your insertion point there. The Data File Merge Bar will be at the top.

3. Key the first sentence in Figure 18-10. Space two times following the period. Then either click the **End Field** button on the Merge Bar or press **Alt+Enter**. WordPerfect will insert an ENDFIELD code and a hard return.

4. Key the second sentence in Figure 18-10. Follow the same procedure until all three sentences have been keyed and are followed by ENDFIELD codes.

5. Check your work and make any necessary corrections. With your insertion point on the line below the third field, open the **Insert** menu and choose **File**. Insert **ziepke.dat** from the student **datafile** folder to give you the other 20 fields in the data file.

6. Check the spacing. Each field should begin on a new line and be followed by an ENDFIELD code.

7. Use **Save As** to save the file as **ziepke 18-9 xxx.dat** and close it.

FIGURE 18-10
Three Fields for the Ziepke Data File

```
Thank you for your phone call
regarding our line of automated
office equipment. ENDFIELD
Thank you for your letter
inquiring about our automated
office equipment. ENDFIELD
Thank you for stopping at our
booth at the recent PC trade
show in your area. ENDFIELD
```

Now let's see how we can use all of this standard text to create letters responding to inquiries by potential customers. In Exercise 18.10 you will prepare a form document that contains four skeleton letters. Each letter will look somewhat like the first letter, which is illustrated in Figure 18-11. The four letters will be separated by hard page breaks. When you merge, all four letters can be merged with the data file at one time. Follow these steps to create your form document.

301

EXERCISE 18.10

1. Beginning in a new document window, create a form document using **ziepke 18-9 xxx.dat** as the associated data file.

2. Use the **Center current and subsequent page(s)** command.

3. Click the **Date** button on the Merge Bar to insert a DATE code. Press **Enter** four times.

4. Key the name and address of the potential customer, as shown in Figure 18-11. Key the greeting as shown and press **Enter** twice.

5. Click the **Insert Field** button on the Merge Bar and insert Fields 1 and 4 for the first paragraph. Do not space between the two FIELD codes. The spaces between sentences were taken care of when the sentences were keyed.

FIGURE 18-11
First Letter in Document Assembly Form Document

```
DATE


Mr. Samuel Sampson
14 Singletary Circle
South Bend, SD 77401

Dear Mr. Sampson:

FIELD(1)FIELD(4)

FIELD(6)FIELD(7)FIELD(11)

FIELD(13)FIELD(19)FIELD(21)

FIELD(23)
```

FIGURE 18-12
Data for Exercise 18.10

```
Miss Sing Ho Lee, 992 Lighthouse Lane, Los Altos, AR 77227
Paragraph 1: Fields 2 and 5
Paragraph 2: Fields 10, 12, and 14
Paragraph 3: Fields 15 and 17
Paragraph 4: Field 23

Mrs. Stella Severson, 17 Sensenbrenner Lane, Sarasota, NC 32413
Paragraph 1: Fields 3 and 5
Paragraph 2: Field 9
Paragraph 3: Fields 18, 20, and 22
Paragraph 4: Field 17
Paragraph 5: Field 23

Mr. James Jillian, 731 Jackman Way, Jonesboro, WI 54911
Paragraph 1: Fields 1 and 10
Paragraph 2: Fields 12, 22, and 11
Paragraph 3: Field 16
Paragraph 4: Field 23
```

6. Press **Enter** twice and insert the FIELD codes for Fields 6, 7, and 11.

7. Repeat the procedure until you have entered the FIELD codes, as shown in Figure 18-11.

8. Press **Ctrl+Enter** to move the insertion point to a new page. Create a letter for Miss Sing Ho Lee using the information in Figure 18-12.

When you finish the letter for Miss Lee, create one for Mrs. Severson and another for Mr. Jillian.

9. When you finish all four form letters, check your work carefully. Then save the file as **ziepke 18-10 xxx.frm**. Play the **pf** macro and close the file, saving it again.

With the form letters prepared, you are ready to merge them with the data file. This will be easy for you. You've merged so many times already.

EXERCISE 18.11

1. Beginning in a new document window, begin a merge. Identify the form document as **ziepke 18-10 xxx.frm** and the data source as **ziepke 18-9 xxx.dat**. In the Perform Merge dialog box, click the **Reset** button unless it is already grayed.

2. When you finish, look at your four letters. Do they look good? Do any adjustments need to be made? If spacing adjustments need to be made in the form document, close your completed merge without saving. Open the form document and make the corrections. Save the form document and close it. Then perform the merge again.

3. Save the merged document as **ziepke 18-11 xxx**. Print your four letters. Then close the document, saving it again when you close it.

Reference Document

The exercise you just completed was easy to prepare because you were told which field numbers to include to suit the request for information from each of the four potential customers. If you were preparing letters on the job, however, you'd need to have the data file in front of you to know which sentences to include. And then you wouldn't know what the sentence numbers were.

For this reason, part of preparing standard text for a document assembly application is to prepare what's known as a *reference document*. That document includes the standard text and the field numbers. With a reference document, anyone can decide which sentences should be used in the form documents. The reference document might be used by the boss or by the administrative assistant. Imagine the scenario of a boss receiving a letter asking for information about a product. He or she could use the reference document to identify the sentences to be used in a "form letter" to be sent back to that prospective customer and jot those numbers on the letter for the assistant. Let's prepare a reference document for the data file in Exercise 18-9.

EXERCISE 18.12

1. Beginning in a new document window, center **ZIEPKE ELECTRONICS**. Center **Standard Sentences** in bold a double space below the title. Press **Enter** twice.

2. Identify the document as a form document with **ziepke 18-9 xxx.dat** as the data source.

3. Key a **1.** at the left margin and press **Tab** for QuickIndent.

4. Click the **Insert Field** button on the Form File Merge Bar and double click **Field 1** to insert the FIELD code after the *1*. Press **Enter** twice. Unless your automatic bullets and numbers are turned off, the next numeral will appear automatically. Insert Field 2. The first part of your form document will look like Figure 18-13.

5. Continue keying numbers, using **Indent**, and entering FIELD codes until you run out of fields. (There are 23 of them.)

6. When you finish, check your work. Then save the file as **ziepke 18-12 xxx.frm**. Play your **pf** macro to insert the Path and Filename code at the bottom of all pages.

7. Save the file again and close it.

8. Use **Merge** to combine **ziepke 18-12 xxx.frm** with **ziepke 18-9 xxx.dat**.

9. When your merge is finished, look over the reference document. Then print it and close it, saving it as **reference 18-12 xxx**.

FIGURE 18-13
Beginning of Exercise 18.12 Form Document

```
         ZIEPKE ELECTRONICS

         Standard Sentences

1.    FIELD(1)

2.    FIELD(2)
```

If the form document is kept, the reference document can be redone each time the standard text in the data file is revised.

Address Book

A feature apart from the data files used in merge applications is the WordPerfect Address Book feature. This feature may be used to keep frequently used addresses, phone numbers, e-mail addresses, etc., together in one place. The information stored in the Address Book can be used on envelopes, letters, labels, mass mailings like those prepared with Merge, and e-mail (if you have a modem or network connection). You can also use the Address Book to dial phone and fax numbers.

The Address Book feature makes it possible for you to have multiple address books. Available books are represented by tabs in the main Address Book window.

Create an Address Book

For practice, let's create an Address Book using the names and addresses you used for the Ziepke letters in Exercises 18.9 through 18.12. Then we'll see how those names and addresses can be used in a merge.

EXERCISE 18.13

1. Beginning in a new document window, open the **Tools** menu and choose **Address Book**.

2. Look at the Corel Address Book dialog box. It should look somewhat like Figure 18-14. Does it have a tab labeled *Ziepke*? If the Ziepke tab appears:
   a. Click that tab and look at the names in the list.
   b. Move the highlight to *Sing Ho Lee* and click the **Edit** button at the bottom of the dialog box.
   c. Look at the kinds of information that may be entered for each person in the Address Book. For this address, you will need the title, first name, last name, address, city, state, and ZIP code. Are all of those parts present? If not, turn to Figure 18-12 and complete the address.
   d. Check the other three addresses for completeness and make any necessary repairs.

3. If no Ziepke tab exists, you will need to create a Ziepke book. Follow these steps:
   a. Click the **Book** menu and choose **New**. Key **Ziepke** and click **OK**. The Ziepke tab should now show at the top of the dialog box.
   b. Click the **Add** button at the bottom of the box to open the New Entry dialog box. With *Person* highlighted, click **OK**.

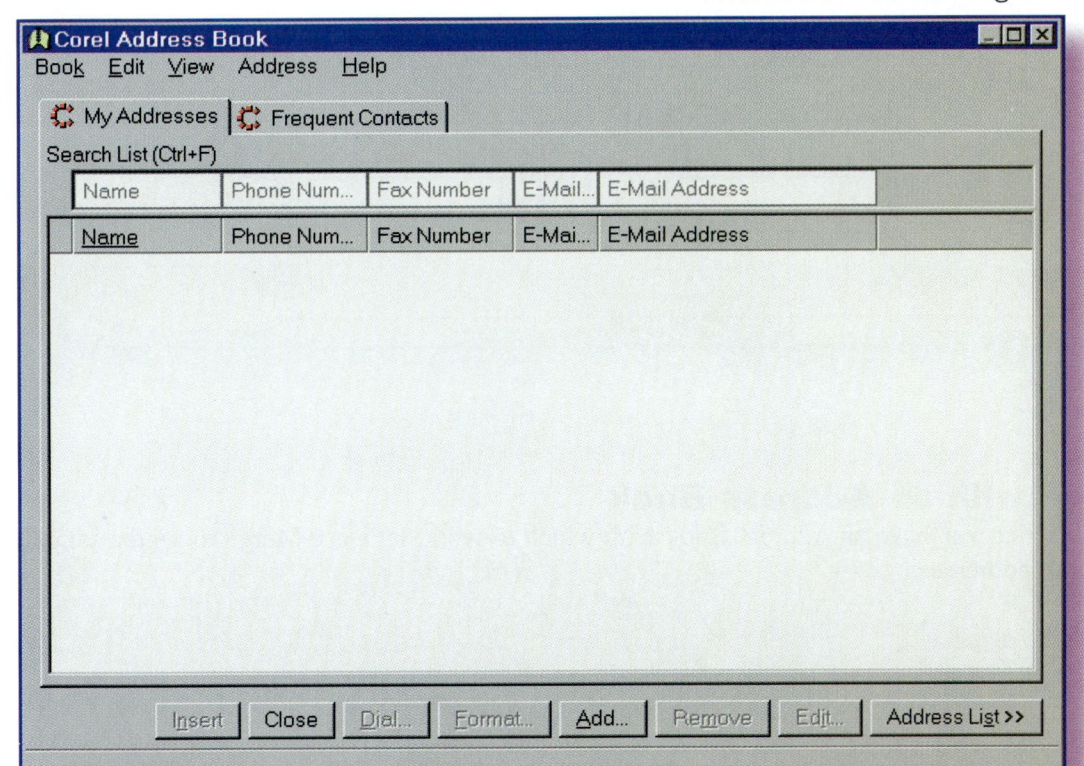

FIGURE 18-14
Corel Address Book Dialog Box

(continued on next page)

EXERCISE 18.13 CONTINUED

c. Look at the New Person Properties dialog box (see Figure 18-15). With the **Personal** tab selected, enter the information about Samuel Sampson in Figure 18-11 into the dialog box. This includes the first and last name and all parts of the address. Include the greeting too, and click **OK**.

d. Follow the procedure in Steps 3b and 3c to add the other four people in Figure 18-12. (Sing Ho Lee's first name is *Sing Ho*.)

4. Close the Address Book.

FIGURE 18-15
New Person Properties Dialog Box

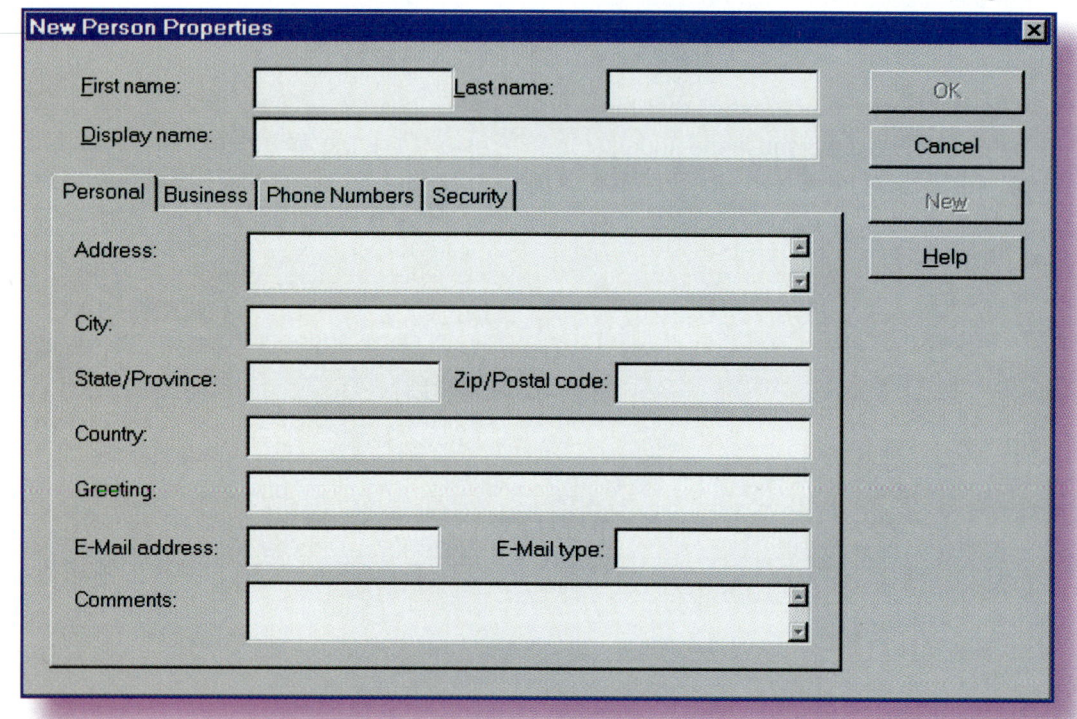

Merge with an Address Book

Now that you have an Address Book with which to work, let's use Merge to send a sample letter to the four addresses.

EXERCISE 18.14

1. Create a form document. In the Associate Form and Data dialog box, click **Associate an address book**.

2. In the drop-down menu beside that choice, change to **Ziepke** (see Figure 18-16). Then click **OK**.

3. In your document window, set up a form document, including the following features:
   a. Center pages vertically.
   b. Insert the DATE code using the Merge Bar.
   c. Insert FIELD codes using the **Insert Field** button. (Note that the available codes match the fields in the Address Book and that the *Greeting* field is near the bottom of the list.)

4. Key the short letter in Figure 18-17.

FIGURE 18-16
Associate Form and Data Dialog Box

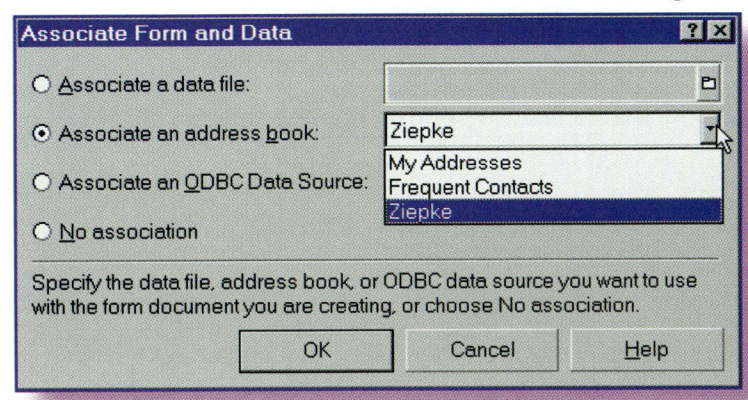

5. When your letter is finished, save it as **ziepke 18-14 xxx.frm**. Play your **pf** macro and save the file again.

6. Click the **Merge** button on the Merge Bar. Note that Form document is Current Document and Data source is Ziepke. Complete the merge.

7. Print the four short letters and close the file, saving it as **interest 18-14 xxx**.

FIGURE 18-17
Letter for Exercise 18.14

```
FIELD(First Name) FIELD(Last Name)
FIELD(Address)
FIELD(City), FIELD(State) FIELD(ZIP Code)

FIELD(Greeting):

Thank you for your interest in our company.  We look forward to doing
business with you.  Please keep in touch.

Sincerely,

ZIEPKE ELECTRONICS



Felix Rodriguez, Manager
```

307

Summary

This lesson took Merge several steps farther than the basics you learned in Lesson 17. In the process of discovering that WordPerfect Merge is a powerful tool, you learned the following:

- Data files can be arranged in a variety of ways.
- The smaller the chunks of data in a data file, the more flexibility you will have in your merge.
- WordPerfect takes care of data missing from a field if the field falls on a line by itself.
- WordPerfect merge codes may be used to deal with missing data if it falls between two other fields on the same line.
- If the ZIP code is in a field by itself, you can include a POSTNET bar code on your envelopes.
- Several special merge codes must be used to merge a data file into a table format.
- Merge can be used for boilerplate, or standard text, letters.
- WordPerfect's Address Book feature can be used for a variety of applications, including merging.

Before leaving Merge, it is important to note that in all of the Merge exercises you've completed in Lessons 17 and 18, you have been instructed to save the data file, the form document, and the completed merge. In actual practice you probably won't ever save the documents that result from the completed merge. Having the form document and the data source makes it simple to remerge the documents, if necessary, and saving the same letter to a number of people uses disk space unnecessarily.

LESSON 18 REVIEW QUESTIONS

FILL IN THE BLANKS

Complete each of the following statements by writing your answer in the blank provided.

1. The smaller the pieces of information in each field, the more flexible your _____ will be.

2. The IFNOTBLANK and _____ commands tell WordPerfect that if information is there, it should be included.

3. After you change options in the Perform Merge Options dialog box, it is important to click the _____ button if you wish to return to the default settings.

4. If you wish to add the POSTNET bar codes to your envelopes in a merge, you must have the _____ in a field by itself when you are setting up your data source.

5. When merging into tables, _____ tells WordPerfect where to loop back to in merging records.

6. When merging into tables, _____ must be in the cell with the final FIELD code.

7. WordPerfect's _____ may be used to keep frequently used addresses, phone numbers, e-mail addresses, etc., together in one place.

TRUE/FALSE

Circle the T if the statement is true. Circle the F if it is false.

T F 8. WordPerfect takes care of missing data from a field if the field falls on a line by itself.

T F 9. In document assembly a reference document is used as the form document.

T F 10. Prerecorded text is sometimes called standard text, or boilerplate.

LESSON 18 PROJECT

SCANS

Keyboard Merge can be combined with document assembly. It involves putting KEYBOARD codes in the fields of the data file prior to the merge. In this project we will revise two of the fields of the Ziepke data file and then merge that data file again with the form document you created for the Ziepke inquiries. Follow along carefully.

1. Open **ziepke 18-9 xxx.dat**. Save the file as **ziepke proj18 xxx.dat**.

2. Move the insertion point to Field 15 (you can see the field numbers at the right on the Application Bar).

3. Position the insertion point following the word *area* and key a comma and a space.

4. Click the Merge Codes button on the Merge Bar and key **keyb** to move the insertion point to the KEYBOARD code. Click Insert and key the prompt, as illustrated in Figure 18-18. Press Enter to enter the code. Key a comma.

FIGURE 18-18
Modified Fields for Lesson 18 Project

```
Our salesperson for your area, KEYBOARD(district salesperson), will
call you within the next few days.

The business card for our salesperson in your area, KEYBOARD(district
salesperson), is enclosed with this letter. Please call
KEYBOARD(him/her) at KEYBOARD(salesperson's telephone number) to
arrange for a demonstration of any of our products.
```

5. Follow the same procedure to put KEYBOARD codes in Field 16. Note that this field gets three KEYBOARD codes.

(continued on next page)

6. Save the file again with the same name and close it.

7. Merge **ziepke proj18 xxx.dat** with **ziepke 18-10 xxx.frm**. During the merge, you will be asked to key the information requested in the KEYBOARD codes. Your document will look like a mess when the prompt appears at the bottom of the window. When a prompt appears, key the required information and press Alt+Enter to move to the next prompt. Following is the information you'll need in the order you should enter it:

District Salesperson:	Joan Jackson
District Salesperson:	Amy Evans at 414-555-6755

8. Save the four letters as **ziepke proj18 letters xxx**. Print only the letters that contain the information about district salespersons and close all files.

NOTE:

With this kind of merge, it is difficult to prepare envelopes. The regular Envelope feature (in the Format menu) can be used for the first letter in the merge. After printing the letters, you could prepare the first envelope and print it, then delete the first letter and prepare an envelope for the next letter, and so on. It doesn't seem to be very efficient, but it is one possible solution.

CRITICAL THINKING ACTIVITY

SCANS

You have recently gone on-line and have access to the Internet. One of the services you are using frequently is e-mail. What WordPerfect feature could be used to enhance your use of e-mail?

Sort, Extract, and Select

LESSON 19

OBJECTIVES

Upon completion of this lesson, you will be able to:

- Use Line Sort.
- Use Paragraph Sort.
- Use Merge Sort.
- Use Table Sort.
- Extract and select records.

Estimated Time: 2 hours

In the last two lessons you've been working with Merge. While a variety of documents might be created using Merge, combining a standard, or shell, document (the form document) with a list of names and addresses is probably one of the most frequently used applications.

If the list of names and addresses to be merged is relatively small, hand sorting the documents for distribution after printing isn't a big problem. When the list is large, however, and post office requirements for ZIP code order are taken into account, hand sorting can be a big job.

With WordPerfect, hand sorting is unnecessary because WordPerfect has a tool called Sort that enables you to sort the records in a data file before it is ever merged with a form document. What's more, you get to direct the sort. The list can be sorted in any number of ways. For instance, a data file can be sorted in alphabetic order by name, in ZIP code order, by ZIP code and alphabetized within each ZIP code grouping, by company name, by amount owed, or by months overdue for payment.

Depending on your needs and the content of the data source, the list can be sorted by just about any other criteria. In addition, WordPerfect can be directed to select certain records from your lists.

Types of Sort

WordPerfect can be used to sort records in the following five formats:

Line	Any groupings of text separated from each other by a hard return or soft return.
Paragraph	Groupings of text separated by two hard returns.
Merge Data File	Rows in data files separated from each other with ENDRECORD codes.
Table Row	Horizontal rows of cells in WordPerfect tables.
Column	Parallel columns separated by hard page breaks.

311

Let's learn about Sort as you practice some examples in each of the types except Column Sort. We didn't prepare any parallel columns because tables do the work so much more easily.

Line Sort

We'll begin with Line Sort. Follow the steps in Exercise 19.1.

EXERCISE 19.1

1. Key the following list of names in a single column at the left margin. Add your name as indicated.

Alberta	**Dale R.**
Carol	**Judy Anne**
Elizabeth	**Pedro**
Walter	**Betty**
Earl	**Carol**
(your name)	

2. With the list showing, open the **Tools** menu and choose **Sort** to display the Sort dialog box, as displayed in Figure 19-1.

3. If it is not already highlighted, select **First word in a line**. Then click **Sort**. Voila! Your list should instantly be alphabetized.

4. Save the list as **sort 19-1 xxx**. Play your **pf** macro to identify the file. Keep it open.

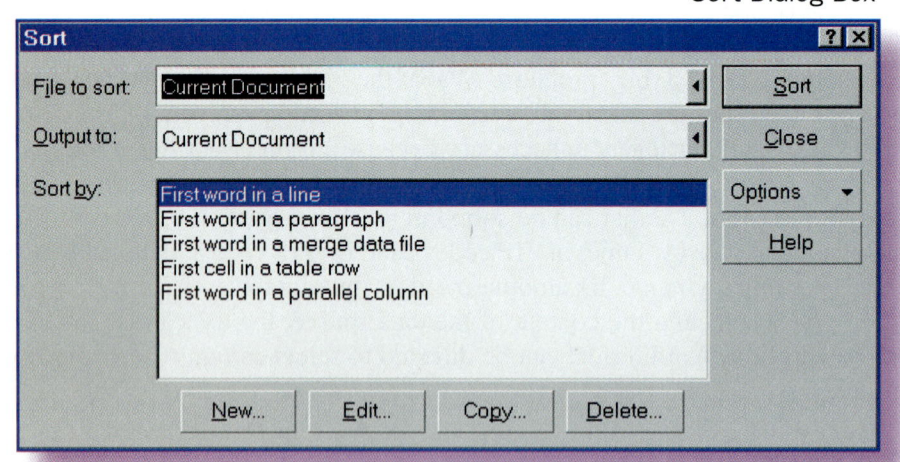

FIGURE 19-1
Sort Dialog Box

That was pretty easy, wasn't it? That's about as basic as Line Sort can be. The people in our list, however, probably wouldn't normally be sorted by first name. Let's give them last names and learn more about Line Sort.

In Exercise 19.2 we'll create a User Defined Sort category that will be edited for each sort in this lesson.

EXERCISE 19.2

FIGURE 19-2
New Sort Dialog Box

1. With **sort 19-1 xxx** open in the window, use **Save As** to save the list as **sort 19-2 xxx**. Amend your list by adding a surname for each of the people in the list as follows:
   Alberta Weigel
   Betty Boneske
   Carol Anderson
   Carol Morgan
   Dale R. Nelson
   Earl Wiesemann
   Elizabeth Reichert
   Judy Anne Boneske
   Pedro DePino
   Walter Anderson

2. Add **Pam Anderson** to the list. Include your own last name.

3. Open the **Tools** menu and choose **Sort** to return to the Sort dialog box. Look at the Sort choices. Note that there is a choice for each type of sort listed at the beginning of this section.

4. Do you see *<User Defined Sort>* in the list? If so, choose it and click **Edit**. If not, click **New**. The Edit Sort or New Sort dialog box, illustrated in Figure 19-2, should appear.

5. Look at the dialog box. The **Line** button should be chosen in the *Sort by* section at the top. In the *Keys* section, only one "Key" should appear. If your dialog box shows more than one, get rid of all but the first by clicking in the *Field* box for any additional Keys and then clicking the **Delete Key** button.

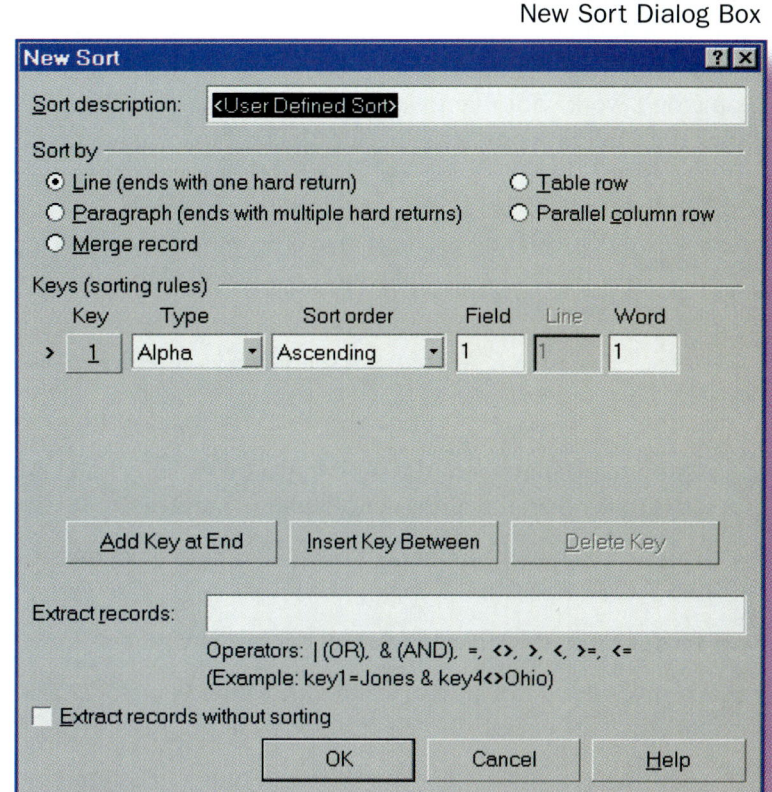

6. In the Key 1 section set Field at **1** and Word at **-1**, and click **OK** and then **Sort**. This will bring you back to your document, and the list should now be alphabetized by last name. (Don't worry about the fact that the Andersons are out of order for now.)

7. Save the list again as **sort 19-2 xxx**. Then open the **Tools** menu and choose **Sort** again so you can look at these dialog boxes as you learn about them.

The *<User Defined Sort>* choice should be highlighted. We'll highlight that choice and choose Edit for all sorting in this course. On the job, you might wish to set the criteria for a specialized kind of sort you use often. Then you can name it so it is easy to choose from the list each time you need it. If you don't use a sort that's listed, it can be deleted to make room for those you DO use.

At the top of the Sort dialog box are a couple of naming options. You don't have to have a document showing in the window to sort it. You can direct WordPerfect to sort a file that is on disk and save it with a different name. Usually you will sort a document that's showing in the window. In that case, you won't work with File to sort and Output.

Now click Edit to open the Edit Sort dialog box. This dialog box is pretty simple, once you get a handle on it. In the *Keys (sorting rules)* section you can make your choices about how you want the document sorted. A "Key" is a term used to tell WordPerfect the priorities regarding how you want the list sorted. The default setting has only one Key, but you may set more Keys.

Because WordPerfect remembers your last sort, the current settings in the *Keys (sorting rules)* section for Key 1 are:

Alpha   Ascending   Field 1   Word -1

- **Type**. You can set your sort to be alphabetic (Alpha) or Numeric.
    - **Alpha** may contain words, a combination of letters and numerals, or numbers of equal length, like Social Security or telephone numbers.
    - **Numeric** includes numbers of unequal length or numbers containing periods or commas, like 3,451 or $5.30.
- **Sort Order**. You may change the order from Ascending (A to Z) to Descending (Z to A).
- **Field**. This is the same kind of field with which you worked in Merge. In Line Sort, fields are separated by tabs or indents. We'll work with fields shortly.
- **Line**. This choice is currently grayed because it is used only with Merge or Paragraph Sort.
- **Word**. *Alberta* is Word 1 and *Weigel* is Word 2, but *Anne* is word 2, also. To be consistent in identifying the last name, count from the right by adding a hyphen. In your list, the last name is always Word -1 of Field 1.

We'll work with some of the other choices in the dialog box shortly. Now we'll learn how to deal with first and last names and more information. Then we'll set some tab stops for exercises coming up.

The names in your list are considered Field 1 of the information to be sorted. The addresses you'll add in Exercise 19.3 will be considered Field 2 information because they will be separated from Field 1 by a tab. Then we'll sort the list—first by ZIP code and then by city. As always, read through the entire exercise before beginning.

EXERCISE 19.3

1. Close the dialog boxes. With **sort 19-2 xxx** open, save the file as **sort 19-3 xxx**.

2. Choose **Tools**, **Sort**, and then **<User Defined Sort>**. Click **Edit**. In the Edit Sort dialog box click the **Add Key at End** button. The criteria is Field 1, Word 1 (the first name).

3. Perform the sort. Are Carol, Pam, and Walter Anderson in order, now? Let's adjust the file and include addresses.

314   UNIT 5: MERGE TOOLS

4. Display the Ruler. Clear all tabs. Set a Left tab at **3.5"** and a Decimal tab at **6.75"**.

5. Each city, state, and ZIP code in Column 2 represents Field 2 of the list. Key the addresses as follows:
   a. Press **End** to move your insertion point to the end of Carol Anderson's name and press **Tab**.
   b. Key Carol's city, state, and ZIP code, as shown in Figure 19-3.
   c. Press the down arrow key and **Tab** to position the insertion point for Pam's information.
   d. Use hard spaces (**Ctrl+space bar**) between the parts of *Butte des Morts*, *Stevens Point*, and *Wisconsin Dells* to make WordPerfect think each of them is all one word.
   e. Include your own address opposite your name.

6. Let's sort by ZIP code. Open the Edit Sort dialog box. Set Key 1 as follows:

Alpha Ascending   Field 2   Word -1

FIGURE 19-3
Addresses for Exercise 19.3 Sort

```
Carol Anderson        Stevens Point, WI 54481
Pam Anderson          Neenah, WI 54956
Walter Anderson       Phoenix, AZ 88471
Betty Boneske         Oshkosh, WI 54901
Judy Anne Boneske     Neenah, WI 54956
Pedro DePino          Butternut, WI 54914
Carol Morgan          Wisconsin Dells, WI 53965
(your name)           (your address)
Dale R. Nelson        Butte des Morts, WI 54927
Elizabeth Reichert    Milwaukee, WI 53211
Alberta Weigel        Hendersonville, NC 18739
Earl Wiesemann        Ladysmith, WI 54848
```

7. Leave Key 2 in place, but change it so the sort is by last name. To do that, change Word to **-1**. (Note that only two people have the same city. If you didn't set Key 2 at **-1**, Boneske might end up before Anderson after the sort.)

8. Click **OK** and then **Sort** to perform the sort. Check your list over to see if it did what you expected. Print it and save it again as **sort 19-3 xxx**. Keep it open.

EXERCISE 19.4

Can you sort this list by the name of the city? You're on your own. (HINT: The city is the first item in Field 2.) When you finish, keep the document open for Exercise 19.5.

Let's take this exercise one step further and use it to learn about a Numeric Sort.

EXERCISE 19.5

1. With your sort from Exercise 19.4 showing in the window, use **Save As** to save the file as **sort 19-5 xxx**.

2. Use a method similar to Exercise 19.3 to add the following dollar amounts at the Decimal tab you set. It doesn't matter who gets which number.

455.00	24.00	110.00
786.00	998.00	2390.00
15.00	567.00	1334.00
1199.00	3.00	1.50

3. Go to the Edit Sort dialog box. Set Key 1 at **Numeric Ascending 3 1**. (This is a Numeric Sort on Word 1 of Field 3. Do you understand that setting? By now, you should. If you don't understand, ask your instructor to help you. It's important!)

4. Click somewhere in the Key 2 line. Click the **Delete Key** button to delete Key 2.

5. Click **OK** and then **Sort** to perform the sort. Did the list rearrange so the person with the smallest debt is at the top?

6. Return to the Edit Sort dialog box. Change Key 1 from *Ascending* to **Descending**. Sort again. Were the results what you expected?

7. Play your **pf** macro to identify the document. Then print it and close it, saving it again as **sort 19-5 xxx** as you close it.

Congratulations! You are now an expert with Line Sort. All of the principles you learned here will be applied in the other kinds of Sort. Be sure you are comfortable with Line Sort before moving on.

Paragraph Sort

Anything separated by two hard returns can be sorted in Paragraph Sort. It can be one line or several, and the lines in the paragraph may end either with a soft return or a hard return. Paragraph Sort may be used to arrange bibliography entries in alphabetic order. You could also use Paragraph Sort for names and addresses. Let's increase the size of the **flowers** data file and merge it with a simple format. Then we'll be able to sort the list using Paragraph Sort.

EXERCISE 19.6

1. Beginning in a new document window, open **flowers 18-1 xxx.dat**. Use **Save As** to save the file as **flowers xxx.dat**.

2. Position the insertion point at the end of the file. Go to the student **datafile** folder and insert **flowers**. You should now have 16 records in your file. Save the large file.

3. Click the **Go to Form** button and create a form document that looks like Figure 19-4. Press **Enter** twice following the *amount due* line.

4. Save the form document as **list 19-6 xxx.frm**. Prepare to merge it with **flowers xxx.dat**. In the Perform Merge dialog box click **Options** and tell WordPerfect not to put the merged records on separate pages.

5. Save the merged file as **flower list 19-6 xxx**. Play your **pf** macro to identify the file.

6. If your file extends to a third page, use **Make It Fit** to squeeze it onto two pages.

FIGURE 19-4
Form Document for Exercise 19.6

```
FIELD(first name) FIELD(last name)
FIELD(company)
FIELD(street)
FIELD(city), FIELD(state)
FIELD(ZIP)
FIELD(amount due)
```

Look at the names, addresses, and amounts in the file. Each of those customers is considered a paragraph with regard to sorting. You can sort by just about any criteria.

EXERCISE 19.7

1. With **flower list 19-6 xxx** showing in the window, go to the Edit Sort dialog box and click the **Paragraph** button at the top. (WordPerfect may have already done that for you.)

2. Set Key 1 to sort by last name. That's Line 1, Field 1, Word -1. Complete the sort and check your work.

3. Sort the list in the following ways:
   a. By amount due with the greatest number at the top (Numeric, Descending, Line -1, Field 1 and Word 1). Note that you can't count the line number from the top because some customers have a company name and others don't.
   b. By ZIP code (Alpha, Ascending, Line -2, Field 1, and Word -1).
   c. By state. (Can you figure it out?)
   d. By city name.

4. Resort the list so the last names of the customers are in alphabetic order.

5. Print the file and close it, saving it again as **flower list 19-6 xxx** as you close it. Close all open files.

That was a simple exercise in Paragraph Sort. Obviously, it can be used for other kinds of paragraphs, as well as for the names and addresses of our blooming customers.

Merge Sort

In the previous exercise using Paragraph Sort you got rid of the merge codes in the original list. In Merge Sort you work with the data files, complete with their merge codes. The ENDFIELD codes separate one field from another.

EXERCISE 19.8

1. Open **flowers xxx.dat**. With the data file showing in the window, open the Edit Sort dialog box. If necessary, change to **Merge record**.

2. Sort alphabetically by the last name of the customer. (That's Field 5.) Check your work. Are Adelbert Aster and Bill Bloom at the top of the list?

3. Insert the correct field number and sort numerically by account number in Ascending order. Are Zola Zinnia and Charles Cosmos at the top of the list?

4. Change to Descending order. Are Mari Gold and Dandi Lyons at the top?

5. Change the field number and sort by the amount owed in Descending order. Are Gary Gardenia and Petunia Peters at the top?

6. Sort by ZIP code number in Ascending order. Are Rose Ramirez and Mari Gold at the top?

7. Close the file without saving it again.

Those sorts were easy because each field only contained one piece of information. Let's try something a little more challenging.

EXERCISE 19.9

1. Open **im spec proj17b xxx.dat**. Save the file as **im spec 19-9 xxx.dat**. Study the fields. Note that the entire inside address is one field.

2. Note, too, that each customer has a company name. Delete the *Bits and Chips* line from Miguel Zedillo's record and close up the space.

3. Sort the list by last name. You should set Field 1, Line 1, and Word -1. You should get Lee, Waldman, and Zedillo.

4. Sort the list by ZIP code. (Because Field 1 has an unequal number of lines, you'll have to use Line -1. Did you remember that the best way to identify the ZIP code number on a line that includes city and state is by using Word -1? You should get Zedillo, Lee, and Waldman.

5. Close the file without saving and open **micro 17-6 xxx.dat**. Look at the way the fields are arranged.

6. Sort the list by last name. You should get Helmke, Noschang, Oppermann, and Weigel.

7. Sort the list by ZIP code. You should get Weigel, Oppermann, Noschang, and Helmke. Close the file without saving it.

As you can see, Merge Sort isn't difficult when you have an understanding of how the merge data files are organized. You should be able to sort any data file now. Let's look at a different kind of sort.

Table Sort

Table Sort is used for sorting the rows in a table. For sort purposes, table rows are divided into columns. Let's create a table to sort. Then we'll practice.

EXERCISE 19.10

1. Beginning in a new document window, merge **flowers 18-8 xxx.frm** with **flowers xxx.dat**. Look at the resulting table. It is unformatted, but that doesn't matter for our sort. Save it as **table 19-10 xxx**.

2. Select the entire table except the first row that contains the column headings. (When you select, the cells should stay all black, not just black in the center. If you drag your insertion point below the bottom of the table when selecting, you'll need to drag it back up into the table so the cells stay black.)

3. Open the Edit Sort dialog box. If necessary, choose the **Table row** button at the top. Then tell WordPerfect to sort the list by the last names of the customers.

4. Select all rows of the table except the first row again. Can you figure out how to sort the customers by amount owed—in Descending order? Do it. Then play your **pf** macro to identify the file. Print it and close it, saving it again.

In Exercise 19.10 you selected the rows to be sorted, so the row containing the column headings wasn't affected. This is an especially useful technique when you want to sort only part of a table. A better way, when you are sorting all of the data in a table, would be to use your table formatting knowledge to set the row containing the column headings as a Header Row. Then WordPerfect knows that the row must always stay at the top. To do this, you would position your insertion point in the row and choose Format, Row, and Header Row.

Now that you're so good with Sort, let's learn how we can work with only part of a list.

Extract

WordPerfect enables you to separate certain records from a list. There are several ways to do this. One of those ways is in the Edit Sort dialog box. Normally you will extract (or select) the records to be used from the data file before completing a merge. Let's work with the **flowers** file and learn to extract based on several criteria.

EXERCISE 19.11

> **NOTE:**
>
> When you extract files, the original list is lost unless you have it saved. In this exercise you will work with the **flowers** list of customers. BE CAREFUL not to save after you use Extract. If you do save, give your file a new name. Otherwise, your partial list will take the place of the complete list of customers on your disk.

1. Beginning in a new document window, open **flowers xxx.dat**. Go to the Edit Sort dialog box and set Key 1 at **Field 10** to point to the ZIP code numbers. Set an Alphabetic sort in Ascending order.

2. In the *Extract records* text box at the bottom, key **Key 1>55000**. (The *greater than* symbol is the shift of the period key.)

3. Perform the sort. You should end up with 8 customers, and the first two are Betty Blum and Lily Larsen. (If you press Ctrl+End and look at the *Pg* indicator, you'll see *10*. One of the records is the blank one in which your insertion point is positioned. The other is the Field Names record at the top.)

4. Close the file without saving and open **flowers xxx.dat** again.

5. This time we'll sort the customers alphabetically, and we'll extract only those customers who owe more than $500.00. Set the sort and extract as follows:
   a. Set Key 1 for last names.
   b. Set Key 2 to identify the field containing amounts due. Remember that it is numeric.
   c. In the *Extract records* text box, key **Key 2>500.00**.
   d. Perform the sort and extract.

6. Check the records. You should have six records, beginning with Adelbert Aster and Bill Bloom. Close the file without saving.

> **NOTE:**
>
> Always check two things in the Edit Sort dialog box before beginning a sort:
>
> - Make sure the setting at the top matches the kind of sort you are performing.
>
> - Check the Extract text box at the bottom. WordPerfect doesn't automatically clear the Extract records text box. If your next sort doesn't involve Extract, the formula must be deleted!

7. Open **flowers xxx.dat** again. Select the accounts where the balance is equal to or greater than 4 months overdue. (HINT: Identify the field to be sorted and put it in any Key. In the *Extract records* text box identify that Key and specify that it should be **=>4**.) Arrange the accounts in Ascending order according to the amount owed. THINK!

8. Check your work. You should end up with Petunia, Zola, Gina, Daisy, and Peter. If you didn't do it right, close the file without saving and try again. If you did it right, congratulate yourself and close the file without saving it.

Select Records

One more method of separating out records for a mailing is Select Records, which may take place during a merge. When you select records during the merge, your data file remains complete, but only the selected records will be used during the merge.

Select Records offers two options. You can specify conditions, like we did when we specified that the amount due should be in excess of $500.00, or you can manually select the records you wish to include. We'll try it both ways.

EXERCISE 19.12

1. Beginning in a new document window, fill in the Perform Merge dialog box to merge **list 19-6 xxx.frm** with **flowers xxx.dat**. Before clicking the **Merge** button, choose **Options** and deselect **Separate each merged document with a page break**. Click **OK**.

2. Back in the Perform Merge dialog box, click the **Select Records** button. Look at the Select Records dialog box. It should look like Figure 19-5.

3. Notice the two round buttons near the top. Click the **Mark records** button. In the *First field to display* box click the down arrow and choose **amount due** from near the bottom of the list. Then click **Update Record List**.

4. Look at the Record List. It should show the amounts due, with the number of months overdue in brackets. Go through the list and click to put an *x* at the left of each account balance that is less than $100.00.

5. Complete the merge. It should include Daisy, Mari, Rose, Peter, Gina, and Dandi. (They might be in a different order. There is no way to arrange the records when you use Select Records.)

6. Save your merged file as **small 19-12 xxx** because it includes customers with small balances. Play the **pf** macro to identify the file, print it, save it again, and close it.

7. Return to the Perform Merge dialog box and choose **Select Records** again. This time, click the **Specify conditions** button. Click the arrow beside the text box under the word *Field* over the first column. Change to **amount due**.

(continued on next page)

321

EXERCISE 19.12 CONTINUED

8. In the *Cond 1* text box key **<100.00** to choose all accounts of less than $100.00. Complete the merge and look at the results. You should have the same six customers.

9. Close the file without saving.

FIGURE 19-5
Select Records Dialog Box

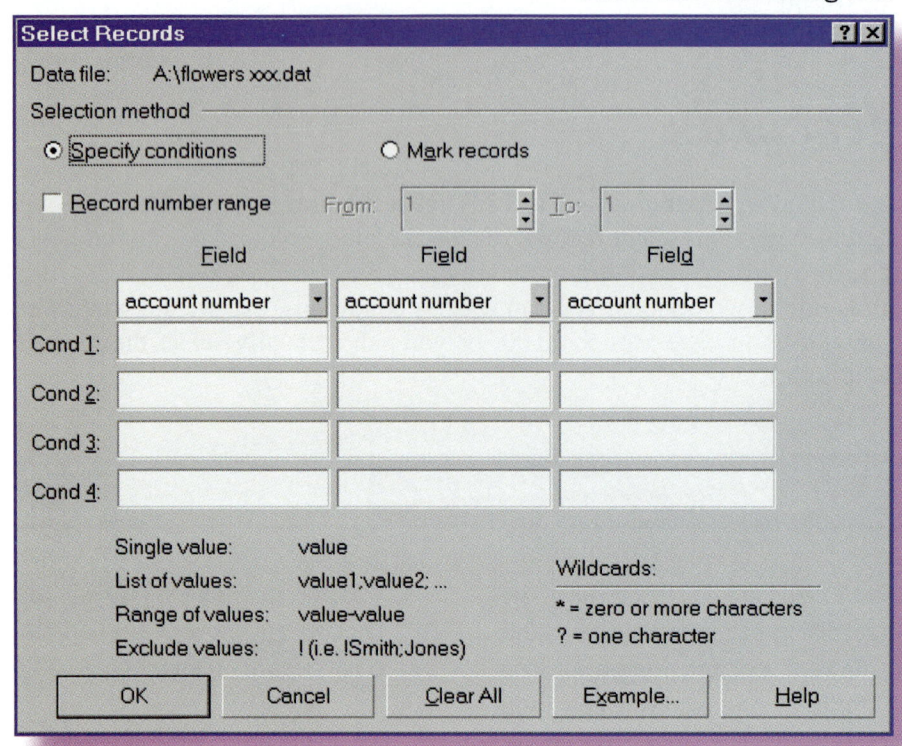

Obviously, this was a brief introduction to Select Records. If you are confused about the different ways to select records, study Figure 19-6. It explains the differences between the two features.

FIGURE 19-6
Feature Comparison

Extract Using Sort	Select Records During Merge
Extract using Sort is done BEFORE the merge.	Select Records takes place when you are setting up the merge.
When the desired records are extracted, all other records are deleted. (Be sure not to save the extracted list over your complete list!)	The complete list of records remains intact, although only the selected records are merged.
During the Extract process, your records can be sorted in a specified order.	Records must be sorted before the merge if you want them in a specified order after the merge.

322   UNIT 5: MERGE TOOLS

Summary

This lesson was mostly about Sort—arranging things in order. You had a lot of practice so you would grasp what Sort is all about. You also learned about selecting records. You learned that:

- Lines of text can be sorted in a number of ways.
- A variety of types of information can be sorted with Paragraph Sort.
- Merge Sort enables you to rearrange data records before the merge, saving hand sorting after the merge.
- Records bearing certain characteristics can be separated out from a complete data file using Extract.
- Select Records enables you to select certain records to be used in a merge during the merge.

You should be an expert at Sort, Extract, and Select by now, but you'll get a little more practice in Project 19.

LESSON 19 REVIEW QUESTIONS

MULTIPLE CHOICE

Use the columns of information about the customers of XYZ Corporation below and circle the best answer to each of the following statements.

Name	Home Office	Amount Owed	Phone Number
Barbara Ann Valette	Tampa, Florida	15.00	813-555-0222
Joni Loock	Madison, Wisconsin	99.00	608-555-2348
Tica Hayes	Knoxville, Tennessee	35.00	423-555-9838
Cherryl Gene Pritts	San Antonio, Texas	44.00	512-555-5560
Jennifer Jarosik	Madison, Wisconsin	76.00	608-555-3348

1. To sort by customer last name, you would set Key 1 at
   - **A.** Field 2, Word 2.
   - **B.** Field 1, Word 2.
   - **C.** Field 1, Word -1.
   - **D.** Field 1, Word 1.

2. To sort by amount owed, you would set Key 1 at
   - **A.** Field 1, Word 1.
   - **B.** Field 2, Word 1.
   - **C.** Field 2, Word -1.
   - **D.** Field 3, Word 1.

3. To sort by name of city, you would set Key 1 at
   - **A.** Field 2, Word 1.
   - **B.** Field 2, Word -1.
   - **C.** Field 1, Word -2.
   - **D.** Field 3, Word 1.

(continued on next page)

4. To sort by state, you would set Key 1 at
   A. Field 2, Word 2.
   B. Field 2, Word -1.
   C. Field 1, Word 2.
   D. Field 1, Word -1.

5. To arrange the third column so that the largest number is on top, you would set
   A. Alpha, Descending.
   B. Alpha, Ascending.
   C. Numeric, Descending.
   D. Numeric, Ascending.

6. To extract only the customers owing more than $25.00, you would set Key 1 to identify the field containing the amounts due and then key _____ in the Extract records text box.
   A. Key 1 = 25.00
   B. Key 1>25.00
   C. Key 1<25.00
   D. Key 1=<25.00

TRUE/FALSE

Circle the T if the statement is true. Circle the F if it is false.

T   F   7. Extract using Sort is done before the merge.

T   F   8. When the desired records are extracted, all other records are deleted.

T   F   9. During the Extract process, your records can be sorted in a specified order.

T   F   10. Select Records during a merge enables you to keep your complete list of records intact while only the selected records are merged.

LESSON 19 PROJECT

SCANS

In this project you will prepare letters for a selected portion of a customer list. All of the data files have been prepared. You must prepare the form document and extract the customers to whom the letters will be sent. Read through the entire exercise before beginning.

1. Open **im spec 17b xxx.dat**. Save the file as **im spec proj19a xxx.dat**.

2. Position the insertion point at the bottom of the file and insert **micro** from the student **datafile** folder.

3. Sort the file by last name of customer. Be sure to remove any extra Keys in the Sort dialog box and remove any Extract commands. After sorting, save the file again with the same name.

4. Using the open file as the associated data file, create a form document for a letter to be sent to selected customers. You get to insert the date, mailing address, and greeting. The body and closing of the letter are illustrated in Figure 19-7. Insert your name in the closing lines.

FIGURE 19-7
Body of Letter for Lesson 19 Project

```
Thank you for choosing Image Specialists to bid on the installation of
imaging equipment in your company offices.  As we agreed in our phone
conversation yesterday, included in the bid will be training for your
employees who will be using the imaging equipment we install if we
should win the contract.

Our consultant for FIELD(area of interest) equipment,
FIELD(representative), will personally bring our bid to you at
FIELD(time) on FIELD(date).  At that time, please ask any questions
you might have about our company and procedures.

Again, the staff of Image Specialists would like to thank you for your
confidence in our organization.  We are looking forward to working
with you should we be selected to install FIELD(area of interest)
equipment at your office.

Sincerely,

IMAGE SPECIALISTS



(your name)
Imaging Manager
```

5. Save the form document as **im spec proj19b xxx.frm**. Play your **pf** macro and save the form again.

6. Merge the form document with the data source. Use either Extract (in the Sort dialog box) or Select Records (in the Perform Merge dialog box) to prepare letters ONLY for those customers interested in *multimedia* systems. (When you merge, use Reset to return the Perform Merge dialog box to the defaults. If you use Select Records, do that AFTER you click the Reset button.)

7. Print the letters and save them as **im spec proj19c xxx**. Close all files.

CRITICAL THINKING ACTIVITY

SCANS

In a list of names you want sorted alphabetically by last name, the name Cindy Van Horne keeps showing up after Robin A. Hood instead of before Reggie Voiers. You have checked the New Sort dialog box and confirmed that Key 1 is set at Field 1, Word -1. What could be causing the problem?

LESSON 20

LABELS

OBJECTIVES

Upon completion of this lesson, you will be able to:

- Key and print labels.
- Prepare merged labels.
- Add the POSTNET bar code to your labels.
- Create name badges.
- Create numbered tickets.

Estimated Time: 2 hours

In Lessons 17 through 19 you've worked with mailing lists. You created lists and sorted them. You created form letters or documents, and you combined those forms with mailing lists. With those tools, you discovered how easy it is to prepare documents to be sent to a number of addresses, whether it is several or several thousands.

All of those letters or documents, however, don't do you or your company much good stacked on your desk. You must come up with a way of distributing them. You have a number of alternatives for distribution:

- facsimile (fax)
- electronic mail
- special courier services (using labels and special packaging)
- the postal service (using envelopes, labels, or window envelopes)

You've already learned how to prepare envelopes—both for individual letters and for bulk mailings. To use window envelopes, you simply need to position the mailing address in a specific location on the letter. Advance works well for locating the address, whether you create individual letters or form letters. As you know, you can even include POSTNET bar codes on your envelopes.

The third alternative in preparing mailings is using labels. There are lots of reasons why a company might choose to use labels for their mailings. By the same token, there are a lot of things you can do with the WordPerfect Labels feature besides creating labels for mailings. For example, you can use the feature to prepare name badges for a meeting. You can also prepare diskette labels, file folder labels, and numbered tickets. We'll try a variety of these uses in this lesson.

Labels for Mailing

WordPerfect comes with definitions for more than 250 labels, tabs, business cards, note cards, and name badges. The predefined labels are listed and described when you open the Format menu and choose Labels. Some of the labels are appropriate for laser printers because they can be printed on a standard size sheet of paper. Others are appropriate for dot matrix printers because they come on a roll or are fanfolded in a box so they can be fed continuously.

On the job you'll choose the definition that fits the labels you can use with your printer. When you've selected the correct label description, you can key the text directly onto the labels or you can define a form document, complete with FIELD codes so you can merge the data source with the label form.

When working with labels, WordPerfect considers each individual label as a logical page. The entire sheet of labels is considered a physical page. If you wish to print only one label, you must print the Current Page. Normally, of course, you will print all of the labels on a page.

One of the most widely used styles of labels has the following characteristics:

- 30 labels per page (3 columns of 10 rows)
- each label measures 1 inch x 2.63 inches
- standard $8^{1}/_{2}$- x 11-inch paper
- specifically manufactured to be printed on a laser printer
- narrow strip at the edges of the page to make allowance for the printer's no-print zone

We'll use a label definition with those characteristics in Exercise 20.1.

EXERCISE 20.1

1. In a new document window, open the **Format** menu and choose **Labels** to display the Labels dialog box.

2. Study the dialog box. Notice that below the Labels window are the details of the label that is highlighted. Move the highlight to *Avery 5160*. Your dialog box should look like Figure 20-1.

3. Look at the description and information about the label. Then click **Select** to choose the label and return to your working window. If you are in Draft view, change to Page view to see how the label looks.

4. Key your name and address. Then press **Ctrl+Enter** to move to a new page, and key the name and address of a friend. Repeat the procedure two more times so you have a total of four labels.

5. Press **Ctrl+Home** to move your insertion point to the beginning of YOUR address. Open the **Format** menu and choose **Page**. Center the current and subsequent pages. Return to your page of labels. Your labels should look like Figure 20-2.

6. Zoom to **Full Page**, if you'd like, to look at the page. Then return to **100%**.

(continued on next page)

EXERCISE 20.1 CONTINUED

FIGURE 20-1
Labels Dialog Box

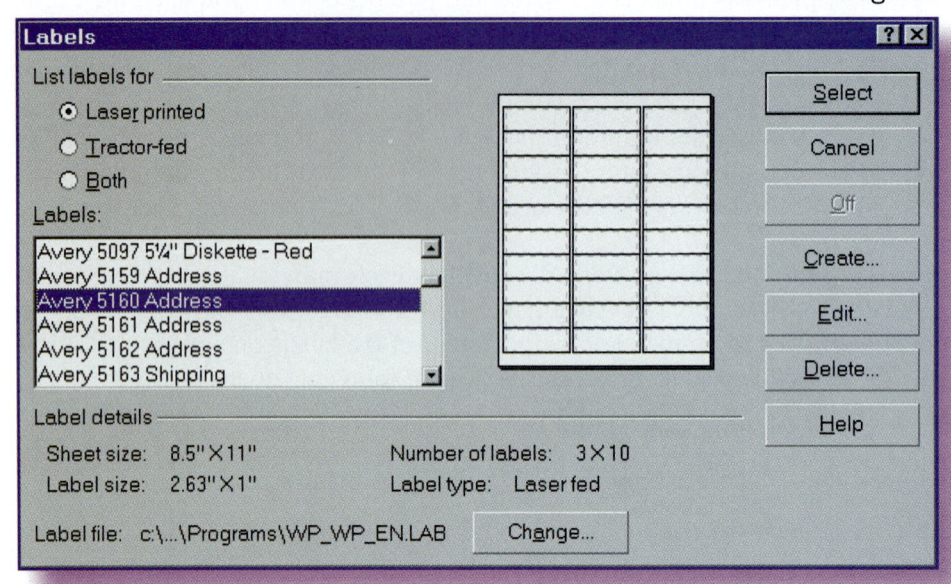

FIGURE 20-2
Sample Labels

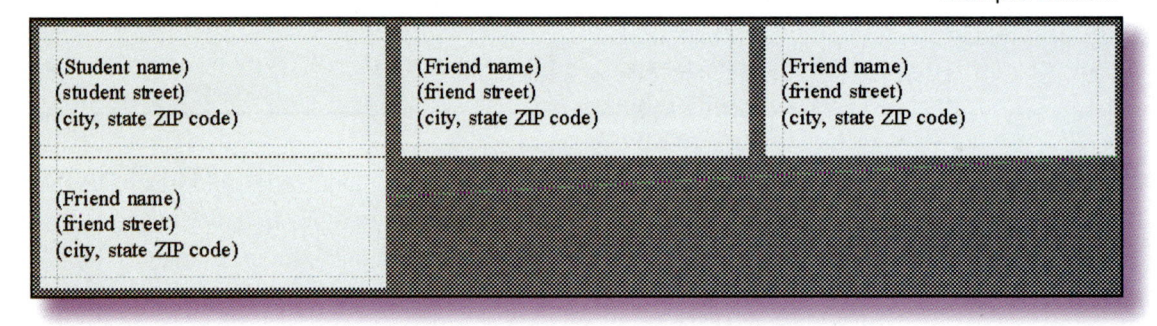

7. Save your labels as **labels 20-1 xxx**. Press **Ctrl+End**. Then press **Ctrl+Enter** to go to Label 5. Insert the Path and Filename code to identify the job.

8. Print the page of labels, save, and close the file.

NOTE:

If you are using a laser printer, the display window in the printer will probably prompt you to manually feed a sheet of labels. Laser printers aren't normally stocked with labels in the feed trays. With most printers, you can feed any sheet of paper through the sheet feed portion of the printer.

UNIT 5: MERGE TOOLS

Now let's use the same label description for merged labels. In this exercise we will put the formatting codes in Current Document Style. This saves time during the merge. It also saves space on your disk when you save the document because the codes are repeated for each label. Read all of the instructions for the exercise before beginning.

EXERCISE 20.2

1. Open the **File** menu and choose **Document**. Then choose **Current Document Style**.

2. In the Styles Editor open the **Format** menu and choose **Labels**. As in the last exercise, choose the **Avery 5160** label description. Still in the Styles Editor, insert the command to center the current and subsequent pages. Look at the codes in the Styles Editor. Then click **OK** to close it.

3. Turn the current document into a form document, using **flowers xxx.dat** as the associated data file.

4. Enter the FIELD codes for the names and addresses on the labels. You don't need the middle initial. Because the FIELD codes are so long, your form document will look like Figure 20-3 when you finish.

5. Save the label form document as **labels 30.frm** because it is for a form document with 30 labels per page.

6. Merge **labels 30.frm** with **flowers xxx.dat**. Look at the labels that result. Zoom to **Full Page** to check them. Then return to **100%**.

7. Save the page of labels as **labels 20-2 xxx**. Position the insertion point in the final label. Press **Ctrl+Enter** to add one more label. Insert the Path and Filename code on that label.

8. Print the page and close it, saving it again.

FIGURE 20-3
Sample Form Document for Exercise 20.2

FIELD(title) FIELD(first name)
FIELD(last name)
FIELD(company)
FIELD(street)

FIELD(city), FIELD(state) FIELD(ZIP)

That was pretty easy, wasn't it? Your sample data file was small, so your sheet of labels was partly empty. You can print hundreds of labels this way. By way of review, following is the basic procedure for preparing labels:

1. Choose the label description. If you are merging, put the code for the labels and the Center Page(s) code in your Current Document Style.

2. Create a form document and name the associated data source. Insert the merge codes.

3. Combine the form document with the data source and print the labels.

329

Before we go to something different, let's amend the label form you prepared in Exercise 20.2 and add a POSTNET bar code to the address. You'll need a label description that provides a larger label than the Avery 5160 label. We'll use the Avery 5162 label description.

EXERCISE 20.3

1. The **labels 30.frm** file should be showing. Go to the Current Document Style dialog box. Delete the Labels Form and Paper Sz/Typ codes. (If it says something about *Ignore*, ignore the reference and delete the code anyhow.)

2. Open the **Format** menu, choose **Labels**, and select **Avery 5162**. Close the Styles Editor and move your insertion point to the line below the FIELD codes for city, state, and ZIP code. (You may need to press Enter.)

3. Click the **Insert Field** button on the Merge Bar to open the Insert Field dialog box. Move it to the lower left corner of your window.

4. Click the **Merge Codes** button on the Merge Bar and key **po** to move to POSTNET(string). Insert it and double click **ZIP** in the Insert Field dialog box to put ZIP between the parentheses. Close both dialog boxes.

5. Look at the code for the POSTNET bar code in your label form. Note that ZIP has two sets of parentheses. That's OK. Use **Save As** to save the labels form as **labels 14.frm**.

6. Merge your files. Because Avery 5162 provides 14 labels per page, the labels will extend to a second page. That's fine.

7. Save your labels as **labels 20-3 xxx**. Add a label at the end and insert the Path and Filename code, as you did in Exercise 20.2.

8. Print your labels. Then save the file again and close all open files.

Name Badges

As mentioned earlier, you can use the same procedure for labels to create name badges for programs and meetings. Let's begin by creating a data file with names and companies for an office demonstration of your equipment. Assume you've invited some customers along with your employees to a demonstration of equipment and software.

EXERCISE 20.4

1. Create a data file using the names and company names in Figure 20-4. Use the following field names: *first name, last name, company*.

2. Sort the list alphabetically by last name and save it as **names 20-4 xxx.dat**.

3. Create a form document to be associated with the data file. In the Current Document Styles Editor, put a code for **Avery 5390** name badges. Include a **Center Page(s)** command and a **Center** justification command. Return to your working window.

FIGURE 20-4
Names and Companies for Exercise 20.4

Miguel Zedillo Bits and Chips	Milton Mason Milty's Millions	Marcus Schmidt Image Specialists
Rosemary Waldman Wally's Wallpaper Shop	Wally Williams Williams Electronics	*B* Pearl Binder East Wisconsin Wire
Kim Lee Lee Electronics	*A* Bertha Bertals	*D* Dick Dawson Dawson, Hughs, & Park
Joshua Jacobs	Nchoua Thor Image Specialists	Mary Winter Winter & Sons Electric
Sandee Simpson Simply Computing	Diego Marchetti Image Specialists	Ruth Anne Remmel Roffler Mfg. Co.
Natasha Nichols Nickelodeon Nightmare	Andreas Werner Image Specialists	Ira Ibsen Ibsen Ink Products
Peggy Perkins Perticular PCs	*C* Pedro Costilla Image Specialists	

4. Enter the FIELD codes for the name badges, as shown in Figure 20-5.
   a. Put each field on a line by itself.
   b. Separate the *last name* field from the *company* field with a double space.
   c. Use a **36-pt.** font size for the first name (it may not fit on one line) and a **14-pt.** font size for the other two lines.

5. Save the form document as **badge xxx.frm**.

6. Merge the form document and the data file. Look at the badges. Save the finished badges as **badge 20-4 xxx**.

7. Go to the end of the file and press **Ctrl+Enter** to create another badge. Insert the Path and Filename code on that badge.

8. Print your badges (all three pages) and close the file, saving it again as **badge 20-4 xxx**.

FIGURE 20-5
Form Document for Exercise 20.4

> FIELD(first name)
> FIELD(last name)
>
> FIELD(company)

Are your name badges beautiful? The different styles of name badges or name tags that can be chosen from the label definition list can be found on the shelves of your favorite office supplies store. It is a good idea to shop for the badges first. Then come back and choose the label definition that matches the badges you've purchased.

Numbered Tickets

You can also number your labels. This procedure requires the use of a couple of merge codes you have not yet used. If you follow along carefully, you shouldn't have any trouble with this procedure.

In this instance you don't need to put your Paper Size code in the Current Document Style because there is no data file. Otherwise, most of the codes for the format will be the same codes you used for the previous exercises.

EXERCISE 20.5

1. Beginning in a new document window, create a form document that has no associated data file.

2. Define a label using **Avery 5390 Name Tag**. Back in your document, choose **Center Page(s)** and **Center** justification.

3. Click the **Merge Codes** button to open the Insert Merge Codes dialog box. Key **fo** and choose **FORNEXT**. The dialog box illustrated in Figure 20-6 will appear.

4. Fill in the following information, pressing **Tab** to move from text box to text box. When you finish, click **OK**. (The Insert Merge Codes dialog box will remain open.)

    Variable = **x**
    Start = **1**
    Stop = **23**
    Step = **1**

(In this set of codes, **x** tells WordPerfect that another **x** will appear somewhere in the document to identify the position for the number. The first **1** tells WordPerfect to start numbering at **1**, while **23** tells WordPerfect to stop numbering at **23**. The final **1** tells WordPerfect to count in increments of **1**. You have the option of setting it to number only even numbers, such as 2, 4, and 6 or only odd numbers, such as 1, 3, and 5.)

FIGURE 20-6
Insert Merge Code Dialog Box

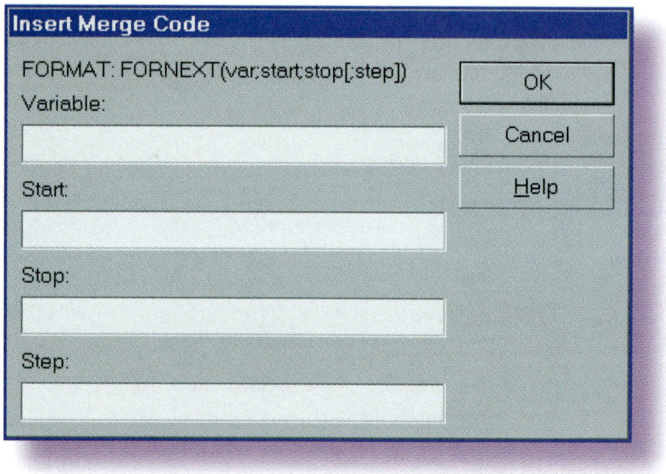

FIGURE 20-7
Text for Exercise 20.5

```
FORNEXT(x;1;23;1) IMAGE SPECIALISTS

         Spring Show
        Monday, April 1
       8 a.m. to 4 p.m.
     (by invitation, only)

       Ticket #VARIABLE(x)
```

5. Back in your document window, you'll see the results of the code you entered. Continue on the same line, keying the first line of the text for the ticket, as illustrated in Figure 20-7. Continue keying the text until you have keyed the number sign (#) after the word *Ticket*.

332   UNIT 5: MERGE TOOLS

6. Click in the Insert Merge Codes dialog box to activate it and key **v** to move to the *Variable* section. Choose **VARIABLE**. At the prompt for the variable, key **x** and click **OK**. Your form should now look like Figure 20-7.

7. Press **Ctrl+Enter** for a hard page break. Your insertion point will move to the next ticket. Then activate the Insert Merge Codes dialog box and choose the **ENDFOR** code. (This code ends the loop that tells Word-Perfect to go back and repeat the text and add the next numeral.)

8. Save your ticket form as **ticket xxx.frm**. Merge the form.

9. When the merge is completed, look at your 23 tickets. (One space is left on the final page for your Path and Filename code.)

10. Save the merged tickets as **show 20-5 xxx**. Go to the blank ticket at the end and insert the Path and Filename code. Print the three pages of tickets and close the file, saving it again.

The tickets you just created are the same size as the name tags you prepared in Exercise 20.4. You could use any of the label definitions if you wished to prepare tickets of a different size. This application was set up for just three pages of tickets. You could print hundreds this way, all numbered, if that was what you needed.

Summary

In this lesson you learned many of the things you can do with the Labels feature. You learned that:

- You can key directly onto the labels after you've defined them.
- You can use labels as a form document to merge with a data source for names and addresses.
- You can add the POSTNET bar code to your labels.
- If one size label doesn't fit, you can try a different size.
- You can use the Labels feature to create name badges.
- Labels can be used to create tickets—even with consecutive numbering.

Quite a number of other tasks can be completed with the Labels feature. As you experiment with it, you will surely have other ideas for its use.

LESSON 20 REVIEW QUESTIONS

FILL IN THE BLANKS

Complete each of the following statements by writing your answer in the blank provided.

1. WordPerfect comes with definitions for more than _250_ labels, tabs, business cards, note cards, and name badges.

(continued on next page)

2. The predefined labels are listed when you open the _Format_ menu and choose Labels.

3. When working with labels, WordPerfect considers each individual label as a _logical_ page.

4. WordPerfect considers the entire sheet of labels a _physical_ page.

5. If you wish to print only one label, you must select _Current Page_ in the Print dialog box.

6. In order to number your labels, tickets, or badges, you first click the Merge Codes button to open the Insert Merge Codes dialog box. Then key fo and choose _ForNext_ to insert the variable, start, stop, and step codes.

7. In preparing tickets, press _Ctrl+Enter_ to move to the next ticket.

WRITTEN QUESTIONS

Write your answers to the following questions.

8. If one size label doesn't fit, what should you do? _Try a different size_

9. How would you use labels in a merge if you wanted to use a list of names and addresses you already have? _Use labels as a form document._

10. Name three things the WordPerfect Labels feature can be used for.
Labels for mailing; Name Badges; Numbered Tickets

LESSON 20 PROJECT

Your instructor is running behind today. He has asked you to make some diskette labels for him to distribute to a class of 16 students that begins this evening. He expected you to write on each label by hand, but you found a box of Avery 5096 Red Diskette Labels that he has given you permission to use if you can prepare them on your own.

Figure 20-8 shows what he would like on the labels. Create the form document and choose the label description. Center the first three lines. For the _Name_ line, key **Name** at the left. Then use Underline Tabs and Alt+F7 to create the line for the students to fill in their names. Save the form document as **diskette xxx.frm**.

To merge the 16 labels, begin the merge. In the Perform Merge dialog box choose Options and set the number of copies at 16. Complete the merge.

When you finish, look at your diskette labels. Create one more label at the end for your Path and Filename code.

Save your diskette labels as **disk proj20 xxx**. Print the labels and close the file.

FIGURE 20-8
Text for Diskette Labels

```
      ADVANCED WORDPERFECT
         November 23, 199x

      Shareware Clipart Files

   Name_____
```

CRITICAL THINKING ACTIVITY

If you wanted to number all advanced-sale tickets up to 1,000 beginning with 100 using only even numbers printed on the tickets, what information would you key in the following text boxes of the Insert Merge Codes dialog box?

Variable = _____
Start = _____
Stop = _____
Step = _____

Command Summary

UNIT 5 REVIEW

FEATURE	MENU CHOICE	KEYBOARD	LESSON
Address Book	Tools, Address Book	—	18
Document Assembly	Tools, Merge, Merge	Shift+F9	18
ENDFIELD Code	Tools, Merge, Data Source	Alt+Enter	17
ENDRECORD Code	Tools, Merge, Data Source	Ctrl+Shift+Enter	17
Envelope (Merge)	Tools, Merge, Merge	—	17
ENDFOR Code	Tools, Merge, Form	—	20
ENDIF Code	Tools, Merge, Form	—	19
Extract	Tools, Sort	Alt+F9	19
Field Names	Tools, Merge, Data Source	—	17
FORNEXT Code	Tools, Merge, Form	—	20
GO(label) Code	Tools, Merge, Form	—	20
IFNOTBLANK Code	Tools, Merge, Form	—	18
KEYBOARD Code	Tools, Merge, Form	—	17
Labels, Create	Format, Labels	—	20
LABEL(label)	Tools, Merge, Form	—	20
Line Sort	Tools, Sort	Alt+F9	19
Merge	Tools, Merge, Merge	Shift+F9	17
Merge Sort	Tools, Sort	Alt+F9	19
Name Badges	Format, Labels	—	20
NEXTRECORD Code	Tools, Merge, Form	—	20
Paragraph Sort	Tools, Sort	Alt+F9	19
POSTNET Bar Code	Tools, Merge, Merge	Shift+F9	18
Select Records	Tools, Merge, Merge	Shift+F9	19
Sort	Tools, Sort	Alt+F9	19
Table Sort	Tools, Sort	Alt+F9	19

UNIT 5 REVIEW QUESTIONS

TRUE/FALSE

On a separate page, key True if the statement below is true or False if it is not. Center *Unit 5 Review Questions* at the top and triple space.

T **(F)** 1. A keyboard merge enables you to enter variable information as the merge takes place.

(T) F 2. If you prepare the form document before you prepare the data source, you can use the field names in the form document.

T F 3. If you are missing information in a data source, the ENDRECORD code must still mark that spot.

T F 4. To extract the records where the ZIP code is larger than 65000 and the ZIP code location is indentified as Key 2, Extract Records should be set at Key2>65000.

(T) F 5. A *physical page* is the term used when referring to an entire sheet of labels.

WRITTEN QUESTIONS

Key your answers to the following questions. Number your answers and double-space between them. Use complete sentences and good grammar.

6. Describe the differences between a data source and a form document.

7. Name four kinds of Sort you learned about in Lesson 19. Which of those is used for merge data files?

8. When performing a sort on a field containing amounts of money, should you set the sort to be Alpha or Numeric?

9. Why must you be careful in saving your data source after you have used Extract?

10. Sometimes when you are working with data files and you are proofreading, the ENDFIELD codes get in the way. Go to WordPerfect Help and find out how you can hide the merge codes so they don't show in your documents. How do you make the codes show again? Go to the data file section and read About Data Files. What are some of the other programs from which you may convert data files?

UNIT 5 APPLICATIONS

Estimated Time: 1½ hours

APPLICATION 1

In Lesson 17 you created a keyboard merge form named **memo.frm**. Use that form for a keyboard merge, and prepare a memo for your instructor with the subject *Merge Topics*. Briefly describe how you feel about the merge tools you learned in Unit 5. Which tools do you like the best? Which do you like the least? Which do you think you could put to use immediately? Save the memo as **memo u5ap1 xxx**. Print the memo. Then close it, saving it again.

APPLICATION 2

Open **seniors** from the student **datafile** folder. Use Save As to save the file on your disk as **seniors u5ap2a xxx**. Play your **pf** macro to identify the file.

You will sort this list in a number of ways. For some of the sorts, you will need to set more than one Key. When you don't need a Key, click in the row of the extra Key and delete it. Always check all parts of the Sort dialog box before you complete a sort.

1. Sort alphabetically by last name. Add Key 2 to sort by first name so the people with the same last name are in alphabetic order. Check your work and print the file. Save it again with the same name.

2. Sort alphabetically by school. Set the sort so if two people are attending the same school, they will be arranged alphabetically by last name and then by first name. (HINT: If you choose the *Insert Key Between* button, the new key will be added above the existing key. Then you just need to set the new Key 1 to point to the schools.) Print the sorted list and save it as **seniors u5ap2b xxx**.

3. Extract the females. (HINT: Identify the school in any Key. In the *Extract records* text box, key **Key?=Female**, substituting the Key number where you have Field 3 for the question mark.) At the same time you extract, sort the list alphabetically by last name. Check your work. Print the list and close it, saving it as **seniors u5ap2c xxx**.

4. Open **seniors u5ap2a xxx** and extract the males. Sort the list alphabetically by school. Print and close, saving this sort as **seniors u5ap2d xxx**.

APPLICATION 3

Assume that you are Manuel Tovar's secretary, and you are tired of preparing an invoice form each time you bill a customer. We'll convert an invoice file to one that can be prepared with Keyboard Merge. Then we'll try it out with a couple of invoices.

Go to your **Units 3 and 4** folder and open **estate 15-8 xxx**. Convert it to a form document, with no associated data source. Save the file as **invoice xxx.frm** and adjust it as follows:

1. Replace the current date and replace it with the DATE code.

2. Delete the billing period information and replace it with a KEYBOARD code prompting the user to key the billing period.

3. Delete the name and address of the customer and replace it with a KEYBOARD code prompting the user to key the name and address of the customer.

4. In the table, delete the first date and replace it with a KEYBOARD code prompting the user to enter the first date of service to be billed. (The entire KEYBOARD code may not show because it's too large for the cell. That's OK.)

5. Delete all of the remaining information in the Date, Description, Hours, and Per Hour columns. DO NOT delete anything in the Total column. Leave the words to the left of the totals near the bottom.

   Save the form again as **invoice xxx.frm** and close it.

APPLICATION 4

Mr. Tovar has given you information for a billing for two clients for the period of September 1, 199x, to October 1, 199x. The information is illustrated in Figure APP-1.

1. Use Keyboard Merge to prepare the first invoice.

2. When you have entered the first date of service, press Alt+Enter to conclude the merge.

3. Then fill in the table in the usual table manner. The calculations should be done automatically.

4. In the row that contains only zeros (00.00), highlight those zeros and delete them.

FIGURE APP-1
Information for Invoices in Application 4

```
Mr. & Mrs. Junior Washington
1776 Cherry Tree Lane
Victoria, NJ 08344

9-6-9x      Office Visit        1 hr. @ 80.00
9-10-9x     Title Search        3 hrs. @ 75.00
9-14-9x     Office Visit        0.5 hrs. @ 80.00
9-28-9x     Office Visit        1 hr. @ 80.00

Ms. Munira Dughish
5723 N. Dexter Street
Victoria, NJ 08344

9-3-9x      Office Visit        1 hr. @ 90.00
9-11-9x     Office Visit        2 hrs. @ 90.00
9-26-9x     Court Appearance    1 hr. @ 90.00
```

When you finish the first invoice, press Ctrl+Enter to go to a new page and merge again. This time, in the Perform Merge dialog box, choose Current Document for Output. Both invoices will be in one document.

Save the finished invoices as **invoice u5ap4 xxx**. Print the invoices and close all files.

(continued on next page)

APPLICATION 5

1. It's housekeeping time again—time to delete some files and move others. Begin by creating a **Units 5 and 6** folder with the **Units 1 and 2** folder and the **Units 3 and 4** folder. Move the files in Figure APP-2 from your normal folder into the **Units 5 and 6** folder.

2. Move the files **seniors u5ap2a**, **memo u5ap1**, and **invoice u5ap4** to the **Applications** folder.

FIGURE APP-2
Files to Move to **Units 5 and 6** Folder

badge xxx.frm	labels 30.frm
diskette xxx.frm	memo.frm
flower list 19-6 xxx	micro 17-4 xxx.frm
flowers 18-8 xxx.frm	micro 17-6 xxx.dat
flowers xxx.dat	micro 17-9a xxx.dat
im spec proj19a xxx.dat	sort 19-5 xxx
invoice xxx.frm	ticket xxx.frm
labels 14.frm	ziepke 18-9 xxx.dat

3. Figure APP-3 lists files that should be deleted. Work carefully. When you finish, your main folder should contain only your macros.

FIGURE APP-3
Files to Delete

accounts 18-8 xxx	interest 18-14 xxx	seniors u5ap2b xxx
badge 20-4 xxx	labels 20-1 xxx	seniors u5ap2c xxx
disk proj20 xxx	labels 20-2 xxx	seniors u5ap2d xxx
flowers 18-1 xxx.dat	labels 20-3 xxx	show 20-5 xxx
flowers 18-1 xxx.frm	list 19-6 xxx.frm	small 19-12 xxx
flowers 18-2 xxx.frm	micro 17-2 xxx.dat	sort 19-1 xxx
flowers 18-4 xxx	micro 17-3 xxx.frm	sort 19-2 xxx
flowers 18-6 xxx.frm	micro 17-5 xxx	sort 19-3 xxx
flowers 18-7 xxx	micro 17-7 xxx	table 19-10 xxx
im spec proj17d xxx	micro 17-8 xxx	ziepke 18-10 xxx.frm
im spec proj17b xxx.dat	micro 17-9b xxx	ziepke 18-11 xxx
im spec proj17c xxx.frm	names 20-4 xxx	ziepke 18-12 xxx.frm
im spec 19-9 xxx.dat	reference 18-12 xxx	ziepke 18-14 xxx.frm
im spec proj19b xxx.frm	referral 17-10 xxx.frm	ziepke proj18 letters
im spec proj19c xxx	referral 17-11 xxx	ziepke proj18 xxx.dat

ON-THE-JOB SIMULATION

JOB 11

Mr. Becker has just handed you the list of customers in Figure J6 who had signed up for the October tour to Disney World. Registrations have been light, and the tour had to be canceled.

He would like you to prepare letters to send to the customers. Create a data file and a form document (see Figure J7) and merge them to complete the letters. Include an envelope with each letter. Save the data file in the **Singing Wheels** folder as **dis job11a xxx.dat** and the form document as **dis job11b xxx.frm**. Save the completed merge as **disney job11 xxx**.

FIGURE J6
Addresses for Job 11

```
Mr. & Mrs. Neverat Holme
773 3rd Street
Manawa, WI 54949

Mrs. Lottie Baggs
22 Sunny Court
Shawano, WI 54166

Miss Norma Nomad
3411 Jonquil Lane
Junction City, WI 54443
```

FIGURE J7
Letter for Job 11

```
(current date)

(Customer)

Dear (greeting):

I am sorry to inform you that the tour you had planned to take with us
to Disney World in Florida beginning on October 22 has been canceled
due to lack of registrations.  A check in the amount of your down
payment is enclosed.

It is extremely rare that we are forced to cancel a tour.  From what
we can tell, registrations were low because so many of our customers
chose instead to go on the November tour to Disney World.  We still
have some openings for that tour and would like to encourage you to
check your calendars.  Perhaps you could go with us on November 15
instead of in October.

Please call within the next week if you are able to arrange to join us
in November.  We would very much like to have you with us at that
time.  Either way, thank you for your business.  It is customers like
you that keep our wheels singing!

Sincerely,

SINGING WHEELS TOURS



Charlie Becker

Enclosure
```

(continued on next page)

JOB 12

Mr. Becker just received three more reservations for the November Disney World trip. The names and addresses of the customers are listed in Figure J8. Use Merge to prepare and print a letter and envelopes for these customers. A letter named **disney** is in the student **datafile** folder for this exercise. (Only the body of the letter and the closing have been prerecorded for you. Insert the merge codes for the date, mailing address, and greeting. Then use Insert to insert the **disney** file.)

Note that the data file includes a field for the middle initial. Not all of the customers have middle initials, so you'll have to set up your merge accordingly for the letters. Include POSTNET bar codes on the envelopes. Do not include middle initials on the envelopes. Save the data file in the **Singing Wheels** folder as **dis job12a xxx.dat** and the form document as **dis job12b xxx.frm**.

After merging, print all three letters and envelopes. Save the merged file as **disney job12 xxx**. Close all files.

FIGURE J8
Customers for Job 12

```
Mr. & Mrs.              Mr.                     Mrs.
Mickey                  Sylvester               Minnie
M.                      A.
Arodent                 Katt                    Marvin
9811 Arkdale Lane       51 Kettleson Creek      3557 Mead Street
Marinette               Kaukauna                Marion
WI                      WI                      WI
54143                   54130                   54950
414-555-7728            414-555-0023            414-555-8893
```

JOB 13

The body and closing of the letter used for Job 12 is generic enough so it could be used each time a registration and deposit arrives for most of the Singing Wheels trips. Open the **disney** document from the student **datafile** folder. Save it in the **Singing Wheels** folder as **deposit.frm**.

Convert the document to a keyboard merge form document, including the DATE code and KEYBOARD codes for the mailing address, the greeting, and the four places where question marks (??) have been inserted in Figure J9. Remove the question marks, of course. Use your **pf** macro to insert the Path and Filename code. Then print the form document and save the file again.

FIGURE J9
Body of **deposit** Keyboard Merge Letter

```
Thank you for your reservation for our trip to ?? leaving on ??.  We
are excited about this trip and hope that it will be everything you
are expecting.  It should be a good time of the year to visit ??.

Your ?? deposit has been recorded, and our usual questionnaire about
your preferences and any possible physical restrictions is enclosed.
Please return the completed questionnaire to us along with your final
payment no less than 30 days before the tour begins.

Again, welcome to what promises to be a fun adventure.  We are looking
forward to having you along for the ride.
```

JOB 14

You finished converting that file to a keyboard merge document just in time. Mr. Becker just received another registration for the trip to Disney World in November. Please prepare a letter like the others for the Disney World tour for Mrs. Lila Lingstrom, 647 3rd Avenue, Larsen, WI 54947. Save the completed file in the **Singing Wheels** folder as **disney job14 xxx**. Include the Path and Filename code in a footer. Prepare an envelope, including the POSTNET bar code. Print the letter and envelope.

JOB 15

Mr. Becker has given you the list of names and addresses of the first ten people who will be on the November bus tour to Disney World. Three of the folks who had signed up for the canceled October tour (Job 11) will be able to go along in November. They are Neverat and Hazel Holme and Mrs. Baggs.

Please use the the name badge form you created in Lesson 20 to make name tags for these three people, as well as for seven other people. (See Figure J10.) You may send friends and relatives—in fact, you get to provide the seven names and addresses. (Position the city and state where the company name was positioned on the name tags in Exercise 20-4. Save the modified form document in the **Singing Wheels** folder as **badge job15 xxx.frm**.)

Prepare the data file for the ten people. Be sure to include the Holmes couple and Mrs. Baggs. Save the data file in the **Singing Wheels** folder as **names job15 xxx.dat**. When you have both files ready, complete the merge. Save the finished document in the **Singing Wheels** folder as **badges job15 xxx**. Add an extra name tag at the end to identify the document. Print the document and save it again. Close all files.

FIGURE J10
Form Document

```
First Name

Last Name


City, State
```

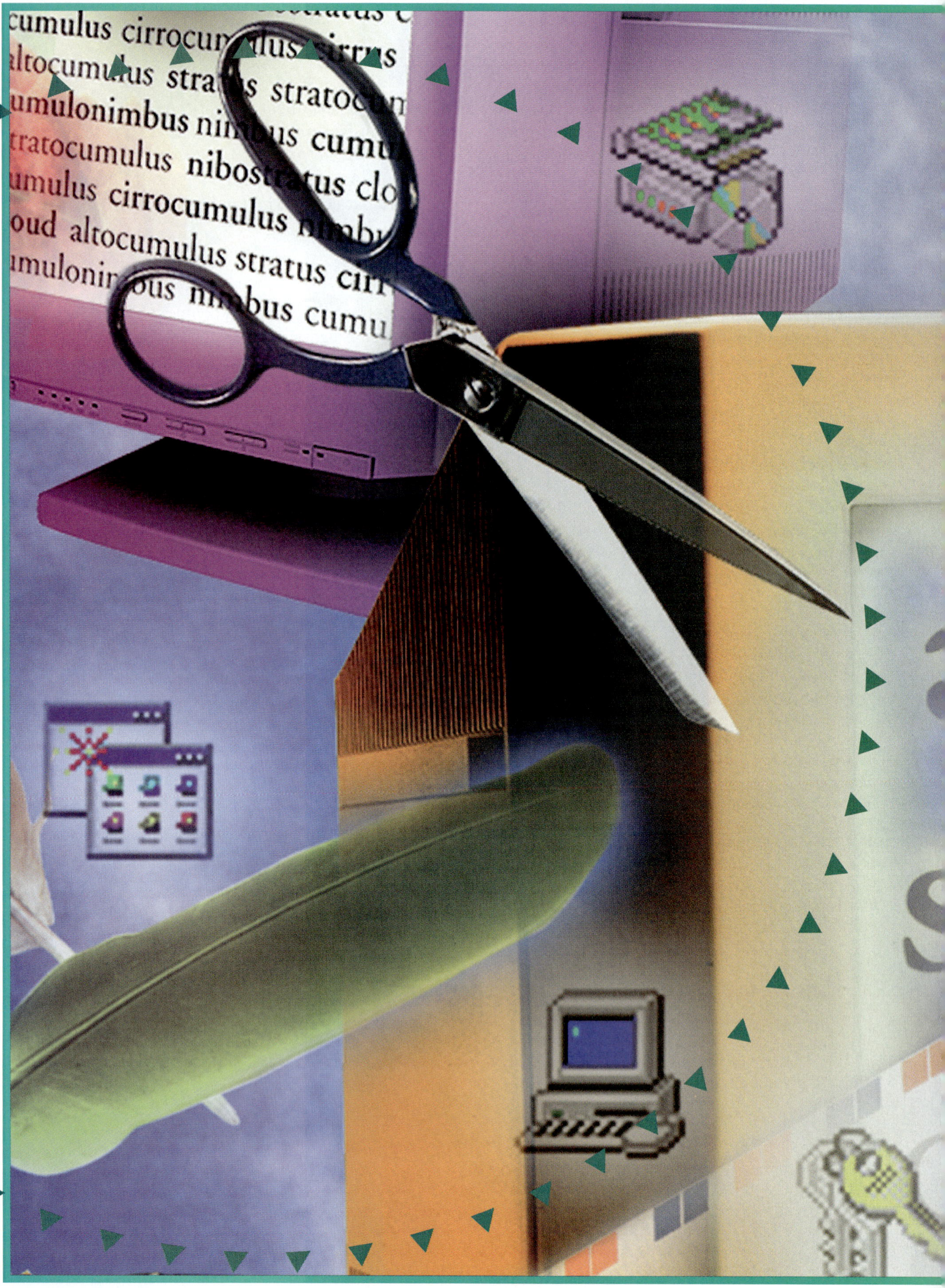

GRAPHICS TOOLS

UNIT 6

lesson 21 — 1.5 hrs.
Graphics Boxes

lesson 22 — 1 hr.
Working with Images

lesson 23 — 1.5 hrs.
Graphics Lines, Borders, and Fill

lesson 24 — 1.5 hrs.
Feature Bonanza

Estimated Time for Unit 6: 7½ hours

LESSON 21: GRAPHICS BOXES

OBJECTIVES

Upon completion of this lesson, you will be able to:

- Insert a graphics box containing an image.
- Select, move, size, and add captions to your graphics boxes.
- Discuss graphics box styles.
- Change the border and fill of your graphics boxes.
- Customize the captions on your boxes.
- Work with wrap options.
- Create and adjust text boxes.
- Use the Drag to Create feature.
- Insert an image From File.

Estimated Time: 1½ hours

Quite often when we think about word processing and graphics, we are thinking about working with page layouts—that is, designing attractive pages for multiple production. The documents might be newsletters, brochures, business reports, resumes, or magazine articles.

Regardless of the final product, the design elements are the same. Page layout is simply the arrangement of type, white space, and graphics. If it is attractive and easy to follow, people will read it. If it is neither attractive nor easy to follow, no matter how interesting, people probably won't read it.

WordPerfect provides you with a number of design elements that enable you to produce attractive documents. These design elements include columns (which you already know how to create), graphics images, graphics lines, borders, and fonts of every imaginable size!

WordPerfect graphics enables you to insert drawings, photos, Clipart images, and a variety of other types of graphics into your documents. In this lesson you'll learn to insert images as well as make changes to the appearance of your images. In the other lessons of this unit you'll work with some of the other graphics elements.

Insert an Image

The first step in working with graphics is to insert an image into your document. Corel WordPerfect comes with more than ten thousand drawings and photos. Only about 60 of those images are copied to your computer when a standard installation is performed. The remainder are on the CD on which the program is shipped. The images are in a compressed format, but if they were saved individually, each would have a .wpg extension, which makes them easy to distinguish from other types of files.

In Exercise 21.1 we'll preview some of the images that come with the program.

EXERCISE 21.1

1. In a new document window open the **Insert** menu, choose **Graphics**, and choose **Clipart**. WordPerfect will display the Scrapbook dialog box, where you can use the scroll bar to preview the images.

2. Move partway through the list, previewing the images.

3. Find **rose2.wpg** and drag the image out of the Scrapbook dialog box to your document. Align the dotted line around the image with the margin guidelines in the upper right corner of the page before releasing the mouse button.

4. Save your document as **rose 21-1 xxx**.

With the rose in the window, let's learn about working with images.

Selecting, Moving, and Sizing Boxes, and Adding Captions

When you insert an image into your document, it is placed in a frame called a graphics box. Unless you place a border around the image or select a certain type of image, that frame doesn't show. You'll learn to work with graphics box frames shortly.

To work with an image, it must be selected. When the image is selected, it is surrounded by black squares called "sizing handles," and they can be dragged to make your image the size or shape you would like it to be. Also when an image is selected, the graphics tools will appear on the Property Bar. This bar is one source of tools for working with images. The other source of tools is the QuickMenu. Most of the same choices are available from these two sources. We'll choose tools from both of these sources in the next few exercises.

Let's begin by exploring the tools available when an image is selected.

EXERCISE 21.2

1. Point to the image and click once to select it. Notice the sizing handles that have appeared.

2. With your mouse pointer, grab the handle at the middle left and drag it to the left about an inch. Look at your rose. Did it get fat? Unless the default settings have been changed, it did.

(continued on next page)

EXERCISE 21.2 CONTINUED

3. Click away from the rose to deselect it and use **Undo** on the Toolbar to return the rose to its original proportions.

4. Select the image again and point to it with your mouse pointer while you right click. The QuickMenu, illustrated in Figure 21-1, should appear. Look at the eight items at the bottom of the Quick-Menu. We'll be concentrating on those items in this lesson.

5. Click away from the QuickMenu to close it. Is your rose still selected? If not, click it to select it. Click the **Graphics** button at the left of the Property Bar. The menu should look like Figure 21-2.

6. If you have a good memory, you'll see that most of the tools at the bottom of the QuickMenu are in the menu in Figure 21-2.

7. Click the **Content** button. Look at the dialog box that appears. This box provides a number of options regarding how the image appears in the area that surrounds it. At the bottom is a check box for preserving the image width/height ratio. If a check mark doesn't appear in that box, click the box so it DOES have a check mark. Then click **OK** to close the Content dialog box.

8. Grab the handle at the middle left and drag about an inch to the left. Did the rose remain the same size and shape? It should have, although it probably moved to the horizontal center of the box area.

9. Click outside of the Image box to deselect it and click the **Undo** button on the Toolbar to return the Image box to its original size and shape.

FIGURE 21-1
Graphics QuickMenu

```
Edit Image
Select Box
Delete Box
Create Caption
Group
Separate
Order           ▶
Image Tools
What's This?
QuickFormat
Caption...
Content...
Position...
Size...
Border/Fill...
Wrap...
Style...
```

FIGURE 21-2
Graphics Menu

```
To Front
To Back
Forward one
Back one
In Front of Text
Behind Text
Flip Left/Right
Flip Top/Bottom
Group
Separate
Size...
Position...
Caption...
Content...
Border/Fill...
Style...
```

Image Width/Height Ratio

The default setting in WordPerfect is that the check box for preserving the ratio of width and height is not selected. Even though you've preserved the ratio of the current image, WordPerfect may not remember when you size your next image. That means that each time you work with an image, you could possibly distort the image. Later in your training you will learn how to permanently change graphics styles.

Since you are probably in a classroom and your preferences might not match those of other students, we won't mess with defaults at this time. Instead, we'll try to remember to go to the Content dialog box and choose that setting for each image with which we work. Remember that if you choose it immediately, you can use Undo to return the image to its original size and shape if you accidentally distort it.

Sizing Graphics Boxes

One way to size graphics boxes is to drag the handles as you did in Exercise 21.2. If you want to set exact measurements for your box, you can choose Size from either the QuickMenu or the Graphics menu. The Box Size dialog box looks like Figure 21-3. When you bring a graphics box into a document, it will always be 1.50" wide. WordPerfect will not distort a box if you leave one of the settings at *Maintain proportions*. Let's practice.

EXERCISE 21.3

1. With **rose 21-1 xxx** showing in your window and the box selected, point to the rose and right click to display the QuickMenu. Choose **Size**.

2. In the Box Size dialog box change the width of the box to **3.0"** and click **OK**. Back in your document window, look at the large rose.

3. With the box selected, click the **Graphics** button on the Property Bar to display the Graphics menu and choose **Size**. Change Width to **Maintain proportions**. Change Height to **Full**. Click **OK**.

4. Zoom to **Full Page** to look. Then return to **100%**.

FIGURE 21-3
Box Size Dialog Box

5. Now return to the Box Size dialog box and change Height to **3.0"**. Click **OK**.

Captions

Now that you've sized the graphics box, let's give it a caption.

EXERCISE 21.4

1. With **rose 21-1 xxx** showing in your window and the box selected, use either the QuickMenu or the Edit menu to choose **Caption**.

2. In the Box Caption dialog box (we'll come back to this box later) click the **Edit** button at the right. *Figure 1* will appear at the bottom left of the box containing the rose.

3. Backspace once to delete the automatic caption and key **A Rose by Any Other Name . . . .** Click outside of the box to deselect it.

349

Moving

When a graphics box is selected, you can drag it to move it to the desired location. The moving tool is a four-headed arrow. You can also set a measured position by choosing Position from either the QuickMenu or Edit menu. We'll move the image by dragging it.

EXERCISE 21.5

1. With the **rose 21-1 xxx** showing in your window and the box selected, point to the rose and use the four-headed arrow to drag the image to the left. Align it at the margin guidelines in the upper left corner of the window.

2. Zoom to **Full Page** so you can see the entire page. Drag the rose to the lower right corner, aligned with the edges of the paper. Note that when you release the mouse button, the image will move about a quarter of an inch away from the edges of the paper. That's the no-print zone, and it will vary according to your printer description.

3. Finally, return it to the upper right corner of the page and return to normal view (100%).

4. Deselect the image and use **Save As** to save the document as **rose 21-5 xxx**. Keep it open.

Graphics Box Styles

Sometimes when you use graphics boxes in your documents, you'd like a different appearance. WordPerfect has saved you formatting time by providing a variety of graphics boxes from which you may choose. Characteristics of the box styles vary, such as location of the caption, whether or not WordPerfect counts the caption for a listing of figures, and whether or not the box is surrounded with a line. The following 14 styles are available:

- *Image.* This is a box with no borders that is best used for images, drawings, and charts.

- *Text.* The Text box usually contains text for information to be set apart from the rest of the text in a document.

- *Equation.* An Equation box is used for formulas and equations.

- *Figure.* A Figure box is like the Image box, but contains the image in a single-line border.

- *Table.* A Table box normally contains a table. In the box, the table can be numbered or rotated. Using boxes, two tables can be placed side by side.

- *User.* The User box is much like a Figure box, but it doesn't have a border.

- *Button.* Button boxes are most often used to put buttons in your document, representing a link to another part of the document. WordPerfect has what's known as Hypertext capabilities. Hypertext links two or more parts of a document so the user can quickly move from one place to another.

- *Watermark.* You've already used Watermark to put an image behind the text of your document.

- *Inline Equation.* This type of box enables you to put an equation right in the line of text that you are keying. It becomes part of the sentence.

- *OLE 2.0 Box.* This type of box is linked to another application. When the object is altered in the other application, it is automatically updated in the linked document. Since we aren't working with other applications, we won't use this type of box.
- *Inline Text.* The Inline Text box allows you to apply special formatting to normal text.
- *Draw Object.* This kind of box is positioned behind the text.
- *Draw Object Text.* This is a box like the Draw Object box, but one that contains text. It is used for grouping text with an image.
- *Sticky Note Text.* This kind of box has a yellow background, and it covers everything behind it.

The kind of work you do will determine which styles of graphics boxes you use most often. Let's look at how the different styles affect the graphics box in your **rose** document and then try some other options.

EXERCISE 21.6

1. Click to select the box. Then right click to display the QuickMenu.

2. Choose **Style** and try some of the other styles as follows:
   a. Change from an Image box to a **Figure** box. Deselect the box and look at the lines and the caption.
   b. Change to a **User** box.
   c. Change to a **Table** box.
   d. Finally, return to an **Image** box.

3. Keep the document open as you read on.

Border/Fill

Another way to change the appearance of the lines surrounding the image is by adjusting those lines with the Box Border/Fill option.

EXERCISE 21.7

1. With your image selected, display the QuickMenu and choose **Border/Fill**. The dialog box in Figure 21-4 will appear. Note that the dialog box has a preview section that shows what your box will look like with the selected border and fill.

2. Scroll to the top of the border choices using the little scroll bar. Choose a heavy black border for your rose.

3. Click the **Fill** tab and choose the third button from the left (10%).

4. Try a couple of other border and fill patterns. Then return to the settings in Steps 2 and 3.

(continued on next page)

EXERCISE 21.7 CONTINUED

5. Click the **Advanced** tab and note that you can give your image a dropped shadow. At the top left, you can set the size of the inside space surrounding your image in the box, as well as the outside space separating your box from the surrounding text.

6. Look at the *Corner radius* section. Change the radius from *0* to **0.2** and notice the round corners on your graphics box.

7. Click **OK** to close the dialog box. Save the document as **rose 21-7 xxx**.

8. Play your **pf** macro to identify the exercise. Then print the document so you can see how the fill and border look around your rose. Keep the document open.

FIGURE 21-4
Box Border/Fill Dialog Box

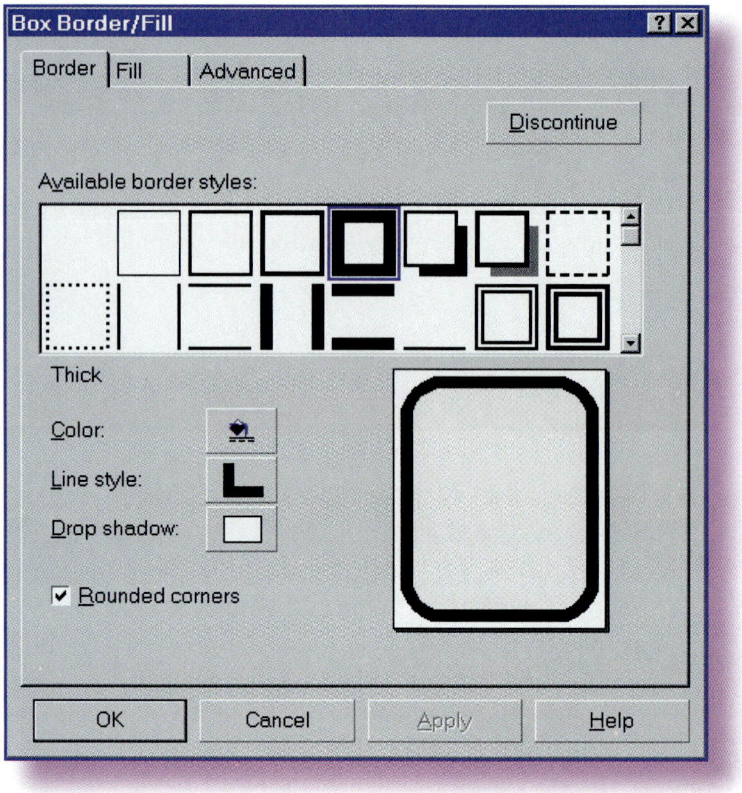

Customizing a Caption

Your graphics box already has a caption, so you don't need to learn to add one. However, you can do many things to customize your captions. Let's adjust the caption for the rose.

EXERCISE 21.8

1. With your rose showing in the window, select the image and go to the Box Border/Fill dialog box. Click **Discontinue** in the upper right corner. This removes the border and the fill.

2. Point to the selected image and display the QuickMenu. Choose **Caption** to display the Box Caption dialog box. It should look much like Figure 21-5.

FIGURE 21-5
Box Caption Dialog Box

3. In the upper left corner, change *Side of box* to **Left** and change *Position* to **Bottom**.

4. Below the preview, rotate the caption **90 degrees**. Click **OK** and look at the way the caption runs along the side of the image.

5. Move the graphics box to the left, aligning it with the top and left guidelines.

6. Return to the Box Caption dialog box. Click the **Edit** button and delete all of the caption except *A Rose . . . .* Click **Close**.

7. Return to the document and use **Save As** to save your file as **rose 21-8 xxx**. Keep it open.

As you can see, the caption is easy to manipulate. Now let's add some text to see how the graphics box works within the document.

Wrap

When text surrounds a graphics box, you have a number of choices regarding how the text wraps around that box. The default is for the text to respect the entire box that contains the image. However, if you prefer, you can tell WordPerfect to forget about the box and wrap the text around the image. What's more, you can designate the sides of the box that the text wraps around. Let's try it.

INTERNET A browser is a software program that gives access to most Internet services. A browser is required to connect to the multimedia documents on the World Wide Web.

EXERCISE 21.9

1. With your rose in the upper left corner of the window and the caption running up the left side of the box, open your **Insert** menu and choose **File**. Go to the student **datafile** folder and choose **columns**.

2. Display the QuickMenu and choose **Wrap**. Look at the Wrap Text dialog box (see Figure 21-6).

3. Choose **Contour** and **Largest side**. Click **OK**. Look at how the text wraps around your image. Move the image to the upper right corner and deselect it.

4. Return your insertion point to the top of the document and change from Left justification to **Full justification**. Note that the words crowd the image a little more with Full justification. Return to **Left justification**.

5. With the insertion point still at the beginning of the text, change to **2 Balanced newspaper columns**.

6. Drag the image to the middle of the page, centered on the gutter.

FIGURE 21-6
Wrap Text Dialog Box

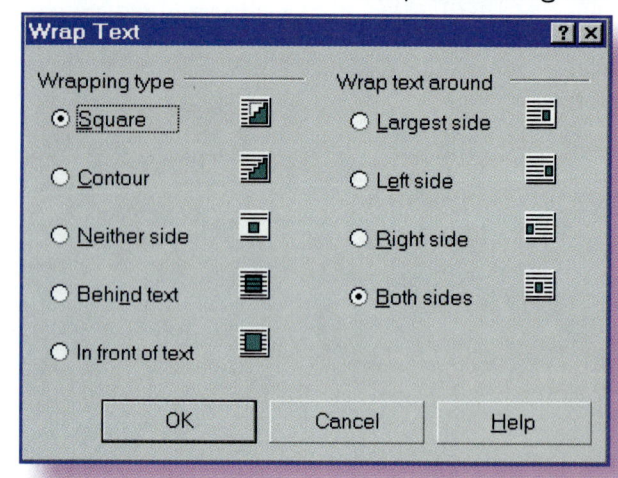

7. Experiment with some of the other Wrap choices. Then return to **Contour** and **Both sides** (although Contour/Largest side would work with columns).

8. Save your document as **rose 21-9 xxx** and print it. Keep it open.

As you can see, you can customize how the image is surrounded by text in a number of ways. Now let's look at how the image is positioned on the page.

Position

A graphics box may be attached, or anchored, in the document in one of three ways. This is called the *Position* of the box. Position affects how the box will react when text is added to or deleted from the page on which the box is located.

- **Paragraph.** When a graphics box is attached to a paragraph, it becomes part of the paragraph. Text added or deleted above the paragraph will cause the paragraph to move on the page. The box will move with the paragraph.

354

UNIT 6: GRAPHICS TOOLS

- **Page**. A graphics box that is attached to the page remains in the same position, regardless of changes to the text surrounding the box.
- **Character**. A graphics box that is anchored to a character is treated as a single character in the line of text. The box moves with the line as changes are made in the text.

The default setting for Position is Page.

EXERCISE 21.10

1. Go to the beginning of **rose 21-9 xxx** and remove the [Col Def] code to return to a single line length.

2. Open the Box Size dialog box and set the Height at **Maintain proportions**. Set the Width at **1"**. Set Wrap at **Contour** and **Largest side**.

3. Move the box to the left margin. Align the top of the box with the beginning of the third paragraph.

4. Select the entire second paragraph (double click in the left margin). Copy the paragraph to the Windows Clipboard.

5. Deselect the paragraph. Position the insertion point at the beginning of the second paragraph and paste the paragraph on the Clipboard into the document at that location. (The second paragraph is now repeated.)

6. Look at what happened with the image. It stayed in the same place on the page. Delete the second paragraph.

7. Select the rose image. Display the QuickMenu and choose **Position**. Change *Attach to* from Page to **Paragraph** (see Figure 21-7).

8. Position the insertion point at the beginning of the second paragraph. Paste the paragraph into the document again. Your image should have moved down, along with the original third paragraph because it is attached to that paragraph.

9. Delete both occurrences of the second paragraph. Now the rose should move up with the paragraph to which it is attached.

10. Select the rose and drag it down. Align the top of the box with the top of the new third paragraph. Keep the document open as you read on.

FIGURE 21-7
Attaching the Image

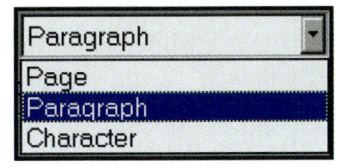

You may not have noticed it, but when the box is attached to the paragraph when you move it, a pushpin at the left identifies the beginning of the paragraph to which it is attached. When you moved from the second to third paragraph, the pushpin moved, too. When the pushpin moves, the [Box] code in Reveal Codes also moves. If you would delete the paragraph to which the box is attached, the [Box] code would also be deleted.

Now let's learn about attaching the box to a character.

EXERCISE 21.11

1. Select the graphics box in your document. Copy the selected image to the Windows Clipboard.

2. Move the insertion point to the end of the document. Paste the copied rose to that position. Make the following changes to the settings of the new box:
   a. Size. Change the Width to **0.3"** and leave the Height set at **Maintain proportions**.
   b. Caption. Go to the Caption dialog box and click the **Reset** button. Word-Perfect will ask if you'd like to delete the caption. Confirm the deletion.
   c. Position. Change the setting so the box is anchored to **Character**.

3. Select the image and use **Cut** to remove it from your document.

4. Position your insertion point at the beginning of the last sentence of the first paragraph. Paste the tiny rose box at that location.

5. Save your practice exercise as **rose 21-11 xxx** and print it. Close the file.

When you attach a graphics box to a character as you did in this exercise, you can expect some strange spacing in your paragraph unless your image is really tiny. In this case, the little rose image pushed the third line of the paragraph down an extra line. If you have occasion to attach graphics boxes to characters, you'll have to work on achieving exactly the right look for your documents.

Text Box

All of the exercises in this lesson have involved an Image box. At one point, you set it to be a User box, but it still contained an image. While any of the box styles can contain images or text, a Text box is created in the keying mode. After keying, click outside of the box to exit the keying mode and deselect the box.

You cannot move the box while you are in the keying mode. If you wish to move the box after keying the text, click outside of the box and then point to the edge of the box until your insertion point becomes a white arrow. When the arrow appears, click once to select the box. The handles will reappear. If you wish to edit or add to the text in the box, click in the box to return to the keying mode.

Text boxes may be used as sticky notes in documents. When formatted as a sticky note, the box will cover the text behind it. The sticky note can be placed anywhere on the page, and is often used to give comments to the reader of an electronic (not paper) document.

EXERCISE 21.12

1. Beginning in a new document window, open the **Insert** menu and choose **Text Box**.

2. Key the sentences in Figure 21-8. Click outside of the box to exit the keying mode. Then point to the line around the box and click to select the box.

3. Choose **Style** from the QuickMenu and change the style to a **User** box. Then change it to a **Figure** box. As you can see, the box contents are unaffected by the box style.

4. Change the Width to **2"** and leave the Height setting at **Maintain proportions**. With the box selected, point to the box border. When the four-headed arrow appears, align the box with the left and top margin guidelines.

5. Click in the text box to edit the contents. Format the words TEXT BOX with **Bold** and **Italic**.

6. Deselect the box and save the file as **box 21-12 xxx**. Play your **pf** macro to identify the document. Keep it open in your window.

7. Go to your student **datafile** folder and open **columns**. With the document open in the window, create a Text box that says:

   This is a sample sticky note.

8. Click outside of the box to exit the edit mode. Then point to the box border and select the box. Display the QuickMenu and choose **Style**. At the bottom of the list, choose **Sticky Note Text**.

9. Position the sticky note in different places on the text. Then close the practice without saving.

FIGURE 21-8
Text for Exercise 21.12

```
This is a TEXT BOX. It is one
of the graphics box styles, and
it is enclosed in a single-line
border.
```

While Text boxes may have different contents than graphics boxes containing images, the theory is the same. All of the things you can do when working with graphics boxes containing images can be done with Text boxes. In fact, you now should be an expert at working with graphics boxes.

Let's learn about another way to create a graphics box.

Drag to Create

Another way to insert a graphics image into your document is by using Drag to Create. When the Shadow Pointer is selected, your pointer turns into a tool that enables you to draw a box in the document window. Then WordPerfect takes you to a QuickMenu from which you may choose a graphics option.

Let's try Drag to Create in our practice document.

EXERCISE 21.13

1. With **box 21-12 xxx** open, click the **Shadow Pointer** button on the Application Bar at the bottom of the window to choose that option.

2. Beginning to the right of the text box, press the left mouse button and hold it. Move the mouse slightly. Your mouse pointer will look like a hand holding a piece of paper.

3. Hold the mouse pointer as you draw a box that is about two inches wide and a half inch high.

4. Release the mouse pointer. A QuickMenu will appear, giving you a choice of graphics options (see Figure 21-9). Choose **Text Box** and key your entire name.

5. Click outside of the box to exit the edit mode. Point to the border and select the box. Use the sizing handles so the border fits snugly around your name.

6. Drag to create another box. (Any size will do.) From the QuickMenu, choose **Clipart**.

7. Select the first Clipart image (**dogholdi.wpg**) and drag it into your document. Center it in the middle of the page, below the Text boxes. Then click the **Shadow Pointer** button again to deselect that option.

8. With the image still selected, display the QuickMenu and choose **Wrap**. At the left of the dialog box, choose **Behind text**. Click **OK**.

9. Back in your document window, deselect the image. Then press **Enter** until the insertion point is at the beginning of the line opposite the paper that the dog is holding. Using **Tab** and the **space bar**, move the insertion point into the box and key **I'm Fido**. (If the words aren't exactly centered, move the Image box until they are and your image looks like Figure 21-10.)

10. Save the file as **box 21-13 xxx**. Print it and close it.

FIGURE 21-9
Drag to Create Options

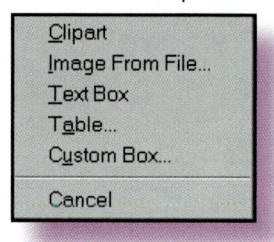

FIGURE 21-10
Graphics Box with Text

Look at your Fido document. The dog image from the Clipart collection is one of only a few images designed so the text will fit within a frame. When you use those images with text placed on the page with hard returns and tabs, the text is firmly positioned on the page. If you wish to move the image, you must also adjust the placement of the text. What's more, in order for this to work, you must tell WordPerfect to put the image behind the text with the Wrap setting. We'll learn another way to combine text with an image in Lesson 22.

Image From File

One of the choices available to you when you open the Insert menu and choose Graphics is to insert an image *From File*. This choice allows you to get images from other sources. (You'll learn about a number of other sources in Lesson 22.) The *From File* choice can also be used to insert WordPerfect graphics images that are stored in places other than the Clipart Scrapbook.

Several WordPerfect images from previous versions of the program have been saved for your use in the student **datafile** folder. Let's use *From File* to insert one of those images.

EXERCISE 21.14

1. Beginning in a new document window, open the **Insert** menu and choose **Graphics**. Then choose **From File**.

2. In the Insert Image dialog box locate your student **datafile** folder and double click to insert the **friends2.wpg** image.

3. Save the file as **friends 21-14 xxx**. Play your **pf** macro to identify the document.

4. Center the word **Friends** as a caption for the image. Format the caption with a **10-pt.** sans serif font using **Italic**.

5. Display the QuickMenu and choose **Position**. Set the Horizontal Position at **Center of Margins**.

6. Display the QuickMenu again and choose **Content**. In the Box Content dialog box click the button displaying the file folder beside the *File name* text box. You will be returned to your **datafile** files. Double click to choose **friends.wpg** and confirm that you would like this image to replace the current contents of the box.

7. Print the file and close it, saving it again with the same name.

Summary

This lesson has provided you with the basics of working with graphics boxes. You learned that the boxes can contain images or text. Specifically, you learned that:

- You can use graphics boxes to dress up documents.
- Graphics boxes can contain text or images.
- WordPerfect comes with several dozen images.
- You can move graphics boxes by dragging them.
- You can size graphics boxes by dragging a sizing handle or by using the Box Size dialog box.
- If you want to preserve the width/height ratio of your graphics images, you must make that choice in the Content dialog box.
- You can manipulate your graphics boxes using the QuickMenu or the Graphics button on the Graphics Property Bar.

- You can enclose your graphics boxes in different border styles and apply different fill options, if you wish.

- Your text can be wrapped around the box in a number of ways.

- A variety of box types are available from which you may choose for the look you want.

- Captions can be manipulated so they appear where you wish and say what you'd like them to say.

- If you prefer to draw a box in your document and fill it with an image or text, you can use the Shadow Pointer for the Drag to Create feature.

- You can insert an image that has been saved as a file.

LESSON 21 REVIEW QUESTIONS

MULTIPLE CHOICE

Circle the best answer to each of the following statements.

1. WordPerfect graphics images have a _____ extension.
    - **A.** cgm
    - **B.** wpg
    - **C.** wcm
    - **D.** sty

2. To insert a graphics image into your document, you must choose _____ from the _____ menu.
    - **A.** Image, Tools
    - **B.** Image, Insert
    - **C.** Graphics, Format
    - **D.** Graphics, Insert

3. When an image is selected, it is surrounded by
    - **A.** a heavy black line.
    - **B.** moving handles.
    - **C.** sizing handles.
    - **D.** a fine black line.

4. When an image is selected, the graphics tools will appear on the _____
    - **A.** Property Bar.
    - **B.** Toolbar.
    - **C.** Application Bar.
    - **D.** Ruler.

5. The other source of tools is the _____
    - **A.** QuickGraphics.
    - **B.** QuickMenu.
    - **C.** QuickFormat.
    - **D.** QuickImages.

6. When you bring a graphics box into a document, it will always be _____ wide.
   A. 1"
   B. 1.25"
   C. 1.50"
   D. 2"

7. You can move a graphics box with the moving tool which is _____
   A. a black square on each corner.
   B. a fat white arrow.
   C. a four-headed arrow.
   D. a dotted square.

MATCHING

Write the letter of the term or phrase from Column 2 that best matches the description in Column 1.

Column 1

____ **8.** Contains text for information to be set apart from the rest of the text in the document.

____ **9.** Used for images but contains the image in a single-line border.

____ **10.** Most often used to put buttons in your document representing a link to another part of the document.

Column 2

A. Image box
B. Text box
C. Equation box
D. Figure box
E. User box
F. Button box
G. OLE 2.0 box

LESSON 21 PROJECT

Let's apply what you've learned about working with graphics boxes in three short projects. Your instructions are more general than specific. Make your documents lovely!

PROJECT 21A

Open the **wind** document from the student **datafile** folder. Save it with your documents as **wind proj21a xxx**. Give the document a title (you get to create it). Position the title 1½" from the top of the page. Format the document with double spacing.

Insert the **Windmill.wpg** graphics image from the student **datafile** folder. Position the image in the lower left corner, and set Wrap to Contour and Right. Make the image 4" wide with Height set to Maintain proportions.

(continued on next page)

Play your **pf** macro to identify the document. Make sure the image doesn't cover the footer. If necessary, use Make It Fit to get the entire document and image on one page. Print the document and close it, saving it again with the same name.

PROJECT 21B

Figure 21-11 illustrates one of the WordPerfect graphics images with text keyed over the image with Wrap set at Behind Text. The image is **call0010.wpg** and it is illustrated with the paper in landscape orientation and the Width set at Full and Height set at Maintain proportions. The text is keyed using 30-pt. Times New Roman, although you can use any font you like.

To get the text in the correct location, deselect the image and press Enter until the insertion point is on the correct line. Then center the text. Because the space for the text in the image is off center, you may wish to use the space bar to push the text a little farther to the right.

When you finish, save the file as **party proj21b xxx**. Play the **pf** macro and print the file. Close it.

FIGURE 21-11
Solution for Project 21B

PROJECT 21C

Open **wind proj21a xxx**. Use Save As to save the document as **wind proj21c xxx**. Change the document so it is formatted with Balanced newspaper columns. Drag the inner column guidelines toward the gutter so each column is 3.13" wide and the gutter is 0.25".

Adjust the size of the graphics box containing the windmill so it is only 3" wide. Maintain the proportions in the Height section. Zoom to Full Page so you can see what you are doing as you move the graphics box to the exact center of the page. Keep the text contoured (largest side) around the box. The document should still be contained on one page. If it isn't, use Make It Fit to adjust it to fit on one page.

CRITICAL THINKING ACTIVITY

SCANS

You have just finished keying the first draft of your small group's report on democratic countries of the world. The report highlights the six largest countries, and with WordPerfect's Clipart capabilities, you have added graphics images of each country's flag plus one or two more images that were appropriate to each country. After adding and deleting text from the suggested revisions, you print the report, but notice that the images are no longer where you inserted them. What could have happened and how would you fix this problem?

LESSON 22
WORKING WITH IMAGES

OBJECTIVES

Upon completion of this lesson, you will be able to:

- Discuss the sources of graphics images to be used in WordPerfect.
- Use the Image Tools palette to edit images.
- Discuss changing defaults for box styles.
- Group graphics boxes and change their order.

Estimated Time: 1 hour

While you might have thought you learned all there was to know about working with graphics boxes in Lesson 21, you'll be pleased to know that a whole set of tools have yet to be explored. These tools are the Image Tools, which can be chosen from either the graphics box QuickMenu or the Graphics button on the Graphics Property Bar.

The tools you used in Lesson 21 were primarily concerned with how and where the graphics box appears in your document. The Image Tools palette concentrates on the image itself and how you can use it to make your documents more attractive.

Before we begin working with the Image Tools, let's briefly discuss images and where you might get the images you need for your work.

Sources of Images

The images you used in your graphics boxes in Lesson 21 were all WordPerfect images. Some of them were from the Corel WordPerfect 8 Suite. Others were from earlier versions of WordPerfect.

Graphics can be acquired from hundreds of sources. Following is a list of some of the sources of graphics images that can be used in your WordPerfect documents:

- You can purchase packages of clip art at any computer supply store or from mail-order catalogs.

- Graphics images can be downloaded from a computer bulletin board or the Internet. (When you download, be sure to check the files for computer viruses.)

- Pictures and images can be scanned from hard copy.

- Digital cameras can be used to take pictures that are recorded on disks. Some digital cameras can be plugged into your computer for transfer of the pictures to your computer.

- You or a talented friend can create images in a draw program.
- Programs are available that allow you to capture images in your window. These programs convert the captured image to a file that can be used in WordPerfect.

When you download images from a bulletin board or the Internet, be careful not to violate copyrights. Most "cute" images like Disney characters shouldn't be used because companies such as Disney own copyrights for those characters.

WordPerfect will recognize images saved in a variety of formats. Some of these include *.wfm*, *.tif*, and *.pcx*. As you already know, all WordPerfect images have a *.wpg* extension.

Corel Images

FIGURE 22-1
Graphics Folders

An obvious source of graphics images is right in your WordPerfect program. When you inserted the rose or dog images, you saw many more images in the **ClipArt** folder. If you choose From File and go to the **WordPerfect Graphics** folder, you'll find another set of folders that includes **Backgrounds**, **Borders**, **ClipArt**, **Pictures**, and **Textures** (see Figure 22-1). Each of these folders contains another set of folders, categorizing the images so it is easier for you to find what you want.

Backgrounds provide continuity to slide shows prepared using the presentations portion of the Corel WordPerfect 8 Suite. *Borders* are useful for page borders. (You'll learn about borders in Lesson 23.) The *Textures* folder contains wood grains, bricks, and a variety of other backgrounds to be used for specific purposes.

Pictures are bitmapped pictures. For some documents, you'll find them to be rather grainy. Let's preview the pictures. (Your instructor may need to help you locate the **Corel Graphics** folder.)

EXERCISE 22.1

1. Beginning in a new document window, open the **Insert** menu and choose **Graphics**. Then choose **From File**.

2. If you have a standard Corel WordPerfect 8 Suite installation, begin at the root. Choose **Corel**, **Suite8**, **Graphics**, and then **Pictures**.

3. Click the **Preview** button on the dialog box Toolbar. Browse through the folders and look at the pictures using the following guidelines:

   a. Time yourself. Don't spend more than 5 minutes looking at the images in the folders.
   b. To select a folder, double click.
   c. To return to the "parent folder," click the folder icon just to the right of the *Look in* text box.
   d. When you finish, click the **Preview** button again to deselect that option.

4. Close your empty document window without saving.

Bitmapped images can be edited a single dot at a time. That's a topic for a graphics course, not a word processing course. If you are interested, WordPerfect Help contains information about editing bitmaps.

Image Tools Palette

The Image Tools palette provides you with a whole set of features to help customize your images. Let's explore the palette using an image from an earlier version of WordPerfect.

Rotate and Move

Let's begin with the tools at the top of the palette.

EXERCISE 22.2

FIGURE 22-2
Image Tools Palette

1. Open the **Insert** menu. Choose **Graphics** and **From File**. Go to your student **datafile** folder and choose **Mallard.wpg**.

2. Display the QuickMenu and choose **Content**. Be sure the image width/height ratio is preserved.

3. With the image selected, choose **Image Tools** from the QuickMenu. The Image Tools palette will look like Figure 22-2.

4. Beginning in the upper left corner, click the **Rotate** button. The selected image will have another set of black squares around it. The new squares with little lines beside them are *rotate* handles.

5. Grab one of the rotate handles and tip the duck forward to the right, as shown in Figure 22-3. When you release the mouse button, part of his head will be hiding behind the edge of the box.

6. Drag the Image Tools palette to the right. Then grab the sizing handle at the center right of the graphics box and drag it so the box containing the duck fills half of the page between the margin guidelines. (The duck will move to the middle of the box.)

7. Click the **Move** button in the Image Tools palette and use the **Move** tool to drag the duck to the right, so its bill is just inside of the graphics box area. If you move too far, move it back.

8. Close the Image Tools palette and deselect the duck. Save the file as **duck 22-2 xxx**. Play your **pf** macro and save the file again.

FIGURE 22-3
Rotating the Duck

366

UNIT 6: GRAPHICS TOOLS

When you enlarged the graphics box, the duck moved to the middle. It didn't get fatter because you told WordPerfect to preserve the width/height ratio. In the last couple of steps you moved the duck to one end of the graphics box. The entire area between the sizing handles is the graphics box. Sometimes you want a box that is larger than the image, and you want part of the box to remain empty. The Move tool enables you to position the image anywhere you want it in the graphics box.

Flip

The two Flip buttons enable you to turn your images around. Good page layout dictates that an image usually faces toward the center of the page, not toward the edge of the page. Rarely will you have an image that you can turn upside down!

EXERCISE 22.3

1. With the **duck 22-2 xxx** document in the window, drag the graphics box from the left margin to the right margin. Align it with the top and right margin guidelines.

2. Display the Image Tools palette and use the **Rotate** tool to make your duck stand upright again (not tipped).

3. Turn your duck upside down with the **Flip** button on the right. Then tip him upright again.

4. Use the **Flip** button on the left to make the duck face the left. With the duck facing the left, use the **Move** tool to move him a little closer to the right edge of the graphics box. Don't lose any tail feathers.

5. Keep him in that position and read on.

Zoom

The Zoom button is three-tiered. Let's try each of the tiers and learn as we work with them.

EXERCISE 22.4

1. With your duck showing and the Image Tools palette displayed, click the **Zoom** button in the Image Tools palette. Compare your pop-out menu with Figure 22-4.

2. Choose the first tool—the one that looks like a magnifying glass with a plus sign in the middle. This turns your mouse pointer into a floating crosshair to be used for drawing an "elastic" box around a part of the image.

FIGURE 22-4
Zoom Portion of Image Tools

3. Draw a box that includes only the duck's head. When you release the mouse pointer, your image will include only the part of the duck around which you made the elastic box.

(continued on next page)

EXERCISE 22.4 CONTINUED

4. Deselect the graphics box. Then save your file as **duck 22-4 xxx** and print it.

5. Display the Image Tools palette again and choose the middle **Zoom** tool. This displays a scroll bar which you can use to increase or decrease the view of the duck. Experiment with it. Then return to the head shot.

6. Choose the third **Zoom** tool. This restores the duck. Finally, click the **Reset Attributes** button at the bottom of the Image Tools palette. This returns the duck to its original proportions, and it will be facing the right again.

7. Keep the duck in the window as you read on.

When you displayed the head of the duck only, you didn't really crop that portion from the duck. The rest of the image was still there. It was just hiding, waiting for you to restore the entire image.

Color

The next four buttons—BW threshold, Contrast, Brightness, and Fill—have to do with the colors of the image and how bright they are. Because the duck is in color, the BW (black/white) threshold is set at None. Contrast and Brightness can move in either direction. The default is the center choice. With a color image, Fill won't be adjusted. The big button at the bottom of that section allows you to invert colors—to look at the colors that are complementary to the regular colors.

EXERCISE 22.5

1. Spend no more than 5 minutes playing with the five color choices on the Image Tools palette. You may choose any settings you wish for your duck.

2. Do NOT click the Edit Contents button. That button takes you to the draw program. It takes a long time to load on most computers, and you need to keep moving.

3. When you have a good idea of what happens with the color choices, click the second button from the bottom—**Edit Attributes**. This displays a dialog box containing all of the tools with which you've been working.

4. Spend a few minutes exploring the choices in that box. Then click **Reset All** to see how easy it is to restore the duck. Close your duck file without saving it again.

As you can see, your options are unlimited regarding what you can do to make the Clipart images fit attractively in your documents.

Box Styles

As discussed earlier, some of the default settings may not be satisfactory as you use WordPerfect on the job and use images in your documents. One of the settings you may decide to change will be the one in the Content dialog box where you told WordPerfect to maintain the width/height ratio. Another is the setting that attaches images to the page rather than to the paragraph.

Whether you need to edit those defaults to make you more efficient on the job will depend on the kind of work you do. In the classroom, however, you don't want to change ANY defaults. Otherwise, it will be confusing to other students.

So that you can learn how easily those defaults can be changed, however, we'll try an exercise in which you DO change the defaults. Then we'll cancel the changes as we return to the working window. Follow along carefully.

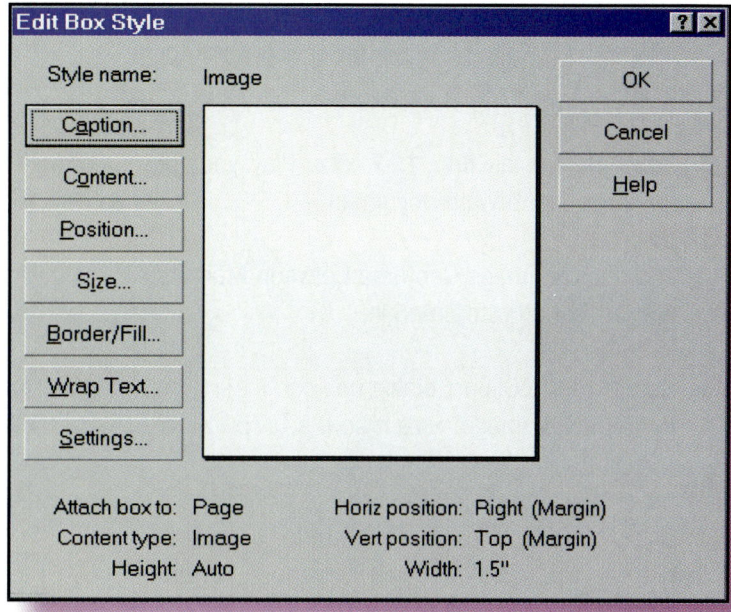

EXERCISE 22.6

FIGURE 22-5
Edit Box Style Dialog Box

1. Beginning in a new document window, open the **Insert** menu. Choose **Graphics**, and then choose **Custom Box**.

2. Be sure **Image** is selected. (When you make changes to box styles, you must change each type individually.)

3. Click **Edit** to display the Edit Box Style dialog box, as illustrated in Figure 22-5.

4. Note that at the top, it reinforces that you are editing the Image style. Look at the buttons at the left. Do they look familiar?

5. Click **Content** and choose the **Preserve...** choice at the bottom. Click **OK**.

6. Click **Position** and change to **Paragraph**. Click **OK**.

7. Now, because you don't want to save those changes, click **Cancel** and then **Close** and **Cancel** to return to your document window.

> **INTERNET**
> In certain browsers and other Internet programs, a bookmark or hotlist is a special file used to save addresses and locations. By saving and recalling addresses, it is easy for you to visit your favorite sites over and over.

Had you accepted the changes you made in those dialog boxes, WordPerfect would have remembered the settings, and you would not have needed to make either of them in your work with future images.

369

Grouping and Arranging Graphics Boxes

When you have more than one graphics box occupying the same space, WordPerfect enables you to decide which box is on top. You can rearrange the order of the boxes as often as you wish. You can also group two or more boxes so that they can be sized or moved together.

Remember Fido? We'll use that same image for practice.

EXERCISE 22.7

1. Beginning in a new document window, insert the **dogholdi.wpg** Clipart image. Size the image to 2" wide. Maintain the proportions for height.

2. Save the file as **fido 22-7 xxx**. Play your **pf** macro to identify the document.

3. Position the image Centered between Margins and 1" from the top margin.

4. Return to the Clipart dialog box and insert the **lightbul.wpg** image. Size it so it's 0.75" wide.

5. Move the lightbulb so the base of it is over the dog's head. With the lightbulb selected, display the QuickMenu and choose **Order**. Choose **To Back**. (The base of the lightbulb should now be behind Fido's head.)

6. Create a Text box that contains the words **I have an idea!**. Press **Enter** after the word *have* so the text is on two lines.

7. Click outside of the box to exit the edit mode. Then point to the border of the box and click to select it (handles only). With the box selected, display the QuickMenu, choose **Border/Fill**, and set the border at **None** (the first choice in the first row of borders). Size the box so the handles are close to the text on all sides.

8. With the Text box still selected, use the moving tool (the four-headed arrow) to move the Text box to the paper in Fido's mouth. For practice, with the box still selected, choose **Order** from the QuickMenu and move the text to the back. Click away from the box to deselect it.

9. Point to the place where the Text box is hiding. When the arrow points toward the upper right, click to select the Text box again. Use the QuickMenu and choose **Order** again to move it to the front.

10. Your file should look like Figure 22-6. Save it again with the same name. Keep it open.

FIGURE 22-6
Layered Graphics Boxes

370

UNIT 6: GRAPHICS TOOLS

Your picture now has three graphics boxes. You aligned them so they look good together. But they are still separate items. If you move one of them, the others will stay in the same place. Let's learn to group the boxes so you can move them as one.

EXERCISE 22.8

1. With **fido 22-7 xxx** showing in the window, save it as **fido 22-8 xxx**. For practice, move the lightbulb away from the dog. Then move it back. It is a separate item.

2. Click the lightbulb to select that image. Hold the **Shift** key while you select the Text box. (One set of sizing handles will surround those two boxes.)

3. Still holding the **Shift** key, click Fido's tail to select the dog. The sizing handles should now contain all three graphics boxes. (If you get dashed lines around the images, click away from them and start again.)

4. Display the QuickMenu and choose **Group**. Point to any part of the grouping and drag it to a different position on the page. All three parts of the grouping should move.

5. Use a corner sizing handle to make the image larger or smaller. The parts should be adjusted together. (If you use the Size dialog box to size a set of grouped boxes, they will fall apart.)

6. Select the grouped images and display the QuickMenu again. Choose **Separate** to change them back into individual boxes.

7. Select the lightbulb and make it 0.5" wide. Reposition it behind Fido's head.

8. Print your practice and save it again with the same name. Close the document.

Summary

This short lesson provided you with additional information about working with graphics images. In this lesson you learned that:

- You can buy Clipart images.
- You can download images from bulletin boards and the Internet.
- Corel WordPerfect Suite 8 comes with a large number of images.
- Images can be rotated and moved within the graphics box area.
- You can flip an image vertically or horizontally.
- Color brightness and intensity can be adjusted.
- After making adjustments to an image, it is easy to return the image to its original size, shape, and color.
- If you find yourself constantly making the same change(s) to graphics boxes, you can change the default settings.

- You can adjust the position of two or several boxes to the front or back.
- Multiple graphics boxes can be grouped to behave as one box.

LESSON 22 REVIEW QUESTIONS

FILL IN THE BLANKS

Complete each of the following statements by writing your answer in the blank provided.

1. The Image Tools can be chosen from either the graphics box QuickMenu or the _____ on the Graphics Property Bar.

2. When you choose From File and go to the WordPerfect Graphics folder, you'll find another set of folders that includes Backgrounds, Borders, ClipArt, _____, and Textures.

3. Click the _____ button on the dialog box Toolbar to browse through the folders and look at the pictures.

4. With the image selected, choose Image Tools and the Image Tools _____ will be displayed.

5. The _____ tool enables you to position the image anywhere you want it in the graphics box.

6. The two _____ buttons enable you to turn your images around.

7. The _____ button is three-tiered; the first one looks like a magnifying glass with a plus sign in the middle.

TRUE/FALSE

Circle the T if the statement is true. Circle the F if it is false.

T F 8. The Textures folder contains images of wood grains, bricks, and a variety of other backgrounds.

T F 9. You can download images from the Internet and use them free of charge because you have already paid for on-line services.

T F 10. You can rearrange the order of the boxes once, from front to back.

LESSON 22 PROJECT

In this project you get to apply your skills with regard to inserting and editing graphics images. You will work on your own, with few directions. Following is the general idea of what you are to do:

1. Open **Brazil** from the student **datafile** folder and save it as **Brazil proj22 xxx**.

2. Use the **pf** macro to identify the file.

3. Increase the size of the top margin on the first page. Format the title and side headings using different font sizes and bold, if you wish. After formatting one side heading, use QuickFormat to apply the formatting to the others, making it easy to reformat if you should change your mind.

4. Use Widow/Orphan control or Block Protect, if necessary, to achieve an attractive page break.

5. Use at least two of the three graphics images listed. Get them from your student **datafile** folder. Position, size, and edit the images so they complement the document, not detract from it. (You may use other graphics images, if you wish. Do not use more than three graphics boxes in a document of this length.)
   a. **Brazil flag.wpg**
   b. **Brazil map.wpg**
   c. **Tropics.wpg**

6. Select the first sentence in the second paragraph about Economics. Copy it to the Clipboard. Then create a Text box. Paste the sentence into that box. Adjust the size of the box so it is 2" wide. Align it at the right margin. Change the text in the box to 14-pt. italic. Go to Border/Fill and choose the fifth border in the second row (Thick Top/Bottom). This type of box that highlights certain information in a document is called a "pull quote." You have no doubt seen pull quotes in magazines and newspapers.

7. When you finish, save the file again, print it, and close it.

CRITICAL THINKING ACTIVITY

You have been working with the red lobster image that you have inserted into your document. With the Image Tools palette displayed, you notice that the BW threshold button has an X in it. Why is that selection unavailable?

LESSON 23
Graphics Lines, Borders, and Fill

OBJECTIVES

Upon completion of this lesson, you will be able to:

- Create and customize horizontal and vertical lines.
- Enclose your paragraphs within Paragraph borders.
- Work with shapes
- Put Page borders around your pages.
- Work with Column borders.
- Use fill to emphasize paragraphs in your documents.

Estimated Time: 1½ hours

Like graphics boxes, graphics lines, borders, and fill are used to enhance the appearance of documents. Much of what you learned in Lesson 21 can be applied to working with lines, borders, and fill. The features are closely related. A graphics border is actually made up of graphics lines. The basic difference is that a border goes all the way around a page, paragraph, or column, while a line simply goes straight from one point to another.

Let's begin by taking a look at graphics lines.

Graphics Lines

WordPerfect will automatically insert horizontal or vertical lines for you if you tell the program what you want. Graphics lines can be chosen from the Insert menu. If you prefer, you can use Ctrl+F11 for a horizontal line and Ctrl+Shift+F11 for a vertical line.

EXERCISE 23.1

1. Beginning in a new document window, press **Ctrl+F11** to insert a horizontal line. Press Enter twice.

2. Open the **Insert** menu and choose **Shape**. Then choose **Horizontal Line**. Look at your two lines. They are identical, except the second is two returns below the first.

3. Press **Ctrl+Shift+F11** to insert a vertical line. Press **Tab** twice.

4. Open the **Insert** menu, choose **Shape**, and choose **Vertical Line**. Look at your two lines.

5. Zoom to **Full Page** to get a bird's-eye view of your lines. Keep the lines showing in the window as you read on.

The lines you created in Exercise 23.1 are the default lines. Each of them extends from margin to margin and is 0.013" thick. If you wish to create a line with any other characteristics, you must create a custom line. Let's practice with custom lines by creating four of them. We'll do all of the formatting and placement of the lines in the Create Graphics Line dialog box.

EXERCISE 23.2

1. Reveal your codes. Look at the line codes. Move your insertion point to the left of one of the codes and look at the description of the line in the code. Record the codes in your list of codes. Close the document without saving it.

2. Open the **Insert** menu, choose **Shape**, and choose **Custom Line**. The Create Graphics Line dialog box should appear, looking like Figure 23-1.

3. We will be creating four lines. The first line is easy. In the buttons at the left is one for *Line thickness*. Click it and look at the selection of lines. At the bottom is a number reporting the current thickness. Change that number to **0.10"**. (That's ten hundredths of an inch or a tenth of an inch.) Click **OK** to return to your document and look at the line. It's thick!

4. Return to the dialog box and make the following changes for the second line:
   a. Near the bottom, click the button beside *Horizontal* and change from Full to **Centered**.
   b. Just below Horizontal is *Vertical*. Change from Baseline to **Set**. In the box to the right key **1.5"** so the second line will be a half inch below the first line.
   c. In the Length box, just above the *Position* section, key **5"**. (The first line was 6.5" long. It went from margin to margin. This line is 1.5" shorter.)
   d. Change thickness to **0.08"**. Click **OK** to return to your document.

5. Create a third line as follows. Then return to your document and look at it.
   a. Set Horizontal at **Centered**.
   b. Set Vertical at **2"** from the top of the page.

(continued on next page)

EXERCISE 23.2 CONTINUED

c. Set Length at **3.5"**.
d. Set thickness at **0.06"**.

6. Finally, create a fourth line. You probably can guess the settings, but here they are:
   a. Set Horizontal at **Centered**.
   b. Set Vertical at **2.5"**.
   c. Set Length at **2"**.
   d. Set thickness at **0.04"**.

7. Back in your document window, look at your lines. They should look like Figure 23-2. Save the file as **lines 23-2 xxx**.

8. Play your **pf** macro to identify the document. Print it and keep it open.

FIGURE 23-1
Create Graphics Line Dialog Box

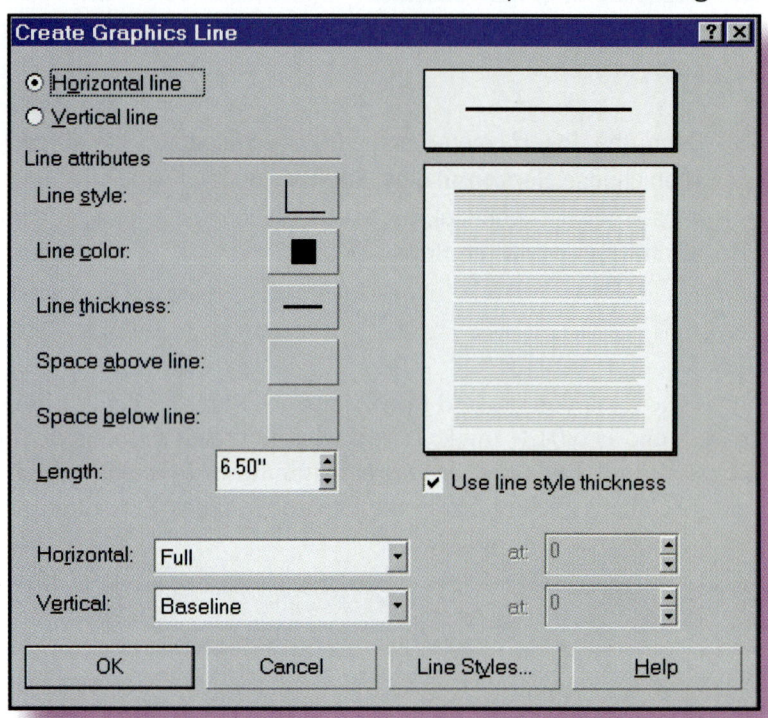

FIGURE 23-2
The Lines for Exercise 23.2

Once you have created a line, you can edit it or move it to a different location. Let's practice editing lines using the lines in your window.

376

UNIT 6: GRAPHICS TOOLS

EXERCISE 23.3

1. Zoom to **Full Page** and save your document, as **lines 23-3 xxx**.

2. Point to the first line carefully. When your white mouse pointer arrow points to the right, drag the line to the bottom of the document. (The line will have sizing handles.) Align it at the top of the footer area. Align the ends of the line with the guidelines at the sides of the page.

3. Point to the middle line at the top and drag it so it's about halfway between the 2-inch line and the 6.5-inch line at the bottom. Then point to the sizing handle at the bottom center of the line and drag it down until the line is about a half inch thick. (Make it BIG and BLACK.)

4. Point to the line that's on top and click to give it handles. Then grab a handle on the left end with a two-headed arrow and drag the end of the line as close to the edge of the page as you can get it. (The line should get longer.)

5. Point to the 2-inch line (the only one you haven't edited) and double click to open the Edit Graphics Line dialog box. Change the color of the line to red.

6. Still in the Edit Graphics Line dialog box, click the button beside **Line Styles** and look at the line styles available. Choose the second line style in the first row. Click **OK** to return to your document.

7. Save your document again as **lines 23-3 xxx**. Print it and close it.

By now you have a pretty good idea of what you can do with horizontal lines. Vertical lines are no different. Simply click the Vertical line radio button in the Create Graphics Line dialog box before setting up the line. Let's create some vertical lines that might be used to dress up a letterhead.

EXERCISE 23.4

1. Beginning in a new document window, create a vertical line that violates the margins of your document. That's OK because the margins will still hold the text. In the Create Graphics Line dialog box, click the button at the top for a **Vertical** line. Set the line up as follows:
    a. Choose **Set** in the Horizontal Position box and key **0.5"** from the left edge of the page.
    b. Choose **Set** in the Vertical Position box and key **0.5"** from the top of the page.
    c. Set the Length at **10"**.
    d. Set thickness at **0.05"**. Click **OK**.

2. Create another vertical line that is the same length, **0.75"** from the left, **0.5"** from the top, and **0.05"** thick. Set the color to a shade of gray. (If you have a color printer, you might want to choose a color that matches your company or school logo.)

3. Return to your document and check your lines. The difference in shading might not be obvious until you print your document.

4. Save the document as **lines 23-4 xxx**. Play your **pf** macro. Then print the document and close it, saving it again.

You can create a different effect by piling your lines up. Look at Figure 23-3. We'll go to the Footer dialog box to position these lines. Then we'll put the Page Number code between them so you can use the whole thing as a fancy footer in your documents.

FIGURE 23-3
Footer Lines

EXERCISE 23.5

1. Beginning in a new document window, open the **Insert** menu and choose **Header/Footer**. Then choose **Footer A** and **Create**.

2. In the Footer A space create four horizontal lines, one at a time. Following are the criteria for those lines:
   a. Line 1   Horizontal Position   **Left**
              Length   **2.5"**
   b. Line 2   Horizontal Position   **Left**
              Length   **1"**
              Thickness   **0.05"**
   c. Line 3   Horizontal Position   **Right**
              Length   **2.5"**
   d. Line 4   Horizontal Position   **Right**
              Length   **1"**
              Thickness   **0.05"**

3. Give the **Center** command and click the **Number** button on the Footer Property Bar. Choose **Page Number**. Your page number should appear between your lines.

4. Click the **Close** button on the Property Bar. Use the scroll bar so you can see your footer at the bottom of the page.

5. Save the file as **footer 23-5 xxx**. With your insertion point at the top of the page, open the **Insert** menu, choose **Other**, and then choose **Path and Filename** to identify this non-document. Print it and close it.

These were just a few short exercises with lines. It should be pretty clear to you at this point that the possibilities for the use of lines in your documents are endless.

Shapes

You may have noticed when you choose to create a custom line that WordPerfect offers you a wide variety of other shapes, such as polygons, polylines, rectangles, circles, and arrows. WordPerfect places these shapes in graphics boxes that can be edited much as you've edited other graphics boxes. Let's practice with a few of the shapes.

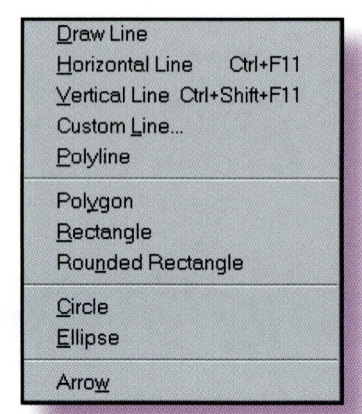

```
Draw Line
Horizontal Line    Ctrl+F11
Vertical Line  Ctrl+Shift+F11
Custom Line...
Polyline

Polygon
Rectangle
Rounded Rectangle

Circle
Ellipse

Arrow
```

378   **UNIT 6: GRAPHICS TOOLS**

EXERCISE 23.6

1. Open **columns** again so you have some text in your window. Then open the **Insert** menu and choose **Shape**. Choose **Rectangle**.

2. Beginning somewhere near the left of the first paragraph, draw a rectangle. When you release the mouse button, the rectangle will be filled with the color that was used last, and the Property Bar will change to include some new tools. (You'll learn about working with those tools in Lesson 29.)

3. With the image selected, display the QuickMenu and choose **Wrap**. Choose **Behind text**.

4. Open the **Insert** menu and choose **Shape** again. This time, choose **Polyline**.

5. Beginning in the upper right corner of the document, draw a diagonal line that extends down and to the left, right over the text of the document. End the line by double clicking.

6. With the line selected, display the QuickMenu and choose **Wrap**. Choose **Contour** and **Both sides**. Note how the line bisects your text.

7. Open the **Insert** menu and choose **Shape** again. Choose **Rounded Rectangle**. Draw a rounded rectangle that fits closely around the word Columns at the beginning of the last paragraph. Choose **Wrap** and position the shape behind the text.

8. Select the rounded rectangle and drag it so it surrounds the last word of the paragraph instead of the first. Size the box so the entire word is enclosed in the rectangle.

9. Save your practice as **shapes 23-6 xxx**. Play your **pf** macro and print the document before closing it.

Borders

Using the Borders feature isn't much different from the Graphics Line feature. Several line styles have been prepared to save you work in defining what the borders should look like and where they should be placed. Unless you have some unusual application, the predefined styles should meet most of your needs. We'll begin with Paragraph borders.

Paragraph Borders

Paragraph borders enclose one or more paragraphs. You have a choice of Paragraph border styles. Let's try a few of them.

> **INTERNET**
> Gopher is a program that uses a series of menus to lead users to files of information. Gopher is named for the Golden Gophers of the University of Minnesota, where the program was developed.

EXERCISE 23.7

FIGURE 23-4
Paragraph Border/Fill Dialog Box

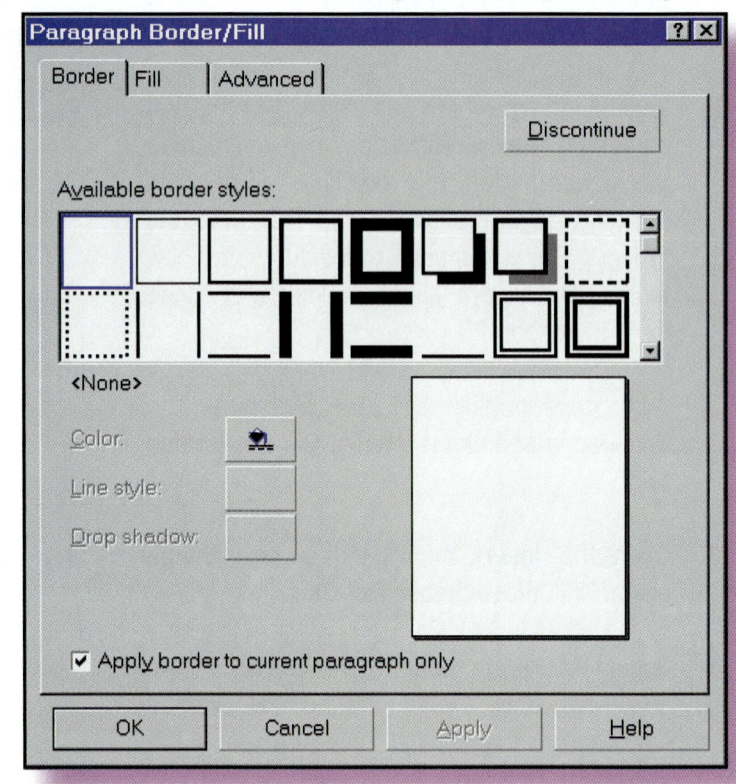

1. Beginning in a new document window, go to the student **datafile** folder and choose **columns**. (This document is beginning to look familiar, isn't it?) Use **Save As** to save the document as **borders 23-7 xxx**.

2. With the insertion point at the beginning of the first paragraph, open the **Format** menu, choose **Paragraph**, and then choose **Border/Fill**. The Paragraph Border/Fill dialog box will open, looking like Figure 23-4.

3. Choose the first border. (It's actually the second button in the first row of borders.) Look at the box at the bottom of the dialog box. The *Apply border to current paragraph only* option should be checked. Click **OK**.

4. Position the insertion point at the beginning of the second paragraph.

5. Choose **Format**, **Paragraph**, and then **Border/Fill**, to return to the Paragraph Border/Fill dialog box.

6. Choose the sixth button in the first row (the one with the black dropped shadow). Click **OK**.

7. Position the insertion point at the beginning of the third paragraph and put a border around that paragraph. This time you'll use the scroll bars so you can choose the second border in the third row. Click **OK**.

8. Your document has two more paragraphs. Select those paragraphs. Then go to the Paragraph Border/Fill dialog box and choose one last border for these two paragraphs. Note that because they were selected, one border contains both paragraphs.

9. Return to your document window. Save the document again as **borders 23-7 xxx**. Play your **pf** macro and print the document. Save it again, and keep it open.

Sometimes you want more space between the text in the paragraph and the border surrounding the paragraph. WordPerfect will put as much space as you'd like. In the process, the border extends into the margin of the document. The text doesn't change. Let's try it.

380 UNIT 6: GRAPHICS TOOLS

EXERCISE 23.8

1. With **borders 23-7 xxx** showing in the window, position the insertion point at the beginning of the first paragraph.

2. Reveal your codes and find the [Para Border] code for the first paragraph. Point to that code and double click. (You could open the dialog box in the normal way, too, to edit the border.)

3. Look at the top of the dialog box. Find the **Advanced** tab and click it. In the *Spacing* section in the upper left corner, click the button beside **Inside**.

4. Point to the first bar in the right-hand column and click to choose it. Watch your paragraph as the dialog box closes and the change is made. You should see the border expand and then move away from the paragraph.

5. Close your document without saving it again.

As you can see, it was easy to adjust the inside space of the border. Most of the time, however, you will probably be satisfied with the default inside space.

Page Borders

Page borders work a lot like Paragraph borders. A major difference is that for Page borders, you get to choose between *Line* borders (like the Paragraph borders) and *Fancy* borders. When you use Line borders, you may choose an option that tells WordPerfect to put the border only on the current page. When you use Fancy borders, the border will appear on all pages of the document following the page where it was inserted. Let's modify our **columns** document and add a Page border that continues to the second page.

EXERCISE 23.9

1. Beginning in a new document window, open the **File** menu, find **columns** in the list at the bottom, and open that file again. Use **Save As** to save the file as **borders 23-9 xxx**.

2. With the insertion point at the beginning of the document, change to double spacing (2.0). Then open the **Format** menu, choose **Page**, and then choose **Border/Fill**.

3. Look at the *Border type* section at the top. If *Fancy* isn't selected, click the button and choose it.

4. Drag the scroll box to the bottom of the scroll bar. Then click above the box once to go up one row. Choose the second border in that row. It looks kind of fluffy when it is in miniature. Click once to select it and then click **OK**, or double click to select the border.

5. Back in your document window, look at the shapes that surround your page. Press **Ctrl+End** to look at the second page of the document. Zoom to **Full Page** to see the page in full. Then return to 100%.

6. Save your document again as **borders 23-9 xxx**. Play your **pf** macro to identify the document. Print the document and keep it open.

If you want the border to appear only on the first page, you can tell WordPerfect to discontinue the border beginning on a particular page. That will turn the border off for the remainder of the document. Let's tell WordPerfect to discontinue the border on the second page.

EXERCISE 23.10

1. Position the insertion point somewhere near the beginning of the second page of **borders 23-9 xxx**.

2. Return to the Page Border dialog box. Click the **Discontinue** button near the upper right corner.

3. Look at both pages of the document. The first should have a border. The second shouldn't. Close your document without saving it.

You probably noticed as you looked through the borders that some of them would work better for announcements than for pages of text. Let's try one of the really fancy ones.

EXERCISE 23.11

1. Beginning in a new document window, go to the Page Border/Fill dialog box and choose the border near the bottom that looks like people in front of a stage.

2. Use **Center** justification and prepare the poster illustrated in Figure 23-5. Use whatever font size looks good. You can customize the words, if you don't happen to know an "Amazing Anne."

3. When you finish, save your flyer as **borders 23-11 xxx**. Press **Ctrl+Home** to move the insertion point to the top of the document. Go to the **Insert** menu and insert the Path and Filename code. It should show through the curtain at the top. Print the flyer, save it, and close it.

FIGURE 23-5
Flyer for Exercise 23.11

Now let's go back to the Page Border/Fill dialog box and look at the Line borders.

EXERCISE 23.12

1. Open **columns** again from the list at the bottom of the **File** menu. Save the file in your normal folder as **borders 23-12 xxx**.

2. With the insertion point at the beginning of the document, set double spacing.

3. Go to the Page Border/Fill dialog box and change *Border type* from *Fancy* to **Line**.

4. Look at the variety of Line borders. Choose the last border on the right of the second row of borders.

5. Look at the bottom of the box. Does a check mark tell WordPerfect to put the border on the current page only? If it doesn't, click that option to select it and click **OK** to return to your document window.

6. Look at the first page. Look at the second page. The border should appear only on the first page.

7. Play your **pf** macro. Print the document and close it, saving it again.

Column Borders

The third kind of border is the Column border. Column borders can only be chosen if your text is in columns. Two styles of Column borders are available—with only a line between the columns, or with the columns completely enclosed within the border.

Let's open our **columns** document yet again and try the two border styles available for columns.

EXERCISE 23.13

1. Beginning in a new document window, go to the **File** menu and open **columns**. Use **Save As** to save the file as **borders 23-13 xxx**.

2. With the insertion point at the beginning of the document, go to the columns dialog box and change to **2 Balanced newspaper columns**. Keep the dialog box open.

3. With the Columns dialog box still displayed, click the **Border/Fill** button.

4. Choose the seventh border style in the last row of borders and look at it in the Preview window. It is simply a line between the columns.

5. Choose the fifth border in the same row. While you are still in the Column Border/Fill dialog box, look at the middle of the dialog box where you have the option of changing the color of the lines and applying a dropped shadow. Click the last drop shadow style.

6. Click the **Advanced** tab and look at the *Drop Shadow* section in the upper right corner. Change the drop shadow color to blue, and set the width at the first choice in the second column.

(continued on next page)

EXERCISE 23.13 CONTINUED

7. While you're there, notice that you can change inside and outside border space for Column borders, just as you did for Paragraph borders.

8. Click **OK** twice to return to your document. Play your **pf** macro. Then print the file and close it, saving it again as **borders 23-13 xxx**.

Actually, you can apply any border style to your columns, but the two with which you experimented in this exercise are the only two that will put a line between the columns.

Fill

Finally, let's take a look at fill. As you know, *fill* is the term that refers to shading the background of something. You used fill in the background of your rose in Lesson 21. The theory is the same. Choose the fill style and/or darkness. Let's work with fill for paragraphs.

EXERCISE 23.14

1. Open the **columns** document from the student **datafile** folder one more time. Use **Save As** to save the file as **borders 23-14 xxx**.

2. Position the insertion point at the beginning of the second paragraph. Choose **Format**, **Paragraph**, and **Border/Fill**. Click the **Fill** tab and look at the variety of Fill styles available.

3. Choose the Fill style third to the right of *None*. Close the Paragraph Border/Fill dialog box.

4. Play your **pf** macro, print the document, save it, and close it.

As you can see, WordPerfect offers you a wide variety of fill styles. In addition, a number of options are available that you can explore at your leisure.

Summary

This lesson was all about dressing up your documents. You learned quite a number of things you can do for that "certain" look. In this lesson you learned that:

- Horizontal, diagonal, and vertical lines, as well as drawn shapes, can be inserted to dress up your documents.

- WordPerfect provides you with a wide variety of borders for paragraphs, pages, and columns.

- You can use fill with or without borders to cause portions of text to stand out from the rest.

LESSON 23 REVIEW QUESTIONS

MULTIPLE CHOICE

Circle the best answer to each of the following statements.

1. If you wish to create a custom line, open the Insert menu, choose _____, and choose Custom Line.
   - **A.** Line
   - **B.** Graphics
   - **C.** Shape
   - **D.** Image

2. The default length of a horizontal graphics line is
   - **A.** 6½ inches.
   - **B.** 8½ inches.
   - **C.** 9 inches.
   - **D.** 11 inches.

3. If you create a vertical line with Ctrl+Shift+F11, your line
   - **A.** can be set at two inches.
   - **B.** will extend from the left margin to the right margin.
   - **C.** will extend from the top margin to the bottom margin.
   - **D.** will extend from the left edge of the page to the right edge.

4. To enclose a paragraph with a border, open the _____ menu, choose Paragraph, and then choose Border/Fill.
   - **A.** Format
   - **B.** Insert
   - **C.** Graphics
   - **D.** Tools

5. When enclosing the text on a page with a Page border,
   - **A.** the text must first be selected.
   - **B.** the insertion point can be anywhere on the page.
   - **C.** the border must be applied before text is keyed.
   - **D.** the border is formatted in a new document and the text is inserted from another file.

6. The third kind of border you learned about in this lesson was the _____ border.
   - **A.** Table
   - **B.** Image
   - **C.** Graphics
   - **D.** Column

WRITTEN QUESTIONS

Write your answers to the following questions.

7. Define the term fill.

(continued on next page)

8. What is the easiest way to move a line?

9. When you choose Page borders, your choices are between what type of borders?

10. What are the two styles of Column borders?

LESSON 23 PROJECT

The project for Lesson 23 consists of several short exercises reviewing what you learned in the lesson. Work quickly and efficiently. See how much you can do without having to look back into the lesson for help.

PROJECT 23A

Open **lighthouses u3t2 xxx**. Save the document as **lighthouses proj23a xxx**. Give the title page of the document a border. You may choose a Line border or a Fancy border. Be sure that the border is on the title page only. If you use a Fancy border, you'll have to discontinue it on the first page of text.

When you finish, save the document again and print the title page only. Close the document.

PROJECT 23B

Use one of the Fancy borders to create a one-page poster, flyer, or handbill. Consider a poster advertising a school dance or party. Perhaps you want to create a flyer urging your classmates to vote for a particular candidate.

When you are satisfied with your work, save the document as **proj23b xxx**. Identify it with the Path and Filename code, either in the footer with the **pf** macro or somewhere else on the page where it will be visible. Print and close the file, saving it again when you close it.

PROJECT 23C

Create a simple letterhead for your home or business using the sample in Figure 23-6 as a guide. Use at least two graphics lines, and vary their width or length to make your letterhead attractive. Vary the font sizes to stress the important parts of your letterhead.

When you finish, save the sample letterhead as **proj23c xxx**. Use your **pf** macro to identify the page. Then print it and close it, saving it again when you close it.

FIGURE 23-6
Sample Letterhead for Project 23C

MYCORP MANUFACTURING
1492 Highland Drive
Hometown, OH 44135

Phone 216-555-2525   Fax 216-555-2526

CRITICAL THINKING ACTIVITY

You have just printed out a document in which you have used Paragraph borders to highlight some of the information. You are not pleased with the appearance of the document because it looks too crowded. You think that if you had more space between the border and the text of the paragraph it would improve the layout. What can you do and how do you do it?

LESSON 24
FEATURE BONANZA

OBJECTIVES

Upon completion of this lesson, you will be able to:

- Use TextArt to create lovely display documents.
- Add drop caps to the beginning of your paragraphs.
- Work with the Equation Editor.
- Rotate the text in a Text box.
- Mark text with Redline and Strikeout.
- Remove the Redline and Strikeout markings.
- Use Compare to compare similar documents.
- Number your lines with Line Numbering.
- Print a document using Booklet Printing.

Estimated Time: 1½ hours

In Lessons 21, 22, and 23 you've learned about a variety of graphics tools to help you dress up your documents. You've worked with graphics boxes, images, lines, borders, and fill. You're probably pretty good with all of those tools.

In this lesson you will be introduced to a set of additional tools. Not much time will be spent on any one of them. Pay attention so you learn as much about each of them as possible.

INTERNET The most efficient form of Internet connection is a direct connection. With communications hardware physically connecting you to the Net, data is transferred between hosts and your computer at the highest possible speeds and with the highest reliability.

TextArt

FIGURE 24-1
Flyer with TextArt

TextArt enables you to turn text into art for display-type documents. To learn about this feature, we'll prepare a one-page flyer that will look much like Figure 24-1 when you are finished. You may prepare the flyer using the information provided in the exercise, or you may prepare an equivalent project using information of interest to you. It's really easy, so enjoy yourself!

EXERCISE 24.1

1. Beginning in a new document window, open the **Insert** menu, choose **Graphics**, and then choose **TextArt**. The TextArt 8 dialog box will appear, looking like Figure 24-2.

2. The largest part of the dialog box reflects what your image will look like with the choices you make. Near the bottom at the left is the place to key. Key **WINNECONNE**.

3. Look at the three black shapes in the *Shapes* section. The shape selected is whichever one was used last.

4. Click the **More** button and look at all the shapes that are available. Click to choose the shape that's third from the right in the first row. The one you are selecting is the shape of *Winneconne* in Figure 24-1.

5. Click **Close** to close the TextArt 8 dialog box. Look at your TextArt image. It has handles like a graphics box—because it IS a graphics box. Drag it so the top of the box is about an inch from the top margin guide-line. Click outside of the graphics box to deselect it.

6. Open the **Insert** menu, choose **Graphics**, and choose **TextArt** again. This time, key **Sovereign State Days**. Choose the shape that's sixth from the right in the first row, and click **Close** to close the TextArt 8 dialog box.

7. Drag the second TextArt box so the text snuggles below the first TextArt box. The boxes will actually be overlapping, but that's OK because no lines surround the TextArt boxes. The text shouldn't touch.

8. Save your emerging flyer as **days 24-1 xxx**. Keep it open as you read on.

Lesson 24 Feature Bonanza

389

FIGURE 24-2
Corel TextArt 8.0 Dialog Box

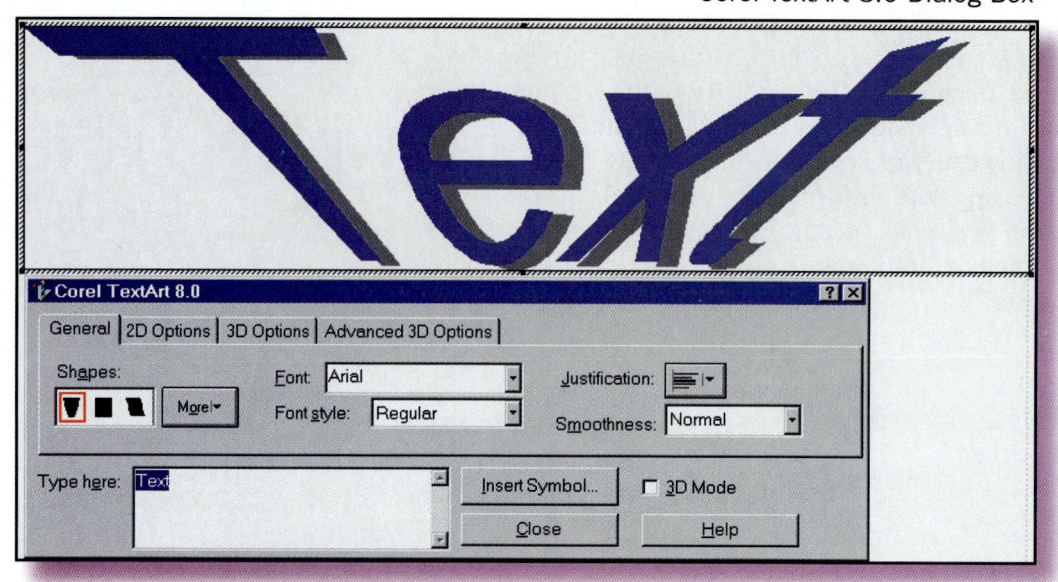

Now let's change the colors and finish the flyer. When working with color, you can adjust four parts of the TextArt letters. Each letter has a body color, an outline, a pattern, and a shadow. We'll look at all four, and you can make some choices. After you've finished, you can explore the options at your leisure.

EXERCISE 24.2

1. Return your insertion point to the top of the flyer. Press **Enter** until your insertion point is a little ways below the second TextArt box.

2. Change to **Center** justification and key the text illustrated in Figure 24-3. You can vary the font faces and font sizes as you wish. When you finish, check your work and save it with the same name.

3. Point to the WINNECONNE TextArt box and double click to select it. Look at the choices available in the TextArt 8 dialog box.

4. Notice *Justification* and *Smoothness* at the right.

FIGURE 24-3
Text for Exercise 24.2

```
Thursday through Sunday
       July 20-24

SCHEDULED EVENTS INCLUDE:
    Venetian Parade
    Pancake Breakfast
 Ecumenical Church Service
    Softball Tournament
  Pie & Ice Cream Social
         Parade
  Carnival & Street Dance
       Toll Bridge

Call 414-555-5822 for Information
  Winneconne, Wisconsin 54986
```

390

UNIT 6: GRAPHIC TOOLS

5. Click the **2D Options** tab and look at the choices. Click the **Pattern** button and change the pattern to **None** (first choice in the second row). Click the **Shadow** button and set a shadow size and location of your choice. Also, in the Shadow box, set the color of the text and the color of the shadow. (You get to choose the colors.)

6. Click the **Outline** button. Set the width of the outline (the first choice below *None* is the default) and the color of the outline. Note that TextArt shows you the letter color here to help you pick a complementing color.

7. Click **Close** to return to your document. Double click the second TextArt box and make the same changes to color and outline that you made in the first box.

8. With your insertion point at the top of the document, play your **pf** macro. Then print the flyer, save it again as **days 24-1 xxx**, and close it.

TextArt boxes are like any other graphics box with regard to sizing and location. In the exercise you just completed you allowed the boxes to fill the space between the margins, but the boxes can be any size you choose. You also may choose the font face and justification, as well as use WordPerfect in your TextArt boxes.

You probably noticed the 3D and Advanced 3D tabs in the Corel TextArt 8.0 dialog box. Those options are not installed in a normal installation, so they are not covered here. If they are available, you may explore them on your own.

Drop Cap

One of the attention-getting devices used in magazine articles is known as a *drop cap*. The first letter of this paragraph has a modified drop cap. A drop cap is simply a large first letter at the beginning of the paragraph or article. Normally, drop caps extend below the line. The one at the beginning of this paragraph extends above the line.

WordPerfect has a flexible Drop Cap feature that creates the drop cap for you and allows you to customize the look of the letter. Let's practice.

EXERCISE 24.3

1. Beginning in a new document window, go to the student **datafile** folder and open **wind**. Save the file as **wind 24-3 xxx**. Play your **pf** macro.

2. Position the insertion point just to the left of the *N* of *Nuclear* in the first paragraph. Open the **Format** menu, choose **Paragraph**, and then choose **Drop Cap**. The beginning of your document should look like Figure 24-4.

3. Normally a paragraph beginning with a drop cap isn't indented. Delete the tab that indents the paragraph.

FIGURE 24-4
Sample with Drop Cap

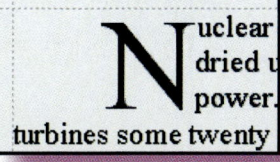

(continued on next page)

EXERCISE 24.3 CONTINUED

4. Look at the Drop Cap Property Bar. Experiment with the different styles and sizes of drop caps.

5. Choose a style and size of drop cap that looks good to you. Click away from the drop cap to close the Property Bar, but keep the document open.

Equation Editor

The Equation Editor in Corel WordPerfect 8 Suite enables you to build complex equations for use in your documents. It doesn't solve equations, but it does enable you to create graphical representations of equations. The Editor is based on a series of more than 100 templates into which you insert the data to create the equation.

When your equation is finished, it is entered into your document as a graphics box. The default setting for the box is an Inline Equation. If you wish to have the equation on a line by itself, simply change the box style to Equation. Let's learn by creating some equations. We'll begin with a simple formula that doesn't involve the use of any of the templates.

EXERCISE 24.4

1. Move your insertion point a double space below the final paragraph in the document. Save the document again as **wind 24-4 xxx**.

2. Open the **Insert** menu and choose **Equation**. The Equation Editor will open, looking much like Figure 24-5. Look at the two rows of buttons across the top of the white space. Each of those buttons contains a number of templates. Browse through a few of them and look at the templates. Whenever you see a gray box, information can be entered at that location.

FIGURE 24-5
Equation Editor

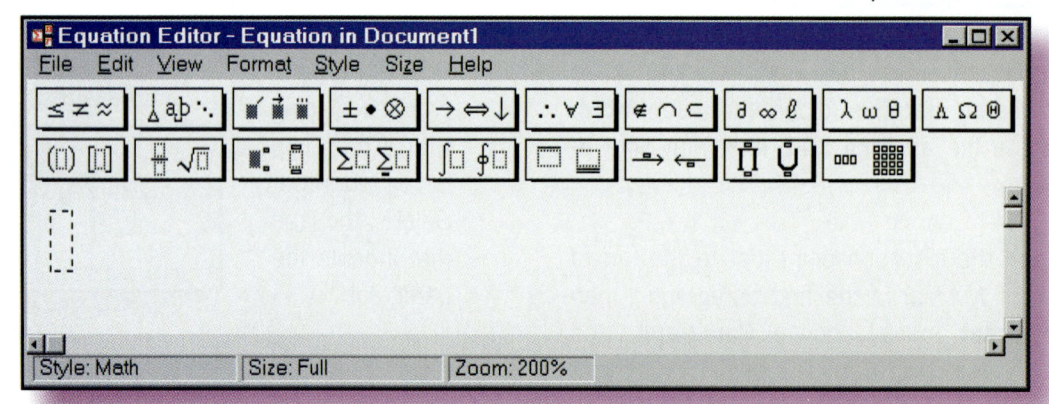

392 UNIT 6: GRAPHIC TOOLS

3. Key **a+b=c**. The equation will appear in the white area. Open the **File** menu and choose **Exit and Return to . . . .** Your equation should appear at the left margin, enclosed in sizing handles. Click away from the equation to deselect the graphics box and press **Enter** twice.

4. Open the **Insert** menu again and choose **Equation** to return to the Equation Editor to create a new equation. Key **at**. Choose the second button in the second row of template buttons and choose the first template on that button.

5. Position your insertion point in the top box and key **b**. Click to position your insertion point in the bottom box and key **d**. Click to the right of the box and key **=c**. Return to your document window.

6. Point to the equation you just completed and double click to return to the Equation Editor. Click to position the insertion point just to the right of the *b*. Choose the first template from the first button on the second row and key **2** in the box.

7. Position the insertion point to the right of the *d* and choose the same template. This time, key **3** in the box. Return to your document. Your equation should look like Figure 24-6.

FIGURE 24-6
Second Equation

$$a + \frac{b^2}{d^3} = c$$

8. Figure 24-7 illustrates a third equation. Can you create it on your own? Here is a little help:
   a. The entire first part of the equation is prepared using the fraction template you used for the *b over d* section of the second equation.

FIGURE 24-7
Third Equation

$$\frac{a + [x^2 y] + b}{d} = c^2$$

   b. The brackets come from the first set of templates on the second row. The square bracket is the second button in the set.
   c. If the equation looks messy, open the **View** menu and choose **Redraw**.

9. When you finish this equation, return to your document. With the equation selected, display the Graphics QuickMenu and choose **Style**. Change to **Equation** so the equation is centered between the margins. (Note that the graphics box extends from margin to margin.)

10. Save the document again as **wind 24-4 xxx**. Keep it open in the window.

This was only a brief introduction to equations. If you use them in your work, you probably already have ideas about how easy it will be to prepare equations using the Corel WordPerfect 8 Equation Editor.

> **NOTE:**
>
> The Equation Editor for WordPerfect versions 5.1 though 7 is also installed with WordPerfect 8. If you are familiar with the earlier version of the Equation Editor and wish to use it, open the Tools menu, choose Settings, and then choose Environment. Click the Graphics tab and select the WordPerfect 5.1 to 7 Equation Editor. A check box can be checked to make a choice of equation editors available each time you wish to create an equation.

Rotate Text

Graphics Text boxes provide you with the unique ability to rotate text. The Rotate choice is in the Content dialog box.

EXERCISE 24.5

1. Position the insertion point below the equations in **wind 24-4 xxx**, and create a Text Box. In the box, key your entire name and address the way you would key it on an envelope or label.

2. Change to a **Figure** box.

3. Choose **Content** from the QuickMenu and choose to rotate the text **90 degrees**. Then size your box so it looks much like Figure 24-8.

4. Drag the box so it's about a half inch below the paragraphs and aligned with the right margin guideline.

5. Save the document as **wind 24-5 xxx**. Print it and close it.

FIGURE 24-8
Graphics Box with Rotated Text

The ability to rotate text in graphics boxes can save you a good deal of time in cutting and pasting. It is easy to do, and you know enough about graphics boxes to create the "look" you want for your documents.

Line Numbering

If you request it, WordPerfect will count the lines on your page and put a number in the left margin opposite each line. This feature is useful in situations where a document must be discussed. The lines can be referred to by number. Give the command to number the lines at the beginning of the document. A code will be placed at that point. To turn Line Numbering off, either deselect the feature or remove the code. We'll practice with Line Numbering in your next exercise.

Redline and Strikeout

Redline and Strikeout are used to prepare suggested corrections to documents so others may have input regarding how the final document will look. Redline is used to mark text to be added. Strikeout is used to mark text to be deleted. After the decisions are made about the changes to the document, one step will remove all text marked with Strikeout and remove the Redline markings from text marked with Redline.

Redline and Strikeout are in the Font dialog box. They are also part of the Legal Toolbar. Accessing them from the Toolbar is easier than continually going to the Font dialog box. In the next exercise we'll display the Legal Toolbar as well as mark a document from an earlier lesson for discussion by company officials.

EXERCISE 24.6

1. Look at Figure 24-9. Note that some of the text has a line through it. That text is marked with Strikeout. Note that some of the text (in addition to the FIELD codes) is in red. That text is marked with Redline.

2. Look at the spaces between words. It is important that when the Redline text is added and the Strikeout text is deleted, the spacing between words is correct.

FIGURE 24-9
Text Marked with Redline and Strikeout

```
Our consultant for FIELD(area of interest) equipment,
FIELD(representative), imaging equipment will personally bring our bid
to you at FIELD(time) on FIELD(date) next week.  Please call 1-800-
555-2345 for an appointment.  At that time, please ask any questions
you might have about our company and procedures.

Again, the staff of Image Specialists would like to thank you for your
confidence in our organization.  We are looking forward to working
with you should we be selected to install FIELD(area of interest)
imaging equipment at your office.
```

(continued on next page)

EXERCISE 24.6 CONTINUED

3. Point to your Toolbar and right click. Choose **Legal** to display the Legal Toolbar below your normal Toolbar. Use Quicktips to find the Redline and Strikeout buttons.

4. Open the **Insert** menu, choose **File**, and insert **im spec.frm** from the student **datafile** folder. Save the file as **redline 24-6 xxx**.

5. With the insertion point at the top of the document, open the **Format** menu and choose **Line**. Then choose **Numbering**. At the top of the large Line Numbering dialog box (which you may study at your leisure), click the **Turn line numbering on** option. Click **OK**. Look at the numbers in the left margin of your document.

6. Working with one chunk of text at a time, click the **Redline** button on the Legal Toolbar and add the text that is shown in red in Figure 24-9.

7. Then, again working with one chunk of text at a time, select the text with a line through it. When exactly the right amount of text is selected, click the **Strikeout** button on the Legal Toolbar.

8. Double-check the spaces around your Redline and Strikeout markings. When everything looks good, save the document again as **redline 24-6 xxx** and print it. Keep it open.

The document has been discussed, and all of the suggested changes have been approved except the one in Line 9. It is the wish of the people who approved the document to leave *and procedures* in the document. Let's remove the markings from that phrase. Then we'll finish what we started with the Redline and Strikeout markings, turn Line Numbering off, and take away the designation of *form document* for the document since it no longer contains any merge codes.

EXERCISE 24.7

1. With **redline 24-6 xxx** showing in your window, click the **Options** button on the Form File Feature Bar and choose **Remove Merge Bar**. A prompt will ask if it's OK to delete the data file association. Confirm your actions. Use **Save As** to save the file as **redline 24-7 xxx**.

2. Reveal your codes and remove the Strikeout markings from Line 9. Open the **File** menu and choose **Document**. Then choose **Remove Compare Markings**. The dialog box illustrated in Figure 24-10 will appear.

3. Make sure the first choice is selected. Then click **OK**. Your document will miraculously be updated. Check spacing and general accuracy. If everything is correct, display your codes and remove the [Ln Num] code.

FIGURE 24-10
Remove Compare Markings Dialog Box

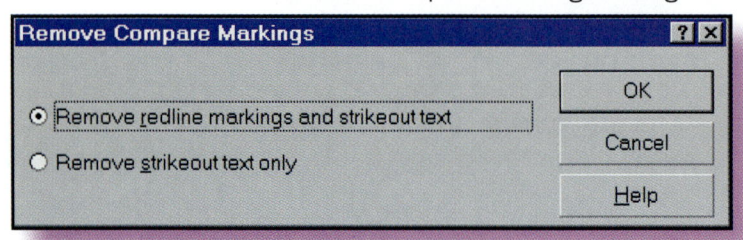

UNIT 6: GRAPHIC TOOLS

4. Print the document. Then close it, saving it again as **redline 24-7 xxx**.

5. Point to the Legal Toolbar and right click. Click **Legal** to deselect the bar.

Compare

WordPerfect will compare two documents that you think may be similar. When it compares the documents, it will add Redline markings for text that has been added and Strikeout markings for text that was deleted. The two documents you just saved present a good opportunity to learn about this feature.

EXERCISE 24.8

1. Open **redline 24-7 xxx**. Then open the **File** menu and choose **Document**. Choose **Add Compare Markings**. The dialog box in Figure 24-11 will appear.

2. Click the file folder button beside the text box and locate **redline 24-6 xxx** in your list of files. Choose the file.

3. Check to be sure WordPerfect will compare by *Word*. Then click **OK**.

4. Look at the resulting document. Word-Perfect has added Strikeout where the variables were located. Note that the FIELD codes are missing.

5. Close the document without saving it. Close all open files.

FIGURE 24-11
Zoom Dialog Box

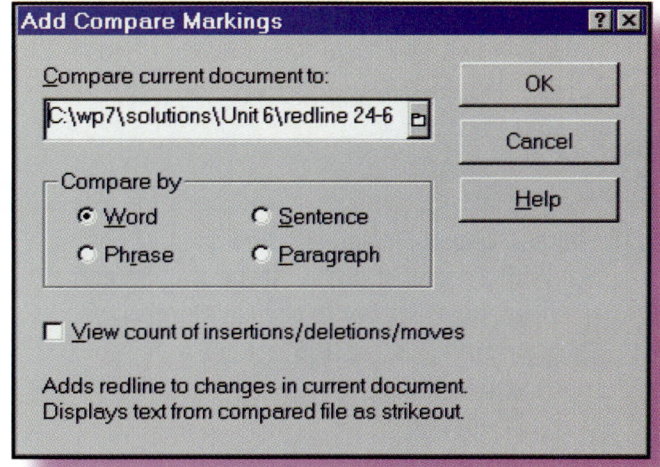

Redline, Strikeout, and Compare are very useful in certain environments. They may be of little use in your work. If you should need them, you now know how easy these features are to use.

Booklet Printing

A very useful feature for some applications is one called *Booklet Printing*. This feature works only when you have your page subdivided into two columns and one row. The purpose of the feature is to arrange the pages in proper booklet order, saving you the trouble of cutting and pasting all the pages of your booklet either before or after printing (to make it ready for mass production). Programs, church

397

bulletins, and a variety of other applications can be easily prepared using Booklet Printing. Let's see how easy it is to use Booklet Printing.

EXERCISE 24.9

1. Beginning in a new document window, open **nasa proj11a xxx**. It is in your **Units 3 and 4** folder. Use **Save As** to save the file as **nasa 24-9 xxx**.

2. With the insertion point at the top of the document, open the **Format** menu, choose **Page**, and choose **Page Setup**. Change to **Landscape** orientation.

3. Then open the **Format** menu again, and choose **Page** and **Page Setup** again. Choose **Divide Page**. Tell WordPerfect you want **2** columns and **1** row.

4. Back in your document window, open the **File** menu, choose **Document**, and then choose **Current Document Style**. Using the **Format** menu in the dialog box to choose **Margins**, set all four margins at **0.5"**. Return to your document window.

5. Give the document a header that includes the word *Page* followed by a space at the flush right position. Use the **Number** button on the Header Property Bar to insert the page number.

6. Move the insertion point out of the header area and use **Suppress** to suppress the header on the first page of the document.

7. Look through your document. If it extends to a fifth page, use **Make It Fit** to make the document fit on four pages. (This doesn't have anything to do with Booklet Printing. It just makes this particular job a little neater.)

8. Open the Print dialog box and choose the **Two-Sided Printing** tab at the top. In the middle at the right is a **Print as booklet** check box. Select that option. Then print your document.

NOTE:

As the document prints, you will be asked to "Reinsert page 1." Click **OK** and put the piece of paper in the bypass tray when it comes out of the printer. If you have trouble with this, ask your instructor to help you.

9. When you have your lovely four-page booklet document, close the document, saving it again as **nasa 24-9 xxx**.

This was a quick introduction to Booklet Printing. If you wanted, you could make a pretty fancy document with this feature. The length of the document doesn't matter. WordPerfect will arrange the pages perfectly for you, whether you have 4 pages or 40.

Summary

You learned about a group of miscellaneous tools in this lesson. Most of them were related in one way or another to graphics images. All of them will probably be useful to you at one time or another. All were easy to use. In this lesson you learned the following:

- The TextArt feature provides many options for putting text into your documents in a decorative manner.

- A Drop Cap can be added to the beginning of any paragraph to add eye appeal and capture the reader's attention.

- The Equation Editor is a flexible tool for anyone who wishes to use equations in their writing.

- Text that is in a Text box can be rotated 90 degrees, 180 degrees, or 270 degrees.

- Redline and Strikeout can be used to indicate text to be added to or deleted from a document.

- Line Numbering puts numbers in the left margin, opposite the lines of the document, to make it easier to discuss a document.

- The WordPerfect Compare feature enables you to compare two similar documents. It puts Strikeout and Redline text in the document to be compared, showing the areas of difference.

- If requested, WordPerfect will print your divided pages in booklet format, arranging the pages in perfect order.

Again, the project consists of several small jobs, enabling you to review some of the features learned in Lesson 24.

LESSON 24 REVIEW QUESTIONS

MULTIPLE CHOICE

Circle the best answer to each of the following statements.

1. To open the TextArt dialog box, first open the _____ menu.
   - **A.** View
   - **B.** Insert
   - **C.** Format
   - **D.** Tools

2. In order to add a drop cap to your work, you must first open the _____ menu.
   - **A.** View
   - **B.** Insert
   - **C.** Format
   - **D.** Tools

3. All of the following statements are true concerning the Equation Editor EXCEPT:
   A. It does enable you to create graphical representations of equations.
   B. It solves the equation you've created.
   C. It enters the equation into your document as a graphics box.
   D. It is based on a series of more than 100 templates.

4. Redline and Strikeout are used primarily for
   A. changing the appearance of your documents.
   B. adding variety to your writing style.
   C. making final changes to a manuscript in preparation for printing.
   D. making suggested changes to a document that other people have to approve.

5. Text marked with Redline will print _____ on a printer that doesn't print in color.
   A. in red tones
   B. with a shaded background
   C. with a box around it
   D. in bold

6. When WordPerfect compares two documents, it
   A. adds Redline and Strikeout markings to show additions and deletions.
   B. adds Redline markings to show additions first time through.
   C. adds Strikeout markings to show deletions first time through.
   D. converts your window to Two Pages view, placing the documents side by side.

7. In order to use the Booklet Printing feature, you must choose _____ in the Print dialog box.
   A. the Details tab
   B. the Multiple Pages tab
   C. the Two-Sided Printing tab
   D. the Print/Booklet tab

TRUE/FALSE

Circle the T if the statement is true. Circle the F if it is false.

T F   8. Booklet Printing works only when you have your page divided into two columns and one row.

T F   9. Normally, a drop cap extends above the line.

T F   10. The Equation Editor inserts an equation into a document as an Inline Equation as the default setting.

LESSON 24 PROJECT

PROJECT 24A

Look at the formula in Figure 24-12. Your boss has given you a document with this formula in it and requested that you prepare a copy. For now, just prepare the formula.

Key the formula in a new document window. When it is perfect, save it as **formula proj24a xxx**. Insert the Path and Filename code a double space below the formula and print the document. Close the file, saving it again.

FIGURE 24-12
Formula for Project 24A

$$\frac{d}{dx}[7y^4]\frac{d}{dx}x^3y + \frac{d}{dx}[x] = 0$$

PROJECT 24B

Go to your **Units 3 and 4** folder and open **cheese proj9 xxx**. Save the file as **cheese proj24b xxx**. Position the insertion point at the beginning of the first paragraph and delete the tab that indents the line. Create a drop cap. Format the drop cap as follows:

- Choose the second style in the last row of the Drop Cap palette.

- Click the Size button and tell WordPerfect to make the drop cap 2 Lines High. The beginning of your paragraph should look like Figure 24-13.

When the document is lovely, print it and close it, saving it again as you close it.

FIGURE 24-13
Beginning of **cheese** Document

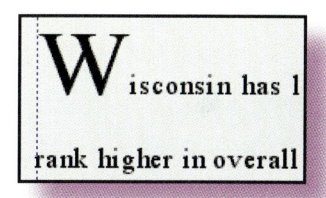

PROJECT 24C

Open **nasa proj11a xxx** again. It is in your **Units 3 and 4** folder. Select the first paragraph and copy it to the Clipboard. Close the file. Paste the paragraph from the Clipboard into a new document window.

Use Redline and Strikeout to mark the changes illustrated in Figure 24-14. Turn on Line Numbering.

FIGURE 24-14
Paragraph for Project 24C

The scientists at the National Aeronautics and Space Administration are continually working to develop technology to help them with issues raised as they progress aid in the space program. Many of their developments have been applied to make life easier or better for the general population populace. A small number of the technologies that have been developed for the space program that have been put to use in other ways developments are discussed in the following sections.

401

Save the file as **nasa proj24c1 xxx**. Insert the Path and Filename code a double space below the paragraph. Print the file.

After discussion among the staff in your office, you decide to NOT change *populace* to *population* in Line 4. Remove the word *population* and the markings around *populace*. Go to the File menu and choose Document. Remove the Compare Markings in such a way that the Redlined text is added and the text marked with Strikeout is removed. Check your work for accuracy. Then save it again, this time as **nasa proj24c2 xxx**, print it, and close it.

CRITICAL THINKING ACTIVITY

SCANS

You are excited about learning to use the Booklet Printing feature of WordPerfect because you have volunteered to prepare the program for this year's Charity Auction. You thought you had all the settings and format correct, but when you printed the first program, the information on the inside was upside down. What could have happened?

Command Summary

UNIT 6 REVIEW

FEATURE	MENU CHOICE	KEYBOARD	LESSON
Booklet Printing	File, Print, Two-Sided Printing	Ctrl+P	24
Column Border	Format, Border/Fill	—	23
Compare	File, Document	—	24
Draw Shapes	Insert, Shape	—	23
Drop Cap	Format, Paragraph	Ctrl+Shift+C	24
Equation	Insert	—	24
Fill	Format, Border/Fill	—	23
Graphics Box	Insert, Image	F11	21
Graphics Line, Custom	Insert, Shape, Custom Line	—	23
Graphics Line, Horizontal	Insert, Shape, Horizontal Line	Ctrl+F11	23
Graphics Line, Vertical	Insert, Shape, Vertical Line	Ctrl+Shift+F11	23
Group Graphic Boxes	QuickMenu, Property Bar	—	22
Horizontal Line	Insert, Shape, Horizontal Line	Ctrl+F11	23
Image Tools	(QuickMenu)	—	22
Inline Equations	Insert, Equation	—	24
Line Numbering	Format, Line	—	24
Page Border	Format, Border/Fill	—	23
Paragraph Border	Format, Border/Fill	—	23
Redline	Format, Font	F9	24
Shapes	Insert, Shape	—	23
Strikeout	Format, Font	F9	24
TextArt	Insert, Graphics, TextArt	—	24
Vertical Line	Insert, Shape, Vertical Line	Ctrl+Shift+F11	23

UNIT 6 REVIEW QUESTIONS

FILL IN THE BLANKS

Complete each of the following statements by keying your answer on a separate page. Center the title, *Unit 6 Review Questions*, followed by a triple space.

1. If you want text to fit around parts of an image, choose _____ in the Wrap Text dialog box.

2. If you want the width/height ratio of a box preserved, choose that option in the _____ dialog box.

3. The _____ tool in the Image Tools palette enables you to tilt and turn an image.

4. The _____ button at the bottom of the Image Tools palette returns the image to all of the default settings.

5. In addition to varying the length, location, color, and style of a line, you can also vary the _____ of a graphics line.

6. _____ is the feature to use to bend text in all kinds of different shapes.

WRITTEN QUESTIONS

Key your answers to the following questions. Number your answers and double-space between them. Use complete sentences and good grammar.

7. What are the two ways you can size a graphics box?

8. When you are wokring with a Text box, how do you get back into edit mode so you can make changes to the text in the box?

9. What is the name of the tool that puts numbers in the left margin opposite the lines of your documents? When might you use this feature?

10. Open the Help menu and go to the section on Images. Find the content, change listing. How do you replace the image in a graphics box with a different image? Go to the section about Booklet Printing and choose print document as a. In that Help box click the book at the bottom about Binding and Two-Sided Printing. How can WordPerfect help you if you want to bind the document?

UNIT 6: GRAPHICS TOOLS

UNIT 6 APPLICATIONS

Estimated Time: 2 hours

APPLICATION 1

Let's combine some of your previously gained skills and create an invitation to a party. Because this application has so many parts, the steps are quite specific. Learn as you go!

1. Change all margins to 0" (or as small as your printer will allow). Then divide the page into 2 columns and 2 rows. (HINT: Choose Format, Page, Page Setup, and then Divide Page.)

2. In the first logical page create a Text box.
   a. Set Center justification and key the text showing in Figure APP-1.
   b. Use a 16-pt. font.
   c. Change to a User box with both Height and Width set at Full.
   d. Choose Content from the QuickMenu and rotate the contents of the box 180 degrees.

3. Save your evolving document as **beach u6ap1 xxx**. Go to the third logical page (press Ctrl+Enter to get there). Create another Text box. In this box key the following partial phrase. Press Enter and insert the Path and Filename code. Both lines should be centered.

   When you care enough . . . .

4. Format the Text box as follows:
   a. Make it a User box and set the Width at Full.
   b. Go to the Box Position dialog box and check to make sure the box is attached to Page.
   c. Set Vertical (at the bottom of the dialog box) at Bottom Margin.
   d. Format the text with a 6- or 8-pt. font size.

5. Press Ctrl+Enter to go to the final logical page and give it a Page border. Select the border that has a crane in the rushes (see Figure APP-2).

6. Using Left justification, key **BEACH PARTY**, as shown in Figure APP-2. You may use the font face and font size of your choice.

7. When you are finished, check your work and print your document. Fold it in quarters like a greeting card. Make any necessary adjustments. Save and close the file.

FIGURE APP-1
Text for Task 1

```
Last Fling of Summer

Sunday, September 2
     2-8 p.m.

Harry's Place on the
     BEACH!

Bring a dish to pass
   and your own
   meat to grill.
```

FIGURE APP-2
Sample Invitation

(continued on next page)

405

APPLICATION 2

Now that you have the idea of the greeting card in your head, create one on your own. Include at least three of the following:

- graphics images
- graphics lines
- graphics borders
- graphics fill
- TextArt
- Drop Cap

Your greeting card may be prepared in quarters like the one in Application 1. Another acceptable alternative is to prepare it using Booklet Printing with Divide Page.

Plan a birthday party, a wedding or baby shower, a corn-husking bee, a quilting party, or make a regular greeting card for one of your friends who is ill or an invitation to a surprise party for someone who is celebrating a birthday. Try your hand at creating a beautiful card!

When you finish, save the card as **greeting u6ap2 xxx**. Put the Path and Filename code in an obscure location. Print the card and close it.

APPLICATION 3

Look at Figure APP-3. It is a suggested letterhead for the attorney for whom you created an invoice form in an earlier lesson. Create a letterhead that looks much like the one in the figure. You may choose a font that appeals to you. The graphics image in the illustration is **Scale.wpg**. It is in the student **datafile** folder.

FIGURE APP-3
Suggested Header for Letterhead in Application 3

Put all of the opening lines and the graphics image in a header so you don't have to deal with them when you use the letterhead. Work efficiently.

Save the letterhead as **tovar u6ap3 xxx**. For identification purposes, insert the Path and Filename code on the first line below the header. Print your letterhead and save it again before closing it.

APPLICATION 4

Open **lighthouses proj23a xxx**. Save the file as **lighthouses u6ap4 xxx**. Prepare the document for Booklet Printing using the following features:

1. Set letter Landscape orientation.

2. Divide the page in 2 columns and 1 row.

3. Insert a hard page break between the title page and the first page of text so the back of the cover will be blank. (Depending on where your insertion point is when you enter the Hard Page

command, you may need to move the footer code to the first page of text and discontinue the watermark.)

4. Set the page number value for the first page of text at 1 (one).

5. Set margins of 0.7" on all four sides in Current Document Style.

6. Remove Footer B (which contains the Path and Filename code) and put the Path and Filename a double space below the last line of the document.

7. Change the indent for paragraphs to a quarter inch.

8. On the first page, open the Insert menu, choose Watermark, and then choose Edit. In the Watermark edit window, display the Image Tools palette. Choose the Move tool and move the image down in the window so it's just inside of the bottom margin guidelines. Return to your document window.

When you have the document formatted to your satisfaction, print it using Booklet Printing. Save and close the document.

APPLICATION 5

It's time to clear your disk of unneeded files and store away those that might be helpful to you at some point in the future. The procedure is the same as in other lessons.

Select the following four files: **Brazil proj22**, **days 24-1**, **lighthouses proj23a**, and **nasa 24-9**. Move them to your **Units 5 and 6** folder. Work carefully.

Select these four files to be moved to your **Applications** folder: **beach u6ap1**, **greeting u6ap2**, **lighthouses u6ap4**, and **tovar u6ap3**.

Figure APP-4 lists the files to be deleted. When you finish, check to see if any random files remain in your main folder. If so, delete those that are of no use to you and file the others in a safe place. Remember to keep the macros (with *.wcm* extensions) in your main folder.

FIGURE APP-4
Files to Delete

borders 23-11	duck 22-4	party proj21b	rose 21-9
borders 23-12	fido 22-8	proj23b	shapes 23-6
borders 23-13	footer 23-5	proj23c	wind 24-3
borders 23-14	formula proj24a	redline 24-6	wind 24-4
borders 23-7	friends 21-14	redline 24-7	wind 24-5
borders 23-9	lines 23-2	rose 21-1	wind proj21a
box 21-12	lines 23-3	rose 21-11	wind proj21c
box 21-13	lines 23-4	rose 21-5	
cheese proj24b	nasa proj24c1	rose 21-7	
duck 22-2	nasa proj24c2	rose 21-8	

ON-THE-JOB SIMULATION

Now that you know how to use all of the graphics tools you learned about in this unit, you can really begin to produce attractive documents for Singing Wheels Tours. We'll create a new type of document in the first job. Then you'll have an opportunity to go back and "pretty up" some of your previous documents.

JOB 16

Go to the student **datafile** folder and open **new england**. Save the file in your **Singing Wheels** folder as **new england job16 xxx**. Add the heading section illustrated in Figure J11.

FIGURE J11
Heading Lines for Job 16

Splendor of New England
September 14-25, 199x—11 days   (Tour #1745)

Format your document in 2 Balanced newspaper columns. Use your **pf** macro to identify the file.

Since you didn't have an opportunity to key the document, read the article about the New England tour to get an idea of what the tourists will do on the tour. With your insertion point at the bottom of the document, go to WordPerfect QuickArt in the **Outdoors** folder and then the **Places** folder. If necessary, change to *.* so you can see all files. Click the Preview button on the Toolbar so you can browse through the images. Choose one of the following four images for your New England tour document: **Lighths**, **Shore**, **Bridge**, or **Sailing**.

Grab the bottom margin guideline and drag it down to approximately 0.5". Set the Width of the image at Full, and line the image up at the bottom margin guidelines. Since you want the entire document on one page, either use Make It Fit or set Wrap at No Wrap (Through). Some of the suggested images will fit better with the document than others. If you can't read the writing where the text goes across the image, display your Image Tools palette and decrease the brightness of the image a little.

When you finish, print your lovely document and close all files.

JOB 17

Open **coach job9 xxx** from your **Singing Wheels** folder. Save it as **coach job17 xxx**. Replace the title of the document with some TextArt that says the same thing. You can create two TextArt images and move them close together like you did in the **Winneconne** document, or you can put the entire heading in one or two lines of a single TextArt image.

Add a couple of horizontal or vertical lines in the heading section. Since the document is already two pages long, you don't need to worry about conserving space. Spend a little time playing with this so it is attractive when you finish. Figure J12 shows one possible solution. Can you make it even more beautiful?

FIGURE J12
Possible Solution for Job 17

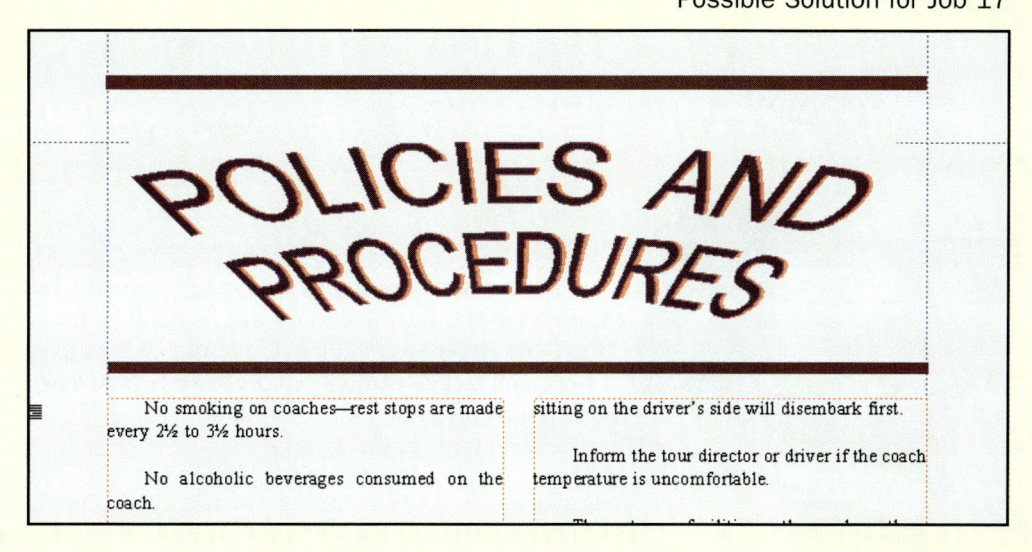

JOB 18

Choose any other document that you created for Singing Wheels. Reformat the document using at least three of the following:

Borders and/or Fill	Drop Caps
Graphics Lines	Booklet Printing
Graphics Boxes and Images	Rotate Text
TextArt	Special Font Faces

When you submit the document to your instructor, include a list of the features you used, including font faces and sizes, kinds of graphics boxes, etc. Make your work look as if it was professionally done. (It was—by you!)

THIS IS THE SIMULATION YOU'VE BEEN LOOKING FOR!

ISBN: 0-538-68538-7

Pathways: Simulation for Word Processing, by Eisch and Voiers, covers the work that must be done by the pro shop staff at the Ohio River Golf Club in Cincinnati, Ohio, to maintain the Par Fore golf league throughout the season. The league plays every Tuesday afternoon for a six-month period. There are 24 two-person teams in this league.

Several times throughout the season, members participate in local area tournaments and also host one invitational tournament at their club. Sponsors help offset the costs of these tournaments with their donations of prizes. Officers of the league are elected in the fall to serve one-year terms starting the following spring. The president, secretary, and treasurer work with the pro shop staff sharing the word processing responsibilities. Sometimes committees are formed to handle special events, but the staff has authority over all communications bearing the letterhead of the club.

Activities include:

1. Maintaining a membership list
2. Handling club and league dues
3. Maintaining records of scores
4. Updating members' local course handicaps
5. Sending regular mailings to the members
6. Creating, formatting, and editing a handbook:
   - local rules
   - bylaws
   - membership list
   - schedule of events
7. Creating labels and name badges
8. Creating and editing forms
9. Arranging an event
10. Preparing invitations to special tournaments
11. Creating prize certificates
12. Maintaining the pro shop inventory
13. Creating an ad for the local yellow pages
14. Preparing an employee's time sheet

For More Information or to Order from
South-Western
Join Us on the Internet

WWW: http://www.swpco.com

South-Western Educational Publishing

Capstone Simulation

SINGING WHEELS TOURS

Introduction

When Mr. Becker discovered that you have a couple of days off from school for vacation, he was delighted! He knows that you have been doing a great job preparing documents for Singing Wheels Tours. One of the administrative assistants in his office has been out and won't be back for a week or more. Mr. Becker has increased your hourly pay and is eager for you to use your WordPerfect skills to prepare some additional documents needed by the company, as well as to catch up on some of the correspondence that has been neglected.

Jobs

Your work will be divided into jobs. The Job Descriptions and Instructions section following this introduction contains a (usually) brief description of each of the jobs and the things you need to know to complete the job. Following the section containing the orders for the jobs is the Job Data section. Read about each job in the Job Descriptions and Instructions section, and study the data in the Job Data section before beginning each new job.

Saving the Files

Use a new disk for these jobs, but keep your old disk handy. You'll be using some of the files created in earlier lessons. (If you are saving your work on the hard drive of your computer, create a new folder to hold the files for this simulation.) Name each job with **sw-job xxx** (for Singing Wheels) and the job number, inserting your initials in place of the *xxx*. For example, Job 1 would be saved as **sw-job1 xxx**. If a job has several parts, attach an **a** or **b** or **c** to identify the parts in chronological order (**sw-job1a xxx**).

Identifying the Files

Find a way to identify each finished job with the Path and Filename code. For most jobs, you'll be able to use your **pf** macro. (If you're saving your work on a different disk than the one you used for your lessons, you'll need to copy that macro to your new disk. An alternative would be to recreate the macro and save it on the new disk.) In the instances where you can't use the macro to identify the file, find a discrete place to put the Path and Filename code.

Envelopes

If this job were for real, you would prepare an envelope to go with each letter that is prepared. Except in rare instances where you will receive special instructions to do so, you don't need to prepare envelopes in this simulation.

Prestored Files

Some parts of the longer documents have been saved in the **singing wheels simulation** folder inside the student **datafile** folder for your convenience so you don't spend so much time keying. Those files will be identified in the instructions for the jobs.

411

As you do this work for Singing Wheels, work efficiently and carefully. Because the office is short staffed, no one has been assigned to double check your work for accuracy. That's your job! Make each document attractive.

Job Descriptions and Instructions

Job 1

Mr. Becker has received the names of some new prospective customers for the company. He has considered developing a form for prospective customers to identify their travel needs and wishes. He has prepared a rough draft of the form. It is illustrated under "Job 1" in the Job Data section, which begins on page 418. You get to prepare the form. Use WordPerfect Symbols for the check boxes. Use Underline Tabs together with Tab and Flush Right to put the lines in the form. Can you create an attractive form?

Job 2

One of the other assistants has been accumulating standard text for nearly repetitive letters. Some sentences need to be added to the data file. Open **inquiries.dat** from the student **datafile** folder. Move your insertion point near the end of the document, to the left of *Sincerely*. Add the three fields shown in the Job 2 section on page 419. Space twice following all periods, and press Alt+Enter to add the ENDFIELD code at the end of each field. When you have finished and proofread your work, save it as **sw-job2 xxx.dat**.

Job 3

With the data file stored, your boss doesn't know which paragraphs are needed for certain letters. He would like a new reference copy so he can choose the paragraphs to be included in the letters.

Create a form document associated with **sw-job2 xxx.dat**. Format the reference document, centering the name of the company at the top and **Inquiry Sentences** as the subtitle. Create a reference copy for all 29 fields that is similar to the one you created in Exercise 18.12. When you finish, save the form document as **sw-job3a xxx.frm**. Merge the files and save the completed merge as **sw-job3b xxx**. Print the reference copy.

Job 4

Create a form document associated with the data file that contains the inquiry sentences. Create letters for the three customers. Print all three letters and envelopes. Include a Tour Preferences Survey with each of the letters. Save the form document as **sw-job4 xxx.frm**. Do not save the merged letters.

Job 5

Create a business card for Mr. Becker. Use Avery Business Card #5371 from the Labels dialog box. Use the **bus-sw.wpg** image from the student **datafile** folder. Use Text boxes to put the text on the card. Attach the graphics boxes to the card using Page position.

When you are satisfied with the appearance of the card, save the file as **sw-job5 xxx**. Go to Merge and tell WordPerfect to merge ten copies of the business card (go to Options to set the number of copies). Those ten copies should fill one physical page. Print the page to duplicate the business cards. You don't need to save the finished document because the form document is saved. (Don't worry about the Path and Filename for this job. Write the job number and your name on the side or back of the page after printing the business cards.)

Job 6

Mr. Becker has determined that it's time to start preparing the tour catalog for next year. He is looking for a two-column layout for each of the tours. You volunteered to use the Mall of America tour and prepare a sample for his approval.

After keying the text, format the title with 20-pt. bold. Format the subtitles with 12-pt. small caps. Format the *day* lines with 16-pt. bold and italic. Use QuickFormat to copy the format to the other days after formatting Day 1. Finally, position the insertion point beside *Day 1* and change the size of the first tab stop to a quarter inch. Then set up the document with Balanced newspaper columns. While setting up the columns, change the spacing between columns (in the lower left corner of the dialog box) to 0.25". Set Full justification for the paragraphs, and turn Hyphenation on. Save the finished file as **sw-job6 xxx**.

Job 7

One of the other office workers at Singing Wheels Tours has been putting the names and addresses of customers into an Address Book so they are readily available when you need to send letters or make phone calls. The people to whom you sent the Tour Preferences Survey should be added to the Address Book, along with a few other customers. The Address Book that has already been prepared is in the student **datafile** folder as **new tourists.abx**. To use that book, you must create a book and import the data into it. Each time you finish with the book, you should export it to the disk or folder where you are keeping your work for this simulation. Since you have not done this before, the other assistant has given you the following steps for importing, adding tourists, and exporting:

NOTE:

If you are using Corel WordPerfect Suite 8 Professional, you'll be asked to choose the Address Book expert to locate the Address Book. Follow the prompts in the dialog box. Either key the filepath and the name of the Address Book, or click the Browse button and change to the drive or folder containing your Singing Wheels data file. A few more steps are involved with the Professional version than with Corel WordPerfect Suite 8.

1. Open the Address Book. Open the Book menu and choose New. Key **tourists** as the name of the book and press Enter to go back to the main Address Book dialog box.

2. Open the Book menu again and choose Import. Identify the location of the student **datafile** folder and then the **singing wheels simulation** folder.

3. Choose **new tourists.abx** and follow the prompts to import the book. It will take a while for the names to be loaded.

4. Use the Add button in the Address Book to add the names, addresses, and phone numbers of the nine people to be added.

5. Export the book to the disk containing your work by choosing Export from the Book menu and specifying the correct location. Call the book **tourists.abx**.

6. When you leave your computer for today, open the Book menu, choose Delete, and choose the Tourists book to remove the book from your computer so it doesn't get in the way of other students.

NOTE:

Whenever you wish to use the **tourists.abx** Address Book you must create a book in the Address Book main dialog box and import the book. When you are finished with it, if you make changes, export it back to your folder. If you haven't made changes, you can simply delete it. If no other students are working with the Singing Wheels simulation, ask your instructor if you may keep the **tourists.abx** book in your Address Book.

Job 8

Apparently Mr. Becker liked the catalog layout for the Mall of America tour that you completed in Job 6. Several more of the trip descriptions have been keyed but need formatting. Since you have a couple of minutes, open **indy** from the student **datafile** folder and apply the same formats as you used in Job 6. Save the formatted file as **sw-job8 xxx**.

Job 9

In working with the Indy file, you discovered that the prices are missing from the Mall of America trip description. You need to open the Mall of America file and add the tour prices. Check the file when you finish. Does it need Block Protect?

Job 10

The agency continues to receive letters about upcoming tours—especially about receiving the newsletter and the catalog. You're intrigued about the possibilities of combining the use of the Address Book with the data file containing the standard text. You have an inquiry from Lottie Baggs, and you decide to see what you can do with one letter.

Create a form document. Click the *Associate an address book* button and choose Tourists from the drop-down menu. Center the current page. Insert the date and the spaces below the date. Open the Address Book and click the Tourists tab. Click the Format button at the bottom and be sure US Standard is chosen. Double click Lottie's name to enter her name and address into your letter. Key the greeting, using Lottie's first name followed by a double space. (Singing Wheels usually refers to its customers by first name—they get to know each other pretty well on their tours.)

Click the Insert Fields button on the Merge Bar and insert standard text paragraphs as follows: Paragraph 1: #16 and #20, Paragraph 2: #19 and #21, Paragraph 3: #29. Click the Merge button on the Merge Bar and your letter should be completed. Remove the Enclosure notation (because nothing is enclosed), print the letter, and close all files, saving the letter as **sw-job10 xxx**. (You don't need to save the form document.)

Job 11

Mr. Becker just told you that he's desperate for a 4" x 4" print ad for the local newspaper. He gave you the information to be included in rough-draft format. Can you prepare an attractive ad?

Job 12

You've just learned that you can create groups of people in the Address Book. Now the start you made to some standard letters in Job 10 looks even better. You want to merge the Address Book with the form letter to get the names and addresses in place. Then you want to add FIELD codes for the standard text and merge the letter forms with the data file containing the standard text sentences. Four people have called about the catalogs. Their letters will be similar.

1. Begin by creating a form document associated with the Address Book.

2. Use Center Page(s) and insert the date.

3. Insert the FIELD codes from the fields in the Address Book for the name, address (street address), city, state, and ZIP code. Insert the greeting, using the customer's first name, and double-space. Save the form document as **sw-job12a xxx.frm**.

4. Click the Merge button to begin the merge. Be sure the Tourists Address Book is chosen. Click the Select Records button to open the Address Book.

5. Look at your Address Book window. Is there a white panel at the right with a Select Address button at the top? Or do you have an Address List button in the lower right corner of the dialog box? If the white panel doesn't show, click the Address List button to display the white panel. Then double click to put the following four names into that panel: *Sheila Goodson, Judy Hallada, Hazel Holme,* and *Deanne Stockwell.*

6. Click OK to complete the merge.

Now that the letters are established, you can make them into a form document and insert the FIELD codes for the standard text.

1. Make the document in the active window a form document, to be associated with the data file (**sw-job2 xxx.dat**).

2. Insert the FIELD codes for the fields listed in the Job Data section. Then complete the merge.

3. Delete the Enclosure notations. Then print your letters, and save the letters as **sw-job12b xxx**. Close all files.

Job 13

Occasionally Singing Wheels Tours goes beyond where a bus can go. One of those tours is a yearly trip to Hawaii, where guests have an opportunity to visit four of the islands and enjoy many of the activities that have made Hawaii a paradise in the Pacific. Since you've always wanted to go to Hawaii, you've offered to prepare the tour brochure for next year's trip.

While you haven't done a brochure before, you don't think it will be difficult, because you have all of the skills that will be used for that project. Here are a few steps to help you along.

1. Go to Page and choose Paper Size. Then choose Letter Landscape.

2. Return to Page and choose Divide Page. Set 3 columns with 1 row.

3. Set all four margins at 0.4". Set an additional tab stop midway between the left margin and the first tab that affects your document. (You'll have a quarter-inch indent.)

4. Insert **Hawaii.wpd** from the student **datafile** folder. You should see text in the first three panels. The remainder of the brochure is on the next page.

5. Save the file with your other documents as **sw-job13 xxx**. Save your work often.

6. Zoom to 65% or 75% to work. You can see all three panels at once if you do this.

7. The student **datafile** folder contains three graphics images you can use in this brochure: **Hula.wpg**, **Island.wpg**, and **Bird-of-paradise.wpg**.

8. Look at the thumbnail illustrations of a possible solution for the brochure in the Job 13 data section. The text for Panel 6 is also included there.

9. Include the company address and phone number in the return address corner of Panel 5. Do this by creating a Text box, keying the information, changing to a User box, and choosing Content to rotate the text 90 degrees. Size the box and move it to the correct corner.

10. Mailing address labels will be used to distribute this brochure to most customers. In the address location create another Text box containing **ALOHA** in 30-pt. letters. Put the Path and Filename code in very small letters on the second line. Rotate the text, size and position the box, and change it to a User box.

When you finish, check your work over carefully and save it again as **sw-job 13 xxx**. Print it and close it.

Job 14

Some of the tour guides incur small expenses during a tour that need to be reimbursed. A couple of the tour guides have given you a list of their expenses and asked you to prepare a memo to Mr. Becker briefly describing the expenses and listing the tours on which the expenses were incurred.

You recall that you have prepared several memos from scratch in your time with the company, and you think that a memo form with KEYBOARD codes might save you some time. You decide to try developing a memo merge form document with KEYBOARD codes.

At the top of the form include the company name and telephone number. You can include the bus image, if you'd like, in letterhead format. Use KEYBOARD codes in the *To:*, *From:*, and *Subject:* lines. Include the DATE merge code for the date. (A sample "unadorned" memo is illustrated in the Job 14 data section.) When you finish, name the form **sw-memo.frm**. Use your **pf** macro to identify the document.

With the form document in the window, click the Merge button on the Merge Bar. Tell WordPerfect to merge (Form document is Current Document and Data source is None). Send the memo to Mr. Becker using the information in the data section. Include the tour number in the *Subject:* line. List the items for reimbursement in a table so you can total the figures with QuickSum.

When you finish the first memo, print it and close it, saving it as **sw-job14a xxx**. When you close it, the memo form will be showing again. Follow the same procedure for the second memo, printing it and saving it as **sw-job14b xxx**.

Job 15

Many of the Singing Wheels customers continue to ask questions about policies and procedures, even though the company policies are clearly stated in each newsletter and catalog. Mr. Becker has asked your advice, and you recommend the preparation of a small booklet containing the general policies and procedures of the company. (You really like booklet printing!) Mr. Becker has asked for a sample.

You have assembled most of the company policies into one large document (**policies** in the **singing wheels simulation** portion of the student **datafile** folder). You need to convert it to a booklet. Use Letter Landscape orientation, and divide your page into two columns and one row. Set all four margins at 0.5".

Use the name of the company as the title on the booklet. Give it a **Policies and Procedures** subtitle. Also on the cover, include a picture of the Singing Wheels bus (from the student **datafile** folder) and the name, address, and phone number of the company. Move the company mission statement from the beginning of the document to the bottom of the cover panel. Make the cover look inviting so the customers will open it to read what's inside. Do not put any text on the inside of the cover, since you're envisioning this booklet with some kind of card stock for the cover.

Number the pages at the bottom center, beginning with the first page of text as page 1. Look through the text and arrange the topics in such a way that the booklet has continuity. Think about what should be first and what should be last. Put one or more topics on a page, and rearrange the material as necessary so that none of the topics carry from one page to the next. It's okay to have some white space on a page, but not too much. Perhaps you can use some decorative graphics to add interest to some of the pages. Another way to add interest is to change the title of each topic to all capital letters.

The Job 15 data section includes information for three more sections to be added to the text of the booklet. Add the extra sections. Then prepare a sample for Mr. Becker, with the understanding that he might want more information included or the current information rearranged in a more desirable order. (Remember to zoom to Full Page to see whole pages at a time as you work.)

Save the booklet as **sw-job 15 xxx**. Find an obscure location on the brochure for the Path and Filename code before printing. Remember that when you use Booklet Printing, you have to reinsert some of the pages.

Job 16

In preparing the materials for the booklet in Job 15, you realized that you didn't include the tour number on the brochure for the Hawaii tour that you prepared in Job 13. Open that document and add the tour number a double space below the days of the tour on the cover of the brochure. It is (**Tour #3712**). Print only the page of the brochure that contains the cover panel.

Job Data

Job 1

SINGING WHEELS TOURS
Tour Preferences Survey

Name _____ Phone _____
Street _____ City _____ State/ZIP _____

Age (optional). Please check one:
☐ 20-29 ☐ 30-39 ☐ 40-49 ☐ 50-59 ☐ 60-69 ☐ 70+

Travel Preferences: Prefer to ☐ travel alone ☐ travel with spouse/friend

Mostly interested in (check all that apply):
☐ 1- to 3-day tours ☐ 4- to 7-day tours ☐ 8- to 14-day tours

Type of tours desired (check all that apply):
☐ Shopping ☐ Sightseeing ☐ Programs/Plays ☐ Musical Events

If Sightseeing, areas to visit (check all that apply):
☐ Florida ☐ Southwest ☐ Northeast ☐ East ☐ Midwest

Accommodations:
☐ Prefer double bed ☐ Prefer king-size bed
☐ Smoking ☐ Nonsmoking

Specific Requests for Tours:
_____
_____
_____

Please return form to:

Singing Wheels Tours
77 Travel Way
Neenah, WI 54956

Job 2

Thank you for stopping at our booth at the recent Fox Cities Chamber of Commerce trade show. ENDFIELD

Please complete the enclosed information form to help us plan tours that will be exactly what you want. ENDFIELD

We are enclosing an information form so we can learn more about your preferences and vacation needs. ENDFIELD

Job 4

Betty Buslaff
8873 Busmann Blvd.
Busseyville, WI 53534

FIELD(1)FIELD(4)

FIELD(7)FIELD(11)

FIELD(15)FIELD(23)

FIELD(29)

Wilbur Williams
22 Wenning Way
Wrightstown, WI 54180

FIELD(16)FIELD(11)

FIELD(8)FIELD(9)

FIELD(19)

FIELD(29)

Ellen Eisenau
14 Scenic Drive
Seymour, WI 54165

FIELD(2)FIELD(6)

FIELD(14)FIELD(11)

FIELD(18)FIELD(24)

FIELD(29)

Job 5

Possible Business Card Layout

Charlie Becker
Singing Wheels Tours

"When you feel the urge to travel."

Singing Wheels Tours
77 Travel Way
Neenah, WI 54956
414-555-7777

Job 6

MALL OF AMERICA SHOPPING

September 1-4, 199x (Tour #2113)
4 Days

Day 1, Tuesday

We spend the day traveling to Minneapolis. Lunch is in Plover at Norma's Nook. Accommodations in the Minneapolis area are at the Happy Haven Hotel in Bloomington. Get in some late afternoon and evening shopping after checking into the motel and resting.

Day 2, Wednesday

You have a full day of shopping today at the mall. Lunch is on your own. In the evening, we have reserved seats for dinner and the theater at the Bloomington Playhouse. The play is the off-Broadway musical Power Shopping Patsy, where guests get a glimpse of what really goes on behind the scenes in our country's largest shopping malls.

Day 3, Thursday

Today is another full day of shopping at the mall. In the evening, you may continue to shop or take an optional tour of the Minneapolis night spots (at a cost of $35 per person). Dinner at the Riverfront is included in the cost of the optional tour.

Day 4, Friday

Today we're covering the miles for the trip home.

Job 7

Here are the phone numbers for the new prospective customers in Job 4. Add all three prospective tourists to the Address Book.

Betty 608-555-7622, Wilbur 414-555-8231, and Ellen 414-555-2311

Here are some former customers to be added to the Address Book:

Neverat Holme
45 Creekside Drive
Manawa, WI 54949
414-555-7853

Hazel Holme
45 Creekside Drive
Manawa, WI 54949
414-555-7853

Lottie Baggs
45 Main Street
Shawano, WI 54166
414-555-7866

Fred Feldman
8722 Farmhill Road
Little Chute, WI 54140
414-555-7869

Kim Kittleson
234 Kiel Street
Kimberly, WI 54136
414-555-7896

Darcy Dobberstein
5693 Township Drive
Darboy, WI 54911
414-555-7879

Job 9

Tour Cost per Person

2 persons/1 bed	$379
2 persons/2 beds	$380
3 persons/2 beds	$340
4 persons/2 beds	$330
1 person/1 bed	$475

CAPSTONE SIMULATION

Job 11

> Charter a Luxury Motor Coach
> For Your Special Event!
>
> ◊ Company Events   ◊ Weddings
> ◊ Club Events   ◊ Sporting Events
> ◊ Conventions   ◊ Church Groups
>
> Luxury Motor Coaches Include:
> - Air Conditioning
> - Reclining Seats
> - Restroom
> - AM/FM Stereo Radio
> - Optional Lounges and Video Cassette Players
>
> Singing Wheels Tours
> 77 Travel Way
> Neenah, WI 54956
> 414-555-7777

Job 12

Deanne Stockwell	Hazel Holme	Judy Hallada	Sheila Goodson
1, 20	26, 4	2, 5	16, 20
17, 19	7, 6	6, 10	12, 13
21	19	11, 19	21
29	29	29	29

Job 13

Panels 1 through 3

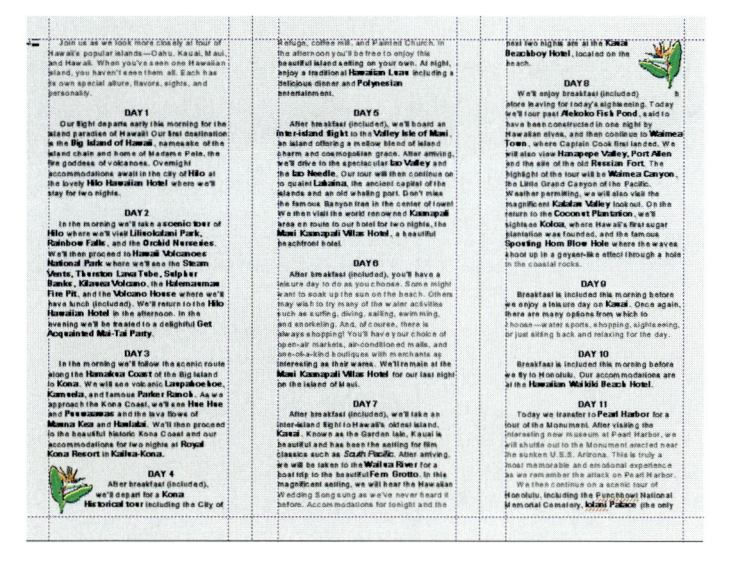

Panels 4 through 6

```
FOUR-ISLAND
HAWAIIAN HOLIDAY

14 Days
January 13-26, 199x

Visit Maui, Kauai, Oahu,
and the Big Island of Hawaii
```

Job 14

Janie Schmohe hosted Tour #5573. Her expenses included the following: soda, $7.28; first aid supplies, $9.65; trash bags, $4.57; and toll fees, $4.40.

Karen Schwark hosted Tour #7833. Her out-of-pocket expenses included toll fees, $6.80, and soda, $9.57.

You get to write the memo.

```
                    MEMORANDUM

     TO:        KEYBOARD

     FROM:      KEYBOARD

     DATE:      DATE

     SUBJECT:   KEYBOARD

     KEYBOARD
```

Job 15

Here are some additional sections for the Singing Wheels policy booklet.

Seat Rotation
Seating is rotated each half day. This system enables everyone to enjoy all locations on the coach.

Luggage
Each person is allowed one large suitcase plus a carry-on bag. It is preferred that the carry-on bag be made of a soft material such as canvas or soft leather. Please limit the size of the carry-on to 15" x 10" x 6". A camcorder is considered a piece of carry-on luggage.

Canadian Border Crossing
A number of our tours involve travel in Canada. Passengers on these tours should have proof of U.S. citizenship in the form of a birth certificate, voter's registration card, or passport. Please carry your proof of citizenship on your person or in your carry-on luggage. Those tours needing proof of citizenship are identified with a Canadian flag pictured near the tour cost. We suggest checking your medical insurance coverage when traveling out of the country.

APPENDIX A

The Hardware

If you have never had any formal training on the computer, it is important that you are comfortable with the parts of the equipment at which you will be working for the duration of this course. Even if you consider yourself "computer literate," it might be a good idea for you to look through the information in this appendix so that you can see how each part of the computer will be used in your WordPerfect training.

Turn to the Start-Up Checklist in the front of this text. Here you will see that a certain level of computer is required for your work with WordPerfect. Your instructor has made sure WordPerfect will run on your computer. You need to be familiar with the computer parts.

Now look at the computer in front of you. It consists of six major hardware components: the video display terminal (VDT or screen), the central processing unit (CPU), the keyboard, the disk drives, the mouse, and the printer. In most classrooms the printer is located in a different part of the room, but it is connected to your computer with a cable. Can you identify the parts of the hardware illustrations in Figures A-1, A-2, and A-3 as they are discussed? Find them on your own computer.

1. **The VDT**. Starting at the top, the *video display terminal* (VDT) is used to show you what you are doing as you use the computer. Look at your VDT. Can you find a power switch and controls for brightness and contrast? You should be familiar with the features of your VDT so that you can adjust the controls for maximum eye comfort.

   FIGURE A-1
   Computer

2. **The CPU**. The brains, or logic center, of the computer is housed in the piece of equipment called the *central processing unit* (CPU). Sometimes the CPU sits on your desk under the VDT. In other cases the CPU might be on the floor beside the desk. Inside of the CPU is a hard drive where WordPerfect has been installed if you are working on a stand-alone machine. In many cases, however, WordPerfect is installed on the file server of a network. That means your PC will be running a program stored on the CPU of a computer in a different part of the room or even in a different room.

   In addition to the hard drive of the computer, the CPU has a temporary memory area called RAM (random access memory) where your work is remembered until you save it on your disk. Find the power switch on your CPU. When the power switch is turned off, any text in RAM is lost.

3. **The Keyboard**. Look at the keyboard. In addition to the alphabetic keys, you should find a set of function keys. The function keys are labeled with *F* and a number, and they may be in a row across the top of the keyboard (there will be 12 of them) or they may be in a double row at the left.

On the right is a series of different keys. You should have a number keypad and some keys with arrows for moving the insertion point. There should also be keys with labels such as **Home**, **End**, **Page Down**, **Page Up**, and **Delete**. (The *insertion point* is the little flashing line in the window showing where you are working at any time.)

4. **The Disk Drives**. In addition to the hard drive of your computer, there are a number of possible configurations for the floppy disk drives. You might have one or two drives that hold $3^{1}/_{2}$-inch disks, or you might have a drive for a CD-ROM. If you are working in a networked environment, you might not have any drives for disks.

   Your instructor will help you determine what kind of drives your computer has and what type of disk you should use for your training. If you have never before used a computer, ask your instructor to give you special instructions regarding the handling of disks and how to insert them into the computer.

5. **The Mouse**. While it is possible to use WordPerfect without a mouse, the use of a mouse is almost imperative. Many features are available only with a mouse. In addition to accessing features with the mouse, the mouse is an efficient means of selecting text, positioning the insertion point, displaying QuickMenus, and moving through your documents. If you have never before used a mouse, specific instructions for the use of a mouse are included in Appendix D.

   FIGURE A-2
   Mouse

6. **The Printer**. There are literally hundreds of printers that might be connected to your classroom computer. Most printers today feed cut sheets of paper from a bin or tray. These printers are either *laser printers* or *ink jet printers*, and the printed pages look like they might have come from a copy machine.

   FIGURE A-3
   Printer

   Some classrooms have printers where the paper is connected in one long sheet. The paper is pushed or pulled through the printer by way of sprocket wheels that fit into the holes of tear strips on the sides of the paper. These are called *dot matrix printers*, and they are noisy.

Network

You may be using a stand-alone version of the software, or your computer might be connected to a number of other computers by way of a network. Whether or not you are using a network won't affect your training, but it may affect how you print and how you save your work. Be sure your instructor gives you the "rules" for your particular classroom so your work is properly saved in a location where you can find it when you need it.

APPENDIX B

The Corel® WordPerfect® Environment

It is important that you are comfortable with the environment in which you are working when you learn a computer program. In the case of Corel WordPerfect 8 for Windows, that includes the WordPerfect working window, as well as the Windows interface.

You must know how to start and exit from the program. You also need to know the parts of the WordPerfect window. In this appendix you will learn about all of those things and more. You will even have some practice exercises to help you learn. Follow along carefully.

Starting and Exiting Corel® WordPerfect®

Look at the Windows 95 desktop. Do you see an icon with a picture that looks somewhat like Figure B-1? The word(s) identifying the icon might be different, but the pen in front of the globe will be the same. The arrow indicates that the icon is a shortcut to the program.

FIGURE B-1
WordPerfect Icon

If you don't see the icon, you may start WordPerfect from the Start button. WordPerfect might be installed in the Corel WordPerfect Suite listed at the top of the Start pop-up menu, or you may select it from the list of programs that appears when you choose Program from the Start pop-up menu. You can also select it by clicking the pen icon if the Desktop Application Director (DAD) is displayed on your desktop.

EXERCISE B.1

SCANS

1. Start WordPerfect using one of the following four methods:
   a. If the icon pictured in Figure B-1 appears on your desktop, point to it and double click to start WordPerfect.
   b. If the icon is not on the desktop, click the **Start** button and look at the short list at the top of the pop-up menu. Is *Corel WordPerfect Suite 8* there? If so, choose it and then choose **Corel WordPerfect 8** to start WordPerfect.
   c. If neither of the first two conditions exist, click the **Start** button and choose **Programs**. Find *WordPerfect 8* in the list of programs. Choose it to start WordPerfect.
   d. Click the pen icon on the DAD bar.

2. Look at the WordPerfect window. Find the parts that are identified in Figure B-2, including the insertion point.

(continued on next page)

427

EXERCISE B.1 CONTINUED

3. Move your mouse around in the window. What does the mouse pointer look like? Key your first name. Note that it begins at the vertical and horizontal guidelines. Move the mouse pointer over the name. What does the pointer look like when it is over text?

4. Press **Enter** several times and watch the *Ln* indicator on the Application Bar at the bottom of the window. The Title Bar will change from *Corel WordPerfect–Document1 (unmodified)* to *Corel WordPerfect–Document 1*. Press the **space bar** several times and watch the *Pos* indicator change.

5. Press **Backspace** until both the *Pos* and *Ln* indicators have returned to 1".

6. Finally, open the **File** menu and choose **Exit**. WordPerfect will ask if you would like to save the document. Click **No**. You should be returned to the Windows desktop.

FIGURE B-2
The Corel WordPerfect 8 Document Window

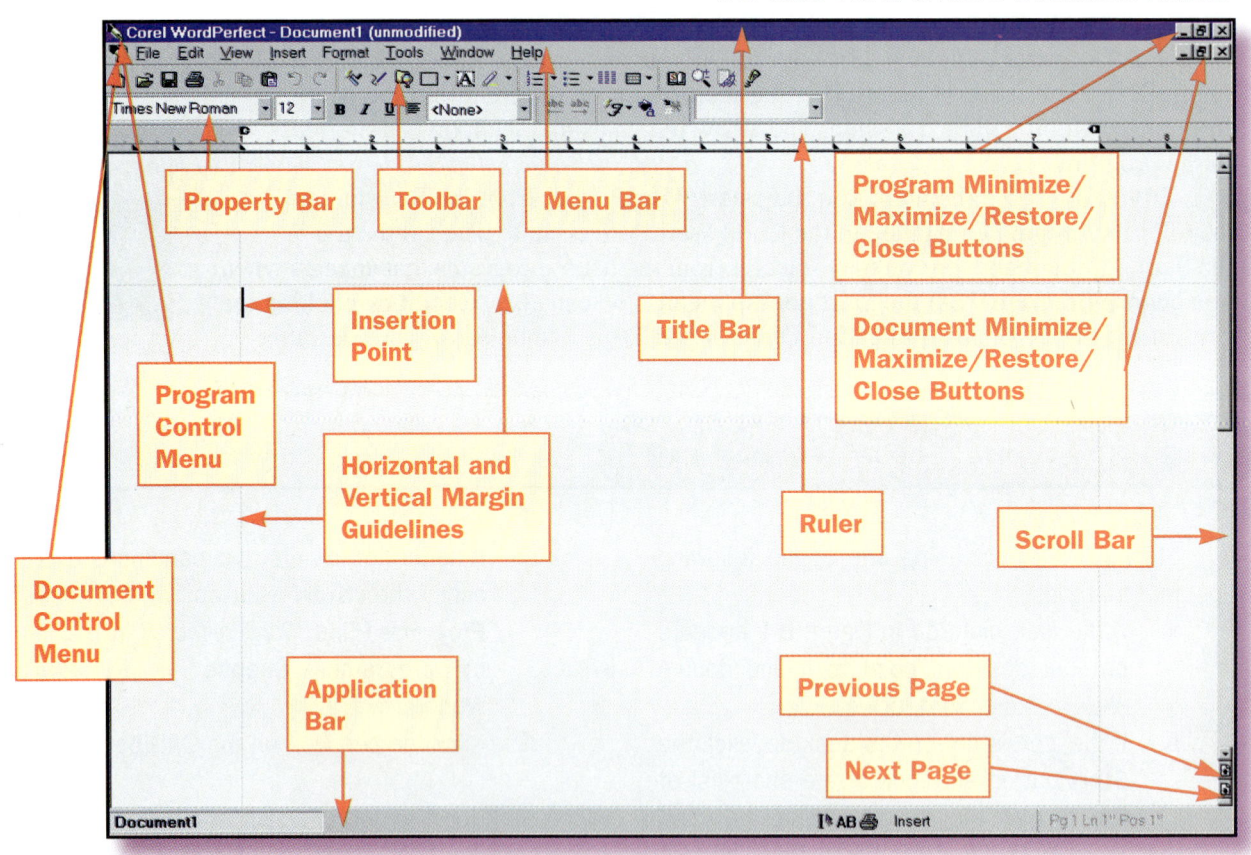

If you have never before worked in a Windows environment, the window may look strange to you and contain a number of parts that look confusing. After using the window for a short time, you'll become quite comfortable with its parts. Work to achieve that comfort zone, so you can begin using WordPerfect efficiently.

Giving Commands

There are two ways for you to give commands to your computer when you're working in Windows. As you've already learned, one of those ways is by making selections with the mouse.

Another way to communicate with the computer is by using the keyboard. You can move the insertion point with the arrow keys. You will enter text and numerals with the keyboard. If you prefer to keep your fingers on the keyboard, you can even use the keyboard to work through the menu system to choose many of your commands.

You can also use the function keys on the keyboard. This set of 12 keys provides access to many of the features available in the WordPerfect menus.

We'll begin to learn about all of these tools for communicating with your computer by starting WordPerfect again and creating a short text document. Then we'll look at some of the parts of the WordPerfect window.

Creating Text

To create text, simply key the information you wish to include in your document. If you make a mistake when you are keying, use the Backspace key to correct the error. Then continue keying as before. Let's practice.

EXERCISE B.2

SCANS

1. Using the steps in Exercise B.1, start WordPerfect. Key your name and press **Enter** twice.

2. Key your name again and press **Enter** two more times. The two occurrences of your name should be separated by a blank line, and the insertion point should be a double space below the second occurrence of your name.

3. Repeat Step 3 so your name appears in the window three times with the insertion point a double space below the third name.

4. Leave the text in the window as you read on.

The Application Bar

You may remember from Figure B-2 that the bar at the bottom of the working WordPerfect window is known as the *Application Bar*. This bar provides important information as you work. Look at the Application Bar in your window. A sample Application Bar is illustrated in Figure B-3. This Application Bar reports the following information:

FIGURE B-3
Sample Application Bar

APPENDIX B

- At the left side of the Application Bar, WordPerfect reports the names of open documents. In this case *Document1* is listed as the document you have open. It has not been saved, so it doesn't have a name.

- The button with the **I** and the arrow may look like it is depressed.

  - When the button is depressed, your mouse pointer looks like an arrow if positioned away from text. The arrow is followed by a Shadow Pointer that helps you locate your position. If you click in an empty portion of the window, the insertion point will be positioned wherever you click. You'll learn more about this later.

  - When the button is NOT depressed, the mouse pointer always looks like a large **I**. With the button in the "up" position, move the mouse pointer over your name. Leave the button in the "up" position, so your insertion point is always an **I**. Keep it that way as you work.

- The AB button is depressed when Caps Lock is turned on.

- The Printer button can be used to print a document.

- The Insert button tells you WordPerfect is working in Insert mode as opposed to Typeover mode, where new characters take the place of existing characters. You should work in Insert mode. (You'll learn to use Typeover in Lesson 2.)

- At the right, the Application Bar reports that the insertion point is on page 1 (*Pg 1*), it is 1" from the top of the page (*Ln 1"*), and it is 1" from the left side of the paper (*Pos 1"*).

The Application Bar can be customized so it might display different information. Compare your Application Bar with the one in Figure B-3. Is it the same? If not, what is different? Does the current date appear on your Application Bar?

You will find the information on the Application Bar to be very useful in your work—especially the part that reports the location of the insertion point in your document. Look at the Application Bar in your window. If your insertion point is below the final keying of your name, it should be somewhere around Ln 2.2". Use the arrow keys on the keyboard to move your insertion point. Does the Application Bar report the new location of your insertion point?

Corel® WordPerfect® Menus

The Menu Bar is the first gray bar at the top of your window. While all Windows programs have a Menu Bar, the menus listed on the Menu Bar vary from program to program. In Corel WordPerfect 8, eight menus are listed. Within these menus, you should be able to find all of the tools needed to create, edit, and format documents, plus a large number of specialized tools to make your work easier.

Each menu has characteristics to help you work. Let's look at a menu and discuss what you see there.

EXERCISE B.3

1. Open the **Edit** menu and compare it to the menu illustrated in Figure B-4.

2. Look at the items that appear in gray. Those items are not available at this time. If you had text selected, more of the choices would be available.

3. Look at the items followed by three dots. If you choose one of these items, a dialog box will be opened. (You'll learn about dialog boxes soon.)

4. Look at the items followed by an arrow pointing to the right (▶). When you choose one of these items, another menu appears, growing from the side of the original menu.

5. Look at the information at the right of some of the menu items in Figure B-4. The menu shows that you can choose Cut, for example, by pressing Ctrl+X, or Find and Replace with Ctrl+F. Your menu may not display this information. You'll learn how to display these shortcuts at the end of this appendix.

6. Use your mouse to click **Convert Case**. Look at the little menu that appears.

FIGURE B-4
Edit Menu

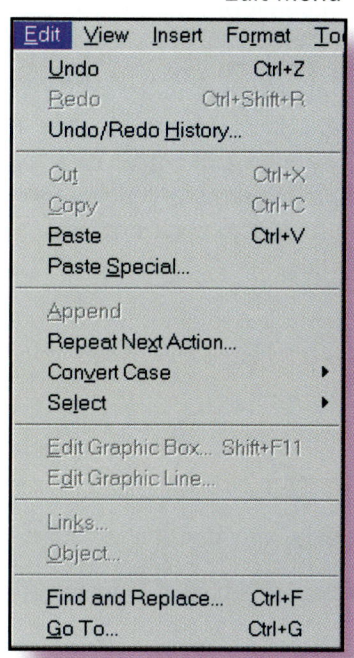

7. Use your mouse to click **Repeat Next Action**. Look at the little dialog box. Click **Cancel** to close the dialog box.

If you open a menu in error or decide you don't wish to make a selection from that menu, you can close it by clicking somewhere outside of the menu in the window. You can also close a menu by pressing the Alt key or by pressing Esc twice. If you open the wrong menu, simply open a different one. The original menu will disappear when the new one is opened.

Now that you know all about menus, let's take a look at dialog boxes and how they make your work easier.

Corel® WordPerfect® Dialog Boxes

Like menus, dialog boxes are used to group features to make them easy to find and choose. While some dialog boxes look complex because they contain many parts, most dialog boxes present choices in a logical manner. Dialog boxes usually contain information about *default* settings (preset conditions in the program). Let's explore a simple dialog box. Then we'll look at one that contains more parts.

APPENDIX B

Figure B-5 illustrates the dialog box used for setting margins. Notice that the default margins are 1" on all sides of the page. While this portion of the dialog box is used only for margins, the dialog box provides a number of options. You can:

FIGURE B-5
Margins Portion of the Page Setup Dialog Box

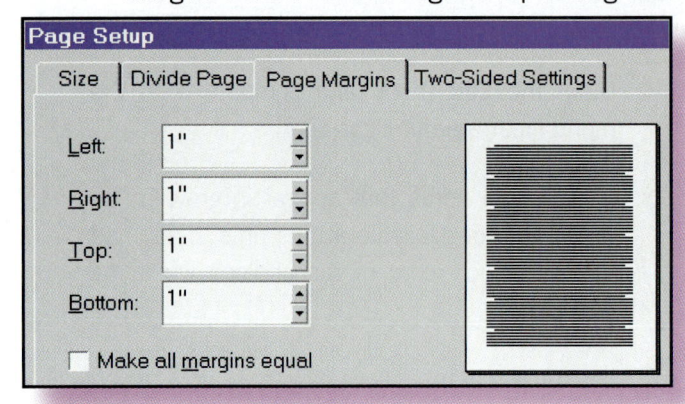

- Key the new setting over the highlighted setting in the white text box area. (It usually works well to use the Tab key to move from one text box to the next, although you can use the mouse to double click into each box, if you prefer.)

- Use the mouse to click the up or down buttons to change any of the four margins.

- Look at the illustration at the right to see how your document would look with the selected margin settings.

- Click the Cancel button to return to your document without making any changes.

- Click the Help button to learn more about setting WordPerfect margins.

- Click OK to accept any setting changes you've made and return to your document.

- Choose a tab at the top to set a different aspect of a page setup.

Now it's time for you to try it.

EXERCISE B.4

SCANS

1. Open the **Format** menu and choose **Margins**.

2. Using the up or down buttons, change all four margins to **2"**.

3. Then change all four margins to **1.5"** by keying **1.5** into each text box.

4. Set the top and bottom margins at **1"** and the side margins at **1.25"**.

5. When you are comfortable with this dialog box, click **Cancel** to cancel any margin changes you made and return to your document.

Some dialog boxes contain additional parts like scroll bars, check boxes, and radio buttons. You will learn about those parts as you encounter them in your exercises.

The Toolbar

Many of the choices you can make from menus have been made more readily available to you on the Toolbar, located just below the Menu Bar. The Toolbar contains a series of buttons, each with an icon to tell you what the button does. The Corel WordPerfect 8 default Toolbar looks like Figure B-6.

When you use the mouse pointer to point at one of the buttons on the Toolbar, a small Quick Tip box will appear, identifying the function of the button. For some of the buttons keystroke equivalents will also be displayed. A variety of Toolbars comes with the program, and they automatically change to fit the feature you are currently using. You can also create your own Toolbars for your particular project needs. You will learn to do this much later in your training. Let's take a quick look at the default Toolbar.

FIGURE B-6
WordPerfect 8 Default Toolbar

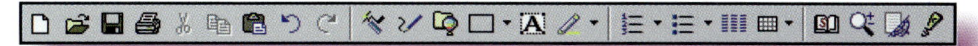

EXERCISE B.5

1. Point to the first button on the Toolbar. Do NOT click the mouse button. The Quick Tip should appear, telling you that button can be used to create a new blank document, and that you can do the same thing with Ctrl+N.

2. Point to the second button. It looks like a file folder. The Quick Tip should tell you it can be used to open a document.

3. The third button looks like a disk. What does the Quick Tip tell you? Of course, it is used for saving a document.

4. The fourth button is supposed to look like a printer. That's probably why the Quick Tip says *Print*.

5. Point to anywhere on the Toolbar and click the RIGHT mouse button. (This is called *right clicking*.)

6. Look through the list of Toolbars to get an idea of what features have their own Toolbars. Click outside of the list to close it.

Are you getting the idea of what the Toolbar can do for you? All of those choices are available in the various menus, but the Toolbar buttons enable you to choose the features more quickly. You will learn about more Toolbar buttons as you continue with your training.

The Property Bar

The Property Bar is just below the Toolbar. It includes a number of miscellaneous choices, some of which will be useful now and others that will be more useful later in your training. The default Property Bar looks like Figure B-7. Let's take a quick look at the buttons on the Property Bar.

FIGURE B-7
WordPerfect 8 Default Property Bar

EXERCISE B.6

1. Use the mouse to point to each of the buttons on the Property Bar and look at the Quick Tip descriptions to see what the button is used for.

2. Use the arrow keys to move your insertion point so it is a double space below the third keying of your name.

3. Click the **Bold** button. It has a dark uppercase *b* on it. The button will look like it is depressed. Key your name. (It should appear in bold.)

4. Click the **Bold** button again to deselect that attribute and press **Enter** twice.

5. With your insertion point a double space below your bolded name, point to the arrow beside the *12* on the Property Bar and click once.

6. When the drop-down menu of font sizes appears, choose **18 pt.** by pointing to *18* and clicking once. Key your name again. It should be quite large.

7. With the insertion point following your large name, display the font size drop-down menu again and choose **12 pt**. Press **Enter** twice. (You may need to use the scroll bar at the right to see the 12.)

QuickMenus

Another way to make choices when you are using a mouse is by using a QuickMenu. A QuickMenu is displayed each time you point somewhere in the text part of your working window and click the right mouse button. (Remember *right clicking*? You used it in the Toolbar to display the list of available Toolbars.) The QuickMenu for the text part of a document window is illustrated in Figure B-8.

The features available in a QuickMenu depend on where the pointer is when you right click. What features are available also depends on what kind of application you are using. A right click in a WordPerfect table, for example, will display a *tables* QuickMenu. A different QuickMenu will appear if you have text blocked, or selected.

When you have right clicked to display a QuickMenu, you can choose options from the menu just like you would from any other kind of menu. If you decide you don't want any of the choices, you can close the QuickMenu by pointing anywhere outside of the QuickMenu and clicking the LEFT mouse button. You will have an opportunity to practice displaying QuickMenus in the next exercise.

FIGURE B-8
Text QuickMenu

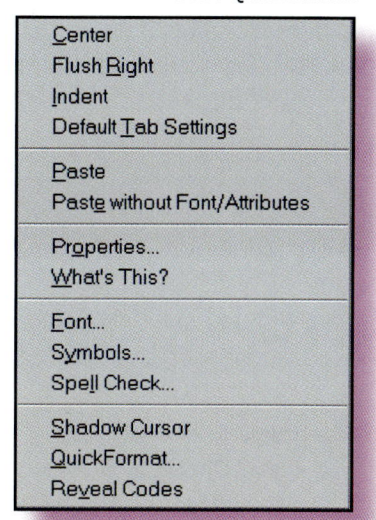

NOTE:

In these learning materials you will click (always with the **left** mouse button), double click (always with the **left** mouse button), and right click (using the **right** mouse button). If you remember that terminology, the mouse won't be a pest to you at all!

The Function Keys

When working with most computer applications programs, features can be chosen using the function keys—those keys across the top of the keyboard that are identified with *F* and a numeral. Word-Perfect uses the 12 function keys to give you access to nearly 70 features. This is done by combining the function key with one or more other keys, such as Alt, Ctrl, or Shift.

Earlier versions of WordPerfect came with a plastic or heavy paper strip to be placed on the keyboard near the function keys to tell you which key to use for which feature. That strip was known as a *function key template*. A function key template does not come with Corel WordPerfect 8, but if you have an old one from WordPerfect 6.0 or 6.1 for Windows, most key assignments have not changed.

In the lessons, when a feature may be chosen with a function key combination more easily than from a menu, your instructions will include that information. The function key assignments you learn will also appear in the Command Summary at the end of each unit and in the Quick Reference at the end of the text.

Closing a Document

Normally when you close a document, you are finished with it and wish to save it on a disk. Sometimes you simply wish to throw it away. To close, open the File menu and choose Close. A dialog box that looks like the one in Figure B-9 will appear.

If you choose No, the document will be closed but not saved. If you choose Cancel, the dialog box will disappear and you will be returned to your document. If you choose Yes and it's a new document, the Save As dialog box will appear so you can name your document and tell WordPerfect where it should be saved.

FIGURE B-9
Close Dialog Box

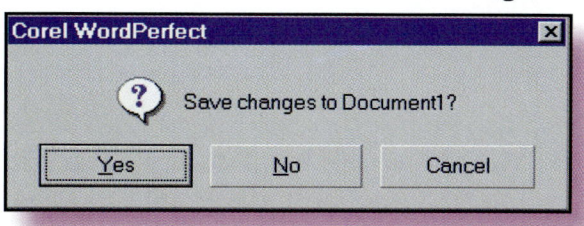

APPENDIX B

435

Note that the Yes button is enclosed with a heavy black line. Any time the button containing the choice you want to make is enclosed with the black line, you may simply press Enter. If you want a different choice, point to that button with the mouse pointer and click. Sometimes it's convenient to use the Tab key to move from one choice in the dialog box to another.

For this exercise we will practice with QuickMenus and then close your document without saving it.

EXERCISE B.7

SCANS

1. With the insertion point a double space below the big version of your name, key **This is fun**.

2. Point to the words you just keyed and right click. Does the QuickMenu that appears look like the one in Figure B-8? Click outside the QuickMenu to close it.

3. Point to somewhere above the blue guideline at the top of your document (in the top margin) and right click. The QuickMenu should have to do with headers, footers, and watermarks. Close the QuickMenu.

4. Point somewhere in the left margin area (to the left of the blue guideline) and right click. The options listed have to do with selecting text and a variety of other things. Close the QuickMenu. (This is enough about Quick-Menus for now. You'll be working with them later.)

5. Open the **File** menu and choose **Close**.

6. When the dialog box illustrated in Figure B-9 appears, either use the mouse to click **No** or press **Tab** to move to **No**, and press **Enter** to affirm the command.

Saving a Document

Now that you are familiar with the parts of the WordPerfect window and you know how to close a document without saving it, you will create some more text to be saved on your disk. In this exercise you will be keying text in a paragraph.

When keying paragraphs on computers, it is important to remember to press Enter only at the end of the paragraph. Let text wrap to the next line when a line is filled (*Word Wrap*). This allows you to key continuously without worrying about line endings. It also makes editing your text much easier.

EXERCISE B.8

SCANS

1. Key the text paragraph in Figure B-10. Press **Tab** to indent the first line. Then key continuously, until the paragraph is complete. Don't worry about errors!

2. Press **Enter** twice at the end of the paragraph.

3. When you finish, keep the paragraph showing in your window as you read on.

FIGURE B-10
Text for Exercise B.8

> Please make a note of the fact that our corporate offices are being moved to a new location at 1234 Washington Avenue. Beginning the first of next month, all of our officers will be making their business contacts in their new offices.

Before you can save your work, you must know where your instructor would like your documents saved. The exercises in this book are written with the assumption that your work will be saved on a diskette in Drive A of your computer. If your instructor would like your work saved elsewhere, you will have to make the proper changes to the instructions as you work. Be sure to ask for help if you need it.

EXERCISE B.9

SCANS

1. Open the **File** menu and choose **Save**, or click the third button on the Toolbar (the one that looks like a disk).

2. The Save File dialog box will open. While the dialog box may not look much like Figure B-11, it will have some of the same characteristics. The parts you will work with here don't change, no matter how the appearance of the box is altered.

3. The insertion point will be at the bottom in the Filename text box. For the name of the document, key **move b-9 xxx** (with your initials taking the place of the xxx portion of the filename). DO NOT PRESS ENTER!

4. Near the top is the Save in text box. That portion of the dialog box has a small arrow beside it. Click the arrow to display the box that enables you to choose the directory or drive. Assuming you are saving your work on the disk in Drive A, use the scroll bar, if necessary, to locate *3½ Floppy (A:)*. The drop-down menu should look much like Figure B-12.

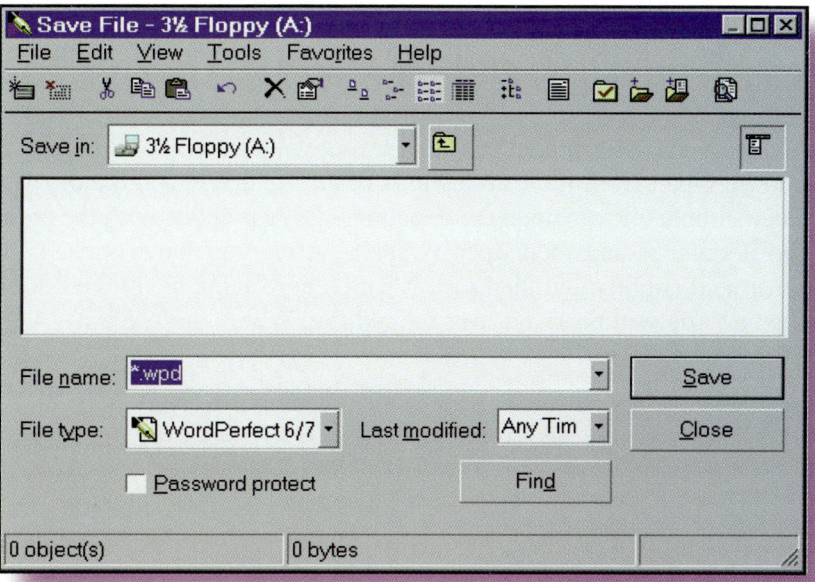

5. Click to select that drive.

FIGURE B-11
Save File Dialog Box

(continued on next page)

APPENDIX B

437

EXERCISE B.9 CONTINUED

FIGURE B-12
Save in Drop-Down List in the Save File Dialog Box

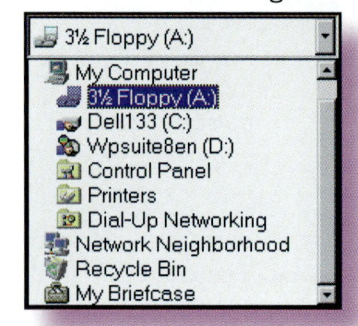

6. Press **Enter** or click **Save** to tell WordPerfect you have made your choices in the dialog box. You will see the light on Drive A as your document is saved on your disk. The document will remain in the window.

A couple of things need to be mentioned at this point. Pressing Enter usually closes a dialog box. If you press Enter before you have made all of the changes in the dialog box, you may get some unwanted results. For example, if you had pressed Enter after keying the name of the document in Exercise B.9, your document might have been saved in a strange place, and you might not have been able to find it again.

Also, had you been finished with your document, you could have chosen Close from the File menu. The same Save File dialog box would have been opened, and your procedure for saving your document would have been the same. The only difference would have been that the document would be cleared from your screen right now if you had used Close.

Opening and Resaving a Document

When a document has been saved, you can reopen it for any reason. To open a document, simply choose Open from the File menu. Locate the drive or directory where the document has been saved. Then double click to open the document. Let's practice with the paragraph you just saved. We will close the document and then open it again. After you have opened the document, you will change the document slightly and then save it with a new name using Save As. (If you save it again with the Save, the new file will be saved over the old file. When you use Save As, you'll end up with both files.)

EXERCISE B.10

SCANS

1. Display the **File** menu and choose **Close**. Your document should disappear.

2. Now display the **File** menu again and choose **Open**.

3. If necessary, change to *3 1/2 Floppy (A:)*, the way you did in Exercise B.9.

4. Click to position the highlight on the **move b-9 xxx** document. You may open the document in one of three ways.
   - With the highlight on the desired document, press **Enter** because the **Open** button is chosen.
   - With the highlight on the desired document, click **Open**.
   - Point to the desired document and double click.

APPENDIX B

Choose a method and do it now. The document should appear in your window.

5. With your insertion point at the beginning of the document (that's where it is when a document is opened), key your complete name and press **Enter** twice to make some room between your name and the paragraph.

6. Choose **Save As** from the **File** menu. The Save As dialog box will appear.

7. In the *Name* text box click to position the insertion point at the end of the word *move*. Key **2**. (The new document name is **move2 b-9 xxx**.)

8. Click **Save** to save the document. Keep the document open as you read on.

Corel® WordPerfect® Help

In the earlier discussions of menus, one of the menus mentioned was the Help menu. A vast resource for help in using WordPerfect is available from the Help menu.

Help looks the same in most programs running under Windows 95. You may access Help from the Help menu or by pressing F1. The Help menu is illustrated in Figure B-13.

The first choice, *Help Topics*, brings up the Help dialog box (see Figure B-14). Note the tabs near the top of the dialog box. The first tab (*Contents*) provides a variety of ways of using Help. A wide variety of topics are available when you choose this tab. The *How Do I* section, for example, contains many topics of Help from which you may choose. You might wish to explore the choices in this dialog box when you have some extra time.

The second tab, *Index*, provides an extensive alphabetized list of topics, much like an encyclopedia or dictionary. To find a particular topic, begin keying the name of the feature. The more you key, the closer WordPerfect will get to the topic you're seeking. When the topic is displayed, double click to go to the Help window for that topic.

FIGURE B-13
Help Menu

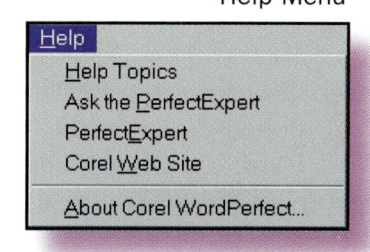

FIGURE B-14
WordPerfect Help

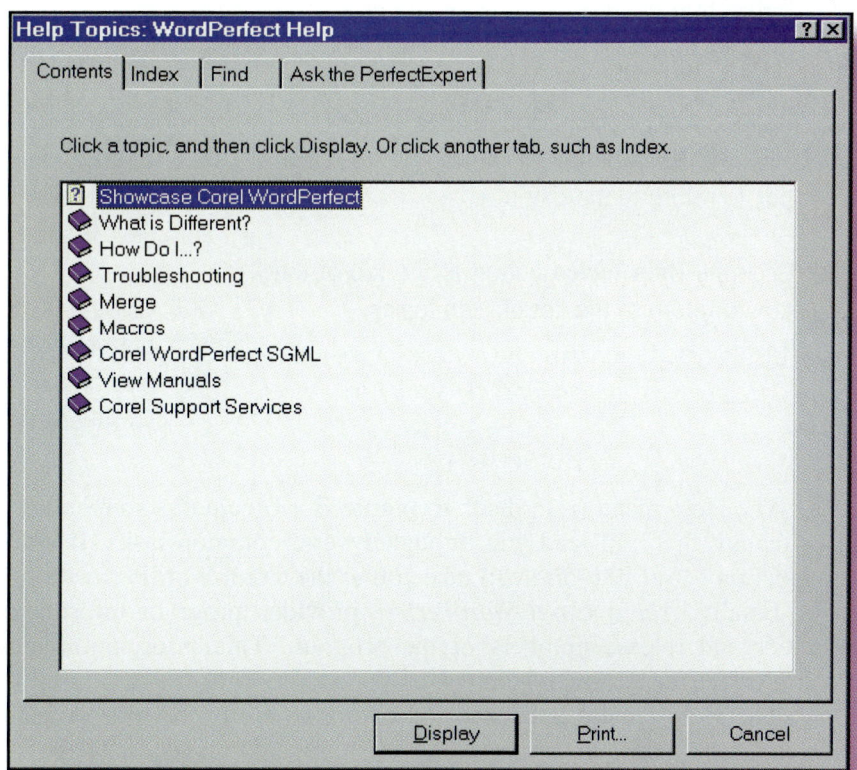

APPENDIX B

439

The third tab, *Find*, sets up a database of words in the Help topics so you can search for Help more efficiently—after the database has been established. You won't work with that feature in this training.

The fourth tab, Ask the PerfectExpert, enables you to ask WordPerfect a question. Then it will display a list of possible locations to answer your question.

Help can also be chosen by pressing F1. The window that appears whenever you choose Help is the same one that was used last time Help was accessed. In other words, WordPerfect remembers which Help window you used last.

EXERCISE B.11

SCANS

1. Open the **Help** menu and click the **Index** tab. We'll use Help to learn to exit from WordPerfect.

2. Key **Exit** and press **Enter**. A list of four topics should appear. Click to highlight *Corel Word-Perfect* and press **Enter** or click the **Display** button. The Help window displayed in Figure B-15 will appear.

3. Read the help provided. Then point to the About Close and Exit icon at the bottom. Notice that the pointer turns into a hand. Click that icon.

4. Read about closing and exiting. Then click the **Back** button at the top of the dialog box to return to the Exit box.

5. Click the **Help Topics** button at the top of the box to return to the list of Help topics.

FIGURE B-15
Help Window

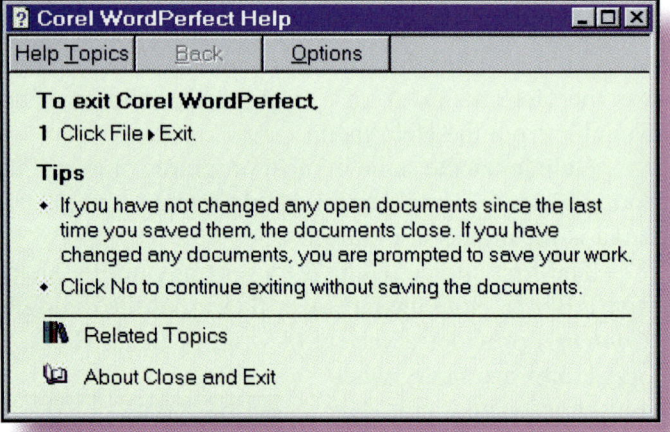

6. Use the scroll bar to go to the bottom of the Help topics. What is the last major topic in the list? It should be *zooming*.

7. Close the dialog box by clicking the **Cancel** button at the bottom right corner of the dialog box and read on. Click the **X** to Close Corel WordPerfect Help

The Help menu (refer back to Figure B-13) contains some other ways to get help. *PerfectExpert* is a feature that will lead you through several common tasks. If you have a modem and an Internet connection *Corel Web-Site* will take you to the Corel WordPerfect 8 home page.

Finally, *About Corel WordPerfect* provides program information about your registered serial number and release numbers of the program. This information may be important when you call WordPerfect for technical help.

The Help feature is packed full of important information. What's more, it is said to be *context-sensitive;* that is, when you are using a feature and you access Help, WordPerfect will often take you to the special Help topics related to the feature with which you are working. You will want to spend some time exploring Help when you've learned a little more about WordPerfect features.

Changing Defaults

As you will learn throughout your training, WordPerfect is set for you to use. That includes many decisions made by the developers of the software regarding what is best for you when you are working. Most of the time, those decisions are fine. Occasionally you'll want to make some changes to help you learn.

In the next exercise you will go to the Settings dialog box to look at where you can make some of those changes. **With your instructor's permission**, you may change a couple of settings. One is to display the keyboard shortcuts in your menus. Another is to change the number of minutes between automatic backup.

Ask your instructor if you should make any changes to WordPerfect in Exercise B.12. If so, go ahead and follow the steps in the exercise. If not, look at the dialog boxes in the exercise, but don't make any changes. (If you are working on a network, WordPerfect may not accept any changes you make in this lesson.)

EXERCISE B.12

(Optional, with instructor's approval)

1. Open the **Tools** menu and choose **Settings** (at the bottom). A dialog box with icons will appear.

2. Double click to choose **Environment** and click the **Interface** tab. At the left are three items regarding what will be displayed in the menus. If *Display shortcut keys* doesn't have a check mark, click to choose that option. Click **OK** to leave this dialog box.

3. In the Settings dialog box, choose **Files**. Look at the choices in the dialog box. It is here that you tell WordPerfect to save your documents with the *.wpd* extension. It is here that you can also set the time for automatic backup. The default is 10 minutes.

4. Change to 5 minutes and click **OK** to close the dialog box. Close the Settings dialog box to return to your document window.

Exiting Corel® WordPerfect®

You are about finished with the exercises in this appendix. Let's practice exiting from WordPerfect. You already did it earlier without a document in the window. This time you have a document open that has already been saved. Note that the Title Bar displays the name and location of the document. The name of the document is also on the Application Bar at the bottom of the window. We'll change the document before exiting so you are asked about saving again. Follow along carefully.

EXERCISE B.13

1. Be sure your insertion point is a double space below your document. If it isn't, hold the **Ctrl** key while you press the **End** key (**Ctrl+End**) to move it there.

2. Key your name.

3. Open the **File** menu and choose **Close**. A dialog box will appear, asking if you would like to save the changes to the document.

4. Press **Enter** (because **Yes** is the selected response) or use your mouse to click **Yes**.

5. Open the **File** menu and choose **Exit**. You will be returned to the Windows desktop.

Summary

This appendix has given you a good introduction to using WordPerfect for creating and saving text. You learned:

- How to start and exit WordPerfect.
- A number of ways to give commands to WordPerfect.
- About the Application Bar.
- About the WordPerfect Toolbar and Property Bar.
- About WordPerfect menus and dialog boxes.
- How to use QuickMenus and function keys.
- How to close and save a document in the desired location.
- How to open a document that has been created and saved.
- How to resave a document.
- How to use WordPerfect Help.

It is important that you have a good understanding of this material before you embark on Lesson 1. If you feel you need additional help with any of the topics covered in this appendix, please ask your instructor for help.

APPENDIX C

File Management

Creating and saving documents (or files) is only part of what a good word processing program can help you do. Managing those files after you've prepared them is an important part of what YOU must do. The computer can help you, but it is your responsibility to manage your files in such a way that they can be located when needed.

Naming Files

A file name may consist of up to 255 characters, spaces, or punctuation marks. For example, both **appendix.c** or **appendix c for WordPerfect 8 text** would be acceptable for the file name of this appendix. When naming your files, you should use consistency and organization. This not only makes naming easier, but it also makes locating the files easier.

Whatever method you choose, be sure that it is indeed a method—not just a haphazard naming of files. To find a file, you need to know exactly "which drawer to open and which file folder to retrieve."

In this training you will be given the names for the files you create or edit and save. These file names will include some information about the topic of the file, the lesson and exercise number of the file, and your initials (in place of *xxx*) to help you and your instructor identify your work. The suggested names make it easier for you and your instructor because they will be the same for all students. As you work with naming files, think about how you might have named the file if given a choice in the matter.

Organizing Files

Visualize an office with no organized paper filing system. When you open the file drawers, you find letters, memos, reports, and contracts piled into the drawers. The same thing can happen when you store files on disks and have no plan for what is stored on which disk or in which folder. File management is as important for computerized files as it is for paper files—maybe even more so because you can't see what's on a disk by looking at it. You must access each file, unless it is very clearly named, to see what that file is about.

Whether you save your files on diskettes or a hard disk, the issue of file management is critical. Let's look at some of the principles of file management.

Filing on Diskettes

If you save your files on diskettes, be organized about what you put on each disk. Think of your disks as file folders in the drawers of a filing cabinet. Organize your work so you can access your files as efficiently as you would be able to access a paper document from the proper file folder in the proper drawer of the filing cabinet.

Plan ahead and organize your disks. In the office you might arrange your files by client and/or matter, case, type of documents (i.e., letters, memos, reports, etc.), or by author.

Filing on a Hard Disk

In most cases with a hard drive system, both your software files and your document files are stored on the same hard disk. With everything stored on one disk, it is especially important to set up a system of organizing files so you can find them when you need them.

When you save on the hard disk, you must group the files into *folders,* as discussed in the next section. The main folder on a hard drive is usually known as **C:**. If you are working on a network, you may have a number of drives, each named with an alphabetic letter. Unless you are a network specialist, you won't mess with those drives.

Regardless of the drive name, the main folder can contain dozens of folders, and each of those folders can contain dozens of folders of their own, and so on. The same is true of diskettes. If the diskette is in Drive A, the main storage area is referred to as **A:**. You can create folders on diskettes, and those folders can contain more folders.

Using Folders

Since it isn't practical to save all files in the same location, the accepted method for separating them is into what are known as *folders*. A folder is a place where related documents are kept together. Sometimes you will create a folder to hold a special kind of work before you begin the work. Then, as the files are created, they will be saved into that folder.

Sometimes you will create the folder for related files after some of the files have been prepared and saved. At that point, you will need to move the files into the folder. In Lesson 8, you will learn to create such a folder and move or copy practice files into that folder.

FIGURE C-1
Folders after Lesson 8

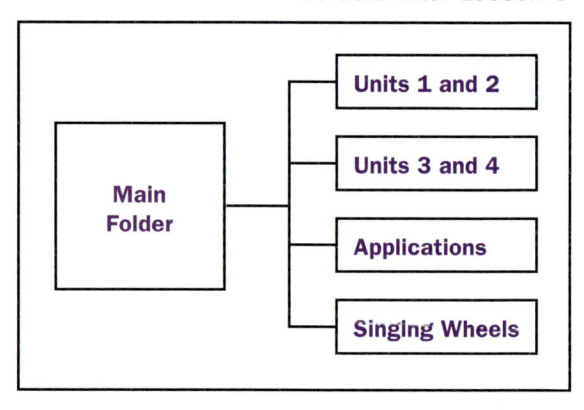

Main Folder
— Units 1 and 2
— Units 3 and 4
— Applications
— Singing Wheels

Figure C-1 illustrates the folder tree structure after you complete the exercises in Lesson 8. Note that you have two levels—the original main level and a set of folders on the second level. The names of the folders on each level must be unique. In other words, you can't have two **Applications** folders on the same level. You could, however, use **Applications** as a folder in the **Units 1 and 2** folder AND the **Units 3 and 4** folder, if you chose.

It is very important that you THINK about the arrangement of your folders so your work is stored logically. If it isn't, you are likely to have trouble finding a file when you need it.

Making Backup Files

One of the most important things you must do when you are filing documents on disk is to make backup files on a regular basis. This prevents loss of important files due to disk damage or problems with the computer. Proper backup procedures also protect your office from theft and natural disaster. Backup disks or tapes may be stored in a fireproof vault or at a different location.

Backup of your files may simply include copying all of the files created during one working day from the file disk or folder you were using that day onto another disk. This gives you two copies of everything you save.

The Disk Operating System (DOS) Copy and Backup commands may be used for making backup copies. Backups can be made from the Windows Explorer. Tape backup systems can be used to back up entire hard drives on a regular basis. This includes document files as well as program files, although most systems allow you to specify which folders are to be backed up.

The method of backup your office uses might determine how you name your files. In any case, it is important that you back up your work regularly and save your backup disks in a safe place.

Purging Files

Regular paper filing cabinets must be cleaned out regularly. A good records management program mandates the disposal of files that are old or no longer needed. Disk files need to be cleaned out on a regular basis, too. Time should be set aside each week, or preferably each day, to go through the files on your disks and "clean house." The Preview feature in the Open dialog box (discussed in Lesson 8) will help you preview files when you can't immediately remember a file name. By limiting the files stored in the main folder on your disks to those currently needed, your retrieval time for accessing files will be improved.

Some files can simply be discarded when they have no further value to you or your firm. You can do that with the Delete option when you are in the Open dialog box. Other files may have value but may be used only once every several months. Those files that are not needed on a regular basis might need to be archived.

Archiving refers to storing seldom-used files in a safe but out-of-the-way place. By copying these seldom-used files to a special disk and deleting them from your working disks, you can improve your retrieval time. In addition, your working disks or folders will have more room for your current work. You will want to have some system for archiving files so that you can find them when you need them.

Disk Capacity

Obviously, the total bytes available on a disk is limited. (A *byte* is approximately equal to a character.) The most commonly used diskette is the high-density $3^1/2$-inch size, which holds 1,440,000 bytes (1.44 megabytes, or Mb). Be careful not to fill a diskette more than three-quarters full. The Open File dialog box reports the number of bytes in the files on a disk or in a folder and the number of bytes remaining unused.

The current capacity of hard drives is much, much greater than that of diskettes, but much of the space on today's hard drives is filled with operating system and program files. This means that you must be as careful with disk space on the hard drives as on diskettes.

In your lessons you will be asked to save some files that have no future importance. Some of the exercises in the lessons involve deleting some files and moving others to related folders. Complete these exercises along with the others in the lessons so you continue to have room to save your files as directed.

Selecting Files

To select a single file, display the Open File dialog box, use the mouse pointer to point to the file to be selected, and click. When a file has been selected, you may open the File menu and choose Delete, Move, Copy, Rename, or a number of other options.

To select a group of files, point to the first file to be selected with the mouse pointer and click to highlight it. Then hold the Shift key while you click the last file in the group to be selected. The first and last file will remain highlighted, and all of the files between the two will also be highlighted. If there are more files to be selected than are showing at one time in the *file name* box, continue to hold the Shift key and use the scroll bar to move the list so you can see the final file to be selected. Click that file and release the Shift key. The Status Bar at the bottom of the Open File dialog box may tell you how many files are selected and how many bytes are in the selected files. If the Status Bar doesn't show, you may choose it from the View menu in the Open File dialog box. With the files selected, you may copy, delete, or move the highlighted files.

To select scattered files, hold the Ctrl key while you click those to be selected. You may use the scroll bar (still holding Ctrl) to move through the list to find the files. When you have highlighted all of the files to be selected, open, delete, move, or copy the files as desired.

APPENDIX D

Using A Mouse

Whenever you use a computer that's working in the Windows environment, you will need a mouse to start programs, move the insertion point, select text, and choose items from menus or dialog boxes. When used properly, the mouse is a helpful little critter.

There is a lot of press these days about using a computer for extended periods of times and remaining physically healthy. One consideration is sitting properly in a good chair. Another consideration is the keyboard—whether you keep your wrists straight when your fingers are busy keying, or if you allow your wrists to rest somewhere in front of the keyboard. The third consideration, although it receives less attention, is the use of a mouse.

Hand Position

The basic guidelines for using the mouse in such a way that it doesn't cause physical problems to your hand, arm, or shoulder are listed here. Use this list to check your hand position:

- Align your thumb along one side of the mouse, with two or three fingers on the other side.
- The mouse should nestle in the palm of your hand, with two or three fingers (depending on whether you have a two-button mouse or a three-button mouse) over the mouse buttons.
- Keep your wrist straight! This means supporting at least a portion of your forearm on the surface where the mouse is positioned. With the wrist straight and the mouse in your palm, you should be able to draw a straight line from your elbow to the cord end of the mouse.
- Position the mouse so you don't have to reach for it. Right beside the keyboard would be good if you have proper arm support with it in that position.
- The mouse should be at about the same height as the keyboard.

The Mouse Buttons

On most personal computers the mouse has either two or three buttons. The button at the left is known as the *primary* mouse button. When you are told to click with the mouse button, the assumption is that you will use the left button.

The button on the right is known as the *secondary* mouse button. In some programs, using the button on the right is becoming much more common for certain tasks. In these learning materials, whenever you are to use the right mouse button, you are told to *right click*.

Sometimes a mouse will have three buttons. When you have a three-button mouse, the mouse driver can be configured to assign special tasks to the middle button. Most often, that assignment is a double click. In other words, when you need to double click, click the middle button one time.

Lefties

Left-handed people can learn to use the mouse with their right hands, if they wish. On a computer that is shared with other workers who are right-handed, this might be the better option.

If the left-handed person wishes to use the mouse with his or her left hand, a couple of options are available. One option is to learn to click the primary mouse button with the middle finger. Then the index finger is used to click the secondary mouse button. That may seem awkward because most of us move our index finger better than any of the others.

It is a simple process to exchange the left and right mouse assignments. This is done in the Windows Control Panel. If you wish to make this change on your home or office machine and you are not familiar with the Control Panel, someone who has had Windows training can help you make this change. Your instructor would probably prefer that you NOT make this change in the classroom.

In the learning materials of this text it is assumed that the primary mouse button is the left button. If you have switched your mouse buttons, keep that change in mind as you proceed.

Clicking and Dragging

When you move the mouse on its mouse pad, the mouse pointer moves in the window. The appearance of the pointer differs, depending on its location in the window. Most of the time, when it is in the document portion of the window, it is a vertical line. When the line is in the position where you want the insertion point, click the left mouse button to position it there.

When the pointer is an arrow, it helps you choose menu items or buttons from one of the many bars or dialog boxes. It also is used with the scroll bars. When the pointer is in the left margin, the fat white arrow points in the opposite direction. Following is a summary of some of the things you will do with the mouse on your computer:

- **Click** once to select an item from the Toolbar, the Property Bar, or a dialog box. You will also click once to position the insertion point in your document. You will always use the left mouse button for this.

- **Right Click** to display the QuickMenu or certain bar preferences.

- **Double Click** to select a word or start a program. In the Open File dialog box, you may need to double click to change drives or folders. Many choices made in dialog boxes may involve clicking to select an item and then clicking OK to close the dialog box. If you double click the item you are selecting, the process often makes the selection and closes the dialog box automatically. Until you get used to working in dialog boxes, you may struggle with WHEN to click and when to double click.

- **Triple Click** to select a sentence. You won't use triple clicking very often.

- **Click and Hold** for some drop-down menus in dialog boxes. If you don't hold the mouse button after pointing to the button and clicking, the menu will close before you have a chance to make your choice.

- **Drag** is when you press the mouse button and hold it while you drag the mouse across the mouse pad, moving the pointer from one location to another. You might use this to select or highlight a block of text. You might also use it to drag selected text from one location to another.

Mouse Pad

It is important that you use a mouse pad under your mouse. This helps the mouse work well for you. It is very frustrating when your mouse doesn't do what you want it to do! The mouse pad provides a better surface "grip" for the ball in the mouse.

Without a mouse pad, the mouse ball picks up all kinds of dirt and needs to be cleaned more often. Also, the bottom of the mouse wears more rapidly when a mouse pad is not used.

Take good care of your mouse. Clean it regularly. With a little practice, you'll develop skill using the mouse that will serve you very well.

APPENDIX E

Codes

As you learn new formatting skills in your lessons, look at the codes in the Reveal Codes window. Then turn to this page and make a note of each code you see. Keep this list up to date so that you can use it as a reference for WordPerfect formatting.

CODE	DESCRIPTION

CODE	DESCRIPTION

APPENDIX F

Working with Type

One of the joys of working with a text editing program on a computer is the capability of using a variety of typefaces and sizes to give your documents a professional appearance. Before you can work knowledgeably with type, however, you should be acquainted with the terminology.

Type Terminology

- **Typeface**. One design of type. A typeface has a name, like Arial, Times New Roman, Swiss, Courier, and Marigold.

- **Style**. A variation within a typeface. Some of the commonly used variations are bold and italic.

- **Typeface Family**. A group of all related sizes and styles derived from a master typeface.

- **Point Size**. The smallest unit of measure in typography is the point. One point equals approximately $1/72$ of a vertical inch. Another way of saying it is that 72-pt. type is approximately one inch tall.

- **Font**. A set of all characters (letters, numbers, and symbols) in a particular typeface in a particular size. When you select a font (e.g., Times New Roman 12 pt.), you are specifying typeface and size.

- **Leading** (pronounced "ledding"). The vertical space between lines of type. The term comes from the days when strips of lead separated the lines of type. In WordPerfect leading is taken care of automatically, although if you wish to force a manual change, you can go to the Typesetting portion of the Formatting menu and choose Word/Letter Spacing.

- **Kerning**. Adjusting the space between individual pairs of letters. Adjustments to spacing can be made in the Word/Letter Spacing dialog box. Kerning is most often used when you are working with very large fonts.

- **Serif**. Type with strokes, or feet, at the ends of the main strokes of letters. Examples of typefaces with serifs include Bitstream Charter, Dutch, and Times New Roman. Serifs contribute to the readability of a typeface by helping the eye quickly differentiate between similar letters. You are reading serif type because it is used for most body text.

- **Sans Serif**. Type without serifs. The letters have no feet or strokes at the ends of the main strokes. Examples of sans serif typefaces include Swiss, Helvetica, Arial, and Univers. Sans serif typefaces are most often used for headings, headers, and any portion of the well-designed page except long passages of text. Can you find an example of sans serif type in this book?

- **Display**. Decorative and novelty typefaces. These typefaces are used for special purposes, like short announcements, but are avoided for body text. They are quite hard to read, especially in all caps. Examples of display typefaces include Script, Marigold, and Shelley Volante, as well as quite a number of other typefaces shipped with Windows and WordPerfect.

- **Monospaced**. Often called fixed-pitch type. Monospaced type requires the same amount of space on the line for each character, regardless of the size of the character. If you measure a horizontal inch in any document prepared in 12-pt. Courier, for example, you'll find that there are exactly ten characters in that inch.

- **Proportional**. Type in which characters take as much space as they need. Proportional type is characterized by the fact that wide characters like *m* and *w* take more space on the line than skinny characters like *i* and *t*. Depending on the text, you can fit one-half to one-third more information on a line with proportional type than with monospaced type, and it's usually easier to read.

As you can readily see, there is much to know about fonts. In WordPerfect you can easily choose a typeface as well as the point size for the document or portion of a document you are creating. Therefore, you can say you are choosing a font. All of the above definitions may be somewhat overwhelming to you. Let's look at some samples.

This is 24-pt. Times New Roman.

This is 16-pt. Times New Roman.

This is 12-pt. Times New Roman. This is a serif typeface. Notice the feet (ending strokes) on the letters. Notice, too, the extra space between lines to make room for the "descenders," like the bottom of the *p*. In WordPerfect that spacing is automatic. All of the characters in this paragraph are the same proportional typeface, but the letters obviously vary in size. Each size is a different font.

This is 24-pt. Arial.

This is 16-pt. Arial.

This is 12-pt. Arial. Note the lack of feet. Arial is a proportional *sans serif* typeface.

```
This is Courier 10cpi (characters per inch) and it looks much
like typewriter spacing.
```
This is Courier 12cpi. Courier is a monospaced font.

Sources of Type

Hundreds of different typefaces are available today. The illustrated typefaces make up only a small sample from which you may choose. You can supplement the built-in fonts of most printers by purchasing interchangeable font cartridges or downloadable soft fonts.

WordPerfect contains a variety of scalable fonts. Most are True Type fonts and are marked with two T's in the font list.

APPENDIX G

Introduction to Windows 95

Welcome to *Microsoft Windows 95®*. Windows 95 provides you with an operating system that encourages you to think of your computer as your desk. It is a working area with quick access to the tools you use daily, such as your calculator, telephone, fax, and filing cabinet. It also enables you to run your favorite applications programs.

The majority of this text is dedicated to helping you learn to use WordPerfect 8, which runs under Windows 95. This appendix will give you a brief glimpse of your operating system and the tools that come with the system.

Benefits of Windows 95

Windows 95 is a popular operating system because it provides a number of important benefits. Following is a list of some of the benefits that are important to most users:

- **Consistent Interface**. All programs that you run under Windows 95 look the same. The window is similar, the dialog boxes are similar, and the menus are similar, along with the other window parts. This makes it easier for you to go from one program to another.

- **Multitasking**. Windows 95 allows you to be running several tasks or applications at the same time, making you a better manager of your time.

- **Plug and Play**. Windows 95 comes with a number of drivers enabling you to install software or hardware in your computer, and Windows will automatically update your system.

- **Internet Access**. Microsoft Network, which comes as part of Windows 95, makes it easy for you to access the Internet, whether you wish to use it for e-mail or research purposes.

- **32-Bit Processing**. In the Windows 95 environment your programs can process data 32 bits at a time, as opposed to the 16-bits-at-a-time standard in earlier Windows and DOS environments.

- **Long Filenames**. In naming your documents in a Windows 95 environment, filenames can be up to 255 characters or spaces long, freeing you from the DOS convention limiting you to an eight-character filename with a three-character extension.

The Desktop

All work in programs running Windows 95 begins at the desktop. Regardless of how your system has been customized, the desktop contains some common tools. If necessary, have your instructor help you to display the Windows 95 desktop. Then find the following tools as they are discussed:

- **Taskbar**. The wide gray bar at the bottom (usually) is known as the taskbar. Your taskbar may contain some buttons indicating that some applications are in use.

- **Start Button**. The Start button is at the left of the taskbar.
- **Clock**. In the lower right corner is a clock, telling you the current time (assuming your computer has been set with the time and date).
- **Icons**. The icons on the desktop will vary. The two you are most likely to see are the *Recycle Bin* and *My Computer*. In addition, a variety of other icons might appear. If the icon contains a bent black arrow in the lower left corner, that icon has been put on the desktop as a shortcut to a program or tool.

The Taskbar

As mentioned in the previous section, the default location for the taskbar is at the bottom of the window, although it can be at any side. When you open a program, document, or window, a button for it appears on the taskbar. You can use this button to quickly switch between the windows or programs you have open. The more programs or tools you have running, the smaller the buttons for those tools are so that they can all be displayed at one time. If necessary, you can make the taskbar deeper so it will hold more buttons.

The Start Button

The Start button opens the Start menu, from which you can choose whatever you need to do your work. Figure G-1 shows the choices in the Start menu and what you can expect from each of those choices.

The Start button always shows in the taskbar, so you can make any choices you wish, even when you have a different window open or a different application running.

Accessories

A wide variety of tools are included in the accessories that come with Windows 95. These tools include a calculator, two simple word processing programs, and some games. If you are using a computer in the classroom, however, the games may have been removed to help keep you on the "straight and narrow." Figure G-2 lists most of the accessories and gives you a brief description of each.

FIGURE G-1
Choices in the Start Menu

- **Programs.** Used to open the Programs submenu. This gives you access to the programs you use most often. An arrow to the right of an item indicates that a submenu will appear.
- **Documents.** Displays the names of the last 15 documents you have opened. Click the document you wish to open. Windows will load the appropriate program and open the document.
- **Settings.** Enables you to access many of the Windows environment settings.
- **Find.** Used to search for files and folders on your computer or on a network.
- **Help.** Opens the Windows Help feature.
- **Run.** Used to start a program.
- **Shut Down.** Used to shut down and restart Windows safely.

FIGURE G-2
Accessories that Come with Windows 95

- **Fax.** Sends and receives faxes if you have the appropriate hardware.
- **Games.** Provides miscellaneous games.
- **Internet Tools.** Contains the Internet Explorer and Internet Setup Tools.
- **Multimedia.** Provides the ability to use video and sound or other media in your work, if you have the appropriate hardware.
- **System Tools.** Includes several utilities you can use to maintain your system's performance.
- **Calculator.** Performs mathematical calculations.
- **Character Map.** Provides a utility for displaying and printing unusual characters not found on the computer keyboard.
- **Dial-Up Networking.** Allows you to connect the computer to other computers and a network by way of a modem.
- **Direct Cable Connection.** Allows you to physically connect two computers that are running Windows 95. The computers don't need to be networked.
- **HyperTerminal.** Allows you to transfer and receive data over telephone lines if you have the appropriate hardware.
- **Notepad.** Provides a simple word processing program for writing and reading text files.
- **Paint.** Provides a drawing program with tools for creating or editing graphics.
- **Phone Dialer.** Stores up to ten phone numbers and speed-dials your calls using a modem.
- **Tips and Tour.** Introduces Windows 95 and displays tips—each time you start the program, if you wish.
- **WordPad.** Provides a simple word processing program for creating and saving text files.

Several of the accessories, such as Fax, Dial-Up Networking, HyperTerminal, and Phone Dialer, require the use of a modem and communications capabilities. Others, such as Calculator, Notepad, Paint, and WordPad are ready for use. With WordPerfect, you don't need most of these accessories, because the same tools are available in the WordPerfect program. Others will be more useful to you, depending on your needs.

My Computer

You can use My Computer to quickly and easily see everything on your computer. Double click the My Computer icon on the desktop to display the My Computer dialog box. It will look much like Figure G-3 with differences, of course, in the type of computer and configuration.

FIGURE G-3
My Computer Dialog Box

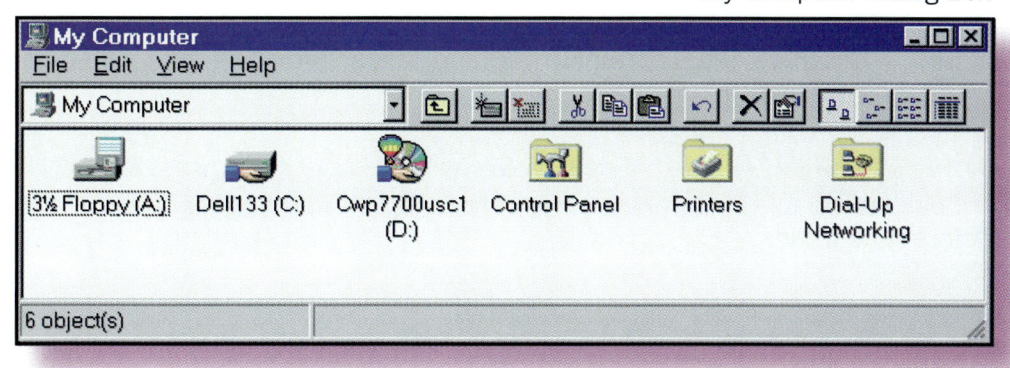

CD-ROM Drive

One of the most important tools in the My Computer dialog box for the WordPerfect user is the CD-ROM drive. If you or your instructor has the Corel WordPerfect Suite 8 CD and your computer has a CD-ROM drive, you can put that CD in the CD-ROM drive and access the *Corel WordPerfect Suite 8 Reference Center*. This is a set of on-line "books" containing detailed instruction for using WordPerfect, Quattro Pro, Presentations, Envoy, and a number of other utilities. Each of these references contains a contents section to help you find what you need, and the Envoy viewer is used to display the pages of the reference as you need them. As you progress with your training in WordPerfect, your instructor may require you to use the *Reference Center* so that you become acquainted with it.

Control Panel

Another important tool in the My Computer dialog box is the Control Panel. When you are using your own computer or you are in charge of the computer at your job, you may find the Control Panel useful for a wide variety of tasks. In the classroom you will probably be asked to not make any changes in the Control Panel. Figure G-4 illustrates the icons for most of the tools in the Control Panel and describes the use of those tools.

FIGURE G-4
The Control Panel Icons

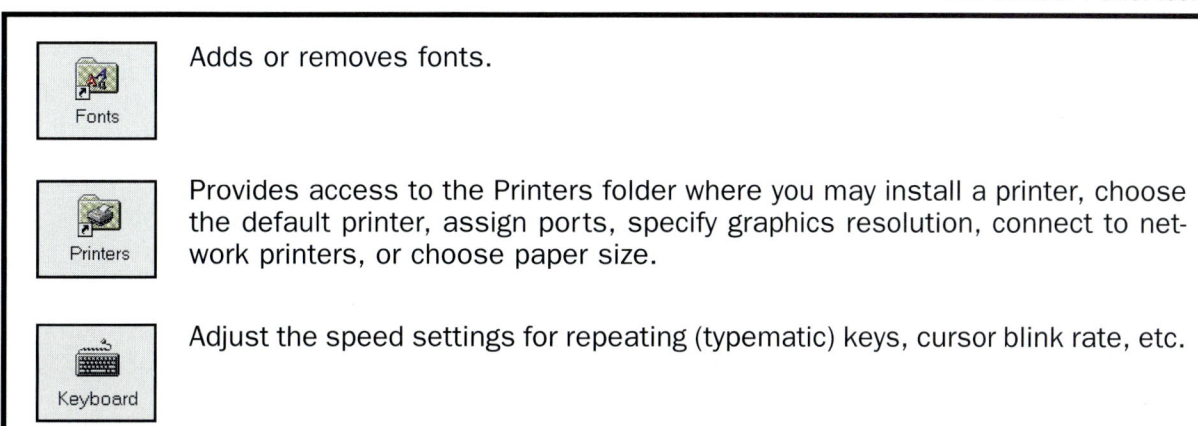

Fonts	Adds or removes fonts.
Printers	Provides access to the Printers folder where you may install a printer, choose the default printer, assign ports, specify graphics resolution, connect to network printers, or choose paper size.
Keyboard	Adjust the speed settings for repeating (typematic) keys, cursor blink rate, etc.

APPENDIX G

FIGURE G-4
The Control Panel Icons (continued)

Icon	Description
Mail and Fax	Sends and receives electronic mail and faxes, providing your equipment is properly equipped.
 Regional Settings	Enables you to set currency, time, date, and other settings for a number of different countries.
 Passwords	Allows you to change the password you use when you log onto Windows.
 Sounds	Enables you to set different sounds for different things that happen when you are using a program.
 Display	Controls the type of video display terminal attached to your system. Allows you to change visual settings.
 Network	Appears only if you are on a network. Is used to control network features. You may also set a user's password.
 Accessibility Options	Opens a dialog box that lets you choose a variety of options to make your system easier to use if you have a visual, dexterity, or hearing impairment.
 Add New Hardware	Helps you get everything working correctly when you install new hardware for your system.
 Add/Remove Programs	Installs or uninstalls parts of the Windows program or installs or removes applications programs.
 Date/Time	Provides the tool for changing the date and time displayed by the system.
 Multimedia	Controls the CD-ROM as well as the available variety of multimedia tools.

FIGURE G-4
The Control Panel Icons (continued)

System	Displays information about CPU, memory, disk drives, monitor, and other system resources.
 Modems	Provides guidance in installing and configuring a modem for transmitting data over telephone lines.
 Mouse	Tailors the way your mouse performs—double clicking and mouse speed. Also used to switch left and right mouse buttons.

File Management

My Computer can be used for file management, although if you use WordPerfect, you will probably do most of your file management from within WordPerfect. One of the things you can't do from WordPerfect is format disks. To **format a disk** using My Computer, follow these steps:

1. In My Computer, click once to select the icon for Drive A.

2. Open the File menu.

3. Choose Format. Follow the prompts to complete the formatting.

To **create a folder** using My Computer, follow these steps:

1. In My Computer, double click to select Drive A.

2. Choose File and then New. Choose folder.

3. Key the folder name and press Enter.

To **rename a folder** using My Computer, follow these steps:

1. Point to the folder to be renamed and right click.

2. Key the new folder name.

To **copy and move folders** using My Computer, use these procedures:

1. To **copy** a folder to a different disk, drag the folder icon on top of the destination disk icon.

APPENDIX G

2. To **copy** a folder to a different location on the same disk, hold Ctrl while you drag the folder icon on top of the destination disk icon.

3. To **move** a folder to a different disk, hold Shift while you drag the folder icon on top of the destination disk icon.

4. To **move** a folder to a different location on the same disk, drag it to the new location.

As you learn file management in WordPerfect, you may find it easier to manage your files from within WordPerfect rather than using the Windows file management tools.

Explorer

All of the same procedures listed for the handling of files in My Computer (except the formatting of disks) can be performed from the Windows 95 Explorer.

Creating Shortcuts

Windows 95 has a number of ways for you to create shortcuts so that you can run the programs or start the desired applications from the desktop. One way is to do it from the Windows Explorer.

To create a shortcut using the Explorer, be sure you can see a portion of the desktop outside of the Explorer dialog box. Then follow these easy steps:

1. Open the Explorer and locate the icon that starts the program to which you would like easier access.

2. Click that icon to select it.

3. Open the File menu in the Explorer and choose Create Shortcut. Windows will make a copy of the icon and drop it to the bottom of the open folder. It will still be highlighted.

4. Drag that icon to the desktop. If you wish to change the text under the icon, click it once to select it. Then right click and choose Rename. Key the new name.

5. If you wish to delete a shortcut from the desktop, click once to select it. Press the Delete key on your keyboard and confirm the deletion.

Summary

This has been a quick introduction to Windows 95. In order to be good with this operating system, you will want to take a class or two. Windows 95 works very well to get you in and out of WordPerfect 8. If all you need is to get in and out of WordPerfect 8, you don't have to be very skilled in the use of Windows 95. You can use WordPerfect for most of your needs.

GLOSSARY

A

Archiving Moving important but seldom-used documents to a safe, out-of-the-way place. (p. 445)

B

Block Protect The feature that enables you to keep a block or section of text together on a page. You can adjust the size of the block to make soft page breaks fall in desirable locations. (p.167)

Bookmark A WordPerfect feature that enables you to mark a location in your document so that you can return to that location quickly. (p.179)

Boot To start a computer or program.

Border A line that extends around parts of a document or sections of text. (p. 351)

Button A rectangular section in a dialog box where you may click to accept or confirm a selection. (p. 430)

Byte The computer measurement of storage—usually representing one character, space, or command such as Tab or Hard Return. (p. 445)

C

Cascade Separate documents in separate windows displayed with parts of windows overlapping other windows. (p. 106)

Case-sensitive A feature, such as Search, where the results vary, depending on whether the letters are uppercase or lowercase. (p. 79)

Cell The intersection of a row and a column in a table or spreadsheet. A cell can hold text, a number, or a formula. (p. 199)

Click To position the mouse pointer on something and then press and quickly release the mouse button. (p. 435)

Codes The hidden commands that cause your document to be formatted. In WordPerfect you can use the Reveal Codes feature to see what codes are formatting your document and the location of those codes. (p. 22)

Context-sensitive A feature that responds differently, depending on what you are doing when you use it. In WordPerfect the Help feature will go directly to the section on Outlining if you are working on an outline when you press F1 for Help. (p. 440)

CPU The working portion of the computer, known as the Central Processing Unit, that contains the processing and memory chips and the circuit boards that enable the computer to process your commands. (p. 425)

D

Data source (Data file) A collection of information to be merged with a form document. Often the data source contains names, addresses, telephone numbers, etc., of customers or clients. (p. 272)

Database A collection of related information, such as a collection of names and addresses of a group of people or a collection of parts in an inventory. In WordPerfect a database is referred to as a *data file*. (p. 272)

Default A setting built into a program that takes effect unless some alternative setting is specified. For example, in WordPerfect, the default margin settings are one inch on all sides of the page. (p. 431)

Desktop The opening window in a graphic environment, where the user may start a program by choosing an icon representing the desired program. (p. 454)

Dialog box A box that appears in the window to provide you with information or to let you select options and settings. (p. 431)

Document Any collection of information stored on a disk. You create a document when you collect graphics and/or text, give it a name, and save it. This term is used interchangeably with *file*. (p. 443)

DOS (Disk Operating System) Software that enables your computer to communicate with your disk drives and your software. (p. 445)

Double click To click the mouse button twice. Some actions can be accessed by clicking once. Others must be double clicked to be accessed. (p. 168)

Download To transfer data from a mainframe computer or network to a smaller unit, like your computer. Downloadable fonts are those fonts being downloaded from the computer hard drive to the printer. (p. 364)

Drag The act of positioning the insertion point in the window and holding the left mouse button while you move the mouse to the end of the section to be selected. (p. 86)

Drop Cap A large letter dropped below the line of writing. It is used to call attention to the beginning of an article in a newsletter or magazine. (p. 391)

E

Em dash A symbol that is used to join two related phrases. It is the longest dash you can key. In WordPerfect you can key it by pressing the hyphen key three times. (p. 74)

Endnotes Endnotes are references to other works or publications. Endnotes are printed as a list on the final page of the document. (p. 152)

Extension The part of a document name following the period. DOS restricts the extension portion of a document name to a maximum of three characters. In WordPerfect it is not imperative that a document name include an extension. Exceptions are macros, style libraries, templates, form documents, data files, and graphics. (p. 454)

F

Field A single piece of information in a data file. Fields are separated by ENDFIELD codes and a hard return. (p. 273)

File Any collection of information stored on a disk. You create a file when you collect graphics and/or text, give it a name, and save it. This term is used interchangeably with *document*. (p. 443)

File name The first part of the name of a document to be saved on a disk. (p. 4)

Filepath The route to where a document is stored on a disk. A filepath includes the use of different levels of directories. For example, a document named *whale* in a folder named *mammals* that is within a main folder named *animals* on the hard drive would have the following filepath: *C:\animals\mammals\whale*.

Fill The background or shading that is present in some graphics or objects. (p. 351)

Find A WordPerfect feature that enables you to key a unique string of characters and then tell WordPerfect to find that text string. (p. 80)

Fixed-pitch font A font that allocates the same amount of space for every character. It is also known as a *monospaced* font. (p. 453)

Floating cell A one-cell table in a WordPerfect document that is attached to a larger table in the same document. When changes are made in the larger table, those changes are reflected in the floating cell. (p. 216)

Flush right The alignment of text at the right margin, leaving the left edges of the text ragged. (p. 127)

Font A set of all characters (letters, numbers, and symbols) in a particular typeface in a particular size. When you select a font (e.g., Times New Roman 12-pt.), you are specifying typeface and size. (p. 452)

Footer A piece of information printed at the bottom of the pages of a multiple-page document to tie the document together. Footers might include page numbers, chapter or unit titles, the title of the publication, or the date, depending on the kind of document being prepared. (p. 140)

Footnotes Footnotes are references to other publications or quotations taken from other publications. Footnotes are usually numbered and positioned at the bottom of the page on which the quoted or referenced text is mentioned. (p. 150)

Form document (Form file) The shell document or file used in a merge that contains the standard text to be merged with the data source. (p. 273)

Format (a disk) To prepare a disk to be used in the computer. When you format a disk, you are setting up the disk so that it can communicate with the computer in which you will be using it. (p. 459)

Formula An equation used to perform a calculation in a spreadsheet or a table. (p. 207)

Function keys The set of 12 *F* keys on the keyboards of IBM and IBM-compatible equipment are referred to as function keys. The function keys are used as an alternative to the menu system in choosing and executing WordPerfect features. (p. 435)

G

Global Find and Replace The ability to locate and change automatically the same word or phrase throughout a document or portion of a document. (p. 82)

GUI (Graphic User Interface) An operating system or program where the documents appear in multiple windows, complete with menus, scroll bars, and icons. Popular examples of operating systems using a graphical user interface are Windows and OS/2.

H

Handle A small box that is displayed on the perimeter of a graphic when a graphic has been selected. Handles can be dragged to size and shape a graphics image. (p. 347)

Hanging indent A paragraph format where the first line of the paragraph begins at the left margin and the remaining paragraph lines are indented to the level of the first tab stop. (p. 66)

Hard copy The printed copy of a document.

Hard disk The high-capacity storage device that is usually permanently affixed inside of the CPU of the computer. Computer programs such as WordPerfect are recorded on the hard disk for easy access. (p. 425)

Hard page break A page break entered manually by the person preparing the document. Hard page breaks always stay in the same position in a document, regardless of text added or deleted. A hard page break is entered by holding Ctrl while pressing Enter. (p. 69)

Hard space A space used between two words or word parts which are not to be separated at the end of the line; e.g., between the first name and the initial in Gail M. Weber. A hard space is entered by holding Ctrl while pressing the space bar. (p. 74)

Headers Pieces of information printed at the top of the pages of a multiple-page document. Headers tie a document together and might include page numbers, chapter or unit titles, the title of the publication, or the date, depending on the kind of document being prepared. (p. 140)

HTML (Hypertext Markup Language) The commands needed to format documents for the Internet. WordPerfect will convert documents to HTML format.

Hyphen character A kind of hyphen used between two word parts which are not to be separated at the end of a line. Hyphen characters might be used as minus signs in formulas or between the parts of a telephone number. A hyphen character is entered by holding Ctrl while pressing the hyphen key. (p. 73)

I

Icon A miniature graphic representing a window, a document, or a program. Icons are most often used on the desktop. (p. 455)

Insertion point The place in a document where something will be added, represented by a blinking vertical bar. (p. 13)

J

Justification How text is aligned at the ends of the lines. The default in WordPerfect is Left Justification (text is aligned at the left margin). Other choices are Full Justification (both the left and the right sides are justified), Center Justification (all lines are centered), and Right Justification (meaning the left margin is ragged and the right margin is even). (p. 127)

K

Kerning Adjusting the space between individual pairs of letters to make the text more visually appealing. (p. 452)

Key A criterion for sorting order when working with WordPerfect Sort. (p. 314)

Keyboard merge To merge a form document with no data source, you key the variable information into the document as the merge progresses. A KEYBOARD code tells WordPerfect to stop for you to key the required information. (p. 284)

Kilobyte A unit of storage consisting of 1,024 bytes.

L

Landscape Page orientation where the long edges of the paper are at the top and bottom of the page and the short edges are at the sides. (p. 247)

Leaders Dots (periods) that direct (lead) your attention from one column of a line of text to another. (p. 35)

Leading A term used in page layout that refers to varying the amount of space between lines of type. In early years of printing, measured strips of lead were inserted between the rows of type when pages were laid out. (p. 452)

Line spacing The vertical distance between two lines of type, measured from baseline to baseline. (p. 125)

List box A box that contains a list of choices, typically in a dialog box. When a list is too long to be completely displayed, it will have a scroll bar so you can view additional choices.

M

Macro A collection of keystrokes that are accumulated because they are used together frequently. Macros are used to simplify and automate repeated sets of commands. (p. 252)

Macro chaining Adding the command to start one macro to the end of another macro so that when the first macro is finished, the second macro will run. (p. 259)

Masthead The large title and date section at the top of a newspaper or newsletter identifying the document, the volume or edition, and the date. Publishers use the same layout for the masthead with each edition so the reader feels comfortable with the look of the publication.

Megabyte A unit of computer storage consisting of 1,024 kilobytes or 1,048,576 bytes. (p. 445)

Menu A list of choices. (p. 430)

Menu Bar The list of menus across the top of the WordPerfect window from which you can choose WordPerfect features. (p. 430)

Merge code A code used to organize the text appropriately when two files are combined. Merge (sometimes called mail merge) is most useful for repetitive documents, such as in combining the names and addresses in a mailing list with a standard letter. (p. 273)

Mnemonics Related letters used to simplify commands, like *b* for *bold* or *u* for *underline*. In WordPerfect menus choices may be made by keying the underlined mnemonic letter.

Modem A device that transmits digital information over telephone lines. Modem is short for *modulator/demodulator*. (p. 440)

Monospaced Spacing in which each character takes up the same amount of space horizontally, regardless of the size of the letter. Courier 10cpi is a monospaced font. (p. 453)

N

Named macro A macro that has a specific name. When a named macro is to be used in WordPerfect, the command to start the macro is given, and the name of the macro must be keyed. (p. 254)

Network A configuration of computers cabled together with one workstation designated as the file server. In a networked environment WordPerfect frequently is loaded on the file server only, and individual workstations access the program from the file server as needed. (p. 426)

No-print zone An area around the outside edges of a sheet of paper where the printer is incapable of printing. The size of the no-print zone varies according to the manufacturer or model of printer. (p. 130)

O

Option A choice in a dialog box. (p. 296)

Orphan The last line of a paragraph that appears by itself at the top of a page of text. (p. 146)

OS/2 An operating system utilizing the graphical user interface which allows a user to have several documents or programs available at any one time and to move easily from one to another without having to exit from a program.

P

Page break An instruction to the printer to start a new page. A *soft page break* is inserted by WordPerfect when a page is full. A *hard page break* is inserted wherever necessary by pressing Ctrl+Enter. (p. 69)

GLOSSARY

Page orientation The way a page is oriented in relation to the printing on it. When the paper is vertical, it is said to be in *portrait orientation*. When the page is horizontal, the orientation is referred to as *landscape*. (p. 247)

Paste To insert text that has been copied or cut from a different location in your document into place at the location of the insertion point. (p. 84)

Path The route or address for a file. The path includes the drive, the main folder, and any folder within the main folder. (p. 17)

Point size The vertical size of a character of type. A 72-pt. character would be approximately an inch tall. A 12-pt. character would be approximately a sixth of an inch tall. The greater the number of points, the taller the letter. (p. 452)

Pointing Using the mouse to move the pointer in the window. Normally, when you have positioned the pointer at the desired location, either the left or right mouse button is used to position the insertion point or make menu choices. (pp. 447-448)

Pop-up list A list of options that appears when a pop-up button is selected. Most pop-up buttons have double arrows or triangles on them.

Portrait The page orientation where the short edges of the paper are at the top and bottom of the page and the long edges are at the sides. (p. 247)

Printer driver The software file that enables a program to communicate with the printer. In WordPerfect, the printer drivers are identified by a *.prs* file extension. (p. 7)

Proportional The method of printing where each printed character takes up only the width it needs, rather than a fixed amount of space. In proportional spacing, for example, a *w* would take considerably more width than would an *I*. (p. 453)

Q

QuickCorrect This feature automatically replaces certain text with other specified text. It will also correct errors and capitalization and can be used to correct predetermined keying and spelling errors. (p. 91)

QuickMenus Context-sensitive menus that appear when you click the right mouse button. (p. 85)

QuickSelect Selecting words, sentences, or paragraphs by double, triple, or quadruple clicking text. (p. 19)

QuickWords Abbreviations set up by the user that expand into complete text. (p. 163)

R

Radio buttons The round option buttons in dialog boxes. Usually only one radio button may be selected at a time. (p. 432)

RAM (Random Access Memory) The temporary storage area or working space for the document you are creating and the program you are using. This storage area is emptied if the computer is turned off or if the electricity supplying it is interrupted. (p. 425)

Record All of the information about a particular customer, client, or product in a data file. It is the complete collection of data about that individual. Records usually are separated by an ENDRECORD code and a Hard Page code. (p. 273)

Redline A feature that enables you to mark text suggested for addition to a document. Text marked with Redline is printed with a shaded background. (p. 395)

Relative tab Tabs set in relation to the left margin; that is, if you change the left margin, the tab will not remain in the original position but will move in relationship to the new margin. (p. 131)

Resident fonts Fonts that are built into the microcircuitry of your printer so you don't have to create the fonts or download them from your hard drive. (p. 453)

S

Sans serif Type without serifs. Letters have no feet, or curves, at the ends of the main strokes. Sans serif type is contrasted with serif type. Sans serif type is best used for headlines and text to which you wish to call attention. (p. 452)

Save (a document) Transferring a document from the memory of the computer to a disk so that it is available at some future time. (p. 4)

Scanning Using a scanner to convert a document on hard copy into a digital image. (p. 364)

Scroll bar The bars on the right side or bottom of the window that provide a tool for moving vertically and/or horizontally through a document or a list. You can move by clicking on the scroll arrows or by dragging the scroll box. (p. 104)

Scrolling Moving through text or a list box using the arrow keys, the Home key together with the arrow keys, the Page Up and Page Down keys, or the scroll bar. (p. 3)

Selected In word processing a section of text that has been blocked or highlighted. You might select text to be moved, copied, or deleted. You might also select text to add a special kind of formatting, like bold, underline, or a new font. (p. 18)

Serif The feet, or curves, at the ends of the main strokes of letters. Serif type is contrasted with sans serif type where there are no feet, or curves, on the letters. Serif type is easy to read in body text. (p. 452)

Size To change the size of an object by dragging the sizing handles that appear when an object is selected. (p. 349)

Soft page break A page break that is automatically inserted by WordPerfect when a page is full. (p. 37)

Spreadsheet Columns and rows forming a grid that contains data, labels, or formulas. Spreadsheets are often used for calculations and accounting purposes. (p. 199)

Strikeout A feature that enables you to mark text suggested for deletion from a document. Text marked with Strikeout is printed with a line drawn through it. (p. 395)

Style A master format for a particular kind of document or document part in WordPerfect. Styles are collections of keystrokes and menu choices to speed up the formatting of documents when the same formats are used repeatedly.

Subdocuments The term used when working with the Master Document feature to describe the individual documents that are to be combined to make up the master document.

Subscript The term used to refer to the position of a character that is printed below the normal line of writing (the baseline). An example is the *2* in H_2O. (p. 75)

Superscript The term used to refer to the position of a character that is printed above the normal line of writing. An example is the *2* in x^2. (p. 75)

Suppress A feature that tells WordPerfect not to include the header, footer, or page number on a specific page of a document. (p. 145)

GLOSSARY

T

Template A master format for a particular kind of document in WordPerfect, or a document part in other brands of word processing software. (p. 50)

Tile To display more than one document in separate windows at the same time. (p. 106)

Toggle key A key on the keyboard that you press once to turn on and again to turn off. Examples are the Caps Lock and Insert keys. (p. 105)

Typeface One design of type. A typeface has a name, like Arial, Arrus, Times New Roman, and Univers. It includes all characters of all sizes in the matching design. (p. 452)

U

URL (Uniform Resource Locator) An address code for finding hypertext or hypermedia documents on World Wide Web (WWW) servers around the world.

V

Variable-pitch font A font that varies the amount of space used by each character. It is another name for a proportional font. (p. 453)

VDT (Video Display Terminal) The screen or monitor of the computer. It is on the VDT that you can watch your work with the computer. (p. 425)

W

Widow A widow is the first line of a paragraph that appears by itself at the bottom of a page. (p. 427)

Wild card A character used to replace one character (?) or a series of characters (*) in a search string. (p. 80)

Window The area where you key a document when using a graphical user interface. (p. 427)

Windows An operating system utilizing the graphical user interface which allows a user to have several documents or programs available at any one time and to move easily from one to another without having to exit from a program. (p. 106)

Word Wrap The feature that causes a word that doesn't fit at the end of one line to drop to the beginning of the next line. (p. 3)

WYSIWYG Acronym for What You See Is What You Get. In a WYSIWYG interface the printed copy will look like what is showing in the window.

Z

Zoom To expand or reduce the size of a document or an image in the window. (p. 6)

NOTE: Some of the terms in this Glossary are terms used when discussing computerized production of documents, but are not used in this text.

INDEX

A

Accessories, Windows, 455
Addition in tables, 209
Address Book
    Merge feature and, 306-308
Adjust column size, 210-211
Adjust column width, 202
Advance dialog box, 159
Advance tool, 158-160
All justification, 127
Alt key combinations. *See* Keystrokes
Applications bar
    double clicking on, 168
Archiving, 445, 461
Arrange Icons By (Open file dialog box View menu) option, 46
Arrow keys, 13-14
Associate dialog box, 276
Asterisk (*), 213
Attributes, 32

B

Backgrounds, 365
Backspace key, 16
Backup files, 444-445
Balanced newspaper columns
    Column borders, 383-384
    creating, 228-229
Block Protect feature, 167, 461
Bold formatting, 28, 54
Booklet Printing feature, 397-398
Bookmark
    defined, 461
    described, 179-180

Bookmark dialog box, 180
Border
    defined, 461
    fancy, 381
    graphics box, 350-351
    Line, 381
    Page, 381-383
    Paragraph, 379-381
Box Border/Fill dialog box, 352
Box Border/Fill dialog box option, 351-352
Box Caption dialog box, 353
Box Size dialog box, 349
Box Styles, 368-369
Bullets and check boxes, 162-163
Bullets & Numbers feature, 68-69
Buttons. *See also* specific buttons and Toolbars
    Button graphics box style, 350
    defined, 461
    previous page, 15
    zoom, 6
Byte, 461

C

Calculations in tables. *See also* Formulas
    for averages of cell values, 212-213
    displaying results in floating cells, 216-217
    keystrokes for arithmetic, 213
    recalculating changes, 212
    summing columns and rows, 209
Caps Lock key, 27-28, 54
Caption, graphics box
    creating, 349

    customizing, 352-353
    styles and position of, 350-351
Cascade, 461
Case
    converting, 32-33
    specifying in searches, 81
Case sensitivity, 461
CD-ROM drive (My Computer) tool, 457
Cells
    defined, 199, 461
    floating, 216-217
    joining, 201
    specifying for calculations, 212-213
Center justification
    defined, 127
    in table column headings, 215
Center Page(s) command
    described, 71
    title pages, 146-147
Center Page(s) dialog box, 71-72
Center tab, 134
Centering
    text between margins, 33-34, 54
Central processing unit (CPU), 425, 461
Changing. *See also* Editing
    fonts, 28-29
    graphics box styles, 350-351, 368-369
    outline levels, 224
    page number values, 149-150
Character
    overview, 355
Check boxes, 162-163
Clicking and dragging, 448

469

ClipArt, 365
Clipboard operations, Windows
   copying, 85
   cutting and pasting, 83-84
   QuickMenu menu choices, 85
   vertical spacing after performing, 86
Close dialog box, 435
Close feature, 54
Closing
   documents, 435
   menus without making selections, 431
Codes. *See also* Document Initial Codes style; Formatting codes
   date, 70
   defined, 461
   double clicking on, 168
   hard page break, 69-70
   Margin Set, 124
   page number, 139
   revealing, 22-23
   searching for and inserting specific, 81-82
   text column, 227
Color
   graphic images, 368
   TextArt letters, 389-391
Column borders, 383-384
Column headings
   adding rows for, 201-202
Column width
   adjusting by dragging, 210-211
   Size Column to Fit feature, 210-211, 215
Columns. *See also* Text columns
   adding to tables, 207
   defined, 199
   number formats, 208-209
   tables vs. tabs, 198
   totalling numbers in, 210
Columns dialog box, 229

Commands
   deleting erroneous, 64-65
   issuing, 429
Comment, 181-182
Comparing documents, 397
Computer hardware components, 425-426
Concordance file, 461
Context-sensitivity
   defined, 461
   of Help feature, 439-440
   of QuickMenus, 434
Control Panel, 457-459
Convert Case feature, 54
Copying
   folders, 459
   formats, 165
   text to Clipboard, 85
Corel WordPerfect Suite 8. *See* WordPerfect
CPU (central processing unit), 461
Create Bookmark dialog box, 179
Create Data File dialog box, 274
Create Graphics Line dialog box, 376
Create Table dialog box, 217
Creating
   bookmarks, 179-180
   borders, 379-381
   captions for graphics boxes, 349
   data files, 273-276
   desktop shortcuts, 460
   drop caps, 391-392
   folders, 108, 459
   footnotes, 151-152
   form files, 276-278
   graphics lines, 374-376
   headers and footers, 140
   labels, 327-331
   lists, 67-68
   outline items, 223-225
   QuickMarks, 178-179

   subdocuments, 467
   tables, 199-202
   text, 3-4
   TextArt, 389-391
   titles, 139
   Toolbars, 103-105
   watermarks, 142-143
Current document style, 170
Customizing
   graphics box captions, 349-350
   graphics lines, 375-376
   Spell Check feature, 94-95
   Toolbars, 104
   view options, 45-46
Cutting text to Clipboard, 83

D

Dash, 74
Data file
   checking for errors, 273
   creating, 273-276
   defined, 273, 461
   editing, 279
   for labels, 327-333
   merging with form document, 278
   planning, 292-293
Data File Merge Feature Bar, 276, 279
Data, missing, 293-294
Database, 461
Data source, 272-273, 461
Date code, 70
Date, inserting, 70-71
Date text, 70
Date/Time dialog box, 70
Decimal justification, 212
Decimal tab, 134
Default font, 169
Default templete, 50
Delete key, 16
Delete Table dialog box, 218

Deleting
    commands made in error, 64-65
    data file associations, 396
    files, 445
    hard page breaks, 69
    outline items, 226
    text
        keystrokes for, 16-17, 54-55
        by selecting, 18-19, 55
Deselecting text, 19
Desktop, Windows 95
    defined, 462
Dialog box. *See also* specific dialog boxes
    closing without making changes, 64
    defined, 462
    described, 431-432
Disk
    capacity of, 445
    formatting, 459
    organizing files on, 443
Disk drive
    described, 426
    selecting for saving documents, 436
Display typeface, 452
Divide page feature
    described, 240
    forms, 240-241
    purpose, 240
Document. *See also* File
    archiving, 461
    closing, 435
    comparing, 397
    default font, 169
    defined, 462
    divide page feature, 240
    formatting entire, 139
    moving insertion point within, 14, 56

printing, 7
viewing, 6-7
Document default font dialog box, 170
Document on Disk dialog box, 111
Document Initial Codes Style, 168-169
Document Initial Font dialog box, 168
DOS, 462
Dot leaders
    command, 54
    Flush right justification and, 35
Double clicking on window, 168, 462
Double indent, 66
Downloading
    defined, 462
Draft view
    command, 54
    described, 5
    header/footer editing window, 140
    opening, 8
Drag to create options, 358
Drag and drop, 86
Draw object box, 351
Draw object text box, 351
Drop caps
    creating, 391-392
    defined, 462

E

Edit Box Style dialog box, 369
Edit menu
    Convert Case, 54
    Copy menu choice, 85
    Cut and Paste menu choices, 83
    Find and Replace feature, 80
    Undo, Redo, and Undelete menu choices, 19-20

Editing
    data files, 279
    graphics lines, 376
    macros, 256-257
    text
        Drag and Drop tool, 86
        Find and Replace feature, 80
        footnotes, 152
        Highlight tool, 87
    text column size, 231-232
    with Select, 83
Em dash
    defined, 462
    inserting, 74
End key, 13-14
ENDFIELD code, 275
Endnote
    creating, 153
    defined, 462
    footnote vs., 150
ENDRECORD, 275
Enter key
    adding extra space using, 37
    Hard Return code and, 22
    word wrap and, 3
Envelope
    creating, 39-40, 54
    preparing for merges, 281-282
    printing
        Envelope dialog box, 39-40
        POSTNET bar codes on, 297
Envelope dialog box, 282
Equation box, 350
Equation Editor, 392-394
Explorer, 460
Extension
    for data files, 286-287
    defined, 462
Extract, 319-321

INDEX

471

F

Favorites list, 47-48, 54
FIELD codes
    entering, 277-278
    preparing envelopes and, 281-282
Fields
    defined, 273, 462
Figure box
    described, 350
File. *See also* Document
    archiving, 461
    backups of, 444-445
    defined, 462
    opening
        methods for, 8-9
    purging, 445
    selecting, 445
File management
    creating folders and moving files, 108
    deleting files, 107
    file transfer, 182-183
    My Computer as tool for, 456-459
    principles of, 443-446
File menu (Open dialog box)
    menu choices, 109
        Open as Copy menu choice, 109
        recent files, 109
File name, 462
File name code, 17
Filepath, 17, 462. *See also* Path code
Fill
    behind portions of text, 384
    defined, 462
Find and Replace feature, 80
Find and Replace dialog box, 80, 82
Find and Replace options, 81

Fixed-pitch font, 463
Floating cells
    creating, 216-217
    defined, 463
Flush right justification
    command, 54
    defined, 463
    described, 33-34
    dot leaders, 35
Folders
    adding to Favorites list, 47-48
    creating, 108, 459
    graphics, 365
    organizing files, 443
Font. *See also* Type terminology
    changing, typeface and size, 28-29
    default font, 29
    defined, 463
    QuickFonts button, 30
Font dialog box, 81
Footer
    defined, 463
    graphic lines over, 378
    left and right hand page numbers, 139-140
    suppressing printing of, 141
Footnote
    creating, 151-152
    defined, 463
    editing, 152
    vs. endnote, 150
Footnote Property Bar Tools, 151
Form document
    creating, 276-278
    defined, 273, 463
    for keyboard merges, 278-279
    for labels, 327-333
Forms
    with tables, 241-245
    with tabs, 237-238
Format (a disk), 463

Format menu
    Border/Fill, 351-352
        Column menu choice, 229
    Drop Cap menu choice, 391
    Envelope feature, 39
    Header/Footer menu choice, 140
    Justification submenu, 124
    Labels menu choice, 327
    Center menu choice, 33
    Hyphenation menu choice, 229
    Make It Fit menu choice, 160-161
    Paragraph command, indenting paragraphs, 66-67
    QuickFormat menu choice, 177
    Styles menu choice, 467
    Watermark, 140
Formatting. *See also* Styles; Template
    character
        changing fonts, 28-29
        selecting text and, 32-33
    dates, 70-71
    default settings, 124-125
    entire document, 167
    guidelines, 121
    QuickFormat tool, 165-167
    tables
        adding fill (shading) to rows, 206
        centering between margins, 203
        justification in columns, 205
        numbers in columns, 207-209
        Table SpeedFormat feature, 215-216
        tools for, 203-204
Formatting codes
    categories of, 31
    deleting, 65
    open vs. paired, 31

Formatting disks, 459
Forms
    organizational charts, 245-247
    Subdivide Page feature, 240-241
    with tables, 241-244
    with tabs, 237-240
Formulas. *See also* Calculations in tables; Formula Bar
    defined, 463
    keying in, 207
.frm extension, 277
Full justification
    of balanced columns, 228
    defined, 127
Full Page view, 6
Full Page zoom, 54
Function keys, 435, 463

G

Global find and replace, 463
Go To Command, 54
Grammatik feature, 91, 97-99
Graphics boxes
    borders and fills, 351-352
    captions, adding, 349-350, 352-353
    image width/height, 348
    inserting an image, 346-347
    moving, 350
    overview, 346
    positioning, 354
    rotating text in, 356-357
    selecting, 354-355
    sizing, 347-348, 349
    styles, 350-351, 368-369
    wrapping text around, 353
Graphics images. *See also* Graphics objects (Draw program)
    colors, 368
    rotating and moving, 356-357
    sources of, 364-365

    watermarks as, 350
    zooming, 367-368
Graphics lines
    creating custom, 375-376
    inserting default, 375
    moving and resizing, 376-377
    shapes, 370-379
Graphics menu
    Drag to Create menu choice, 357
    Equation menu choice, 392-394
    Horizontal Line menu choice, 374-377
    Image menu choice, 348
    Text box menu choice, 350
    TextArt menu choice, 389-391
    Vertical Line menu choice, 374-377
Graphics QuickMenu, 348
Gridlines. *See* Table gridlines
GUI, 463
Gutter, editing text column size by dragging, 231

H

Handles, 463. *See also* Sizing
Hanging Indent
    endnotes, 152
    QuickIndent feature, 66-67
Hard page break, 69-70, 463
Hard Return (HRt) code, 22
Hard space, 74-75
Hardware, computer, 425-426
Header
    defined, 464
    described, 140
    page numbers in, 140, 143
    suppressing printing of, 141
    viewing, 6
Header/Footer Property bar tools, 140
Headers/Footers dialog box, 140

Help, WordPerfect, 439-440
Highlight feature, 87
Home key, 13, 14
Horizontal graphics lines
    creating custom, 375-376
    inserting default, 375
    resizing and moving, 376-377
Hyphen character, 73, 464. *See also* Hyphenation feature
Hyphen code, 73
Hyphenation feature, 229-231

I

Icon
    defined, 464
Image box, 350
Image Tools palette
    color and brightness buttons, 368
    flip button, 367
    Rotate and Move buttons, 366
    Zoom button, 367
Image width/height ratio
    default settting, 348
Import data dialog box, 219
Indenting paragraphs
    Indent feature, 66-67
    QuickIndent feature, 67
    Ruler Bar, 130-131
Inline equation box, 350
Inline Text box, 350
Insert Columns/Rows dialog box, 201
Insert Field Name or Number dialog box, 277
Insert key, 15
Insert menu
    Bookmarks, 179-180
    Date/Time dialog box, 70-71
    footnotes, 151-152
    Outline/Bullets & Numbering, 68-69
    QuickMarks, 178-179

Insert Merge Codes dialog box, 332
Insert Page Number dialog box, 144
Inserting
   codes using Find and Replace Codes dialog box, 81-82
   dates, 70-71
   Equation boxes, 392-394
   graphics images, 359
   graphics lines, 375
   path and filename codes, 17
   text, 15
Insertion point
   defined, 464
   moving, 14, 56, 200
Italic formatting, 28, 54

J

Justification
   default setting, 124
   defined, 464
   described, 127
   flush right, 33-34, 54, 463
   full, 127, 228
   graphics box text wrapping and, 354
   in tables, 205

K

Keep Text Together dialog box, 146
Kerning, 452, 464
Key (sorting), 314, 464
Keyboard
   as computer system component, 425-426
   as means of issuing commands, 429
Keyboard merge, 464
Keyboard shortcuts, 28

Keystrokes
   aligning text, 33-34
   arrow keys, 13
   calculations in tables, 212-213
   cancelling erroneous commands, 64-65
   changing outline levels, 223-225
   closing feature, 54
   copying text, 85
   dates, 70-71
   deleting text, 16
   em dashes, 74
   Find and Replace feature, 81
   graphic lines, inserting, 375
   hard page breaks, 69-70
   Help, 439-440
   hyphen character, 73
   indenting paragraphs, 66-67
   justification, 124
   moving insertion point, 14, 56, 200
   Open file dialog box, 8
   outlines, 224
   playing macros, 254-256
   Print dialog box, 7
   QuickMarks, 178-179
   soft hyphens, 230
   Undo, Redo, and Undelete features, 19

L

Labels
   creating
      for mailing, 327-330
      as name badges, 330-331
      as numbered tickets, 332-333
   distribution of, 326
Labels dialog box, 328
Landscape orientation
   defined, 464
Last modified box, 45

Leaders, 464
Leading, 452
Left justfication, 127
Left tab, 134
Legal document. *See* Table of Authorities
Line Hyphenation dialog box, 230
Line numbering, 395
Line spacing
   default settings, 124-126
   defined, 464
Line Spacing dialog box, 125
List box, 464
Lists
   families, 47
Logical page, 240
Lowercase characters, converting to uppercase, 54

M

Macro
   defined, 465
   default, 252
   described, 252
   editing, 256-257
   playing, 254-256
   recording, 253-254
   setting location for, 252
Macro chaining, 465
Mail merge. *See* Merge
Make It Fit dialog box, 161
Make It Fit feature, 160-161
Margin Set codes, 126
Margins
   default settings, 124
   justifying text at right, 33-34
      page numbers and bottom, 147-148
   setting
      for entire document, 139
      guidelines, 128
      Margins dialog box, 126
      Ruler Bar, 129-130

Margins portion of Page Setup dialog box, 129
Mass mailing. *See* Merge
Masthead style, 465
Menu. *See also* specific menus
   closing without making choices, 64
   defined, 465
Menu Bar, 465
Menus, 430-431
Merge codes
   defined, 465
   for merging into tables, 299-300
   most common, 273
   for numbered tickets, 337-339
Merge dialog box, 274
Merge Feature Bar, 49-50
Merging files
   Address Book feature, 304-307
   for document assembly, 301-303
   editing data files, 279
   envelopes, 281-282
   into tables, 299-300
   from keyboard, 284-286
   mass mailing, 49-50
   missing data, 293-296
   multiple-line fields, 279-281
   options for, 296-297
   overview, 274
   planning data files, 292-293
   POSTNET bar codes, 297-299
   table data files, 283
   terminology, 272
   troubleshooting, 284
Minus sign (-)
   calculations in tables, 212
Monospaced type, 453, 465
Mouse. *See also* QuickSelect options
   buttons, 447
   clicking and dragging, 448

   double clicking on window components, 168, 462
   hand position, 447
   importance in using WordPerfect, 447
   left-handed users, 448
   moving insertion point using, 14-15
   text, selecting, 83
Mouse buttons
   described, 447
Mouse pad, 449
Moving
   graphics boxes, 350
   graphics images, 356-357
   graphics lines, 376-377
   insertion point, 13, 56, 200
   text
      Clipboard operations, 83-84
Multiple-line fields, 279-281
My Computer dialog box, 457
My Computer tools
   CD-ROM drive, 457
   Control Panel, 457-459
   file management, 459-460

N

Name badges, 330
Named macro, 465
Naming files, 443
Network, 426, 465
New Sort dialog box, 313
New page, 69
No-print zone, 465
Numbered ticket, 332-333
Numbers. *See also* Calculations in tables; Formulas
   formatting in table columns, 207, 209
   for outline items, 223, 225

O

OLE 2.0 box, 351
Open as Copy, 109
Open codes, 31
Open file dialog box, 8
   Favorites list, 47-48
   features, 45
   rearranging order of files in, 176-177
   selecting files in, 445
   view menu, 46
Opening
   documents, 8-9
Organizational charts, 245-247
Organizing files, 443-444
Orphan, 465. *See also* Widow/Orphan feature
OS/2, 465
Outline
   adding and deleting items, 226
   creating, 223-225
   ending, 226
   styles, 226-228
Outline/Bullets and numbering, 68
Outline Tools on Property bar
   described, 224
   Hide Body Text button, 225

P

Page
   centering text on, 71
   dividing into equal sections for forms, 240-241
   graphics box positioning relative to, 355
   orientation of text on, 247-249
   printing current or multiple, 110
Page Border, 381-383

Page break
   defined, 465
   hard, 69-70
   soft, 37, 467
Page Down key, 13-14
Page numbers
   changing value of, 149-150
   in footers, 139-140
   in headers, 140, 143
   inserting in text, 147-148
   suppressing printing of, 145-146
Page orientation, 466. *See also* Landscape orientation
Page Setup dialog box, 129, 241
Page Up key, 13-14
Page view
   described, 5
   footnotes in, 151
Paired codes, 31
Paper, selecting size of, 242
Paragraph
   Block Protect tool, 167
      graphics box positioning relative to, 354
      widow/orphan control, 146
Paragraph Border/Fill dialog box, 380
Paragraph Borders, 379-380
Paragraph Sort, 316-317
Pasting text, 84, 466
Path, 466
Path code, inserting, 17
Pausing macros, 257-258
Perform Merge dialog box, 278
Physical page, 240
Playing macros, 254-256
Plus sign (+)
   calculations in tables, 212
Point size
   defined, 452, 466
Pointing, 466
Pop-up list, 466
Portrait orientation, 247, 466

Position Hyphen dialog box, 230
POSTNET bar codes, 297
   on envelopes, 297
Preview (Open file dialog box View menu) option, 45
Print dialog box, 7
Print job, checking status of, 105
Printer
   described, 426
   feeding labels into, 328
   selecting, 7
Printing
   booklets, 397-398
   documents, 7
   envelopes
      Envelope dialog box, 39-40
      POSTNET bar codes, 297
   labels, 327-328
Prompt-As-You-Go, 91
Proofreaders' marks, 58
Properties for Table Format dialog box, 205-206
Properties for Table Numeric Format dialog box, 208
Property Bar
   Columns button, 229
   described, 105
   double clicking on, 168
   Font dialog box, 29-30
   QuickJoin button, 202
   Tables button, 197
   Zoom button, 6
Proportional type, 453, 466

Q

QuickCorrect, 91
QuickCorrect dialog box, 92, 164
QuickCorrect feature, 91-93, 466
QuickFinder feature, 177-178
QuickFonts, 29-30
QuickFormat dialog box, 165
QuickFormat feature, 165-167

QuickIndent feature, 67
QuickMark feature, 178-179
QuickMenus, 85, 434, 466
   defined, 466
   Graphics, 348
   Tab, 134
   Table, 201
QuickSelect, 19, 466
QuickSplit column button, 204
QuickSplit row button, 204
QuickSum button, 210
QuickWords, 91, 163, 466

R

Radio Buttons, 466
RAM (random access memory), 425, 466
Readability, document, 91
Reading grade level, 91
Recalculation, 212
Recent files, 109
Recording macros, 253
Records
   defined, 273, 466
Redline and strikeout feature
   defined, 466, 467
   described, 395-397
   in document comparisons, 397
Redo feature, 19
Reference document, 303-304
Relative tab, 466
Remove Compare Markings dialog box, 396
Renaming folders, 459
Renegade lines. *See* Widow/Orphan feature
Replacing text
   Find and Replace Text dialog box, 82
   misspelled words, 94-95
Resaving documents, 438
Reveal Codes feature, 22-23, 54
Right justification, 127

Right tab, 134
Rotating
   graphics images, 356-357
   text, 394
Rows
   adding, 201-202
   defined, 199
   sum of numbers in, 208-209
Ruler Bar
   double clicking on, 168
   setting tabs, 131-132

S

Sans serif typeface, 452, 467
Saving
   data files, 276
Scroll bars
   on custom Toolbars, 104-105
   defined, 467
Searching
   for text. *See* Find and Replace Text dialog box
Select Page Numbering Format dialog box, 148
Select Records dialog box, 322
Selecting
   records for sorts, 321
   text
      for applying attributes, 32-33
      for deleting, 18-19
      formating, 169
Sentence, selecting entire, 18-19
Serif typeface, 452, 467
Shadow pointer, 172
Shortcuts, 460
Size Column to Fit feature, 210-211, 215
Sizing objects
   defined, 467
   graphical lines, 376-377

graphics boxes
   with exact measurements, 349
   with sizing handles, 347
   when rotating and moving, 350
Slash (/), 212
Soft hyphens, 230
Soft page break, 37, 54, 69-70, 467
Sort dialog box, 312
Sorting
   Line Sort, 312-316
   Merge Sort, 317-319
   Paragraph Sort, 316-317
   Table Sort, 319
   types of sorts, 311
Space code, 73-74
Spell Check feature, 91, 94-95
Spell-As-You-Go feature, 91, 93-94
Spreadsheet
   defined, 467
   importing into tables, 218-219
Starting WordPerfect, 3
Status Bar (Open file dialog box View menu), 45
Sticky Note Text, 351
Strikeout feature
   defined, 467
   described, 395-397
   in document comparisons, 397
Style, typeface, 452
Styles
   defined, 467
   graphics box, 350-351, 368-369
   outline, 225
Styles Editor dialog box, 171
Subdocument
   defined, 467
Superscripts and supscripts, 75, 467

Suppress dialog box, 145
Suppress feature
   defined, 467
Symbols. *See* WordPerfect symbols

T

Tab key
   inserting tabs using, 36-37
   QuickIndent feature and, 67
Tab QuickMenu, 134
Tab Set dialog box, 131
Tab stops
   default setting, 124
Tab types, 134
Table. *See also* Calculations in tables; Cells; Columns; Formulas; Rows
   add rows, 201-202
   adjusting column width, 202
   creating, 199-202
   formatting
      adding fill (shading) to rows, 206
      centering between margins, 203
      justification in columns, 205
      lines grid, 206
      numbers in columns, 207-209
      Table SpeedFormat feature, 215-216
      tools for, 203-204
   in forms, 241-244
   joining cells, 201-202
   merging into, 283
   terminology, 199
Table box, 350
Table formulas, 207, 210
Table gridlines, 203

Table menu
   QuickFill and size columns to fit, 215
   Table Property bar, 203
Table QuickMenu, 201
Table Row Sort, 316, 324
Table SpeedFormat feature, 215-216
   QuickFill button, 215
   Size Column to Fit button, 215
   SpeedFormat button, 215
Tabs
   default standard template settings, 50
   in forms, 237-238
   setting
      Ruler Bar, 131-132
      Tab Set dialog box, 131
   tables vs., 198-199
   types of, 134
Text
   aligning and justifying, 33-34
   applying attributes, 32
   converting to table format, 217
   creating
      in documents, 3-4
   cutting, 83
   deleting, 16-19
   enhancement, 27
   highlighting, 87
   inserting, 15
   marking
      with Redline and Strikeout features, 395-397
   moving
      Clipboard operations, 83-84
      insertion point, 56
   pasting, 84
   printing selected, 110
   selecting, 55
   standard or boilerplate, 308
   wrapping around graphics boxes, 353-354

Text box
   changing graphics box style to, 358
   creating, 357-358
   described, 350, 357
   rotating text in, 394-395
Text columns
   balanced newspaper, 228-229
   creating, 227-228
   editing size of, 231-232
   in portion of document, 232
TextArt 8 dialog box, 390
TextArt, 389-391
Thesaurus feature, 91, 96-97
Tickets, numbered, 332-333
Title
   document, 141
Title page, 146-147
Toggle key, 468
Toolbar (Open file dialog box View menu) option, 45
Toolbar. *See also* Property Bar
   creating and customizing, 103, 104
   default
      Bold, Italic, and Underline buttons, 32
      Copy button, 85
      Cut and Paste buttons, 83
      described, 433
      Highlight button, 87
      location, 103
      New Blank Document button, 80
      Open button, 8
      Print button, 7
      scroll bar, 104-105
      Spell Check button, 95
Tools menu. *See* specific menu
Troubleshooting merges, 284
Two Page view, 55
Type terminology, 452-453

Typeface. *See also* Font
   defined, 452, 468
   sources of, 453
Typeover mode, 18, 55

U

Undelete dialog box, 21
Undelete feature, 19, 21, 55
Underline formatting, 28, 55
Underline Tabs feature, 238
Undo feature, 19, 21, 55
Uppercase characters, converting to lowercase, 54
USPS bar codes. *See* POSTNET bar codes

V

Values dialog box, 150
Variable-pitch font, 468
VDT (video display terminal), 468
Vertical graphics lines, inserting, 374-375
Video display terminal (VDT), 468
View menu (Open file dialog box) menu options, 44-45
View page feature, 55
Viewing
   documents, 5-6
   extensions, 286-287
   graphics folders, 365
   graphics images before inserting, 346-347
   history of edits using Undo and Redo, 19, 21
   outline levels, 223-225
   templates in Styles Editor dialog box, 171

W

Watermark
    creating, 142-143
    defined, 140
    Watermark graphics box style, 350
Watermark Property Bar, 142
Whole word, 81
Widow/Orphan feature
    described, 146
Wild card, 468
Window, 468
Window menu, 106-107
Windows 95
    accessories, 455-456
    benefits of, 454
    clock, 455
    Explorer, 460
    icons, 455
    My Computer, 456-459
    Start button, 455
    taskbar, 455
Word division rules, 229
Word wrap
    defined, 468
    Enter key and, 3
WordPerfect
    changing defaults, 441
    closing a document, 435
    creating text, 3, 429
    dialog box, 431-432
    editing in, 12
    environment, 427
    exiting, 427-428, 441-442
    function keys, 435
    giving commands, 429
    help, 439-440
    images, 365
    quick menus, 434
    saving a document, 436-437
    starting, 3, 427-428
WordPerfect symbols dialog box, 161-162
.wpd extension
    Open file dialog box and, 45
    as WordPerfect default, 4
Wrapping text
    around graphics boxes, 353-354
Writing Tools dialog box
    Grammatik tab, 91, 97-99
    Spell Checker, 95-96
    Thesaurus tab, 96-97

Z

Zoom dialog box, 6, 397
Zoom feature
    command, 54-55
    defined, 468
    graphics images, 367-368

Progress Record

Name _____

UNIT 1   GETTING STARTED

		Printed[1]	Score	Date Completed	Instructor
Lesson 1	education 1-2	....	_____	_____	_____
	matter proj1a	....	_____	_____	_____
	matter proj1b	....	_____	_____	_____
	Lesson 1 Quiz	....	_____	_____	_____
Lesson 2	foreign 2-7	....	_____	_____	_____
	working 2-10	....	_____	_____	_____
	nasa proj2	3 pages	_____	_____	_____
	Lesson 2 Quiz	....	_____	_____	_____
Lesson 3	appearance 3-3	....	_____	_____	_____
	appearance 3-4	....	_____	_____	_____
	foreign 3-6	....	_____	_____	_____
	music 3-8	....	_____	_____	_____
	gifts 3-10	....	_____	_____	_____
	sasoot 3-11	letter & env.	_____	_____	_____
	skeleton proj3	....	_____	_____	_____
	Lesson 3 Quiz	....	_____	_____	_____
Lesson 4	gifts 4-3	....	_____	_____	_____
	seasons 4-4	....	_____	_____	_____
	gifts proj4b	....	_____	_____	_____
	Lesson 4 Quiz	....	_____	_____	_____
	quality u1ap1a	....	_____	_____	_____
	quality u1ap1b	....	_____	_____	_____
	gifts u1ap2	....	_____	_____	_____
	canada u1ap3	....	_____	_____	_____
	schedule job1	....	_____	_____	_____
	schedule job2	....	_____	_____	_____
	Unit 1 Quiz	....	_____	_____	_____
	Unit 1 Production Test	....	_____	_____	_____

[1]All printed exercises are one page unless otherwise indicated.

UNIT 2 COREL® WORDPERFECT® BASICS

		Printed	Score	Date Completed	Instructor
Lesson 5	indent 5-3	....	_____	_____	
	online 5-4	....	_____	_____	
	numbers 5-6	....	_____	_____	
	dates 5-9	....	_____	_____	
	sasoot 5-10	....	_____	_____	
	codes 5-11	....	_____	_____	
	gifts proj5a	....	_____	_____	
	online proj5b	....	_____	_____	_____
	Lesson 5 Quiz	....	_____	_____	_____
Lesson 6	pc-tv 6-6	....	_____	_____	
	gifts proj6	....	_____	_____	_____
	Lesson 6 Quiz	....	_____	_____	_____
Lesson 7	fix 7-3	....	_____	_____	
	errors 7-4	....	_____	_____	
	errors 7-5	....	_____	_____	
	gifts proj7a	....	_____	_____	
	gifts proj7b	....	_____	_____	_____
	Lesson 7 Quiz	....	_____	_____	_____
Lesson 8	nasa proj2	page 3	_____	_____	
	nasa proj2	2 paragraphs	_____	_____	
	proj8a	last page	_____	_____	
	proj8b	....	_____	_____	_____
	Lesson 8 Quiz	....	_____	_____	_____
	quality u2ap1	....	_____	_____	
	desktop u2ap2a	....	_____	_____	
	desktop u2ap2b	....	_____	_____	
	quality u2ap3	....	_____	_____	
	opinion u2ap4	....	_____	_____	
	schedule job3	....	_____	_____	
	houston job4	....	_____	_____	_____
	Unit 2 Quiz	....	_____	_____	_____
	Unit 2 Production Test	....	_____	_____	_____

UNIT 3 — FORMATTING TOOLS

		Printed	Score	Date Completed	Instructor
Lesson 9	record 9-2	....	_____	_____	
	record 9-3	....	_____	_____	
	record 9-4	....	_____	_____	
	record 9-5	....	_____	_____	
	salad 9-7	....	_____	_____	
	hostas 9-8	....	_____	_____	
	record 9-9	....	_____	_____	
	Mildred 9-10	....	_____	_____	
	cheese proj9	....	_____	_____	_____
	Lesson 9 Quiz	....	_____	_____	_____
Lesson 10	pcug 10-1	....	_____	_____	
	pcug 10-2	....	_____	_____	
	wind 10-7	2 pages	_____	_____	
	wind 10-8	title page	_____	_____	
	gifts 10-10	....	_____	_____	
	wind 10-11	last page	_____	_____	
	footnote 10-12	....	_____	_____	
	footnote 10-13	....	_____	_____	
	wind 10-15	4 pages	_____	_____	
	pc proj10a	2 pages	_____	_____	
	pc proj10b	page 2	_____	_____	_____
	Lesson 10 Quiz	....	_____	_____	_____
Lesson 11	gifts 11-3	....	_____	_____	
	char 11-5	....	_____	_____	
	pc 11-9	3 pages	_____	_____	
	pc 11-10	3 pages	_____	_____	
	pcug 11-13	....	_____	_____	
	nasa proj11a	3 pages	_____	_____	
	nasa proj11b	3 pages	_____	_____	_____
	Lesson 11 Quiz	....	_____	_____	
Lesson 12	pc proj12	3 pages	_____	_____	
	Lesson 12 Quiz	....	_____	_____	
	sasoot u3ap1	2 pages	_____	_____	
	lighthouses u3ap2	3 pages	_____	_____	
	boxes u3ap3	....	_____	_____	
	mall job6	2 pages	_____	_____	
	coach job7	2 pages	_____	_____	_____
	Unit 3 Quiz	....	_____	_____	_____
	Unit 3 Production Test	....	_____	_____	_____

UNIT 4 — SPECIAL LAYOUT TOOLS

	Printed	Score	Date Completed	Instructor
Lesson 13 Bombay 13-4	....	_____	_____	
Bombay 13-7	....	_____	_____	
sales 13-12	....	_____	_____	
sales 13-13	....	_____	_____	
patty 13-16	....	_____	_____	
patty 13-17	....	_____	_____	
patty 13-19	....	_____	_____	
schneider proj13a	....	_____	_____	
schneider proj13b	....	_____	_____	_____
Lesson 13 Quiz	....	_____	_____	_____
Lesson 14 outline 14-1	....	_____	_____	
columns 14-7	....	_____	_____	
columns 14-8	....	_____	_____	
columns 14-9	....	_____	_____	
columns 14-10	....	_____	_____	
columns 14-11	....	_____	_____	
wind proj14	....	_____	_____	
nasa proj14a	....	_____	_____	
nasa proj14b	....	_____	_____	_____
Lesson 14 Quiz	....	_____	_____	_____
Lesson 15 intake 15-2	....	_____	_____	
intake 15-4	....	_____	_____	
time 15-6	....	_____	_____	
estate 15-8	....	_____	_____	
boss 15-10	....	_____	_____	
landscape 15-11	....	_____	_____	
message proj15	....	_____	_____	_____
Lesson 15 Quiz	....	_____	_____	_____

		Printed	Score	Date Completed	Instructor
Lesson 16	berry 16-5	letter & env.	____	_____	_____
	fax 16-8	. . . .	____	_____	_____
	sasoot proj16	2 pages	____	_____	_____
	Lesson 16 Quiz	. . . .	____	_____	_____
	sasoot u4ap1	2 pages	____	_____	_____
	fax form u4ap2	. . . .	____	_____	_____
	release u4ap3	. . . .	____	_____	_____
	online u4ap4	. . . .	____	_____	_____
	schedule job8	. . . .	____	_____	_____
	coach job9	2 pages	____	_____	_____
	coach job10	2 pages	____	_____	_____
	Unit 4 Quiz	. . . .	____	_____	_____
	Unit 4 Production Test	. . . .	____	_____	_____

UNIT 5 — MERGE TOOLS

		Printed	Score	Date Completed	Instructor
Lesson 17	micro 17-5	3 letters	____	_____	_____
	micro 17-7	letters 2 & 4	____	_____	_____
	micro 17-8	1 envelope	____	_____	_____
	micro 17-9b	2 letters	____	_____	_____
	referral 17-11	2 referrals	____	_____	_____
	im spec proj17d	3 let. & env.	____	_____	_____
	Lesson 17 Quiz	. . . .	____	_____	_____
Lesson 18	flowers 18-4	. . . .	____	_____	_____
	flowers 18-7	3 let. & env.	____	_____	_____
	accounts 18-8	. . . .	____	_____	_____
	ziepke 18-11	4 letters	____	_____	_____
	reference 18-12	2 pages	____	_____	_____
	interest 18-14	4 letters	____	_____	_____
	ziepke proj18	letters 2 & 4	____	_____	_____
	Lesson 18 Quiz	. . . .	____	_____	_____
Lesson 19	sort 19-3	. . . .	____	_____	_____
	sort 19-5	. . . .	____	_____	_____
	flower list 19-6	2 pages	____	_____	_____
	table 19-10	. . . .	____	_____	_____
	small 19-12	. . . .	____	_____	_____
	im spec proj19c	. . . .	____	_____	_____
	Lesson 19 Quiz	. . . .	____	_____	_____

Lesson 20 labels 20-1 . . . . _____ _____
   labels 20-2 . . . . _____ _____
   labels 20-3 . . . . _____ _____
   badge 20-4 3 pages _____ _____
   show 20-5 3 pages _____ _____
   disk proj20 2 pages _____ _____ _____
   Lesson 20 Quiz . . . . _____ _____
   memo u5ap1 . . . . _____ _____
   seniors u5ap2a . . . . _____ _____
   seniors u5ap2b . . . . _____ _____
   seniors u5ap2c . . . . _____ _____
   seniors u5ap2d . . . . _____ _____
   invoice u5ap4 2 pages _____ _____
   disney job11 3 let. & env. _____ _____
   disney job12 3 let. & env. _____ _____
   deposit.frm . . . . _____ _____
   disney job14 letter & env. _____ _____
   badges job15 . . . . _____ _____ _____
   Unit 5 Quiz . . . . _____ _____ _____
   Unit 5 Production Test . . . . _____ _____ _____

UNIT 6 GRAPHICS TOOLS

	Printed	**Score**	**Date Completed**	**Instructor**
Lesson 21 rose 21-7	. . . .	_____	_____	
rose 21-9	. . . .	_____	_____	
rose 21-11	. . . .	_____	_____	
box 21-13	. . . .	_____	_____	
friends 21-14	. . . .	_____	_____	
wind proj21a	. . . .	_____	_____	
party proj21b	. . . .	_____	_____	
wind proj21c	. . . .	_____	_____	_____
Lesson 21 Quiz	. . . .	_____	_____	
Lesson 22 duck 22-4	. . . .	_____	_____	
fido 22-8	. . . .	_____	_____	
Brazil proj22	2 pages	_____	_____	_____
Lesson 22 Quiz	. . . .	_____	_____	

	Printed	Score	Date Completed	Instructor
Lesson 23 lines 23-2	....	_____	_____	
lines 23-3	....	_____	_____	
lines 23-4	....	_____	_____	
footer 23-5	....	_____	_____	
borders 23-6	....	_____	_____	
borders 23-8	2 pages	_____	_____	
borders 23-10	....	_____	_____	
borders 23-11	2 pages	_____	_____	
borders 23-12	....	_____	_____	
borders 23-13	....	_____	_____	
lighthouses proj23a	title page	_____	_____	
proj 23b	....	_____	_____	
proj 23c	....	_____	_____	_____
Lesson 23 Quiz	....	_____	_____	_____
Lesson 24 days 24-1	....	_____	_____	
wind 24-5	....	_____	_____	
redline 24-6	....	_____	_____	
redline 24-7	....	_____	_____	
nasa 24-9	2 pages	_____	_____	
formula proj24a	....	_____	_____	
cheese proj24b	....	_____	_____	
nasa proj24c1	....	_____	_____	
nasa proj24c2	....	_____	_____	_____
Lesson 24 Quiz	....	_____	_____	_____
beach u6ap1	....	_____	_____	
greeting u6ap2	....	_____	_____	
tovar u6ap3	....	_____	_____	
lighthouses u6ap4	3 pages	_____	_____	
new england job16	....	_____	_____	
coach job17	2 pages	_____	_____	
job18	....	_____	_____	_____
Unit 6 Quiz	....	_____	_____	_____
Unit 6 Production Test	....	_____	_____	_____

APPENDIX B — THE COREL® WORDPERFECT® ENVIRONMENT

	Printed	Score	Date Completed	Instructor
move 6-9 xxx	....	_____	_____	
move2 6-9 xxx	....	_____	_____	_____

QUICK REFERENCE

FEATURE	MENU CHOICE	KEYBOARD	LESSON
Address Book	Tools	—	18
Advance	Format, Typesetting	—	11
All Justification	Format, Justification (Property Bar)	—	9
Application Bar	—	—	1, Appendix B
Balanced Newspaper Columns	Format, Columns (Toolbar)	—	14
Block Protect	Format, Keep Text Together	—	12
Bold	Format, Font (Property Bar)	Ctrl+B or F9	3
Booklet Printing	File, Print, Two-Sided Printing	Ctrl+P	24
Bookmark	Tools, Bookmark	—	12
Bulleted List	Insert, Outline/Bullets & Numbering	—	5
Bullets & Numbers	Insert	Ctrl+Shift+B	5
Caps Lock	—	Caps Lock	3
Cascade Windows	Window, Cascade	—	8
Center	Format, Line	Shift+F7	3
Center Justification	Format, Justification (Property Bar)	Ctrl+E	9
Center Page(s)	Format, Page	—	5
Chart	Insert, Graphics, Chart	—	**
Close	File	Ctrl+F4	1, Appendix B
Column Border	Format, Border/Fill	—	23
Columns	Format, Columns (Toolbar)	—	14
Comment	Insert, Comment	—	12
Compare	File, Document	—	24
Condense Master	File, Document	—	**
Convert Case	Edit	Ctrl+K	3
Copy	Edit (Toolbar)	Ctrl+C	6
Copy Files	File, Open (Toolbar)	Ctrl+O	4
Create Data File	Tools, Merge, Data File	Shift+F9	17
Create Folder	File, Open	Ctrl+O	8
Create Form Document	Tools, Merge, Form	Shift+F9	17
Current Document Style	File, Document	—	11
Cut	Edit (Toolbar)	Ctrl+X	6
Dash (em dash)	—	---	5
Data Source, Create	Tools, Merge, Data Source	Shift+F9	17

**Not covered in this book.

Corel® WordPerfect® 8 Tutorial by Mary Alice Eisch
Quick Reference ©1999 by South-Western Educational Publishing

FEATURE	MENU CHOICE	KEYBOARD	LESSON
Date Code		Ctrl+Shift+D	5
Date Text	Insert, Date/Time	Ctrl+D	5
Default Font	File, Document	—	11
Define Index	Tools, Reference, Index	—	**
Define T. of Auth.	Tools, Reference, T. of Auth.	—	**
Define T. of Cont.	Tools, Reference, T. of Cont.	—	**
Delay Codes	Format, Page	—	**
Delete Line	—	Ctrl+Delete	2
Delete Word	—	Ctrl+Backspace	2
Divide Page	Format, Page, Page Setup	—	15
Document Assembly	Tools, Merge, Merge	Shift+F9	18
Dot Leaders	—	Alt+F7, Alt+F7	3
Double Indent	Format, Paragraph	Ctrl+Shift+F7	5
Draft View	View, Draft	Ctrl+F5	1
Drag and Drop	—	—	6
Draw	Insert, Graphics, Draw	—	**
Drop Cap	Format, Paragraph	Ctrl+Shift+C	24
Em Dash	—	---	5
ENDFIELD Code	Tools, Merge, Data Source	Alt+Enter	17
ENDFOR Code	Tools, Merge, Form	—	20
ENDIF Code	Tools, Merge, Form	—	19
Endnote	Insert, Footnote/Endnote	—	10
ENDRECORD Code	Tools, Merge, Data Source	Ctrl+Shift+Enter	17
Envelope (Merge)	Tools, Merge, Merge	—	17
Envelope (Single)	Format, Envelope	—	3
Equations	Insert, Equation	—	24
Exit	File	Alt+F4	1, Appendix B
Expand Master	File, Document	—	**
Extract	Tools, Sort	Alt+F9	19
Favorites	File, Open (Toolbar)	F4 or Ctrl+O	4
Field Names	Tools, Merge, Data Source	—	17
Fill	Format, Border/Fill	—	23
Find	Edit, Find	F2 or Ctrl+F	6
Flush Right	Format, Line	Alt+F7	3
Font Face	Format, Font (Property Bar)	F9	3
Font Size	Format, Font (Property Bar)	F9	3

Corel® WordPerfect® 8 Tutorial by Mary Alice Eisch
Quick Reference ©1999 by South-Western Educational Publishing

FEATURE	MENU CHOICE	KEYBOARD	LESSON
Footers	Insert, Header/Footer	—	10
Footnote	Insert, Footnote/Endnote	—	10
Form Document, Create	Tools, Merge, Form	Shift+F9	17
FORNEXT Code	Tools, Merge, Form	—	20
Full Justification	Format, Justification (Property Bar)	Ctrl+J	9
Full Page Zoom	View (Toolbar)	—	1
Generate	Tools	Ctrl+F9	**
Go To	Edit	Ctrl+G	2
GO(label) Code	Tools, Merge, Form	—	20
Grammatik	Tools	Alt+Shift+F1	7
Graphics Box	Insert, Image	F11	21
Graphics Line, Custom	Insert, Shape, Custom Line	—	23
Group Graphics Boxes	Quick Menu or Property Bar	—	22
Hanging Indent	Format, Paragraph	Ctrl+F7	5
Hard Page Break	Insert, New Page	Ctrl+Enter	5
Hard Space	Format, Line, Other Codes	Ctrl+Space Bar	5
Headers	Insert, Header/Footer	—	10
Help	Help, Help Topics	F1	Appendix B
Highlight	Tools (Toolbar)	—	6
Horizontal Line	Insert Shape, Horizontal Line	Ctrl+F11	23
Hypertext	Tools, Reference	—	**
Hyphen Character	Format, Line, Other Codes	Ctrl+–	5
Hyphenation	Tools, Language, Hyphenation	—	14
IFNOTBLANK Code	Tools, Merge, Form	—	18
Image Tools	(QuickMenu)	—	22
Images, Draw	Insert, Graphics, Draw	—	**
Images, Edit	Insert, Draw	—	**
Indent	Format, Paragraph	F7	5
Index	Tools, Reference	—	**
Insert	—	Insert	2
Insert File	Insert, File	—	4
Insert Image	Insert, Graphics, Clipart	—	21
Internet Publisher	File, Internet Publisher	—	**
Italic	Format, Font (Property Bar)	Ctrl+I or F9	3
Justification	Format, Justification	—	9
KEYBOARD Code	Tools, Merge, Form	—	17
Keyboard Map	Tools, Settings, Customize	—	**

Corel® WordPerfect® 8 Tutorial by Mary Alice Eisch
Quick Reference ©1999 by South-Western Educational Publishing

FEATURE	MENU CHOICE	KEYBOARD	LESSON
LABEL(label)	Tools, Merge, Form	—	20
Labels, Create	Format, Labels	—	20
Landscape Orientation	Format, Page, Page Setup	—	15
Left Justification	Format, Justification (Property Bar)	Ctrl+L	9
Line Numbering	Format, Line	—	24
Line Spacing	Format, Line (Property Bar)	—	9
Lists	Tools, Reference	—	**
Macro, Edit	Tools, Macro	—	16
Macro, Play	Tools, Macro	Alt+F10	16
Macro, Record	Tools, Macro	Ctrl+F10	16
Make It Fit	Format	—	11
Margins	Format, Margins	Ctrl+F8	9
Master Document	File, Document	—	**
Merge	Tools, Merge, Merge	Shift+F9	4, 17
Move Files	File, Open (Toolbar)	Ctrl+O	4
Name Badges	Format, Labels	—	20
New Blank Page	(Toolbar)	Ctrl+N	6
New Page Number	Format, Page, Numbering	—	10
Newspaper Columns	Format, Columns (Toolbar)	—	14
NEXTRECORD Code	Tools, Merge, Form	—	20
Open	File (Toolbar)	F4 or Ctrl+O	1, Appendix B
Open as Copy	File, Open	Ctrl+O	8
Orientation	Format, Page, Page Setup	—	15
Outline/Bullets & Numbering	Insert	—	5
Page Border	Format, Border/Fill	—	23
Page Break	Insert, New Page	Ctrl+Enter	5
Page Numbering	Format, Page, Numbering	—	10
Page Size	Format, Page, Page Setup	—	15
Page View	View, Page	Alt+F5	1
Paragraph Border	Format, Border/Fill	—	23
Paste	Edit (Toolbar)	Ctrl+V	6
Path and Filename	Insert, Other	—	2
PerfectExpert	Help	—	**
Portrait Orientation	Format, Page, Page Size	—	15
POSTNET Bar Code	Tools, Merge, Merge	Shift+F9	18
Print	File (Toolbar)	Ctrl+P	1

Corel® WordPerfect® 8 Tutorial by Mary Alice Eisch
Quick Reference ©1999 by South-Western Educational Publishing

FEATURE	MENU CHOICE	KEYBOARD	LESSON
Prompt-As-You-Go	(Property Bar)	—	7
Property Bar	View	—	8, Appendix B
Proofreaders' Marks	—	—	4
QuickCorrect	Tools	—	7
QuickFinder	File, Open	Ctrl+O	12
QuickFormat	Format, QuickFormat (Toolbar)	—	11
QuickMark, Find	Tools, Bookmark	Ctrl+Q	12
QuickMark, Insert	Tools, Bookmark	Ctrl+Shift+Q	12
QuickMenu	—	—	6, Appendix B
QuickWords	Tools	—	11
Redline	Format, Font	F9	24
Redo	Edit (Toolbar)	Ctrl+Shift+R	2
Reference	Tools	—	**
Replace	Edit, Replace	F2	6
Reveal Codes	View	Alt+F3	2
Right Justification	Format, Justification (Property Bar)	Ctrl+R	9
Ruler	View, Ruler	Alt+Shift+F3	9
Save	File	Shift+F3, Ctrl+S	1, Appendix B
Select All	Edit, Select	Ctrl+A	15
Select Records	Tools, Merge, Merge	Shift+F9	19
Select Text	Edit, Select	F8	2
Settings	Tools, Settings	—	16, Appendix B
Shadow Pointer	(Application Bar)	—	11
Shapes	Insert, Shape	—	**
Soft Hyphen	Format, Line, Other Codes	Ctrl+Shift+–	14
Soft Page Break	Automatic	—	3, 5
Sort	Tools, Sort	Alt+F9	19
Spell Check	Tools (Toolbar)	Ctrl+F1	7
Spell-As-You-Go	Tools (Property Bar)	Alt+Ctrl+F1	7
Strikeout	Format, Font	F9	24
Styles	Format, Styles	Alt+F8	**
Subscript	Format, Font	F9	5
Superscript	Format, Font	F9	5
Suppress	Format, Page	—	10
Symbols	Insert	Ctrl+W	11
Tab	—	Tab	3

Corel® WordPerfect® 8 Tutorial by Mary Alice Eisch
Quick Reference ©1999 by South-Western Educational Publishing

FEATURE	MENU CHOICE	KEYBOARD	LESSON
Tab Set	Format, Line (Ruler)	—	9
Table, Create	Table, Create (Toolbar)	—	13
Table of Authorities	Tools, Reference, T. of Auth.	—	**
Table of Contents	Tools, Reference, T. of Cont.	—	**
Templates	File, New	Ctrl+T	**
TextArt	Insert, Graphics, TextArt	—	24
Thesaurus	Tools	Alt+F1	7
Tile Windows	Window, Tile	—	8
Toolbar	View, Toolbars	—	8, Appendix B
Two Pages View	View, Two Pages	—	1
Typeover	—	Insert	2
Undelete		Ctrl+Shift+Z	2
Underline	Format, Font (Property Bar)	Ctrl+U or F9	3
Underline Tabs	Format, Font	F9	15
Undo	Edit (Toolbar)	Ctrl+Z	3
Vertical Line	Insert, Shape, Vertical Line	Ctrl+Shift+F11	23
View Page	View	Alt+F5	1
Watermark	Insert, Watermark	—	10
Web Page	File, New or File, Internet Publisher	—	**
Widow/Orphan	Format, Keep Text Together	—	10
Zoom	View (Toolbar)	—	1

Corel® WordPerfect® 8 Tutorial by Mary Alice Eisch
Quick Reference ©1999 by South-Western Educational Publishing